FOUNDATIONS

OF

WESTERN THOUGHT

SIX MAJOR PHILOSOPHERS

EDITED AND INTRODUCED BY

JAMES GORDON CLAPP

MORRIS PHILIPSON

HENRY M. ROSENTHAL

HUNTER COLLEGE,

THE CITY UNIVERSITY OF NEW YORK

1 9   6 2

FOUNDATIONS OF WESTERN THOUGHT

SIX MAJOR PHILOSOPHERS

NEW YORK : ALFRED·A·KNOPF

ACKNOWLEDGMENTS

THE EDITORS wish to acknowledge with gratitude
the permission of the following publishers to reprint
in this book material from the following copyright
works controlled by them.

Cambridge University Press, London and New York:
from Aristotle, *De Anima*, translated by R. D. Hicks,
copyright 1907; and from *The Philosophical Works
of Descartes*, translated by Elizabeth S. Haldane and
G. R. T. Ross, copyright 1911, reprinted with
corrections, 1931.

Harvard University Press: from Aristotle, *Metaphysics*, translated by Hugh Tredennick, Loeb Classical Library editions, copyright 1933, 1936; and
from Aristotle, *Nichomachean Ethics*, translated by
H. Rackham, Loeb Classical Library editions,
copyright 1926, new and revised edition, 1934.

Random House, Inc.: from *The Philosophy of
Kant*, edited and translated by Carl J. Friedrich,
copyright 1949 by Random House, Inc.

THIS IS A BORZOI BOOK,
PUBLISHED BY ALFRED A. KNOPF, INC.

FIRST EDITION

PREFACE FOR THE
Reader

There are many ways to introduce a reader to philosophy. With will enough and sufficient care and time, one can begin anywhere and end up everywhere. The classic way whereby men have become versed in philosophy has been the careful study of some of the great philosophers of the past. This has been the high road into the city of philosophy.

The considerations which governed the selection of readings in this book are greatness, wholeness, and philosophic depth. No one surely will dispute the greatness either of the philosophers (Plato, Aristotle, Descartes, Berkeley, Hume, and Kant), or of the works which are reproduced here. That is not to say that there are not other, perhaps equally important authors and other major philosophy books to be read and studied. It is to say that no one can be judged to be fully competent in philosophy without a knowledge and understanding of the authors and works included in these readings. Their greatness has been attested to by time and the continued attention paid to them today. One may be certain that they will continue to be read as long as men are concerned with philosophical inquiry.

To read these philosophers of the past is not to retreat from present issues and problems into preoccupation with antiquated intellectual endeavors; it is to encounter some of the most lively and penetrating examinations of the perennial questions of mankind. Plato and Aristotle, as well as the others, have something important to say to us, something relevant, timely, and thought-provoking. If philosophy begins in wonder, it also ends in wonder, but the wonder at the end is not the wonder at the beginning. If finally we are ignorant still, our ignorance is conscious

and aware both of itself and of the possibilities of wisdom and knowledge. Without wonder in the beginning we cannot ever ask questions
about anything, without wonder at the end we cannot fail to be deceived. Among the objects of perennial concern are God, man, and the
world; the true, the good, and the beautiful; appearance and reality;
freedom and necessity. Men have discoursed about them in many ways,
and these discourses have led to agreements and disagreements. It is
these agreements and disagreements—frequently passionate in feeling,
often profound in thought, and almost invariably total in commitment
—which generate the essential intellectual life of men, societies, and
cultures. The men and their thought are serious, and one does well to
take them seriously.

Frequently failure to be serious about each philosopher, as well as
the fact that there are certain broad similarities among certain philosophers, has encouraged a classification of philosophies under general
rubrics such as materialism, idealism, positivism, realism, and nominalism. Equally general are terms such as Platonism, Aristotelianism, and
Thomism. The terms themselves do little damage if they are seen for
what they are—loose and vague categories for easy reference.

To read Plato is to come closer to his mind than to read about
Platonism. There is far more in the interrelation and interplay between
body and mind in Descartes' philosophy than is suggested by the offhand
label of "dualism." To call Berkeley and Kant "idealists" creates confusions and invites inattention to what they actually said and thought.
In short, it is better to read a philosopher than to read books about him.
With few exceptions, the readings in this book are complete works. The
thought of a great mind expressed in a book represents the author's
judgment of the completed statement he wished to make. Whenever
possible his book should be respected in its wholeness.

The whole of a particular work, however, is not the whole of a
man's philosophy, for a single work may be far from representative of
the range and depth of his thought. The completeness of a single book
must therefore be balanced against the counterweight of the remainder
of each philosopher's total range and depth. Each must be independently evaluated.

Plato wrote many Dialogues over a long career, and in their totality
they reveal both the extraordinary range of his interests and the successive stages of his intellectual development. Dialogues other than those
we have chosen have a considerable claim for our attention. Nonetheless,
the *Symposium*, the *Phaedo*, and the *Sophist*, which are reproduced in
their entirety in this book, are collectively more representative of Plato's
philosophy than any other three we might have chosen.

Aristotle is the most difficult of all, for his works are many and most of the important ones are long. The *De Anima* is presented in its entirety in the admirable Hicks translation, which has been out of print for some time. Aristotle's naturalistic view of life and the cosmos, as well as his positive scientific interest, are well displayed in the *De Anima*. The work is pivotal for it points in one way or another to virtually all his other works. The *De Anima*, however, does not cover the range of Aristotle's interests. The *Ethics* and the *Metaphysics* are necessary to indicate in some measure the extent and diversity of his philosophic inquiry. We have compromised here with our purpose to present whole works. Space would not allow us to include the whole of each work, and to include one of them at the expense of the other would present a distorted picture of Aristotle. Nonetheless, very large portions of each work are presented.

Descartes is represented by the *Meditations,* which is undoubtedly his most mature philosophic statement, even though it does not cover the full range of his intellectual interests. Some effort has been made in the Introduction to the Descartes section to indicate the variety and extent of his inquiries and writings. Similarly, Berkeley's *Three Dialogues between Hylas and Philonus* is truly representative of his thought in the most beautiful and expressive form in which he stated it. There is merit in comparing the dialogue as a form of philosophic expression in Plato, Berkeley, and Hume, and in comparing this form with the expository form of philosophic statements as exemplified by Aristotle, Descartes, and Kant.

In the instance of David Hume, the whole of the *Dialogues Concerning Natural Religion* was for us a preferable choice to fragments of his *Treatise of Human Nature,* or fragments of the *Inquiry Concerning Human Understanding* and the *Inquiry Concerning the Principles Of Morals.* The dialogues make use of the principles which Hume formulated in his longer and more difficult philosophic writings, and they make visible the bent of his critical mind.

Kant, like Plato and Aristotle, presents some problems. He wrote extensively on many subjects, and his major works, the three critiques,[1] are long and difficult. The *Prolegomena To Every Future Metaphysics That May Be Presented As A Science* and the *Metaphysical Foundations Of Morals* represent the two most accessible works to the philosophy of Kant. We have used the translations of both works by Carl J. Friedrich because we believe they are the most reliable as well as the most readable English translations of these works. The *Metaphysical Foundations Of Morals* is virtually complete; only a few passages are omitted. Of the *Prolegomena To Every Future Metaphysics* Professor Friedrich has

---

[1] *Critique Of Pure Reason; Critique Of Practical Reason; Critique Of Judgment.*

translated very large sections, indeed most of it. All that he has translated is included here.

Our third consideration, depth, is not the same as difficulty, even
though they have frequently gone together in philosophy. The readings
included in this book have all in one way or another probed deeply into
some of the most fundamental questions which have beset and continue to beset the minds of men. Whatever answers may finally be given
to these questions, one dare not fail to take into account the various
answers which are advanced in the works presented here. If it be true,
as Whitehead has suggested, that philosophy never returns to its previous position after the impact of a great philosopher, it is equally true
that it is at one's peril that anyone ignores the great predecessors.

The understanding of the selections in this book requires intellectual effort. They are not too difficult, however, for a beginning
student or reader. The challenge which serious inquiry presents demands
a serious and mature effort on the part of any reader not only in philosophy but in any area of human endeavor.

Many philosophers of importance have been omitted from this
book of selections. But to have included some of them would have
drastically cut into the selections we have presented, and to have included many of them would have left us with tattered fragments of
each. The basis upon which we decided to include certain philosophic
works and omit others is a personal commitment on how to introduce
a reader to philosophy.

The "history of philosophy" approach has proved for us largely to
be a failure, because it left the reader with little more than a series of
names, dates, and a few pat generalities about each philosopher read or
studied. Even when this approach is followed in a college course over a
period of a year, there is hardly time or incentive to probe, reflect, and
move about in the philosophy of any one man. Being superficial, such
treatment hardly gives the reader time to become engaged with any
thinker or any thought.

Our own method is "historical" in the sense that it presents the
philosophies of past great figures. However, it makes possible a thorough
examination in depth of philosophic problems as they are presented by
pivotal philosophers whose positions are nonetheless quite distinct.
Whoever has studied Plato and Aristotle may with profit move further
into the past to study the pre-Socratics as well as forward into the future
to examine the philosophers of the Hellenistic and medieval periods,
the modern and contemporary.

So too a knowledge of Descartes, Berkeley, Hume, and Kant is
fundamental for the study of virtually all philosophy which comes after
them, including the most contemporary. If there is, as many contend,

a great philosophic revolution going on in our own day, one must study what it is revolting from and why it is doing so. Without this no revolution can be clear about itself.

The material contained in this book is far more than anyone can possibly cover in one semester. Where this book is used for a college course it can serve two purposes. It can offer the basic readings for a year's course in philosophy. Where a semester course constitutes the basic course in philosophy, it offers an instructor considerable choice of readings without sacrifice of quality or thoroughness.

It remains but to say a word or two about the introductions to each philosopher. They are individual statements and reflect personal differences of style, manner, and approach. No effort has been made to bring them under any formula defining what is the best way to introduce a particular philosopher. Had any of the editors written the introductory essay for a given philosopher other than the one for whom he did write it, the essay would have been somewhat different than it presently appears. Yet this is not quite so relative and personal as it may seem. These differences are a reflection of the various problems each philosopher presents.

An instructor in any case will do what he wishes with them. He may use them as references so that he may go on to other things himself, he may argue with and dispute them to generate his own dialectic, or he may ignore them altogether to replace them with his own introduction. All represent different ways of philosophizing and all are, in principle, legitimate.

JAMES GORDON CLAPP

CONTENTS

PLATO

INTRODUCTION TO

Plato

Plato was born 428/7 B.C. and died 348/7 B.C. He stands at the head-waters of the philosophic tradition. The several streams of the pre-Socratic and the Socratic traditions come together in his activity to form what for European philosophy is the main stream; and after him the main stream divides again into its several branches, major and minor: "Peripatetic" or Aristotelian, Stoic and Epicurean, neo-Platonic, medieval, the syntheses of scholasticism and Renaissance philosophy, and the modern schools.

Plato's philosophic activity may be taken (a) as a reinterpretation and theoretical resynthesis of the original formative influences of philosophy, from Miletus to Elea, from Ionia to Sicily,[1] from physics to metaphysics; (b) as a sustained sociopsychological inquiry into the causes of the Athenian decline and catastrophic collapse in the thirty-year war with Sparta; (c) as a long threnody on the death of Socrates, "wisest and best of men"; (d) as a series of pioneer explorations in philosophical anthropology, or inquiry into the status of man in the general scheme of things and investigation of the limits and possibilities of human existence.

Traces of all these types of interest, and their possibilities for the interpretation of Plato, are to be found in the Dialogues here selected, as they would be, to some extent, in any group of others.

---

[1] These are geographical areas which represent different pre-Socratic schools of philosophy. The major features of these earlier traditions, as Plato had them, arise for relevant evaluation in each of the three Platonic Dialogues included in this selection and are marked for identification in the appropriate places. A more systematic review of the same traditions, as Aristotle had them, and what he had included Plato, is partly given in the First Book of *De Anima* and in Book Alpha of Aristotle's *Metaphysics*.

One may say of Plato, in a word that has some special present currency, that he was totally *engagé*, by mind, temperament, and aptitude.
His philosophic activity, taken as a whole, is thus the model and paradigm of the philosophic genius: to be totally engaged while totally conscious and totally clear.

The outward facts of his life shrink to triviality against the totality
of his engagement in his work and the totality of its involvement in the
whole range of the human problem.

Plato was born in Athens; he died there. He descends from an
Athenian family of high distinction.[2] His entire youth and early manhood were spent under the shadow of the war with Sparta. He was a
witness of the trial of Socrates—an aftermath of that war, its revolutions
and counterrevolutions, its betrayals and countertreacheries. He traveled
as far as Sicily, and perhaps to Egypt, and tried to give advice to tyrants, or politicians. He founded an academy—the first European university, it is sometimes called—and lectured there. He was a teacher of
Aristotle, who studied there. He wrote dialogues and founded philosophy.

Much or little may be made of the question how much of Plato's
philosophy is Socratic and how much Platonic, strictly. Opinions and
estimations differ among authorities, depending on the Dialogue, the
time at which written, and the interpretation to which it may be subjected.[3]

In the following presentation of the philosophy of Plato—as exhibited in three of his Dialogues—this question counts for little. The
character of the ideas—their nature and definition, the disposition of
the ideas within the Dialogues themselves, and their destiny in the history of ideas after Plato's work is done—engages our concern sufficiently
to overshadow the nicer question of responsibility for particular accents
of them, whether Socratic or Platonic.

It is assumed in the Dialogues that anybody may have these ideas,
and that at one time or other anybody has, although, for concreteness's
sake, in argument an idea is often assigned to a contemporary spokesman of it as if he were the author. A good example is the *Theaetetus*,
where Protagoras stands for a relativistic and humanistic doctrine of

---

[2] An excellent short account of Plato's life will be found in John Burnet:
Greek Philosophy: Thales to Plato (London: Macmillan; 1914), ch. XII, which
also indicates and evaluates the main sources upon which subsequent accounts of
his life are based. See also W. Jaeger: *Paideia: The Ideals of Greek Culture* (New
York: Oxford University Press; 1945), vols. 2 and 3; A. E. Taylor: *Plato: the Man &
His Work* (London: Methuen; 1949) and *Socrates* (Boston: Beacon Press; 1951);
and Burnet: op. cit., ch. VIII, for a discussion of the "historical Socrates."

[3] The variety of views on the question is briefly surveyed in the second chapter
of vol. II of W. Jaeger: op. cit.

knowledge ("man is the measure of things") that was widely and even anonymously held.

It is difficult to imagine the pre-Platonic Socrates entertaining or cultivating all the "Platonic" ideas of the Dialogues in their unbridled complexity and in all their possible ramifications. It is difficult to imagine the post-Socratic Plato having come upon them all by himself. In short, the question of authorship, pushed to its extremity, becomes the question of the origin of ideas; and that is precisely one of the questions which Plato examines in his Dialogues, though he does not examine it as much historically as Aristotle later does.

The strictly *historical* relationship of ideas—as distinct from their intrinsic and nontemporal relations—becomes important in and after Aristotle.

If, as has been often observed,[4] the history of European philosophy is a commentary on Plato, Plato's Dialogues are the scriptures of that history.

A "scriptural" type of document, in any given cultural tradition, has two characteristics: (a) It tends to become the focus of retrospective ideas, so that it is no longer possible—or if possible, it is not always of first importance—to determine whether the ideas that have become associated with the text were intended by the text's author or have simply taken up permanent residence in that text and can no longer be evicted from it. (b) Any *part* of the document as "scripture" now inevitably tends to reflect the whole of it, as if the whole cluster of meanings were subject to multiple refraction in the several facets of the whole.

This does not mean, for instance, that *any* idea can be justified in the text that has arbitrarily found its way into it. The current popular notion of "Platonic love," for instance, has very little, if anything, to do with the complex meaning of the *Symposium's* dialectic.

But it does mean that there are latencies of thought in almost every line of the Platonic "scripture" that make it almost impossible to exclude with finality certain ideas that reached their fuller development, and explicit formulation, in much later thinkers.

Whitehead, for example, finds it plausible to read Plato's *Timaeus* as a prescient anticipation, in archaic symbols, of the mathematical cosmologies of our day. That the language is from our point of view circumlocutory or archaic does not affect the substance of the meaning. After all, it might be said, Isaac Newton was still (in 1685) writing "X^2" as "the quadrature of X."

By the same token, therefore, it is impossible to exclude a priori,

---

[4] Thus, for example, A. N. Whitehead: "The safest general characterization of the European philosophical tradition is that it consists of a series of footnotes to Plato." *Process and Reality* (New York: Macmillan; 1929), p. 63.

or in any case with finality, the problems of modern politics from Plato's
Republic, or the issues of Bertrand Russell's "logic of description" from
the analysis of ordinary statements as given toward the end of the
Sophist.

How much or how little of those later issues belong in Plato—not
by extrapolation into him, but by genuine finding there—and how
much such issues gain or lose in depth and meaning by being turned up
in Plato, this is for the student to discover, decide, and justify—with the
text and its argument as the ultimate controls.

In this sense, the "problem" approach to the study of philosophy,
and the "textual" one may properly coincide; and their coincidence is
never greater, or more rewarding, than in Plato.

THE DIALOGUES

Plato's power consists in the ability to beguile, to puzzle, and to exalt.
The *Symposium* beguiles, the *Phaedo* exalts, and the *Sophist* puzzles,
but all three Dialogues do all these things together. The beguilement is
in any case puzzling, and the puzzlement is exalting, if one follows it
through.

Plato presumably did not invent the dialogue form, any more than
Socrates invented the form of instructive conversation; and if he did
invent it, he presumably had an earlier invention before him for guide
and inspiration. But he created it—by which is meant that he established it for all time as the peculiar inner, if not outward, mode of the
activity called philosophy. After Plato, all philosophy is dialectical, and
the first form of dialectic is the dialogue. The presiding genius of
Aristotle's expository analysis—in the *Metaphysics* and *De Anima* no
less than in the *Ethics*—is the genius of the dialogue, or the argument
with another person interiorized, as it is of Descartes' *Meditations* and
Kant's *Prolegomena*.

In reading works which are strictly expository in form—such as those
just mentioned—the experienced reader learns to ask the same question
as is proper to the dialogue—namely, Whom is the writer now rebutting,
with whom is he arguing, and what has given him his cue?

If the student should eventually proceed beyond the confines of
this introductory textbook to examine Hegel's *Logic* or, perhaps, Sartre's
Being and Nothingness, he will find the felt presence of the dialogue
there too.

The essence of the dialogue is, of course, dramatic: it has a dramatis personae, or masks in action, and these masks are ideas. Plato's discovery was that ideas have a life of their own. It is necessary to identify them. The difficulty of identifying them is that they do not stand still. And yet they have to be engaged. A convenient way of engaging them is very boldly to commit what in logic is called the fallacy of *ad hominem*, which consists in attacking the person rather than the thought. But when the thought and the person have been merged, when the idea is allowed to live the life to which it is by its own nature committed, and the person is wholly intellectualized, or absorbed with the idea he stands for, then this fallacy disappears.

The war of persons—the civil conflict of "all against all," the Hobbesian state of nature, which constituted a good deal of Greek political history—is transformed into the clash of ideas.

In the reading of the Dialogues a distinction soon appears between the *ostensible* theme and the *real* theme. The progress of the Dialogue is often precisely this effort to precipitate the real theme out of the deceptive or ostensible ones.

There are Dialogues where the effort sometimes has to be abandoned as not feasible within the framework set, and so the real theme is only discovered in a subsequent Dialogue. Whether or no the subsequent Dialogue—in this logical sense—was actually written later is of secondary importance, for Plato may be assumed to be willing to "weave" the pattern of his thought, in and out, backwards and forwards, and, like the artist that he is, to be less concerned with the linear sequence of his ideas, than with the fullness and completeness of the picture.

In Plato what is last in the order of exposition is sometimes first in the order of motivation. His "final causes" (to borrow the Aristotelian term) are sometimes his concealed and even uncompleted "first causes."

THE SYMPOSIUM

(Note: the numbers in parentheses correspond to the marginal numbers in the text of the Dialogues. They are the page numbers of the standard Greek edition.)

The ostensible theme of the *Symposium* is "love," or "eros"; its real theme is human *paideia*, or self-education toward whatever is the "absolute."

The *Symposium* beguiles, puzzles, and exalts by turn. It beguiles, first, as gossip does: I am going to tell you something, Apollodorus says, and I am sure you want to know; or don't you? You have already asked for it, and so here goes.

There follows—as if by total recall, and not a word is missing—a story that Apollodorus was not himself a witness of but heard at second hand from Aristodemus, who was there and heard it all and then told him. The entire Dialogue subdivides into a proper introduction, telling how and where Apollodorus got his story of the symposium, or banquet; the banquet itself, with its full-length dialectical competition on the ostensible subject of love; and an epilogue telling how at long last the party broke up, or was practically broken up by Alcibiades, making it possible for the Dialogue to end and therefore to be recalled.

This technique of recall is the device Plato uses in most, though not all, of his Dialogues to start matters off. It may be a technique transposed from Plato's early apprenticeship—according to tradition—in Greek "poetry"—that is, playwrighting, where chorus and other supernumeraries of the action set the remembered scene for the audience by telling them how and when the story got to the point at which the play began. It may, on the other hand, be a device—conscious or unconscious—that comes out of Plato's deeper self and more ultimate commitment—namely, his conviction, alluded to in the *Symposium* and briefly expounded in the *Phaedo*,[5] that "knowledge is recollection," whatever that may mean. One of the things it apparently means is that the most important events have already taken place (not necessarily in the "past" but possibly in "eternity") and that those events had witnesses, with whom it would be worthwhile to establish a lively and preferred association. Among those witnesses of memorable, "eternal" events might be Aristodemus—since Apollodorus couldn't make it—or it might be one's own "soul" was such a witness, if one could get it to undertake recall.

There is now recalled, then, what the speakers said on Love.

Besides Socrates, whose profession is that of stonemason, the speakers include two dilettanti, Phaedrus and Pausanias; two playwrights, Aristophanes and Agathon, the latter both host and celebrant; one doctor, Eryximachus; and one man who is difficult to describe since he was all things to all men—politician, playboy, soldier, sailor, wit, Athenian "man of the year," and within that same year renegade from Athens to her mortal enemy, Sparta. This man is the brilliant and notorious Alcibiades, who, corrupt though he be, yet bears for Socrates the greatest love of all, because it is the love of appreciation.

There was a sense in which the term "sophist" could be applied to each of the six who stand apart from Socrates;[6] for they are all inter-

---

[5] And somewhat more fully expounded in the *Meno*, where it is also "demonstrated."

[6] As, for instance, in the meaning claimed for the term by Protagoras in Plato's Dialogue of that name (*Protagoras*, 316).

preters and purveyors of current "wisdom" and masters, one way or another, of the tricks of the trade of achievement. A possible exception is Aristophanes, who is gifted with the comic poet's peculiar double vision—the capacity to purvey common wisdom while seeing through and beyond it.

Phaedrus and Pausanias tell us what we already know: that the love of a man for a man had a status among the Greeks, or among some Greeks, midway between vice and virtue. It was a daring thing to do, and was presumably a mark of manhood; at the same time one got no laurel wreaths for being the passionate or devoted "lover" of such-and-such a citizen: the minstrelsy of homosexual love in the "Greek anthology" is not impressive for quantity or quality. The homosexual lover tries hard to be heroic; he often succeeds, it seems, in being ridiculous. Whether homosexuality is considered socially "normal" or not in parts of ancient Greece, the line taken about homosexual love is usually a defensive one, as in the speeches here of Phaedrus and Pausanias; for underneath their eloquent transvaluations one detects, perhaps, a faint note of hysteria.

But what Plato wishes to do with their speeches is clear enough, and they do it for him perhaps better than he himself could do, since he has not done it with equal effectiveness anywhere else in his Dialogues. He and they wish to desexualize the emotion of love. The "right true end of love" is more than love.

This will be the burden and the theme of the great Socratic utterance that comes later. But already it is intimated in the twistings and turnings, the divisions and discardings, the primitive mythologizing "dialectic" of the two dilettanti,[7] who argue, though perhaps they do not wholly mean to, that the turning away from the "earthly" love of women is merely the first step in the going beyond the love of "lovers" altogether, and a first purchase on the love of souls and the goods thereof.

Now Eryximachus, the man of medicine, speaks.

Greek medical science in the fifth century was not merely a specialty —though it was that, too, of course—but one of the basic "wisdoms." It was a knowledge of the body, a knowledge of nature, and a knowledge of "life." A mixture of pharmacological, psychosomatic, and physical-therapy techniques—many of them sophisticated and effective—it also aimed at being a philosophy, or even a cosmology: understand the body, and you understand the spheres. The better doctors of the time stopped short, to be sure, of reversing this claim, and proposing that if you understood the planets you understood the "humors."

Eryximachus pulls all the stops.

---

[7] The one is a follower of the sophist Hippias, and the other of Prodicus. These two leading sophists of the day and their company of faithful in Athens are identified for us in *Protagoras* (315).

First he cures Aristophanes' hiccups, and then he "cosmologizes" the theme of love. Overeducated and, no doubt, bursting to communicate, he will not let go of his captive audience until he has given them a short, predigested history of pre-Socratic philosophy. It is, of course, considerably rubbed up for popular consumption. Heracleitus, and his "process" philosophy are mentioned (187). Pythagoras and his "harmonic" philosophy seem to be there, though not mentioned by name. The Hesiodic theory of propitious seasons, all subject to the power and cajolery of love, comes limping in, and so Eryximachus goes on to his rickety ladder of love: from agronomy to astronomy, from sacrifices and ceremonies to the more esoteric art of divination, from divination to piety, from piety to happiness, and from happiness to friendship between gods and men, all by love.

It is Aristophanes' turn.

One would give something to know what brought on the hiccups from which he has now recovered. Which of these pompous mouthings that he has had to listen to has been parodied where—in *The Birds, The Frogs, The Clouds, Lysistrata*, or in all of them?

The wild fable and its admonitory epilogue—that a worse fate awaits us if we do not mend our ways—are familiar to all. We were once one, though we were three types of one, all man, all woman, or all both, and given to locomotion by gigantic somersaultings; until the gods, taking fright at our "hybris," or impudence, split us down the middle and set us to seek our reconstituted wholes by happenstance. We embrace whom we can. But what we are looking for is merely to be one.

The unabashed buffoonery does not wholly disguise the subtlety of Aristophanes' contribution. Love is doomed to frustration, in whatever form; yet it cannot cease. The unity that it seeks is in our primal being. Our ontogenetic struggles seek to recover a phylogenetic fact. Is this phylogenetic fact also an "ontological" one, as it later came to be known—that is, a fact of "being"? Is this what Socrates intimates, as he heard it from Diotima?

There is one more yet to go.

It takes a more than ordinary courtesy to listen to Agathon, host and celebrant though he be, for he appears to be the greatest bore of all. What he tells us might well have been learned from a handbook of afterdinner speeches. "Love is not the eldest god" or child of nature—as Phaedrus had alleged—"he is indeed the youngest," and the prettiest, and the tenderest, and so on.

And yet, as if in the Socratic presence even the silliest tongue cannot help but stumble on a fragment of the truth—as had Phaedrus and Pausanias, and Eryximachus, and clear-eyed Aristophanes—even Agathon holds the issue up closer to the light before he runs away from it.

This exaltation of the issue takes place at once: the correct thing to do, says Agathon, is to praise a thing's *nature*, before you go on to celebrate its results.

It is as if this insight were the one that Socrates was waiting for. All he has to do is show that Agathon misused it. This he will do by the question-and-answer method; once that method is established, dialectic is in charge, and the long, labored speeches will give birth to their theme.

The stages are as follows:

1. It is established that love's nature is not the *having* but the *wanting* or *being deprived*. Love *has none* of the attributes previously ascribed to it. This is the first truth delivered.

2. The rest comes from Diotima, and what she once told to Socrates, what he now remembers, is a summary forecast of "Platonism."

In this "Platonism" that she reveals there are three guilding notions: (a) There is a world of "being" where "absolutes," or "essential natures," and all deathless things reside—the beautiful, for example, and wisdom and the good. (b) There is a world that "wants" being, or is deprived of it. In this world are all things that "generate," and in generating grow and die. The worlds of (a) and (b) are linked by (c), the intermediary agents, or processes, or principles, such as love.

Now "intermediation" has a character that is itself twofold. With reference to "being" it is obviously "lack." But with reference to itself, or to the "generating" world, it is the *energy* in it, or the impulse of that world toward its source in "being."

We have the same situation in the case of human knowledge, where the role of "right opinion"—or "recollective" learning, as Plato will have it—is like that of love. Both learning and love are dialectical recoveries of the sources of our being.

The "phenomenology" of love is particularly instructive, for the workings of the "daimon," as Diotima names it, are expressed everywhere, in all of "generation." The aim of the passion love is the same everywhere, in beasts as well as men: it aims at "immortality." But this immortality is grasped in experience not only procreatively, and not only by the body, but by the soul's generation of its forms of the good.

The pursuit of the beautiful is merely that desire for the secure possession of the immortal good. This leads to *paideia*, or education of self.

3. That *paideia* Diotima now applies, without transition, to the *polis* and to its claim that "the greatest and fairest sort of wisdom by far is that which is concerned with the ordering of states and families, and which is called temperance and justice" (208); but in this case,

as in the *Republic*, the political and social *paideia* is both paradigm and prolegomenon to the more intimate *paideia*, of the individual soul—whose ladder of ascent in love is from the single fair Form to the plurality of Forms in life, art, and knowledge; an ordinary passage to extraordinary existence in the vision of the good.

The rest of the Dialogue is anticlimactic to the argument, but it perfects it by showing Socrates as the living embodiment of the argument's theme.

Alcibiades bursts in, roistering as usual, stumbles to a seat between Socrates and Agathon—his "heavenly" and his "earthly" love—and sends the company far into the forgetful night with the unforgettable portrait of Socrates as the man, so it seems, about whom all the tale was told. For it is he, it appears, who is outwardly ugly and inwardly so fair as to be divine. He that stood at Potidaea—as he stood on the very threshold of the banquet, a few hours and pages before—in a deathless trance of communication with some essential things—absolutes or gods, or daimonic intermediaries—that they have been trying to find out about all this while.

At the end Socrates is still arguing a thesis for Plato's sake: that the "comic" and the "tragic" genius are one and the same. One wonders how he would have worked that out. But we leave them there.

THE PHAEDO

The ostensible theme of the *Phaedo* is the immortality of the soul; its real theme is the nature of human knowledge, or understanding.

On his last day Socrates has just had the chains removed from his legs. This occasions a reflection on the peculiar relation of pleasure to pain. He is asked by Cebes why in prison he has turned to versifying. Socrates explains that his versifying—or "making music"—was in obedience to a dream he has had, which is recounted. Then he sends a message to Evenus, who sent the question. "Tell this to Evenus," says Socrates, "and bid him be of good cheer; say that I would have him come after me if he be a wise man, and not tarry . . ."

This broaches the first issue: the paradox of dying.

On the one hand dying is a good, since it is a pilgrimage to a better place than the one we now occupy; but on the other hand we have no right to accelerate this pilgrimage by suicide, for we do not belong to ourselves, and it is an impudence to go faster than we are meant to. (The script, so to speak, is given us to read at a certain tempo, and to run away with it is the action of a bad actor who insists on stealing the show.) But if suicide is forbidden, says Cebes, then why this song about the delightfulness of dying? Why not stay with our masters (the gods) and the lines they have appointed us in this life? is not that, rather, the choice of wisdom? Is not dying itself either pitiable or foolish?

Socrates is pleased with this challenge. It gives him an opportunity to justify dying to the living. All he has to do now is show the immortality of the soul.

(Before he goes into this, there is a brief but humble complaint from the jailer, who stands ready to administer the poison, that Socrates will please not talk too much; if he overdoes it, he might have to take a second helping.)

The peculiarity of the arguments that now follow lies in the fact that they progressively transform the issue. They do not prove what one set out to prove, but they change the original view of the question. To feel this as a disappointment or disillusionment with the issue is to misunderstand the nature of Socratic "proof," and its intentions.

Rarely, if ever, does a Socratic "proof" aim at a verdict. There is that in Plato which suggests that imposing a verdict is the business of "persuasion" rather than of "reason." The business of reason is to see. What is to be seen here, in the *Phaedo*, is what it means to die, and therefore what it means to live. Socrates is at this moment close enough to both states to see more clearly than is usual, and all he really wants to do is get his loving friends to share his present view.

Everyone will readily agree to the following elementary points:

1. that dying is quite real: "we believe that there is such a thing . . ." (64).

2. that what is real about it is separation.

3. that what are separated are soul and body.

(This looks like "begging the question"—or assuming what is to be proved; but it is not necessarily that. All we have said need not amount to more than saying that when you open an envelope you separate the flap from the back. We are not yet committed to very exacting assumptions about the "flap" or the "back.")

But now we are going to make a more grievous assumption. The separation has also to do with "pleasure." In short, it is no "fun" to die; and dying is farewell to all that.

But the philosopher does it gladly and continually. If "separating" from the possibility of pleasure is what dying is—and that seems a reasonable interpretation, certainly in conformity with common sense, which never "wants to die"—the philosopher knows what "dying" is all the time, and he has always been in love with it.

There is a certain amount of playing with words here, but somewhat more than that is involved, because behind the words are attitudes (such as "who wants to die?" and "Oh, what fun it is to live!" etc.), and the attitudes are being true to themselves.

We are "proving" something—that is to say, seeing it—but it does not yet seem very important. It becomes important when "knowledge" does.

In sum: Pleasure and body are identified. Whatever takes flight from the one takes flight from the other. The flight of the soul from the body and the well-known life-long flight of the philosopher from pleasure (Socrates was thinking about it after they took his chains off) suggest the close relation between these two separations. There is therefore a presumption that they come to some kind of fusion in a common climactic moment, which is dying. The further presumption is that the philosopher's farther flight beyond that moment will share whatever qualities the soul enjoys in the same beyond.

It would be reassuring if we could now prove that what the soul enjoys is immortality.

Let us strengthen our previous presumptions by considering the case not negatively but positively.

The flight from pleasure is a flight from the senses; but this flight from the senses, considered positively, is the "actual acquirement of knowledge" (65).

Here again the paths of the philosopher and of the soul appear to coincide. They both acquire knowledge under the same conditions, and these conditions seem to have their optimal fulfilment at the same moment: death. (We still do not know whether the soul is immortal. Of course, if the soul is, then the philosopher would be too, in so far as he will be content to be altogether a soul.[8])

Our next clue about the soul is from the nature of its knowledge. Knowledge is *of* "being," and in some sense knowledge *is* "being." (What is already implicit here is the doctrine of "participation," but we do not yet have that doctrine except in so far as we may "recollect," from the *Symposium*, that mortal things by love "partake of immortality.")

Simmias now has to answer a series of very simple questions. Are there absolutes, asks Socrates, such as justice, beauty, good? Yes, of course. What knows them, soul or body? Soul. Again, what are the optimal conditions of such knowing? When the soul is separated from the body.

The previous proof has been restated with this addition: that the

---

[8] This raises a further question as to the status not merely of the soul but of the *human being* after death. That question is touched on in the *Phaedo*, not dialectically, but in terms of the eschatological hypothesis, or myth, at the end (110–15). With this may be compared the myth of Er at the end of the *Republic*.

existential status of the objects of knowledge has been made the subject of an emphatic reminder. It is in the realm of "being" that the objects of knowledge are, and that is where the soul will be when it knows them. To be "in" that realm is to constitute that realm. The soul and the things it knows share that constitution of being.

The knowing process is now mapped out as a negative, or reverse, form of the *paideia* of the *Symposium*.

In the *paideia* which is death, one love must give way to another. Separate the loves—the higher from the lower; the love of money from the love of truth or ideas. That is what the philosopher does when he dies, and that is also what he lives for.

How easily, too, the death *paideia* relates to the familiar civic virtues —such as courage and temperance—which have already been celebrated by Phaedrus and Pausanias, by Alcibiades and Aristophanes, at an earlier banquet. It trips off the tongue of Socrates—obviously indifferent to the jailer's warning not to talk too much—like a remembered poem: the beauty of being temperate or courageous, when you are dead, is that it is absolutely without contradiction; it has cast off that double nature of love's *paideia* and is now itself, without admixture of its opposite, uncompounded by recipe of greater and less. Dying does what initiation into the mysteries does (69), only it does it better and does it absolutely; once for all.

Cebes is deeply impressed, only not convinced. Will Socrates please try to convince him? All that has been said still depends on a very simple thing, namely whether the soul does exist when a man is dead.

Socrates will try to found the argument on stronger "probabilities." The following "probabilities" are now encompassed (70–2):

1. There is an "ancient doctrine" that the souls of the living are born from the dead. The least the doctrine implies is that the souls must "exist" in the other world.

2. This doctrine seems to gain credibility from the familiar Heracleitean notion that "all things which have opposites [are] generated out of their opposites." [9]

3. This "universal opposition of all things" is a process manifested in stages or intermediate degrees.

4. If we assume the truth of the foregoing and apply it to the life process, the conclusions then are: (a) That the life process is not linear but cyclical; that is, the wheel of life-death always turns up "life"

---

[9] The mechanical frequency with which the Heracleitean doctrine enters into the Platonic arguments makes it seem that the doctrine was part of conversational ritual in those days. As a cliché of explanation it is not seriously examined until transformed by Aristotle into the new, though derivative, categories of his own "contraries."

at one point or other. (b) For if the life process *were* linear, then all things would by this time have passed into death—the end of the line; and nothing would be alive.

It is now "probable" that "the living spring from the dead," that "the souls of the dead are in existence"; and that "the good souls have a better portion than the evil." (But the last point was not among the questions raised).

It is clear the force of the argument depends upon the value of the Heracleitean doctrine, generalized and applied to the life process. So applied, that process would presumably have three terms: two opposites, and an intermediate third term. The opposites are "life" and "death" (whatever they may be). What is the third, or intermediate, term? It must be the "biologic process," or the "ordinary living," which lies between being born and dying, as it also lies between the two *real* opposites ("life" and "death"). Ordinary life has some of both in it.

But in that case, what *is* the difference between "life" and "death," and what were we trying to prove? ("The way up and the way down are one and the same," Heracleitus said.) Is the difference merely the relative one between "up" and "down," which is obliterated by standing on one's head or living at the antipodes? No; there must be some more vital difference. We may as well begin to take it up.

The old physics of Heracleitus has allowed the crucial distinctions to elude us; but Platonic "psychology," or theory of knowledge, might pin them down.

Cebes draws in Simmias (73–6).

Isn't there a doctrine of "recollection," of which one has heard before? Isn't there such a thing as impressions or experiences associating in the mind; and when they associate, isn't there a third thing that links them, which third thing is never the impression or experience itself; that is to say, neither hot nor cold, neither lover nor lyre, neither like nor unlike; but an abstraction or conception? And is it not true that your perceiving and interpreting, and therefore your knowing, must depend on that abstraction?

For Plato the abstraction is not a mere formality, like the "equal" sign in an equation, but contains and signifies an original grasp on the sources of our knowledge.

In knowing anything, we are therefore making a return to origins. This origin is *before* any actual experience by the senses; and this "beforeness" signifies, in the argument, an absolute distinctiveness of nature: between idea and sense experience; therefore between soul and body; therefore, by extension, between life and death.

Socrates' belief in immortality is thus dependent on his theory of knowledge.

But the proof has now been pointed backwards: not that the soul goes on, but that it pre-exists. "Yes, Socrates," says Simmias, "I am convinced that there is precisely the same necessity for the one as for the other; and the argument retreats successfully to the position that the existence of the soul before birth cannot be separated from the existence of the essence of which you speak . . ." (77).

Now it is only necessary to complete the proof in the other direction: "before" has to be supplemented by "after," and then the resulting sum will be "forever."

The most provoking puzzle in the *Phaedo* lies in this shift from the proof of "before" to the proof of "after," a shift which coincides with the shift of interlocutors from Simmias back to Cebes.

If the company has swallowed this camel of "before," why should it strain at this gnat of "after"?

For the proof of "before" is of incomparably greater difficulty and, what is more, is proposed and accepted as a satisfying "proof," almost to be taken literally, whereas the proof of "after" is exalted hypothesis, rendered as brilliantly, as concretely, and as exhaustively as the circumstances permit; but never rested on, always a mere delaying action against the jailer's cup, and by delaying, transcending it. But the proof of "before" does not have that justifying occasion or obstacle.

We may now recapitulate, as Socrates does in the long central passage (77–85) that follows.

Plato has been weaving together two major doctrinal contributions to the theme, and giving to each a Platonic cast:

1. He uses the Heracleitean doctrine of the blending of the opposites, but he recognizes in the biologic opposites of "life" and "death" a qualitatively superior first term,—that is, "life."

2. Incorporating the old doctrine of metempsychosis into his theory of knowledge, he makes the intermediary flux of valid sense experience dependent on "recollection" of knowledge.

3. The superior first term in knowledge, as in all derivative or dependent forms of it (such as seeing and believing), is the abstraction, essence, absolute, essential nature, form, or idea.

4. Qualitatively first terms, wherever they occur, in knowledge and in existence, both come before and outlast all other terms.

There is no reason whatsoever to question the good faith of Simmias or Cebes in at first assenting so readily to these complexities, even though the host and author of them is a man about to die. The best reason for their assenting lies not in the courtesies of the situation, but in the fact that they cannot refute them.

The refutation is still as difficult as the demonstration, or even more so.

The difficulty of the argument may be seen if we note how Socrates has shifted the questions from (a) a temporal ("before and after") type of question, to (b) a quasi-spatial type ("visible" vs. "invisible," "corporeal" vs. "incorporeal," "here" vs. "there") to (c) a logical ("superior knowledge" vs. "derivative sense") type of question. The last, by fusing the first two, purports to transcend them.[1]

In short, the soul lives on because she *must*. She must—if what? If the whole previous argument—the beguilement, the "solution" of the puzzlement, and the exaltation along the way—is to make any sense. They would be very large matters to sacrifice in the interests of mere and proper logic; and in any case, no one seems inclined to retrace the arduous way. The time is coming near.

After a moment's silence and a profound bow to the pregnancy of the occasion, Simmias takes the argument up again. He has a very simple question.

Suppose, he says, O Socrates, you take all those glowing terms of yours, which you have applied to the soul—the "invisible," the "incorporeal," the "perfect," the "divine," all those metaphors of power and persuasion—and suppose you apply them to the musical situation. Would you not say, for instance, that the harmony or the tune produced from the lyre is all that you claim for the soul, when contrasted with the mud and glue, the sticks and stone of which the lyre is made? But what of it? However "divine" and "invisible" the harmony is, does it live on when the lyre is broken?

Obviously it does not, and neither does the soul, if we suppose that the soul is merely a "harmony."

Let me put it this way, Cebes adds. If we grant that the soul is "stronger and more lasting" than the body, all that this proves, if anything, is that the soul ought to "outlast" the body; it does not prove that it will last "forever" or is immortal. Suppose, for instance, I weave a coat and that I outlast it, as I expect to do. That doesn't prove that I will outlast the last coat I weave. (On the contrary, one might be buried in it.) Suppose we assume that the soul constantly reweaves the body during a man's lifetime, or that it weaves many bodies and will enter them successively. But will it not, at long last, and inevitably, weary of the labor and dissolve in death?

What now of immortality?

The company feels that a "wound" has been delivered to the

---

[1] The difference in the order of merit in these types of questions is partly the difference between philosophers; between Plato and Aristotle, Aristotle and Hume, Descartes and Berkeley, Plato and Kant; and among those divergences, the disciplines of philosophy and science, science and religion, religion and art find their different ways.

argument. The drama of the issue is overshadowed by the drama of the moment.

Socrates, moved by love of those who are opposing him, warns against "misology" (89), or letting disillusionment with an argument lead to disillusionment with the truth; and he reveals what we have known, that he is not a "partisan" on the present issue; he is trying to convince, not his hearers, but himself (91), of the truth.

Returning to the argument, Socrates divides it into two.

First, the "harmony" argument of Simmias:

1. Of Socrates' previous argument Simmias has found the "recollection" and "pre-existence" arguments acceptable (91).

2. But if he accepts "recollection" and "pre-existence" and what they imply about the nature of the soul, then he cannot argue that the soul is a "harmony" in the musical sense of the term.

3. Because, in the musical sense, the "harmony" is simply the organized musical *result, ex post facto* to the instrument and to the musical parts, such as tones, and always admitting of "degrees"—that is, of more or less successful organization as music. Moreover, the musical "harmony" can never be said to be in opposition to the instrument.

4. Whereas, the soul is not a *result* but, according to the doctrine of "recollection," is prior to the body; it is always soul, not "more or less"; and if it is still to be taken as "harmony," then all souls must be equally "harmony" in the same sense; which can only mean that there is no difference between one soul and another with respect to virtue and vice; which is manifestly not the case.

Finally, it is notorious that the soul is often in opposition to the body. The soul is therefore not a "harmony" (92).

The argument now turns to Cebes, and in so doing approaches its uttermost of gravity and seriousness. "And whether the soul enters into the body once only or many times," says Socrates to Cebes, "does not, as you say, make any difference in the fears of individuals. For any man, who is not devoid of sense, must fear, if he has no knowledge, and can give no account of the soul's immortality. This, or something like this, I suspect to be your notion, Cebes; and I designedly recur to it in order that nothing may escape us, and that you may, if you wish, add or subtract anything" (95).

"But," says Cebes, "as far as I see at present, I have nothing to add or subtract: I mean what you say that I mean" (95).

In other words: we return to our starting point, that the soul has an "after" existence *because* it has had a "before" existence. And all you have to do, Socrates, is persuade me of the force of that "because." I am not so very convinced thus far; not enough to overcome my fear, for my own death and yours.

In other words, Socrates, I am not really concerned that you may
have lived "before" (pre-existence, or metempsychosis, or reincarnation,
and all that). I am concerned, very simply, that you are going to die; and
that that will be the end.

"Socrates paused a while, and seemed to be absorbed in reflection." (96)

There will be no further hesitation before the issue, or flirtation
with it, in the mere dance of dialectic.

The mask is off: the argument has to do with *causes*; with the true
and proper *explanation* of anything; and not with the "where" or the
"when" or the "how" of generation and corruption, of living and dying,
or of anything that happens (because all that happens is a living and a
dying of a something), but with the "why" of it. That is all, says
Socrates, that Cebes wants to know. That is all that Socrates ever
wanted to know. (Not "how" we die, but "why" we do it; and if we
knew, in the Platonic sense of knowing, the answer to that, the soul
would be immortal!)

That is a child's question—if not a childish one—and Socrates
is quite cheerful about it: it is the only thing he ever wanted to
know.

The quest of this child's grail—the eternal "why"—led him to the
so-called "theory of Ideas," or the Forms. And he tells about it through
the medium of a short and pointed intellectual autobiography (97).

He went from childish questions about one and two, adding and
dividing, to science questions and some ancient science fiction. None of
the unfinished cosmologies of his predecessors the great Ionian nature-
philosophers, detained him very long. He made a longer pause over the
doctrine that had come his way of a man called Anaxagoras, who explained in a book that "mind was the disposer and cause of all."
Socrates was attracted, as one might expect, to any doctrine upholding
"mind."

But this book of Anaxagoras proved to be the greatest, though the
last, disillusionment of all. For the "mind" that Anaxagoras taught,
when it came right down to it, was not the mind of "cause" but merely
the sum of "conditions," which Anaxagoras mislabeled "mind."

Socrates offers a test case. All he wants, for example, from any
explanatory doctrine would be an answer to the question: why am I in
jail? That is what he means by "cause"—not this parody of "cause" that
would allege the reason to lie in Socrates' bones and his joints, his
cartilaginous tissue, and, perhaps, his neural and fleshly layers—for these
are merely the histological and mechanical "conditions" of his being
there—but rather the one true cause of his being about to die, namely,
that the judges of Athens ("How you, O Athenians, have been affected

by my accusers . . . !") have condemned him to death, and he, Socrates, has already declined the opportunity readied for him to escape.[2]

"There is surely a strange confusion of cause and conditions in all this," says Socrates. "It may be said, indeed, that without bones and muscles and all the other parts of the body I cannot execute my purposes. But to say that I do as I do because of them, and that this is the way in which the mind acts, and not from the choice of the best, is a very careless and idle mode of speaking. I wonder that they cannot distinguish the causes from the condition, which the many, feeling about in the dark, are always mistaking and misnaming" (99).

Not the mechanisms of the world, but "the obligatory and containing power of the good" is what Socrates means by cause.

All this, so far, sounds like a grand disgression, that a man might be entitled to who is about to die.

Socrates' audience does not think so.

They know that what Socrates is confessing is not a success story, the culmination of his researches, but his hypothesis of last resort. That hypothesis is: that there exists an "absolute," the Form or Idea or essential nature of goodness or beauty in itself. Socrates came to the theory of the Forms as the "why," or "because," of his being in jail. He will no longer "prove" it; he will simply "assume" it.

What is being explained? Practically everything: all appearances or phenomena, and the differences between them.

We have to remember that these differences *are* the phenomena and all the phenomena, both sensuous and ethical. The differences between the beautiful and the ugly, the greater and the lesser, the better and the worse, these and their varieties constitute the whole spectrum of what you see, hear, touch, and otherwise encounter in the realm of encountering, and this is what we mean by experience or phenomena.

There is, therefore, only one thing to explain, and when you have explained that you have explained all: namely, *why* the difference? Why is it *better*, for example, for Socrates to have *more* jail and *less* freedom of one sort, to face *more* "death" and look forward to *less* "life," inasmuch as the *greater* bulk of the men of Athens have chosen differences of precisely another sort, namely, *more* of their sort of freedom and *less* of Socrates' kind?

Granted the hypothesis—namely, that there is an absolute or an essential Form, by whatever name, and that it has all the "immortal" attributes which have been ascribed to it, of invisibility, indivisibility, intangibility, timelessness, and the like—the explanation is very simple,

---

[2] As recorded in the Dialogue *Crito*. The account of the trial is in the *Apology*.

and it is contained in one word: *participation.* That is, the "differences" in the world, the varieties of encountering—chairs, tables, jails, love, and death—these are explainable as degrees of participation.[3]

The dialectic of participation is the grand finale of the Dialogue (100–6).

As usual with such a dialectic in Plato, it both reviews the phenomena and interprets them. But the descriptive review, which is also a recapitulation of the main threads of previous argument, is now attached to and dependent on a position which nothing in the Dialogue has succeeded in shaking, but which, on the contrary, has towered higher, as if on ever firmer foundations, with every shift and turn, and that is the theory of Ideas.

In sum: The Platonic theory of knowledge has been shown to be the only feasible explanation of cause. The cause of phenomena is participation in the Forms. The cause of the dissolution of certain kinds of phenomena is the approach of incompatible or opposite Forms.

Thus, snow has formed a union with "cold," so that the approach of "heat," the incompatible opposite of "cold," leads to melting—in other words, the flight of "cold."

And the number three has formed that kind of union with the idea of the "odd," so that the approach of "even" to the three is similarly incompatible. In such a case, the incompatibility expresses itself not as the sense experience of "melting" but as the logical experience of absurdity.

We have no other kind of causal explanation of *anything,* Plato says. We must therefore apply it to the case of body and soul, life and death, which are surely not immune to causal explanation, but, on the contrary, the situation where such explanation is most urgent or most required. The soul, by hypothesis, is of the form "life." Life, by definition, is "deathless." At the approach of death, the soul departs the body and remains as it was, forever "deathless."

If we challenge this conclusion, we can only henceforth do so by challenging the most innocent feature of our existence: the simple understanding of simple situations, such as melting and multiplying.

We have, in the Platonic phrase, "saved the appearances." And by doing so we could not help but prove the immortality of the soul.

The time remaining is only sufficient for some cosmological specu-

---

[3] Participation is a two-way street. There is the farther end, where the participation takes place or is aimed at. And there is right here where you start from, the world of what is commonly called things. There are thus two problems: why things participate in the Forms, and why the Forms got entangled with things. The *Phaedo* deals only with the first question. The second is dealt with to some extent in Plato's *Timaeus* and *Parmenides* and—from a different, more "Aristotelian," perspective—in the *Philebus.*

lation about the soul's *paideia* after death, which need by no means
turn out exactly as described but may serve to point the moral: that
the soul had better know once for all, and all through life, just what
her "opposites" are and what the penalty is for flirtation with the in-
compatibles of her true nature—that is, with injustice or corruption or
ugliness or falsehood.

The company agrees. What choice has it? The jailer comes with
the cup. And Socrates' last words are to his friend. "Crito," he says, "I
owe a cock to Asclepius; please remember to pay it."

Asclepius was the god of healing.

THE SOPHIST

The ostensible theme of this Dialogue is the definition of the sophist;
but its real theme is language and existence, or the nature and function
of the philosopher.

The explicit characterization of the latter would presumably have
been given in a later Dialogue, which Plato never wrote—perhaps because it did not really need to be written. For the philosopher has already been limned in his living model in the *Symposium*, sketched in
the quality of his moral and metaphysical passion in the *Phaedo*, and
assigned to his social, administrative, and educational function in the
Republic. Other Dialogues of Plato fill out the picture, both in its details and in its broad outlines.

In the *Sophist* the nature of the philosopher arises, as it were, by
negation. He is that which the sophist is not. But the two are very
closely allied—more closely, perhaps, than is comfortable for either, both
with respect to the common source in method from which they spring
and with respect to the function which they both elect to exercise. The
sophist exercises that function perversely, and therefore with disreputable
results. The philosopher exercises it nobly, and with results akin to the
divine. But though the sophist is the philosopher's obverse, he has made
the nature of philosophy's essential problems clearer than anybody else
has done.

The argument of the *Sophist* develops in the following stages.

1. Without prologue or the customary devices of recall,[4] four
people suddenly stand before us: Theodorus, Socrates, a Stranger from

---

[4] It is not clear whether the *Sophist*, though presented as a continuation of
"yesterday's" *Theaetetus*, is also part of the same manuscript "roll" which at the
beginning of the *Theaetetus* gives us Euclid's "recollection" of the latter Dialogue.

Elea, and the young Theaetetus. Socrates proposes to the Stranger the theme of discussion—namely, the nature of the "sophist, statesman, and philosopher"—and nominates Theaetetus to be the Stranger's interlocutor, so that he may avoid the tedium of long speeches (216–18). Having set the dialectic up, Socrates plays no further role in the Dialogue.

2. There follows a long and complex demonstration of the pursuit of a definition by "division" or "dichotomizing."

This demonstration is tedious; it is obviously in part satirical and shows some of the excess of the overdevelopment of an angry point (as in Swift's *Gulliver's Travels*, where the reader perhaps gets the idea of what can be done with the contrast of big and little long before the author has finished developing it). Who or what is the object of the satire?

There are the following possibilities: (a) the historical sophists of Socrates' day, during the latter half of the fifth century; (b) the rival philosophic schools, contemporary with the writing of this Dialogue, of which the school of Isocrates is possibly an example; (c) a "sociological" type, constructed by Plato (no doubt derived from hints both historical and contemporary), to serve as whipping boy or object lesson in this discussion; (d) the philosophic method itself, as perhaps practiced by some members of the Platonic Academy, including Plato himself. This would mean that the Dialogue is in part self-satire, and therefore meant therapeutically.

Of the above possibilities, the first seems too remote as an object for such heavy satire. Plato is, after all, writing at a distance of fifty to sixty years from the contemporaries of Socrates. This possibility may therefore be dismissed. Possibility (b) is intrinsically plausible, but has no other evidence to support it.[5] Possibility (c) seems to conform to a general intention in all the Dialogues, namely to give to ideas and problems of universal import a local and topical application. Possibility (d) is what we ought to assume a thinker like Plato was capable of—namely, some self-directed irony—and what he may have been driven to by observation of the growing professionalism of the ambitious young philosophers in the Academy.

The method of "division" as practiced in this instance seeks to find a class of objects, situations, or actions that is on the face of it com-

---

[5] The possibility that Isocrates is specifically the target of the satire may or may not be rendered more plausible by the fact, pointed out by Burnet, op. cit., pp. 273 ff., that the "influence of Isokrates is strongly marked for the first time" in this Dialogue. In the absence of external evidence, estimating such a possibility depends to some extent on one's view of the psychology of satire. Ernest Hemingway's early work, *Torrents of Spring*, is a satire to the point of parody on the style of Sherwood Anderson. It could be read to show the "marked influence of Sherwood Anderson on Ernest Hemingway."

parable to the thing being defined. The objects must have at least one feature in common in order to make the comparison possible at all. In the Platonic world of thought it would be hard to find any two activities which do not at least share the common feature of being "arts": which means merely that they are systematic activities aiming at an end. Thus, "sophism" is an art and so is hunting, both belong to the acquisitive-coercive arts, and so forth.

The method which is being satirized is, then, comparison (or analogizing) and "division" as the primitive, or regressive, form of dialectic. When dialectic does not rise above its mere mechanics of operation, then it is no better than the game of "twenty questions," an exploratory guessing at how to classify things that might just as well remain unclassified.

If one substitutes the phrase "disputatious triviality" for "sophism," Plato's attack becomes of wide-ranging application, and the chips are entitled to fall where they may.

In the application of the method of "dichotomy" in the first part of the *Sophist* (218–27), it is not possible to "sift" or "winnow" the method as meant seriously from the method as satirized.

Its first phase culminates in a fivefold classification of the sophist, as (1) "a paid hunter after wealth and youth"; (2) "a merchant in the goods of the soul"; (3) "a retailer" of the same; (4) "a manufacturer" of the same; (5) a "controversialist," or "Eristic" professional.

A sixth classification follows, but it turns out to be quite inconsistent with the previous five. For at the sixth turn, we arrive at an "art" which seems to be also practiced by the sophist, but which is in its own nature too good to be allowed to him. This is the subart called "purification." The sophist is now not a "hunter" or "fisher" of men, but the "purifier" of their minds or souls by the therapeutic art of "cross-examination" (231). The sophist, it would appear, offers men the tragic catharsis of philosophy itself.

3. We have arrived at the point where the enemy of the good has turned into its spokesman. There is something misleading in any classification that leads to definition of the sophist as "purifier."

He cannot be a real purifier because he makes the indiscriminate claim to know "all things." But this is impossible. (It is Socrates' claim to uniqueness, in the *Apology*, that he alone knows that he does not know.) The case of the sophist—who has suddenly and illegitimately emerged on the side of the angels—must therefore be re-examined.

The man who claims to know "all things" is a "magician" or conjurer—a "juggler and *imitator*," in a word, a dealer in illusion or likenesses of reality; and we must therefore re-examine the case from the standpoint of a new enterprise of "dichotomy": the subdivision of the art of *imitation*. (231–6).

4. The various arts of imitation—both good and bad—have to do with the problem of things that *appear* or *seem* to exist but do not really do so. They do not have real *being*; what they have is *not-being*.

What does this mean, and how is it possible? How can something have, or exemplify, *not-being*, or nonexistence, and yet be a something in any sense at all?

It was Parmenides—the man whom the Eleatic Stranger refers to as his "father" in philosophy—who denied that this was possible and issued the admonition, which the Stranger quotes, against occupying oneself with the dangerous and repellent idea that the nonexistent *is*.

But if there is no such thing as the nonexistent, then everything in some sense is, and what is the difference between a fact and a non-fact, and how does one establish the difference between them or speak of it?

We see, then, how the "many headed sophist" has performed a service to philosophy, compelling us, quite against our will, to admit the existence of not-being (240).

That is what comes of forcing a man into a corner: we have convicted him of dealing in illusions. But then he does deal in *something*, doesn't he? What is the status in *being* or *existence* of the nonthings in which he deals?

The sophist has forced us not to be so cheerful about it all. When we convict him of being a mere opinionator, or "falsifier" and "deceiver," we had better supply, if we can, a criterion of the distinction between *knowledge* and *opinion*, between *true* statements and *false* ones, between things that are and things that *are not*. There has to be some status for *error* if we are going to save the possibility of *truth*.

The Stranger asks: "Does false opinion think that things which are *are not*, or that in a certain sense they are?" (240).

The latter, says Theaetetus; and the reverse would be also true; that is, that false opinion must also think that things that do exist *do not*. So that "there is no other way in which a false proposition can arise," except by finding a meaning to the paradox that *not-being is*. How else could we determine that a false proposition "is not" true?

In this exchange the Stranger and Theaetetus point up a standing problem for philosophy, from Parmenides to F. H. Bradley, from Zeno to Wittgenstein.

5. We are thus led to the problem of being.

The Eleatic Stranger now shows a genius for generalizing synthesis that is at least the equal of, and is less tedious than, the analytic "dividing" which has gone before. He sums up three great historical views on the problem.

a. The Eleatic and Ionian views may be grouped together, exemplifying a common concern with being as the problem of the one and the many or the whole and the part. The question would be whether part as well as whole has a status in existence and, if so, how the part achieves the negative status of *not* being the whole. And how do they come together and go apart in those physical *processes* which the Ionians made so much of? Parmenides crushed the question out of existence. The "all is one," he said. But then it turned out that there were "many" names, or characterizations, for that "one," and so that question was reborn as that of "the one and the many."

The Eleatics and Ionians rode roughshod over the contradictions in the problem, the former with transcendentalizing metaphors and the latter with psycho-chemical ones, and on the whole they merely left it for the sophist to make the most of it. The Eleatics seem to have denied, or made unintelligible, the possibility of error; the Ionians perhaps gave it, though inadvertently, a status equal, though opposite, to truth.

What the Stranger calls the "war of the gods and the giants" on the issue advanced it somewhat farther.

b. The "giants" are the mechanists or materialists of Socrates' day and later. They are more sophisticated than they used to be in the days when they were simple metaphysical atomists; at least they no longer insist on simple "tangibility" (or "squeezability") as the one and only proof of existence. But from their more sophisticated views we may extract an intelligible, if not conclusive, definition of being: let the "power to produce effects" henceforth be their definition of real existence (247).

c. The "gods" are the "friends of the ideas."

The position taken up is that of Socrates in the *Phaedo*, though not the same in all its accents and ramifications. It goes beyond the *Phaedo* and at the same time comes closer to home; for when the argument is over and done with, we are back with the problems of common-sense assertion that the *Phaedo* had vaulted over. The final preoccupation will be with the laws of meaningful speech, whatever source and origin those laws may have, whether in the timeless realm of ideas above or in the restless generation of things below.

The premises of the "idealists" are: that there is a world of being, which knowledge knows; and that there is a world of bodies, which generation is. The former is the *Symposium's* absolute, and the source and guide of its *paideia*. The latter is the stumbling block of the *Phaedo*, which it is necessary to remove by showing its inessential status or separating it from the soul so that the soul can know itself in deathless truth.

In the *Phaedo* the polarities of body and being, of generation and essence, were brought together by a type of process called "participation," and it is by the participation of bodies in the *ideas* that are, that knowledge knows the *things* that are, and, presumably, those which are not, as when snow *is not* cold any longer.

It is this Socratic grasp at knowledge and its theory which gives us here the clue to the answer to the sophist and to his paradoxes of being. For if intelligence or mind knows "being," when it knows at all, then, at least, being is acted upon, or moved, in so far as it is known.

"Being" is, in this respect, the passive subject of that *power* which, whether active or passive, the materialists agreed was the mark of true existence. But from the point of view of its intrinsic, qualitative superiority, "being" can have no less life or activity than mind which is seeking to know it. It is inconceivable, in other words, to leave "being" in the state of mere passivity.

But the obverse of this argument now asserts itself: "being" that is activity must also be in some sense at rest; how else could we get and retain the *changelessness* of the "equal," the "beautiful," the "long" and the "short" of it, which we needed in order to know anything at all?

We have now shown that being both *is* and *is not* in motion; *is* and *is not* at rest; and therefore *is* and *is not* what it is.

The problem that was provoked by the facts and exigencies of "participation" can only be *solved* by the same. "Participation" has limits; different wave lengths, as it were; and built-in *rules*, by which the universal participants must abide.

The science of dialectic, it now appears, is the science of those limits and their rules. Sophism, it will later appear, consists in acknowledging them, no less than dialectic does, but it does so by flouting and perverting them. Sophism is dialectic trivialized and corrupted (246–54).

6. We are now ready to lay down the rules, even if only provisionally.

These are the rules of classes and genera, of things that will mingle or participate and things that will not, of the built-in restraints and attractions of the world. Both logic and things, both the physical opposites of the *Phaedo's* beginning and the logical opposites of the *Phaedo's* end, seem to have a common structure. That structure is sought by Plato in his "categories of being."

Plato himself has sought other types of categorial structure, in the *Philebus*, for instance, and in the *Timaeus*. The search persists in Aristotle, in the medieval thinkers, and in Kant, and still goes on in the mathematical logicians, the existentialists, and the linguistic philosophers of our day.

There are, the Stranger says, five provisional rules or categories of knowing, five basic ways of relation among all things. They are: being itself; rest; motion; the same; and the other.

Not-being is *other* than (any particular form of) being. But insofar as any particular is itself distinguishable, it partakes of otherness, or is the *same* as not-being. And the *otherness* of things pervades the whole of being; so that not-being always *is*, even in things that are otherwise the *same. Identity* and *difference* are both *absolute* and *relative.*

The philosopher has helped the sophist to his feet. The latter had stumbled on the validity—in fact, the necessity—of making distinctions if we are to speak and act at all; only the sophist, through perversity, got entangled in the project and vulgarized it to the point of no return. For, says the Stranger, "the attempt at universal separation," an attempt which has characterized the endless fragmentation of sophistry, "is the final annihilation of all reasoning; for only by the union of conceptions with one another do we attain to discourse of reason" (259).

7. Our final goal is, "to assert discourse to be a kind of being; for if we could not, the worst of all consequences would follow; we should have no philosophy" (260).

Discourse, here, is not in the heavens above or the waters beneath, neither where the "giants" dig nor where the "gods" survey, but in the mouths of men. And that is where the "soul" is, presumably still as deathless as it ever was.

Is it not evident, the Stranger says, that "thought, opinion, and imagination . . . exist in our minds both as false and true?" (263). And "thought," the first of these classes, the thing that has to do with the Ideas or the Forms, as well as with being and the categories just established, "thought and speech are the same; with this exception, that what is called thought is the unuttered conversation of the soul with itself . . . But the stream of thought which flows through the lips and is audible, is called speech." [6]

All we need, then, in order to establish the *being* of thought and speech, is a science of what can be truly said and what cannot. Such a science would later come to be called "theory of predication."

---

[6] "At another time she [the young Helen Keller] asked, 'What is a soul?' 'No one knows,' I replied; 'but we know it is not the body, and it is that part of us which thinks and loves and hopes . . . [and] is invisible.' 'But if I write what my soul thinks,' she said, 'it will be visible, and the words will be its body.' " From Anne Sullivan's account, 1891, of the education of Helen Keller, in *The Story of My Life,* by Helen Keller (New York: Doubleday; 1954), p. 372.

So far as Plato is concerned, the basic equipment is already before us, partly in the theory of Ideas or Forms and the mind's relation to them and partly in that refinement of the theory of participation (or proper and improper mingling) which has just been worked out in the five categories of being and not-being.

To that equipment we now add the theory of the sentence—its basic and inalienable parts of noun and verb, or subject and predicate, and the way in which they properly hang together. "Theaetetus sits," is now a true sentence because the being of what the sentence says is the *same* as the being of Theaetetus and his action at this particular moment; and "Theaetetus flies" is a false sentence, because the being of what it says is *other* than what Theaetetus is now doing. And we verify the status in being of both the saying and the doing by investigation of that mixture of "sensation and opinion" which is what supplies our knowledge of events.

If our investigation has to go that far—that is to say, if we have any actual problem about what our thought and sensation actually are or have been with reference to a particular situation—the Platonic modes of investigation are before us: being, motion, rest, same, and other.

If we chose, for example, to concentrate on the investigation of "motion and rest," we might be led to the psychology and physiology, or even to the physics, of our knowing processes; or to their history, in motivation and in relation to "other minds." Or if we chose to concentrate on the being proper of the self, we might confront the difficulty of the self in remaining what it is (the same) or in trying *not* to be it.

Complications and paradoxes lie latent in these categories, which it has been partly the business of later chapters in the history of philosophy to name (for if they have no name they cannot be talked about) and, so far as possible, to clarify: theory of predication; the "calculus" of sentences and their predicates that symbolic logic has added to the categories of traditional logic; ontological arguments, or arguments about being, with reference to God and man; the Hegelian thesis and antithesis of "sameness" and "otherness" in the historical interplay of man with society and nature; the absoluteness of the claim of not-being in contemporary existentialist philosophies; the claims of sensation to be the final arbiter of "sameness" vs. "otherness," of true and false, of affirmation and negation, in the empiricist tradition; all these and others lie latent in the final arguments here. There was no reason for the Eleatic Stranger to have gone on and on. There is no way of certainly telling what he, or Plato through him, would have said on these and sundry other related matters.

Other philosophers have had, and will have, their say.

It remains only to round out the argument by formulating the farewell definition for the sophist. He has performed his constructive function in the earlier argument in two major ways: by showing us how, if you simply obvert him, he might be the true philosopher, who "purifies" by cross-questioning; and by calling attention to the pervasiveness and even universality of not-being. But "the corruption of the best is always the worst." [7] And the sophist has corrupted the two aspects of the good that discourse is: both cross-questioning and the category of the *not*.

He practices an art of manipulating abstractions, such as "the figure or form of justice and virtue in general" (267), and he does so without any knowledge of their true being or with perverse indifference to the distinction between when the form of justice *is* and when it is *not*. He does this "in private, and in short speeches compels the person who is conversing with him to contradict himself" (268). This, it should be remembered, is doing something to the soul. He has thus earned his final epitaph, which seems considerably milder at the end of the Dialogue than much of what has gone before. But that is because as an adversary figure he has been cut down to size. His surviving role is as a foil to right speech and true philosophy.

Henry M. Rosenthal

SELECTED BIBLIOGRAPHY

Works

The Dialogues of Plato. Translated into English by B. Jowett; the third and last edition, with marginal notes by the translator; in 2 vols. New York: Random House; 1937. The complete Dialogues are also available in the Plato section of the Loeb Classical Library, Harvard University Press. The volumes of the Loeb translations contain the Greek text on facing pages.

Thirteen Epistles of Plato. Translated with introduction and notes by L. A. Post. Oxford: Clarendon Press; 1925.

The Platonic Epistles. Translated with introduction and notes by J. Harward. Cambridge: Cambridge University Press; 1932.

Single Dialogues, and groups of them, are available in a great variety of editions, both paperback and hard-cover. Some of these editions contain extensive scholarly introductions and notes bearing on particular points of interpretation. Especially helpful are the translations of and commentaries on the *Phaedo* by R. Hackforth (Cambridge: Cambridge University Press; 1955) and R. S. Bluck (London: Rout-

---

[7] Cf. Aristotle, *Nichomachean Ethics*, Bk. VIII, ch. 10.

ledge & Kegan Paul; 1955) and on the *Sophist* by F. M. Cornford (London: Routledge & Kegan Paul; 1951). An attractive translation of the *Symposium* is by W. Hamilton, in a Penguin paperback.

About Plato

Bluck, R. S.: *Plato's Life and Thought*. Boston: Beacon Press; 1951.

Burnet, John: *Early Greek Philosophy*. Fourth edition. London: Adam and Charles Black; 1930.

————: *Greek Philosophy: Thales to Plato*. London: Macmillan; 1914.

————: *Platonism*. Berkeley: University of California Press; 1928.

Field, G. C.: *Plato and His Contemporaries*. London: Methuen; 1930.

Gauss, H.: *Plato's Conception of Philosophy*. London: Macmillan; 1937.

Jaeger, W.: *Paideia: The Ideals of Greek Culture*. Translated from the second German edition by Gilbert Highet; 3 vols.; second English edition. New York: Oxford University Press; 1945.

Lodge, R. C.: *Plato's Theory of Art*. London: Routledge & Kegan Paul; 1953.

————: *Plato's Theory of Ethics: The Moral Criterion and the Highest Good*. New York: Harcourt, Brace; 1928.

Ross, W. D.: *Plato's Theory of Ideas*. Oxford: The Clarendon Press; 1953.

Shorey, Paul: *Platonism, Ancient and Modern*. Second edition. Berkeley: University of California Press; 1938.

————: *What Plato Said*. Chicago: University of Chicago Press; 1933.

Stace, Walter T.: *A Critical History of Greek Philosophy*. London: Macmillan; 1920.

Taylor, A. E.: *Plato: The Man and His Work*. Sixth edition. London: Methuen; 1949.

————: *Socrates*. Boston: Beacon Press; 1951.

Zeller, E.: *Outlines of the History of Greek Philosophy*. Thirteenth edition; revised by W. Nestle; translated by L. R. Palmer. New York: Humanities Press; 1951.

Backgrounds

Bury, J. B.: *A History of Greece to the Death of Alexander the Great*. London: Macmillan; 1913. New York: Modern Library; 1937.

The Cambridge Ancient History. New York: Cambridge University Press; 1927. Relevant chapters in vols. V and VI.

Hadas, M.: *A History of Greek Literature*. New York: Columbia University Press; 1950.

SYMPOSIUM

PERSONS OF THE DIALOGUE

APOLLODORUS, *who repeats to his companion the dialogue which he had heard from Aristodemus, and had already once narrated to Glaucon*

PHAEDRUS
PAUSANIAS
ERYXIMACHUS
ARISTOPHANES
AGATHON
SOCRATES
ALCIBIADES
A TROOP OF REVELLERS

SCENE:—*The House of Agathon*

Concerning the things about which you ask to be informed I believe that I am not ill-prepared with an answer. For the day before [172 yesterday I was coming from my own home at Phalerum to the city, and one of my acquaintance, who had caught a sight of me from behind, calling out playfully in the distance, said: Apollodorus, O thou Phalerian [1] man, halt! So I did as I was bid; and then he said, I was looking for you, Apollodorus, only just now, that I might ask you about the speeches in praise of love, which were delivered by Socrates, Alcibiades, and others, at Agathon's supper. Phoenix, the son of Philip, told another person who told me of them; his narrative was very indistinct, but he said that you knew, and I wish that you would give me an account of them. Who, if not you, should be the reporter of the words

---

[1] Probably a play of words on φαλαρός, 'bald-headed.'

of your friend? And first tell me, he said, were you present at this
meeting?

Your informant, Glaucon, I said, must have been very indistinct
indeed, if you imagine that the occasion was recent; or that I could have
been of the party.

Why, yes, he replied, I thought so.

Impossible: I said. Are you ignorant that for many years Agathon
has not resided at Athens; and not three have elapsed since I became
acquainted with Socrates, and have made it my daily business to know
all that he says and does. There was a time when I was running   [173
about the world, fancying myself to be well employed, but I was really
a most wretched being, no better than you are now. I thought that I
ought to do anything rather than be a philosopher.

Well, he said, jesting apart, tell me when the meeting occurred.

In our boyhood, I replied, when Agathon won the prize with his
first tragedy, on the day after that on which he and his chorus offered
the sacrifice of victory.

Then it must have been a long while ago, he said; and who told
you—did Socrates?

No indeed, I replied, but the same person who told Phoenix;—
he was a little fellow, who never wore any shoes, Aristodemus, of the
deme of Cydathenaeum. He had been at Agathon's feast; and I think
that in those days there was no one who was a more devoted admirer
of Socrates. Moreover, I have asked Socrates about the truth of some
parts of his narrative, and he confirmed them. Then, said Glaucon, let
us have the tale over again; is not the road to Athens just made for
conversation? And so we walked, and talked of the discourses on love;
and therefore, as I said at first, I am not ill-prepared to comply with
your request, and will have another rehearsal of them if you like. For
to speak or to hear others speak of philosophy always gives me the
greatest pleasure, to say nothing of the profit. But when I hear another
strain, especially that of you rich men and traders, such conversation
displeases me; and I pity you who are my companions, because you think
that you are doing something when in reality you are doing nothing.
And I dare say that you pity me in return, whom you regard as an unhappy creature, and very probably you are right. But I certainly know of
you what you only think of me—there is the difference.

Companion. I see, Apollodorus, that you are just the same—always
speaking evil of yourself, and of others; and I do believe that you pity
all mankind, with the exception of Socrates, yourself first of all, true in
this to your old name, which, however deserved, I know not how you
acquired, of Apollodorus the madman; for you are always raging against
yourself and everybody but Socrates.

Apollodorus. Yes, friend, and the reason why I am said to be mad, and out of my wits, is just because I have these notions of myself and you; no other evidence is required.

Companion. No more of that, Apollodorus; but let me renew my request that you would repeat the conversation.

Apollodorus. Well, the tale of love was on this wise:—But perhaps I had better begin at the beginning, and endeavour to give you   [174 the exact words of Aristodemus:

He said that he met Socrates fresh from the bath and sandalled; and as the sight of the sandals was unusual, he asked him whither he was going that he had been converted into such a beau:—

To a banquet at Agathon's, he replied, whose invitation to his sacrifice of victory I refused yesterday, fearing a crowd, but promising that I would come to-day instead; and so I have put on my finery, because he is such a fine man. What say you to going with me unasked?

I will do as you bid me, I replied.

Follow then, he said, and let us demolish the proverb:—

'*To the feasts of inferior men the good unbidden go;*'

instead of which our proverb will run:—

'*To the feasts of the good the good unbidden go;*'

and this alteration may be supported by the authority of Homer himself, who not only demolishes but literally outrages the proverb. For, after picturing Agamemnon as the most valiant of men, he makes Menelaus, who is but a faint-hearted warrior, come unbidden [2] to the banquet of Agamemnon, who is feasting and offering sacrifices, not the better to the worse, but the worse to the better.

I rather fear, Socrates, said Aristodemus, lest this may still be my case; and that, like Menelaus in Homer, I shall be the inferior person, who

'*To the feasts of the wise unbidden goes.*'

But I shall say that I was bidden of you, and then you will have to make an excuse.

'*Two going together,*'

he replied, in Homeric fashion, one or other of them may invent an excuse by the way.[3]

This was the style of their conversation as they went along. Socrates dropped behind in a fit of abstraction, and desired Aristodemus, who

[2] Iliad ii. 408, and xvii. 588.
[3] Iliad x. 224.

was waiting, to go on before him. When he reached the house of
Agathon he found the doors wide open, and a comical thing happened.
A servant coming out met him, and led him at once into the banqueting-
hall in which the guests were reclining, for the banquet was about to
begin. Welcome, Aristodemus, said Agathon, as soon as he appeared—
you are just in time to sup with us; if you come on any other matter
put it off, and make one of us, as I was looking for you yesterday and
meant to have asked you, if I could have found you. But what have you
done with Socrates?

I turned round, but Socrates was nowhere to be seen; and I had to
explain that he had been with me a moment before, and that I came
by his invitation to the supper.

You were quite right in coming, said Agathon; but where is he
himself?

He was behind me just now, as I entered, he said, and I   [175
cannot think what has become of him.

Go and look for him, boy, said Agathon, and bring him in; and
do you, Aristodemus, meanwhile take the place by Eryximachus.

The servant then assisted him to wash, and he lay down, and presently another servant came in and reported that our friend Socrates had
retired into the portico of the neighbouring house. 'There he is fixed,'
said he, 'and when I call to him he will not stir.'

How strange, said Agathon; then you must call him again, and keep
calling him.

Let him alone, said my informant; he has a way of stopping anywhere and losing himself without any reason. I believe that he will soon
appear; do not therefore disturb him.

Well, if you think so, I will leave him, said Agathon. And then,
turning to the servants, he added, 'Let us have supper without waiting
for him. Serve up whatever you please, for there is no one to give you
orders; hitherto I have never left you to yourselves. But on this occasion
imagine that you are our hosts, and that I and the company are your
guests; treat us well, and then we shall commend you.' After this, supper was served, but still no Socrates; and during the meal Agathon several times expressed a wish to send for him, but Aristodemus objected;
and at last when the feast was about half over—for the fit, as usual,
was not of long duration—Socrates entered. Agathon, who was reclining alone at the end of the table, begged that he would take the place
next to him; that 'I may touch you,' he said, 'and have the benefit of
that wise thought which came into your mind in the portico, and is
now in your possession; for I am certain that you would not have come
away until you had found what you sought.'

How I wish, said Socrates, taking his place as he was desired, that wisdom could be infused by touch, out of the fuller into the emptier man, as water runs through wool out of a fuller cup into an emptier one; if that were so, how greatly should I value the privilege of reclining at your side! For you would have filled me full with a stream of wisdom plenteous and fair; whereas my own is of a very mean and questionable sort, no better than a dream. But yours is bright and full of promise, and was manifested forth in all the splendour of youth the day before yesterday, in the presence of more than thirty thousand Hellenes.

You are mocking, Socrates, said Agathon, and ere long you and I will have to determine who bears off the palm of wisdom—of this Dionysus shall be the judge; but at present you are better occupied with supper.

Socrates took his place on the couch, and supped with the   [176 rest; and then libations were offered, and after a hymn had been sung to the god, and there had been the usual ceremonies, they were about to commence drinking, when Pausanias said, And now, my friends, how can we drink with least injury to ourselves? I can assure you that I feel severely the effect of yesterday's potations, and must have time to re-cover; and I suspect that most of you are in the same predicament, for you were of the party yesterday. Consider then: How can the drinking be made easiest?

I entirely agree, said Aristophanes, that we should, by all means, avoid hard drinking, for I was myself one of those who were yesterday drowned in drink.

I think that you are right, said Eryximachus, the son of Acumenus; but I should still like to hear one other person speak: Is Agathon able to drink hard?

I am not equal to it, said Agathon.

Then, said Eryximachus, the weak heads like myself, Aristodemus, Phaedrus, and others who never can drink, are fortunate in finding that the stronger ones are not in a drinking mood. (I do not include Socrates, who is able either to drink or to abstain, and will not mind, whichever we do.) Well, as none of the company seem disposed to drink much, I may be forgiven for saying, as a physician, that drinking deep is a bad practice, which I never follow, if I can help, and certainly do not recom-mend to another, least of all to any one who still feels the effects of yes-terday's carouse.

I always do what you advise, and especially what you prescribe as a physician, rejoined Phaedrus the Myrrhinusian, and the rest of the company, if they are wise, will do the same.

It was agreed that drinking was not to be the order of the day, but that they were all to drink only so much as they pleased.

Then, said Eryximachus, as you are all agreed that drinking is to be voluntary, and that there is to be no compulsion, I move, in the next place, that the flute-girl, who has just made her appearance, be told to go away and play to herself, or, if she likes, to the women who are within.[4] To-day let us have conversation instead; and, if you will allow me, I will tell you what sort of conversation. This proposal   [177 having been accepted, Eryximachus proceeded as follows:—

I will begin, he said, after the manner of Melanippe in Euripides,

'Not mine the word'

which I am about to speak, but that of Phaedrus. For often he says to me in an indignant tone:—'What a strange thing it is, Eryximachus, that, whereas other gods have poems and hymns made in their honour, the great and glorious god, Love, has no encomiast among all the poets who are so many. There are the worthy sophists too—the excellent Prodicus for example, who have descanted in prose on the virtues of Heracles and other heroes; and, what is still more extraordinary, I have met with a philosophical work in which the utility of salt has been made the theme of an eloquent discourse; and many other like things have had a like honour bestowed upon them. And only to think that there should have been an eager interest created about them, and yet that to this day no one has ever dared worthily to hymn Love's praises! So entirely has this great deity been neglected.' Now in this Phaedrus seems to me to be quite right, and therefore I want to offer him a contribution; also I think that at the present moment we who are here assembled cannot do better than honour the god Love. If you agree with me, there will be no lack of conversation; for I mean to propose that each of us in turn, going from left to right, shall make a speech in honour of Love. Let him give us the best which he can; and Phaedrus, because he is sitting first on the left hand, and because he is the father of the thought, shall begin.

No one will vote against you, Eryximachus, said Socrates. How can I oppose your motion, who profess to understanding nothing but matters of love; nor, I presume, will Agathon and Pausanias; and there can be no doubt of Aristophanes, whose whole concern is with Dionysus and Aphrodite; nor will any one disagree of those whom I see around me. The proposal, as I am aware, may seem rather hard upon us whose place is last; but we shall be contented if we hear some good speeches first. Let Phaedrus begin the praise of Love, and good luck to him. All the company expressed their assent, and desired him to do as Socrates bade him.   [178

Aristodemus did not recollect all that was said, nor do I recollect

---

[4] Cp. Prot. 347.

all that he related to me; but I will tell you what I thought most worthy of remembrance, and what the chief speakers said.

Phaedrus began by affirming that Love is a mighty god, and wonderful among gods and men, but especially wonderful in his birth. For he is the eldest of the gods, which is an honour to him; and a proof of his claim to this honour is, that of his parents there is no memorial; neither poet nor prose-writer has ever affirmed that he had any. As Hesiod says:—

> 'First Chaos came, and then broad-bosomed Earth,
> The everlasting seat of all that is,
> And Love.'

In other words, after Chaos, the Earth and Love, these two, came into being. Also Parmenides sings of Generation:

> 'First in the train of gods, he fashioned Love.'

And Acusilaus agrees with Hesiod. Thus numerous are the witnesses who acknowledge Love to be the eldest of the gods. And not only is he the eldest, he is also the source of the greatest benefits to us. For I know not any greater blessing to a young man who is beginning life than a virtuous lover, or to the lover than a beloved youth. For the principle which ought to be the guide of men who would nobly live—that principle, I say, neither kindred, nor honour, nor wealth, nor any other motive is able to implant so well as love. Of what am I speaking? Of the sense of honour and dishonour, without which neither states nor individuals ever do any good or great work. And I say that a lover who is detected in doing any dishonourable act, or submitting through cowardice when any dishonour is done to him by another, will be more pained at being detected by his beloved than at being seen by his father, or by his companions, or by any one else. The beloved too, when he is found in any disgraceful situation, has the same feeling about his lover. And if there were only some way of contriving that a state or an army should be made up of lovers and their loves [5], they would be the very best governors of their own city, abstaining from all dishonour, and emulating one another in honour; and when fighting at   [179 each other's side, although a mere handful, they would overcome the world. For what lover would not choose rather to be seen by all mankind than by his beloved, either when abandoning his post or throwing away his arms? He would be ready to die a thousand deaths rather than endure this. Or who would desert his beloved or fail him in the hour of danger? The veriest coward would become an inspired hero, equal to

---

[5] Cp. Rep. v. 468 D.

the bravest, at such a time; Love would inspire him. That courage which, as Homer says, the god breathes into the souls of some heroes, Love of his own nature infuses into the lover.

Love will make men dare to die for their beloved—love alone; and women as well as men. Of this, Alcestis, the daughter of Pelias, is a monument to all Hellas; for she was willing to lay down her life on behalf of her husband, when no one else would, although he had a father and mother; but the tenderness of her love so far exceeded theirs, that she made them seem to be strangers in blood to their own son, and in name only related to him; and so noble did this action of hers appear to the gods, as well as to men, that among the many who have done virtuously she is one of the very few to whom, in admiration of her noble action, they have granted the privilege of returning alive to earth; such exceeding honour is paid by the gods to the devotion and virtue of love. But Orpheus, the son of Oeagrus, the harper, they sent empty away, and presented to him an apparition only of her whom he sought, but herself they would not give up, because he showed no spirit; he was only a harp-player, and did not dare like Alcestis to die for love, but was contriving how he might enter Hades alive; moreover, they afterwards caused him to suffer death at the hands of women, as the punishment of his cowardliness. Very different was the reward of the true love of Achilles towards his lover Patroclus—his lover and not his love (the notion that Patroclus was the beloved one is a foolish error into which Aeschylus has fallen, for Achilles was surely the fairer of the two, fairer also than all the other heroes; and, as Homer informs us, he was still beardless, and younger far). And greatly as the gods   [180 honour the virtue of love, still the return of love on the part of the beloved to the lover is more admired and valued and rewarded by them, for the lover is more divine; because he is inspired by God. Now Achilles was quite aware, for he had been told by his mother, that he might avoid death and return home, and live to a good old age, if he abstained from slaying Hector. Nevertheless he gave his life to revenge his friend, and dared to die, not only in his defence, but after he was dead. Wherefore the gods honoured him even above Alcestis, and sent him to the Islands of the Blest. There are my reasons for affirming that Love is the eldest and noblest and mightiest of the gods, and the chiefest author and giver of virtue in life, and of happiness after death.

This, or something like this, was the speech of Phaedrus; and some other speeches followed which Aristodemus did not remember; the next which he repeated was that of Pausanias. Phaedrus, he said, the argument has not been set before us, I think, quite in the right form;—we should not be called upon to praise Love in such an indiscriminate manner. If there were only one Love, then what you said would be well

enough; but since there are more Loves than one, you should have
begun by determining which of them was to be the theme of our praises.
I will amend this defect; and first of all I will tell you which Love is
deserving of praise, and then try to hymn the praiseworthy one in a
manner worthy of him. For we all know that Love is inseparable from
Aphrodite, and if there were only one Aphrodite there would be only
one Love; but as there are two goddesses there must be two Loves. And
am I not right in asserting that there are two goddesses? The elder one,
having no mother, who is called the heavenly Aphrodite—she is the
daughter of Uranus; the younger, who is the daughter of Zeus and Dione
—her we call common; and the Love who is her fellow-worker is rightly
named common, as the other love is called heavenly. All the gods ought
to have praise given to them, but not without distinction of their natures; and therefore I must try to distinguish the characters of the two
Loves. Now actions vary according to the manner of their performance. Take, for example, that which we are now doing,   [181
drinking, singing and talking—these actions are not in themselves either
good or evil, but they turn out in this or that way according to the mode
of performing them; and when well done they are good, and when
wrongly done they are evil; and in like manner not every love, but only
that which has a noble purpose, is noble and worthy of praise. The Love
who is the offspring of the common Aphrodite is essentially common,
and has no discrimination, being such as the meaner sort of men feel,
and is apt to be of women as well as of youths, and is of the body rather
than of the soul—the most foolish beings are the objects of this love
which desires only to gain an end, but never thinks of accomplishing
the end nobly, and therefore does good and evil quite indiscriminately.
The goddess who is his mother is far younger than the other, and she
was born of the union of the male and female, and partakes of both.
But the offspring of the heavenly Aphrodite is derived from a mother in
whose birth the female has no part,—she is from the male only; this
is that love which is of youths, and the goddess being older, there is
nothing of wantonness in her. Those who are inspired by this love turn
to the male, and delight in him who is the more valiant and intelligent
nature; any one may recognise the pure enthusiasts in the very character
of their attachments. For they love not boys, but intelligent beings
whose reason is beginning to be developed, much about the time at
which their beards begin to grow. And in choosing young men to be
their companions, they mean to be faithful to them, and pass their whole
life in company with them, not to take them in their inexperience, and
deceive them, and play the fool with them, or run away from one to
another of them. But the love of young boys should be forbidden by
law, because their future is uncertain; they may turn out good or bad,

either in body or soul, and much noble enthusiasm may be thrown away
upon them; in this matter the good are a law to themselves, and the
coarser sort of lovers ought to be restrained by force, as we restrain or
attempt to restrain them from fixing their affections on women   [182
of free birth. These are the persons who bring a reproach on love; and
some have been led to deny the lawfulness of such attachments because
they see the impropriety and evil of them; for surely nothing that is
decorously and lawfully done can justly be censured. Now here and in
Lacedaemon the rules about love are perplexing, but in most cities
they are simple and easily intelligible; in Elis and Boeotia, and in
countries having no gifts of eloquence, they are very straightforward;
the law is simply in favour of these connexions, and no one, whether
young or old, has anything to say to their discredit; the reason being,
as I suppose, that they are men of few words in those parts, and therefore the lovers do not like the trouble of pleading their suit. In Ionia
and other places, and generally in countries which are subject to the
barbarians, the custom is held to be dishonourable; loves of youths share
the evil repute in which philosophy and gymnastics are held, because
they are inimical to tyranny; for the interests of rulers require that
their subjects should be poor in spirit [6] and that there should be no
strong bond of friendship or society among them, which love, above all
other motives, is likely to inspire, as our Athenian tyrants learned by experience; for the love of Aristogeiton and the constancy of Harmodius
had a strength which undid their power. And, therefore, the ill-repute
into which these attachments have fallen is to be ascribed to the evil
condition of those who make them to be ill-reputed; that is to say, to
the self-seeking of the governors and the cowardice of the governed;
on the other hand, the indiscriminate honour which is given to them
in some countries is attributable to the laziness of those who hold this
opinion of them. In our own country a far better principle prevails, but,
as I was saying, the explanation of it is rather perplexing. For, observe
that open loves are held to be more honourable than secret ones, and
that the love of the noblest and highest, even if their persons are less
beautiful than others, is especially honourable. Consider, too, how great
is the encouragement which all the world gives to the lover; neither is
he supposed to be doing anything dishonourable; but if he succeeds he
is praised, and if he fail he is blamed. And in the pursuit of his love
the custom of mankind allows him to do many strange things, which
philosophy would bitterly centure if they were done from any   [183
motive of interest, or wish for office or power. He may pray, and entreat, and supplicate, and swear, and lie on a mat at the door, and

---

[6] Cp. Arist. Politics, v. 11. § 15.

endure a slavery worse than that of any slave—in any other case friends and enemies would be equally ready to prevent him, but now there is no friend who will be ashamed of him and admonish him, and no enemy will charge him with meanness or flattery; the actions of a lover have a grace which ennobles them; and custom has decided that they are highly commendable and that there is no loss of character in them; and, what is strangest of all, he only may swear and forswear himself (so men say), and the gods will forgive his transgression, for there is no such thing as a lover's oath. Such is the entire liberty which gods and men have allowed the lover, according to the custom which prevails in our part of the world. From this point of view a man fairly argues that in Athens to love and to be loved is held to be a very honourable thing. But when parents forbid their sons to talk with their lovers, and place them under a tutor's care, who is appointed to see to these things, and their companions and equals cast in their teeth anything of the sort which they may observe, and their elders refuse to silence the reprovers and do not rebuke them—any one who reflects on all this will, on the contrary, think that we hold these practices to be most disgraceful. But, as I was saying at first, the truth as I imagine is, that whether such practices are honourable or whether they are dishonourable is not a simple question; they are honourable to him who follows them honourably, dishonourable to him who follows them dishonourably. There is dishonour in yielding to the evil, or in an evil manner; but there is honour in yielding to the good, or in an honourable manner. Evil is the vulgar lover who loves the body rather than the soul, inasmuch as he is not even stable, because he loves a thing which is in itself unstable, and therefore when the bloom of youth which he was desiring is over, he takes wing and flies away, in spite of all his words and promises; whereas the love of the noble disposition is lifelong, for it becomes one with the everlasting. The custom of our country would have both of them proven well and truly, and would   [184 have us yield to the one sort of lover and avoid the other, and therefore encourages some to pursue, and others to fly; testing both the lover and beloved in contests and trials, until they show to which of the two classes they respectively belong. And this is the reason why, in the first place, a hasty attachment is held to be dishonourable, because time is the true test of this as of most other things; and secondly there is a dishonour in being overcome by the love of money, or of wealth, or of political power, whether a man is frightened into surrender by the loss of them, or, having experienced the benefits of money and political corruption, is unable to rise above the seductions of them. For none of these things are of a permanent or lasting nature; not to mention that no generous friendship ever sprang from them. There remains, then, only one way of honourable attachment which custom allows in the beloved, and this is the way of virtue; for as we admitted that any service which the lover does to him is not to be accounted flattery or a dishonour to himself, so the beloved has one way only of voluntary service which is not dishonourable, and this is virtuous service.

For we have a custom, and according to our custom any one who does service to another under the idea that he will be improved by him either in wisdom, or in some other particular of virtue—such a voluntary service, I say, is not to be regarded as a dishonour, and is not open to the charge of flattery. And these two customs, one the love of youth, and the other the practice of philosophy and virtue in general, ought to meet in one, and then the beloved may honourably indulge the lover. For when the lover and beloved come together, having each of them a law, and the lover thinks that he is right in doing any service which he can to his gracious loving one; and the other that he is right in showing any kindness which he can to him who is making him wise and good; the one capable of communicating wisdom and virtue, the other seeking to acquire them with a view to education and wisdom; when the two laws of love are fulfilled and meet in one—then, and then only, may the beloved yield with honour to the lover. Nor when love is of this disinterested sort is there any disgrace in being deceived, but in every other case there is equal disgrace in being or not being deceived. For he who is gracious to his lover under the impression that he is rich,   [185 and is disappointed of his gains because he turns out to be poor, is disgraced all the same: for he has done his best to show that he would give himself up to any one's 'uses base' for the sake of money; but this is not honourable. And on the same principle he who gives himself to a lover because he is a good man, and in the hope that he will be improved by his company, shows himself to be virtuous, even though the object of his affection turn out to be a villain, and to have no virtue; and if he is deceived he has committed a noble error. For he has proved that for his part he will do anything for anybody with a view to virtue and improvement, than which there can be nothing nobler. Thus noble in every case is the acceptance of another for the sake of virtue. This is that love which is the love of the heavenly goddess, and is heavenly, and of great price to individuals and cities, making the lover and the beloved alike eager in the work of their own improvement. But all other loves are the offspring of the other, who is the common goddess. To you, Phaedrus, I offer this my contribution in praise of love, which is as good as I could make extempore.

Pāusănĭăs cāme tŏ ă pāuse—this is the balanced way in which I have been taught by the wise to speak; and Aristodemus said that the turn of Aristophanes was next, but either he had eaten too much, or from some other cause he had the hiccough, and was obliged to change turns with Eryximachus the physician, who was reclining on the couch below him. Eryximachus, he said, you ought either to stop my hiccough, or to speak in my turn until I have left off.

I will do both, said Eryximachus: I will speak in your turn, and do you speak in mine; and while I am speaking let me recommend you to hold your breath, and if after you have done so for some time the hiccough is no better, then gargle with a little water; and if it still continues, tickle your nose with something and sneeze; and if you sneeze once or twice, even the most violent hiccough is sure to go. I will do as you prescribe, said Aristophanes, and now get on.

Eryximachus spoke as follows: Seeing that Pausanias made a fair beginning, and but a lame ending, I must endeavour to supply   [186 his deficiency. I think that he has rightly distinguished two kinds of love. But my art further informs me that the double love is not merely an affection of the soul of man towards the fair, or towards anything, but is to be found in the bodies of all animals and in productions of the earth, and I may say in all that is; such is the conclusion which I seem to have gathered from my own art of medicine, whence I learn how great and wonderful and universal is the deity of love, whose empire extends over all things, divine as well as human. And from medicine I will begin that I may do honour to my art. There are in the human body these two kinds of love, which are confessedly different and unlike, and being unlike, they have loves and desires which are unlike; and the desire of the healthy is one, and the desire of the diseased is another; and as Pausanias was just now saying that to indulge good men is honourable, and bad men dishonourable:—so too in the body the good and healthy elements are to be indulged, and the bad elements and the elements of disease are not to be indulged, but discouraged. And this is what the physician has to do, and in this the art of medicine consists: for medicine may be regarded generally as the knowledge of the loves and desires of the body, and how to satisfy them or not; and the best physician is he who is able to separate fair love from foul, or to convert one into the other; and he who knows how to eradicate and how to implant love, whichever is required, and can reconcile the most hostile elements in the constitution and make them loving friends, is a skilful practitioner. Now the most hostile are the most opposite, such as hot and cold, bitter and sweet, moist and dry, and the like. And my ancestor, Asclepius, knowing how to implant friendship and accord in these elements, was the creator of our art, as our friends the poets here tell us, and I believe them; and not only medicine in every branch, but the arts of gymnastic and husbandry are under his dominion. Any one who pays the least attention to   [187

the subject will also perceive that in music there is the same reconciliation of opposites; and I suppose that this must have been the meaning of Heracleitus, although his words are not accurate; for he says that
The One is united by disunion, like the harmony of the bow and the
lyre. Now there is an absurdity in saying that harmony is discord or is
composed of elements which are still in a state of discord. But what he
probably meant was, that harmony is composed of differing notes of
higher or lower pitch which disagreed once, but are now reconciled by
the art of music; for if the higher and lower notes still disagreed, there
could be no harmony,—clearly not. For harmony is a symphony, and
symphony is an agreement; but an agreement of disagreements while
they disagree there cannot be; you cannot harmonize that which
disagrees. In like manner rhythm is compounded of elements short and
long, once differing and now in accord; which accordance, as in the
former instance, medicine, so in all these other cases, music implants,
making love and unison to grow up among them; and thus music, too,
is concerned with the principles of love in their application to harmony
and rhythm. Again, in the essential nature of harmony and rhythm
there is no difficulty in discerning love which has not yet become double. But when you want to use them in actual life, either in the composition of songs or in the correct performance of airs or metres composed already, which latter is called education, then the difficulty begins,
and the good artist is needed. Then the old tale has to be repeated of
fair and heavenly love—the love of Urania the fair and heavenly muse,
and of the duty of accepting the temperate, and those who are as yet
intemperate only that they may become temperate, and of preserving
their love; and again, of the vulgar Polyhymnia, who must be used
with circumspection that the pleasure be enjoyed, but may not generate
licentiousness; just as in my own art it is a great matter so to regulate
the desires of the epicure that he may gratify his tastes without the
attendant evil of disease. Whence I infer that in music, in medicine,
in all other things human as well as divine, both loves ought to be
noted as far as may be, for they are both present.   [188

The course of the seasons is also full of both these principles; and
when, as I was saying, the elements of hot and cold, moist and dry,
attain the harmonious love of one another and blend in temperance
and harmony, they bring to men, animals, and plants health and plenty,
and do them no harm; whereas the wanton love, getting the upper hand
and affecting the seasons of the year, is very destructive and injurious,
being the source of pestilence, and bringing many other kinds of diseases on animals and plants; for hoar-frost and hail and blight spring
from the excesses and disorders of these elements of love, which to
know in relation to the revolutions of the heavenly bodies and the sea-

sons of the year is termed astronomy. Furthermore all sacrifices and the whole province of divination, which is the art of communion between gods and men—these, I say, are concerned only with the preservation of the good and the cure of the evil love. For all manner of impiety is likely to ensue if, instead of accepting and honouring and reverencing the harmonious love in all his actions, a man honours the other love, whether in his feelings towards gods or parents, towards the living or the dead. Wherefore the business of divination is to see to these loves and to heal them, and divination is the peacemaker of gods and men, working by a knowledge of the religious or irreligious tendencies which exist in human loves. Such is the great and mighty, or rather omnipotent force of love in general. And the love, more especially, which is concerned with the good, and which is perfected in company with temperance and justice, whether among gods or men, has the greatest power, and is the source of all our happiness and harmony, and makes us friends with the gods who are above us, and with one another. I dare say that I too have omitted several things which might be said in praise of Love, but this was not intentional, and you, Aristophanes, may now supply the omission or take some other line of commendation; for I perceive that you are rid of the hiccough.

Yes, said Aristophanes, who followed, the hiccough is [189 gone; not, however, until I applied the sneezing; and I wonder whether the harmony of the body has a love of such noises and ticklings, for I no sooner applied the sneezing than I was cured.

Eryximachus said: Beware, friend Aristophanes, although you are going to speak, you are making fun of me; and I shall have to watch and see whether I cannot have a laugh at your expense, when you might speak in peace.

You are quite right, said Aristophanes, laughing. I will unsay my words; but do you please not to watch me, as I fear that in the speech which I am about to make, instead of others laughing with me, which is to the manner born of our muse and would be all the better, I shall only be laughed at by them.

Do you expect to shoot your bolt and escape, Aristophanes? Well, perhaps if you are very careful and bear in mind that you will be called to account, I may be induced to let you off.

Aristophanes professed to open another vein of discourse; he had a mind to praise Love in another way, unlike that either of Pausanias or Eryximachus. Mankind, he said, judging by their neglect of him, have never, as I think, at all understood the power of Love. For if they had understood him they would surely have built noble temples and altars, and offered solemn sacrifices in his honour; but this is not done, and most certainly ought to be done: since of all the gods he is the best friend of men, the helper and the healer of the ills which are the great impediment to the happiness of the race. I will try to describe his power to you, and you shall teach the rest of the world what I am teaching you. In the first place, let me treat of the nature of man and what has happened to it; for the original human nature was not like the present, but different. The sexes were not two as they are now, but originally three in number; there was man, woman, and the union of the two, having a name corresponding to this double nature, which had once a real existence, but is now lost, and the word 'Androgynous' is only preserved as a term of reproach. In the second place, the primeval man was round, his back and sides forming a circle; and he had four hands and four feet, one head with two faces, looking opposite ways, set on a round neck and precisely alike; also four ears, two   [190 privy members, and the remainder to correspond. He could walk upright as men now do, backwards or forwards as he pleased, and he could also roll over and over at a great pace, turning on his four hands and four feet, eight in all, like tumblers going over and over with their legs in the air; this was when he wanted to run fast. Now the sexes were three, and such as I have described them; because the sun, moon, and earth are three; and the man was originally the child of the sun, the woman of the earth, and the man-woman of the moon, which is made up of sun and earth, and they were all round and moved round and round like their parents. Terrible was their might and strength, and the thoughts of their hearts were great, and they made an attack upon the gods; of them is told the tale of Otys and Ephialtes who, as Homer says, dared to scale heaven, and would have laid hands upon the gods. Doubt reigned in the celestial councils. Should they kill them and annihilate the race with thunderbolts, as they had done the giants, then there would be an end of the sacrifices and worship which men offered to them; but, on the other hand, the gods could not suffer their insolence to be unrestrained. At last, after a good deal of reflection, Zeus discovered a way. He said: 'Methinks I have a plan which will humble their pride and improve their manners; men shall continue to exist, but I will cut them in two and then they will be diminished in strength and increased in numbers; this will have the advantage of making them more profitable to us. They shall walk upright on two legs, and if they continue insolent and will not be quiet, I will split them again and they shall hop about on a single leg.' He spoke and cut men in two, like a sorb-apple which is halved for pickling, or as you might divide an egg with a hair; and as he cut them one after another, he bade Apollo give the face and the half of the neck a turn in order that the man might contemplate the section of himself: he would thus learn a lesson of humility. Apollo was also bidden to heal their wounds and compose their forms. So he gave a turn to the face and pulled the skin from the sides all over that which in our language is called the belly, like the purses which draw in, and he made one mouth at the centre, which he fastened in a knot (the same which is called   [191 the navel); he also moulded the breast and took out most of the wrinkles, much as a shoemaker might smooth leather upon a last; he left a few, however, in the region of the belly and navel, as a memorial of the primeval state. After the division the two parts of man, each desiring his other half, came together, and throwing their arms about one another, entwined in mutual embraces, longing to grow into one, they were on the point of dying from hunger and self-neglect, because they did not like to do anything apart; and when one of the halves dies and the other survived, the survivor sought another mate, man or woman as we call them,—being the sections of entire men or women,—and clung to that. They were being destroyed, when Zeus in pity of them invented a new plan: he turned the parts of generation round to the front, for this had not been always their position, and they sowed the seed no longer as hitherto like grasshoppers in the ground, but in one another; and after the transposition the male generated in the female in order that by the mutual embraces of man and woman they might breed, and the race might continue; or if man came to man they might be satisfied, and rest, and go their ways to the business of life: so ancient is the desire of one another which is implanted in us, reuniting our original nature, making one of two, and healing the state of man. Each of us when separated, having one side only, like a flat fish, is but the indenture of a man, and he is always looking for his other half. Men who are a section of that double nature which was once called Androgynous are lovers of women; adulterers are generally of this breed, and also adulterous women who lust after men: the women who are a section of the woman do not care for men, but have female attachments; the female companions are of this sort. But they who are a section of the male follow the male, and while they are young, being slices of the original   [192 man, they hang about men and embrace them, and they are themselves the best of boys and youths, because they have the most manly nature. Some indeed assert that they are shameless, but this is not true; for they do not act thus from any want of shame, but because they are valiant and manly, and have a manly countenance, and they embrace that which is like them. And these when they grow up become our statesmen, and these only, which is a great proof of the truth of what I am saying. When they reach manhood they are lovers of youth, and are not naturally inclined to marry or beget children,—if at all, they do so only in obedience to the law; but they are satisfied if they may be allowed to live with one another unwedded; and such a nature is prone to love and ready to return love, always embracing that which is akin to him. And when one of them meets with his other half, the actual half of himself, whether he be a lover of youth or a lover of another sort, the pair are lost in an amazement of love and friendship and intimacy, and will not be out of the other's sight, as I may say, even for a moment: these are the people who pass their whole lives together; yet they could not explain what they desire of one another. For the intense yearning which each of them has towards the other does not appear to be the desire of lover's intercourse, but of something else which the soul of either evidently desires and cannot tell, and of which she had only a dark and doubtful presentiment. Suppose Hephaestus, with his instruments, to come to the pair who are lying side by side and to say to them, 'What do you people want of one another?' they would be unable to explain. And suppose further, that when he saw their perplexity he said: 'Do you desire to be wholly one; always day and night to be in one another's company? for if this is what you desire, I am ready to melt you into one and let you grow together, so that being two you shall become one, and while you live a common life as if you were a single man, and after your death in the world below still be one departed soul instead of two—I ask whether this is what you lovingly desire, and whether you are satisfied to attain this?'—there is not a man of them who when he heard the proposal would deny or would not acknowledge that this meeting and melting into one another, this becoming one instead of two, was the very expression of his ancient need [7]. And the reason is that human nature was originally one and we   [193 were a whole, and the desire and pursuit of the whole is called love. There was a time, I say, when were were one, but now because of the wickedness of mankind God has dispersed us, as the Arcadians were dispersed into villages by the Lacedaemonians [8]. And if we are not obedient to the gods, there is a danger that we shall be split up again and go about in basso-relievo, like the profile figures having only half a nose which are sculptured on monuments, and that we shall be like tallies. Wherefore let us exhort all men to piety, that we may avoid evil, and obtain the good, of which Love is to us the lord and minister; and let no one oppose him—he is the enemy of the gods who oppose him. For if we are friends of the God and at peace with him we shall find our own true loves, which rarely happens in this world at present. I am serious, and therefore I must beg Eryximachus not to make fun or to find any allusion in what I am saying to Pausanias and Agathon, who, as I suspect, are both of the manly nature, and belong to the class which I have been describing. But my words have a wider application—

[7] Cp. Arist. Pol. ii. 4, § 6.
[8] Cp. Arist. Pol. ii. 2, § 3.

they include men and women everywhere; and I believe that if our loves were perfectly accomplished, and each one returning to his primeval nature had his original true love, then our race would be happy. And if this would be best of all, the best in the next degree and under present circumstances must be the nearest approach to such an union; and that will be the attainment of a congenial love. Wherefore, if we would praise him who has given to us the benefit, we must praise the god Love, who is our greatest benefactor, both leading us in this life back to our own nature, and giving us high hopes for the future, for he promises that if we are pious, he will restore us to our original state, and heal us and make us happy and blessed. This, Eryximachus, is my discourse of love, which, although different to yours, I must beg you to leave unassailed by the shafts of your ridicule, in order that each may have his turn; each, or rather either, for Agathon and Socrates are the only ones left.

Indeed, I am not going to attack you, said Eryximachus, for I thought your speech charming, and did I not know that Agathon and Socrates are masters in the art of love, I should be really afraid that they would have nothing to say, after the world of things which have been said already. But, for all that, I am not without hopes.

Socrates said: You played your part well, Eryximachus; but [194 if you were as I am now, or rather as I shall be when Agathon has spoken, you would, indeed, be in a great strait.

You want to cast a spell over me, Socrates, said Agathon, in the hope that I may be disconcerted at the expectation raised among the audience that I shall speak well.

I should be strangely forgetful, Agathon, replied Socrates, of the courage and magnanimity which you showed when your own compositions were about to be exhibited, and you came upon the stage with the actors and faced the vast theatre altogether undismayed, if I thought that your nerves could be fluttered at a small party of friends.

Do you think, Socrates, said Agathon, that my head is so full of the theatre as not to know how much more formidable to a man of sense a few good judges are than many fools?

Nay, replied Socrates, I should be very wrong in attributing to you, Agathon, that or any other want of refinement. And I am quite aware that if you happened to meet with any whom you thought wise, you would care for their opinion much more than for that of the many. But then we, having been a part of the foolish many in the theatre, cannot be regarded as the select wise; though I know that if you chanced to be in the presence, not of one of ourselves, but of some really wise man, you would be ashamed of disgracing yourself before him—would you not?

Yes, said Agathon.

But before the many you would not be ashamed, if you thought that you were doing something disgraceful in their presence?

Here Phaedrus interrupted them, saying: Do not answer him, my dear Agathon; for if he can only get a partner with whom he can talk, especially a good-looking one, he will no longer care about the completion of our plan. Now I love to hear him talk; but just at present I must not forget the encomium on Love which I ought to receive from him and from every one. When you and he have paid your tribute to the god, then you may talk.

Very good, Phaedrus, said Agathon; I see no reason why I should not proceed with my speech, as I shall have many other opportunities of conversing with Socrates. Let me say first how I ought to speak, and then speak:—

The previous speakers, instead of praising the god Love, or unfolding his nature, appear to have congratulated mankind on the benefits which he confers upon them. But I would rather praise   [195 the god first, and then speak of his gifts; this is always the right way of praising everything. May I say without impiety or offence, that of all the blessed gods he is the most blessed because he is the fairest and best? And he is the fairest: for, in the first place, he is the youngest, and of his youth he is himself the witness, fleeing out of the way of age, who is swift enough, swifter truly than most of us like:—Love hates him and will not come near him; but youth and love live and move together— like to like, as the proverb says. Many things were said by Phaedrus about Love in which I agree with him; but I cannot agree that he is older than Iapetus and Kronos:—not so; I maintain him to be the youngest of the gods, and youthful ever. The ancient doings among the gods of which Hesiod and Parmenides spoke, if the tradition of them be true, were done of Necessity and not of Love; had Love been in those days, there would have been no chaining or mutilation of the gods, or other violence, but peace and sweetness, as there is now in heaven, since the rule of Love began. Love is young and also tender; he ought to have a poet like Homer to describe his tenderness, as Homer says of Ate, that she is a goddess and tender:—

> 'Her feet are tender, for she sets her steps,
> Not on the ground but on the heads of men:'

herein is an excellent proof of her tenderness,—that she walks not upon the hard but upon the soft. Let us adduce a similar proof of the tenderness of Love; for he walks not upon the earth, nor yet upon the skulls of men, which are not so very soft, but in the hearts and souls of both gods and men, which are of all things the softest: in them he walks and dwells and makes his home. Not in every soul without exception, for where there is hardness he departs, where there is softness there he dwells; and nestling always with his feet and in all manner of ways in the softest of soft places, how can he be other than the softest [196 of all things? Of a truth he is the tenderest as well as the youngest, and also he is of flexible form; for if he were hard and without flexure he could not enfold all things, or wind his way into and out of every soul of man undiscovered. And a proof of his flexibility and symmetry of form is his grace, which is universally admitted to be in an especial manner the attribute of Love; ungrace and love are always at war with one another. The fairness of his complexion is revealed by his habitation among the flowers; for he dwells not amid bloomless or fading beauties, whether of body or soul or aught else, but in the place of flowers and scents, there he sits and abides. Concerning the beauty of the god I have said enough; and yet there remains much more which I might say. Of his virtue I have now to speak: his greatest glory is that he can neither do nor suffer wrong to or from any god or any man; for he suffers not by force if he suffers; force comes not near him, neither when he acts does he act by force. For all men in all things serve him of their own free will, and where there is voluntary agreement, there, as the laws which are the lords of the city say, is justice. And not only is he just but exceedingly temperate, for Temperance is the acknowledged ruler of the pleasures and desires, and no pleasure ever masters Love; he is their master and they are his servants; and if he conquers them he must be temperate indeed. As to courage, even the God of War is no match for him; he is the captive and Love is the lord, for love, the love of Aphrodite, masters him, as the tale runs; and the master is stronger than the servant. And if he conquers the bravest of all others, he must be himself the bravest. Of his courage and justice and temperance I have spoken, but I have yet to speak of his wisdom; and according to the measure of my ability I must try to do my best. In the first place he is a poet (and here, like Eryximachus, I magnify my art), and he is also the source of poesy in others, which he could not be if he were not himself a poet. And at the touch of him every one becomes a poet,[9] even even though he had no music in him before [9]; this also is a proof that Love is a good poet and accomplished in all the fine arts; for no one can give to another that which he has not himself, or teach that of which he has no knowledge. Who will deny that the creation of the animals is his doing? Are they not all the works of his wisdom, born and [197 begotten of him? And as to the artists, do we not know that he only of them whom love inspires has the light of fame?—he whom Love

---

[9] A fragment of the Sthenoboea of Euripides.

touches not walks in darkness. The arts of medicine and archery and divination were discovered by Apollo, under the guidance of love and desire; so that he too is a disciple of Love. Also the melody of the Muses, the metallurgy of Hephaestus, the weaving of Athene, the empire of Zeus over gods and men, are all due to Love, who was the inventor of them. And so Love set in order the empire of the gods—the love of beauty, as is evident, for with deformity Love has no concern. In the days of old, as I began by saying, dreadful deeds were done among the gods, for they were ruled by Necessity; but now since the birth of Love, and from the Love of the beautiful, has sprung every good in heaven and earth. Therefore, Phaedrus, I say of Love that he is the fairest and best in himself, and the cause of what is fairest and best in all other things. And there comes into my mind a line of poetry in which he is said to be the god who

> 'Gives peace on earth and calms the stormy deep,
> Who stills the winds and bids the sufferer sleep.'

This is he who empties men of disaffection and fills them with affection, who makes them to meet together at banquets such as these: in sacrifices, feasts, dances, he is our lord—who sends courtesy and sends away discourtesy, who gives kindness ever and never gives unkindness; the friend of the good, the wonder of the wise, the amazement of the gods; desired by those who have no part in him, and precious to those who have the better part in him; parent of delicacy, luxury, desire, fondness, softness, grace; regardful of the good, regardless of the evil: in every word, work, wish, fear—saviour, pilot, comrade, helper; glory of gods and men, leader best and brightest: in whose footsteps let every man follow, sweetly singing in his honour and joining in that sweet strain with which love charms the souls of gods and men. Such is the speech, Phaedrus, half-playful, yet having a certain measure of serious-ness, which, according to my ability, I dedicate to the god.

When Agathon had done speaking, Aristodemus said that   [198 there was a general cheer; the young man was thought to have spoken in a manner worthy of himself, and of the god. And Socrates, looking at Eryximachus, said: Tell me, son of Acumenus, was there not reason in my fears? and was I not a true prophet when I said that Agathon would make a wonderful oration, and that I should be in a strait?

The part of the prophecy which concerns Agathon, replied Eryxi-machus, appears to me to be true; but not the other part—that you will be in a strait.

Why, my dear friend, said Socrates, must not I or any one be in a strait who has to speak after he has heard such a rich and varied dis-course? I am especially struck with the beauty of the concluding words

—who could listen to them without amazement? When I reflected on the immeasurable inferiority of my own powers, I was ready to run away for shame, if there had been a possibility of escape. For I was reminded of Gorgias, and at the end of his speech I fancied that Agathon was shaking at me the Gorginian or Gorgonian head of the great master of rhetoric, which was simply to turn me and my speech into stone, as Homer says [1], and strike me dumb. And then I perceived how foolish I had been in consenting to take my turn with you in praising love, and saying that I too was a master of the art, when I really had no conception how anything ought to be praised. For in my simplicity I imagined that the topics of praise should be true, and that this being presupposed, out of the true the speaker was to choose the best and set them forth in the best manner. And I felt quite proud, thinking that I knew the nature of true praise, and should speak well. Whereas I now see that the intention was to attribute to Love every species of greatness and glory, whether really belonging to him or not, without regard to truth or falsehood—that was no matter; for the original proposal seems to have been not that each of you should really praise Love, but only that you should appear to praise him. And so you attribute to Love every imaginable form of praise which can be gathered anywhere; and you say that 'he is all this,' and 'the cause of all   [199 that,' making him appear the fairest and best of all to those who know him not, for you cannot impose upon those who know him. And a noble and solemn hymn of praise have you rehearsed. But as I misunderstood the nature of the praise when I said that I would take my turn, I must beg to be absolved from the promise which I made in ignorance, and which (as Euripides would say [2]) was a promise of the lips and not of the mind. Farewell then to such a strain: for I do not praise in that way; no, indeed, I cannot. But if you like to hear the truth about love, I am ready to speak in my own manner, though I will not make myself ridiculous by entering into any rivalry with you. Say then, Phaedrus, whether you would like to have the truth about love, spoken in any words and in any order which may happen to come into my mind at the time. Will that be agreeable to you?

Aristodemus said that Phaedrus and the company bid him speak in any manner which he thought best. Then, he added, let me have your permission first to ask Agathon a few more questions, in order that I may take his admissions as the premisses of my discourse.

I grant the permission, said Phaedrus: put your questions. Socrates then proceeded as follows:—

---

[1] Odyssey, λ. 632.
[2] Eurip. Hyppolytus, l. 612.

In the magnificent oration which you have just uttered, I think that you were right, my dear Agathon, in proposing to speak of the nature of Love first and afterwards of his works—that is a way of beginning which I very much approve. And as you have spoken so eloquently of his nature, may I ask you further, Whether love is the love of something or of nothing? And here I must explain myself: I do not want you to say that love is the love of a father or the love of a mother—that would be ridiculous; but to answer as you would, if I asked is a father a father of something? to which you would find no difficulty in replying, of a son or daughter: and the answer would be right.

Very true, said Agathon.

And you would say the same of a mother?

He assented.

Yet let me ask you one more question in order to illustrate my meaning: Is not a brother to be regarded essentially as a brother of something?

Certainly, he replied.

That is, of a brother or sister?

Yes, he said.

And now, said Socrates, I will ask about Love:—Is Love of something or of nothing?

Of something, surely, he replied. [200

Keep in mind what this is, and tell me what I want to know—whether Love desires that of which love is.

Yes, surely.

And does he possess, or does he not possess, that which he loves and desires?

Probably not, I should say.

Nay, replied Socrates, I would have you consider whether 'necessarily' is not rather the word. The inference that he who desires something is in want of something, and that he who desires nothing is in want of nothing, is in my judgment, Agathon, absolutely and necessarily true. What do you think?

I agree with you, said Agathon.

Very good. Would he who is great, desire to be great, or he who is strong, desire to be strong?

That would be inconsistent with our previous admissions.

True. For he who is anything cannot want to be that which he is?

Very true.

And yet, added Socrates, if a man being strong desired to be strong, or being swift desired to be swift, or being healthy desired to be healthy, in that case he might be thought to desire something which he already has or is. I give the example in order that we may avoid misconception. For the possessors of these qualities, Agathon, must be supposed to have their respective advantages at the time, whether they choose or not; and who can desire that which he has? Therefore, when a person says, I am well and wish to be well, or I am rich and wish to be rich, and I desire simply to have what I have—to him we shall reply: 'You, my friend, having wealth and health and strength, want to have the continuance of them; for at this moment, whether you choose or no, you have them. And when you say, I desire that which I have and nothing else, is not your meaning that you want to have what you now have in the future?' He must agree with us—must he not?

He must, replied Agathon.

Then, said Socrates, he desires that what he has at present may be preserved to him in the future, which is equivalent to saying that he desires something which is non-existent to him, and which as yet he has not got.

Very true, he said.

Then he and every one who desires, desires that which he has not already, and which is future and not present, and which he has not, and is not, and of which he is in want;—these are the sort of things which love and desire seek?

Very true, he said.

Then now, said Socrates, let us recapitulate the argument. First, is not love of something, and of something too which is wanting to a man?

Yes, he replied.   [201

Remember further what you said in your speech, or if you do not remember I will remind you: you said that the love of the beautiful set in order the empire of the gods, for that of deformed things there is no love—did you not say something of that kind?

Yes, said Agathon.

Yes, my friend, and the remark was a just one. And if this is true, Love is the love of beauty and not of deformity?

He assented.

And the admission has been already made that Love is of something which a man wants and has not?

True, he said.

Then Love wants and has not beauty?

Certainly, he replied.

And would you call that beautiful which wants and does not possess beauty?

Certainly not.

Then would you still say that love is beautiful?

Agathon replied: I fear that I did not understand what I was saying.

You made a very good speech, Agathon, replied Socrates; but there is yet one small question which I would fain ask:—Is not the good also the beautiful?

Yes.

Then in wanting the beautiful, love wants also the good?

I cannot refute you, Socrates, said Agathon:—Let us assume that what you say is true.

Say rather, beloved Agathon, that you cannot refute the truth; for Socrates is easily refuted.

And now, taking my leave of you, I will rehearse a tale of love which I heard from Diotima of Mantineia [3], a woman wise in this and in many other kinds of knowledge, who in the days of old, when the Athenians offered sacrifice before the coming of the plague, delayed the disease ten years. She was my instructress in the art of love, and I shall repeat to you what she said to me, beginning with the admissions made by Agathon, which are nearly if not quite the same which I made to the wise woman when she questioned me: I think that this will be the easiest way, and I shall take both parts myself as well as I can [4]. As you, Agathon, suggested [5], I must speak first of the being and nature of Love, and then of his works. First I said to her in nearly the same words which he used to me, that Love was a mighty god, and likewise fair; and she proved to me as I proved to him that, by my own showing, Love was neither fair nor good. 'What do you mean, Diotima,' I said, 'is love then evil and foul?' 'Hush,' she cried; 'must that be foul which is not fair? 'Certainly,' I said. 'And is that which is not wise, ig-   [202 norant? do you not see that there is a mean between wisdom and ignorance?' 'And what may that be?' I said. 'Right opinion,' she replied; 'which, as you know, being incapable of giving a reason, is not knowledge (for how can knowledge be devoid of reason? nor again, ignorance, for neither can ignorance attain the truth), but is clearly something which is a mean between ignorance and wisdom.' 'Quite true,' I replied. 'Do not then insist,' she said, 'that what is not fair is of necessity foul, or what is not good evil; or infer that because love is not fair and good he is therefore foul and evil; for he is in a mean between them.' 'Well,' I said, 'Love is surely admitted by all to be a great god.' 'By those who know or by those who do not know?' 'By all.' 'And how, Socrates,' she said with a smile, 'can Love be acknowledged to be a great

---

[3] Cp. I. Alcibiades.
[4] Cp. Gorgias, 505 E.
[5] Supra, 195 A.

god by those who say that he is not a god at all?' 'And who are they?' I said. 'You and I are two of them,' she replied. 'How can that be?' I said. 'It is quite intelligible,' she replied; 'for you yourself would acknowledge that the gods are happy and fair—of course you would—would you dare to say that any god was not?' 'Certainly not,' I replied. 'And you mean by the happy, those who are the possessors of things good or fair?' 'Yes.' 'And you admitted that Love, because he was in want, desires those good and fair things of which he is in want?' 'Yes, I did.' 'But how can he be a god who has no portion in what is either good or fair?' 'Impossible.' 'Then you see that you also deny the divinity of Love.'

'What then is Love?' I asked; 'Is he mortal?' 'No.' 'What then?' 'As in the former instance, he is neither mortal nor immortal, but in a mean between the two.' 'What is he, Diotima?' 'He is a great spirit (δαίμων), and like all spirits he is intermediate between the divine and the mortal.' 'And what,' I said, 'is his power?' 'He interprets,' she replied, 'between gods and men, conveying and taking across to the gods the prayers and sacrifices of men, and to men the commands and replies of the gods; he is the mediator who spans the chasm which divides them, and therefore in him all is bound together, and through him the arts of the prophet and the priest, their sacrifices and mysteries and   [203 charms, and all prophecy and incantation, find their way. For God mingles not with man; but through Love all the intercourse and converse of god with man, whether awake or asleep, is carried on. The wisdom which understands this is spiritual; all other wisdom, such as that of arts and handicrafts, is mean and vulgar. Now these spirits or intermediate powers are many and diverse, and one of them is Love.' 'And who,' I said, 'was his father, and who his mother?' 'The tale,' she said, 'will take time; nevertheless I will tell you. On the birthday of Aphrodite there was a feast of the gods, at which the god Poros or Plenty, who is the son of Metis or Discretion, was one of the guests. When the feast was over, Penia or Poverty, as the manner is on such occasions, came about the doors to beg. Now Plenty, who was the worse for nectar (there was no wine in those days), went into the garden of Zeus and fell into a heavy sleep; and Poverty considering her own straitened circumstances, plotted to have a child by him, and accordingly she lay down at his side and conceived Love, who partly because he is naturally a lover of the beautiful, and because Aphrodite is herself beautiful, and also because he was born on her birthday, is her follower and attendant. And as his parentage is, so also are his fortunes. In the first place he is always poor, and anything but tender and fair, as the many imagine him; and he is rough and squalid, and has no shoes, nor a house to dwell in; on the bare earth exposed he lies under the open heaven, in the streets, or at the doors of houses, taking his rest; and like his mother he is always in distress. Like his father too, whom he also partly resembles, he is always plotting against the fair and good; he is bold, enterprising, strong, a mighty hunter, always weaving some intrigue or other, keen in the pursuit of wisdom, fertile in resources; a philosopher at all times, terrible as an enchanter, sorcerer, sophist. He is by nature neither mortal nor immortal, but alive and flourishing at one moment when he is in plenty, and dead at another moment, and again alive by reason of his father's nature. But that which is always flowing in is always flowing out, and so he is never in want and never in wealth; and, further, he is in a mean between ignorance and knowledge. The truth of the matter is this: No god is a philosopher or seeker after wisdom, for he is wise already; nor does any man who is wise seek after wisdom. Neither do the ignorant seek after wisdom. For herein is the evil of ignorance, that he   [204 who is neither good nor wise is nevertheless satisfied with himself: he has no desire for that of which he feels no want.' 'But who then, Diotima,' I said, 'are the lovers of wisdom, if they are neither the wise nor the foolish?' 'A child may answer that question,' she replied; 'they are those who are in a mean between the two; Love is one of them. For wisdom is a most beautiful thing, and Love is of the beautiful; and therefore Love is also a philosopher or lover of wisdom, and being a lover of wisdom is in a mean between the wise and the ignorant. And of this too his birth is the cause; for his father is wealthy and wise, and his mother poor and foolish. Such, my dear Socrates, is the nature of the spirit Love. The error in your conception of him was very natural, and as I imagine from what you say, has arisen out of a confusion of love and the beloved, which made you think that love was all beautiful. For the beloved is the truly beautiful, and delicate, and perfect, and blessed; but the principle of love is of another nature, and is such as I have described.'

I said: 'O thou stranger woman, thou sayest well; but, assuming Love to be such as you say, what is the use of him to men?' 'That, Socrates,' she replied, 'I will attempt to unfold: of his nature and birth I have already spoken; and you acknowledge that love is of the beautiful. But some one will say: Of the beautiful in what, Socrates and Diotima?—or rather let me put the question more clearly, and ask: When a man loves the beautiful, what does he desire?' I answered her 'That the beautiful may be his.' 'Still,' she said, 'the answer suggests a further question: What is given by the possession of beauty?' 'To what you have asked,' I replied, 'I have no answer ready.' 'Then,' she said, 'let me put the word "good" in the place of the beautiful, and repeat the question once more: If he who loves loves the good, what is it then that he loves?' 'The possession of the good,' I said. 'And what does he gain who possesses the good?' 'Happiness,' I replied; 'there is less diffi-

culty in answering that question.' 'Yes,' she said, 'the happy   [205
are made happy by the acquisition of good things. Nor is there any
need to ask why a man desires happiness; the answer is already final.'
'You are right,' I said. 'And is this wish and this desire common to all?
and do all men always desire their own good, or only some men?—
what say you?' 'All men,' I replied; 'the desire is common to all.' 'Why,
then,' she rejoined, 'are not all men, Socrates, said to love, but only
some of them? whereas you say that all men are always loving the same
things.' 'I myself wonder,' I said, 'why this is.' 'There is nothing to
wonder at,' she replied; 'the reason is that one part of love is separated
off and receives the name of the whole, but the other parts have other
names.' 'Give an illustration,' I said. She answered me as follows:
'There is poetry, which, as you know, is complex and manifold. All
creation or passage of non-being into being is poetry or making, and
the processes of all art are creative; and the masters of arts are all poets
or makers.' 'Very true.' 'Still,' she said, 'you know that they are not
called poets, but have other names; only that portion of the art which
is separated off from the rest, and is concerned with music and metre,
is termed poetry, and they who possess poetry in this sense of the word
are called poets.' 'Very true,' I said. 'And the same holds of love. For you
may say generally that all desire of good and happiness is only the great
and subtle power of love; but they who are drawn towards him by any
other path, whether the path of money-making or gymnastics or
philosophy, are not called lovers—the name of the whole is appropriated to those whose affection takes one form only—they alone are
said to love, or to be lovers.' 'I dare say,' I replied, 'that you are right.'
'Yes,' she added, 'and you hear people say that lovers are seeking for
their other half; but I say that they are seeking neither for the half of
themselves, nor for the whole, unless the half or the whole be also a
good. And they will cut off their own hands and feet and cast them
away, if they are evil; for they love not what is their own, unless perchance there be some one who calls what belongs to him the   [206
good, and what belongs to another the evil. For there is nothing which
men love but the good. Is there anything?' 'Certainly, I should say,
that there is nothing.' 'Then,' she said, 'the simple truth is, that men
love the good.' 'Yes,' I said. 'To which must be added that they love
the possession of the good?' 'Yes, that must be added.' 'And not only
the possession, but the everlasting possession of the good?' 'That must
be added too.' 'Then love,' she said, 'may be described generally as the
love of the everlasting possession of the good?' 'That is most true.'

'Then if this be the nature of love, can you tell me further,' she
said, ' what is the manner of the pursuit? what are they doing who show
all this eagerness and heat which is called love? and what is the object

which they have in view? Answer me.' 'Nay, Diotima,' I replied, 'if I had known, I should not have wondered at your wisdom, neither should I have come to learn from you about this very matter.' 'Well,' she said, 'I will teach you:—The object which they have in view is birth in beauty, whether of body or soul.' 'I do not understand you,' I said; 'the oracle requires an explanation.' 'I will make my meaning clearer,' she replied. 'I mean to say, that all men are bringing to the birth in their bodies and in their souls. There is a certain age at which human nature is desirous of procreation—procreation which must be in beauty and not in deformity; and this procreation is the union of man and woman, and is a divine thing; for conception and generation are an immortal principle in the mortal creature, and in the inharmonious they can never be. But the deformed is always inharmonious with the divine, and the beautiful harmonious. Beauty, then, is the destiny or goddess of parturition who presides at birth, and therefore, when approaching beauty, the conceiving power is propitious, and diffusive, and benign, and begets and bears fruit: at the sight of ugliness she frowns and contracts and has a sense of pain, and turns away, and shrivels up, and not without a pang refrains from conception. And this is the reason why, when the hour of conception arrives, and the teeming nature is full, there is such a flutter and ecstasy about beauty whose approach is the alleviation of the pain of travail. For love, Socrates, is not, as you imagine, the love of the beautiful only.' 'What then?' 'The love of generation and of birth in beauty.' 'Yes,' I said. 'Yes, indeed,' she replied. 'But why of generation?' 'Because to the mortal creature, generation is a sort of eternity and immortality,' she replied; 'and if, as has been already admitted, love is of the everlasting possession of the good, all men will necessarily desire immortality together with good: [207 Wherefore love is of immortality.'

All this she taught me at various times when she spoke of love. And I remember her once saying to me, 'What is the cause, Socrates, of love, and the attendant desire? See you not how all animals, birds, as well as beasts, in their desire of procreation, are in agony when they take the infection of love, which begins with the desire of union; whereto is added the care of offspring, on whose behalf the weakest are ready to battle against the strongest even to the uttermost, and to die for them, and will let themselves be tormented with hunger or suffer anything in order to maintain their young. Man may be supposed to act thus from reason; but why should animals have these passionate feelings? Can you tell me why?' Again I replied that I did not know. She said to me: 'And do you expect ever to become a master in the art of love, if you do not know this?' 'But I have told you already, Diotima, that my ignorance is the reason why I come to you; for I am conscious that I want a teacher; tell me then the cause of this and of the other mysteries of love.' 'Marvel not,' she said, 'if you believe that love is of the immortal, as we have several times acknowledged; for here again, and on the same principle too, the mortal nature is seeking as far as is possible to be everlasting and immortal: and this is only to be attained by generation, because generation always leaves behind a new existence in the place of the old. Nay even in the life of the same individual there is succession and not absolute unity: a man is called the same, and yet in the short interval which elapses between youth and age, and in which every animal is said to have life and identity, he is undergoing a perpetual process of loss and reparation—hair, flesh, bones, blood, and the whole body are always changing. Which is true not only of the body, but also of the soul, whose habits, tempers, opinions, desires, pleasures, pains, fears, never remain the same in any one of us, but are always coming and going; and equally true of knowledge, and what is still more surprising to us mortals, not only do the sciences in   [208 general spring up and decay, so that in respect of them we are never the same; but each of them individually experiences a like change. For what is implied in the word "recollection," but the departure of knowledge, which is ever being forgotten, and is renewed and preserved by recollection, and appears to be the same although in reality new, according to that law of succession by which all mortal things are preserved, not absolutely the same, but by substitution, the old worn-out mortality leaving another new and similar existence behind—unlike the divine, which is always the same and not another? And in this way, Socrates, the mortal body, or mortal anything, partakes of immortality; but the immortal in another way. Marvel not then at the love which all men have of their offspring; for that universal love and interest is for the sake of immortality.'

I was astonished at her words, and said: 'Is this really true, O thou wise Diotima?' And she answered with all the authority of an accomplished sophist: 'Of that, Socrates, you may be assured;—think only of the ambition of men, and you will wonder at the senselessness of their ways, unless you consider how they are stirred by the love of an immortality of fame. They are ready to run all risks greater far than they would have run for their children, and to spend money and undergo any sort of toil, and even to die, for the sake of leaving behind them a name which shall be eternal. Do you imagine that Alcestis would have died to save Admetus, or Achilles to avenge Patroclus, or your own Codrus in order to preserve the kingdom for his sons, if they had not imagined that the memory of their virtues, which still survives among us, would be immortal? Nay,' she said, 'I am persuaded that all men do all things, and the better they are the more they do them, in hope of the glorious fame of immortal virtue; for they desire the immortal.

'Those who are pregnant in the body only, betake themselves to women and beget children—this is the character of their love; their offspring, as they hope, will preserve their memory and give them the blessedness and immortality which they desire in the future. But souls which are pregnant—for there certainly are men who are more　　[209 creative in their souls than in their bodies—conceive that which is proper for the soul to conceive or contain. And what are these conceptions?— wisdom and virtue in general. And such creators are poets and all artists who are deserving of the name inventor. But the greatest and fairest sort of wisdom by far is that which is concerned with the ordering of states and families, and which is called temperance and justice. And he who in youth has the seed of these implanted in him and is himself inspired, when he comes to maturity desires to beget and generate. He wanders about seeking beauty that he may beget offspring—for in deformity he will beget nothing—and naturally embraces the beautiful rather than the deformed body; above all when he finds a fair and noble and well-nurtured soul, he embraces the two in one person, and to such an one he is full of speech about virtue and the nature and pursuits of a good man; and he tries to educate him; and at the touch of the beautiful which is ever present to his memory, even when absent, he brings forth that which he had conceived long before, and in company with him tends that which he brings forth; and they are married by a far nearer tie and have a closer friendship than those who beget mortal children, for the children who are their common offspring are fairer and more immortal. Who, when he thinks of Homer and Hesiod and other great poets, would not rather have their children than ordinary human ones? Who would not emulate them in the creation of children such as theirs, which have preserved their memory and given them everlasting glory? Or who would not have such children as Lycurgus left behind him to be the saviours, not only of Lacedaemon, but of Hellas, as one may say? There is Solon, too, who is the revered father of Athenian laws; and many others there are in many other places, both among Hellenes and barbarians, who have given to the world many noble works, and have been the parents of virtue of every kind; and many temples have been raised in their honour for the sake of children such as theirs; which were never raised in honour of any one, for the sake of his mortal children.

'These are the lesser mysteries of love, into which even you, Socrates, may enter; to the greater and more hidden ones which　　[210 are the crown of these, and to which, if you pursue them in a right spirit, they will lead, I know not whether you will be able to attain. But I will do my utmost to inform you, and do you follow if you can. For he who would proceed aright in this matter should begin in youth to visit beautiful forms; and first, if he be guided by his instructor aright, to love one such form only—out of that he should create fair thoughts; and soon he will of himself perceive that the beauty of one form is akin to the beauty of another; and then if beauty of form in general is his pursuit, how foolish would he be not to recognize that the beauty in every form is one and the same! And when he perceives this he will abate his violent love of the one, which he will despise and deem a small thing, and will become a lover of all beautiful forms; in the next stage he will consider that the beauty of the mind is more honourable than the beauty of the outward form. So that if a virtuous soul have but a little comeliness, he will be content to love and tend him, and will search out and bring to the birth thoughts which may improve the young, until he is compelled to contemplate and see the beauty of institutions and laws, and to understand that the beauty of them all is of one family, and that personal beauty is a trifle; and after laws and institutions he will go on to the sciences, that he may see their beauty, being not like a servant in love with the beauty of one youth or man or institution, himself a slave mean and narrow-minded, but drawing towards and contemplating the vast sea of beauty, he will create many fair and noble thoughts and notions in boundless love of wisdom; until on that shore he grows and waxes strong, and at last the vision is revealed to him of a single science, which is the science of beauty everywhere. To this I will proceed; please to give me your very best attention:

'He who has been instructed thus far in the things of love, and who has learned to see the beautiful in due order and succession, when he comes toward the end will suddenly perceive a nature of wondrous beauty (and this, Socrates, is the final cause of all our former   [211 toils)—a nature which in the first place is everlasting, not growing and decaying, or waxing and waning; secondly, not fair in one point of view and foul in another, or at one time or in one relation or at one place fair, at another time or in another relation or at another place foul, as if fair to some and foul to others, or in the likeness of a face or hands or any other part of the bodily frame, or in any form of speech or knowledge, or existing in any other being, as for example, in an animal, or in heaven, or in earth, or in any other place; but beauty absolute, separate, simple, and everlasting, which without diminution and without increase, or any change, is imparted to the ever-growing and perishing beauties of all other things. He who from these ascending under the influence of true love, begins to perceive that beauty, is not far from the end. And the true order of going, or being led by another, to the things of love, is to begin from the beauties of earth and mount upwards for the sake of that other beauty, using these as steps only, and from one going on to two, and from two to all fair forms, and from fair forms to fair practices, and from fair practices to fair notions, until from fair notions he arrives at the notion of absolute beauty, and at last knows what the essence of beauty is. This, my dear Socrates,' said the stranger of Mantineia, 'is that life above all others which man should live, in the contemplation of beauty absolute; a beauty which if you once beheld, you would see not to be after the measure of gold, and garments, and fair boys and youths, whose presence now entrances you; and you and many a one would be content to live seeing them only and conversing with them without meat or drink, if that were possible—you only want to look at them and to be with them. But what if man had eyes to see the true beauty—the divine beauty, I mean, pure and clear and unalloyed, not clogged with the pollutions of mortality and all the colours and vanities of human life—thither looking, and holding converse with the true beauty simple and divine? Remember how in that   [212 communion only, beholding beauty with the eye of the mind, he will be enabled to bring forth, not images of beauty, but realities (for he has hold not of an image but of a reality), and bringing forth and nourishing true virtue to become the friend of God and be immortal, if mortal man may. Would that be an ignoble life?'

Such, Phaedrus—and I speak not only to you, but to all of you—were the words of Diotima; and I am persuaded of their truth. And being persuaded of them, I try to persuade others, that in the attainment of this end human nature will not easily find a helper better than love. And therefore, also, I say that every man ought to honour him as I myself honour him, and walk in his ways, and exhort others to do the same, and praise the power and spirit of love according to the measure of my ability now and ever.

The words which I have spoken, you, Phaedrus, may call an encomium of love, or anything else which you please.

When Socrates had done speaking, the company applauded, and Aristophanes was beginning to say something in answer to the allusion which Socrates had made to his own speech [6], when suddenly there was a great knocking at the door of the house, as of revellers, and the sound of a flute-girl was heard. Agathon told the attendants to go and see who were the intruders. 'If they are friends of ours,' he said, 'invite them in, but if not, say that the drinking is over.' A little while afterwards they heard the voice of Alcibiades resounding in the court; he was in a great state of intoxication, and kept roaring and shouting 'Where is Agathon? Lead me to Agathon,' and at length, supported by

---

[6] p. 205 E.

the flute-girl and some of his attendants, he found his way to them.
'Hail, friends,' he said, appearing at the door crowned with a massive
garland of ivy and violets, his head flowing with ribands. 'Will you have
a very drunken man as a companion of your revels? Or shall I crown
Agathon, which was my intention in coming, and go away? For I was unable to come yesterday, and therefore I am here to-day, carrying on my
head these ribands, that taking them from my own head, I may
crown the head of this fairest and wisest of men, as I may be allowed
to call him. Will you laugh at me because I am drunk? Yet I know
very well that I am speaking the truth, although you may laugh.   [213
But first tell me; if I come in shall we have the understanding of which
I spoke [7]? Will you drink with me or not?'

The company were vociferous in begging that he would take his
place among them, and Agathon specially invited him. Thereupon he
was led in by the people who were with him; and as he was being led,
intending to crown Agathon, he took the ribands from his own head and
held them in front of his eyes; he was thus prevented from seeing Socrates, who made way for him, and Alcibiades took the vacant place
between Agathon and Socrates, and in taking the place he embraced
Agathon and crowned him. Take off his sandals, said Agathon, and let
him make a third on the same couch.

By all means; but who makes the third partner in our revels? said
Alcibiades, turning round and starting up as he caught sight of Socrates.
By Heracles, he said, what is this? here is Socrates always lying in wait
for me, and always, as his way is, coming out at all sorts of unsuspected
places: and now, what have you to say for yourself, and why are you
lying here, where I perceive that you have contrived to find a place, not
by a joker or lover of jokes, like Aristophanes, but by the fairest of the
company?

Socrates turned to Agathon and said: I must ask you to protect me,
Agathon; for the passion of this man has grown quite a serious matter
to me. Since I became his admirer I have never been allowed to speak to
any other fair one, or so much as to look at them. If I do, he goes wild
with envy and jealousy, and not only abuses me but can hardly keep his
hands off me, and at this moment he may do me some harm. Please to
see to this, and either reconcile me to him, or, if he attempts violence,
protect me, as I am in bodily fear of his mad and passionate attempts.

There can never be reconciliation between you and me, said
Alcibiades; but for the present I will defer your chastisement. And I
must beg you, Agathon, to give me back some of the ribands that I
may crown the marvellous head of this universal despot—I would not

---

[7] Supra 212 D. Will you have a very drunken man? etc.

have him complain of me for crowning you, and neglecting him, who in conversation is the conqueror of all mankind; and this not only once, as you were the day before yesterday, but always. Whereupon, taking some of the ribands, he crowned Socrates, and again reclined.

Then he said: You seem, my friends, to be sober, which is a thing not to be endured; you must drink—for that was the agreement under which I was admitted—and I elect myself master of the feast until you are well drunk. Let us have a large goblet, Agathon, or rather, he said, addressing the attendant, bring me that wine-cooler. The wine-cooler which had caught his eye was a vessel holding more than two   [214 quarts—this he filled and emptied, and bade the attendant fill it again for Socrates. Observe, my friends, said Alcibiades, that this ingenious trick of mine will have no effect on Socrates, for he can drink any quantity of wine and not be at all nearer being drunk. Socrates drank the cup which the attendant filled for him.

Eryximachus said: What is this, Alcibiades? Are we to have neither conversation nor singing over our cups; but simply to drink as if we were thirsty?

Alcibiades replied: Hail, worthy son of a most wise and worthy sire!

The same to you, said Eryximachus; but what shall we do?

That I leave to you, said Alcibiades.

'The wise physician skilled our wounds to heal [8]'

shall prescribe and we will obey. What do you want?

Well, said Eryximachus, before you appeared we had passed a resolution that each one of us in turn should make a speech in praise of love, and as good a one as he could: the turn was passed round from left to right; and as all of us have spoken, and you have not spoken but have well drunken, you ought to speak, and them impose upon Socrates any task which you please, and he on his right hand neighbour, and so on.

That is good, Eryximachus, said Alcibiades; and yet the comparison of a drunken man's speech with those of sober men is hardly fair; and I should like to know, sweet friend, whether you really believe what Socrates was just now saying; for I can assure you that the very reverse is the fact, and that if I praise any one but himself in his presence, whether God or man, he will hardly keep his hands off me.

For shame, said Socrates.

Hold your tongue, said Alcibiades, for by Poseidon, there is no one else whom I will praise when you are of the company.

Well then, said Eryximachus, if you like praise Socrates.

---

[8] From Pope's Homer, Il. xi. 514.

What do you think, Eryximachus? said Alcibiades: shall I attack him and inflict the punishment before you all?

What are you about? said Socrates; are you going to raise a laugh at my expense? Is that the meaning of your praise?

I am going to speak the truth, if you will permit me.

I not only permit, but exhort you to speak the truth.

Then I will begin at once, said Alcibiades, and if I say anything which is not true, you may interrupt me if you will, and say 'that is a lie,' though my intention is to speak the truth. But you must not wonder if I speak any how as things come into my mind; for the fluent and orderly enumeration of all your singularities is not a task which is easy to a man in my condition.

And now, my boys, I shall praise Socrates in a figure which   [215 will appear to him to be a caricature, and yet I speak, not to make fun of him, but only for the truth's sake. I say, that he is exactly like the busts of Silenus, which are set up in the statuaries' shops, holding pipes and flutes in their mouths; and they are made to open in the middle, and have images of gods inside them. I say also that he is like Marsyas the satyr. You yourself will not deny, Socrates, that your face is like that of a satyr. Aye, and there is a resemblance in other points too. For example, you are a bully, as I can prove by witnesses, if you will not confess. And are you not a flute-player? That you are, and a performer far more wonderful than Marsyas. He indeed with instruments used to charm the souls of men by the powers of his breath, and the players of his music do so still: for the melodies of Olympus [9] are derived from Marsyas who taught them, and these, whether they are played by a great master or by a miserable flute-girl, have a power which no others have; they alone possess the soul and reveal the wants of those who have need of gods and mysteries, because they are divine. But you produce the same effect with your words only, and do not require the flute; that is the difference between you and him. When we hear any other speaker, even a very good one, he produces absolutely no effect upon us, or not much, whereas the mere fragments of you and your words, even at second-hand, and however imperfectly repeated, amaze and possess the souls of every man, woman, and child who comes within hearing of them. And if I were not afraid that you would think me hopelessly drunk, I would have sworn as well as spoken to the influence which they have always had and still have over me. For my heart leaps within me more than that of any Corybantian reveller, and my eyes rain tears when I hear them. And I observe that many others are affected in the same manner. I have heard Pericles and other great orators, and I

---

[9] Cp. Arist. Pol. viii. 5. 16.

thought that they spoke well, but I never had any similar feeling; my soul was not stirred by them, nor was I angry at the thought of my own slavish state. But this Marsyas has often brought me to such a pass, that I have felt as if I could hardly endure the life which I am lead-   [216 ing (this, Socrates, you will admit); and I am conscious that if I did not shut my ears against him, and fly as from the voice of the siren, my fate would be like that of others,—he would transfix me, and I should grow old sitting at his feet. For he makes me confess that I ought not to live as I do, neglecting the wants of my own soul, and busying myself with the concerns of the Athenians; therefore I hold my ears and tear myself away from him. And he is the only person who ever made me ashamed, which you might think not to be in my nature, and there is no one else who does the same. For I know that I cannot answer him or say that I ought not to do as he bids, but when I leave his presence the love of popularity gets the better of me. And therefore I run away and fly from him, and when I see him I am ashamed of what I have confessed to him. Many a time have I wished that he were dead, and yet I know that I should be much more sorry than glad, if he were to die: so that I am at my wit's end.

And this is what I and many others have suffered from the flute-playing of this satyr. Yet hear me once more while I show you how exact the image is, and how marvellous his power. For let me tell you; none of you know him; but I will reveal him to you; having begun, I must go on. See you how fond he is of the fair? He is always with them and is always being smitten by them, and then again he knows nothing and is ignorant of all things—such is the appearance which he puts on. Is he not like a Silenus in this? To be sure he is: his outer mask is the carved head of the Silenus; but, O my companions in drink, when he is opened, what temperance there is residing within! Know you that beauty and wealth and honour, at which the many wonder, are of no account with him, and are utterly despised by him: he regards not at all the persons who are gifted with them; mankind are nothing to him; all his life is spent in mocking and flouting at them. But when I opened him, and looked within at his serious purpose, I saw in him divine and golden images of such fascinating beauty that I was ready to do in a   [217 moment whatever Socrates commanded: they may have escaped the observation of others, but I saw them. Now I fancied that he was seriously enamoured of my beauty, and I thought that I should therefore have a grand opportunity of hearing him tell what he knew, for I had a wonderful opinion of the attractions of my youth. In the prosecution of this design, when I next went to him, I sent away the attendant who usually accompanied me (I will confess the whole truth, and beg you to listen; and if I speak falsely, do you, Socrates, expose the falsehood). Well,

he and I were alone together, and I thought that when there was nobody with us, I should hear him speak the language which lovers use
to their loves when they are by themselves, and I was delighted.
Nothing of the sort; he conversed as usual, and spent the day with me
and then went away. Afterwards I challenged him to the palaestra; and
he wrestled and closed with me several times when there was no one
present; I fancied that I might succeed in this manner. Not a bit; I
made no way with him. Lastly, as I had failed hitherto, I thought that
I must take stronger measures and attack him boldly, and, as I had begun, not give him up, but see how matters stood between him and me.
So I invited him to sup with me, just as if he were a fair youth, and I a
designing lover. He was not easily persuaded to come; he did, however,
after a while accept the invitation, and when he came the first time,
he wanted to go away at once as soon as supper was over, and I had
not the face to detain him. The second time, still in pursuance of my
design, after we had supped, I went on conversing far into the night,
and when he wanted to go away, I pretended that the hour was late and
that he had much better remain. So he lay down on the couch next to
me, the same on which he had supped, and there was no one but ourselves sleeping in the apartment. All this may be told without shame
to any one. But what follows I could hardly tell you if I were sober. Yet
as the proverb says, 'In vino veritas,' whether with boys, or without
them [1]; and therefore I must speak. Nor, again, should I be justified in
concealing the lofty actions of Socrates when I come to praise him.
Moreover I have felt the serpent's sting; and he who has suffered, as
they say, is willing to tell his fellow-sufferers only, as they alone will be
likely to understand him, and will not be extreme in judging of   [218
the sayings or doings which have been wrung from his agony. For I have
been bitten by a more than viper's tooth; I have known in my soul, or
in my heart, or in some other part, that worst of pangs, more violent
in ingenuous youth than any serpent's tooth, the pang of philosophy,
which will make a man say or do anything. And you whom I see
around me, Phaedrus and Agathon and Eryximachus and Pausanias and
Aristodemus and Aristophanes, all of you, and I need not say Socrates
himself, have had experience of the same madness and passion in
your longing after wisdom. Therefore listen and excuse my doings then
and my sayings now. But let the attendants and other profane and un-
mannered persons close up the doors of their ears.

When the lamp was put out and the servants had gone away, I
thought that I must be plain with him and have no more ambiguity.

---

[1] In allusion to the two proverbs, οἶνος καὶ παῖδες ἀληθεῖς, and οἶνος καὶ
ἀλήθεια.

So I gave him a shake, and I said: "Socrates, are you asleep?" "No," he said. "Do you know what I am meditating?" "What are you meditating?" he said. "I think," I replied, "that of all the lovers whom I have ever had you are the only one who is worthy of me, and you appear to be too modest to speak. Now I feel that I should be a fool to refuse you this or any other favour, and therefore I come to lay at your feet all that I have and all that my friends have, in the hope that you will assist me in the way of virtue, which I desire above all things, and in which I believe that you can help me better than any one else. And I should certainly have more reason to be ashamed of what wise men would say if I were to refuse a favour to such as you, than of what the world, who are mostly fools, would say of me if I granted it." To these words he replied in the ironical manner which is so characteristic of him:—"Alcibiades, my friend, you have indeed an elevated aim if what you say is true, and if there really is in me any power by which you may become better; truly you must see in me some rare beauty of a kind infinitely higher than any which I see in you. And therefore, if you mean to share with me and to exchange beauty for beauty, you will have greatly the advantage of me; you will gain true beauty in return for appearance—like Diomede, gold in exchange for brass. But [219 look again, sweet friend, and see whether you are not deceived in me. The mind begins to grow critical when the bodily eye fails, and it will be a long time before you get old." Hearing this, I said: "I have told you my purpose, which is quite serious, and do you consider what you think best for you and me." "That is good," he said; "at some other time then we will consider and act as seems best about this and about other matters." Whereupon, I fancied that he was smitten, and that the words which I had uttered like arrows had wounded him, and so without waiting to hear more I got up, and throwing my coat about him crept under his threadbare cloak, as the time of year was winter, and there I lay during the whole night having this wonderful monster in my arms. This again, Socrates, will not be denied by you. And yet, notwithstanding all, he was so superior to my solicitations, so contemptuous and derisive and disdainful of my beauty—which really, as I fancied, had some attractions—hear, O judges; for judges you shall be of the haughty virtue of Socrates—nothing more happened, but in the morning when I awoke (let all the gods and goddesses be my witnesses) I arose as from the couch of a father or an elder brother.

What do you suppose must have been my feelings, after this rejection, at the thought of my own dishonour? And yet I could not help wondering at his natural temperance and self-restraint and manliness. I never imagined that I could have met with a man such as he is in wisdom and endurance. And therefore I could not be angry with him or renounce his company, any more than I could hope to win him. For I well knew that if Ajax could not be wounded by steel, much less he by money; and my only chance of captivating him by my personal attractions had failed. So I was at my wit's end; no one was ever more hopelessly enslaved by another. All this happened before he and I went on the expedition to Potidaea; there we messed together, and I had the opportunity of observing his extraordinary power of sustaining fatigue. His endurance was simply marvellous when, being   [220 cut off from our supplies, we were compelled to go without food—on such occasions, which often happen in time of war, he was superior not only to me but to everybody; there was no one to be compared to him. Yet at a festival he was the only person who had any real powers of enjoyment; though not willing to drink, he could if compelled beat us all at that,—wonderful to relate! no human being had ever seen Socrates drunk; and his powers, if I am not mistaken, will be tested before long. His fortitude in enduring cold was also surprising. There was a severe frost, for the winter in that region is really tremendous, and everybody else either remained indoors, or if they went out had on an amazing quantity of clothes, and were well shod, and had their feet swathed in felt and fleeces: in the midst of this, Socrates with his bare feet on the ice and in his ordinary dress marched better than the other soldiers who had shoes, and they looked daggers at him because he seemed to despise them.

I have told you one tale, and now I must tell you another, which is worth hearing,

'Of the doings and sufferings of the enduring man'

while he was on the expedition. One morning he was thinking about something which he could not resolve; he would not give it up, but continued thinking from early dawn until noon—there he stood fixed in thought; and at noon attention was drawn to him, and the rumour ran through the wondering crowd that Socrates had been standing and thinking about something ever since the break of day. At last, in the evening after supper, some Ionians out of curiosity (I should explain that this was not in winter but in summer), brought out their mats and slept in the open air that they might watch him and see whether he would stand all night. There he stood until the following morning; and with the return of light he offered up a prayer to the sun, and went his way.[2] I will also tell, if you please—and indeed I am bound to tell— of his courage in battle; for who but he saved my life? Now this was the engagement in which I received the prize of valour: for I was

---

[2] Cp. supra, 175 B.

wounded and he would not leave me, but he rescued me and my arms; and he ought to have received the prize of valour which the generals wanted to confer on me partly on account of my rank, and I told them so (this, again, Socrates will not impeach or deny), but he was more eager than the generals that I and not he should have the prize. There was another occasion on which his behaviour was very remark- [221 able—in the flight of the army after the battle of Delium, where he served among the heavy-armed,—I had a better opportunity of seeing him than at Potidaea, for I was myself on horseback, and therefore comparatively out of danger. He and Laches were retreating, for the troops were in flight, and I met them and told them not to be discouraged, and promised to remain with them; and there you might see him, Aristophanes, as you describe[3], just as he is in the streets of Athens, stalking like a pelican, and rolling his eyes, calmly contemplating enemies as well as friends, and making very intelligible to anybody, even from a distance, that whoever attacked him would be likely to meet with a stout resistance; and in this way he and his companion escaped—for this is the sort of man who is never touched in war; those only are pursued who are running away headlong. I particularly observed how superior he was to Laches in presence of mind. Many are the marvels which I might narrate in praise of Socrates; most of his ways might perhaps be paralleled in another man, but his absolute unlikeness to any human being that is or ever has been is perfectly astonishing. You may imagine Brasidas and others to have been like Achilles; or you may imagine Nestor and Antenor to have been like Pericles; and the same may be said of other famous men, but of this strange being you will never be able to find any likeness, however remote, either among men who now are or who ever have been—other than that which I have already suggested of Silenus and the satyrs; and they represent in a figure not only himself, but his words. For, although I forgot to mention this to you before, his words are like the images of Silenus which open; they are ridiculous when you first hear them; he clothes himself in language that is like the skin of the wanton satyr—for his talk is of pack-asses and smiths and cobblers and curriers, and he is always repeating the same things in the same words[4], so that any ignorant or inexperienced person might feel disposed to laugh at him; but he who opens [222 the bust and sees what is within will find that they are the only words which have a meaning in them, and also the most divine, abounding in fair images of virtue, and of the widest comprehension, or rather extending to the whole duty of a good and honourable man.

---

[3] Aristoph. Clouds, 362.
[4] Cp. Gorg. 490, 491, 517.

This, friends, is my praise of Socrates. I have added my blame of him for his ill-treatment of me; and he has ill-treated not only me, but Charmides the son of Glaucon, and Euthydemus the son of Diocles, and many others in the same way—beginning as their lover he has ended by making them pay their addresses to him. Wherefore I say to you, Agathon, "Be not deceived by him; learn from me and take warning, and do not be a fool and learn by experience, as the proverb says."

When Alcibiades had finished, there was a laugh at his outspokenness; for he seemed to be still in love with Socrates. You are sober, Alcibiades, said Socrates, or you would never have gone so far about to hide the purpose of your satyr's praises, for all this long story is only an ingenious circumlocution, of which the point comes in by the way at the end; you want to get up a quarrel between me and Agathon, and your notion is that I ought to love you and nobody else, and that you and you only ought to love Agathon. But the plot of this Satyric or Silenic drama has been detected, and you must not allow him, Agathon, to set us at variance.

I believe you are right, said Agathon, and I am disposed to think that his intention in placing himself between you and me was only to divide us; but he shall gain nothing by that move; for I will go and lie on the couch next to you.

Yes, yes replied Socrates, by all means come here and lie on the couch below me.

Alas, said Alcibiades, how I am fooled by this man; he is determined to get the better of me at every turn. I do beseech you, allow Agathon to lie between us.

Certainly not, said Socrates, as you praised me, and I in turn ought to praise my neighbour on the right, he will be out of order in praising me again when he ought rather to be praised by me, and I must entreat you to consent to this, and not be jealous, for I have a great desire to praise the youth.

Hurrah! cried Agathon, I will rise instantly, that I may be praised by Socrates.

The usual way, said Alcibiades; where Socrates is, no one else has any chance with the fair; and now how readily has he invented a specious reason for attracting Agathon to himself.

Agathon arose in order that he might take his place on the couch by Socrates, when suddenly a band of revellers entered, and spoiled the order of the banquet. Some one who was going out having left the door open, they had found their way in, and made themselves at home; great confusion ensued, and every one was compelled to drink large quantities of wine. Aristodemus said that Eryximachus,

Phaedrus, and others went away—he himself fell asleep, and as the nights were long took a good rest: he was awakened towards daybreak by a crowing of cocks, and when he awoke, the others were either asleep, or had gone away; there remained only Socrates, Aristophanes, and Agathon, who were drinking out of a large goblet which they passed round, and Socrates was discoursing to them. Aristodemus was only half awake, and he did not hear the beginning of the discourse; the chief thing which he remembered was Socrates compelling the other two to acknowledge that the genius of comedy was the same with that of tragedy, and that the true artist in tragedy was an artist in comedy also. To this they were constrained to assent, being drowsy, and not quite following the argument. And first of all Aristophanes dropped off, then, when the day was already dawning, Agathon. Socrates, having laid them to sleep, rose to depart; Aristodemus, as his manner was, following him. At the Lyceum he took a bath, and passed the day as usual. In the evening he retired to rest at his own home.

PHAEDO

PERSONS OF THE DIALOGUE

PHAEDO, *who is the narrator of the Dialogue to Echecrates of Phlius*
SOCRATES
ATTENDANT OF THE PRISON
APOLLODORUS
SIMMIAS
CEBES
CRITO

SCENE:—*The Prison of Socrates*

PLACE OF THE NARRATION:—*Phlius*

Echecrates. Were you yourself, Phaedo, in the prison with Socrates on the day when he drank the poison?   [57

Phaedo. Yes, Echecrates, I was.

Echecrates. I should so like to hear about his death. What did he say in his last hours? We were informed that he died by taking poison, but no one knew anything more; for no Phliasian ever goes to Athens now, and it is a long time since any stranger from Athens has found his way hither; so that we had no clear account.

Phaedo. Did you not hear of the proceedings at the trial?   [58

Echecrates. Yes: some one told us about the trial, and we could not understand why, having been condemned, he should have been put to death, not at the time, but long afterwards. What was the reason of this?

Phaedo. An accident, Echecrates: the stern of the ship which the Athenians send to Delos happened to have been crowned on the day before he was tried.

Echecrates. What is this ship?

Phaedo. It is the ship in which, according to Athenian tradition, Theseus went to Crete when he took with him the fourteen youths, and was the saviour of them and of himself. And they are said to have vowed to Apollo at the time, that if they were saved they would send a yearly mission to Delos. Now this custom still continues, and the whole period of the voyage to and from Delos, beginning when the priest of Apollo crowns the stern of the ship, is a holy season, during which the city is not allowed to be polluted by public executions; and when the vessel is detained by contrary winds, the time spent in going and returning is very considerable. As I was saying, the ship was crowned on the day before the trial, and this was the reason why Socrates lay in prison and was not put to death until long after he was condemned.

Echecrates. What was the manner of his death, Phaedo? What was said or done? And which of his friends were with him? Or did the authorities forbid them to be present—so that he had no friends near him when he died?

Phaedo. No; there were several of them with him.

Echecrates. If you have nothing to do, I wish that you would tell me what passed, as exactly as you can.

Phaedo. I have nothing at all to do, and will try to gratify your wish. To be reminded of Socrates is always the greatest delight to me, whether I speak myself or hear another speak of him.

Echecrates. You will have listeners who are of the same mind with you, and I hope that you will be as exact as you can.

Phaedo. I had a singular feeling at being in his company. For I could hardly believe that I was present at the death of a friend, and therefore I did not pity him, Echecrates; he died so fearlessly, and his words and bearing were so noble and gracious, that to me he appeared blessed. I thought that in going to the other world he could not be without a divine call, and that he would be happy, if any man ever was, when he arrived there; and therefore I did not pity him as might have seemed natural at such an hour. But I had not the pleasure which I usually feel in philosophical discourse (for philosophy was the theme of which we spoke). I was pleased, but in the pleasure there was also a strange admixture of pain; for I reflected that he was soon to die, and this double feeling was shared by us all; we were laughing and weeping by turns, especially the excitable Apollodorus— you know the sort of man?

Echecrates. Yes.

Phaedo. He was quite beside himself; and I and all of us were greatly moved.

Echecrates. Who were present?

Phaedo. Of native Athenians there were, besides Apollodorus, Critobulus and his father Crito, Hermogenes, Epigenes, Aeschines, Antisthenes; likewise Ctesippus of the deme of Paeania, Menexenus, and some others; Plato, if I am not mistaken, was ill.

Echecrates. Were there any strangers?

Phaedo. Yes, there were; Simmias the Theban, and Cebes, and Phaedondes; Euclid and Terpsion, who came from Megara.

Echecrates. And was Aristippus there, and Cleombrotus?

Phaedo. No, they were said to be in Aegina.

Echecrates. Any one else?

Phaedo. I think that these were nearly all.

Echecrates. Well, and what did you talk about?

Phaedo. I will begin at the beginning, and endeavour to repeat the entire conversation. On the previous days we had been in the habit of assembling early in the morning at the court in which the trial took place, and which is not far from the prison. There we used to wait talking with one another until the opening of the doors (for they were not opened very early); then we went in and generally passed the day with Socrates. On the last morning we assembled sooner than usual, having heard on the day before when we quitted the prison in the evening that the sacred ship had come from Delos; and so we arranged to meet very early at the accustomed place. On our arrival the jailer who answered the door, instead of admitting us, came out and told us to stay until he called us. "For the Eleven," he said, "are now with Socrates; they are taking off his chains, and giving orders that he is to die to-day." He soon returned and said that we might come [60 in. On entering we found Socrates just released from chains, and Xanthippè, whom you know, sitting by him, and holding his child in her arms. When she saw us she uttered a cry and said, as women will: "O Socrates, this is the last time that either you will converse with your friends, or they with you." Socrates turned to Crito and said: "Crito, let some one take her home." Some of Crito's people accordingly led her away, crying out and beating herself. And when she was gone, Socrates, sitting up on the couch, bent and rubbed his leg, saying, as he was rubbing: How singular is the thing called pleasure, and how curiously related to pain, which might be thought to be the opposite of it; for they are never present to a man at the same instant, and yet he who pursues either is generally compelled to take the other; their bodies are two, but they are joined by a single head. And I cannot help thinking that if Aesop had remembered them, he would have made a fable about God trying to reconcile their strife, and how, when he could not, he fastened their heads together; and this is the reason why when one comes the other follows: as I know by my own experience now, when after the pain in my leg which was caused by the chain pleasure appears to succeed.

Upon this Cebes said: I am glad, Socrates, that you have mentioned the name of Aesop. For it reminds me of a question which has been asked by many, and was asked of me only the day before yesterday by Evenus the poet—he will be sure to ask it again, and therefore if you would like me to have an answer ready for him, you may as well tell me what I should say to him:—he wanted to know why you, who never before wrote a line of poetry, now that you are in prison are turning Aesop's fables into verse, and also composing that hymn in honour of Apollo.

Tell him, Cebes, he replied, what is the truth—that I had no idea of rivalling him or his poems; to do so, as I knew, would be no easy task. But I wanted to see whether I could purge away a scruple which I felt about the meaning of certain dreams. In the course of my life I have often had intimations in dreams "that I should compose music." The same dream came to me sometimes in one form, and sometimes in another, but always saying the same or nearly the same words: "Cultivate and make music," said the dream. And hitherto I had imagined that this way was only intended to exhort and encourage me in the study of philosophy, which has been the pursuit of my life, and is the noblest and best of music. The dream was bidding me   [61 do what I was already doing, in the same way that the competitor in a race is bidden by the spectators to run when he is already running. But I was not certain of this; for the dream might have meant music in the popular sense of the word, and being under sentence of death, and the festival giving me a respite, I thought that it would be safer for me to satisfy the scruple, and, in obedience to the dream, to compose a few verses before I departed. And first I made a hymn in honour of the god of the festival, and then considering that a poet, if he is really to be a poet, should not only put together words, but should invent stories, and that I have no invention, I took some fables of Aesop, which I had ready at hand and which I knew—they were the first I came upon—and turned them into verse. Tell this to Evenus, Cebes, and bid him be of good cheer; say that I would have him come after me if he be a wise man, and not tarry; and that to-day I am likely to be going, for the Athenians say that I must.

Simmias said: What a message for such a man! having been a frequent companion of his I should say that, as far as I know him, he will never take your advice unless he is obliged.

Why, said Socrates,—is not Evenus a philosopher?

I think that he is, said Simmias.

Then he, or any man who has the spirit of philosophy, will be willing to die; but he will not take his own life, for that is held to be unlawful.

Here he changed his position, and put his legs off the couch on to the ground, and during the rest of the conversation he remained sitting.

Why do you say, enquired Cebes, that a man ought not to take his own life, but that the philosopher will be ready to follow the dying?

Socrates replied: And have you, Cebes and Simmias, who are the disciples of Philolaus, never heard him speak of this?

Yes, but his language was obscure, Socrates.

My words, too, are only an echo; but there is no reason why I should not repeat what I have heard: and indeed, as I am going to another place, it is very meet for me to be thinking and talking of the nature of the pilgrimage which I am about to make. What can I do better in the interval between this and the setting of the sun?

Then tell me, Socrates, why is suicide held to be unlawful? as I have certainly heard Philolaus, about whom you were just now asking, affirm when he was staying with us at Thebes; and there are others who say the same, although I have never understood what was meant by any of them.

Do not lose heart, replied Socrates, and the day may come   [62 when you will understand. I suppose that you wonder why, when other things which are evil may be good at certain times and to certain persons, death is to be the only exception, and why, when a man is better dead, he is not permitted to be his own benefactor, but must wait for the hand of another.

Fery true, said Cebes, laughing gently and speaking in his native Boeotian.

I admit the appearance of inconsistency in what I am saying; but there may not be any real inconsistency after all. There is a doctrine whispered in secret that man is a prisoner who has no right to open the door and run away; this is a great mystery which I do not quite understand. Yet I too believe that the gods are our guardians, and that we men are a possession of theirs. Do you not agree?

Yes, I quite agree, said Cebes.

And if one of your own possessions, an ox or an ass, for example, took the liberty of putting himself out of the way when you had given no intimation of your wish that he should die, would you not be angry with him, and would you not punish him if you could?

Certainly, replied Cebes.

Then, if we look at the matter thus, there may be reason in saying that a man should wait, and not take his own life until God summons him, as he is now summoning me.

Yes, Socrates, said Cebes, there seems to be truth in what you say. And yet how can you reconcile this seemingly true belief that God is our guardian and we his possessions, with the willingness to die which you were just now attributing to the philosopher? That the wisest of men should be willing to leave a service in which they are ruled by the gods who are the best of rulers, is not reasonable; for surely no wise man thinks that when set at liberty he can take better care of himself than the gods take of him. A fool may perhaps think so—he may argue that he had better run away from his master, not considering that his duty is to remain to the end, and not to run away from the good, and that there would be no sense in his running away. The wise man will want to be ever with him who is better than himself. Now this, Socrates, is the reverse of what was just now said; for upon this view the wise man should sorrow and the fool rejoice at passing out of life.

The earnestness of Cebes seemed to please Socrates. Here, [63 said he, turning to us, is a man who is always enquiring, and is not so easily convinced by the first thing which he hears.

And certainly, added Simmias, the objection which he is now making does appear to me to have some force. For what can be the meaning of a truly wise man wanting to fly away and lightly leave a master who is better than himself? And I rather imagine that Cebes is referring to you; he thinks you are too ready to leave us, and too ready to leave the gods whom you acknowledge to be our good masters.

Yes, replied Socrates; there is reason in what you say. And so you think that I ought to answer your indictment as if I were in a court?

We should like you to do so, said Simmias.

Then I must try to make a more successful defence before you than I did before the judges. For I am quite ready to admit, Simmias and Cebes, that I ought to be grieved at death, if I were not persuaded in the first place that I am going to other gods who are wise and good (of which I am as certain as I can be of any such matters), and secondly (though I am not so sure of this last) to men departed, better than those whom I leave behind; and therefore I do not grieve as I might have done, for I have good hope that there is yet something remaining for the dead, and as has been said of old, some far better thing for the good than for the evil.

But do you mean to take away your thoughts with you, Socrates? said Simmias. Will you not impart them to us?—for they are a benefit in which we too are entitled to share. Moreover, if you succeed in convincing us, that will be an answer to the charge against yourself.

I will do my best, replied Socrates. But you must first let me hear what Crito wants; he has long been wishing to say something to me.

Only this, Socrates, replied Crito:—the attendant who is to give you the poison has been telling me, and he wants me to tell you, that you are not to talk much; talking, he says, increases heat, and this is apt to interfere with the action of the poison; persons who excite themselves are sometimes obliged to take a second or even a third dose.

Then, said Socrates, let him mind his business and be prepared to give the poison twice or even thrice if necessary; that is all.

I knew quite well what you would say, replied Crito; but I was obliged to satisfy him.

Never mind him, he said.

And now, O my judges, I desire to prove to you that the real philosopher has reason to be of good cheer when he is about to die, and that after death he may hope to obtain the greatest good in   [64 the other world. And how this may be, Simmias and Cebes, I will endeavour to explain. For I deem that the true votary of philosophy is likely to be misunderstood by other men; they do not perceive that he is always pursuing death and dying; and if this be so, and he has had the desire of death all his life long, why when his time comes should he repine at that which he has been always pursuing and desiring?

Simmias said laughingly: Though not in a laughing humour, you have made me laugh, Socrates; for I cannot help thinking that the many when they hear your words will say how truly you have described philosophers, and our people at home will likewise say that the life which philosophers desire is in reality death, and that they have found them out to be deserving of the death which they desire.

And they are right, Simmias, in thinking so, with the exception of the words 'they have found them out;' for they have not found out either what is the nature of that death which the true philosopher deserves, or how he deserves or desires death. But enough of them:—let us discuss the matter among ourselves. Do we believe that there is such a thing as death?

To be sure, replied Simmias.

Is it not the separation of soul and body? And to be dead is the completion of this; when the soul exists in herself, and is released from the body and the body is released from the soul, what is this but death?

Just so, he replied.

There is another question, which will probably throw light on our present enquiry if you and I can agree about it:—Ought the philosopher to care about the pleasures—if they are to be called pleasures—of eating and drinking?

Certainly not, answered Simmias.

And what about the pleasures of love—should he care for them?
By no means.

And will he think much of the other ways of indulging the body,
for example, the acquisition of costly raiment, or sandals, or other
adornments of the body? Instead of caring about them, does he not
rather despise anything more than nature needs? What do you say?

I should say that the true philosopher would despise them.

Would you not say that he is entirely concerned with the soul
and not with the body? He would like, as far as he can, to get away from
the body and to turn to the soul.

Quite true.

In matters of this sort philosophers, above all other men, may be
observed in every sort of way to dissever the soul from the com-   [65
munion of the body.

Very true.

Whereas, Simmias, the rest of the world are of opinion that to him
who has no sense of pleasure and no part in bodily pleasure, life is not
worth having; and that he who is indifferent about them is as good
as dead.

That is also true.

What again shall we say of the actual acquirement of knowledge?—is the body, if invited to share in the enquiry, a hinderer or
a helper? I mean to say, have sight and hearing any truth in them? Are
they not, as the poets are always telling us, inaccurate witnesses? and
yet, if even they are inaccurate and indistinct, what is to be said of the
other senses?—for you will allow that they are the best of them?

Certainly, he replied.

Then when does the soul attain truth?—for in attempting to
consider anything in company with the body she is obviously deceived.

True.

Then must not true existence be revealed to her in thought, if at
all?

Yes.

And thought is best when the mind is gathered into herself and
none of these things trouble her—neither sounds nor sights nor pain
nor any pleasure,—when she takes leave of the body, and has as little
as possible to do with it, when she has no bodily sense or desire, but is
aspiring after true being?

Certainly.

And in this the philosopher dishonours the body; his soul runs
away from his body and desires to be alone and by herself?

That is true.

Well, but there is another thing, Simmias: Is there or is there not an absolute justice?

Assuredly there is.

And an absolute beauty and absolute good?

Of course.

But did you ever behold any of them with your eyes?

Certainly not.

Or did you ever reach them with any other bodily sense?—and I speak not of these alone, but of absolute greatness, and health, and strength, and of the essence or true nature of everything. Has the reality of them ever been perceived by you through the bodily organs? or rather, is not the nearest approach to the knowledge of their several natures made by him who so orders his intellectual vision as to have the most exact conception of the essence of each thing which he considers?

Certainly.

And he attains to the purest knowledge of them who goes to each with the mind alone, not introducing or intruding in the act of thought sight or any other sense together with reason, but with the very light of the mind in her own clearness searches into the very truth   [66 of each; he who has got rid, as far as he can, of eyes and ears and, so to speak, of the whole body, these being in his opinion distracting elements which when they infect the soul hinder her from acquiring truth and knowledge—who, if not he, is likely to attain to the knowledge of true being?

What you say has a wonderful truth in it, Socrates, replied Simmias.

And when real philosophers consider all these things, will they not be led to make a reflection which they will express in words something like the following? 'Have we not found,' they will say, 'a path of thought which seems to bring us and our argument to the conclusion, that while we are in the body, and while the soul is infected with the evils of the body, our desire will not be satisfied? and our desire is of the truth. For the body is a source of endless trouble to us by reason of the mere requirement of food; and is liable also to diseases which overtake and impede us in the search after true being: it fills us full of loves, and lusts, and fears, and fancies of all kinds, and endless foolery, and in fact, as men say, takes away from us the power of thinking at all. Whence come wars, and fightings, and factions? whence but from the body and the lusts of the body? Wars are occasioned by the love of money, and money has to be acquired for the sake and in the service of the body; and by reason of all these impediments we have no time to give to philosophy; and, last and worst of all, even if we are at leisure and betake ourselves to some speculation, the body is always breaking in upon us, causing turmoil and confusion in our enquiries, and so amazing us that we are prevented from seeing the truth. It has been proved to us by experience that if we would have pure knowledge of anything we must be quit of the body—the soul in herself must behold things in themselves: and then we shall attain the wisdom which we desire, and of which we say that we are lovers; not while we live, but after death; for if while in company with the body, the soul cannot have pure knowledge, one of two things follows—either knowledge is not to be attained at all, or, if at all, after death. For then, and   [67 not till then, the soul will be parted from the body and exist in herself alone. In this present life, I reckon that we make the nearest approach to knowledge when we have the least possible intercourse or communion with the body, and are not surfeited with the bodily nature, but keep ourselves pure until the hour when God himself is pleased to release us. And thus having got rid of the foolishness of the body we shall be pure and hold converse with the pure, and know of ourselves the clear light everywhere, which is no other than the light of truth.' For the impure are not permitted to approach the pure. These are the sort of words, Simmias, which the true lovers of knowledge cannot help saying to one another, and thinking. You would agree; would you not?

Undoubtedly, Socrates.

But, O my friend, if this be true, there is great reason to hope that, going whither I go, when I have come to the end of my journey, I shall attain that which has been the pursuit of my life. And therefore I go on my way rejoicing, and not I only, but every other man who believes that his mind has been made ready and that he is in a manner purified.

Certainly, replied Simmias.

And what is purification but the separation of the soul from the body, as I was saying before; the habit of the soul gathering and collecting herself into herself from all sides out of the body; the dwelling in her own place alone, as in another life, so also in this, as far as she can;—the release of the soul from the chains of the body?

Very true, he said.

And this separation and release of the soul from the body is termed death?

To be sure, he said.

And the true philosophers, and they only, are ever seeking to release the soul. Is not the separation and release of the soul from the body their especial study?

That is true.

And, as I was saying at first, there would be a ridiculous contradiction in men studying to live as nearly as they can in a state of death, and yet repining when it comes upon them.

Clearly.

And the true philosophers, Simmias, are always occupied in the practice of dying, wherefore also to them least of all men is death terrible. Look at the matter thus:—if they have been in every way the enemies of the body, and are wanting to be alone with the soul, when this desire of theirs is granted, how inconsistent would they be if they trembled and repined, instead of rejoicing at their departure to that place where, when they arrive, they hope to gain that which in life they desired—and this was wisdom—and at the same   [68 time to be rid of the company of their enemy. Many a man has been willing to go to the world below animated by the hope of seeing there an earthly love, or wife, or son, and conversing with them. And will he who is a true lover of wisdom, and is strongly persuaded in like manner that only in the world below he can worthily enjoy her, still repine at death? Will he not depart with joy? Surely he will, O my friend, if he be a true philosopher. For he will have a firm conviction that there, and there only, he can find wisdom in her purity. And if this be true, he would be very absurd, as I was saying, if he were afraid of death.

He would indeed, replied Simmias.

And when you see a man who is repining at the approach of death, is not his reluctance a sufficient proof that he is not a lover of wisdom, but a lover of the body, and probably at the same time a lover of either money or power, or both?

Quite so, he replied.

And is not courage, Simmias, a quality which is specially characteristic of the philosopher?

Certainly.

There is temperance again, which even by the vulgar is supposed to consist in the control and regulation of the passions, and in the sense of superiority to them—is not temperance a virtue belonging to those only who despise the body, and who pass their lives in philosophy?

Most assuredly.

For the courage and temperance of other men, if you will consider them, are really a contradiction.

How so?

Well, he said, you are aware that death is regarded by men in general as a great evil.

Very true, he said.

And do not courageous men face death because they are afraid of yet greater evils?

That is quite true.

Then all but the philosophers are courageous only from fear, and because they are afraid; and yet that a man should be courageous from fear, and because he is a coward, is surely a strange thing.

Very true.

And are not the temperate exactly in the same case? They are temperate because they are intemperate—which might seem to be a contradiction, but is nevertheless the sort of thing which happens with this foolish temperance. For there are pleasures which they are afraid of losing; and in their desire to keep them, they abstain from some pleasures, because they are overcome by others; and although to be conquered by pleasure is called by men intemperance, to them   [69 the conquest of pleasure consists in being conquered by pleasure. And that is what I mean by saying that, in a sense, they are made temperate through intemperance.

Such appears to be the case.

Yet the exchange of one fear or pleasure or pain for another fear or pleasure or pain, and of the greater for the less, as if they were coins, is not the exchange of virtue. O my blessed Simmias, is there not one true coin for which all things ought to be exchanged?—and that is wisdom; and only in exchange for this, and in company with this, is anything truly bought or sold, whether courage or temperance or justice. And is not all true virtue the companion of wisdom, no matter what fears or pleasures or other similar goods or evils may or may not attend her? But the virtue which is made up of these goods, when they are severed from wisdom and exchanged with one another, is a shadow of virtue only, nor is there any freedom or health or truth in her; but in the true exchange there is a purging away of all these things, and temperance, and justice, and courage, and wisdom herself are the purgation of them. The founders of the mysteries would appear to have had a real meaning, and were not talking nonsense when they intimated in a figure long ago that he who passes unsanctified and uninitiated into the world below will lie in a slough, but that he who arrives there after initiation and purification will dwell with the gods. For 'many,' as they say in the mysteries, 'are the thyrsus-bearers, but few are the mystics,'—meaning, as I interpret the words, 'the true philosophers.' In the number of whom, during my whole life, I have been seeking, according to my ability, to find a place;—whether I have sought in a right way or not, and whether I have succeeded or not, I shall truly know in a little while, if God will, when I myself arrive in the other world—such is my belief. And therefore I maintain that I am right, Simmias and Cebes, in not grieving or repining at parting from you and my masters in this world, for I believe that I shall equally find good masters and friends in another world. But most men do not believe this saying; if then I succeed in convincing you by my defence better than I did the Athenian judges, it will be well.

Cebes answered: I agree, Socrates, in the greater part of what you say. But in what concerns the soul, men are apt to be incred- [70 ulous; they fear that when she has left the body her place may be nowhere, and that on the very day of death she may perish and come to an end—immediately on her release from the body, issuing forth dispersed like smoke or air and in her flight vanishing away into nothingness. If she could only be collected into herself after she has obtained release from the evils of which you were speaking, there would be good reason to hope, Socrates, that what you say is true. But surely it requires a great deal of argument and many proofs to show that when the man is dead his soul yet exists, and has any force or intelligence.

True, Cebes, said Socrates; and shall I suggest that we converse a little of the probabilities of these things?

I am sure, said Cebes, that I should greatly like to know your opinion about them.

I reckon, said Socrates, that no one who heard me now, not even if he were one of my old enemies, the Comic poets, could accuse me of idle talking about matters in which I have no concern:—If you please, then, we will proceed with the enquiry.

Suppose we consider the question whether the souls of men after death are or are not in the world below. There comes into my mind an ancient doctrine which affirms that they go from hence into the other world, and returning hither, are born again from the dead. Now if it be true that the living come from the dead, then our souls must exist in the other world, for if not, how could they have been born again? And this would be conclusive, if there were any real evidence that the living are only born from the dead; but if this is not so, then other arguments will have to be adduced.

Very true, replied Cebes.

Then let us consider the whole question, not in relation to man only, but in relation to animals generally, and to plants, and to everything of which there is generation, and the proof will be easier. Are not all things which have opposites generated out of their opposites? I mean such things as good and evil, just and unjust—and there are innumerable other opposites which are generated out of opposites. And I want to show that in all opposites there is of necessity a similar alternation; I mean to say, for example, that anything which becomes greater must become greater after being less.

True.

And that which becomes less must have been once greater and then have become less.   [71

Yes.

And the weaker is generated from the stronger, and the swifter from the slower.

Very true.

And the worse is from the better, and the more just is from the more unjust.

Of course.

And is this true of all opposites? and are we convinced that all of them are generated out of opposites?

Yes.

And in this universal opposition of all things, are there not also two intermediate processes which are ever going on, from one to the other opposite, and back again; where there is a greater and a less there is also an intermediate process of increase and diminution, and that which grows is said to wax, and that which decays to wane?

Yes, he said.

And there are many other processes, such as division and composition, cooling and heating, which equally involve a passage into and out of one another. And this necessarily holds of all opposites, even though not always expressed in words—they are really generated out of one another, and there is a passing or process from one to the other of them?

Very true, he replied.

Well, and is there not an opposite of life, as sleep is the opposite of waking?

True, he said.

And what is it?

Death, he answered.

And these, if they are opposites, are generated the one from the other, and have their two intermediate processes also?

Of course.

Now, said Socrates, I will analyze one of the two pairs of opposites which I have mentioned to you, and also its intermediate processes, and you shall analyze the other to me. One of them I term sleep, the other waking. The state of sleep is opposed to the state of waking, and out of sleeping waking is generated, and out of waking, sleeping; and the process of generation is in the one case falling asleep, and in the other waking up. Do you agree?

I entirely agree.

Then, suppose that you analyze life and death to me in the same manner. Is not death opposed to life?

Yes.

And they are generated one from the other?

Yes.

What is generated from the living?

The dead.

And what from the dead?

I can only say in answer—the living.

Then the living, whether things or persons, Cebes, are generated from the dead?

That is clear, he replied.

Then the inference is that our souls exist in the world below?

That is true.

And one of the two processes or generations is visible—for surely the act of dying is visible?

Surely, he said.

What then is to be the result? Shall we exclude the opposite process? and shall we suppose nature to walk on one leg only? Must we not rather assign to death some corresponding process of generation?

Certainly, he replied.

And what is that process?

Return to life.

And return to life, if there be such a thing, is the birth of the dead into the world of the living?   [72

Quite true.

There here is a new way by which we arrive at the conclusion that the living come from the dead, just as the dead come from the living; and this, if true, affords a most certain proof that the souls of the dead exist in some place out of which they come again.

Yes, Socrates, he said; the conclusion seems to flow necessarily out of our previous admissions.

And that these admissions were not unfair, Cebes, he said, may be shown, I think, as follows: If generation were in a straight line only, and there were no compensation or circle in nature, no turn or return of elements into their opposites, then you know that all things would at last have the same form and pass into the same state, and there would be no more generation of them.

What do you mean? he said.

A simple thing enough, which I will illustrate by the case of sleep, he replied. You know that if there were no alternation of sleeping and waking, the tale of the sleeping Endymion would in the end have no meaning, because all other things would be asleep too, and he would not be distinguishable from the rest. Or if there were composition only, and no division of substances, then the chaos of Anaxagoras would come again. And in like manner, my dear Cebes, if all things which partook of life were to die, and after they were dead remained in the form of death, and did not come to life again, all would at last die, and nothing would be alive—what other result could there be? For if the living spring from any other things, and they too die, must not all things at last be swallowed up in death? [1]

There is no escape, Socrates, said Cebes; and to me your argument seems to be absolutely true.

Yes, he said, Cebes, it is and must be so, in my opinion; and we have not been deluded in making these admissions; but I am confident that there truly is such a thing as living again, and that the living spring from the dead, and that the souls of the dead are in existence, and that the good souls have a better portion than the evil.

Cebes added: Your favourite doctrine, Socrates, that knowledge is simply recollection, if true, also necessarily implies a previous time in which we have learned that which we now recollect. But this would be impossible unless our soul had been in some place before existing   [73 in the form of man; here then is another proof of the soul's immortality.

But tell me, Cebes, said Simmias, interposing, what arguments are urged in favour of this doctrine of recollection. I am not very sure at the moment that I remember them.

One excellent proof, said Cebes, is afforded by questions. If you put a question to a person in a right way, he will give a true answer of himself, but how could he do this unless there were knowledge and right reason already in him? And this is most clearly shown when he is taken to a diagram or to anything of that sort.[2]

But if, said Socrates, you are still incredulous, Simmias, I would ask you whether you may not agree with me when you look at the matter in another way;—I mean, if you are still incredulous as to whether knowledge is recollection?

Incredulous I am not, said Simmias; but I want to have this doctrine of recollection brought to my own recollection, and, from what Cebes has said, I am beginning to recollect and be convinced: but I should still like to hear what you were going to say.

This is what I would say, he replied:—We should agree, if I am not mistaken, that what a man recollects he must have known at some previous time.

Very true.

And what is the nature of this knowledge or recollection? I mean to ask, Whether a person who, having seen or heard or in any way perceived anything, knows not only that, but has a conception of something else

---

[1] But cp. Rep. x. 611 A.
[2] Cp. Meno 83 ff.

which is the subject, not of the same but of some other kind of knowledge, may not be fairly said to recollect that of which he has the conception?

What do you mean?

I mean what I may illustrate by the following instance:—The
knowledge of a lyre is not the same as the knowledge of a man?

True.

And yet what is the feeling of lovers when they recognize a lyre,
or a garment, or anything else which the beloved has been in the habit
of using? Do not they, from knowing the lyre, form in the mind's eye
an image of the youth to whom the lyre belongs? And this is recollection. In like manner any one who sees Simmias may remember Cebes;
and there are endless examples of the same thing.

Endless, indeed, replied Simmias.

And recollection is most commonly a process of recovering that
which has been already forgotten through time and inattention.

Very true, he said.

Well; and may you not also from seeing the picture of a house or
a lyre remember a man? and from the picture of Simmias, you may
be led to remember Cebes;

True.

Or you may also be led to the recollection of Simmias himself?

Quite so.   [74

And in all these cases, the recollection may be derived from things
either like or unlike?

It may be.

And when the recollection is derived from like things, then another
consideration is sure to arise, which is—whether the likeness in any degree falls short or not of that which is recollected?

Very true, he said.

And shall we proceed a step further, and affirm that there is such
a thing as equality, not of one piece of wood or stone with another,
but that, over and above this, there is absolute equality? Shall we say so?

Say so, yes, replied Simmias, and swear to it, with all the confidence
in life.

And do we know the nature of this absolute essence?

To be sure, he said.

And whence did we obtain our knowledge? Did we not see equali-
ties of material things, such as pieces of wood and stones, and gather
from them the idea of an equality which is different from them? For
you will acknowledge that there is a difference. Or look at the matter
in another way:—Do not the same pieces of wood or stone appear at
one time equal, and at another time unequal?

That is certain.

But are real equals ever equal? or is the idea of equality the same as of inequality?

Impossible, Socrates.

Then these (so-called) equals are not the same with the idea of equality?

I should say, clearly not, Socrates.

And yet from these equals, although differing from the idea of equality, you conceived and attained that idea?

Very true, he said.

Which might be like, or might be unlike them?

Yes.

But that makes no difference: whenever from seeing one thing you conceived another, whether like or unlike, there must surely have been an act of recollection?

Very true.

But what would you say of equal portions of wood and stone, or other material equals? and what is the impression produced by them? Are they equals in the same sense in which absolute equality is equal? or do they fall short of this perfect equality in a measure?

Yes, he said, in a very great measure too.

And must we not allow, that when I or any one, looking at any object, observes that the thing which he sees aims at being some other thing, but falls short of, and cannot be, that other thing, but is inferior, he who makes this observation must have had a previous knowledge of that to which the other, although similar, was inferior.

Certainly.

And has not this been our own case in the matter of equals and of absolute equality?

Precisely.

Then we must have known equality previously to the time when we first saw the material equals, and reflected that all these ap-   [75 parent equals strive to attain absolute equality, but fall short of it?

Very true.

And we recognize also that this absolute equality has only been known, and can only be known, through the medium of sight or touch, or of some other of the senses, which are all alike in this respect?

Yes, Socrates, as far as the argument is concerned, one of them is the same as the other.

From the senses then is derived the knowledge that all sensible things aim at an absolute equality of which they fall short?

Yes.

Then before we began to see or hear or perceive in any way, we must have had a knowledge of absolute equality, or we could not have referred to that standard the equals which are derived from the senses? —for to that they all aspire, and of that they fall short.

No other inference can be drawn from the previous statements.

And did we not see and hear and have the use of our other senses as soon as we were born?

Certainly.

Then we must have acquired the knowledge of equality at some previous time?

Yes.

That is to say, before we were born, I suppose?

True.

And if we acquired this knowledge before we were born, and were born having the use of it, then we also knew before we were born and at the instant of birth not only the equal or the greater or the less, but all other ideas; for we are not speaking only of equality, but of beauty, goodness, justice, holiness, and of all which we stamp with the name of essence in the dialectical process, both when we ask and when we answer questions. Of all this we may certainly affirm that we acquired the knowledge before birth?

We may.

But if, after having acquired, we have not forgotten what in each case we acquired, then we must always have come into life having knowledge, and shall always continue to know as long as life lasts—for knowing is the acquiring and retaining knowledge and not forgetting. Is not forgetting, Simmias, just the losing of knowledge?

Quite true, Socrates.

But if the knowledge which we acquired before birth was lost by us at birth, and if afterwards by the use of the senses we recovered what we previously knew, will not the process which we call learning be a recovering of the knowledge which is natural to us, and may not this be rightly termed recollection?

Very true.

So much is clear—that when we perceive something,   [76 either by the help of sight, or hearing, or some other sense, from that perception we are able to obtain a notion of some other thing like or unlike which is associated with it but has been forgotten. Whence, as I was saying, one of two alternatives follows:—either we had this knowledge at birth, and continued to know through life; or, after birth, those who are said to learn only remember, and learning is simply recollection.

Yes, that is quite true, Socrates.

And which alternative, Simmias, do you prefer? Had we the knowledge at our birth, or did we recollect the things which we knew previously to our birth?

I cannot decide at the moment.

At any rate you can decide whether he who has knowledge will or will not be able to render an account of his knowledge? What do you say?

Certainly, he will.

But do you think that every man is able to give an account of these very matters about which we are speaking?

Would that they could, Socrates, but I rather fear that to-morrow, at this time, there will no longer be any one alive who is able to give an account of them such as ought to be given.

Then you are not of opinion, Simmias, that all men know these things?

Certainly not.

They are in process of recollecting that which they learned before?

Certainly.

But when did our souls acquire this knowledge?—not since we were born as men?

Certainly not.

And therefore, previously?

Yes.

Then, Simmias, our souls must also have existed without bodies before they were in the form of man, and must have had intelligence.

Unless indeed you suppose, Socrates, that these notions are given us at the very moment of birth; for this is the only time which remains.

Yes, my friend, but if so, when do we lose them? for they are not in us when we are born—that is admitted. Do we lose them at the moment of receiving them, or if not at what other time?

No, Socrates, I perceive that I was unconsciously talking nonsense.

Then may we not say, Simmias, that if, as we are always repeating, there is an absolute beauty, and goodness, and an absolute essence of all things; and if to this, which is now discovered to have existed in our former state, we refer all our sensations, and with this compare them, finding these ideas to be pre-existent and our inborn possession—then our souls must have had a prior existence, but if not, there would be no force in the argument? There is the same proof that these ideas must have existed before we were born, as that our souls existed before we were born; and if not the ideas, then not the souls.

Yes, Socrates; I am convinced that there is precisely the same necessity for the one as for the other; and the argument retreats successfully to the position that the existence of the soul before birth cannot   [77 be separated from the existence of the essence of which you speak. For there is nothing which to my mind is so patent as that beauty, goodness, and the other notions of which you were just now speaking, have a most real and absolute existence; and I am satisfied with the proof.

Well, but is Cebes equally satisfied? for I must convince him too.

I think, said Simmias, that Cebes is satisfied: although he is the most incredulous of mortals, yet I believe that he is sufficiently convinced of the existence of the soul before birth. But that after death the soul will continue to exist is not yet proven even to my own satisfaction. I cannot get rid of the feeling of the many to which Cebes was referring —the feeling that when the man dies the soul will be dispersed, and that this may be the extinction of her. For admitting that she may have been born elsewhere, and framed out of other elements, and was in existence before entering the human body, why after having entered in and gone out again may she not herself be destroyed and come to an end?

Very true, Simmias, said Cebes; about half of what was required has been proven; to wit, that our souls existed before we were born:— that the soul will exist after death as well as before birth is the other half of which the proof is still wanting, and has to be supplied; when that is given the demonstration will be complete.

But that proof, Simmias and Cebes, has been already given, said Socrates, if you put the two arguments together—I mean this and the former one, in which we admitted that everything living is born of the dead. For if the soul exists before birth, and in coming to life and being born can be born only from death and dying, must she not after death continue to exist, since she has to be born again?—Surely the proof which you desire has been already furnished. Still I suspect that you and Simmias would be glad to probe the argument further. Like children, you are haunted with a fear that when the soul leaves the body, the wind may really blow her away and scatter her; especially if a man should happen to die in a great storm and not when the sky is calm.

Cebes answered with a smile: Then, Socrates, you must argue us out of our fears—and yet, strictly speaking, they are not our fears, but there is a child within us to whom death is a sort of hobgoblin: him too we must persuade not to be afraid when he is alone in the dark.

Socrates said: Let the voice of the charmer be applied daily until you have charmed away the fear.

And where shall we find a good charmer of our fears, Soc- [78 rates, when you are gone?

Hellas, he replied, is a large place, Cebes, and has many good men, and there are barbarous races not a few: seek for him among them all, far and wide, sparing neither pains nor money; for there is no better way of spending your money. And you must seek among yourselves too; for you will not find others better able to make the search.

The search, replied Cebes, shall certainly be made. And now, if you please, let us return to the point of the argument at which we digressed.

By all means, replied Socrates; what else should I please?

Very good.

Must we not, said Socrates, ask ourselves what that is which, as we imagine, is liable to be scattered, and about which we fear? and what again is that about which we have no fear? And then we may proceed further to enquire whether that which suffers dispersion is or is not of the nature of soul—our hopes and fears as to our own souls will turn upon the answers to these questions.

Very true, he said.

Now the compound or composite may be supposed to be naturally capable, as of being compounded, so also of being dissolved; but that which is uncompounded, and that only, must be, if anything is, indissoluble.

Yes; I should imagine so, said Cebes.

And the uncompounded may be assumed to be the same and unchanging, whereas the compound is always changing and never the same.

I agree, he said.

Then now let us return to the previous discussion. Is that idea or essence, which in the dialectical process we define as essence or true existence—whether essence of equality, beauty, or anything else—are these essences, I say, liable at times to some degree of change? or are they each of them always what they are, having the same simple self-existent and unchanging forms, not admitting of variation at all, or in any way, or at any time?

They must be always the same, Socrates, replied Cebes.

And what would you say of the many beautiful—whether men or horses or garments or any other things which are named by the same names and may be called equal or beautiful,—are they all unchanging and the same always, or quite the reverse? May they not rather be described as almost always changing and hardly ever the same, either with themselves or with one another?

The latter, replied Cebes; they are always in a state of change.

And these you can touch and see and perceive with the   [79 senses, but the unchanging things you can only perceive with the mind—they are invisible and are not seen?

That is very true, he said.

Well then, added Socrates, let us suppose that there are two sorts of existences—one seen, the other unseen.

Let us suppose them.

The seen is the changing, and the unseen is the unchanging?

That may be also supposed.

And, further, is not one part of us body, another part soul?

To be sure.

And to which class is the body more alike and akin?

Clearly to the seen—no one can doubt that.

And is the soul seen or not seen?

Not by man, Socrates.

And what we mean by 'seen' and 'not seen' is that which is or is not visible to the eye of man?

Yes, to the eye of man.

And is the soul seen or not seen?

Not seen.

Unseen then?

Yes.

Then the soul is more like to the unseen, and the body to the seen?

That follows necessarily, Socrates.

And were we not saying long ago that the soul when using the body as an instrument of perception, that is to say, when using the sense of sight or hearing or some other sense (for the meaning of perceiving through the body is perceiving through the senses)—were we not saying that the soul too is then dragged by the body into the region of the changeable, and wanders and is confused; the world spins round her, and she is like a drunkard, when she touches change?

Very true.

But when returning into herself she reflects, then she passes into the other world, the region of purity, and eternity, and immortality, and unchangeableness, which are her kindred, and with them she ever lives, when she is by herself and is not let or hindered; then she ceases from her erring ways, and being in communion with the unchanging is unchanging. And this state of the soul is called wisdom?

That is well and truly said, Socrates, he replied.

And to which class is the soul more nearly alike and akin, as far as may be inferred from this argument, as well as from the preceding one?

I think, Socrates, that, in the opinion of every one who follows the argument, the soul will be infinitely more like the unchangeable—even the most stupid person will not deny that.

And the body is more like the changing?

Yes.

Yet once more consider the matter in another light: When the soul and the body are united, then nature orders the soul to rule and   [80 govern, and the body to obey and serve. Now which of these two functions is akin to the divine? and which to the mortal? Does not the divine appear to you to be that which naturally orders and rules, and the mortal to be that which is subject and servant?

True.

And which does the soul resemble?

The soul resembles the divine, and the body the mortal—there can be no doubt of that, Socrates.

Then reflect, Cebes: of all which has been said is not this the conclusion?—that the soul is in the very likeness of the divine, and immortal, and intellectual, and uniform, and indissoluble, and unchangeable; and that the body is in the very likeness of the human, and mortal, and unintellectual, and multiform, and dissoluble, and changeable. Can this, my dear Cebes, be denied?

It cannot.

But if it be true, then is not the body liable to speedy dissolution? and is not the soul almost or altogether indissoluble?

Certainly.

And do you further observe, that after a man is dead, the body, or visible part of him, which is lying in the visible world, and is called a corpse, and would naturally be dissolved and decomposed and dissipated, is not dissolved or decomposed at once, but may remain for some time, nay even for a long time, if the constitution be sound at the time of death, and the season of the year favourable? For the body when shrunk and embalmed, as the manner is in Egypt, may remain almost entire through infinite ages; and even in decay, there are still some portions, such as the bones and ligaments, which are practically indestructible:—Do you agree?

Yes.

And is it likely that the soul, which is invisible, in passing to the place of the true Hades, which like her is invisible, and pure, and noble, and on her way to the good and wise God, whither, if God will, my soul is also soon to go,—that the soul, I repeat, if this be her nature and origin, will be blown away and destroyed immediately on quitting the body, as the many say? That can never be, my dear Simmias and Cebes. The truth rather is, that the soul which is pure at departing and draws after her no bodily taint, having never voluntarily during life had connection with the body, which she is ever avoiding, herself gathered into herself;—and making such abstraction her perpetual study—which means that she has been a true disciple of philosophy; and   [81 therefore has in fact been always engaged in the practice of dying? For is not philosophy the study of death?—

Certainly—

That soul, I say, herself invisible, departs to the invisible world—to the divine and immortal and rational; thither arriving, she is secure of bliss and is released from the error and folly of men, their fears and wild passions and all other human ills, and for ever dwells, as they say of the initiated, in company with the gods [3]. Is not this true, Cebes?

Yes, said Cebes, beyond a doubt.

But the soul which has been polluted, and is impure at the time of her departure, and is the companion and servant of the body always, and is in love with and fascinated by the body and by the desires and pleasures of the body, until she is led to believe that the truth only exists in a bodily form, which a man may touch and see and taste, and use for the purposes of his lusts,—the soul, I mean, accustomed to hate and fear and avoid the intellectual principle, which to the bodily eye is dark and invisible, and can be attained only by philosophy;—do you suppose that such a soul will depart pure and unalloyed?

Impossible, he replied.

She is held fast by the corporeal, which the continual association and constant care of the body have wrought into her nature.

Very true.

And this corporeal element, my friend, is heavy and weighty and earthy, and is that element of sight by which a soul is depressed and dragged down again into the visible world, because she is afraid of the invisible and of the world below—prowling about tombs and sepulchres, near which, as they tell us, are seen certain ghostly apparitions of souls which have not departed pure, but are cloyed with sight and therefore visible.[4]

That is very likely, Socrates.

---

[3] Cp. Apol. 40 E.
[4] Compare Milton, Comus, 463 foll.:—

'But when lust,
By unchaste looks, loose gestures, and foul talk,
But most by lewd and lavish act of sin,
Lets in defilement to the inward parts,
The soul grows clotted by contagion,
Imbodies, and imbrutes, till she quite lose,
The divine property of her first being.
Such are those thick and gloomy shadows damp
Oft seen in charnel vaults and sepulchres,
Lingering, and sitting by a new made grave,
As loath to leave the body that it lov'd,
And linked itself by carnal sensuality
To a degenerate and degraded state.'

Yes, that is very likely, Cebes; and these must be the souls, not of the good, but of the evil, which are compelled to wander about such places in payment of the penalty of their former evil way of life; and they continue to wander until through the craving after the corporeal which never leaves them, they are imprisoned finally in another body. And they may be supposed to find their prisons in the same natures which they have had in their former lives.

What natures do you mean, Socrates?

What I mean is that men who have followed after gluttony, and wantonness, and drunkenness, and have had no thought of avoiding them, would pass into asses and animals of that sort. What do   [82 you think?

I think such an opinion to be exceedingly probable.

And those who have chosen the portion of injustice, and tyranny, and violence, will pass into wolves, or into hawks and kites;—whither else can we suppose them to go?

Yes, said Cebes; with such natures, beyond question.

And there is no difficulty, he said, in assigning to all of them places answering to their several natures and propensities?

There is not, he said.

Some are happier than others; and the happiest both in themselves and in the place to which they go are those who have practised the civil and social virtues which are called temperance and justice, and are acquired by habit and attention without philosophy and mind [5].

Why are they the happiest?

Because they may be expected to pass into some gentle and social kind which is like their own, such as bees or wasps or ants, or back again into the form of man, and just and moderate men may be supposed to spring from them.

Very likely.

No one who has not studied philosophy and who is not entirely pure at the time of his departure is allowed to enter the company of the Gods, but the lover of knowledge only. And this is the reason, Simmias and Cebes, why the true votaries of philosophy abstain from all fleshly lusts, and hold out against them and refuse to give themselves up to them,—not because they fear poverty or the ruin of their families, like the lovers of money, and the world in general; nor like the lovers of power and honour, because they dread the dishonour or disgrace of evil deeds.

No, Socrates, that would not become them, said Cebes.

No indeed, he replied; and therefore they who have any care of

---

[5] Cp. Rep. x. 619 C.

their own souls, and do not merely live moulding and fashioning the body, say farewell to all this; they will not walk in the ways of the blind: and when philosophy offers them purification and release from evil, they feel that they ought not to resist her influence, and whither she leads they turn and follow.

What do you mean, Socrates?

I will tell you, he said. The lovers of knowledge are conscious that the soul was simply fastened and glued to the body—until philosophy received her, she could only view real existence through the bars of a prison, not in and through herself; she was wallowing in the mire of every sort of ignorance, and by reason of lust had become the principal accomplice in her own captivity. This was her original state; and   [83 then, as I was saying, and as the lovers of knowledge are well aware, philosophy, seeing how terrible was her confinement, of which she was to herself the cause, received and gently comforted her and sought to release her, pointing out that the eye and the ear and the other senses are full of deception, and persuading her to retire from them, and abstain from all but the necessary use of them, and be gathered up and collected into herself, bidding her trust in herself and her own pure apprehension of pure existence, and to mistrust whatever comes to her through other channels and is subject to variation; for such things are visible and tangible, but what she sees in her own nature is intelligible and invisible. And the soul of the true philosopher thinks that she ought not to resist this deliverance, and therefore abstains from pleasures and desires and pains and fears, as far as she is able; reflecting that when a man has great joys or sorrows or fears or desires, he suffers from them, not merely the sort of evil which might be anticipated—as for example, the loss of his health or property which he has sacrificed to his lusts—but an evil greater far, which is the greatest and worst of all evils, and one of which he never thinks.

What is it, Socrates? said Cebes.

The evil is that when the feeling of pleasure or pain is most intense, every soul of man imagines the objects of this intense feeling to be then plainest and truest: but this is not so, they are really the things of sight.

Very true.

And is not this the state in which the soul is most enthralled by the body?

How so?

Why, because each pleasure and pain is a sort of nail which nails and rivets the soul to the body, until she becomes like the body, and believes that to be true which the body affirms to be true; and from agreeing with the body and having the same delights she is obliged to have the same habits and haunts, and is not likely ever to be pure at her departure to the world below, but is always infected by the body; and so she sinks into another body and there germinates and grows, and has therefore no part in the communion of the divine and pure and simple.

Most true, Socrates, answered Cebes.

And this, Cebes, is the reason why the true lovers of knowledge are temperate and brave; and not for the reason which the world gives.

Certainly not.   [84

Certainly not! The soul of a philosopher will reason in quite another way; she will not ask philosophy to release her in order that when released she may deliver herself up again to the thraldom of pleasures and pains, doing a work only to be undone again, weaving instead of unweaving her Penelope's web. But she will calm passion, and follow reason, and dwell in the contemplation of her, beholding the true and divine (which is not matter of opinion), and thence driving nourishment. Thus she seeks to live while she lives, and after death she hopes to go to her own kindred and to that which is like her, and to be freed from human ills. Never fear, Simmias and Cebes, that a soul which has been thus nurtured and has had these pursuits, will at her departure from the body be scattered and blown away by the winds and be nowhere and nothing.

When Socrates had done speaking, for a considerable time there was silence; he himself appeared to be meditating, as most of us were, on what had been said; only Cebes and Simmias spoke a few words to one another. And Socrates observing them asked what they thought of the argument, and whether there was anything wanting? For, said he, there are many points still open to suspicion and attack, if any one were disposed to sift the matter thoroughly. Should you be considering some other matter I say no more, but if you are still in doubt do not hesitate to say exactly what you think, and let us have anything better which you can suggest; and if you think that I can be of any use, allow me to help you.

Simmias said: I must confess, Socrates, that doubts did arise in our minds, and each of us was urging and inciting the other to put the question which we wanted to have answered but which neither of us liked to ask, fearing that our importunity might be troublesome at such a time.

Socrates replied with a smile: O Simmias, what are you saying? I am not very likely to persuade other men that I do not regard my present situation as a misfortune, if I cannot even persuade you that I am no worse off now than at any other time in my life. Will you not allow that I have as much of the spirit of prophecy in me as the swans?

For they, when they perceive that they must die, having sung all their life long, do then sing more lustily than ever, rejoicing in the thought that they are about to go away to the god whose ministers they   [85 are. But men, because they are themselves afraid of death, slanderously affirm of the swans that they sing a lament at the last, not considering that no bird sings when cold, or hungry, or in pain, not even the night-ingale, nor the swallow, nor yet the hoopoe; which are said indeed to tune a lay of sorrow, although I do not believe this to be true of them any more than of the swans. But because they are sacred to Apollo, they have the gift of prophecy, and anticipate the good things of another world; wherefore they sing and rejoice in that day more than ever they did before. And I too, believing myself to be the consecrated servant of the same God, and the fellow-servant of the swans, and thinking that I have received from my master gifts of prophecy which are not inferior to theirs, would not go out of life less merrily than the swans. Never mind then, if this be your only objection, but speak and ask anything which you like, while the eleven magistrates of Athens allow.

Very good, Socrates, said Simmias; then I will tell you my diffi-culty, and Cebes will tell you his. I feel myself (and I daresay that you have the same feeling), how hard or rather impossible is the attainment of any certainty about questions such as these in the present life. And yet I should deem him a coward who did not prove what is said about them to the uttermost, or whose heart failed him before he had ex-amined them on every side. For he should persevere until he has achieved one of two things: either he should discover, or be taught the truth about them; or, if this be impossible, I would have him take the best and most irrefragable of human theories, and let this be the raft upon which he sails through life—not without risk, as I admit, if he cannot find some word of God which will more surely and safely carry him. And now, as you bid me, I will venture to question you, and then I shall not have to reproach myself hereafter with not having said at the time what I think. For when I consider the matter, either alone or with Cebes, the argument does certainly appear to me, Socrates, to be not sufficient.

Socrates answered: I dare say, my friend, that you may be right, but I should like to know in what respect the argument is insufficient.

In this respect, replied Simmias:—Suppose a person to use the same argument about harmony and the lyre—might he not say that harmony is a thing invisible, incorporeal, perfect, divine, exist-   [86 ing in the lyre which is harmonized, but that the lyre and the strings are matter and material, composite, earthy, and akin to mortality? And when some one breaks the lyre, or cuts and rends the strings, then he who takes this view would argue as you do, and on the same analogy, that the harmony survives and has not perished—you cannot imagine, he would say, that the lyre without the strings, and the broken strings themselves which are mortal remain, and yet that the harmony, which is of heavenly and immortal nature and kindred, has perished—perished before the mortal. The harmony must still be somewhere, and the wood and strings will decay before anything can happen to that. The thought, Socrates, must have occurred to your own mind that such is our conception of the soul; and that when the body is in a manner strung and held together by the elements of hot and cold, wet and dry, then the soul is the harmony or due proportionate admixture of them. But if so, whenever the strings of the body are unduly loosened or overstrained through disease or other injury, then the soul, though most divine, like other harmonies of music or of works of art, of course perishes at once; although the material remains of the body may last for a considerable time, until they are either decayed or burnt. And if any one maintains that the soul, being the harmony of the elements of the body, is first to perish in that which is called death, how shall we answer him?

Socrates looked fixedly at us as his manner was, and said with a smile: Simmias has reason on his side; and why does not some one of you who is better able than myself answer him? for there is force in his attack upon me. But perhaps, before we answer him, we had better also hear what Cebes has to say that we may gain time for reflection, and when they have both spoken, we may either assent to them, if there is truth in what they say, or if not, we will maintain our position. Please to tell me then, Cebes, he said, what was the difficulty which troubled you?

Cebes said: I will tell you. My feeling is that the argument is where it was, and open to the same objections which were urged before; for I am ready to admit that the existence of the soul be-   [87 fore entering into the bodily form has been very ingeniously, and, if I may say so, quite sufficiently proven; but the existence of the soul after death is still, in my judgment, unproven. Now my objection is not the same as that of Simmias; for I am not disposed to deny that the soul is stronger and more lasting than the body, being of opinion that in all such respects the soul very far excels the body. Well then, says the argument to me, why do you remain unconvinced?—When you see that the weaker continues in existence after the man is dead, will you not admit that the more lasting must also survive during the same period of time? Now I will ask you to consider whether the objection, which, like Simmias, I will express in a figure, is of any weight. The

analogy which I will adduce is that of an old weaver, who dies, and
after his death somebody says:—He is not dead, he must be alive;—
see, there is the coat which he himself wove and wore, and which
remains whole and undecayed. And then he proceeds to ask of some
one who is incredulous, whether a man lasts longer, or the coat which
is in use and wear; and when he is answered that a man lasts far
longer, thinks that he has thus certainly demonstrated the survival of
the man, who is the more lasting, because the less lasting remains.
But that, Simmias, as I would beg you to remark, is a mistake; any
one can see that he who talks thus is talking nonsense. For the truth
is, that the weaver aforesaid, having woven and worn many such coats,
outlived several of them; and was outlived by the last; but a man is
not therefore proved to be slighter and weaker than a coat. Now the
relation of the body to the soul may be expressed in a similar figure;
and any one may very fairly say in like manner that the soul is lasting,
and the body weak and shortlived in comparison. He may argue in
like manner that every soul wears out many bodies, especially if a man
live many years. While he is alive the body deliquesces and decays,
and the soul always weaves another garment and repairs the waste.
But of course, whenever the soul perishes, she must have on her last
garment, and this will survive her; and then at length, when the soul
is dead, the body will show its native weakness, and quickly decom-
pose and pass away. I would therefore rather not rely on the argument
from superior strength to prove the continued existence of the   [88
soul after death. For granting even more than you affirm to be possible, and acknowledging not only that the soul existed before birth,
but also that the souls of some exist, and will continue to exist after
death, and will be born and die again, and that there is a natural
strength in the soul which will hold out and be born many times
—nevertheless, we may be still inclined to think that she will weary
in the labours of successive births, and may at last succumb in one
of her deaths and utterly perish; and this death and dissolution of the
body which brings destruction to the soul may be unknown to any
of us, for no one of us can have had any experience of it: and if so,
then I maintain that he who is confident about death has but a foolish
confidence, unless he is able to prove that the soul is altogether immortal and imperishable. But if he cannot prove the soul's immortality, he who is about to die will always have reason to fear that
when the body is disunited, the soul also may utterly perish.

All of us, as we afterwards remarked to one another, had an unpleasant feeling at hearing what they said. When we had been so
firmly convinced before, now to have our faith shaken seemed to in-

troduce a confusion and uncertainty, not only into the previous argument, but into any future one; either we were incapable of forming a judgment, or there were no grounds of belief.

Echecrates. There I feel with you—by heaven I do, Phaedo, and when you were speaking, I was beginning to ask myself the same question: What argument can I ever trust again? For what could be more convincing than the argument of Socrates, which has now fallen into discredit? That the soul is a harmony is a doctrine which has always had a wonderful attraction for me, and, when mentioned, came back to me at once, as my own original conviction. And now I must begin again and find another argument which will assure me that when the man is dead the soul survives. Tell me, I implore you, how did Socrates proceed? Did he appear to share the unpleasant feeling which you mention? or did he calmly meet the attack? And did he answer forcibly or feebly? Narrate what passed as exactly as you can.

Phaedo. Often, Echecrates, I have wondered at Socrates, but never more than on that occasion. That he should be able to answer   [89 was nothing, but what astonished me was, first, the gentle and pleasant and approving manner in which he received the words of the young men, and then his quick sense of the wound which had been inflicted by the argument, and the readiness with which he healed it. He might be compared to a general rallying his defeated and broken army, urging them to accompany him and return to the field of argument.

Echecrates. What followed?

Phaedo. You shall hear, for I was close to him on his right hand, seated on a sort of stool, and he on a couch which was a good deal higher. He stroked my head, and pressed the hair upon my neck— he had a way of playing with my hair; and then he said: To-morrow, Phaedo, I suppose that these fair locks of yours will be severed.

Yes, Socrates, I suppose that they will, I replied.

Not so, if you will take my advice.

What shall I do with them? I said.

To-day, he replied, and not to-morrow, if this argument dies and we cannot bring it to life again, you and I will both shave our locks: and if I were you, and the argument got away from me, and I could not hold my ground against Simmias and Cebes, I would myself take an oath, like the Argives, not to wear hair any more until I had renewed the conflict and defeated them.

Yes, I said; but Heracles himself is said not to be a match for two.

Summon me then, he said, and I will be your Iolaus until the sun goes down.

I summon you rather, I rejoined, not as Heracles summoning Iolaus, but as Iolaus might summon Heracles.

That will do as well, he said. But first let us take care that we avoid a danger.

Of what nature? I said.

Lest we become misologists, he replied: no worse thing can happen to a man than this. For as there are misanthropists or haters of men, there are also misologists or haters of ideas, and both spring from the same cause, which is ignorance of the world. Misanthropy arises out of the too great confidence of inexperience;—you trust a man and think him altogether true and sound and faithful, and then in a little while he turns out to be false and knavish; and then another and another, and when this has happened several times to a man, especially when it happens among those whom he deems to be his own most trusted and familiar friends, and he has often quarrelled with them, he at last hates all men, and believes that no one has any good in him at all. You must have observed this trait of character?

I have.

And is not the feeling discreditable? Is it not obvious that such an one having to deal with other men, was clearly without any experience of human nature; for experience would have taught him the true state of the case, that few are the good and few the evil, and that [90] the great majority are in the interval between them.

What do you mean? I said.

I mean, he replied, as you might say of the very large and very small—that nothing is more uncommon than a very large or very small man; and this applies generally to all extremes, whether of great and small, or swift and slow, or fair and foul, or black and white: and whether the instances you select be men or dogs or anything else, few are the extremes, but many are in the mean between them. Did you never observe this?

Yes, I said, I have.

And do you not imagine, he said, that if there were a competition in evil, the worst would be found to be very few?

Yes, that is very likely, I said.

Yes, that is very likely, he replied; although in this respect arguments are unlike men—there I was led on by you to say more than I had intended; but the point of comparison was, that when a simple man who has no skill in dialectics believes an argument to be true which he afterwards imagines to be false, whether really false or not, and then another and another, he has no longer any faith left, and great disputers, as you know, come to think at last that they have grown to be the wisest of mankind; for they alone perceive the utter unsoundness and instability of all arguments, or indeed, of all things,

which, like the currents in the Euripus, are going up and down in
never-ceasing ebb and flow.

That is quite true, I said.

Yes, Phaedo, he replied, and how melancholy, if there be such
a thing as truth or certainty or possibility of knowledge—that a man
should have lighted upon some argument or other which at first seemed
true and then turned out to be false, and instead of blaming himself
and his own want of wit, because he is annoyed, should at last be too
glad to transfer the blame from himself to arguments in general: and
for ever afterwards should hate and revile them, and lose truth and
the knowledge of realities.

Yes, indeed, I said; that is very melancholy.

Let us then, in the first place, he said, be careful of allowing or
of admitting into our souls the notion that there is no health or soundness in any arguments at all. Rather say that we have not yet attained
to soundness in ourselves, and that we must struggle manfully and
do our best to gain health of mind—you and all other men having
regard to the whole of your future life, and I myself in the prospect of
death. For at this moment I am sensible that I have not the tem-   [91
per of a philosopher; like the vulgar, I am only a partisan. Now the
partisan, when he is engaged in a dispute, cares nothing about the
rights of the question, but is anxious only to convince his hearers of his
own assertions. And the difference between him and me at the present
moment is merely this—that whereas he seeks to convince his hearers
that what he says is true, I am rather seeking to convince myself; to
convince my hearers is a secondary matter with me. And do but
see much I gain by the argument. For if what I say is true, then I
do well to be persuaded of the truth; but if there be nothing after
death, still, during the short time that remains, I shall not distress
my friends with lamentations, and my ignorance will not last, but will
die with me, and therefore no harm will be done. This is the state
of mind, Simmias and Cebes, in which I approach the argument. And I
would ask you to be thinking of the truth and not of Socrates: agree
with me, if I seem to you to be speaking the truth; or if not, withstand
me might and main, that I may not deceive you as well as myself in my
enthusiasm, and like the bee, leave my sting in you before I die.

And now let us proceed, he said. And first of all let me be sure
that I have in my mind what you were saying. Simmias, if I remember rightly, has fears and misgivings whether the soul, although a
fairer and diviner thing than the body, being as she is in the form
of harmony, may not perish first. On the other hand, Cebes appeared
to grant that the soul was more lasting than the body, but he said
that no one could know whether the soul, after having worn out

many bodies, might not perish herself and leave her last body behind her; and that this is death, which is the destruction not of the body but of the soul, for in the body the work of destruction is ever going on. Are not these, Simmias and Cebes, the points which we have to consider?

They both agreed to this statement of them.

He proceeded: And did you deny the force of the whole preceding argument, or of a part only?

Of a part only, they replied.

And what did you think, he said, of that part of the argument in which we said that knowledge was recollection, and hence inferred that the soul must have previously existed somewhere else   [92 before she was enclosed in the body?

Cebes said that he had been wonderfully impressed by that part of the argument, and that his conviction remained absolutely unshaken. Simmias agreed, and added that he himself could hardly imagine the possibility of his ever thinking differently.

But, rejoined Socrates, you will have to think differently, my Theban friend, if you still maintain that harmony is a compound, and that the soul is a harmony which is made out of strings set in the frame of the body; for you will surely never allow yourself to say that a harmony is prior to the elements which compose it.

Never, Socrates.

But do you not see that this is what you imply when you say that the soul existed before she took the form and body of man, and was made up of elements which as yet had no existence? For harmony is not like the soul, as you suppose; but first the lyre, and the strings, and the sounds exist in a state of discord, and then harmony is made last of all, and perishes first. And how can such a notion of the soul as this agree with the other?

Not at all, replied Simmias.

And yet, he said, there surely ought to be harmony in a discourse of which harmony is the theme?

There ought, replied Simmias.

But there is no harmony, he said, in the two propositions that knowledge is recollection, and that the soul is a harmony. Which of them will you retain?

I think, he replied, that I have a much stronger faith, Socrates, in the first of the two, which has been fully demonstrated to me, than in the latter, which has not been demonstrated at all, but rests only on probable and plausible grounds; and is therefore believed by the many. I know too well that these arguments from probabilities are impostors, and unless great caution is observed in the use of them, they are apt to be deceptive—in geometry, and in other things too. But the doctrine of knowledge and recollection has been proven to me on trustworthy grounds: and the proof was that the soul must have existed before she came into the body, because to her belongs the essence of which the very name implies existence. Having, as I am convinced, rightly accepted this conclusion, and on sufficient grounds, I must, as I suppose, cease to argue or allow others to argue that the soul is a harmony.

Let me put the matter, Simmias, he said, in another point of view: Do you imagine that a harmony or any other composi- [93 tion can be in a state other than that of the elements, out of which it is compounded?

Certainly not.

Or do or suffer anything other than they do or suffer?

He agreed.

Then a harmony does not, properly speaking, lead the parts or elements which make up the harmony, but only follows them.

He assented.

For harmony cannot possibly have any motion, or sound, or other quality which is opposed to its parts.

That would be impossible, he replied.

And does not the nature of every harmony depend upon the manner in which the elements are harmonized?

I do not understand you, he said.

I mean to say that a harmony admits of degrees, and is more of a harmony, and more completely a harmony, when more truly and fully harmonized, to any extent which is possible; and less of a harmony, and less completely a harmony, when less truly and fully harmonized.

True.

But does the soul admit of degrees? or is one soul in the very least degree more or less, or more or less completely, a soul than another?

Not in the least.

Yet surely of two souls, one is said to have intelligence and virtue, and to be good, and the other to have folly and vice, and to be an evil soul: and this is said truly?

Yes, truly.

But what will those who maintain the soul to be a harmony say of this presence of virtue and vice in the soul?—will they say that here is another harmony, and another discord, and that the virtuous soul is harmonized, and herself being a harmony has another

harmony within her, and that the vicious soul is inharmonical and
has no harmony within her?

I cannot tell, replied Simmias; but I suppose that something of
the sort would be asserted by those who say that the soul is a harmony.

And we have already admitted that no soul is more a soul than
another; which is equivalent to admitting that harmony is not more
or less harmony, or more or less completely a harmony?

Quite true.

And that which is not more or less a harmony is not more or less
harmonized?

True.

And that which is not more or less harmonized cannot have
more or less of harmony, but only an equal harmony?

Yes, an equal harmony.

Then one soul not being more or less absolutely a soul than another, is not more or less harmonized?

Exactly.

And therefore has neither more nor less of discord, nor yet of
harmony?

She has not.

And having neither more nor less of harmony or of discord, one
soul has no more vice or virtue than another, if vice be discord and
virtue harmony?

Not at all more.

Or speaking more correctly, Simmias, the soul, if she is a   [94
harmony, will never have any vice; because a harmony, being absolutely a harmony, has no part in the inharmonical.

No.

And therefore a soul which is absolutely a soul has no vice?

How can she have, if the previous argument holds?

Then, if all souls are equally by their nature souls, all souls of all
living creatures will be equally good?

I agree with you, Socrates, he said.

And can all this be true, think you? he said; for these are the consequences which seem to follow from the assumption that the soul is
a harmony?

It cannot be true.

Once more, he said, what ruler is there of the elements of human
nature other than the soul, and especially the wise soul? Do you know
of any?

Indeed, I do not.

And is the soul in agreement with the affections of the body? or is she at variance with them? For example, when the body is hot and thirsty, does not the soul incline us against drinking? and when the body is hungry, against eating? And this is only one instance out of ten thousand of the opposition of the soul to the things of the body.

Very true.

But we have already acknowledged that the soul, being a harmony, can never utter a note at variance with the tensions and relaxations and vibrations and other affections of the strings out of which she is composed; she can only follow, she cannot lead them?

It must be so, he replied.

And yet do we not now discover the soul to be doing the exact opposite—leading the elements of which she is believed to be composed; almost always opposing and coercing them in all sorts of ways throughout life, sometimes more violently with the pains of medicine and gymnastic; then again more gently; now threatening, now admonishing the desires, passions, fears, as if talking to a thing which is not herself, as Homer in the Odyssey represents Odysseus doing in the words—

> 'He beat his breast, and thus reproached his heart:
> Endure, my heart; far worse hast thou endured!'

Do you think that Homer wrote this under the idea that the soul is a harmony capable of being led by the affections of the body, and not rather of a nature which should lead and master them—herself a far diviner thing than any harmony?

Yes, Socrates, I quite think so.

Then, my friend, we can never be right in saying that the soul is a harmony, for we should contradict the divine Homer, and [95 contradict ourselves.

True, he said.

Thus much, said Socrates, of Harmonia, your Theban goddess, who has graciously yielded to us; but what shall I say, Cebes, to her husband Cadmus, and how shall I make peace with him?

I think that you will discover a way of propitiating him, said Cebes; I am sure that you have put the argument with Harmonia in a manner that I could never have expected. For when Simmias was mentioning his difficulty, I quite imagined that no answer could be given to him, and therefore I was surprised at finding that his argument could not sustain the first onset of yours, and not impossibly the other, whom you call Cadmus, may share a similar fate.

Nay, my good friend, said Socrates, let us not boast, lest some evil eye should put to flight the word which I am about to speak. That, however, may be left in the hands of those above; while I draw near in Homeric fashion, and try the mettle of your words. Here lies the point:—You want to have it proven to you that the soul is imperishable and immortal, and the philosopher who is confident in death appears to you to have but a vain and foolish confidence, if he believes that he will fare better in the world below than one who has led another sort of life, unless he can prove this: and you say that the demonstration of the strength and divinity of the soul, and of her existence prior to our becoming men, does not necessarily imply her immortality. Admitting the soul to be longlived, and to have known and done much in a former state, still she is not on that account immortal; and her entrance into the human form may be a sort of disease which is the beginning of dissolution, and may at last, after the toils of life are over, end in that which is called death. And whether the soul enters into the body once only or many times, does not, as you say, make any difference in the fears of individuals. For any man, who is not devoid of sense, must fear, if he has no knowledge and can give no account of the soul's immortality. This, or something like this, I suspect to be your notion, Cebes; and I designedly recur to it in order that nothing may escape us, and that you may, if you wish, add or subtract anything.

But, said Cebes, as far as I see at present, I have nothing to add or subtract: I mean what you say that I mean.

Socrates paused awhile, and seemed to be absorbed in reflection. At length he said: You are raising a tremendous question, Cebes, involving the whole nature of generation and corruption, about which,   [96 if you like, I will give you my own experience; and if anything which I say is likely to avail towards the solution of your difficulty you may make use of it.

I should very much like, said Cebes, to hear what you have to say.

Then I will tell you, said Socrates. When I was young, Cebes, I had a prodigious desire to know that department of philosophy which is called the investigation of nature; to know the causes of things, and why a thing is and is created or destroyed appeared to me to be a lofty profession; and I was always agitating myself with the consideration of questions such as these:—Is the growth of animals the result of some decay which the hot and cold principle contracts, as some have said? Is the blood the element with which we think, or the air, or the fire? or perhaps nothing of the kind—but the brain may be the originating power of the perceptions of hearing and sight and smell, and memory and opinion may come from them, and science may be based on memory and opinion when they have attained fixity. And then I went on to examine the corruption of them, and then to the things of heaven and earth, and at last I concluded myself to be utterly and absolutely incapable of these enquiries, as I will satisfactorily prove to you. For I was fascinated by them to such a degree that my eyes grew blind to things which I had seemed to myself, and also to others, to know quite well; I forgot what I had before thought self-evident truths; e.g. such a fact as that the growth of man is the result of eating and drinking; for when by the digestion of food flesh is added to flesh and bone to bone, and whenever there is an aggregation of congenial elements, the lesser bulk becomes larger and the small man great. Was not that a reasonable notion?

Yes, said Cebes, I think so.

Well; but let me tell you something more. There was a time when I thought that I understood the meaning of greater and less pretty well; and when I saw a great man standing by a little one, I fancied that one was taller than the other by a head; or one horse would appear to be greater than another horse: and still more clearly did I seem to perceive that ten is two more than eight, and that two cubits are more than one, because two is the double of one.

And what is now your notion of such matters? said Cebes.

I should be far enough from imagining, he replied, that I knew the cause of any of them, by heaven I should; for I cannot satisfy myself that, when one is added to one, the one to which the addition   [97 is made becomes two, or that the two units added together make two by reason of the addition. I cannot understand how, when separated from the other, each of them was one and not two, and now, when they are brought together, the mere juxtaposition or meeting of them should be the cause of their becoming two: neither can I understand how the division of one is the way to make two; for then a different cause would produce the same effect,—as in the former instance the addition and juxtaposition of one to one was the cause of two, in this the separation and subtraction of one from the other would be the cause. Nor am I any longer satisfied that I understand the reason why one or anything else is either generated or destroyed or is at all, but I have in my mind some confused notion of a new method, and can never admit the other.

Then I heard some one reading, as he said, from a book of Anaxagoras, that mind was the disposer and cause of all, and I was delighted at this notion, which appeared quite admirable, and I said to myself: If mind is the disposer, mind will dispose all for the best, and put each particular in the best place; and I argued that if any one desired to find out the cause of the generation or destruction or existence of anything, he must find out what state of being or doing or suffering was best for that thing, and therefore a man had only to consider the best for himself and others, and then he would also know the worse, since the same science comprehended both. And I rejoiced to think that I had found in Anaxagoras a teacher of the causes of existence such as I desired, and I imagined that he would tell me first whether the earth is flat or round; and whichever was true, he would proceed to explain the cause and the necessity of this being so, and then he would teach me the nature of the best and show that this was best; and if he said that the earth was in the centre, he would further explain that this position was the best, and I should be satisfied with the explanation given, and not want any other sort of cause. And I   [98 thought that I would then go on and ask him about the sun and moon and stars, and that he would explain to me their comparative swiftness, and their returnings and various states, active and passive, and how all of them were for the best. For I could not imagine that when he spoke of mind as the disposer of them, he would give any other account of their being as they are, except that this was best; and I thought that when he had explained to me in detail the cause of each and the cause of all, he would go on to explain to me what was best for each and what was good for all. These hopes I would not have sold for a large sum of money, and I seized the books and read them as fast as I could in my eagerness to know the better and the worse.

What expectations I had formed, and how grievously was I disappointed! As I proceeded, I found my philosopher altogether forsaking mind or any other principle of order, but having recourse to air, and ether, and water, and other eccentricities. I might compare him to a person who began by maintaining generally that mind is the cause of the actions of Socrates, but who, when he endeavoured to explain the causes of my several actions in detail, went on to show that I sit here because my body is made up of bones and muscles; and the bones, as he would say, are hard and have joints which divide them, and the muscles are elastic, and they cover the bones, which have also a covering or environment of flesh and skin which contains them; and as the bones are lifted at their joints by the contraction or relaxation of the muscles, I am able to bend my limbs, and this is why I am sitting here in a curved posture—that is what he would say; and he would have a similar explanation of my talking to you, which he would attribute to sound, and air, and hearing, and he would assign ten thousand other causes of the same sort, forgetting to mention the true cause, which is, that the Athenians have thought fit to condemn me, and accordingly I have thought it better and more right to remain here and undergo my sentence; for I am inclined to think that   [99 these muscles and bones of mine would have gone off long ago to Megara or Boeotia—by the dog, they would, if they had been moved only by their own idea of what was best, and if I had not chosen the better and nobler part, instead of playing truant and running away, of enduring any punishment which the state inflicts. There is surely a strange confusion of causes and conditions in all this. It may be said, indeed, that without bones and muscles and the other parts of the body I cannot execute my purposes. But to say that I do as I do because of them, and that this is the way in which mind acts, and not from the choice of the best, is a very careless and idle mode of speaking. I wonder that they cannot distinguish the cause from the condition, which the many, feeling about in the dark, are always mistaking and misnaming. And thus one man makes a vortex all round and steadies the earth by the heaven; another gives the air as a support to the earth, which is a sort of broad trough. Any power which in arranging them as they are arranges them for the best never enters into their minds; and instead of finding any superior strength in it, they rather expect to discover another Atlas of the world who is stronger and more everlasting and more containing than the good;—of the obligatory and containing power of the good they think nothing; and yet this is the principle which I would fain learn if any one would teach me. But as I have failed either to discover myself, or to learn of any one else, the nature of the best, I will exhibit to you, if you like, what I have found to be the second best mode of enquiring into the cause.

I should very much like to hear, he replied.

Socrates proceeded:—I thought that as I had failed in the contemplation of true existence, I ought to be careful that I did not lose the eye of my soul; as people may injure their bodily eye by observing and gazing on the sun during an eclipse, unless they take the precaution of only looking at the image reflected in the water, or in some similar medium. So in my own case, I was afraid that my soul might be blinded altogether if I looked at things with my eyes or tried to apprehend them by the help of the senses. And I thought that I had better have recourse to the world of mind and seek there the truth of existence. I dare say that the simile is not perfect—for I am   [100 very far from admitting that he who contemplates existences through the medium of thought, sees them only 'through a glass darkly,' any more than he who considers them in action and operation. However, this was the method which I adopted: I first assumed some principle which I judged to be the strongest, and then I affirmed as true whatever seemed to agree with this, whether relating to the cause or to anything else; and that which disagreed I regarded as untrue. But I should like to explain my meaning more clearly, as I do not think that you as yet understand me.

No indeed, replied Cebes, not very well.

There is nothing new, he said, in what I am about to tell you; but only what I have been always and everywhere repeating in the previous discussion and on other occasions: I want to show you the nature of that cause which has occupied my thoughts. I shall have to go back to those familiar words which are in the mouth of every one, and first of all assume that there is an absolute beauty and goodness and greatness, and the like; grant me this, and I hope to be able to show you the nature of the cause, and to prove the immortality of the soul.

Cebes said: You may proceed at once with the proof, for I grant you this.

Well, he said, then I should like to know whether you agree with me in the next step; for I cannot help thinking, if there be anything beautiful other than absolute beauty should there be such, that it can be beautiful only in so far as it partakes of absolute beauty—and I should say the same of everything. Do you agree in this notion of the cause?

Yes, he said, I agree.

He proceeded: I know nothing and can understand nothing of any other of those wise causes which are alleged; and if a person says to me that the bloom of colour, or form, or any such thing is a source of beauty, I leave all that, which is only confusing to me, and simply and singly, and perhaps foolishly, hold and am assured in my own mind that nothing makes a thing beautiful but the presence and participation of beauty in whatever way or manner obtained; for as to the manner I am uncertain, but I stoutly contend that by beauty all beautiful things become beautiful. This appears to me to be the safest answer which I can give, either to myself or to another, and to this I cling, in the persuasion that this principle will never be overthrown, and that to myself or to any one who asks the question, I may safely reply, That by beauty beautiful things become beautiful. Do you not agree with me?

I do.

And that by greatness only great things become great and greater greater, and by smallness the less become less?

True.

Then if a person were to remark that A is taller by a head than B, and B less by a head than A, you would refuse to admit his [101 statement, and would stoutly contend that what you mean is only that the greater is greater by, and by reason of, greatness, and the less is less only by, and by reason of, smallness; and thus you would avoid the danger of saying that the greater is greater and the less less by the measure of the head, which is the same in both, and would also avoid the monstrous absurdity of supposing that the greater man is greater by reason of the head, which is small. You would be afraid to draw such an inference, would you not?

Indeed, I should, said Cebes, laughing.

In like manner you would be afraid to say that ten exceeded eight by, and by reason of, two; but would say by, and by reason of, number; or you would say that two cubits exceed one cubit not by a half, but by magnitude?—for there is the same liability to error in all these cases.

Very true, he said.

Again, would you not be cautious of affirming that the addition of one to one, or the division of one, is the cause of two? And you would loudly asseverate that you know of no way in which anything comes into existence except by participation in its own proper essence, and consequently, as far as you know, the only cause of two is the participation in duality—this is the way to make two, and the participation in one is the way to make one. You would say: I will let alone puzzles of division and addition—wiser heads than mine may answer them; inexperienced as I am, and ready to start, as the proverb says, at my own shadow, I cannot afford to give up the sure ground of a principle. And if any one assails you there, you would not mind him, or answer him until you had seen whether the consequences which follow agree with one another or not, and when you are further required to give an explanation of this principle, you would go on to assume a higher principle, and a higher, until you found a resting-place in the best of the higher; but you would not confuse the principle and the consequences in your reasoning, like the Eristics—at least if you wanted to discover real existence. Not that this confusion signifies to them, who never care or think about the matter at all, for they have the wit to be well pleased with themselves however great may be the turmoil of their   [102 ideas. But you, if you are a philosopher, will certainly do as I say.

What you say is most true, said Simmias and Cebes, both speaking at once.

Echecrates. Yes, Phaedo; and I do not wonder at their assenting. Any one who has the least sense will acknowledge the wonderful clearness of Socrates' reasoning.

Phaedo. Certainly, Echecrates; and such was the feeling of the whole company at the time.

Echecrates. Yes, and equally of ourselves, who were not of the company, and are now listening to your recital. But what followed?

Phaedo. After all this had been admitted, and they had agreed that ideas exist, and that other things participate in them and derive their names from them, Socrates, if I remember rightly, said:—

This is your way of speaking; and yet when you say that Simmias is greater than Socrates and less than Phaedo, do you not predicate of Simmias both greatness and smallness?

Yes, I do.

But still you allow that Simmias does not really exceed Socrates, as the words may seem to imply, because he is Simmias, but by reason of the size which he has; just as Simmias does not exceed Socrates because he is Simmias, any more than because Socrates is Socrates, but because he has smallness when compared with the greatness of Simmias?

True.

And if Phaedo exceeds him in size, this is not because Phaedo is Phaedo, but because Phaedo has greatness relatively to Simmias, who is comparatively smaller?

That is true.

And therefore Simmias is said to be great, and is also said to be small, because he is in a mean between them, exceeding the smallness of the one by his greatness, and allowing the greatness of the other to exceed his smallness. He added, laughing, I am speaking like a book, but I believe that what I am saying is true.

Simmias assented.

I speak as I do because I want you to agree with me in thinking, not only that absolute greatness will never be great and also small, but that greatness in us or in the concrete will never admit the small or admit of being exceeded: instead of this, one of two things will happen, either the greater will fly or retire before the opposite, which is the less, or at the approach of the less has already ceased to exist; but will not, if allowing or admitting of smallness, be changed by that; even as I, having received and admitted smallness when compared with Simmias, remain just as I was, and am the same small person. And as the idea of greatness cannot condescend ever to be or become small, in like manner the smallness in us cannot be or become great; nor can any other oppo- site which remains the same ever be or become its own oppo-   [103 site, but either passes away or perishes in the change.

That, replied Cebes, is quite my notion.

Hereupon one of the company, though I do not exactly remember which of them, said: In heaven's name, is not this the direct contrary of what was admitted before—that out of the greater came the less and out of the less the greater, and that opposites were simply generated from opposites; but now this principle seems to be utterly denied.

Socrates inclined his head to the speaker and listened. I like your courage, he said, in reminding us of this. But you do not observe that there is a difference in the two cases. For then we were speaking of opposites in the concrete, and now of the essential opposite which, as is affirmed, neither in us nor in nature can ever be at variance with itself:

then, my friend, we were speaking of things in which opposites are inherent and which are called after them, but now about the opposites which are inherent in them and which give their name to them; and these essential opposites will never, as we maintain, admit of generation into or out of one another. At the same time, turning to Cebes, he said: Are you at all disconcerted, Cebes, at our friend's objection?

No, I do not feel so, said Cebes; and yet I cannot deny that I am often disturbed by objections.

Then we are agreed after all, said Socrates, that the opposite will never in any case be opposed to itself?

To that we are quite agreed, he replied.

Yet once more let me ask you to consider the question from another point of view, and see whether you agree with me:—There is a thing which you term heat, and another thing which you term cold?

Certainly.

But are they the same as fire and snow?

Most assuredly not.

Heat is a thing different from fire, and cold is not the same with snow?

Yes.

And yet you will surely admit, that when snow, as was before said, is under the influence of heat, they will not remain snow and heat; but at the advance of the heat, the snow will either retire or perish?

Very true, he replied.

And the fire too at the advance of the cold will either retire or perish; and when the fire is under the influence of the cold, they will not remain as before, fire and cold.

That is true, he said.

And in some cases the name of the idea is not only attached to the idea in an eternal connection, but anything else which, not being the idea, exists only in the form of the idea, may also lay claim to it. I will try to make this clearer by an example:—The odd number is always called by the name of odd?

Very true.

But is this the only thing which is called odd? Are there not other things which have their own name, and yet are called   [104 odd, because, although not the same as oddness, they are never without oddness?—that is what I mean to ask—whether numbers such as the number three are not of the class of odd. And there are many other examples: would you not say, for example, that three may be called by its proper name, and also be called odd, which is not the same with three? and this may be said not only of three but also of five, and of every alternate number—each of them without being oddness is odd;

and in the same way two and four, and the other series of alternate numbers, has every number even, without being evenness. Do you agree?

Of course.

Then now mark the point at which I am aiming:—not only do essential opposites exclude one another, but also concrete things, which, although not in themselves opposed, contain opposites; these, I say, likewise reject the idea which is opposed to that which is contained in them, and when it approaches them they either perish or withdraw. For example; Will not the number three endure annihilation or anything sooner than be converted into an even number, while remaining three?

Very true, said Cebes.

And yet, he said, the number two is certainly not opposed to the number three?

It is not.

Then not only do opposite ideas repel the advance of one another, but also there are other natures which repel the approach of opposites.

Very true, he said.

Suppose, he said, that we endeavour, if possible, to determine what these are.

By all means.

Are they not, Cebes, such as compel the things of which they have possession, not only to take their own form, but also the form of some opposite?

What do you mean?

I mean, as I was just now saying, and as I am sure that you know, that those things which are possessed by the number three must not only be three in number, but must also be odd.

Quite true.

And on this oddness, of which the number three has the impress, the opposite idea will never intrude?

No.

And this impress was given by the odd principle?

Yes.

And to the odd is opposed the even?

True.

Then the idea of the even number will never arrive at three?

No.

Then three has no part in the even?

None.

Then the triad or number three is uneven?

Very true.

To return then to my distinction of natures which are not opposed, and yet do not admit opposites—as, in the instance given, three, although not opposed to the even, does not any the more admit of the even, but always brings the opposite into play on the other side;   [105 or as two does not receive the odd, or fire the cold—from these examples (and there are many more of them) perhaps you may be able to arrive at the general conclusion, that not only opposites will not receive opposites, but also that nothing which brings the opposite will admit the opposite of that which it brings, in that to which it is brought. And here let me recapitulate—for there is no harm in repetition. The number five will not admit the nature of the even, any more than ten, which is the double of five, will admit the nature of the odd. The double has another opposite, and is not strictly opposed to the odd, but nevertheless rejects the odd altogether. Nor again will parts in the ratio 3:2, nor any fraction in which there is a half, nor again in which there is a third, admit the notion of the whole, although they are not opposed to the whole: You will agree?

Yes, he said, I entirely agree and go along with you in that.

And now, he said, let us begin again; and do not you answer my question in the words in which I ask it: let me have not the old safe answer of which I spoke at first, but another equally safe, of which the truth will be inferred by you from what has been just said. I mean that if any one asks you "what that is, of which the inherence makes the body hot," you will reply not heat (this is what I call the safe and stupid answer), but fire, a far superior answer, which we are now in a condition to give. Or if any one asks you "why a body is diseased," you will not say from disease, but from fever; and instead of saying that oddness is the cause of odd numbers, you will say that the monad is the cause of them: and so of things in general, as I dare say that you will understand sufficiently without my adducing any further examples.

Yes, he said, I quite understand you.

Tell me, then, what is that of which the inherence will render the body alive?

The soul, he replied.

And is this always the case?

Yes, he said, of course.

Then whatever the soul possesses, to that she comes bearing life?

Yes, certainly.

And is there any opposite to life?

There is, he said.

And what is that?

Death.

Then the soul, as has been acknowledged, will never receive the opposite of what she brings.

Impossible, replied Cebes.

And now, he said, what did we just now call that principle which repels the even?

The odd.

And that principle which repels the musical or the just?

The unmusical, he said, and the unjust.

And what do we call that principle which does not admit of death?

The immortal, he said.

And does the soul admit of death?

No.

Then the soul is immortal?

Yes, he said.

And may we say that this has been proven?

Yes, abundantly proven, Socrates, he replied.

Supposing that the odd were imperishable, must not three   [106 be imperishable?

Of course.

And if that which is cold were imperishable, when the warm principle came attacking the snow, must not the snow have retired whole and unmelted—for it could never have perished, nor could it have remained and admitted the heat?

True, he said.

Again, if the uncooling or warm principle were imperishable, the fire when assailed by cold would not have perished or have been extinguished, but would have gone away unaffected?

Certainly, he said.

And the same may be said of the immortal: if the immortal is also imperishable, the soul when attacked by death cannot perish; for the preceding argument shows that the soul will not admit of death, or ever be dead, any more than three or the odd number will admit of the even, or fire, or the heat in the fire, of the cold. Yet a person may say: "But although the odd will not become even at the approach of the even, why may not the odd perish and the even take the place of the odd?" Now to him who makes this objection, we cannot answer that the odd principle is imperishable; for this has not been acknowledged, but if this had been acknowledged, there would have been no difficulty in contending that at the approach of the even the odd principle and the number three took their departure; and the same argument would have held good of fire and heat and any other thing.

Very true.

And the same may be said of the immortal: if the immortal is also imperishable, then the soul will be imperishable as well as immortal; but if not, some other proof of her imperishableness will have to be given.

No other proof is needed, he said; for if the immortal, being eternal, is liable to perish, then nothing is imperishable.

Yes, replied Socrates, and yet all men will agree that God, and the essential form of life, and the immortal in general, will never perish.

Yes, all men, he said—that is true; and what is more, gods, if I am not mistaken, as well as men.

Seeing then that the immortal is indestructible, must not the soul, if she is immortal, be also imperishable?

Most certainly.

Then when death attacks a man, the mortal portion of him may be supposed to die, but the immortal retires at the approach of death and is preserved safe and sound?

True.

Then, Cebes, beyond question, the soul is immortal and imperishable, and our souls will truly exist in another world!   [107

I am convinced, Socrates, said Cebes, and have nothing more to object; but if my friend Simmias, or any one else, has any further objection to make, he had better speak out, and not keep silence, since I do not know to what other season he can defer the discussion, if there is anything which he wants to say or to have said.

But I have nothing more to say, replied Simmias; nor can I see any reason for doubt after what has been said. But I still feel and cannot help feeling uncertain in my own mind, when I think of the greatness of the subject and the feebleness of man.

Yes, Simmias, replied Socrates, that is well said: and I may add that first principles, even if they appear certain, should be carefully considered; and when they are satisfactorily ascertained, then, with a sort of hesitating confidence in human reason, you may, I think, follow the course of the argument; and if that be plain and clear, there will be no need for any further enquiry.

Very true.

But then, O my friends, he said, if the soul is really immortal, what care should be taken of her, not only in respect of the portion of time which is called life, but of eternity! And the danger of neglecting her from this point of view does indeed appear to be awful. If death had only been the end of all, the wicked would have had a good bargain in dying, for they would have been happily quit not only of their body, but of their own evil together with their souls. But now, inasmuch as the soul is manifestly immortal, there is no release or salvation from evil except the attainment of the highest virtue and wisdom. For the soul when on her progress to the world below takes nothing with her but nurture and education; and these are said greatly to benefit or greatly to injure the departed, at the very beginning of his journey thither.

For after death, as they say, the genius of each individual, to whom he belonged in life, leads him to a certain place in which the dead are gathered together, whence after judgment has been given they pass into the world below, following the guide, who is appointed to conduct them from this world to the other: and when they have there received their due and remained their time, another guide brings them back again after many revolutions of ages. Now this way to the other world   [108 is not, as Aeschylus says in the Telephus, a single and straight path—if that were so no guide would be needed, for no one could miss it; but there are many partings of the road, and windings, as I infer from the rites and sacrifices which are offered to the gods below in places where three ways meet on earth. The wise and orderly soul follows in the straight path and is conscious of her surroundings; but the soul which desires the body, and which, as I was relating before, has long been fluttering about the lifeless frame and the world of sight, is after many struggles and many sufferings hardly and with violence carried away by her attendant genius; and when she arrives at the place where the other souls are gathered, if she be impure and have done impure deeds, whether foul murders or other crimes which are the brothers of these, and the works of brothers in crime—from that soul every one flees and turns away; no one will be her companion, no one her guide, but alone she wanders in extremity of evil until certain times are fulfilled, and when they are fulfilled, she is borne irresistibly to her own fitting habitation; as every pure and just soul which has passed through life in the company and under the guidance of the gods has also her own proper home.

Now the earth has divers wonderful regions, and is indeed in nature and extent very unlike the notions of geographers, as I believe on the authority of one who shall be nameless.

What do you mean, Socrates? said Simmias. I have myself heard many descriptions of the earth, but I do not know, and I should very much like to know, in which of these you put faith.

And I, Simmias, replied Socrates, if I had the art of Glaucus would tell you; although I know not that the art of Glaucus could prove the truth of my tale, which I myself should never be able to prove, and even if I could, I fear, Simmias, that my life would come to and end before the argument was completed. I may describe to you, however, the form and regions of the earth according to my conception of them.

That, said Simmias, will be enough.

Well then, he said, my conviction is, that the earth is a round body in the centre of the heavens, and therefore has no need of air or of any similar force to be a support, but is kept there and hindered   [109 from falling or inclining any way by the equability of the surrounding heaven and by her own equipoise. For that which, being in equipoise, is in the centre of that which is equably diffused, will not incline any way in any degree, but will always remain in the same state and not deviate. And this is my first notion.

Which is surely a correct one, said Simmias.

Also I believe that the earth is very vast, and that we who dwell in the region extending from the river Phasis to the Pillars of Heracles inhabit a small portion only about the sea, like ants or frogs about a marsh, and that there are other inhabitants of many other like places; for everywhere on the face of the earth there are hollows of various forms and sizes, into which the water and the mist and the lower air collect. But the true earth is pure and situated in the pure heaven—there are the stars also; and it is the heaven which is commonly spoken of by us as the ether, and of which our own earth is the sediment gathering in the hollows beneath. But we who live in these hollows are deceived into the notion that we are dwelling above on the surface of the earth; which is just as if a creature who was at the bottom of the sea were to fancy that he was on the surface of the water, and that the sea was the heaven through which he saw the sun and the other stars, he having never come to the surface by reason of his feebleness and sluggishness, and having never lifted up his head and seen, nor ever heard from one who had seen, how much purer and fairer the world above is than his own. And such is exactly our case: for we are dwelling in a hollow of the earth, and fancy that we are on the surface; and the air we call heaven, in which we imagine that the stars move. But the fact is, that owing to our feebleness and sluggishness we are prevented from reach- ing the surface of the air: for if any man could arrive at the exter- ior limit, or take the wings of a bird and come to the top, then like a fish who puts his head out of the water and sees this world, he would see a world beyond; and, if the nature of man could sustain the sight, he would acknowledge that this other world was the place of the true heaven and the true light and the true earth. For our earth, and   [110 the stones, and the entire region which surrounds us, are spoilt and cor- roded, as in the sea all things are corroded by the brine, neither is there any noble or perfect growth, but caverns only, and sand, and an endless slough of mud; and even the shore is not to be compared to the fairer sights of this world. And still less is this our world to be compared with the other. Of that upper earth which is under the heaven, I can tell you a charming tale, Simmias, which is well worth hearing.

And we, Socrates, replied Simmias, shall be charmed to listen to you.

The tale, my friend, he said, is as follows:—In the first place, the earth, when looked at from above, is in appearance streaked like one of those balls which have leather coverings in twelve pieces, and is decked with various colours, of which the colours used by painters on earth are in a manner samples. But there the whole earth is made up of them, and they are brighter far and clearer than ours; there is a purple of wonderful lustre, also the radiance of gold, and the white which is in the earth is whiter than any chalk or snow. Of these and other colours the earth is made up, and they are more in number and fairer than the eye of man has ever seen; the very hollows (of which I was speaking) filled with air and water have a colour of their own, and are seen like light gleaming amid the diversity of the other colours, so that the whole presents a single and continuous appearance of variety in unity. And in this fair region everything that grows—trees, and flowers, and fruits—are in a like degree fairer than any here; and there are hills, having stones in them in a like degree smoother, and more transparent, and fairer in colour than our highly-valued emeralds and sardonyxes and jaspers, and other gems, which are but minute fragments of them: for there all the stones are like our precious stones, and fairer still [6]. The reason is, that they are pure, and not, like our precious stones, infected or corroded by the corrupt briny elements which coagulate among us, and which breed foulness and disease both in earth and stones, as well as in animals and plants. They are the jewels of the upper earth, which also shines with gold and silver and the like, and they are set in the light of day and are large and abundant   [111 and in all places, making the earth a sight to gladden the beholder's eye. And there are animals and men, some in a middle region, others dwelling about the air as we dwell about the sea; others in islands which the air flows round, near the continent; and in a word, the air is used by them as the water and the sea are by us, and the ether is to them what the air is to us. Moreover, the temperament of their seasons is such that they have no disease, and live much longer than we do, and have sight and hearing and smell, and all the other senses, in far greater perfection, in the same proportion that air is purer than water or the ether than air. Also they have temples and sacred places in which the gods really dwell, and they hear their voices and receive their answers, and are conscious of them and hold converse with them; and they see the sun, moon, and stars as they truly are, and their other blessedness is of a piece with this.

Such is the nature of the whole earth, and of the things which are around the earth; and there are divers regions in the hollows on the face of the globe everywhere, some of them deeper and more extended than that which we inhabit, others deeper but with a narrower opening than

---

[6] Cp. Rev., esp. c. xxi. v. 18 ff.

ours, and some are shallower and also wider. All have numerous per-
forations, and there are passages broad and narrow in the interior of the
earth, connecting them with one another; and there flows out of and
into them, as into basins, a vast tide of water, and huge subterranean
streams of perennial rivers, and springs hot and cold, and a great fire, and
great rivers of fire, and streams of liquid mud, thin or thick (like the
rivers of mud in Sicily, and the lava streams which follow them), and the
regions about which they happen to flow are filled up with them. And
there is a swinging or see-saw in the interior of the earth which moves
all this up and down, and is due to the following cause:—There is a
chasm which is the vastest of them all, and pierces right through
the whole earth; this is that chasm which Homer describes in   [112
the words.—

 'Far off, where is the inmost depth beneath the earth;'

and which he in other places, and many other poets, have called
Tartarus. And the see-saw is caused by the streams flowing into and out
of this chasm, and they each have the nature of the soil through which
they flow. And the reason why the streams are always flowing in and
out, is that the watery element has no bed or bottom, but is swinging
and surging up and down, and the surrounding wind and air do the
same; they follow the water up and down, hither and thither, over the
earth—just as in the act of respiration the air is always in process of
inhalation and exhalation;—and the wind swinging with the water in
and out produces fearful and irresistible blasts: when the waters retire
with a rush into the lower parts of the earth, as they are called, they
flow through the earth in those regions, and fill them up like water
raised by a pump, and then when they leave those regions and rush back
hither, they again fill the hollows here, and when these are filled, flow
through subterranean channels and find their way to their several
places, forming seas, and lakes, and rivers, and springs. Thence they
again enter the earth, some of them making a long circuit into many
lands, others going to a few places and not so distant; and again fall
into Tartarus, some at a point a good deal lower than that at which
they rose, and others not much lower, but all in some degree lower than
the point from which they came. And some burst forth again on the
opposite side, and some on the same side, and some wind round the
earth with one or many folds like the coils of a serpent, and descend
as far as they can, but always return and fall into the chasm. The rivers
flowing in either direction can descend only to the centre and no further, for opposite to the rivers is a precipice.

 Now these rivers are many, and mighty, and diverse, and there are
four principal ones, of which the greatest and outermost is that called

Oceanus, which flows round the earth in a circle; and in the opposite direction flows Acheron, which passes under the earth through desert places into the Acherusian lake: this is the lake to the shores   [113 of which the souls of the many go when they are dead, and after waiting an appointed time, which is to some a longer and to some a shorter time, they are sent back to be born again as animals. The third river passes out between the two, and near the place of outlet pours into a vast region of fire, and forms a lake larger than the Mediterranean Sea, boiling with water and mud; and proceeding muddy and turbid, and winding about the earth, comes, among other places, to the extremities of the Acherusian lake, but mingles not with the waters of the lake, and after making many coils about the earth plunges into Tartarus at a deeper level. This is that Pyriphlegethon, as the stream is called, which throws up jets of fire in different parts of the earth. The fourth river goes out on the opposite side, and falls first of all into a wild and savage region, which is all of a dark blue colour, like lapis lazuli; and this is that river which is called the Stygian river, and falls into and forms the Lake Styx, and after falling into the lake and receiving strange powers in the waters, passes under the earth, winding round in the opposite direction, and comes near the Acherusian lake from the opposite side to Pyriphlegethon. And the water of this river too mingles with no other, but flows round in a circle and falls into Tartarus over against Pyriphlegethon; and the name of the river, as the poets say, is Cocytus.

Such is the nature of the other world; and when the dead arrive at the place to which the genius of each severally guides them, first of all, they have sentence passed upon them, as they have lived well and piously or not. And those who appear to have lived neither well nor ill, go to the river Acheron, and embarking in any vessels which they may find, are carried in them to the lake, and there they dwell and are purified of their evil deeds, and having suffered the penalty of the wrongs which they have done to others, they are absolved, and receive the rewards of their good deeds, each of them according to his deserts. But those who appear to be incurable by reason of the greatness of their crimes—who have committed many and terrible deeds of sacrilege, murders foul and violent, or the like—such are hurled into Tartarus which is their suitable destiny, and they never come out. Those again who have committed crimes, which, although great, are not irremediable—who in a moment of anger, for example, have done some violence to a father or a mother, and have repented for the re-   [114 mainder of their lives, or, who have taken the life of another under the like extenuating circumstances—these are plunged into Tartarus, the pains of which they are compelled to undergo for a year, but at the end of the year the wave casts them forth—mere homicides by way of Cocytus, parricides and matricides by Pyriphlegethon—and they are borne to the Acherusian lake, and there they lift up their voices and call upon the victims whom they have slain or wronged, to have pity on them, and to be kind to them, and let them come out into the lake. And if they prevail, then they come forth and cease from their troubles; but if not, they are carried back again into Tartarus and from thence into the rivers unceasingly, until they obtain mercy from those whom they have wronged: for that is the sentence inflicted upon them by their judges. Those too who have been pre-eminent for holiness of life are released from this earthly prison, and go to their pure home which is above, and dwell in the purer earth; and of these, such as have duly purified themselves with philosophy live henceforth altogether without the body, in mansions fairer still, which may not be described, and of which the time would fail me to tell.

Wherefore, Simmias, seeing all these things, what ought not we to do that we may obtain virtue and wisdom in this life? Fair is the prize, and the hope great!

A man of sense ought not to say, nor will I be very confident, that the description which I have given of the soul and her mansions is exactly true. But I do say that, inasmuch as the soul is shown to be immortal, he may venture to think, not improperly or unworthily, that something of the kind is true. The venture is a glorious one, and he ought to comfort himself with words like these, which is the reason why I lengthen out the tale. Wherefore, I say, let a man be of good cheer about his soul, who having cast away the pleasures and ornaments of the body as alien to him and working harm rather than good, has sought after the pleasures of knowledge; and has arrayed the soul, not in some foreign attire, but in her own proper jewels, temperance, and justice, and courage, and nobility, and truth—in these adorned   [115 she is ready to go on her journey to the world below, when her hour comes. You, Simmias and Cebes, and all other men, will depart at some time or other. Me already, as a tragic poet would say, the voice of fate calls. Soon I must drink the poison; and I think that I had better repair to the bath first, in order that the women may not have the trouble of washing my body after I am dead.

When he had done speaking, Crito said: And have you any commands for us, Socrates—anything to say about your children, or any other matter in which we can serve you?

Nothing particular, Crito, he replied: only, as I have always told you, take care of yourselves; that is a service which you may be ever rendering to me and mine and to all of us, whether you promise to do so or not. But if you have no thought for yourselves, and care not to walk

according to the rule which I have prescribed for you, not now for the
first time, however much you may profess or promise at the moment, it
will be of no avail.

We will do our best, said Crito: And in what way shall we bury
you?

In any way that you like; but you must get hold of me, and take
care that I do not run away from you. Then he turned to us, and
added with a smile:—I cannot make Crito believe that I am the same
Socrates who have been talking and conducting the argument; he
fancies that I am the other Socrates whom he will soon see, a dead
body—and he asks, How shall he bury me? And though I have spoken
many words in the endeavour to show that when I have drunk the
poison I shall leave you and go to the joys of the blessed,—these
words of mine, with which I was comforting you and myself, have had,
as I perceive, no effect upon Crito. And therefore I want you to be
surety for me to him now, as at the trial he was surety to the judges
for me: but let the promise be of another sort; for he was surety for me
to the judges that I would remain, and you must be my surety to him
that I shall not remain, but go away and depart; and then he will
suffer less at my death, and not be grieved when he sees my body being
burned or buried. I would not have him sorrow at my hard lot, or say at
the burial, Thus we lay out Socrates, or, Thus we follow him to the
grave or bury him; for false words are not only evil in themselves, but
they infect the soul with evil. Be of good cheer then, my dear Crito, and
say that you are burying my body only, and do with that what-   [116
ever is usual, and what you think best.

When he had spoken these words, he arose and went into a
chamber to bathe; Crito followed him and told us to wait. So we
remained behind, talking and thinking of the subject of discourse,
and also of the greatness of our sorrow; he was like a father of whom
we were being bereaved, and we were about to pass the rest of our
lives as orphans. When he had taken the bath his children were
brought to him—(he had two young sons and an elder one); and the
women of his family also came, and he talked to them and gave them
a few directions in the presence of Crito; then he dismissed them and
returned to us.

Now the hour of sunset was near, for a good deal of time had
passed while he was within. When he came out, he sat down with us
again after his bath, but not much was said. Soon the jailer, who was
the servant of the Eleven, entered and stood by him, saying:—To you,
Socrates, whom I know to be the noblest and gentlest and best of all
who ever came to this place, I will not impute the angry feelings of
other men, who rage and swear at me, when, in obedience to the

authorities, I bid them drink the poison—indeed, I am sure that you will not be angry with me; for others, as you are aware, and not I, are to blame. And so fare you well, and try to bear lightly what must needs be —you know my errand. Then bursting into tears he turned away and went out.

Socrates looked at him and said: I return your good wishes, and will do as you bid. Then turning to us, he said, How charming the man is: since I have been in prison he has always been coming to see me, and at times he would talk to me, and was as good to me as could be, and now see how generously he sorrows on my account. We must do as he says, Crito; and therefore let the cup be brought, if the poison is prepared: if not, let the attendant prepare some.

Yet, said Crito, the sun is still upon the hill-tops, and I know that many a one has taken the draught late, and after the announcement has been made to him, he has eaten and drunk, and enjoyed the society of his beloved; do not hurry—there is time enough.

Socrates said: Yes, Crito, and they of whom you speak are right in so acting, for they think that they will be gainers by the delay; but I am right in not following their example, for I do not think that I should gain anything by drinking the poison a little later; I   [117 should only be ridiculous in my own eyes for sparing and saving a life which is already forfeit. Please then to do as I say, and not to refuse me.

Crito made a sign to the servant, who was standing by; and he went out, and having been absent for some time, returned with the jailer carrying the cup of poison. Socrates said: You, my good friend, who are experienced in these matters, shall give me directions how I am to proceed. The man answered: You have only to walk about until your legs are heavy, and then to lie down, and the poison will act. At the same time he handed the cup to Socrates, who in the easiest and gentlest manner, without the least fear or change of colour or feature, looking at the man with all his eyes, Echecrates, as his manner was, took the cup and said: What do you say about making a libation out of this cup to any god? May I, or not? The man answered: We only prepare, Socrates, just so much as we deem enough. I understand, he said: but I may and must ask the gods to prosper my journey from this to the other world—even so—and so be it according to my prayer. Then raising the cup to his lips, quite readily and cheerfully he drank off the poison. And hitherto most of us had been able to control our sorrow; but now when we saw him drinking, and saw too that he had finished the draught, we could no longer forbear, and in spite of my-self my own tears were flowing fast; so that I covered my face and wept, not for him, but at the thought of my own calamity in having to part from such a friend. Nor was I the first; for Crito, when he found himself unable to restrain his tears, had got up, and I followed; and at that moment, Apollodorus, who had been weeping all the time, broke out in a loud and passionate cry which made cowards of us all. Socrates alone retained his calmness: What is this strange outcry? he said. I sent away the women mainly in order that they might not misbehave in this way, for I have been told that a man should die in peace. Be quiet then, and have patience. When we heard his words we were ashamed, and refrained our tears; and he walked about until, as he said, his legs began to fail, and then he lay on his back, according to the directions; and the man who gave him the poison now and then looked at his feet and legs; and after a while he pressed his foot hard, and asked him if he could feel; and he said, No; and then his leg,   [118 and so upwards and upwards, and showed us that he was cold and stiff. And he felt them himself, and said: When the poison reaches the heart, that will be the end. He was beginning to grow cold about the groin, when he uncovered his face, for he had covered himself up, and said—they were his last words—he said: Crito, I owe a cock to Asclepius; will you remember to pay the debt? The debt shall be paid, said Crito; is there anything else? There was no answer to this question; but in a minute or two a movement was heard, and the attendants uncovered him; his eyes were set, and Crito closed his eyes and mouth.

Such was the end, Echecrates, of our friend; concerning whom I may truly say, that of all the men of his time whom I have known, he was the wisest and justest and best.

SOPHIST

>>>->>><<<-<<<

PERSONS OF THE DIALOGUE

An Eleatic Stranger, *whom Theodorus and Theaetetus*
bring with them. The younger Socrates, *who is a*
silent auditor.
Theodorus
Theaetetus
Socrates

Theodorus. Here we are, Socrates, true to our agreement of yesterday;
and we bring with us a stranger from Elea, who is a disciple of
Parmenides and Zeno, and a true philosopher.   [216

   Socrates. Is he not rather a god, Theodorus, who comes to us in
the disguise of a stranger? For Homer says that all the gods, and
especially the god of strangers, are companions of the meek and just,
and visit the good and evil among men. And may not your companion
be one of those higher powers, a cross-examining deity, who has come
to spy out our weakness in argument, and to cross-examine us?

   Theodorus. Nay, Socrates, he is not one of the disputatious sort—
he is too good for that. And, in my opinion, he is not a god at all; but
divine he certainly is, for this is a title which I should give to all
philosophers.

   Socrates. Capital, my friend! and I may add that they are almost as
hard to be discerned as the gods. For the true philosophers, and
such as are not merely made up for the occasion, appear in various
forms unrecognized by the ignorance of men, and they 'hover about
cities,' as Homer declares, looking from above upon human life; and
some think nothing of them, and others can never think enough; and
sometimes they appear as statesmen, and sometimes as sophists; and

then, again, to many they seem to be no better than madmen. I should like to ask our Eleatic friend, if he would tell us, what is thought about them in Italy, and to whom the terms are applied.   [217

Theodorus. What terms?

Socrates. Sophist, statesman, philosopher.

Theodorus. What is you difficulty about them, and what made you ask?

Socrates. I want to know whether by his countrymen they are regarded as one or two; or do they, as the names are three, distinguish also three kinds, and assign one to each name?

Theodorus. I dare say that the Stranger will not object to discuss the question. What do you say, Stranger?

Stranger. I am far from objecting, Theodorus, nor have I any difficulty in replying that by us they are regarded as three. But to define precisely the nature of each of them is by no means a slight or easy task.

Theodorus. You have happened to light, Socrates, almost on the very question which we were asking our friend before we came hither, and he excused himself to us, as he does now to you; although he admitted that the matter had been fully discussed, and that he remembered the answer.

Socrates. Then do not, Stranger, deny us the first favour which we ask of you: I am sure that you will not, and therefore I shall only beg of you to say whether you like and are accustomed to make a long oration on a subject which you want to explain to another, or to proceed by the method of question and answer. I remember hearing a very noble discussion in which Parmenides employed the latter of the two methods, when I was a young man, and he was far advanced in years.[1]

Stranger. I prefer to talk with another when he responds pleasantly, and is light in hand; if not, I would rather have my own say.

Socrates. Any one of the present company will respond kindly to you, and you can choose whom you like of them; I should recommend you to take a young person—Theaetetus, for example—unless you have a preference for some one else.

Stranger. I feel ashamed, Socrates, being a new-comer into your society, instead of talking a little and hearing others talk, to be spinning out a long soliloquy or address, as if I wanted to show off. For the true answer will certainly be a very long one, a great deal longer than might be expected from such a short and simple question. At the same time, I fear that I may seem rude and ungracious

---

[1] Cp. Parm., 137 ff.

if I refuse your courteous request, especially after what you have   [218
said. For I certainly cannot object to your proposal, that Theaetetus
should respond, having already conversed with him myself, and being
recommended by you to take him.

Theaetetus. But are you sure, Stranger, that this will be quite
so acceptable to the rest of the company as Socrates imagines?

Stranger. You hear them applauding, Theaetetus; after that, there
is nothing more to be said. Well then, I am to argue with you, and if
you tire of the argument, you may complain of your friends and
not of me.

Theaetetus. I do not think that I shall tire, and if I do, I shall get
my friend here, young Socrates, the namesake of the elder Socrates, to
help; he is about my own age, and my partner at the gymnasium, and is
constantly accustomed to work with me.

Stranger. Very good; you can decide about that for yourself as we
proceed. Meanwhile you and I will begin together and enquire into
the nature of the Sophist, first of the three: I should like you to make
out what he is and bring him to light in a discussion; for at present we
are only agreed about the name, but of the thing to which we both apply
the name possibly you have one notion and I another; whereas we
ought always to come to an understanding about the thing itself in
terms of a definition, and not merely about the name minus the definition. Now the tribe of Sophists which we are investigating is not
easily caught or defined; and the world has long ago agreed, that if
great subjects are to be adequately treated, they must be studied in the
lesser and easier instances of them before we proceed to the greatest
of all. And as I know that the tribe of Sophists is troublesome and hard
to be caught, I should recommend that we practise beforehand the
method which is to be applied to him on some simple and smaller
thing, unless you can suggest a better way.

Theaetetus. Indeed I cannot.

Stranger. Then suppose that we work out some lesser example
which will be a pattern of the greater?

Theaetetus. Good.

Stranger. What is there which is well known and not great, and
is yet as susceptible of definition as any larger thing? Shall I say an
angler? He is familiar to all of us, and not a very interesting or important person.

Theaetetus. He is not.

Stranger. Yet I suspect that he will furnish us with the sort   [219
of definition and line of enquiry which we want.

Theaetetus. Very good.

Stranger. Let us begin by asking whether he is a man having art or not having art, but some other power.

Theaetetus. He is clearly a man of art.

Stranger. And of arts there are two kinds?

Theaetetus. What are they?

Stranger. There is agriculture, and the tending of mortal creatures, and the art of constructing or moulding vessels, and there is the art of imitation—all these may be appropriately called by a single name.

Theaetetus. What do you mean? And what is the name?

Stranger. He who brings into existence something that did not exist before is said to be a producer, and that which is brought into existence is said to be produced.

Theaetetus. True.

Stranger. And all the arts which were just now mentioned are characterized by this power of producing?

Theaetetus. They are.

Stranger. Then let us sum them up under the name of productive or creative art.

Theaetetus. Very good.

Stranger. Next follows the whole class of learning and cognition; then comes trade, fighting, hunting. And since none of these produces anything, but is only engaged in conquering by word or deed, or in preventing others from conquering, things which exist and have been already produced—in each and all of these branches there appears to be an art which may be called acquisitive.

Theaetetus. Yes, that is the proper name.

Stranger. Seeing, then, that all arts are either acquisitive or creative, in which class shall we place the art of the angler?

Theaetetus. Clearly in the acquisitive class.

Stranger. And the acquisitive may be subdivided into two parts: there is exchange, which is voluntary and is effected by gifts, hire, purchase; and the other part of acqusitive, which takes by force of word or deed, may be termed conquest?

Theaetetus. That is implied in what has been said.

Stranger. And may not conquest be again subdivided?

Theaetetus. How?

Stranger. Open force may be called fighting, and secret force may have the general name of hunting?

Theaetetus. Yes.

Stranger. And there is no reason why the art of hunting should not be further divided.

Theaetetus. How would you make the division?

Stranger. Into the hunting of living and of lifeless prey.

Theaetetus. Yes, if both kinds exist.

Stranger. Of course they exist; but the hunting after lifeless   [220 things having no special name, except some sorts of diving, and other small matters, may be omitted; the hunting after living things may be called animal hunting.

Theaetetus. Yes.

Stranger. And animal hunting may be truly said to have two divisions, land-animal hunting, which has many kinds and names, and water-animal hunting, or the hunting after animals who swim?

Theaetetus. True.

Stranger. And of swimming animals, one class lives on the wing and the other in the water?

Theaetetus. Certainly.

Stranger. Fowling is the general term under which the hunting of all birds is included.

Theaetetus. True.

Stranger. The hunting of animals who live in the water has the general name of fishing.

Theaetetus. Yes.

Stranger. And this sort of hunting may be further divided also into two principal kinds?

Theaetetus. What are they?

Stranger. There is one kind which takes them in nets, another which takes them by a blow.

Theaetetus. What do you mean, and how do you distinguish them?

Stranger. As to the first kind—all that surrounds and encloses anything to prevent egress, may be rightly called an enclosure.

Theaetetus. Very true.

Stranger. For which reason twig baskets, casting-nets, nooses, creels, and the like may all be termed 'enclosures'?

Theaetetus. True.

Stranger. And therefore this first kind of capture may be called by us capture with enclosures, or something of that sort?

Theaetetus. Yes.

Stranger. The other kind, which is practised by a blow with hooks and three-pronged spears, when summed up under one name, may be called striking, unless you, Theaetetus, can find some better name?

Theaetetus. Never mind the name—what you suggest will do very well.

Stranger. There is one mode of striking, which is done at night, and by the light of a fire, and is by the hunters themselves called firing, or spearing by firelight.

Theaetetus. True.

Stranger. And the fishing by day is called by the general name of barbing, because the spears, too, are barbed at the point.

Theaetetus. Yes, that is the term.

Stranger. Of this barb-fishing, that which strikes the fish who is below from above is called spearing, because this is the way in which the three-pronged spears are mostly used.

Theaetetus. Yes, it is often called so.

Stranger. Then now there is only one kind remaining.

Theaetetus. What is that?

Stranger. When a hook is used, and the fish is not struck in any chance part of his body, as he is with the spear, but only about the head and mouth, and is then drawn out from below upwards   [221 with reeds and rods:—What is the right name of that mode of fishing, Theaetetus?

Theaetetus. I suspect that we have now discovered the object of our search.

Stranger. Then now you and I have come to an understanding not only about the name of the angler's art, but about the definition of the thing itself. One half of all art was acquisitive—half of the acquisitive art was conquest or taking by force, half of this was hunting, and half of hunting was hunting animals, half of this was hunting water animals —of this again, the under half was fishing, half of fishing was striking; a part of striking was fishing with a barb, and one half of this again, being the kind which strikes with a hook and draws the fish from below upwards, is the art which we have been seeking, and which from the nature of the operation is denoted angling or drawing up (ἀσπαλιευτικὴ, ἀνασπᾶσθαι).

Theaetetus. The result has been quite satisfactorily brought out.

Stranger. And now, following this pattern, let us endeavour to find out what a Sophist is.

Theaetetus. By all means.

Stranger. The first question about the angler was, whether he was a skilled artist or unskilled?

Theaetetus. True.

Stranger. And shall we call our new friend unskilled, or a thorough master of his craft?

Theaetetus. Certainly not unskilled, for his name, as, indeed, you imply, must surely express his nature.

Stranger. Then he must be supposed to have some art.

Theaetetus. What art?

Stranger. By heaven, they are cousins! it never occurred to us.

Theaetetus. Who are cousins?

Stranger. The angler and the Sophist.

Theaetetus. In what way are they related?

Stranger. They both appear to me to be hunters.

Theaetetus. How the Sophist? Of the other we have spoken.

Stranger. You remember our division of hunting, into hunting after swimming animals and land animals?

Theaetetus. Yes.

Stranger. And you remember that we subdivided the swimming and left the land animals, saying that there were many kinds of them?

Theaetetus. Certainly.   [222

Stranger. Thus far, then, the Sophist and the angler, starting from the art of acquiring, take the same road?

Theaetetus. So it would appear.

Stranger. Their paths diverge when they reach the art of animal hunting; the one going to the sea-shore, and to the rivers and to the lakes, and angling for the animals which are in them.

Theaetetus. Very true.

Stranger. While the other goes to land and water of another sort— rivers of wealth and broad meadow-lands of generous youth; and he also is intending to take the animals which are in them.

Theaetetus. What do you mean?

Stranger. Of hunting on land there are two principal divisions.

Theaetetus. What are they?

Stranger. One is the hunting of tame, and the other of wild animals.

Theaetetus. But are tame animals ever hunted?

Stranger. Yes, if you include man under tame animals. But if you like you may say that there are no tame animals, or that, if there are, man is not among them; or you may say that man is a tame animal but is not hunted—you shall decide which of these alternatives you prefer.

Theaetetus. I should say, Stranger, that man is a tame animal, and I admit that he is hunted.

Stranger. Then let us divide the hunting of tame animals into two parts.

Theaetetus. How shall we make the division?

Stranger. Let us define piracy, man-stealing, tyranny, the whole military art, by one name, as hunting with violence.

Theaetetus. Very good.

Stranger. But the art of the lawyer, of the popular orator, and the art of conversation may be called in one word the art of persuasion.

Theaetetus. True.

Stranger. And of persuasion, there may be said to be two kinds?

Theaetetus. What are they?

Stranger. One is private, and the other public.

Theaetetus. Yes; each of them forms a class.

Stranger. And of private hunting, one sort receives hire, and the other brings gifts.

Theaetetus. I do not understand you.

Stranger. You seem never to have observed the manner in which lovers hunt.

Theaetetus. To what do you refer?

Stranger. I mean that they lavish gifts on those whom they hunt in addition to other inducements.

Theaetetus. Most true.

Stranger. Let us admit this, then, to be the amatory art.

Theaetetus. Certainly.

Stranger. But that sort of hireling whose conversation is pleasing and who baits his hook only with pleasure and exacts nothing but his maintenance in return, we should all, if I am not mistaken, describe as possessing flattery or an art of making things pleasant. [223

Theaetetus. Certainly.

Stranger. And that sort, which professes to form acquaintances only for the sake of virtue, and demands a reward in the shape of money, may be fairly called by another name?

Theaetetus. To be sure.

Stranger. And what is the name? Will you tell me?

Theaetetus. It is obvious enough; for I believe that we have discovered the Sophist: which is, as I conceive, the proper name for the class described.

Stranger. Then now, Theaetetus, his art may be traced as a branch of the appropriative [2], acquisitive family—which hunts animals,—living—land—tame animals; which hunts man,—privately—for hire,—taking money in exchange—having the semblance of education; and this is termed Sophistry, and is a hunt after young men of wealth and rank—such is the conclusion.

Theaetetus. Just so.

Stranger. Let us take another branch of his genealogy; for he is a professor of a great and many-sided art; and if we look back at what has preceded we see that he presents another aspect, besides that of which we are speaking.

Theaetetus. In what respect?

---

[2] Omitting χειρωτικῆς and πεζοθηρίας.

Stranger. There were two sorts of acquisitive art; the one concerned with hunting, the other with exchange.

Theaetetus. There were.

Stranger. And of the art of exchange there are two divisions, the one of giving, and the other of selling.

Theaetetus. Let us assume that.

Stranger. Next, we will suppose the art of selling to be divided into two parts.

Theaetetus. How?

Stranger. There is one part which is distinguished as the sale of a man's own productions; another, which is the exchange of the works of others.

Theaetetus. Certainly.

Stranger. And is not that part of exchange which takes place in the city, being about half of the whole, termed retailing?

Theaetetus. Yes.

Stranger. And that which exchanges the goods of one city for those of another by selling and buying is the exchange of the merchant?

Theaetetus. To be sure.

Stranger. And you are aware that this exchange of the merchant is of two kinds: it is partly concerned with food for the use of the body, and partly with the food of the soul which is bartered and received in exchange for money.

Theaetetus. What do you mean?

Stranger. You want to know what is the meaning of food for the soul; the other kind you surely understand.

Theaetetus. Yes.

Stranger. Take music in general and painting and marionette playing and many other things, which are purchased in one city, [224 and carried away and sold in another—wares of the soul which are hawked about either for the sake of instruction or amusement;—may not he who takes them about and sells them be quite as truly called a merchant as he who sells meats and drinks?

Theaetetus. To be sure he may.

Stranger. And would you not call by the same name him who buys up knowledge and goes about from city to city exchanging his wares for money?

Theaetetus. Certainly I should.

Stranger. Of this merchandise of the soul, may not one part be fairly termed the art of display? And there is another part which is certainly not less ridiculous, but being a trade in learning must be called by some name germane to the matter?

Theaetetus. Certainly.

Stranger. The latter should have two names,—one descriptive of the sale of the knowledge of virtue, and the other of the sale of other kinds of knowledge.

Theaetetus. Of course.

Stranger. The name of art-seller corresponds well enough to the latter; but you must try and tell me the name of the other.

Theaetetus. He must be the Sophist, whom we are seeking; no other name can possibly be right.

Stranger. No other; and so this trader in virtue again turns out to be our friend the Sophist, whose art may now be traced from the art of acquisition through exchange, trade, merchandise, to a merchandise of the soul which is concerned with speech and the knowledge of virtue.

Theaetetus. Quite true.

Stranger. And there may be a third reappearance of him;—for he may have settled down in a city, and may fabricate as well as buy these same wares, intending to live by selling them, and he would still be called a Sophist?

Theaetetus. Certainly.

Stranger. Then that part of acquisitive art which exchanges, and of exchange which either sells a man's own productions or retails those of others, as the case may be, and in either way sells the knowledge of virtue, you would again term Sophistry?

Theaetetus. I must, if I am to keep pace with the argument.

Stranger. Let us consider once more whether there may not be yet another aspect of sophistry.

Theaetetus. What is it?

Stranger. In the acquisitive there was a subdivision of the [225 combative or fighting art.

Theaetetus. There was.

Stranger. Perhaps we had better divide it.

Theaetetus. What shall be the divisions?

Stranger. There shall be one division of the competitive, and another of the pugnacious.

Theaetetus. Very good.

Stranger. That part of the pugnacious which is a contest of bodily strength may be properly called by some such name as violent.

Theaetetus. True.

Stranger. And when the war is one of words, it may be termed controversy?

Theaetetus. Yes.

Stranger. And controversy may be of two kinds.

Theaetetus. What are they?

Stranger. When long speeches are answered by long speeches, and there is public discussion about the just and unjust, that is forensic controversy.

Theaetetus. Yes.

Stranger. And there is a private sort of controversy, which is cut up into questions and answers, and this is commonly called disputation?

Theaetetus. Yes, that is the name.

Stranger. And of disputation, that sort which is only a discussion about contracts, and is carried on at random, and without rules of art, is recognized by the reasoning faculty to be a distinct class, but has hitherto had no distinctive name, and does not deserve to receive one from us.

Theaetetus. No; for the different sorts of it are too minute and heterogeneous.

Stranger. But that which proceeds by rules of art to dispute about justice and injustice in their own nature, and about things in general, we have been accustomed to call argumentation (Eristic)?

Theaetetus. Certainly.

Stranger. And of argumentation, one sort wastes money, and the other makes money.

Theaetetus. Very true.

Stranger. Suppose we try and give to each of these two classes a name.

Theaetetus. Let us do so.

Stranger. I should say that the habit which leads a man to neglect his own affairs for the pleasure of conversation, of which the style is far from being agreeable to the majority of his hearers, may be fairly termed loquacity: such is my opinion.

Theaetetus. That is the common name for it.

Stranger. But now who the other is, who makes money out of private disputation, it is your turn to say.

Theaetetus. There is only one true answer: he is the wonderful Sophist, of whom we are in pursuit, and who reappears again for the fourth time.

Stranger. Yes, and with a fresh pedigree, for he is the   [226 money-making species of the Eristic, disputatious, controversial, pugnacious, combative, acquisitive family, as the argument has already proven.

Theaetetus. Certainly.

Stranger. How true was the observation that he was a many-sided animal, and not to be caught with one hand, as they say!

Theaetetus. Then you must catch him with two.

Stranger. Yes, we must, if we can. And therefore let us try another track in our pursuit of him: You are aware that there are certain menial occupations which have names among servants?

Theaetetus. Yes, there are many such; which of them do you mean?

Stranger. I mean such as sifting, straining, winnowing, threshing [3].

Theaetetus. Certainly.

Stranger. And besides these there are a great many more, such as carding, spinning, adjusting the warp and the woof; and thousands of similar expressions are used in the arts.

Theaetetus. Of what are they to be patterns, and what are we going to do with them all?

Stranger. I think that in all of these there is implied a notion of division.

Theaetetus. Yes.

Stranger. Then if, as I was saying, there is one art which includes all of them, ought not that art to have one name?

Theaetetus. And what is the name of the art?

Stranger. The art of discerning or discriminating.

Theaetetus. Very good.

Stranger. Think whether you cannot divide this.

Theaetetus. I should have to think a long while.

Stranger. In all the previously named processes either like has been separated from like or the better from the worse.

Theaetetus. I see now what you mean.

Stranger. There is no name for the first kind of separation; of the second, which throws away the worse and preserves the better, I do know a name.

Theaetetus. What is it?

Stranger. Every discernment or discrimination of that kind, as I have observed, is called a purification.

Theaetetus. Yes, that is the usual expression.

Stranger. And any one may see that purification is of two kinds.

Theaetetus. Perhaps so, if he were allowed time to think; but I do not see at this moment.

Stranger. There are many purifications of bodies which may with propriety be comprehended under a single name.

Theaetetus. What are they, and what is their name?

Stranger. There is the purification of living bodies in their   [227 inward and in their outward parts, of which the former is duly effected by medicine and gymnastic, the latter by the not very dignified art of the bath-man; and there is the purification of inanimate substances—to

---

[3] Reading δίνειν, a conjecture of Professor Campbell's.

this the arts of fulling and of furbishing in general attend in a number of minute particulars, having a variety of names which are thought ridiculous.

Theaetetus. Very true.

Stranger. There can be no doubt that they are thought ridiculous, Theaetetus; but then the dialectical art never considers whether the benefit to be derived from the purge is greater or less than that to be derived from the sponge, and has not more interest in the one than in the other; her endeavour is to know what is and is not kindred in all arts, with a view to the acquisition of intelligence; and having this in view, she honours them all alike, and when she makes comparisons, she counts one of them not a whit more ridiculous than another; nor does she esteem him who adduces as his example of hunting, the general's art, at all more decorous than another who cites that of the vermin-destroyer, but only as the greater pretender of the two. And as to your question concerning the name which was to comprehend all these arts of purification, whether of animate or inanimate bodies, the art of dialectic is in no wise particular about fine words, if she may be only allowed to have a general name for all other purifications, binding them up together and separating them off from the purification of the soul or intellect. For this is the purification at which she wants to arrive, and this we should understand to be her aim.

Theaetetus. Yes, I understand; and I agree that there are two sorts of purification, and that one of them is concerned with the soul, and that there is another which is concerned with the body.

Stranger. Excellent; and now listen to what I am going to say, and try to divide further the first of the two.

Theaetetus. Whatever line of division you suggest, I will endeavour to assist you.

Stranger. Do we admit that virtue is distinct from vice in the soul?

Theaetetus. Certainly.

Stranger. And purification was to leave the good and to cast out whatever is bad?

Theaetetus. True.

Stranger. Then any taking away of evil from the soul may be properly called purification?

Theaetetus. Yes.

Stranger. And in the soul there are two kinds of evil.

Theaetetus. What are they?

Stranger. The one may be compared to disease in the   [228 body, the other to deformity.

Theaetetus. I do not understand.

Stranger. Perhaps you have never reflected that disease and discord are the same.

Theaetetus. To this, again, I know not what I should reply.

Stranger. Do you not conceive discord to be a dissolution of kindred elements, originating in some disagreement?

Theaetetus. Just that.

Stranger. And is deformity anything but the want of measure, which is always unsightly?

Theaetetus. Exactly.

Stranger. And do we not see that opinion is opposed to desire, pleasure to anger, reason to pain, and that all these elements are opposed to one another in the souls of bad men?

Theaetetus. Certainly.

Stranger. And yet they must all be akin?

Theaetetus. Of course.

Stranger. Then we shall be right in calling vice a discord and disease of the soul?

Theaetetus. Most true.

Stranger. And when things having motion, and aiming at an appointed mark, continually miss their aim and glance aside, shall we say that this is the effect of symmetry among them, or of the want of symmetry?

Theaetetus. Clearly of the want of symmetry.

Stranger. But surely we know that no soul is voluntarily ignorant of anything?

Theaetetus. Certainly not.

Stranger. And what is ignorance but the aberration of a mind which is bent on truth, and in which the process of understanding is perverted?

Theaetetus. True.

Stranger. Then we are to regard an unintelligent soul as deformed and devoid of symmetry?

Theaetetus. Very true.

Stranger. Then there are these two kinds of evil in the soul—the one which is generally called vice, and is obviously a disease of the soul . . .

Theaetetus. Yes.

Stranger. And there is the other, which they call ignorance, and which, because existing only in the soul [4], they will not allow to be vice.

Theaetetus. I certainly admit what I at first disputed—that there

---

[4] Or, 'although there is no other vice in the soul but this.'

are two kinds of vice in the soul, and that we ought to consider cowardice, intemperance, and injustice to be all alike forms of disease
in the soul, and ignorance, of which there are all sorts of varieties,
to be deformity.

Stranger. And in the case of the body are there not two arts which
have to do with the two bodily states?

Theaetetus. What are they?

Stranger. There is gymnastic, which has to do with deformity, and
medicine, which has to do with disease.

Theaetetus. True.

Stranger. And where there is insolence and injustice and   [229
cowardice, is not chastisement the art which is most required [5]?

Theaetetus. That certainly appears to be the opinion of mankind.

Stranger. Again, of the various kinds of ignorance, may not instruction be rightly said to be the remedy?

Theaetetus. True.

Stranger. And of the art of instruction, shall we say that there is
one or many kinds? At any rate there are two principal ones. Think.

Theaetetus. I will.

Stranger. I believe that I can see how we shall soonest arrive at the
answer to this question.

Theaetetus. How?

Stranger. If we can discover a line which divides ignorance into
two halves. For a division of ignorance into two parts will certainly imply that the art of instruction is also two-fold, answering to the two
divisions of ignorance.

Theaetetus. Well, and do you see what you are looking for?

Stranger. I do seem to myself to see one very large and bad sort of
ignorance which is quite separate, and may be weighed in the scale
against all other sorts of ignorance put together.

Theaetetus. What is it?

Stranger. When a person supposes that he knows, and does not
know; this appears to be the great source of all the errors of the intellect.

Theaetetus. True.

Stranger. And this, if I am not mistaken, is the kind of ignorance
which specially earns the title of stupidity.

Theaetetus. True.

Stranger. What name, then, shall be given to the sort of instruction
which gets rid of this?

Theaetetus. The instruction which you mean, Stranger, is, I should
imagine, not the teaching of handicraft arts, but what, thanks to us,
has been termed education in this part of the world.

---

[5] Omitting δίκη , or reading δίκῃ.

Stranger. Yes, Theaetetus, and by nearly all Hellenes. But we have still to consider whether education admits of any further division.

Theaetetus. We have.

Stranger. I think that there is a point at which such a division is possible.

Theaetetus. Where?

Stranger. Of education, one method appears to be rougher, and another smoother.

Theaetetus. How are we to distinguish the two?

Stranger. There is the time-honoured mode which our fathers commonly practised towards their sons, and which is still adopted by many —either of roughly reproving their errors, or of gently advising   [230 them; which varieties may be correctly included under the general term of admonition.

Theaetetus. True.

Stranger. But whereas some appear to have arrived at the conclusion that all ignorance is involuntary, and that no one who thinks himself wise is willing to learn any of those things in which he is conscious of his own cleverness, and that the admonitory sort of instruction gives much trouble and does little good——

Theaetetus. There they are quite right.

Stranger. Accordingly, they set to work to eradicate the spirit of conceit in another way.

Theaetetus. In what way?

Stranger. They cross-examine a man's words, when he thinks that he is saying something and is really saying nothing, and easily convict him of inconsistencies in his opinions; these they then collect by the dialectical process, and placing them side by side, show that they contradict one another about the same things, in relation to the same things, and in the same respect. He, seeing this, is angry with himself, and grows gentle towards others, and thus is entirely delivered from great pejudices and harsh notions, in a way which is most amusing to the hearer, and produces the most lasting good effect on the person who is the subject of the operation. For as the physician considers that the body will receive no benefit from taking food until the internal obstacles have been removed, so the purifier of the soul is conscious that his patient will receive no benefit from the application of knowledge until he is refuted, and from refutation learns modesty; he must be purged of his prejudices first and made to think that he knows only what he knows, and no more.

Theaetetus. That is certainly the best and wisest state of mind.

Stranger. For all these reasons, Theaetetus, we must admit that refutation is the greatest and chiefest of purifications, and he who has not been refuted, though he be the Great King himself, is in an awful state of impurity; he is uninstructed and deformed in those things in which he who would be truly blessed ought to be fairest and purest.

Theaetetus. Very true.

Stranger. And who are the ministers of this art? I am afraid to say the Sophists. [231

Theaetetus. Why?

Stranger. Lest we should assign to them too high a prerogative.

Theaetetus. Yet the Sophist has a certain likeness to our minister of purification.

Stranger. Yes, the same sort of likeness which a wolf, who is the fiercest of animals, has to a dog, who is the gentlest. But he who would not be found tripping, ought to be very careful in this matter of comparisons, for they are most slippery things. Nevertheless, let us assume that the Sophists are the men. I say this provisionally, for I think that the line which divides them will be marked enough if proper care is taken.

Theaetetus. Likely enough.

Stranger. Let us grant, then, that from the discerning art comes purification, and from purification let there be separated off a part which is concerned with the soul; of this mental purification instruction is a portion, and of instruction education, and of education, that refutation of vain conceit which has been discovered in the present argument; and let this be called by you and me the nobly-descended art of Sophistry.

Theaetetus. Very well; and yet, considering the number of forms in which he has presented himself, I begin to doubt how I can with any truth or confidence describe the real nature of the Sophist.

Stranger. You naturally feel perplexed; and yet I think that he must be still more perplexed in his attempt to escape us, for as the proverb says, when every way is blocked, there is no escape; now, then, is the time of all others to set upon him.

Theaetetus. True.

Stranger. First let us wait a moment and recover breath, and while we are resting, we may reckon up in how many forms he has appeared. In the first place, he was discovered to be a paid hunter after wealth and youth.

Theaetetus. Yes.

Stranger. In the second place, he was a merchant in the goods of the soul.

Theaetetus. Certainly.

Stranger. In the third place, he has turned out to be a retailer of the same sort of wares.

Theaetetus. Yes; and in the fourth place, he himself manufactured the learned wares which he sold.

Stranger. Quite right; I will try and remember the fifth myself. He belonged to the fighting class, and was further distinguished as a hero of debate, who professed the eristic art.

Theaetetus. True.

Stranger. The sixth point was doubtful, and yet we at last agreed that he was a purger of souls, who cleared away notions obstructive to knowledge.

Theaetetus. Very true.

Stranger. Do you not see that when the professor of any   [232 art has one name and many kinds of knowledge, there must be something wrong? The multiplicity of names which is applied to him shows that the common principle to which all these branches of knowledge are tending, is not understood.

Theaetetus. I should imagine this to be the case.

Stranger. At any rate we will understand him, and no indolence shall prevent us. Let us begin again, then, and re-examine some of our statements concerning the Sophist; there was one thing which appeared to me especially characteristic of him.

Theaetetus. To what are you referring?

Stranger. We were saying of him, if I am not mistaken, that he was a disputer?

Theaetetus. We were.

Stranger. And does he not also teach others the art of disputation?

Theaetetus. Certainly he does.

Stranger. And about what does he profess that he teaches men to dispute? To begin at the beginning—Does he make them able to dispute about divine things, which are invisible to men in general?

Theaetetus. At any rate, he is said to do so.

Stranger. And what do you say of the visible things in heaven and earth, and the like?

Theaetetus. Certainly he disputes, and teaches to dispute about them.

Stranger. Then, again, in private conversation, when any universal assertion is made about generation and essence, we know that such persons are tremendous argufiers, and are able to impart their own skill to others.

Theaetetus. Undoubtedly.

Stranger. And do they not profess to make men able to dispute about law and about politics in general?

Theaetetus. Why, no one would have anything to say to them, if they did not make these professions.

Stranger. In all and every art, what the craftsman ought to say in answer to any question is written down in a popular form, and he who likes may learn.

Theaetetus. I suppose that you are referring to the precepts of Protagoras about wrestling and the other arts?

Stranger. Yes, my friend, and about a good many other things. In a word, is not the art of disputation a power of disputing about all things?

Theaetetus. Certainly; there does not seem to be much which is left out.

Stranger. But oh! my dear youth, do you suppose this possible? for perhaps your young eyes may see things which to our duller sight do not appear.

Theaetetus. To what are you alluding? I do not think that   [233 I understand your present question.

Stranger. I ask whether anybody can understand all things.

Theaetetus. Happy would mankind be if such a thing were possible!

Stranger. But how can any one who is ignorant dispute in a rational manner against him who knows?

Theaetetus. He cannot.

Stranger. Then why has the sophistical art such a mysterious power?

Theaetetus. To what do you refer?

Stranger. How do the Sophists make young men believe in their supreme and universal wisdom? For if they neither disputed nor were thought to dispute rightly, or being thought to do so were deemed no wiser for their controversial skill, then, to quote your own observation, no one would give them money or be willing to learn their art.

Theaetetus. They certainly would not.

Stranger. But they are willing.

Theaetetus. Yes, they are.

Stranger. Yes, and the reason, as I should imagine, is that they are supposed to have knowledge of those things about which they dispute?

Theaetetus. Certainly.

Stranger. And they dispute about all things?

Theaetetus. True.

Stranger. And therefore, to their disciples, they appear to be all-wise?

Theaetetus. Certainly.

Stranger. But they are not; for that was shown to be impossible.

Theaetetus. Impossible, of course.

Stranger. Then the Sophist has been shown to have a sort of conjectural or apparent knowledge only of all things, which is not the truth?

Theaetetus. Exactly; no better description of him could be given.

Stranger. Let us now take an illustration, which will still more clearly explain his nature.

Theaetetus. What is it?

Stranger. I will tell you, and you shall answer me, giving your very closest attention. Suppose that a person were to profess, not that he could speak or dispute, but that he knew how to make and do all things, by a single art.

Theaetetus. All things?

Stranger. I see that you do not understand the first word that I utter, for you do not understand the meaning of 'all.'

Theaetetus. No, I do not.

Stranger. Under all things, I include you and me, and also animals and trees.

Theaetetus. What do you mean?

Stranger. Suppose a person to say that he will make you and me, and all creatures.

Theaetetus. What would he mean by 'making'? He can-   [234 not be a husbandman;—for you said that he is a maker of animals.

Stranger. Yes; and I say that he is also the maker of the sea, and the earth, and the heavens, and the gods, and of all other things; and, further, that he can make them in no time, and sell them for a few pence.

Theaetetus. That must be a jest.

Stranger. And when a man says that he knows all things, and can teach them to another at a small cost, and in a short time, is not that a jest?

Theaetetus. Certainly.

Stranger. And is there any more artistic or graceful form of jest than imitation?

Theaetetus. Certainly not; and imitation is a very comprehensive term, which includes under one class the most diverse sorts of things.

Stranger. We know, of course, that he who professes by one art to make all things is really a painter, and by the painter's art makes resemblances of real things which have the same name with them; and he can deceive the less intelligent sort of young children, to whom he shows his pictures at a distance, into the belief that he has the absolute power of making whatever he likes.

Theaetetus. Certainly.

Stranger. And may there not be supposed to be an imitative art of reasoning? Is it not possible to enchant the hearts of young men by words poured through their ears, when they are still at a distance from the truth of facts, by exhibiting to them fictitious arguments, and making them think that they are true, and that the speaker is the wisest of men in all things?

Theaetetus. Yes; why should there not be another such art?

Stranger. But as time goes on, and their hearers advance in years, and come into closer contact with realities, and have learnt by sad experience to see and feel the truth of things, are not the greater part of them compelled to change many opinions which they formerly entertained, so that the great appears small to them, and the easy difficult, and all their dreamy speculations are over turned by the facts of life?

Theaetetus. That is my view, as far as I can judge, although, at my age, I may be one of those who see things at a distance only.

Stranger. And the wish of all of us, who are your friends, is and always will be to bring you as near to the truth as we can with-   [235 out the sad reality. And now I should like you to tell me, whether the Sophist is not visibly a magician and imitator of true being; or are we still disposed to think that he may have a true knowledge of the various matters about which he disputes?

Theaetetus. But how can he, Stranger? Is there any doubt, after what has been said, that he is to be located in one of the divisions of children's play?

Stranger. Then we must place him in the class of magicians and mimics.

Theaetetus. Certainly we must.

Stranger. And now our business is not to let the animal out, for we have got him in a sort of dialectical net, and there is one thing which he decidedly will not escape.

Theaetetus. What is that?

Stranger. The inference that he is a juggler.

Theatetus. Precisely my own opinion of him.

Stranger. Then, clearly, we ought as soon as possible to divide the image-making art, and go down into the net, and, if the Sophist does not run away from us, to seize him according to orders and deliver him over to reason, who is the lord of the hunt, and proclaim the capture of him; and if he creeps into the recesses of the imitative art, and secretes himself in one of them, to divide again and follow him up until in some sub-section of imitation he is caught. For our method of tackling each and all is one which neither he nor any other creature will ever escape in triumph.

Theaetetus. Well said; and let us do as you propose.

Stranger. Well, then, pursuing the same analytic method as before, I think that I can discern two divisions of the imitative art, but I am not as yet able to see in which of them the desired form is to be found.

Theaetetus. Will you tell me first what are the two divisions of which you are speaking?

Stranger. One is the art of likeness-making;—generally a likeness of anything is made by producing a copy which is executed according to the proportions of the original, similar in length and breadth and depth, each thing receiving also its appropriate colour.

Theaetetus. Is not this always the aim of imitation?

Stranger. Not always; in works either of sculpture or of painting, which are of any magnitude, there is a certain degree of decep- [236 tion; for if artists were to give the true proportions of their fair works, the upper part, which is farther off, would appear to be out of proportion in comparison with the lower, which is nearer; and so they give up the truth in their images and make only the proportions which appear to be beautiful, disregarding the real ones.

Theaetetus. Quite true.

Stranger. And that which being other is also like, may we not fairly call a likeness or image?

Theaetetus. Yes.

Stranger. And may we not, as I did just now, call that part of the imitative art which is concerned with making such images the art of likeness-making?

Theaetetus. Let that be the name.

Stranger. And what shall we call those resemblances of the beautiful, which appear such owing to the unfavourable position of the spectator, whereas if a person had the power of getting a correct view of works of such magnitude, they would appear not even like that to which they profess to be like? May we not call these 'appearances,' since they appear only and are not really like?

Theaetetus. Certainly.

Stranger. There is a great deal of this kind of thing in painting, and in all imitation.

Theaetetus. Of course.

Stranger. And may we not fairly call the sort of art, which produces an appearance and not an image, phantastic art?

Theaetetus. Most fairly.

Stranger. These then are the two kinds of image-making—the art of making likenesses, and phantastic or the art of making appearances?

Theaetetus. True.

Stranger. I was doubtful before in which of them I should place the Sophist, nor am I even now able to see clearly; verily he is a wonderful and inscrutable creature. And now in the cleverest manner he has got into an impossible place.

Theaetetus. Yes, he has.

Stranger. Do you speak advisedly, or are you carried away at the moment by the habit of assenting into giving a hasty answer?

Theaetetus. May I ask to what you are referring?

Stranger. My dear friend, we are engaged in a very difficult speculation—there can be no doubt of that; for how a thing can appear and seem, and not be, or how a man can say a thing which is not true, has always been and still remains a very perplexing question. Can   [237 any one say or think that falsehood really exists, and avoid being caught in a contradiction? Indeed, Theaetetus, the task is a difficult one.

Theaetetus. Why?

Stranger. He who says that falsehood exists has the audacity to assert the being of not-being; for this is implied in the possibility of falsehood. But, my boy, in the days when I was a boy, the great Parmenides protested against this doctrine, and to the end of his life he continued to inculcate the same lesson—always repeating both in verse and out of verse:

'Keep your mind from this way of enquiry, for never will you
     show [6] that not being is.'

Such is his testimony, which is confirmed by the very expression when sifted a little. Would you object to begin with the consideration of the words themselves?

Theaetetus. Never mind about me; I am only desirous that you should carry on the argument in the best way, and that you should take me with you.

Stranger. Very good; and now say, do we venture to utter the forbidden word 'not-being'?

Theaetetus. Certainly we do.

Stranger. Let us be serious then, and consider the question neither in strife nor play: suppose that one of the hearers of Parmenides was asked, 'To what is the term "not-being" to be applied?'—do you know what sort of object he would single out in reply, and what answer he would make to the enquirer?

Theaetetus. That is a difficult question, and one not to be answered at all by a person like myself.

Stranger. There is at any rate no difficulty in seeing that the predicate 'not-being' is not applicable to any being.

Theaetetus. None, certainly.

Stranger. And if not to being, then not to something.

Theaetetus. Of course not.

---

[6] Reading τοῦτο φανῇ.

Stranger. It is also plain, that in speaking of something we speak of being, for to speak of an abstract something naked and isolated from all being is impossible.

Theaetetus. Impossible.

Stranger. You mean by assenting to imply that he who says something must say some one thing?

Theaetetus. Yes.

Stranger. Some in the singular (τὶ) you would say is the sign of one, some in the dual (τινὲ) of two, some in the plural (τινὲς) of many?

Theaetetus. Exactly.

Stranger. Then he who says 'not something' must say absolutely nothing.

Theaetetus. Most assuredly.

Stranger. And as we cannot admit that a man speaks and says nothing, he who says 'not-being' does not speak at all.

Theaetetus. The difficulty of the argument can no further go.

Stranger. Not yet, my friend, is the time for such a word;   [238 for there still remains of all perplexities the first and greatest, touching the very foundation of the matter.

Theaetetus. What do you mean? Do not be afraid to speak.

Stranger. To that which is, may be attributed some other thing which is?

Theaetetus. Certainly.

Stranger. But can anything which is, be attributed to that which is not?

Theaetetus. Impossible.

Stranger. And all number is to be reckoned among things which are?

Theaetetus. Yes, surely number, if anything, has a real existence.

Stranger. Then we must not attempt to attribute to not-being number either in the singular or plural?

Theaetetus. The argument implies that we should be wrong in doing so.

Stranger. But how can a man either express in words or even conceive in thought things which are not or a thing which is not without number?

Theaetetus. How indeed?

Stranger. When we speak of things which are not, are we not attributing plurality to not-being?

Theaetetus. Certainly.

Stranger. But, on the other hand, when we say 'what is not,' do we not attribute unity?

Theaetetus. Manifestly.

Stranger. Nevertheless, we maintain that you may not and ought not to attribute being to not-being?

Theaetetus. Most true.

Stranger. Do you see, then, that not-being in itself can neither be spoken, uttered, or thought, but that it is unthinkable, unutterable, unspeakable, indescribable?

Theaetetus. Quite true.

Stranger. But, if so, I was wrong in telling you just now that the difficulty which was coming is the greatest of all.

Theaetetus. What! is there a greater still behind?

Stranger. Well, I am surprised, after what has been said already, that you do not see the difficulty in which he who would refute the notion of not-being is involved. For he is compelled to contradict himself as soon as he makes the attempt.

Theaetetus. What do you mean? Speak more clearly.

Stranger. Do not expect clearness from me. For I, who maintain that not-being has no part either in the one or many, just now spoke and am still speaking of not-being as one; for I say 'not-being.' Do you understand?

Theaetetus. Yes.

Stranger. And a little while ago I said that not-being is unutterable, unspeakable, indescribable: do you follow?

Theaetetus. I do after a fashion.

Stranger. When I introduced the word 'is,' did I not contradict what I said before?

Theaetetus. Clearly.   [239

Stranger. And in using the singular verb, did I not speak of not-being as one?

Theaetetus. Yes.

Stranger. And when I spoke of not-being as indescribable and unspeakable and unutterable, in using each of these words in the singular, did I not refer to not-being as one?

Theaetetus. Certainly.

Stranger. And yet we say that, strictly speaking, it should not be defined as one or many, and should not even be called 'it,' for the use of the word 'it' would imply a form of unity.

Theaetetus. Quite true.

Stranger. How, then, can any one put any faith in me? For now, as always, I am unequal to the refutation of not-being. And therefore, as I was saying, do not look to me for the right way of speaking about not-being; but come, let us try the experiment with you.

Theaetetus. What do you mean?

Stranger. Make a noble effort, as becomes youth, and endeavour with all your might to speak of not-being in a right manner, without introducing into it either existence or unity or plurality.

Theaetetus. It would be a strange boldness in me which would attempt the task when I see you thus discomfited.

Stranger. Say no more of ourselves; but until we find some one or other who can speak of not-being without number, we must acknowledge that the Sophist is a clever rogue who will not be got out of his hole.

Theaetetus. Most true.

Stranger. And if we say to him that he professes an art of making appearances, he will grapple with us and retort our argument upon ourselves; and when we call him an image-maker he will say, 'Pray what do you mean at all by an image?'—and I should like to know, Theaetetus, how we can possibly answer the younker's question?

Theaetetus. We shall doubtless tell him of the images which are reflected in water or in mirrors; also of sculptures, pictures, and other duplicates.

Stranger. I see, Theaetetus, that you have never made the acquaintance of the Sophist.

Theaetetus. Why do you think so?

Stranger. He will make believe to have his eyes shut, or to have none.

Theaetetus. What do you mean?

Stranger. When you tell him of something existing in a mirror, or in sculpture, and address him as though he had eyes, he will   [240 laugh you to scorn, and will pretend that he knows nothing of mirrors and streams, or of sight at all; he will say that he is asking about an idea.

Theaetetus. What can he mean?

Stranger. The common notion pervading all these objects, which you speak of as many, and yet call by the single name of image, as though it were the unity under which they were all included. How will you maintain your ground against him?

Theaetetus. How, Stranger, can I describe an image except as something fashioned in the likeness of the true?

Stranger. And do you mean this something to be some other true thing, or what do you mean?

Theaetetus. Certainly not another true thing, but only a resemblance.

Stranger. And you mean by true that which really is?

Theaetetus. Yes.

Stranger. And the not true is that which is the opposite of the true?

Theaetetus. Exactly.

Stranger. A resemblance, then, is not really real, if, as you say, not true?

Theaetetus. Nay, but it is in a certain sense.

Stranger. You mean to say, not in a true sense?

Theaetetus. Yes; it is in reality only an image.

Stranger. Then what we call an image is in reality really unreal.

Theaetetus. In what a strange complication of being and not-being we are involved!

Stranger. Strange! I should think so. See how, by his reciprocation of opposites, the many-headed Sophist has compelled us, quite against our will, to admit the existence of not-being.

Theaetetus. Yes, indeed, I see.

Stranger. The difficulty is how to define his art without falling into a contradiction.

Theaetetus. How do you mean? And where does the danger lie?

Stranger. When we say that he deceives us with an illusion, and that his art is illusory, do we mean that our soul is led by his art to think falsely, or what do we mean?

Theaetetus. There is nothing else to be said.

Stranger. Again, false opinion is that form of opinion which thinks the opposite of the truth:—You would assent?

Theaetetus. Certainly.

Stranger. You mean to say that false opinion thinks what is not?

Theaetetus. Of course.

Stranger. Does false opinion think that things which are not are not, or that in a certain sense they are?

Theaetetus. Things that are not must be imagined to exist in a certain sense, if any degree of falsehood is to be possible.

Stranger. And does not false opinion also think that things which most certainly exist do not exist at all?

Theaetetus. Yes.

Stranger. And here, again, is falsehood?

Theaetetus. Falsehood—yes.

Stranger. And in like manner, a false proposition will be deemed to be one which asserts the non-existence of things which are, and the existence of things which are not.

Theaetetus. There is no other way in which a false proposition can arise.

Stranger. There is not; but the Sophist will deny these [241] statements. And indeed how can any rational man assent to them, when the very expressions which we have just used were before acknowledged by us to be unutterable, unspeakable, indescribable, unthinkable? Do you see his point, Theaetetus?

Theaetetus. Of course he will say that we are contradicting ourselves when we hazard the assertion, that falsehood exists in opinion and in words; for in maintaining this, we are compelled over and over again to assert being of not-being, which we admitted just now to be an utter impossibility.

Stranger. How well you remember! And now it is high time to hold a consultation as to what we ought to do about the Sophist; for if we persist in looking for him in the class of false workers and magicians, you see that the handles for objection and the difficulties which will arise are very numerous and obvious.

Theaetetus. They are indeed.

Stranger. We have gone through but a very small portion of them, and they are really infinite.

Theaetetus. If that is the case, we cannot possibly catch the Sophist.

Stranger. Shall we then be so faint-hearted as to give him up?

Theaetetus. Certainly not, I should say, if we can get the slightest hold upon him.

Stranger. Will you then forgive me, and, as your words imply, not be altogether displeased if I flinch a little from the grasp of such a sturdy argument?

Theaetetus. To be sure I will.

Stranger. I have a yet more urgent request to make.

Theaetetus. Which is—?

Stranger. That you will promise not to regard me as a parricide.

Theaetetus. And why?

Stranger. Because, in self-defence, I must test the philosophy of my father Parmenides, and try to prove by main force that in a certain sense not-being is, and that being, on the other hand, is not.

Theaetetus. Some attempt of the kind is clearly needed.

Stranger. Yes, a blind man, as they say, might see that, and, unless these questions are decided in one way or another, no one when he speaks of false words, or false opinion, or idols, or images, or imitations, or appearances, or about the arts which are concerned with them, can avoid falling into ridiculous contradictions.

Theaetetus. Most true.

Stranger. And therefore I must venture to lay hands on my   [242 father's argument; for if I am to be over-scrupulous, I shall have to give the matter up.

Theaetetus. Nothing in the world should ever induce us to do so.

Stranger. I have a third little request which I wish to make.

Theaetetus. What is it?

Stranger. You heard me say what I have always felt and still feel—
that I have no heart for this argument?

Theaetetus. I did.

Stranger. I tremble at the thought of what I have said, and expect
that you will deem me mad, when you hear of my sudden changes
and shiftings; let me therefore observe, that I am examining the question entirely out of regard for you.

Theaetetus. There is no reason for you to fear that I shall impute
any impropriety to you, if you attempt this refutation and proof; take
heart, therefore, and proceed.

Stranger. And where shall I begin the perilous enterprise? I think
that the road which I must take is—

Theaetetus. Which?—Let me hear.

Stranger. I think that we had better, first of all, consider the points
which at present are regarded as self-evident, lest we may have fallen
into some confusion, and be too ready to assent to one another, fancying that we are quite clear about them.

Theaetetus. Say more distinctly what you mean.

Stranger. I think that Parmenides, and all who ever yet undertook
to determine the number and nature of existences, talked to us in rather
a light and easy strain.

Theaetetus. How?

Stranger. As if we had been children, to whom they repeated each
his own mythus or story;—one said that there were three principles,
and that at one time there was war between certain of them; and then
again there was peace, and they were married and begat children, and
brought them up; and another spoke of two principles,—a moist
and a dry, or a hot and a cold, and made them marry and cohabit. The
Eleatics, however, in our part of the world, say that all things are
many in name, but in nature one; this is their mythus, which goes back
to Xenophanes, and is even older. Then there are Ionian, and in more
recent times Sicilian muses, who have arrived at the conclusion that
to unite the two principles is safer, and to say that being is one and
many, and that these are held together by enmity and friendship, ever
parting, ever meeting, as the severer Muses assert, while the gentler
ones do not insist on the perpetual strife and peace, but admit   [243
a relaxation and alternation of them; peace and unity sometimes prevailing under the sway of Aphrodite, and then again plurality and war,
by reason of a principle of strife. Whether any of them spoke the
truth in all this is hard to determine; besides, antiquity and famous men

should have reverence, and not be liable to accusations so serious. Yet one thing may be said of them without offence—

Theaetetus. What thing?

Stranger. That they went on their several ways disdaining to notice people like ourselves; they did not care whether they took us with them, or left us behind them.

Theaetetus. How do you mean?

Stranger. I mean to say, that when they talk of one, two, or more elements, which are or have become or are becoming, or again of heat mingling with cold, assuming in some other part of their works separations and mixtures,—tell me, Theaetetus, do you understand what they mean by these expressions? When I was a younger man, I used to fancy that I understood quite well what was meant by the term 'not-being,' which is our present subject of dispute; and now you see in what a fix we are about it.

Theaetetus. I see.

Stranger. And very likely we have been getting into the same perplexity about 'being,' and yet may fancy that when anybody utters the word, we understand him quite easily, although we do not know about not-being. But we may be equally ignorant of both.

Theaetetus. I dare say.

Stranger. And the same may be said of all the terms just mentioned.

Theaetetus. True.

Stranger. The consideration of most of them may be deferred; but we had better now discuss the chief captain and leader of them.

Theaetetus. Of what are you speaking? You clearly think that we must first investigate what people mean by the word 'being.'

Stranger. You follow close at my heels, Theaetetus. For the right method, I conceive, will be to call into our presence the dualistic philosophers and to interrogate them. 'Come,' we will say, 'Ye, who affirm that hot and cold or any other two principles are the universe, what is this term which you apply to both of them, and what do you mean when you say that both and each of them "are"? How are we to understand the word "are"? Upon your view, are we to suppose that there is a third principle over and above the other two,—three in all, and not two? For clearly you cannot say that one of the two principles is being, and yet attribute being equally to both of them; for, if you did, whichever of the two is identified with being, will comprehend the other; and so they will be one and not two.'

Theaetetus. Very true.

Stranger. But perhaps you mean to give the name of 'being' to both of them together?

Theaetetus. Quite likely.

Stranger. 'Then, friends,' we shall reply to them, 'the an-   [244
swer is plainly that the two will still be resolved into one.'

Theaetetus. Most true.

Stranger. 'Since then, we are in a difficulty, please to tell us what
you mean, when you speak of being; for there can be no doubt that
you always from the first understood your own meaning, whereas we
once thought that we understood you, but now we are in a great
strait. Please to begin by explaining this matter to us, and let us no
longer fancy that we understand you, when we entirely misunderstand
you.' There will be no impropriety in our demanding an answer to this
question, either of the dualists or of the pluralists?

Theaetetus. Certainly not.

Stranger. And what about the assertors of the oneness of the all—
must we not endeavour to ascertain from them what they mean by
'being'?

Theaetetus. By all means.

Stranger. Then let them answer this question: One, you say,
alone is? 'Yes,' they will reply.

Theaetetus. True.

Stranger. And there is something which you call 'being'?

Theaetetus. 'Yes.'

Stranger. And is being the same as one, and do you apply two
names to the same thing?

Theaetetus. What will be their answer, Stranger?

Stranger. It is clear, Theaetetus, that he who asserts the unity of
being will find a difficulty in answering this or any other question.

Theaetetus. Why so?

Stranger. To admit of two names, and to affirm that there is nothing but unity, is surely ridiculous?

Theaetetus. Certainly.

Stranger. And equally irrational to admit that a name is anything?

Theaetetus. How so?

Stranger. To distinguish the name from the thing, implies duality.

Theaetetus. Yes.

Stranger. And yet he who identifies the name with the thing will
be compelled to say that it is the name of nothing, or if he says that
it is the name of something, even then the name will only be the name
of a name, and of nothing else.

Theaetetus. True.

Stranger. And the one will turn out to be only one of one,[7] and being absolute unity, will represent a mere name [7].

---

[7] Reading with the MSS. καὶ τοῦ ὀνόματος αὐτὸ ἓν ὄν.

Theaetetus. Certainly.

Stranger. And would they say that the whole is other than the one that is, or the same with it?

Theaetetus. To be sure they would, and they actually say so.

Stranger. If being is a whole, as Parmenides sings,—

> 'Every way like unto the fullness of a well-rounded sphere,
> Evenly balanced from the centre on every side,
> And must needs be neither greater nor less in any way,
> Neither on this side nor on that—'

then being has a centre and extremes, and, having these, must also have parts.

Theaetetus. True.

Stranger. Yet that which has parts may have the attribute [245] of unity in all the parts, and in this way being all and a whole, may be one?

Theaetetus. Certainly.

Stranger. But that of which this is the condition cannot be absolute unity?

Theaetetus. Why not?

Stranger. Because, according to right reason, that which is truly one must be affirmed to be absolutely indivisible.

Theaetetus. Certainly.

Stranger. But this indivisible, if made up of many parts, will contradict reason.

Theaetetus. I understand.

Stranger. Shall we say that being [8] is one and a whole, because it has the attribute of unity? Or shall we say that being is not a whole at all?

Theaetetus. That is a hard alternative to offer.

Stranger. Most true; for being, having in a certain sense the attribute of one, is yet proved not to be the same as one, and the all is therefore more than one.

Theaetetus. Yes.

Stranger. And yet if being be not a whole, through having the attribute of unity, and there be such a thing as an absolute whole, being lacks something of its own nature?

Theaetetus. Certainly.

Stranger. Upon this view, again, being, having a defect of being, will become not-being?

Theaetetus. True.

---

[8] Reading τὸ ὄν.

Stranger. And, again, the all becomes more than one, for being and the whole will each have their separate nature.

Theaetetus. Yes.

Stranger. But if the whole does not exist at all, all the previous difficulties remain the same, and there will be the further difficulty, that besides having no being, being can never have come into being.

Theaetetus. Why so?

Stranger. Because that which comes into being always comes into being as a whole, so that he who does not give whole a place among beings, cannot speak either of essence or generation as existing.

Theaetetus. Yes, that certainly appears to be true.

Stranger. Again; how can that which is not a whole have any quantity? For that which is of a certain quantity must necessarily be the whole of that quantity.

Theaetetus. Exactly.

Stranger. And there will be innumerable other points, each of them causing infinite trouble to him who says that being is either one or two.

Theaetetus. The difficulties which are dawning upon us prove this; for one objection connects with another, and they are always involving what has preceded in a greater and worse perplexity.

Stranger. We are far from having exhausted the more exact thinkers who treat of being and not-being. But let us be content to leave them, and proceed to view those who speak less precisely; and   [246 we shall find as the result of all, that the nature of being is quite as difficult to comprehend as that of not-being.

Theaetetus. Then now we will go to the others.

Stranger. There appears to be a sort of war of Giants and Gods going on amongst them; they are fighting with one another about the nature of essence.

Theaetetus. How is that?

Stranger. Some of them are dragging down all things from heaven and from the unseen to earth, and they literally grasp in their hands rocks and oaks; of these they lay hold, and obstinately maintain, that the things only which can be touched or handled have being or essence, because they define being and body as one, and if any one else says that what is not a body exists they altogether despise him, and will hear of nothing but body.

Theaetetus. I have often met with such men, and terrible fellows they are.

Stranger. And that is the reason why their opponents cautiously defend themselves from above, out of an unseen world, mightily contending that true essence consists of certain intelligible and incorporeal ideas; the bodies of the materialists, which by them are maintained to be the very truth, they break up into little bits by their arguments, and affirm them to be, not essence, but generation and motion. Between the two armies, Theaetetus, there is always an endless conflict raging concerning these matters.

Theaetetus. True.

Stranger. Let us ask each party in turn, to give an account of that which they call essence.

Theaetetus. How shall we get it out of them?

Stranger. With those who make being to consist in ideas, there will be less difficulty, for they are civil people enough; but there will be very great difficulty, or rather an absolute impossibility, in getting an opinion out of those who drag everything down to matter. Shall I tell you what we must do?

Theaetetus. What?

Stranger. Let us, if we can, really improve them; but if this is not possible, let us imagine them to be better than they are, and more willing to answer in accordance with the rules of argument, and then their opinion will be more worth having; for that which better men acknowledge has more weight than that which is acknowledged by inferior men. Moreover we are no respecters of persons, but seekers after truth.

Theaetetus. Very good.

Stranger. Then now, on the supposition that they are improved, let us ask them to state their views, and do you interpret them.

Theaetetus. Agreed.

Stranger. Let them say whether they would admit that there is such a thing as a mortal animal.

Theaetetus. Of course they would.

Stranger. And do they not acknowledge this to be a body having a soul?

Theaetetus. Certainly they do.

Stranger. Meaning to say the soul is something which exists?

Theaetetus. True.   [247

Stranger. And do they not say that one soul is just, and another unjust, and that one soul is wise, and another foolish?

Theaetetus. Certainly.

Stranger. And that the just and wise soul becomes just and wise by the possession of justice and wisdom [9], and the opposite under opposite circumstances?

Theaetetus. Yes, they do.

Stranger. But surely that which may be present or may be absent will be admitted by them to exist?

---

[9] Reading with Professor Campbell δικαιοσύνης ἕξει καὶ φρονήσεως.

Theaetetus. Certainly.

Stranger. And, allowing that justice, wisdom, the other virtues, and their opposites exist, as well as a soul in which they inhere, do they affirm any of them to be visible and tangible, or are they all invisible?

Theaetetus. They would say that hardly any of them are visible.

Stranger. And would they say that they are corporeal?

Theaetetus. They would distinguish: the soul would be said by them to have a body; but as to the other qualities of justice, wisdom, and the like, about which you asked, they would not venture either to deny their existence, or to maintain that they were all corporeal.

Stranger. Verily, Theaetetus, I perceive a great improvement in them; the real aborigines, children of the dragon's teeth, would have been deterred by no shame at all, but would have obstinately asserted that nothing is which they are not able to squeeze in their hands.

Theaetetus. That is pretty much their notion.

Stranger. Let us push the question; for if they will admit that any, even the smallest particle of being, is incorporeal, it is enough; they must then say what that nature is which is common to both the corporeal and incorporeal, and which they have in their mind's eye when they say of both of them that they 'are.' Perhaps they may be in a difficulty; and if this is the case, there is a possibility that they may accept a notion of ours respecting the nature of being, having nothing of their own to offer.

Theaetetus. What is the notion? Tell me, and we shall soon see.

Stranger. My notion would be, that anything which possesses any sort of power to affect another, or to be affected by another, if only for a single moment, however trifling the cause and however slight the effect, has real existence; and I hold that the definition of *being is* simply *power*.

Theaetetus. They accept your suggestion, having nothing better of their own to offer.

Stranger. Very good; perhaps we, as well as they, may one day change our minds; but, for the present, this may be regarded   [248 as the understanding which is established with them.

Theaetetus. Agreed.

Stranger. Let us now go to the friends of ideas; of their opinions, too, you shall be the interpreter.

Theaetetus. I will.

Stranger. To them we say—You would distinguish essence from generation?

Theaetetus. 'Yes,' they reply.

Stranger. And you would allow that we participate in generation with the body, and through perception, but we participate with the soul through thought in true essence; and essence you would affirm to be always the same and immutable, whereas generation or becoming varies?

Theaetetus. Yes; that is what we should affirm.

Stranger. Well, fair sirs, we say to them, what is this participation, which you assert of both? Do you agree with our recent definition?

Theaetetus. What definition?

Stranger. We said that being was an active or passive energy, arising out of a certain power which proceeds from elements meeting with one another. Perhaps your ears, Theaetetus, may fail to catch their answer, which I recognize because I have been accustomed to hear it.

Theaetetus. And what is their answer?

Stranger. They deny the truth of what we were just now saying to the aborigines about existence.

Theaetetus. What was that?

Stranger. Any power of doing or suffering in a degree however slight was held by us to be a sufficient definition of being?

Theaetetus. True.

Stranger. They deny this, and say that the power of doing or suffering is confined to becoming, and that neither power is applicable to being.

Theaetetus. And is there not some truth in what they say?

Stranger. Yes; but our reply will be that we want to ascertain from them more distinctly, whether they further admit that the soul knows, and that being or essence is known.

Theaetetus. There can be no doubt that they say so.

Stranger. And is knowing and being known doing or suffering, or both, or is the one doing and the other suffering, or has neither any share in either?

Theaetetus. Clearly, neither has any share in either; for if they say anything else, they will contradict themselves.

Stranger. I understand; but they will allow that if to know is active, then, of course, to be known is passive. And on this view being, in so far as it is known, is acted upon by knowledge, and is therefore in motion; for that which is in a state of rest cannot be acted upon, as we affirm.

Theaetetus. True.

Stranger. And, O heavens, can we ever be made to believe [249 that motion and life and soul and mind are not present with perfect being? Can we imagine that being is devoid of life and mind, and exists in awful unmeaningness an everlasting fixture?

Theaetetus. That would be a dreadful thing to admit, Stranger.

Stranger. But shall we say that being has mind and not life?

Theaetetus. How is that possible?

Stranger. Or shall we say that both inhere in perfect being, but that it has no soul which contains them?

Theaetetus. And in what other way can it contain them?

Stranger. Or that being has mind and life and soul, but although endowed with soul remains absolutely unmoved?

Theaetetus. All three suppositions appear to me to be irrational.

Stranger. Under being, then, we must include motion, and that which is moved.

Theaetetus. Certainly.

Stranger. Then, Theaetetus, our inference is, that if there is no motion, neither is there any mind anywhere, or about anything or belonging to any one.

Theaetetus. Quite true.

Stranger. And yet this equally follows, if we grant that all things are in motion—upon this view too mind has no existence.

Theaetetus. How so?

Stranger. Do you think that sameness of condition and mode and subject could ever exist without a principle of rest?

Theaetetus. Certainly not.

Stranger. Can you see how without them mind could exist, or come into existence anywhere?

Theaetetus. No.

Stranger. And surely contend we must in every possible way against him who would annihilate knowledge and reason and mind, and yet ventures to speak confidently about anything.

Theaetetus. Yes, with all our might.

Stranger. Then the philosopher, who has the truest reverence for these qualities, cannot possibly accept the notion of those who say that the whole is at rest, either as unity or in many forms: and he will be utterly deaf to those who assert universal motion. As children say entreatingly 'Give us both,' so he will include both the moveable and immoveable in his definition of being and all.

Theaetetus. Most true.

Stranger. And now, do we seem to have gained a fair notion of being?

Theaetetus. Yes truly.

Stranger. Alas, Theaetetus, methinks that we are now only beginning to see the real difficulty of the enquiry into the nature of it.

Theaetetus. What do you mean?

Stranger. O my friend, do you not see that nothing can exceed our ignorance, and yet we fancy that we are saying something good?

Theaetetus. I certainly thought that we were; and I do not at all understand how we never found out our desperate case.

Stranger. Reflect: after having made these admissions, may   [250 we not be justly asked the same questions which we ourselves were asking of those who said that all was hot and cold?

Theaetetus. What were they? Will you recall them to my mind?

Stranger. To be sure I will, and I will remind you of them, by putting the same questions to you which I did to them, and then we shall get on.

Theaetetus. True.

Stranger. Would you not say that rest and motion are in the most entire opposition to one another?

Theaetetus. Of course.

Stranger. And yet you would say that both and either of them equally are?

Theaetetus. I should.

Stranger. And when you admit that both or either of them are, do you mean to say that both or either of them are in motion?

Theaetetus. Certainly not.

Stranger. Or do you wish to imply that they are both at rest, when you say that they are?

Theaetetus. Of course not.

Stranger. Then you conceive of being as some third and distinct nature, under which rest and motion are alike included; and, observing that they both participate in being, you declare that they are.

Theaetetus. Truly we seem to have an intimation that being is some third thing, when we say that rest and motion are.

Stranger. Then being is not the combination of rest and motion, but something different from them.

Theaetetus. So it would appear.

Stranger. Being, then, according to its own nature, is neither in motion nor at rest.

Theaetetus. That is very much the truth.

Stranger. Where, then, is a man to look for help who would have any clear or fixed notion of being in his mind?

Theaetetus. Where, indeed?

Stranger. I scarcely think that he can look anywhere; for that which is not in motion must be at rest, and again, that which is not at rest must be in motion; but being is placed outside of both these classes. Is this possible?

Theaetetus. Utterly impossible.

Stranger. Here, then, is another thing which we ought to bear in mind.

Theaetetus. What?

Stranger. When we were asked to what we were to assign the appellation of not-being, we were in the greatest difficulty:—do you remember?

Theaetetus. To be sure.

Stranger. And are we not now in as great a difficulty about being?

Theaetetus. I should say, Stranger, that we are in one which is, if possible, even greater.

Stranger. Then let us acknowledge the difficulty; and as being and not-being are involved in the same perplexity, there is hope that when the one appears more or less distinctly, the other will equally   [251 appear; and if we are able to see neither, there may still be a chance of steering our way in between them, without any great discredit.

Theaetetus. Very good.

Stranger. Let us enquire, then, how we come to predicate many names of the same thing.

Theaetetus. Give an example.

Stranger. I mean that we speak of man, for example, under many names—that we attribute to him colours and forms and magnitudes and virtues and vices, in all of which instances and in ten thousand others we not only speak of him as a man, but also as good, and having numberless other attributes, and in the same way anything else which we originally supposed to be one is described by us as many, and under many names.

Theaetetus. That is true.

Stranger. And thus we provide a rich feast for tyros, whether young or old; for there is nothing easier than to argue that the one cannot be many, or the many one; and great is their delight in denying that a man is good; for man, they insist, is man and good is good. I dare say that you have met with persons who take an interest in such matters—they are often elderly men, whose meagre sense is thrown into amazement by these discoveries of theirs, which they believe to be the height of wisdom.

Theaetetus. Certainly, I have.

Stranger. Then, not to exclude any one who has ever speculated at all upon the nature of being, let us put our questions to them as well as to our former friends.

Theaetetus. What questions?

Stranger. Shall we refuse to attribute being to motion and rest, or anything to anything, and assume that they do not mingle, and are incapable of participating in one another? Or shall we gather all into one class of things communicable with one another? Or are some things communicable and others not?—Which of these alternatives, Theaetetus, will they prefer?

Theaetetus. I have nothing to answer on their behalf. Suppose that you take all these hypotheses in turn, and see what are the consequences which follow from each of them.

Stranger. Very good, and first let us assume them to say that nothing is capable of participating in anything else in any respect; [252 in that case rest and motion cannot participate in being at all.

Theaetetus. They cannot.

Stranger. But would either of them be if not participating in being?

Theaetetus. No.

Stranger. Then by this admission everything is instantly overturned, as well the doctrine of universal motion as of universal rest, and also the doctrine of those who distribute being into immutable and everlasting kinds; for all these add on a notion of being, some affirming that things 'are' truly in motion, and others that they 'are' truly at rest.

Theaetetus. Just so.

Stranger. Again, those who would at one time compound, and at another resolve all things, whether making them into one and out of one creating infinity, or dividing them into finite elements, and forming compounds out of these; whether they suppose the processes of creation to be successive or continuous, would be talking nonsense in all this if there were no admixture.

Theaetetus. True.

Stranger. Most ridiculous of all will the men themselves be who want to carry out the argument and yet forbid us to call anything, because participating in some affection from another, by the name of that other.

Theaetetus. Why so?

Stranger. Why, because they are compelled to use the words 'to be,' 'apart,' 'from others,' 'in itself,' and ten thousand more, which they cannot give up, but must make the connecting links of discourse; and therefore they do not require to be refuted by others, but their enemy, as the saying is, inhabits the same house with them; they are always carrying about with them an adversary, like the wonderful ventriloquist, Eurycles, who out of their own bellies audibly contradicts them.

Theaetetus. Precisely so; a very true and exact illustration.

Stranger. And now, if we suppose that all things have the power of communion with one another—what will follow?

Theaetetus. Even I can solve that riddle.

Stranger. How?

Theaetetus. Why, because motion itself would be at rest, and rest again in motion, if they could be attributed to one another.

Stranger. But this is utterly impossible.

Theaetetus. Of course.

Stranger. Then only the third hypothesis remains.

Theaetetus. True.

Stranger. For, surely, either all things have communion with all; or nothing with any other thing; or some things communicate with some things and others not.

Theaetetus. Certainly.

Stranger. And two out of these three suppositions have been found to be impossible.

Theaetetus. Yes.

Stranger. Every one then, who desires to answer truly, will adopt the third and remaining hypothesis of the communion of some with some.

Theaetetus. Quite true.

Stranger. This communion of some with some may be il-   [253 lustrated by the case of letters; for some letters do not fit each other, while others do.

Theaetetus. Of course.

Stranger. And the vowels, especially, are a sort of bond which pervades all the other letters, so that without a vowel one consonant cannot be joined to another.

Theaetetus. True.

Stranger. But does every one know what letters will unite with what? Or is art required in order to do so [1]?

Theaetetus. Art is required.

Stranger. What art?

Theaetetus. The art of grammar.

Stranger. And is not this also true of sounds high and low?—Is not he who has the art to know what sounds mingle, a musician, and he who is ignorant, not a musician?

Theaetetus. Yes.

Stranger. And we shall find this to be generally true of art or the absence of art.

Theaetetus. Of course.

Stranger. And as classes are admitted by us in like manner to be some of them capable and others incapable of intermixture, must not

---

[1] Reading δρᾶν ἱκανῶς αὐτά (? αὐτό).

he who would rightly show what kinds will unite and what will not, proceed by the help of science in the path of argument? And will he not ask if the connecting links are universal, and so capable of intermixture with all things; and again, in divisions, whether there are not other universal classes, which make them possible?

Theaetetus. To be sure he will require science, and, if I am not mistaken, the very greatest of all sciences.

Stranger. How are we to call it? By Zeus, have we not lighted unwittingly upon our free and noble science, and in looking for the Sophist have we not entertained the philosopher unawares?

Theaetetus. What do you mean?

Stranger. Should we not say that the division according to classes, which neither makes the same other, nor makes other the same, is the business of the dialectical science?

Theaetetus. That is what we should say.

Stranger. Then, surely, he who can divide rightly is able to see clearly one form pervading a scattered multitude, and many different forms contained under one higher form; and again, one form knit together into a single whole and pervading many such wholes, and many forms, existing only in separation and isolation. This is the knowledge of classes which determines where they can have communion with one another and where not.

Theaetetus. Quite true.

Stranger. And the art of dialectic would be attributed by you only to the philosopher pure and true?

Theaetetus. Who but he can be worthy?

Stranger. In this region we shall always discover the philosopher, if we look for him; like the Sophist, he is not easily discovered,   [254 but for a different reason.

Theaetetus. For what reason?

Stranger. Because the Sophist runs away into the darkness of not-being, in which he has learned by habit to feel about, and cannot be discovered because of the darkness of the place. Is not that true?

Theaetetus. It seems to be so.

Stranger. And the philosopher, always holding converse through reason with the idea of being, is also dark from excess of light; for the souls of the many have no eye which can endure the vision of the divine.

Theaetetus. Yes; that seems to be quite as true as the other.

Stranger. Well, the philosopher may hereafter be more fully considered by us, if we are disposed; but the Sophist must clearly not be allowed to escape until we have had a good look at him.

Theaetetus. Very good.

Stranger. Since, then, we are agreed that some classes have a communion with one another, and others not, and some have communion with a few and others with many, and that there is no reason why some should not have universal communion with all, let us now pursue the enquiry, as the argument suggests, not in relation to all ideas, lest the multitude of them should confuse us, but let us select a few of those which are reckoned to be the principal ones, and consider their several natures and their capacity of communion with one another, in order that if we are not able to apprehend with perfect clearness the notions of being and not-being, we may at least not fall short in the consideration of them, so far as they come within the scope of the present enquiry, if peradvanture we may be allowed to assert the reality of not-being, and yet escape unscathed.

Theaetetus. We must do so.

Stranger. The most important of all the genera are those which we were just now mentioning—being and rest and motion.

Theaetetus. Yes, by far.

Stranger. And two of these are, as we affirm, incapable of communion with one another.

Theaetetus. Quite incapable.

Stranger. Whereas being surely has communion with both of them, for both of them are?

Theaetetus. Of course.

Stranger. That makes up three of them.

Theaetetus. To be sure.

Stranger. And each of them is other than the remaining two, but the same with itself.

Theaetetus. True.

Stranger. But then, what is the meaning of these two words, 'same' and 'other'? Are they two new kinds other than the three, and yet always of necessity intermingling with them, and are we to have five kinds instead of three; or when we speak of the same and other, are we unconsciously speaking of one of the three first kinds?   [255

Theaetetus. Very likely we are.

Stranger. But, surely, motion and rest are neither the other nor the same.

Theaetetus. How is that?

Stranger. Whatever we attribute to motion and rest in common, cannot be either of them.

Theaetetus. Why not?

Stranger. Because motion would be at rest and rest in motion, for either of them, being predicated of both, will compel the other to change into the opposite of its own nature, because partaking of its opposite.

Theaetetus. Quite true.

Stranger. Yet they surely both partake of the same and of the other?

Theaetetus. Yes.

Stranger. Then we must not assert that motion, any more than rest, is either the same or the other.

Theaetetus. No; we must not.

Stranger. But are we to conceive that being and the same are identical?

Theaetetus. Possibly.

Stranger. But if they are identical, then again in saying that motion and rest have being, we should also be saying that they are the same.

Theaetetus. Which surely cannot be.

Stranger. Then being and the same cannot be one.

Theaetetus. Scarcely.

Stranger. Then we may suppose the same to be a fourth class, which is now to be added to the three others.

Theaetetus. Quite true.

Stranger. And shall we call the other a fifth class? Or should we consider being and other to be two names of the same class?

Theaetetus. Very likely.

Stranger. But you would agree, if I am not mistaken, that existences are relative as well as absolute?

Theaetetus. Certainly.

Stranger. And the other is always relative to other?

Theaetetus. True.

Stranger. But this would not be the case unless being and the other entirely differed; for, if the other, like being, were absolute as well as relative, then there would have been a kind of other which was not other than other. And now we find that what is other must of necessity be what it is in relation to some other.

Theaetetus. That is the true state of the case.

Stranger. Then we must admit the other as the fifth of our selected classes.

Theaetetus. Yes.

Stranger. And the fifth class pervades all classes, for they all differ from one another, not by reason of their own nature, but because they partake of the idea of the other.

Theaetetus. Quite true.

Stranger. Then let us now put the case with reference to each of the five.

Theaetetus. How?

Stranger. First there is motion, which we affirm to be absolutely 'other' than rest: what else can we say?

Theaetetus. It is so.

Stranger. And therefore is not rest.

Theaetetus. Certainly not.

Stranger. And yet is, because partaking of being.

Theaetetus. True.

Stranger. Again, motion is other than the same?

Theaetetus. Just so.

Stranger. And is therefore not the same.

Theaetetus. It is not.

Stranger. Yet, surely, motion is the same, because all things partake of the same.

Theaetetus. Very true.

Stranger. Then we must admit, and not object to say, that motion is the same and is not the same, for we do not apply the terms 'same' and 'not the same,' in the same sense; but we call it the 'same,' in relation to itself, because partaking of the same; and not the same, because having communion with the other, it is thereby severed from the same, and has become not that but other, and is therefore rightly spoken of as 'not the same.'

Theaetetus. To be sure.

Stranger. And if absolute motion in any point of view partook of rest, there would be no absurdity in calling motion stationary.

Theaetetus. Quite right,—that is, on the supposition that some classes mingle with one another, and others not.

Stranger. That such a communion of kinds is according to nature, we had already proved [2] before we arrived at this part of our discussion.

Theaetetus. Certainly.

Stranger. Let us proceed, then. May we not say that motion is other than the other, having been also proved by us to be other than the same and other than rest?

Theatetus. That is certain.

Stranger. Then, according to this view, motion is other and also not other?

Theaetetus. True.

Stranger. What is the next step? Shall we say that motion is other than the three and not other than the fourth,—for we agreed that there are five classes about and in the sphere of which we proposed to make enquiry?

---

[2] Cp. supra, 252.

Theaetetus. Surely we cannot admit that the number is less than it appeared to be just now.

Stranger. Then we may without fear contend that motion is other than being?

Theaetetus. Without the least fear.

Stranger. The plain result is that motion, since it partakes of being, really is and also is not?

Theaetetus. Nothing can be plainer.

Stranger. Then not-being necessarily exists in the case of motion and of every class; for the nature of the other entering into them all, makes each of them other than being, and so non-existent; and therefore of all of them, in like manner, we may truly say that they are not; and again, inasmuch as they partake of being, that they are and are existent.

Theaetetus. So we may assume.

Stranger. Every class, then, has plurality of being and infinity of not-being.

Theaetetus. So we must infer.   [257

Stranger. And being itself may be said to be other than the other kinds.

Theaetetus. Certainly.

Stranger. Then we may infer that being is not, in respect of as many other things as there are; for not being these it is itself one, and is not the other things, which are infinite in number.

Theaetetus. That is not far from the truth.

Stranger. And we must not quarrel with this result, since it is of the nature of classes to have communion with one another; and if any one denies our present statement [viz. that being is not, etc.], let him first argue with our former conclusion [i.e., respecting the communion of ideas], and then he may proceed to argue with what follows.

Theaetetus. Nothing can be fairer.

Stranger. Let me ask you to consider a further question.

Theaetetus. What question?

Stranger. When we speak of not-being, we speak, I suppose, not of something opposed to being, but only different.

Theaetetus. What do you mean?

Stranger. When we speak of something as not great, does the expression seem to you to imply what is little any more than what is equal?

Theaetetus. Certainly not.

Stranger. The negative particles, οὖ and μή, when prefixed to words, do not imply opposition, but only difference from the words, or more correctly from the things represented by the words, which follow them.

Theaetetus. Quite true.

Stranger. There is another point to be considered, if you do not object.

Theaetetus. What is it?

Stranger. The nature of the other appears to me to be divided into fractions like knowledge.

Theaetetus. How so?

Stranger. Knowledge, like the other, is one; and yet the various parts of knowledge have each of them their own particular name, and hence there are many arts and kinds of knowledge.

Theaetetus. Quite true.

Stranger. And is not the case the same with the parts of the other, which is also one?

Theaetetus. Very likely; but will you tell me how?

Stranger. There is some part of the other which is opposed to the beautiful?

Theaetetus. There is.

Stranger. Shall we say that this has or has not a name?

Theaetetus. It has; for whatever we call not-beautiful is other than the beautiful, not than something else.

Stranger. And now tell me another thing.

Theaetetus. What?

Stranger. Is the not-beautiful anything but this—an existence parted off from a certain kind of existence, and again from another point of view opposed to an existing something?

Theaetetus. True.

Stranger. Then the not-beautiful turns out to be the opposition of being to being?

Theaetetus. Very true.

Stranger. But upon this view, is the beautiful a more real and the not-beautiful a less real existence?

Theaetetus. Not at all.

Stranger. And the not-great may be said to exist, equally   [258 with the great?

Theaetetus. Yes.

Stranger. And, in the same way, the just must be placed in the same category with the not-just—the one cannot be said to have any more existence than the other.

Theaetetus. True.

Stranger. The same may be said of other things; seeing that the nature of the other has a real existence, the parts of this nature must equally be supposed to exist.

Theaetetus. Of course.

Stranger. Then, as would appear, the opposition of a part of the other, and of a part of being, to one another, is, if I may venture to say so, as truly essence as being itself, and implies not the opposite of being, but only what is other than being.

Theaetetus. Beyond question.

Stranger. What then shall we call it?

Theaetetus. Clearly, not being; and this is the very nature for which the Sophist compelled us to search.

Stranger. And has not this, as you were saying, as real an existence as any other class? May I not say with confidence that not-being has an assured existence, and a nature of its own? Just as the great was found to be great and the beautiful beautiful, and the not-great not-great, and the not-beautiful not-beautiful, in the same manner not-being has been found to be and is not-being, and is to be reckoned one among the many classes of being. Do you, Theaetetus, still feel any doubt of this?

Theaetetus. None whatever.

Stranger. Do you observe that our scepticism has carried us beyond the range of Parmenides' prohibition?

Theaetetus. In what?

Stranger. We have advanced to a further point, and shown him more than he forbad us to investigate.

Theaetetus. How is that?

Stranger. Why, because he says—

'Not-being never is [3], and do thou keep thy thoughts from this way of enquiry.'

Theaetetus. Yes, he says so.

Stranger. Whereas, we have not only proved that things which are not are, but we have shown what form of being not-being is; for we have shown that the nature of the other is, and is distributed over all things in their relations to one another, and whatever part of the other is contrasted with being, this is precisely what we have ventured to call not-being.

Theatetetus. And surely, Stranger, we were quite right.

Stranger. Let not any one say, then, that while affirming the opposition of not-being to being, we still assert the being of not-being; for as to whether there is an opposite of being, to that enquiry we have [259 long said good-bye—it may or may not be, and may or may not be capable of definition. But as touching our present account of not-being, let a man either convince us of error, or, so long as he cannot, he too must say, as we are saying, that there is a communion of classes, and that being, and difference or other, traverse all things and mutually

---

[3] Reading τοῦτο φανῇ.

interpenetrate, so that the other partakes of being, and by reason of this participation is, and yet is not that of which it partakes, but other, and being other than being, it is clearly a necessity that not-being should be. And again, being, through partaking of the other, becomes a class other than the remaining classes, and being other than all of them, is not each one of them, and is not all the rest, so that undoubtedly there are thousands upon thousands of cases in which being is not, and all other things, whether regarded individually or collectively, in many respects are, and in many respects are not.

Theaetetus. True.

Stranger. And he who is sceptical of this contradiction, must think how he can find something better to say; or if he sees a puzzle, and his pleasure is to drag words this way and that, the argument will prove to him, that he is not making a worthy use of his faculties; for there is no charm in such puzzles, and there is no difficulty in detecting them; but we can tell him of something else the pursuit of which is noble and also difficult.

Theaetetus. What is it?

Stranger. A thing of which I have already spoken;—letting alone these puzzles as involving no difficulty, he should be able to follow and criticize in detail every argument, and when a man says that the same is in a manner other, or that other is the same, to understand and refute him from his own point of view, and in the same respect in which he asserts either of these affections. But to show that somehow and in some sense the same is other, or the other same, or the great small, or the like unlike; and to delight in always bringing forward such contradictions, is no real refutation, but is clearly the newborn babe of some one who is only beginning to approach the problem of being.

Theaetetus. To be sure.

Stranger. For certainly, my friend, the attempt to separate all existences from one another is a barbarism and utterly unworthy of an educated or philosophical mind.

Theaetetus. Why so?

Stranger. The attempt at universal separation is the final annihilation of all reasoning; for only by the union of conceptions with   [260 one another do we attain to discourse of reason.

Theaetetus. True.

Stranger. And, observe that we were only just in time in making a resistance to such separatists, and compelling them to admit that one thing mingles with another.

Theaetetus. Why so?

Stranger. Why, that we might be able to assert discourse to be a kind of being; for if we could not, the worst of all consequences would follow; we should have no philosophy. Moreover, the necessity for determining the nature of discourse presses upon us at this moment; if utterly deprived of it, we could no more hold discourse; and deprived of it we should be if we admitted that there was no admixture of natures at all.

Theaetetus. Very true, But I do not understand why at this moment we must determine the nature of discourse.

Stranger. Perhaps you will see more clearly by the help of the following explanation.

Theaetetus. What explanation?

Stranger. Not-being has been acknowledged by us to be one among many classes diffused over all being.

Theaetetus. True.

Stranger. And thence arises the question, whether not-being mingles with opinion and language.

Theaetetus. How so?

Stranger. If not-being has no part in the proposition, then all things must be true; but if not-being has a part, then false opinion and false speech are possible, for to think or to say what is not—is falsehood, which thus arises in the region of thought and in speech.

Theaetetus. That is quite true.

Stranger. And where there is falsehood surely there must be deceit.

Theaetetus. Yes.

Stranger. And if there is deceit, then all things must be full of idols and images and fancies.

Theaetetus. To be sure.

Stranger. Into that region the Sophist, as we said, made his escape, and, when he had got there, denied the very possibility of falsehood; no one, he argued, either conceived or uttered falsehood, inasmuch as not-being did not in any way partake of being.

Theaetetus. True.

Stranger. And now, not-being has been shown to partake of being, and therefore he will not continue fighting in this direction, but he will probably say that some ideas partake of not-being, and some not, and that language and opinion are of the non-partaking class; and he will still fight to the death against the existence of the image-making and phantastic art, in which we have placed him, because, as he will say, opinion and language do not partake of not-being, and unless this participation exists, there can be no such thing as falsehood. And, with the view of meeting this evasion, we must begin by enquiring into the nature of language, opinion, and imagination, in order that when we find them we may find also that they have communion with [261 not-being, and, having made out the connection of them, may thus prove that falsehood exists; and therein we will imprison the Sophist, if he deserves it, or, if not, we will let him go again and look for him in another class.

Theaetetus. Certainly, Stranger, there appears to be truth in what was said about the Sophist at first, that he was of a class not easily caught, for he seems to have abundance of defences, which he throws up, and which must every one of them be stormed before we can reach the man himself. And even now, we have with difficulty got through his first defence, which is the not-being of not-being, and lo! here is another; for we have still to show that falsehood exists in the sphere of language and opinion, and there will be another and another line of defence without end.

Stranger. Any one, Theaetetus, who is able to advance even a little ought to be of good cheer, for what would he who is dispirited at a little progress do, if he were making none at all, or even undergoing a repulse? Such a faint heart, as the proverb says, will never take a city: but now that we have succeeded thus far, the citadel is ours, and what remains is easier.

Theaetetus. Very true.

Stranger. Then, as I was saying, let us first of all obtain a conception of language and opinion, in order that we may have clearer grounds for determining, whether not-being has any concern with them, or whether they are both always true, and neither of them ever false.

Theaetetus. True.

Stranger. Then, now, let us speak of names, as before we were speaking of ideas and letters; for that is the direction in which the answer may be expected.

Theaetetus. And what is the question at issue about names?

Stranger. The question at issue is whether all names may be connected with one another, or none, or only some of them.

Theaetetus. Clearly the last is true.

Stranger. I understand you to say that words which have a meaning when in sequence may be connected, but that words which have no meaning when in sequence cannot be connected?

Theaetetus. What are you saying?

Stranger. What I thought that you intended when you gave your assent; for there are two sorts of intimation of being which are given by the voice.

Theaetetus. What are they?

Stranger. One of them is called nouns, and the other verbs.

Theaetetus. Describe them.

Stranger. That which denotes action we call a verb.   [262

Theaetetus. True.

Stranger. And the other, which is an articulate mark set on those who do the actions, we call a noun.

Theaetetus. Quite true.

Stranger. A succession of nouns only is not a sentence, any more than of verbs without nouns.

Theaetetus. I do not understand you.

Stranger. I see that when you gave your assent you had something else in your mind. But what I intended to say was, that a mere succession of nouns or of verbs is not discourse.

Theaetetus. What do you mean?

Stranger. I mean that words like 'walks,' 'runs,' 'sleeps,' or any other words which denote action, however many of them you string together, do not make discourse.

Theaetetus. How can they?

Stranger. Or, again, when you say 'lion,' 'stag,' 'horse,' or any other words which denote agents—neither in this way of stringing words together do you attain to discourse; for there is no expression of action or inaction, or of the existence of existence or non-existence indicated by the sounds, until verbs are mingled with nouns; then the words fit, and the smallest combination of them forms language, and is the simplest and least form of discourse.

Theaetetus. Again I ask, What do you mean?

Stranger. When any one says 'A man learns,' should you not call this the simplest and least of sentences?

Theaetetus. Yes.

Stranger. Yes, for he now arrives at the point of giving an intimation about something which is, or is becoming, or has become, or will be. And he not only names, but he does something, by connecting verbs with nouns; and therefore we say that he discourses, and to this connection of words we give the name of discourse.

Theaetetus. True.

Stranger. And as there are some things which fit one another, and other things which do not fit, so there are some vocal signs which do, and others which do not, combine and form discourse.

Theaetetus. Quite true.

Stranger. There is another small matter.

Theaetetus. What is it?

Stranger. A sentence must and cannot help having a subject.

Theaetetus. True.

Stranger. And must be of a certain quality.

Theaetetus. Certainly.

Stranger. And now let us mind what we are about.

Theaetetus. We must do so.

Stranger. I will repeat a sentence to you in which a thing and an action are combined, by the help of a noun and a verb; and you shall tell me of whom the sentence speaks.

Theaetetus. I will, to the best of my power.

Stranger. 'Theaetetus sits'—not a very long sentence.   [263

Theaetetus. Not very.

Stranger. Of whom does the sentence speak, and who is the subject? that is what you have to tell.

Theaetetus. Of me; I am the subject.

Stranger. Or this sentence, again—

Theaetetus. What sentence?

Stranger. 'Theaetetus, with whom I am now speaking, is flying.'

Theaetetus. That also is a sentence which will be admitted by every one to speak of me, and to apply to me.

Stranger. We agreed that every sentence must necessarily have a certain quality.

Theaetetus. Yes.

Stranger. And what is the quality of each of these two sentences?

Theaetetus. The one, as I imagine, is false, and the other true.

Stranger. The true says what is true about you?

Theaetetus. Yes.

Stranger. And the false says what is other than true?

Theaetetus. Yes.

Stranger. And therefore speaks of things which are not as if they were?

Theaetetus. True.

Stranger. And says that things are real of you which are not; for, as we were saying, in regard to each thing or person, there is much that is and much that is not.

Theaetetus. Quite true.

Stranger. The second of the two sentences which related to you was first of all an example of the shortest form consistent with our definition.

Theaetetus. Yes, this was implied in our recent admission.

Stranger. And, in the second place, it related to a subject?

Theaetetus. Yes.

Stranger. Who must be you, and can be nobody else?

Theaetetus. Unquestionably.

Stranger. And it would be no sentence at all if there were no subject, for, as we proved, a sentence which has no subject is impossible.

Theaetetus. Quite true.

Stranger. When other, then, is asserted of you as the same, and not-being as being, such a combination of nouns and verbs is really and truly false discourse.

Theaetetus. Most true.

Stranger. And therefore thought, opinion, and imagination are now proved to exist in our minds both as true and false.

Theaetetus. How so?

Stranger. You will know better if you first gain a knowledge of what they are, and in what they severally differ from one another.

Theaetetus. Give me the knowledge which you would wish me to gain.

Stranger. Are not thought and speech the same, with this exception, that what is called thought is the unuttered conversation of the soul with herself?

Theaetetus. Quite true.

Stranger. But the stream of thought which flows through the lips and is audible is called speech?

Theaetetus. True.

Stranger. And we know that there exists in speech . . .

Theaetetus. What exists?

Stranger. Affirmation.

Theaetetus. Yes, we know it. [264

Stranger. When the affirmation or denial takes place in silence and in the mind only, have you any other name by which to call it but opinion?

Theaetetus. There can be no other name.

Stranger. And when opinion is presented, not simply, but in some form of sense, would you not call it imagination?

Theaetetus. Certainly.

Stranger. And seeing that language is true and false, and that thought is the conversation of the soul with herself, and opinion is the end of thinking, and imagination or phantasy is the union of sense and opinion, the inference is that some of them, since they are akin to language, should have an element of falsehood as well as of truth?

Theaetetus. Certainly.

Stranger. Do you perceive, then, that false opinion and speech have been discovered sooner than we expected?—For just now we seemed to be undertaking a task which would never be accomplished.

Theaetetus. I perceive.

Stranger. Then let us not be discouraged about the future; but now having made this discovery, let us go back to our previous classification.

Theaetetus. What classification?

Stranger. We divided image-making into two sorts; the one likeness-making, the other imaginative or phantastic.

Theaetetus. True.

Stranger. And we said that we were uncertain in which we should place the Sophist.

Theaetetus. We did say so.

Stranger. And our heads began to go round more and more when it was asserted that there is no such thing as an image or idol or appearance, because in no manner or time or place can there ever be such a thing as falsehood.

Theaetetus. True.

Stranger. And now, since there has been shown to be false speech and false opinion, there may be imitations of real existences, and out of this condition of the mind an art of deception may arise.

Theaetetus. Quite possible.

Stranger. And we have already admitted, in what preceded, that the Sophist was lurking in one of the divisions of the likeness-making art?

Theaetetus. Yes.

Stranger. Let us, then, renew the attempt, and in dividing any class, always take the part to the right, holding fast to that which holds the Sophist, until we have stripped him of all his common properties, and reached his difference or peculiar. Then we may exhibit   [265 him in his true nature, first to ourselves and then to kindred dialectical spirits.

Theaetetus. Very good.

Stranger. You may remember that all art was originally divided by us into creative and acquisitive.

Theaetetus. Yes.

Stranger. And the Sophist was flitting before us in the acquisitive class, in the subdivisions of hunting, contests, merchandize, and the like.

Theaetetus. Very true.

Stranger. But now that the imitative art has enclosed him, it is clear that we must begin by dividing the art of creation; for imitation is a kind of creation—of images, however, as we affirm, and not of real things.

Theaetetus. Quite true.

Stranger. In the first place, there are two kinds of creation.

Theaetetus. What are they?

Stranger. One of them is human and the other divine.

Theaetetus. I do not follow.

Stranger. Every power, as you may remember our saying originally, which causes things to exist, not previously existing, was defined by us as creative.

Theaetetus. I remember.

Stranger. Looking, now, at the world and all the animals and plants, at things which grow upon the earth from seeds and roots, as well as at inanimate substances which are formed within the earth, fusile or non-fusile, shall we say that they come into existence—not having existed previously—by the creation of God, or shall we agree with vulgar opinion about them?

Theaetetus. What is it?

Stranger. The opinion that nature brings them into being from some spontaneous and unintelligent cause. Or shall we say that they are created by a divine reason and a knowledge which comes from God?

Theaetetus. I dare say that, owing to my youth, I may often waver in my view, but now when I look at you and see that you incline to refer them to God, I defer to your authority.

Stranger. Nobly said, Theaetetus, and if I thought that you were one of those who would hereafter change your mind, I would have gently argued with you, and forced you to assent; but as I perceive that you will come of yourself and without any argument of mine, to that belief which, as you say, attracts you, I will not forestall the work of time. Let me suppose, then, that things which are said to be made by nature are the work of divine art, and that things which are made by man out of these are work of human art. And so there are two kinds of making and production, the one human and the other divine.

Theaetetus. True.

Stranger. Then, now, subdivide each of the two sections which we have already.

Theaetetus. How do you mean?

Stranger. I mean to say that you should make a vertical di-   [266 vision of production or invention, as you have already made a lateral one.

Theaetetus. I have done so.

Stranger. Then, now, there are in all four parts or segments—two of them have reference to us and are human, and two of them have reference to the gods and are divine.

Theaetetus. True.

Stranger. And, again, in the division which was supposed to be made in the other way, one part in each subdivision is the making of the things themselves, but the two remaining parts may be called the making of likenesses; and so the productive art is again divided into two parts.

Theaetetus. Tell me the divisions once more.

Stranger. I suppose that we, and the other animals, and the elements out of which things are made—fire, water, and the like—are known by us to be each and all the creation and work of God.

Theaetetus. True.

Stranger. And there are images of them, which are not them, but which correspond to them; and these are also the creation of a wonderful skill.

Theaetetus. What are they?

Stranger. The appearances which spring up of themselves in sleep or by day, such as a shadow when darkness arises in a fire, or the reflection which is produced when the light in bright and smooth objects meets on their surface with an external light, and creates a perception the opposite of our ordinary sight.

Theaetetus. Yes; and the images as well as the creation are equally the work of a divine hand.

Stranger. And what shall we say of human art? Do we not make one house by the art of building, and another by the art of drawing, which is a sort of dream created by man for those who are awake?

Theaetetus. Quite true.

Stranger. And other products of human creation are also twofold and go in pairs; there is the thing, with which the art of making the thing is concerned, and the image, with which imitation is concerned.

Theaetetus. Now I begin to understand, and am ready to acknowledge that there are two kinds of production, and each of them twofold; in the lateral division there is both a divine and a human production; in the vertical there are realities and a creation of a kind of similitudes.

Stranger. And let us not forget that of the imitative class the one part was to have been likeness-making, and the other phantastic, if it could be shown that falsehood is a reality and belongs to the class of real being.

Theaetetus. Yes.

Stranger. And this appeared to be the case; and therefore now, without hesitation, we shall number the different kinds as two.

Theaetetus. True.

Stranger. Then, now, let us again divide the phantastic   [267 art.

Theaetetus. Where shall we make the division?

Stranger. There is one kind which is produced by an instrument, and another in which the creator of the appearance is himself the instrument.

Theaetetus. What do you mean?

Stranger. When any one makes himself appear like another in his figure or his voice, imitation is the name for this part of the phantastic art.

Theaetetus. Yes.

Stranger. Let this, then, be named the art of mimicry, and this the province assigned to it; as for the other division, we are weary and will give that up, leaving to some one else the duty of making the class and giving it a suitable name.

Theaetetus. Let us do as you say—assign a sphere to the one and leave the other.

Stranger. There is a further distinction, Theaetetus, which is worthy of our consideration, and for a reason which I will tell you.

Theaetetus. Let me hear.

Stranger. There are some who imitate, knowing what they imitate, and some who do not know. And what line of distinction can there possibly be greater than that which divides ignorance from knowledge?

Theaetetus. There can be no greater.

Stranger. Was not the sort of imitation of which we spoke just now the imitation of those who know? For he who would imitate you would surely know you and your figure?

Theaetetus. Naturally.

Stranger. And what would you say of the figure or form of justice or of virtue in general? Are we not well aware that many, having no knowledge of either, but only a sort of opinion, do their best to show that this opinion is really entertained by them, by expressing it, as far as they can, in word and deed?

Theaetetus. Yes, that is very common.

Stranger. And do they always fail in their attempt to be thought just, when they are not? Or is not the very opposite true?

Theaetetus. The very opposite.

Stranger. Such a one, then, should be described as an imitator—to be distinguished from the other, as he who is ignorant is distinguished from him who knows?

Theaetetus. True.

Stranger. Can we find a suitable name for each of them? This is clearly not an easy task; for among the ancients there was some confusion of ideas, which prevented them from attempting to divide genera into species; wherefore there is no great abundance of names. Yet, for the sake of distinctness, I will make bold to call the imitation which coexists with opinion, the imitation of appearance—that which coexists with science, a scientific or learned imitation.

Theaetetus. Granted.

Stranger. The former is our present concern, for the Sophist was classed with imitators indeed, but not among those who have knowledge.

Theaetetus. Very true.

Stranger. Let us, then, examine our imitator of appearance, and see whether he is sound, like a piece of iron, or whether there is still some crack in him.

Theaetetus. Let us examine him.

Stranger. Indeed there is a very considerable crack; for if you look, you find that one of the two classes of imitators is a simple creature, who thinks that he knows that which he only fancies; the   [268 other sort has knocked about among arguments, until he suspects and fears that he is ignorant of that which to the many he pretends to know.

Theaetetus. There are certainly the two kinds which you describe.

Stranger. Shall we regard one as the simple imitator—the other as the dissembling or ironical imitator?

Theaetetus. Very good.

Stranger. And shall we further speak of this latter class as having one or two divisions?

Theaetetus. Answer yourself.

Stranger. Upon consideration, then, there appear to me to be two; there is the dissembler, who harangues a multitude in public in a long speech, and the dissembler, who in private and in short speeches compels the person who is conversing with him to contradict himself.

Theaetetus. What you say is most true.

Stranger. And who is the maker of the longer speeches? Is he the statesman or the popular orator?

Theaetetus. The latter.

Stranger. And what shall we call the other? Is he the philosopher or the Sophist?

Theaetetus. The philosopher he cannot be, for upon our view he is ignorant; but since he is an imitator of the wise he will have a name which is formed by an adaptation of the word σοφός. What shall we name him? I am pretty sure that I cannot be mistaken in terming him the true and very Sophist.

Stranger. Shall we bind up his name as we did before, making a chain from one end of his genealogy to the other?

Theaetetus. By all means.

Stranger. He, then [4], who traces the pedigree of his art as follows— who, belonging to the conscious or dissembling section of the art of causing self-contradiction, is an imitator of appearance, and is separated from the class of phantastic which is a branch of image-making into that further division of creation, the juggling of words, a creation human, and not divine—any one who affirms the real Sophist to be of this blood and lineage will say the very truth.

Theaetetus. Undoubtedly.

---

[4] Reading τὸν δή.

ARISTOTLE

INTRODUCTION TO

Aristotle

LIFE

Aristotle was born in 384 B.C. in Stagira, a small Macedonian town. His father, Nicomachus, was physician and probably friend to Amyntas II; according to some reports, he served in the same capacity to the son of Amyntas, Philip of Macedonia. Aristotle's deep interest in and extensive writings about biology have often been attributed to his sense of the tradition into which he was born. Professions in the ancient world generally were hereditary, and all physicians claimed a common descent from Asclepius, god of healing and son of Apollo.

After the death of his father, Aristotle was raised by a relative until his seventeenth or eighteenth year, whereupon he was sent to Athens to study at the flourishing and famous Academy of Plato. He remained there for twenty years. What Aristotle did during these twenty years is a subject of much speculation but of very little solid information, even as there is no firm knowledge with respect to his personal and intellectual relations with Plato. Nonetheless, there is considerable reason to believe that in his maturer years at the Academy he taught, engaged in scientific research, and wrote several dialogues in the Platonic manner.[1]

Speusippus, a nephew of Plato, became the leader of the Academy after the death of his uncle. Shortly thereafter Aristotle departed from the Academy and Athens. His reasons for leaving are not known. He may have been piqued at his failure to succeed Plato. Certainly even at that early date he could have had little sympathy with the extreme

---

[1] Werner Jaeger: *Aristotle* (New York: Oxford University Press; 1934).

metaphysical position of Speusippus. Many of Aristotle's barbs and criticisms of the "friends of Forms" are aimed at Speusippus and his friends, not at Plato.

Whatever the reason for his leaving, Aristotle went to Assos, a city in Asia Minor. There Hermeias, also a former member of the Academy, ruled with unchallenged power. During his years in Assos Aristotle almost certainly taught, studied, and wrote. That the relationship between Hermeias and Aristotle was a close one is indicated by the fact that Aristotle married Pythias, niece of the tyrant.

Philip of Macedonia and Hermeias formed an alliance which aimed at a conquest of Persia. Hermias, however, was assassinated, and Aristotle fled to Lesbos. Subsequently, in 343–2 Philip invited him to return to Macedon to become tutor to the young prince, Alexander. How long Aristotle remained in the position of tutor is not known, but he did not return to Athens until 335–4, after the death of Philip.

In Athens once again, where he remained for the next twelve years, Aristotle opened his school, the Lyceum, outside the city itself. Much of the teaching took place along the walks and amid the colonnades of what today would be called the campus. Hence Aristotelians became known as peripatetics (*peripatein*, to walk about). That the school was dedicated to Apollo and the muses may be a filial tribute to his father's mythological genealogy.

Whatever the development of Aristotle's thought was in the years between his departure from and return to Athens, it seems certain that during the twelve years at the Lyceum he became Aristotelian.

In 323 Alexander died. His death was the cue for strong anti-Macedonian feelings in Athens to burst into expression. Aristotle's long association with the royal family of Macedon made him a ready target. A charge of impiety was raised against him. Prudently he turned over to his pupil, Theophrastus, the direction of the Lyceum and fled from Athens. He is reputed to have remarked that he would not give the Athenians a second chance to sin against philosophy. Yet they may have done so unwittingly, for he died a year later, 322 B.C., in Chaldis, a city of Euboea, where he had sought protection.

WRITINGS

Many problems attend the works of Aristotle with which the beginner in philosophy need not be deeply concerned, but about which he should be informed. Ancient report has it that the works of Aristotle were far more extensive than those that have come down to us. Though it is extremely unlikely that any of the lost writings will be discovered, there is no reason to believe that a recovery of them would cause a radical reappraisal of his mature philosophical position.

There is some reason to believe, however, that a recovery of the lost writings might throw light on his intellectual development. Several dialogues in the Platonic manner, which are quoted by Cicero and others, suggest that they were written during his later years at the Academy and shortly thereafter—possibly when he resided in Assos. It comes as a surprise to read that there are several ancient references to the beauty and elegance of Aristotle's style; most likely these comments are in reference to his dialogues. More important, however, the recovery of Aristotle's dialogues might disclose the degree of Aristotle's closeness to Plato—the Plato of the later Dialogues— as well as how and where he differed from other members of the Academy.[2] It well may be that Aristotle believed himself to be the truest disciple of Plato, for many of the arguments Aristotle brings to bear on certain interpretations of the theory of Ideas are already to be found, at least in germ, in the later Dialogues of Plato.

Whatever the case may be, more information would be of considerable historical and philosophical value for the understanding of the development of the mind of Aristotle, as well as for the appraisal of the philosophical relationship between what have come to be called Platonism and Aristotelianism.

Aristotle's relation to all his predecessors has become an important scholarly problem because he made it so. Jaeger has stated it well: "He was the inventor of the notion of intellectual development in time." [3] It is part of Aristotle's method of inquiry to make extensive comment on his predecessors with respect to whatever subject is under discussion. An excellent instance of this will be found in the *De Anima*. He summarizes previous thought on the subject to which he addresses himself, and then advances his own position by disputatious examination of the thought and evidence at hand. In doing this he calls forth arguments and facts to show that some thesis either must be, cannot be, or probably is or is not warranted.

By the foregoing method he virtually wrote the first history of philosophy incidentally to his main projects. He thus became one of the prime sources of information about previous philosophers. Always, however, he proceeded from his own categorical scheme. This last fact

---

[2] Ibid. Jaeger writes that his own work is an attempt to discover "the half obliterated traces of his [Aristotle's] mental progress."

[3] Ibid., p. 3.

has often led some scholars to the conclusion that Aristotle either misunderstood or misrepresented many of his predecessors.

The merits of this last thesis need not be entered into here. Rather,
it is more to the point to note that Aristotle, although he saw philosophic and scientific inquiry as part of a continuing process, was persuaded that his own philosophy superseded all previous philosophies. A
reappraisal of them was therefore in order. He did not hesitate to use
what he found adequate and relevant in previous thought, but he
hardly felt bound by it. His primary enterprise was not history but philosophy. Plato, Bacon, Descartes, Hegel, Whitehead, Russell, all have
written on their predecessors for the purpose of expounding their own
philosophies. In short, history, particularly the history of philosophy, is always read from some point of view. As such, it should be
respected.

Quite another question has been raised about the works of
Aristotle. The range of interest and the extent of knowledge manifest
in even the extant works have raised the issue, Are these the works of
one man or of a group of men? The consensus of contemporary opinion is that, setting aside a few minor works the authenticity of which is
questioned, the unity of thought evident in Aristotle's writings is such
that it can be the product of only one mind, albeit one which apparently
knew virtually all that was known in his time. This was still a human
possibility in antiquity.

There are three other questions which are distinguishable but
closely related concerning the extant texts of Aristotle: (1) In what
order were these works written? (2) Who organized into one whole,
and when, the various books which comprise the works such as the
Metaphysics, the *Physics*, and the *Nichomachean Ethics*? (3) Who
wrote and how did he or they write the texts? Answers to each one of
these questions entail answers to the other two.

To ask in what order the several works of Aristotle were written is to
raise a question which defies an answer; they contain so many cross
references that each work suggests that most of the others were written
before it. We can hardly suppose that all of his works sprang whole
from the mind of Aristotle as mythology tells us Athena did from the
brow of Zeus. This fact that the *Nichomachean Ethics*, the *Metaphysics*, and the *De Anima* each refer to the other two suggests part of
the answer to our third question.

The foregoing facts can be explained if we assume that the extant
works are the result of material worked and reworked over a number of
years. This is further supported by the fact that the state and form of
Aristotle's writings appear to be that of notes, rather than of a book or
books meant for publication. Frequently Aristotle presents many diffi-

cult and complex issues in a quick and summary fashion, much as one might do either in a set of lecture notes or in addressing an audience already well familiar with his philosophy. Elsewhere, on the other hand, he examines problems with a most scrupulous concern for every minute detail and possible alternative, as though he wished to have everything kept in mind. All this fits in well with the hypothesis that what we have are notes of some kind rather than carefully worked-out books.

One theory suggests that the works which we now possess are but the notes taken by Aristotle's students during his lectures. Quite apart from the rude implications of this thesis, it has not found much serious support in recent years. A second view which has much wider acceptance is that we have Aristotle's own lecture notes which he worked and reworked over the years. This hypothesis accounts for most of the facts and may well be correct. It has not, however, been definitely proved or disproved. Several other explanations have been offered which are too complex to go into here.[4]

If no question can be made of which work of Aristotle was written before another, many questions can be raised about the parts of what have been taken to be whole works. Werner Jaeger has argued that certain parts of the Metaphysics, Nichomachean Ethics, and the Physics were written much earlier than others and represent different stages of Aristotle's intellectual development. If true, then it may be that these books cannot be taken as wholes which represent Aristotle's mature thought. The essential problem, difficult to answer, is, Did Aristotle in maturity reject his earlier thought? If he did so, what was rejected and what retained? Jaeger's thesis entails the proposition that ancient editors, long after Aristotle's death, put the various works of Aristotle together in the form in which we now have them.

While there is much evidence to support Jaeger's central argument, many accredited scholars dispute it on the grounds that the parts of Aristotle's works hold together well enough. One well may argue that Aristotle might have approved the organization of his extant writings as we now have them.

The foregoing considerations are important to advanced students of Aristotle. They should not confuse nor upset the beginning student, because the works of Aristotle are simply there—to be read and studied. They constitute the primary data for the understanding of his thought. Moreover, there emerges from his writings a clear and recognizable philosophy, despite the many refined problems attending it.

---

[4] Philip Wheelright: Aristotle (New York: The Odyssey Press; 1951) pp. xvii–xxv.

PHILOSOPHY: *Living Substance*

The philosophy of Aristotle is fundamentally simple and comparatively easy to understand in its broad and main outlines, but the works
of Aristotle are extremely complex in every respect. It is the interplay
of the simplicity of his philosophy and the complexity of his writing
which has given many scholars so much difficulty in understanding
Aristotle. These statements must appear to be somewhat paradoxical
and therefore require an explanation.

Aristotle is fond of distinguishing between "what is better known
to us and what is more knowable in itself," or asserting that "as it is
from the things which are naturally obscure, though more easily recognised by us, that we proceed to what is clear and, in the order of
thought, more knowable" [5] or distinguishing between experience and
knowledge. It is in this distinction that the above paradox is resolved.

The study of Aristotle may begin at almost any point. Nonetheless,
his inquiries into living things have a special claim as a useful introduction to his thought. He was a great biologist, writing on many aspects of
life and vital functions, and he developed many of his fundamental
philosophic categories in terms of his analysis of the primary data of
living beings. If the key to understanding Aristotle lies in comprehending all that he means by substance (*ousia*) and what it entails,
then we should begin with living things, for he observes in the *Metaphysics* that they "are substances if anything is." [6] We shall proceed then
from living things to nature in general. After a brief comment on language and logic, we shall turn to the *Metaphysics* and conclude with a
discussion of the *Ethics*. Other works shall have to go untouched except
for the briefest mention.

Let us begin, then, with what seems to be better known to us, more
observable, and a matter of common experience of living things.

Everything that lives has a beginning and an end in birth and
death. Other things as well begin and end. In life, however, the transition at each terminus is dramatic and radical. A corpse of any kind of
creature retains generally for a while the gross physical structure of the
living being; it is a body. Nonetheless, it is not a man, horse, or dog, as
the case may be, for it is incapable of performing any of the vital functions which characterize life. Socrates dead neither hungers nor thirsts,
sees nor hears, wakes nor sleeps; neither does his corpse talk, argue,

---

[5] *De Anima*, II, 2.
[6] *Metaphysics*, Book Z (7); 1032; 19–20 (Ross translation; Oxford University
Press. Tredennick translates, "substance in the highest degree.")

reason, love, or hate. In the language of the Greeks the soul has departed from the body. A man is called a man, and correspondingly each other kind of creature is named and defined in virtue of the capacity to perform the characteristic functions of its kind or species (*eidos*).

It is evident that there are two factors here: (1) the body in which the powers and functions reside—this Aristotle will call matter (*hyle*) or proximate matter (*prote hyle*)—and (2) the power to function in a certain way or ways—this power actually residing in a particular body Aristotle calls form (*morphe* or *eidos*). When form and matter are united in a functioning living creature, there then exists a substance (*ousia*) in the highest degree. The distinguishing mark of substance we shall see is that it is "a this" (*tode ti*)—for example, this man, this tree, this house. Nonetheless, we can also call "form" substance, for it is that in virtue of which we call each thing "this—". Again we may call the "matter" substance, for it has some form of definiteness both before and after the life span of the living organism. Nonetheless, considered apart from form or the individual, it is never "a this."

"Matter" (*hyle*) is used by Aristotle in a way which may appear to be unfamiliar. He often calls it "that out of which," much as we use the word "material" in the following sentences: "The wood is that out of which the table is made." "The cloth is that out of which the suit or dress is made." "Oxygen and hydrogen are that out of which water is made." It is evident then that, setting prime matter aside, there are many different matters or kinds of matters. Aristotle even speaks of the "passive intellect" as matter with respect to the active intellect. In virtue of their inherent characteristics, different matters have different potentialities.

Before there is an organism, there is something from which it comes to be. Thus oak trees come to be from acorns; fish and animals, including man, from fertilized ova.[7] In each case the potentiality of these several matters is singular in that, for example, an acorn alone can become an oak tree; a walnut never can do so. It is Aristotle's contention that each kind of matter has a certain impulsion in itself to move toward a fulfillment in actuality. The Greek word *dynamis* conveys more than the English "potentiality" does. It implies not merely capability or possibility, but tendency as well. The acorn has within itself an "internal principle or cause" whereby it strives to become an oak tree if external conditions facilitate it. This process (*energeia*) which constitutes its growth and development is always towards an end (*telos*) which is, speaking formally, an ideal limit. If achieved, this

---

[7] Aristotle believed that the form of an animal came from the male and the matter from the female menstrum.

telos would be the actual perfection of the organism, which then would be all that it perfectly could be—a healthy flourishing oak tree in one case, a perfect man in all aspects of his being in another. Aristotle's position here is, of course, teleological: "Nature always acts toward an end." This teleology must not, however, be conceived either in supernatural or in anthropomorphic terms.

Aristotle holds that there is a radical distinction between generation (*genesis*, coming to be) and destruction on one hand and other kinds of change such as growth and development, qualitative change, locomotion, and quantitative change. He asserts that only substances come to be in an unqualified sense.[8]

In speaking of the soul (*psyche*) Aristotle defines it as the form (*morphe*) of a natural body potentially having life within it. By this he means that it is the capacity or power of that substance to function in the characteristic way of its species. It is for logical purposes that we simply call man a "rational animal." Much more is intended in nature, however, when Aristotle says that the soul is the actuality (*entelecheia*) of the body. As such, it is the organizing and integrating force which unites the parts of the body and the organs into a functioning integral whole, and which governs growth and development throughout a continuous life history. The mere presence of this power of functioning in a body leads Aristotle to call the soul the "first degree of actuality of the body." However, in that this same actuality, soul, moves toward a fulfillment and self-realization, the attainment of it constitutes the highest degree of actuality (*entelecheia*). Aristotle's writings are full of examples to illustrate this distinction. It is one thing to be able to think or to see; it is another to exercise the power to think or to see. The student must keep in mind these various senses of actuality.

From the foregoing it follows that the parts of the body of a living organism are organs (literally "instruments"). The most cursory examination of life reinforces this conclusion. An eye, heart, liver, lungs do not exist as such apart from the organism in which they function, nor can we define any of them apart from their instrumentality in the whole. It is not the eye that sees, but the whole man, by or with his eyes; it is not the lungs which breathe but the whole man with or by means of his lungs. Always Aristotle insists on the absolute substantial

---

[8] *Physica* I, 7; see also *Physica* V, 1: *De Generatione et Corruptione*. It is true that Aristotle includes genesis and passing away under change (kinesis) in *Physica* III, 1 and several other places, but for the most part he distinguishes them. For a most detailed discussion of the problems of change, genesis and becoming see Friedrich Solmsen, *Aristotle's System of the Physical World*. Ithaca, N.Y.: Cornell University Press; 1960). It is sufficient here to observe that there is prima facie evidence to support the thesis that substantial change, coming into being (*genesis*), and passing away (*pythora*) differ from other kinds of change.

unity of the whole, the organism as the essential fact in life. It is only by analogy with the whole that he speaks of the eyes as the matter and sight as the form in which the function or activity of seeing resides.

With the same insistence he maintains the unity of form and matter, for the unity of a potentiality to an actuality is primary, and there is no existence of one without the other. Soul and body are one. He makes an exception only in the case of the active intellect.

From the foregoing it should be clear that Aristotle means by form (*eidos*) something quite different from the so-called Platonic Ideas, Forms, or Archetypes. Certainly Aristotle holds that form is intelligible. He will not, however, reify form apart from matter; neither will he accept the notion of "participation." His point may be stated as follows: Insofar as "sphericity" is a concept in the mind of the mathematician, it is an abstraction which appears to have the characteristics of an Idea, but "spherical" as a characteristic of a body is one of the factors determining how the body acts or behaves in relation to other bodies. Form, in its primary instance is, in a natural substance, correlative to the matter of which it is the form and a condition or cause of its being (hence acting) the kind of thing it is. Thus, of things in nature definition must state the matter as well as the form. Of this, more later.

The notion of species has for Aristotle both a logical and a naturalistic sense. The two are related but distinct. Turning again to living things, let us look at species in nature. Living substances appear to be different in kind from nonliving things because they act quite differently from nonliving things. To be sure, they are like other physical entities in many respects—indeed, they are physical entities. Nevertheless, something additional is present. Living things nourish themselves and, as a class, are capable of reproducing other individuals similar to themselves. Furthermore, the growth and development of living organisms are quite different from the accretion or piling up of inanimate bodies. Virtually all living things appear to be capable of some self-motion as well as some selectivity in their action.[9] Among living creatures there also appear to be differences of kind. There are some living beings which possess only what Aristotle calls the nutritive soul.[1] By this he means that they are capable of no biological function higher than those which pertain to the fundamental life process. They do not sense, in the proper meaning of this term, nor do they remember, imagine, think, or reason.

Other creatures have in addition to the nutritive soul the power of

---

[9] Fire, for example, seems to move of its own nature upward to its natural place in the heavens and therefore it has a nature (an internal cause or principle of change), but there appears to be no selectivity in its action.

[1] Some translators use the term "vegetative soul."

sensing, and usually what goes with it, imagination (*phantasia*) [2], memory, and the capacity to learn in some degree. The capacity to sense in an organism Aristotle calls the "sensitive" or "animal soul." One must not suppose that Aristotle believes that any creature has two souls; the higher capacity simply presupposes or rests upon the lower. The ability to sense is different in *kind*, not degree, from the capacity for self-nutrition and growth. This is evident if we consider the difference between eating and seeing food. To eat, food must be taken physically and materially into the stomach; to see, the object seen must remain materially outside of the eyes. Again, nutrition requires no awareness of an object; sensing occurs when there is perception of color, sound, odor, and so on. This is the very essence of sensing. Nutrition and sensing are simply different organic functions and cannot be reduced one to another, nor to a common factor. This is fundamental in the *De Anima*.

In the case of man there is a new and additional power—that of mind (*nous*). It is the mind's capacity to totally abstract from sense experience [3] the intelligible character of existing things and to form concepts which then may be joined in judgments and reasoned discourse that sets man apart from other things and makes him a different kind (species) of being from other living creatures. Even if only one man existed and differed in kind from all other creatures, he would nonetheless constitute a species. There is then a certain sense in which each man is the species man. As it is, however, there are other men, creatures of the same kind as ourselves.

It must be noted here that there are no essential differences between men, no subspecies of man. Mankind constitutes an *infima species*. There are, of course, differences between men which are of an accidental or circumstantial nature. There are many criteria for establishing this, but the most important one lies in the fact that no man or men have inherent capacities which differ in kind from other men. The differences can all be accounted for in other terms.

Let us examine what is entailed in the notion of *kind* or *species*, by contrasting it with a familiar kind of materialism. A materialist reductionist, ancient or modern, would hold that the differences between living and nonliving things as well as the differences between the species of living beings are differences of degree, however great, and

---

[2] Imagination in the sense used here must not be confused with creative imagination. The second rests upon the first which is the capacity to form images as contrasted with seeing or hearing. It therefore includes dreams, memory objects, afterimages, etc.

[3] See the first few pages of the *Metaphysics* for a summary account of how this takes place. Also the *De Anima*, III, 4–6.

not differences of kind. On this view it would follow that when we know enough, or if we knew enough of physico-chemical processes, we could explain in terms of these processes all the so-called higher order processes of living creatures. There would not be then any really new force in living things, however complex, which could not be reduced to the lower-order ones. Species in that case would not be real, and the distinctions of Aristotle would have only nominal value. Without entering into the merits of such a controversy, it must be noted that this reductionism is precisely what Aristotle would deny. We have already seen that Aristotle holds that the soul is an active force, a way of functioning, and an irreducible factor organizing and integrating the organs of the body into one integral unity. This is the basis on which he defends the reality of species.

In logical terms the species is defined by genus and differentia. In the case of man, if he be a "rational animal," "rational" tells us what characteristic differentiates him from other species of the same genus, whereas "animal" informs us of what characteristics he shares with other species. In one sense then the genus denotes the *matter*—the first condition of becoming a man. Similarly, the differentia denotes the *form*, for it denotes that essential and singular trait in virtue of which one is called a man and not some other kind of animal. The concept of species applies to inanimate substances as well as to living things. Aristotle held that the elements were earth, air, fire, and water. They differ from each other qualitatively and are the physical elements of all bodies whatsoever. Each element therefore is a separate kind of substance (*ousia*). The same holds for every compound. It does not hold for mixtures or collections of substances. It is by an extension of the term "substance," or by an analogy, that artifacts may also be called substances. They lack a nature in themselves—that is they, or the matter out of which they are made, have no internal cause or principle of change. Wood becomes a chair only when it is worked by a cabinetmaker. Form is imposed on it. Nonetheless, when made, it has a certain kind of character and in some sense satisfies the essential condition for being a substance; it is "a this" (*tode ti*). Such kinds of entities may be regarded as if they were species, but they are actually not because they have no "nature."

The insistence on the reality of species is important because it is essential to so many other concepts for Aristotle. Without it his notion of substance collapses—as it did in the seventeenth century in the philosophies of Descartes, Locke, and others—into an entirely different meaning. We shall pursue it further in different contexts in the following pages.

NATURE

The Greek word *physikê* (φυσική), from which the English word
"physics" derives, has a variety of shaded meanings. Most prominent
among them are the following: natural, produced or caused by nature,
inborn, native, belonging to the nature of (for example, a plant), of or
concerning the order of external nature. The work of Aristotle called
Physica (The Physics) is an inquiry into the nature, conditions, and
varieties of changes in natural substances. It is not an experimental
science, but a theoretical or contemplative one. It is prior to any empirical science in so far as all empirical sciences presuppose the subject
matter examined in *Physica*.

Aristotle dismisses the thesis that there is no real change as irrelevant to inquiry into nature, because if this thesis were valid, a science
of nature would be vapid. The naturalist takes change for granted,
leaving it to another science, presumably *first philosophy*, to demonstrate its reality. The problems of the reality and nature of change
Aristotle inherited from his predecessors. Although he drew upon
their several proposed solutions, he believed that he had solved many,
if not most, of the fundamental problems which beset earlier answers.

All change, he held, requires that there be a substratum
(*hypokeimenon*),[4] something which endures and persists throughout

---

[4] It is a misfortune for the understanding of Aristotle, dating as far back as
Cicero, that the Greek word *ousia* came to be translated "substance" (in Latin
substare, to be under or to stand under.) There is no Latin or English equivalent
for *ousia* and one would do well to become habituated to using the Greek word
ousia where it applies rather than the misleading "substance." In Greek *hypokeimenon* (ὑποκείμενον) means "to lie under" or "to stand under." It is clear that
"substance" is a translation of *hypokeimenon* and not of *ousia*. Aristotle in a variety
of contexts applies the term *hypokeimenon* to *ousia*. This plus the fact that there
is in Latin no equivalent for *ousia* almost certainly accounts for the term "substance"
in most current translations of Aristotle.

It will be of some value to indicate the senses in which *ousia* is said to "stand
under." In the *Categories* Aristotle calls *ousia* an *hypokeimenon* in the linguistic
sense that the subject stands under the predicate. "Socrates" is always a subject,
never a predicate. The term which stands in discourse for the individual referred to
is constant in a series of statements such as "Socrates is a man," "Socrates is mortal,"
"Socrates is brave." He extends this usage to species, such as *man*, and to genus,
such as *animal* for the species is predicable only of the individual, and the genus
only of the individual and the species.

In a quite different sense *ousia* may be said to "stand under" when an existent
being endures through change of an accidental or incidental kind, as when the
sitting Socrates stands up or the hot iron becomes cold. In both instances the
essential being remains identical in its being and so may be said to "stand under"
the change. Again in so far as a particular being remains identical throughout a life
history, as Socrates may be said to do from birth to death, he may be said to "stand

the change. This must be a particular concrete *ousia*. In addition, there must be a pair of contraries or opposites. These three, substratum and each contrary, he calls the first principles (*arche*) of change which always entail a "that from which" and "a that to which" a thing changes. Thus, a body may move from one place to another (locomotion), or from being hot to being cool (qualitative change), or from being smaller to being larger (quantity), or from being ignorant (a state of privation) to knowing (fulfillment). There are as many types of change as there are categories.

We have already seen that "Only *ousiai* are said to 'come to be' in the unqualified sense." [5] In genesis and destruction alone do new *ousiai* come into existence and pass out of existence, although even here there is some substratum. Aristotle, as we have already noted, for the most part, sets substantive change aside and does not consider it under the category of change (*kinesis*), but under *metabole*, a term broad enough to include genesis and *kinesis*.[6]

In all that Aristotle calls change it can be observed that the thing which changes remains substantively identical while changing in some other respect. The problem turns on the question, How can something change and be the same? The hot iron, both when cooling and when cooled, remains iron—that is, identical in its essential nature; the body that moves from one place to another continues its identity throughout and at the end of change; the man who becomes ill or well, who learns or forgets, remains one identical essential being. Were this not so, change would be unintelligible, for it would be impossible to say *what* changes. It is in this sense that the thing which changes is a substratum (*hypokeimenon*) to the contraries. This solution rests on the distinction between essential becoming and other kinds of change. It has been noted earlier that the difference is radical and therefore one of kind. If it were merely a difference of degree all the old problems of identity and difference would re-emerge.

To maintain the foregoing distinctions, Aristotle affirms the absolute priority of *ousia* to every other category in nature, in being, and in thought. Apart from *ousia* or *ousiai*, nothing exists. Thus Aristotle

---

under" all the changes in his life whether these changes be developmental or accidental.

In still another sense matter may be called an *hypokeimenon* in that it "stands under" the form which organizes it, that is, it is subordinate to form, and underpins it. The precise meanings of *hypokeimenon* as well as *ousia* can be discovered only in the context in which they are used.

From this point on *ousia* and the plural *ousiai* will be used in place of the word "substance."

[5] *Physica* I, 7.
[6] Solmsen: Op. cit., pp. 178–9.

insists that all change is the change of some entity or *thing* and that
every attribute has existential reality only as it is related to, characterizes, or is predicable of some *ousia* or *ousiai*. In this connection we note that he defines time as "the measure of motion with respect to before and after." [7] It need hardly be added that the motion
must be the motion of some *ousia*.

Similarly he dismisses the notion of empty space—or "the void,"
as Democritus had called it—as absurd, for it suggests that there may
exist a spatially extended nothingness. In Aristotle's view space is an
abstraction of mathematicians which some of them subsequently reified.
On the contrary, he argues that actual spatial extension is the extension of some body or bodies. "Place" (*topos*) is the concept he
substitutes for the abstraction "space." He defines "place" as "the inner-
most motionless boundary of that which contains." [8] Thus to state the
place where a body is, requires relating it to some frame of reference of
another body or bodies. The foregoing should indicate how Aristotle
relates everything ultimately to *ousia*. It is also evident that there are
different kinds of change, such as quantitative and qualitative changes,
and changes in place, position, and time.

There are other considerations about change to be raised. Since
there are different kinds of *ousiai*, characterized by different natures,
we must consider them in more general terms than was done with
living things. Aristotle defines nature as an internal principle of motion
or change. [9] This primarily refers to that process (*energeia*) whereby
an *ousia* fulfills itself in moving toward the highest actuality
(*entelecheia*) it can attain. This applies to all natural *ousiai*—the elements, compounds, living things, the heavenly bodies. His definition of
motion "the fulfillment of what exists potentially, in so far as it exists
potentially" [1] also has its first reference to the aforementioned kind of
change.

Since things change in other respects as well, and the making of
artifacts is a kind of change, Aristotle extends the definition to cover all
other changes. Fire may ascend by nature to the heavens, or by nature
the infant develops into an adult. However, it hardly seems that iron
tends to become either hot or cold, though it can become either. Neither
does it appear that wood strives to become a bench or a bed. We may
say these things are *potentially* one of the contraries, but we must limit

---

[7] *Physica* IV, 11.

[8] Ibid. IV, 4.

[9] Ibid. II, 1: "nature is a source or cause of being moved and of being at rest
in that to which it belongs primarily, in virtue of itself and not in virtue of a concomitant attribute" (translated by R. P. Hardie and R. K. Gaye).

[1] Ibid. III, 1.

the meaning to "can become." How is this possible in terms of what we have already said about Aristotle?

The answer lies in what Aristotle calls accident (*symbebekos*). As many terms do for Aristotle, "accident" has a number of delicately graded meanings. It may mean any of the following: what may or may not be predicated of a subject; what is incidental to something else; what exists in a subject, not in virtue of the nature or essential form of the subject, but due to some other cause. A few examples will make this clear. Polyclitus may be a sculptor and also white. One fact is incidental to the other, and each is due to a different cause. There is no single causal order whereby one accidental trait may be deduced or inferred from the other. Being a sculptor cannot be deduced from the nature of Polyclitus even though being rational is a precondition of being a sculptor. Being white can be accounted for in terms of certain chemical traits of the body of Polyclitus, not in terms of his being a man. Similarly, one cannot infer where or when an *ousia* is in a given place from the knowledge of the essential form, and vice versa. It follows, then, for Aristotle, that there are plural orders and causes as well as plural kinds of *ousiai*. Aristotle does not mean that an accident is something uncaused. It is caused, but not by the thing in its nature to which it is said to be accidental; and there is no single common causal order to which the accidental can be reduced. There are a considerable number of respects—which cannot be gone into here— in which one thing may be said to be accidental to another.

There are a few additional points, however, which must be considered. The existence of the accidental excludes the possibility of a single science which can account for all change or being under one causal order. If there is to be knowledge of many kinds of things, a plurality of sciences is necessary, for there can be no science of the accidental. It also follows that accidents allow the possibility of chance and spontaneity. It is also possible that the accidental may be a cause: when two causal orders cross at some place and time, the conjunction of them may lead to a new and unexpected consequence, as when a man journeys to a distant city to buy rugs, he ransoms a friend who by chance he discovers is about to be sold into slavery. In nature, taken as a whole, many such coincidences may occur.

We have left to the last in this section on *nature* consideration of the so-called "four causes." The word "cause" is misleading to the modern mind and is unfortunate as a translation of Aristotle's terms (*aitia, aition*). Wheelwright [2] has substituted with some merit for "causes" the expressions "determining factors" or "conditions" (*aitia, aition*). Aristotle asserts that every scientific inquiry must raise and an-

---

[2] Wheelwright: Op. cit.

swer four essential questions if it is to win secure and adequate knowledge of the subject: (1) Out of what is it made, or from what does it
come into being? The answer to this indicates the matter (*hyle*) or
material cause. (2) What is it? This answer gives the essential form
("formal cause," *eidos, morphe*) or the meaning (logos). (3) To what
end does it exist? The answer to this instance states the end ("final
cause," *telos*) or the purpose. (4) What, or who brought it about?
The answer to this question informs us of the "efficient cause" (*othen*).

The first three of these questions and answers have already been
discussed in other terms. The fourth requires some comment. The
efficient cause is, of the four, most nearly like the contemporary concept
of cause. Aristotle gives the example that the carpenter is the efficient
cause of the table. He admits that one can find an indefinite number of
efficient causes—for example, body A may move B, B move C, and so
on. The material, formal, and final causes are internal to *ousia*, but the
efficient cause appears to be, for the most part, external. The exception
is soul, which is an efficient cause as well as a formal cause. Apart from
this, one is tempted to extrapolate and say that efficient causes are the
external causes or conditions which bring about change—that is, set
things in motion. The soul is then a special kind of efficient cause in
that it is in itself the origin (*othen*) of motion.[3]

The student must observe that Aristotle employs the concepts of the
four causes or conditions throughout his works. The shifting nuances of
these terms require attention, for the meaning in each use is disclosed
only in the context in which it is employed.

So much for our comments on Aristotle's conception of nature.

THE LOGICAL WORKS

The collection of works on language and logic in the *Organon* is the
first systematic philosophical examination of almost all aspects of language to appear in the ancient world. By no means was Aristotle the
first to discover all of the principles he enunciates; Plato is rich with the
analysis of language and its use. Nonetheless, the thorough examination
which Aristotle gave to it stands even today as a monument of philosophic inquiry.

The word *organon* means "instrument." This is what Aristotle
takes logic to be: an instrument for thought and inquiry without which

---

[3] *De Anima* II, 4: "the soul is the cause of animate bodies as being in itself
the origin of motion" (Hicks translation).

there cannot be either science or communication. As such it must be inquired into in itself. Only a brief statement about each of the works included in the *Organon* is possible here.

The first of these treatises, the *Categories*, discusses words in so far as they are terms of propositions or statements. Literally the word category means "predicate." There are ten predicates, of which one stands out in sharp distinction from the rest—namely, substance, thing, or *ousia*. This, as we well know, is an ambiguous word, but it has one clear meaning: it signifies that which is individual. "Socrates" denotes one man and stands in discourse for a single individual *ousia*. Moreover, Socrates can never be predicated of any other subject or be the trait of another thing. He and other individuals are the ultimate subjects of discourse. In a secondary and tertiary sense, respectively, species, such as man or horse, and genus, such as animal, also are termed *ousiai*. Although they are predicable of more than one thing, species is predicable only of particular individuals, and genus only of species and individuals. Species and genus signify what kind of being—say, Socrates—is, whereas "white" or "tall" do not. *Ousia* is recognized by the following marks: it has no contrary; it does not admit of variation of degree (each man is equally a man); and, while remaining numerically one and the same, it is capable of admitting contrary qualities. The other categories signify ways of being other than *ousia*, and all of them are predicable of *ousiai*. They are quantity, quality, relation, activity, passivity, place, time, state, and position. It is worth noting that this list is descriptive, unlike Kant's categorical scheme, which is deductive and presumably exhaustive. From this list of terms we can see that for Aristotle "being" or "to be" is a most ambiguous word. "Being" cannot be a highest genus under which each category is a species, for to be a quality is quite different from being a quantity, or an *ousia*. Aristotle was constantly aware of the ambiguity of words and held that much of the confusion about "being" in earlier philosophies was due to confusions about meanings.

The second logical work, *On Interpretation*, is closely related to the *Categories*. It examines propositions and their relations to each other when all the terms are the same, as in the following statements: "All men are mortal." "No men are mortal." "Some men are mortal." "Some men are not mortal." In these statements only the words "men" and "mortal" are terms, or categorical. The other words are not. Out of the relationships between these statements Aristotle formulated the principle of contradiction and other principles of equal importance for logic.

In the *Prior Analytics* Aristotle developed the theory and form of the syllogism and syllogistic reasoning. In essence he showed how propositions may be related to each other in valid deductive reasoning.

The *Posterior Analytics* formulated the principles which must hold for all deductive and theoretical (theoretikos) sciences—of which there are but three, mathematics, metaphysics, and physics (natural philosophy as we have discussed it earlier.)

In the *Topics* Aristotle worked out a theory of dialectical reasoning of a kind which proceeds not so much from science as from accredited opinion. It might well be said to deal with probability reasoning about matters not firmly established.

In the final work of the *Organon, De Sophisticis Elenchis*, Aristotle examined a number of the more common forms of fallacious arguments. It is a veritable handbook of the devices and sophistries of deceptive propaganda.

Subjects inquired into in the *Organon* have been constantly before the minds of philosophers throughout the history of Western thought. Never more than today have philosophers given their attention to language and logic, for they are indispensable tools of philosophy and scientific inquiry, as well as of our ordinary discourse. For Aristotle it is important to remember that, while his logical work is an instrument of philosophy, it is indivisibly related to his philosophy. It is also important to note and distinguish when and where he uses such terms as *ousia*, species, genus, form, and cause in a logical sense, in a metaphysical sense, and in a naturalistic sense. There are shifting nuances in these various uses, and Aristotle frequently makes use of all of them in the same work.

METAPHYSICS

The *Metaphysics* was not given its present title by Aristotle. *Meta ta physica* means after or beyond the physics, and first was used as a title for the work by a later editor, possibly Eudemus. Aristotle's own designation for the subject matter of the *Metaphysics* is sometimes "first philosophy"; elsewhere he calls it theology. He defines "first philosophy" as an inquiry into "being *quâ* being." This is different from the special sciences, for they are concerned with some special part or kind of being.

Is a science of first philosophy possible? This question is particularly difficult for Aristotle, because he holds that the word being (*to on*) is equivocal, as we saw in the *Categories*. At the same time Aristotle contends that every science examines a single subject matter. Since being is not a highest genus of which the categories are species, how then can one science treat being in its diverse and irreducibly distinct senses? Aristotle answers these questions through his analysis of *ousia*.

Aristotle proceeds from the criticisms Plato made of earlier philosophers, most notably Heraclitus and Parmenides. He carries his own views further than Plato and rejects the primacy which Plato gave to the ideas or Archetypes. He does, however, agree with Plato that being must be intelligible or there can be no science of it. He argues that the principle of contradiction and the principle of excluded middle have ontological reality as well as logical validity.[4] This entails the conclusion that mind (*nous*) in some sense is at the ultimate heart of being.

Though "being" is an ambiguous term, it has one sense which is primary—namely, *ousia*. We have already examined this term in three contexts. We must approach it again in the most universal way possible.

The criteria by which Aristotle judges something to be an *ousia* are "thisness" (*tode ti*) and the possession of a certain intelligible character, function, or form. Whatever is advanced as a claimant for the title *ousia* must meet these criteria in at least some respect or degree. Universals cannot meet the test of "thisness," for they are predicable of many. The Idea "man," though it be intelligible, cannot be more real than a man for many reasons. In the first place the definition of man must include the matter as well as the form. This the Idea "man" cannot do without contradiction. Secondly, if the Idea is an *ousia*, then it is "a this," and subsists in itself. How then could the many men "participate" in the one Idea? Would it not diffuse itself in multiplicity? Even if this difficulty could be overcome, there is another consequence which goes against common sense. All existing men would be second rate, for they would be at best imperfect copies of the real man, the prototype or Idea.

Aristotle proposes as an alternative that the universal is derivative, not primary. Existing men are primary in nature, their *substantial form*[5] is immersed in matter. Nonetheless, existence is intelligible, and the mind in its reflective act may, by abstraction from experience, come to

---

[4] The principle of contradiction stated logically is, "Two contradictory propositions cannot both be true at the same time." Stated ontologically, "The same thing cannot both be and not be at the same time, in the same place, and in the same respect." The law of excluded middle logically stated is, "Of two contradictory propositions one or the other must be true; a third or "middle" proposition is excluded." Ontologically this means that there is no third state possible between, say, Socrates existing and Socrates nonexisting.

[5] Ellen Stone Haring: "Substantial Form in Aristotle's *Metaphysics* Z" (in 3 parts), *Review of Metaphysics*, Vol. X, no. 2, Vol. X, no. 3, and Vol. X, no. 4 (1956–7). Dr. Haring freely admits that the term "substantial form" is not used by Aristotle. However, she uses it to differentiate the form studied in Z (7) of the *Metaphysics* from accidents, for only substantial form makes a substantial being what it is. She writes, "It is the principle of determinacy and intelligibility in such individuals as humans or plants." Her detailed analysis of the complex argument in Book Z (7) justifies her use of "substantial form." I have followed her usage and argument. Advanced students will find this article extremely valuable for the understanding of the *Metaphysics*.

"think the form apart from matter,"—that is, to know what it is to be a man. Thus Aristotle reverses the order of knowledge with respect to Plato's theory of reminiscence. Sense experience is not the occasion of the mind's recollection, it is the source from which the mind draws its thought. Indeed, Aristotle shares with Plato the conviction that there is an intelligible order and structure in existence, but it is immanent, not transcendent.

Whatever *substantial form* may be, it is not an Idea. It has the character of being "a this" as well as being intelligible. Its claims to being *ousia* in the primary sense outweigh others. These claims must be considered in relation to all other claims. In one sense matter may be called *ousia* in that it apparently individuates each existing thing. Yet it is but a potentiality considered as a matter, and consequently something is lacking to it. If we consider natural substances, we find, according to Aristotle, a hierarchy of them. Let us assume that the four elements—earth, air, fire, and water—are the lowest in the order of natural substances. As such, they possess some character of definiteness, some substantial form. Aristotle's analysis requires that we differentiate the form from the matter. What then is the matter of the elements? It is what Aristotle calls "prime matter." This is the ultimate substratum of all natural substances. Nothing much can be said about it other than that it is "that out of which" of all things. Two remarks may be made about this. *Prime matter* never exists, nor can it ever exist apart from some substantial form, some form of definiteness. It eternally exists as organized in one way or another. The second point is that prime matter is the ultimate limit of analysis. As such, one cannot go beyond it, define it. It is a terminus of analysis in one direction of being. Therefore it can only be named and pointed to. This then cannot be *ousi* in the primary sense.

If we turn to the *proximate matters* of particular substances, we discover that they are *ousiai* in that they have a nature or form of definiteness, but in so far as they are potential for some higher actuality, they are not fully qualified *ousiai*. Anything then, in so far as it is a matter, will not satisfy the conditions of being primary *ousia*.

Can the individual being—Socrates, for example—be an *ousia* in the primary sense? The answer is, Yes and no. In so far as the individual is a composite of matter and substantial form, he is derivative and therefore not a primary *ousia*. In so far as he is this singular existing subject, he is an *ousia*. He appears to satisfy the criteria. From what, however, does he derive his "thisness" and his intelligibility? It is from substantial form. The individual is called "this man," "this dog," and so forth, in virtue of the substantial form present in the composite being. This argument is valid only if substantial form is neither an Idea nor a universal but "a this," an active force organizing the matter and the parts of an existing entity into a whole. In living things soul alone satisfies these conditions. Souls are constitutive of things, universals are not. Substantial forms then are factors determining the nature and functions of particular things.

If *ousia* is the primary sense of "being," how then do the characteristics signified by the other categories have their "being," and how does one science deal with all of them? The answer lies in the fact that they constitute characteristics, orders, and relations of *ousiai* and have no real existence apart from them. Some, such as qualities, are constitutive of certain *ousiai* as hot, light, and dry are essential attributes of fire but are accidental to some higher substance in which fire is present as matter. Others, such as time, are relations or orders of *ousiai*.[6]

Everything that is comprehended under each category may become a subject matter of inquiry. We then may speak of these attributes in a manner analogous to that in which we discourse about *ousiai*. Moreover, the categories always have their reference to *ousiai* and cannot be conceived to exist apart. These facts then justify the place of the categories other than *ousia* in the science of first philosophy.

There remains but to say a few words about the first cause. The cosmos and the continual motion and processes in the universe require an eternal and primal source. Since the universe is, according to Aristotle, knowable, eternal in time, and forever in motion, a cause both of the eternity of motion and the intelligibility of being is required. God is an unmoved mover. He moves all else without being moved Himself by anything else. He moves as the object of love moves the lover. He alone is pure immaterial substantial form. Whether or not He is the soul or entelechy of the universe, is moot, and cannot be explored here. God is at the same time "the thought of thought," an immaterial spiritual being who eternally thinks Himself. Aristotle intends that He is an active living intellect and not a mere realm of essences. Whether He is immanent or transcendent is difficult to say. Whether He is the active intellect which Aristotle says is that alone in man which is immortal, or the individual active intellect of each man is also immortal cannot be clearly gathered from the extant texts. Certainly He is the guarantor of the intelligibility of the universe in some sense. Just as Aristotle says little about matter at one extreme of existence, so he says little that is definitively clear about the highest extreme of existence, God.

---

[6] *Metaphysics* VII, 16–17.

ETHICS[7]

Aristotle divides all knowledge into three classes. The first is contemplative knowledge (*theoretikos*), which aims primarily at knowledge and
understanding for its own sake, and is concerned with what is necessary
or probable. The objects of this knowledge are independent of human
deliberation and desire. The second class of knowledge is concerned
with human action, most notably in politics and ethics. This he calls
practical (*praktikos*). The third is art (*techne*) and is concerned with
the making of things such as painting, carpentry, or poetry.

Manifestly, ethics comes under the heading of practical knowledge
for it is concerned with human action and passion. Aristotle observes
that man is a political animal and adds that only a beast or a god can
live alone. Human society with its mores, institutions, and laws is the
soil in which man may, under favorable conditions, achieve his highest
fulfillment. The highest end of the *polis*[8] is to provide the means
whereby men may live the good life. Reason is the inherent character
in man which makes moral and political existence possible. Conversely,
the full range of human reason could never come into play if society did
not provide the accumulated wealth necessary for leisure, science, and
art. Without language and the funded knowledge in arts, science, and
practical wisdom, each man would begin where the first man began.
Because rational society is lacking to them it has been said that each
ape is the first ape. Man, however, inherits the past of other men and
may build upon it.

Ethics is that part of the master science, politics (*politike*), which is
concerned with the good for the individual man. Aristotle takes it for
granted that human good is also social or political. The ground work for
Aristotle's *Nichomachean Ethics* has been laid by the *Metaphysics*, *Natural Philosophy*, and the *De Anima*. We already know that everything
aims at some good. The good which man aims at is happiness (*eudaimonia*). A better translation of the term *eudaimonia* would be "fulfillment" were it not for tradition. Happiness consists of the highest possible realization of our powers in a life of reason, a life in which
reason expresses itself in every respect of our being—animal, intellectual,
political, and social. Aristotle is cognizant of the irrational elements in
man. Nonetheless, he is persuaded that these elements are amenable to

---

[7] Because the *Nichomachean Ethics* is a work of somewhat lesser difficulties
than those we have already discussed, our remarks on it will be comparatively brief
and largely confined to a few points which might otherwise be confusing.

[8] *polis* = city.

reason by training and habituation. It is not his purpose to eradicate the irrational elements of our being; they are part of our animal nature and require expression. On the contrary, they can be perfected and sublimated when brought under the deliberate desire of the life of reason.

Aristotle dismisses the notion of an absolute good as irrelevant to human happiness. He recognizes many things to be good, some better than others. The search is for the highest good—that life which, if we were wise, we all should seek. Among the claimants for the position of highest good are wealth, pleasure (sensuous pleasure particularly), and honor (position, status, fame). While all of them are good, and no man could be called happy without them in some measure, they cannot meet the requisite conditions to be the highest good. Only virtue (*arete*) will prove to be the highest good. *Arete* originally meant courage or manliness but came in time to mean excellence or perfection in a thing or action, according to its kind. Therefore, Aristotle without difficulty or embarrassment writes of the intellectual virtues (modes of perfection in the mind) as well as moral virtues (modes of perfection in human action).

The terms "virtue" and "happiness" are consequently closely linked in Aristotle through the conception of entelechy, for together they imply that fulfillment is achieved in its many aspects through the pursuit of excellence. Pleasure, then, is an accompaniment, an outcome, and a sign of the highest happiness.

Reflection on the human condition in the world discloses that virtues, such as courage or justice, which appear to entail pain, discomfort, or displeasure at certain times and under certain conditions nevertheless are essential to a good life taken as a whole. It is impossible to see how a life could be lived well if a man feared everything or nothing, or was unjust in all things. The consequences in each case would nullify every hope of happiness.

Aristotle's assertion that one becomes virtuous by being virtuous sounds paradoxical on first hearing; yet it is the way one becomes a tennis player, a musician, a scientist, or temperate. It is also the way one acquires vices. Virtues and vices are habits, not in the sense of mechanically conditioned responses, but in the sense that they are characteristic dispositional traits to act in a certain manner in certain typical situations. Thus a friendly man tends to be friendly in most situations that call for friendliness.

The term "mean" in Aristotle's definition of virtue calls for some comment, since it has frequently been misunderstood. It is borrowed from the discourse of mathematics and is used analogically in the *Nichomachean Ethics*. In practical science we are concerned with "what is true on the whole and for the most part." Mathematical exactitude is not to be expected. Aristotle's use of the word "mean" is intended to convey the notion "what is called for," or "what is appropriate in the particular situation." Manifestly certain things are never called for, appropriate, or a *mean* in any situation. In others the mean varies with time, place, circumstances, and persons. Thus what is temperate in food and drink depends on matters such as age, health, the occasion (for example, a feast, or the aftermath of strain or shock), and the variable circumstances of life. It may be difficult to know precisely what the right choice is in a given situation. Nonetheless, some choices are clearly better than others; and one is best of all, even when we cannot be certain of which one it is. Appropriate choices in particular situations are learned through experience and habit.

Comment on the remainder of the *Nichomachean Ethics* is not called for here. To give it would require a far more extensive essay than is allowable in these pages. One personal comment may be excusable, however. The *Nichomachean Ethics* has endured the test of time and may well be still the greatest work on ethics ever written. Other books have appeared to be more brilliant or startling. However, they either passed out of fashion, acquired an aesthetic or literary status, or became the subjects of special scholarly studies. Aristotle's ethics remains a living part of practical wisdom. His thought has become part of the fabric of our lives so deeply that familiarity may lead us not to see its greatness.

JAMES GORDON CLAPP

SELECTED BIBLIOGRAPHY

Translations

The Works of Aristotle. Translated into English under the editorship of Sir David Ross; 11 vols. New York and London: Oxford University Press.
Loeb Classical Library. Cambridge, Mass.: Harvard University Press (with English and Greek texts).
There are numerous other translations of individual works of Aristotle.

Commentaries

Barker, Ernest: The Political Thought of Plato and Aristotle. New York: G. P. Putnam's Sons; 1901.
Cherniss, Harold F.: Aristotle's Criticism of Plato and the Academy. Baltimore, Md.: Johns Hopkins University Press; 1944.
Cooper, Lane: The Poetics of Aristotle: Its Meaning and Influence. London: Longmans, Green; 1927.

Grote, George: *Aristotle*. 2 vols. London: John Murry; 1883.

Jaeger, Werner: *Aristotle: Fundamentals of the History of his Development*. New York and London: Oxford University Press; 1934.

Randall, John H.: *Aristotle*. New York: Columbia University Press; 1960.

Shute, Clarence W.: *The Psychology of Aristotle*. New York: Columbia University Press; 1941.

Solmsen, Friedrich: *Aristotle's System of the Physical World*. Ithaca, N.Y.: Cornell University Press; 1960.

Mure, G. R. G.: *Aristotle*. London: Oxford University Press; 1932.

Ross, Sir David: *Aristotle*. London: Methuen; 1930.

Spicer, Eulalie E.: *Aristotle's Conception of the Soul*. London: University of London Press; 1934.

St. Thomas Aquinas, *Aristotle's De Anima with the Commentaries of St. Thomas Aquinas*. Translated by Kenelm Foster and Sylvester Humphries. New Haven, Conn.: Yale University Press; 1954.

Wheelright, Philip, *Aristotle*. New York: The Odyssey Press; 1951.

DE ANIMA

❧ ⟫⟫⟫⟫⟪⟪⟪⟪ ❧

Book · I

Cognition is in our eyes a thing of beauty and worth, and [ch. 1 402a
this is true of one cognition more than another, either because it is
exact or because it relates to more important and remarkable objects. On
both these grounds we may with good reason claim a high place for the
enquiry concerning the soul. It would seem, too, than an acquaintance
with the subject contributes greatly to the whole domain of truth and,
more particularly, to the study of nature, the soul being virtually the
principle of all animal life.

Our aim is to discover and ascertain the nature and essence of soul
and, in the next place, all the accidents belonging to it; of which some
are thought to be attributes peculiar to the soul itself, while others, it is
held, belong to the animal also, but owe their existence to the soul. But
everywhere and in every way it is extremely difficult to arrive at any
trustworthy conclusion on the subject. It is the same here as in many
other enquiries. What we have to investigate is the essential nature of
things and the What. It might therefore be thought that there is a single
procedure applicable to all the objects whose essential nature we wish to
discover, as demonstration is applicable to the properties which go
along with them: in that case we should have to enquire what this
procedure is. If, however, there is no single procedure common to all
sciences for defining the What, our task becomes still more difficult, as
it will then be necessary to settle in each particular case the method
to be pursued. Further, even if it be evident that it consists in demonstration of some sort or division or some other procedure, there is still
room for much perplexity and error, when we ask from what premises
our enquiry should start, for there are different premises for different
sciences; for the science of numbers, for example, and plane geometry.

The first thing necessary is no doubt to determine under which of the summa genera soul comes and what it is; I mean, whether it is a particular thing, i.e. substance, or is quality or is quantity, or falls under any other of the categories already determined. We must further ask whether it is amongst things potentially existent or is rather a sort of actuality, the distinction being all-important. Again, we must consider whether it is divisible or indivisible; whether, again, all and   [402b every soul is homogeneous or not; and, if not, whether the difference between the various souls is a difference of species or a difference of genus: for at present discussions and investigations about soul would appear to be restricted to the human soul. We must take care not to overlook the question whether there is a single definition of soul answering to a single definition of animal; or whether there is a different definition for each separate soul, as for horse and dog, man and god: animal, as the universal, being regarded either as non-existent or, if existent, as logically posterior. This is a question which might equally be raised in regard to any other common predicate. Further, on the assumption that there are not several souls, but merely several different parts in the same soul, it is a question whether we should begin by investigating soul as a whole or its several parts. And here again it is difficult to determine which of these parts are really distinct from one another and whether the several parts, or their functions, should be investigated first. Thus, e.g. should the process of thinking come first or the mind that thinks, the process of sensation or the sensitive faculty? And so everywhere else. But, if the functions should come first, again will arise the question whether we should first investigate the correlative objects. Shall we take, e.g., the sensible object before the faculty of sense and the intelligible object before the intellect?

It would seem that not only is the knowledge of a thing's essential nature useful for discovering the causes of its attributes, as, e.g., in mathematics the knowledge of what is meant by the terms straight or curved, line or surface, aids us in discovering to how many right angles the angles of a triangle are equal: but also, conversely, a knowledge of the attributes is a considerable aid to the knowledge of what a thing is. For when we are able to give an account of all, or at any rate most, of the attributes as they are presented to us, then we shall be in a position to define most exactly the essential nature of the thing. In fact, the starting point of every demonstration is a definition of what something is. Hence the definitions which lead to no information about attributes and do not facilitate even conjecture respecting   [403a them have clearly been framed for dialectic and are void of content, one and all.

A further difficulty arises as to whether all attributes of the soul are also shared by that which contains the soul or whether any of them are peculiar to the soul itself: a question which it is indispensable, and yet by no means easy, to decide. It would appear that in most cases soul neither acts nor is acted upon apart from the body: as, e.g., in anger, confidence, desire and sensation in general. Thought, if anything, would seem to be peculiar to the soul. Yet, if thought is a sort of imagination, or not independent of imagination, it will follow that even thought cannot be independent of the body. If, then, there be any of the functions or affections of the soul peculiar to it, it will be possible for the soul to be separated from the body: if, on the other hand, there is nothing of the sort peculiar to it, the soul will not be capable of separate existence. As with the straight line, so with it. The line, *quâ* straight, has many properties; for instance, it touches the brazen sphere at a point; but it by no means follows that it will so touch it if separated. In fact it is inseparable, since it is always conjoined with body of some sort. So, too, the attributes of the soul appear to be all conjoined with body: such attributes, viz., as anger, mildness, fear, pity, courage; also joy, love and hate; all of which are attended by some particular affection of the body. This indeed is shown by the fact that sometimes violent and palpable incentives occur without producing in us exasperation or fear, while at other times we are moved by slight and scarcely perceptible causes, when the blood is up and the bodily condition that of anger. Still more is this evident from the fact that sometimes even without the occurrence of anything terrible men exhibit all the symptoms of terror. If this be so, the attributes are evidently forms or notions realised in matter. Hence they must be defined accordingly: anger, for instance, as a certain movement in a body of a given kind, or some part or faculty of it, produced by such and such a cause and for such and such an end. These facts at once bring the investigation of soul, whether in its entirety or in the particular aspect described, within the province of the natural philosopher. But every such attribute would be differently defined by the physicist and the dialectician or philosopher. Anger, for instance, would be defined by the dialectician as desire for retaliation or the like, by the physicist as a ferment of the blood or heat which is about the heart: [403b the one of them gives the matter, the other the form or notion. For the notion is the form of the thing, but this notion, if it is to be, must be realised in matter of a particular kind; just as in the case of a house. The notion or definition of a house would be as follows: a shelter to protect us from harm by wind or rain or scorching heat; while another will describe it as stones, bricks and timbers; and again another as the form realised in these materials and subserving given ends. Which then of these is the true physicist? Is it he who confines himself to the matter, while ignoring the form? Or he who treats of the form exclusively? I answer, it is rather he who in his definition takes account of both. What then of each of the other two? Or shall we rather say that there is no one who deals with properties which are not separable nor yet treated as separable, but the physicist deals with all the active properties or passive affections belonging to body of a given sort and the corresponding matter? All attributes not regarded as so belonging he leaves to someone else: who in certain cases is an expert, a carpenter, for instance, or a physician. The attributes which, though inseparable, are not regarded as properties of body of a given sort, but are reached by abstraction, fall within the province of the mathematician: while attributes which are regarded as having separate existence fall to the first philosopher or metaphysician. But to return to the point of digression. We were saying that the attributes of the soul are as such,—I mean, as anger and fear, inseparable from the physical matter of the animals to which they belong, and not, like line and surface, separable in thought.

In our enquiry concerning soul it is necessary to state the   [ch. 2 problems which must be solved as we proceed, and at the same time to collect the views of our predecessors who had anything to say on the subject, in order that we may adopt what is right in their conclusions and guard against their mistakes. Our enquiry will begin by presenting what are commonly held to be in a special degree the natural attributes of soul. Now there are two points especially wherein that which is animate is held to differ from the inanimate, namely, motion and the act of sensation: and these are approximately the two characteristics of soul handed down to us by our predecessors. There are some who maintain that soul is preeminently and primarily the cause of movement. But they imagined that that which is not itself in motion cannot move anything else, and thus they regarded the soul as a thing which is in motion. Hence Democritus affirms the soul to be a sort of   [404a fire or heat. For the "shapes" or atoms are infinite and those which are spherical he declares to be fire and soul: they may be compared with the so-called motes in the air, which are seen in the sunbeams that enter through our windows. The aggregate of such seeds, he tells us, forms the constituent elements of the whole of nature (and herein he agrees with Leucippus), while those of them which are spherical form the soul, because such figures most easily find their way through everything and, being themselves in motion, set other things in motion. The atomists assume that it is the soul which imparts motion to animals. It is for this reason that they make life depend upon respiration. For, when the surrounding air presses upon bodies and tends to extrude those atomic shapes which, because they are never at rest themselves, impart motion to animals, then they are reinforced from outside by the entry of other like atoms in respiration, which in fact, by helping to check compression and solidification, prevent the escape of the atoms already contained in the animals; and life, so they hold, continues so long as there is strength to do this. The doctrine of the Pythagoreans seems also to contain the same thought. Some of them identified soul with the motes in the air, others with that which sets these motes in motion: and as to these motes it has been stated that they are seen to be in incessant motion, even though there be a perfect calm. The view of others who describe the soul as that which moves itself tends in the same direction. For it would seem that all these thinkers regard motion as the most distinctive characteristic of the soul. Everything else, they think, is moved by the soul, but the soul is moved by itself: and this because they never see anything cause motion without itself being in motion. Similarly the soul is said to be the moving principle by Anaxagoras and all others who have held that mind sets the universe in motion; but not altogether in the same sense as by Democritus. The latter, indeed, absolutely identified soul and mind, holding that the presentation to the senses is the truth: hence, he observed, Homer had well sung of Hector in his swoon that he lay 'with other thoughts.' Democritus, then, does not use the term mind to denote a faculty conversant with truth, but regards mind as indentical with soul. Anaxagoras, however, is [404b] less exact in his use of the terms. In many places he speaks of mind as the cause of goodness and order, but elsewhere he identifies it with the soul: as where he attributes it to all animals, both great and small, high and low. As a matter of fact, however, mind in the sense of intelligence would not seem to be present in all animals alike, nor even in all men.

Those, then, who have directed their attention to the motion of the animate being, conceived the soul as that which is most capable of causing motion: while those who laid stress on its knowledge and perception of all that exists identified the soul with the ultimate principles, whether they recognised a plurality of these or only one. Thus Empedocles compounded soul out of all the elements, while at the same time regarding each one of them as a soul. His words are "With earth we see earth, with water water, with air bright air, but ravaging fire by fire, love by love, and strife by gruesome strife." In the same manner Plato in the *Timaeus* constructs the soul out of the elements. Like, he there maintains, is known by like, and the things we know are composed of the ultimate principles. In like manner it was explained in the lectures on philosophy, that the self-animal or universe is made up of the idea of One, and of the idea-numbers Two, or primary length, Three, primary breadth, and Four, primary depth, and similarly with all the rest of the ideas. And again this has been put in another way as follows: reason is the One, knowledge is the Two, because it proceeds by a single road to one conclusion, opinion is the number of a surface, Three, and sensation the number of a solid, Four. In fact, according to them the numbers, though they are the ideas themselves, or the ultimate principles, are nevertheless derived from elements. And things are judged, some by reason, others by knowledge, others again by opinion and others by sensation: while these idea-numbers are forms of things. And since the soul was held to be thus cognitive as well as capable of causing motion, some thinkers have combined the two and defined the soul as a self-moving number.

But there are differences of opinion as to the nature and number of the ultimate principles, especially between those thinkers who make the principles corporeal and those who make them incorporeal; and again between both of these and others who combine the two and   [405a take their principles from both. But, further, they differ also as to their number: some assuming a single principle, some a plurality. And, when they come to give an account of the soul, they do so in strict accordance with their several views. For they have assumed, not unnaturally, that the soul is that primary cause which in its own nature is capable of producing motion. And this is why some identified soul with fire, this being the element which is made up of the finest particles and is most nearly incorporeal, while further it is preeminently an element which both moves and sets other things in motion. Democritus has expressed more neatly the reason for each of these facts. Soul he regards as identical with mind, and this he makes to consist of the primary indivisible bodies and considers it to be a cause of motion from the fineness of its particles and their shape. Now the shape which is most susceptible of motion is the spherical; and of atoms of this shape mind, like fire, consists. Anaxagoras, while apparently understanding by mind something different from soul, as we remarked above, really treats both as a single nature, except that it is preeminently mind which he takes as his first principle; he says at any rate that mind alone of things that exist is simple, unmixed, pure. But he refers both knowledge and motion to the same principle, when he says that mind sets the universe in motion. Thales, too, apparently, judging from the anecdotes related of him, conceived soul as a cause of motion, if it be true that he affirmed the loadstone to possess soul, because it attracts iron. Diogenes, however, as also some others, identified soul with air. Air, they thought, is made up of the finest particles and is the first principle: and this explains the fact that the soul knows and is a cause of motion, knowing by virtue of being the primary element from which all else is derived, and causing motion by the extreme fineness of its parts. Heraclitus takes soul for his first principle, as he identifies it with the vapour from which he derives all other things, and further says that it is the least corporeal of things and in ceaseless flux; and that it is by something in motion that what is in motion is known; for he, like most philosophers, conceived all that exists to be in motion. Alcmaeon, too, seems to have had a similar conception. For soul, he maintains, is immortal because it is like the beings which are immortal; and it has this attribute in virtue of being ever in motion: for he attributes continuous and unending motion to everything which is divine, moon, sun, stars and the whole heaven. Among   [405b cruder thinkers there have been some, like Hippon, who have even asserted the soul to be water. The reason for this view seems to have been the fact that in all animals the seed is moist: in fact, Hippon refutes those who make the soul to be blood by pointing out that the seed is not blood, and that this seed is the rudimentary soul. Others, again, like Critias, maintain the soul to be blood, holding that it is sentience which is most distinctive of soul and that this is due to the nature of blood. Thus each of the four elements except earth has found its supporter. Earth, however, has not been put forward by anyone, except by those who have explained the soul to be derived from, or identical with, all the elements.

Thus practically all define the soul by three characteristics, motion, perception and incorporeality; and each of these characteristics is referred to the ultimate principles. Hence all who define soul by its capacity for knowledge either make it an element or derive it from the elements, being on this point, with one exception, in general agreement. Like, they tell us, is known by like; and therefore, since the soul knows all things, they say it consists of all the ultimate principles. Thus those thinkers who admit only one cause and one element, as fire or air, assume the soul also to be one element; while those who admit a plurality of principles assume plurality also in the soul. Anaxagoras alone says that mind cannot be acted upon and has nothing in common with any other thing. How, if such be its nature, it will know anything and how its knowledge is to be explained, he has omitted to state; nor do his utterances afford a clue. All those who introduce pairs of opposites among their principles make the soul also to consist of opposites; while those who take one or other of the two opposites, either hot or cold or something else of the sort, reduce the soul also to one or other of these elements. Hence, too, they etymologise according to their theories; some identify soul with heat, deriving $\zeta\tilde{\eta}\nu$ [1] from $\zeta\epsilon\tilde{\iota}\nu$ [2], and contend that this identity accounts for the word for life; others say that what is cold is

---

[1] $\zeta\tilde{\eta}\nu$ = to live.
[2] $\zeta\epsilon\tilde{\iota}\nu$ = to boil.

called soul from the respiratory process and consequent "cooling down," deriving ψυχή [3] from ψύχειν.[4] Such, then, are the views regarding soul which have come down to us and the grounds on which they are held.

We have to consider in the first place the subject of mo-   [ch. 3 tion. For, unless I am mistaken, the definition of soul as the self-moving, or as that which is capable of self-motion, misrepresents its es-   [406a sential nature: nay, more; it is quite impossible for soul to have the attribute of motion at all. To begin with, it has been already stated that a thing may cause motion without necessarily being moved itself. A thing is always moved in one of two ways; that is, either indirectly, through something else, or directly, of and through itself. We say things are moved through something else when they are in something else that is moved: as, for instance, sailors on board a ship: for they do not move in the same sense as the ship, for the ship moves of itself, they because they are in something else which is moved. This is evident if we consider the members of the body: for the motion proper to the feet and so to men also is walking, but it is not attributable to our sailors in the case supposed. There being thus two senses in which the term "to be moved" is used, we are now enquiring whether it is of and through itself that the soul is moved and partakes of motion.

Of motion there are four species, change of place or locomotion, change of quality or alteration, diminution and augmentation. It is, then, with one or more or all of these species that the soul will move. If it is not indirectly or *per accidens* that it moves, motion will be a natural attribute of soul; and, if this be so, it will also have position in space, since all the aforesaid species of motion are in space. But, if it be the essential nature of soul to move itself, motion will not be an accidental attribute of soul, as it is of whiteness or the length of three cubits; for these are also moved, but *per accidens*, viz. by the motion of the body to which these attributes belong. This, too, is why these attributes have no place belonging to them; but the soul will have a place, if indeed motion is its natural attribute.

Further, if it moves naturally, then it will also move under constraint; and, if under constraint, then also naturally. So likewise with rest. For, as it remains at rest naturally in any state into which it moves naturally, so similarly it remains at rest by constraint in any state into which it moves by constraint. But what is meant by constrained motions or states of rest of the soul it is not easy to explain, even though we give free play to fancy. Again, if its motion tends upward, it will be fire; if downward, earth; these being the motions proper to these natu-

---

[3] ψυχή = soul.
[4] ψύχειν = cooling down (souls); respiration.

ral bodies. And the same argument applies to directions of motion which are intermediate.

Again, since it appears that the soul sets the body in motion, it may reasonably be supposed to impart to it the motions which it has itself: and if so, then conversely it is true to say that the motion which the soul has itself is the motion which the body has. Now the [406b motion of the body is motion in space: therefore the motion of the soul is also motion in space, whether the whole soul so move, or only the parts, the whole remaining at rest. But if this is admissible, the soul might also conceivably quit the body and re-enter; and this would involve the consequence that dead animals may rise again.

To return now to motion *per accidens,* soul might certainly thus be moved by something external as well:—for the animal might be thrust by force. But a thing which has self-motion as part of its essential nature cannot be moved from without except incidentally; any more than that which is good in itself can be means to an end, or that which is good for its own sake can be so for the sake of something else. But, supposing the soul to be moved at all, one would say that sensible things would be the most likely to move it.

Again, even if soul does move itself, this is equivalent to saying that it is moved; and, all motion being defined as displacement of the thing moved *quâ* moved, it will follow that the soul will be displaced from its own essential nature, if it be true that its self-movement is not an accident, but that motion belongs to the essence of soul in and of itself. Some say that the soul in fact moves the body, in which it is, in the same way in which it moves itself. So, for example, Democritus; and herein he resembled Philippus, the comic poet, who tells us that Daedalus endowed the wooden Aphrodite with motion, simply by pouring in quicksilver: this is very similar to what Democritus says. For according to him the spherical atoms, which from their nature can never remain still, being moved, tend to draw the whole body after them and thus set it in motion. But do these same atoms, we shall ask in our turn, produce rest, as well as motion? How this should be, it is difficult, if not impossible, to say. And, speaking generally, it is not in this way that the soul would seem to move the animal, but by means of purpose of some sort, that is, thought.

In the same way the Platonic *Timaeus* explains on physical grounds that the soul sets the body in motion, for by its own motion it sets the body also in motion, because it is closely interwoven with it. For when it had been made out of the elements and divided in harmonical ratios in order that it might have a native perception of proportion and that the universe might move in harmonic revolutions, he, the creator, proceeded to bend the straight line into a circle; and then to split the

one circle into two, intersecting at two points; and one of   [407a
the two circles he split into seven, the revolutions of heaven being regarded as the motions of the soul. In the first place, it is not right to
call the soul a magnitude. For by the soul of the universe Timaeus
clearly intends something of the same sort as what is known as mind:
he can hardly mean that it is like the sensitive or appetitive soul, whose
movements are not circular. But the thinking mind is one and continuous in the same sense as the process of thinking. Now thinking consists of thoughts. But the unity of these thoughts is a unity of succession, the unity of a number, and not the unity of a magnitude. This
being so, neither is mind continuous in this latter sense, but either it
is without parts or else it is continuous in a different sense from an
extended magnitude. For how can it possibly think if it be a magnitude?
Will it think with some one or other of its parts: such parts being taken
either in the sense of magnitudes or in the sense of points, if a point
can be called a part? If it be with parts in the sense of points, and
there is an infinity of these, clearly mind will never reach the end of
them; while, if they be taken in the sense of magnitudes, mind will have
the same thoughts times without end. But experience shows that we
can think a thought once and no more. Again, if it be enough for the
soul to apprehend with one or other of its parts, what need is there
for it to be moving in a circle or to have magnitude at all? But, if
it is necessary to thought that the mind should bring the whole circle
into contact, what does the contact of the several parts mean? Again,
how will it think that which is divisible by means of that which is without parts, or that which is without parts by means of that which is
divisible? It must be mind which is meant by the circle in question.
For when mind moves it thinks; when a circle moves it revolves.
If, then, thought is a revolution, the circle which has such a revolution must be mind. But then it will go on thinking of something forever, for this is required by the eternity of the revolution. To practical
thinking there are limits, for it always implies an external end; while
speculative thinking is determined in the same way as the logical explanations which express it. Now every explanation consists either in
definition or in demonstration. But demonstrations have a premiss for
starting-point and reach a kind of goal in the inference or conclusion; while, even if they never reach a conclusion, at all events they
do not revert to the starting-point, but with the aid of a succession of
middle terms and extremes advance in a straight line. But circular movement returns to the point from which it started. Definitions, too, are
all determinate. Besides, if the same revolution recurs again and again,
the mind will be obliged to think the same thing again and again. Further, it is a sort of rest or coming to a halt, and not motion, which

thinking resembles: and we may say the same of the syllogism. Nor, again, will that which does not move easily, but under constraint, even realise happiness. If the motion of soul be not its essence, it [407b will be an unnatural motion. And the entanglement of the mind in the body without the possibility of release is painful; nay, it is to be avoided, if indeed it is really better for mind to be independent of body, a view commonly expressed and widely accepted. Also it is not clear why the heaven revolves in a circle; seeing that circular motion is neither implied by the essence of soul (that form of movement being indeed merely accidental to it), nor due to the body: on the contrary it is rather the soul which causes the motion of the body. Besides, we are not even told that it is better so: yet surely the reason why God made the soul revolve in a circle ought to have been that movement was better for it than rest, and this form of movement better than any other.

But such an enquiry as this belongs more appropriately to a different subject: so let us dismiss it for the present. We may, however, note here another absurdity which is involved in this as in most other theories concerning the soul. They attach the soul to, and enclose it in, body, without further determining why this happens and what is the condition of the body. And yet some such explanation would seem to be required, as it is owing to their relationship that the one acts, the other is acted upon, that the one is moved, and the other causes it to move; and between two things taken at random no such mutual relations exist. The supporters of such theories merely undertake to explain the nature of the soul. Of the body which is to receive it they have nothing more to say: just as if it were possible for any soul taken at random, according to the Pythagorean stories, to pass into any body. This is absurd, for each body appears to have a distinctive form or shape of its own. It is just like talking of a transmigration of carpentry into flutes: for the craft must employ the right tools and the soul the right body.

There is yet another opinion concerning soul which has [ch. 4 come down to us, commending itself to many minds as readily as any that is put forward, although it has been severely criticised even in the popular discussions of the present day. The soul is asserted to be a kind of harmony, for harmony is on this view a blending or combining of opposites, and the components of the body are opposites. And yet this harmony must mean either a certain proportion in the components or else the combining of them; and the soul cannot possibly be either of these. Furthermore, to cause motion is no attribute of a harmony: yet this function more than any other is all but universally as- [408a signed to soul. Again, it is more in harmony with the facts to apply the term harmony to health or bodily excellence generally than to soul, as is very clearly seen when we try to assign to a harmony of whatever kind the affections or functions of the soul: it is difficult to harmonise them.

Further, if we use the word harmony with a twofold application; first, and in its most natural sense, of those magnitudes which have motion and position, to denote the combining of them into a whole, when they are so closely fitted together that they do not admit between them anything of the same kind; and then in a secondary sense to denote the proportion subsisting between the components of a mixture: in neither sense is it reasonable to call soul a harmony. The view which regards it as a combining of the parts of the body is singularly open to criticism. For there are many combinings of the parts, and they combine in many ways. What part, then, is that whose combining with the rest we must assume to be the intellect, and in what way does it combine? Or again, what of the sensitive and appetitive faculties? But it is equally absurd to regard the soul as the proportion determining the mixture. For the elements are not mixed in the same proportion in flesh as in bone. Thus it will follow that there are many souls, and that, too, all over the body, if we assume that all members consist of the elements variously commingled and that the proportion determining the mixture is a harmony, that is, soul. This is a question we might ask Empedocles; who says that each of the parts is determined by a certain proportion. Is the soul, then, this proportion, or is it rather developed in the frame as something distinct? And, further, is it a mixture at random or a mixture in the right proportion which he ascribes to Love: and, if the latter, is Love the proportion itself or something other than the proportion and distinct from it? Such, then, are the difficulties involved in this view. On the other hand, if soul is something distinct from the mixture, how comes it that it is destroyed simultaneously with the disappearance of the quiddity of the flesh and of the other parts of the animal? And, further, assuming that each of the separate parts has not a soul of its own, unless the soul be the proportion of their admixture, what is it that perishes when the soul quits the body?

From what has been said it is clear that the soul cannot be a harmony and cannot revolve in a circle. But incidentally it can, as we have seen, move and set itself in motion: for instance; the body in which it is may move, and be set in motion by the soul: otherwise it cannot possibly move from place to place. The question whether the soul is moved would more naturally arise in view of such facts as the   [408b following. The soul is said to feel pain and joy, confidence and fear, and again to be angry, to perceive and to think; and all these states are held to be movements: which might lead one to infer that soul itself is moved. But this is no necessary inference. For suppose it ever so true that to feel pain or joy and to think are movements, that to experience each of these is to be moved and that the movement is due to the soul: suppose that to be angry, for instance, or to be afraid means a particular movement of the heart, and that to think means a movement of this or of some other part, some of these movements being movements of locomotion, others of qualitative change (of what sort and how produced does not concern us here): yet, even then, to speak of the soul as feeling anger is as if one should say that the soul weaves or builds. Doubtless it would be better not to say that the soul pities or learns or thinks, but that the man does so with the soul: and this, too, not in the sense that the motion occurs in the soul, but in the sense that motion sometimes reaches to, sometimes starts from, the soul. Thus, sensation originates in particular objects, while recollection, starting from the soul, is directed towards the movements or traces of movements in the sense-organs. But intellect would seem to be developed in us as a self-existing substance and to be imperishable. For, if anything could destroy it, it would be the feebleness of age. But, as things are, no doubt what occurs is the same as in the case of the sense-organs. If an aged man could procure an eye of the right sort, he would see just as well as a young man. Hence old age must be due to an affection or state not of the soul as such, but of that in which the soul resides, just as in the case in intoxication and disease. In like manner, then, thought and the exercise of knowledge are enfeebled through the loss of something else within, but are in themselves impassive. But reasoning, love and hatred are not attributes of the thinking faculty but of its individual possessor, in so far as he possesses it. Hence when this possessor perishes, there is neither memory nor love: for these never did belong to the thinking faculty, but to the composite whole which has perished, while the intellect is doubtless a thing more divine and is impassive.

From the foregoing it is clear that the soul is incapable of motion; and, if it is not moved at all, clearly it does not move itself. Now of all the views that have been put forward by far the most irrational is that which makes the soul a self-moving number. Its supporters are involved in many impossibilities, not only in those which arise from attributing motion to the soul, but also in others of a special character due to calling it a number. For how are we to conceive of   [409a a unit, a thing which is without parts or differences, as in motion? By what would it be moved, and in what way? For if it is capable of imparting motion as well as of being moved, it must admit differences. Further, since they say that a line by its motion generates a surface and that a point by its motion generates a line, the movements of the units will also be lines, for a point is a unit having position. But the number of the soul must, from the nature of the case, be somewhere and have position. Again, if you subtract a number or unit from a number, a different number remains: whereas plants and many animals continue to live when divided and seem to have specifically the same soul in each segment. Besides, it would seem to make no difference whether we say units or tiny particles. For if the little round atoms of Democritus be converted into points and only their sum-total be retained, in such sum-total there will still be a part which moves and a part which is moved, just as there is in that which is extended. The truth of this statement does not depend upon the size of the atoms, whether great or small, but upon the fact that there is a sum-total or quantity of them. Hence there must be something to set the units in motion. But if in the animal the part which causes motion is the soul, then it is so likewise in the number: so that it will not be both that which causes motion and that which is moved which is the soul, but that which causes motion only. How then can this cause of motion be a unit? For if it were so there must be some difference between it and the other units. But what is there to differentiate points which are units, except position? If, then, the units, that is the points, in the body are distinct from the units of soul, the units of soul will be in the same place as the points, for each unit will occupy the space of a point. And yet if two things can be in the same place, why not an infinite number? When the place which things occupy is indivisible, the things themselves are also indivisible. If, on the other hand, the number of the soul consists of the points in the body, or if the soul is the number of such points, why are not all bodies possessed of soul? For in all bodies there would seem to be points: nay, an infinity of points. And, further, how can the points be separated and set free from the bodies to which they belong; unless, indeed, we are prepared to resolve lines into points?

It comes to this, then, as we have said, first, that this [ch. 5 view coincides with that which makes of the soul a body composed of fine particles; next, that its agreement with Democritus as [409b to the manner in which he makes the body to be moved by the soul gives it an especial absurdity of its own. If the soul resides in the whole sentient body, on the assumption that the soul is a sort of body it necessarily follows that two bodies occupy the same space. Those who call the soul a number have to assume many points in the one point, or else that everything corporeal has a soul; unless the number that comes to exist in the body is a different number, quite distinct from the sum of the points already present in the body. Hence it follows that the animal is moved by the number in the same way precisely as we said Democritus moved it. For what difference does it make whether we speak of small round atoms or large units, or indeed of units in spatial motion at all? Either way it is necessary to make the motion of the animal depend on the motion of these atoms or units. Such, then, are some of the difficulties confronting those who join motion and number: and there are many others, since it is impossible that the conjunction of motion with number should form even an attribute, much less the definition, of soul. This will be evident if we try to deduce from this definition the affections and functions of the soul; its reasonings, perceptions, pleasures, pains, and so forth. For, as we said above, from the account given it is difficult even to divine what these functions are.

Three modes of defining the soul have come down to us: some defined it as that which, in virtue of its self-motion, is most capable of causing motion; others as the body which consists of the finest particles, or which is more nearly incorporeal than anything else. And we have pretty fully explained what difficulties and inconsistencies these views present. It remains to consider what is meant by saying that the soul is composed of the elements. Soul, we are told, is composed of the elements in order that it may perceive and know each several thing. But this theory necessarily involves many impossibilities. For it is assumed that like is known by like; which implies that soul is identical with the things that it knows. These elements, however, are not all that exists: there are a great, or perhaps we should say rather, an infinite number of other things as well, namely, those which are compounded of the elements. Granted, then, that it is possible for the soul to know and to perceive the constituent elements of all these composite things, with what will it know or perceive the compound itself? I mean, what God or man is; what flesh or bone is: and so likewise with regard to any other composite thing. For it is not elements   [410a taken anyhow which constitute this or that thing, but only those which are united in a given proportion or combination, as Empedocles says of bone:—

"Then did the bounteous earth in broad-bosomed crucibles win out of eight parts two from the sheen of moisture and four from the fire-god; and the bones came into being all white."

It is therefore of no use for the elements to be in the soul, unless it also contains their proportions and the mode of combining them. For each element will know its like, but there will be nothing to know bone or man, unless these also are to be present in the soul: which, I need hardly say, is impossible. Who would ask if stone or man resides in the soul? And similarly with that which is good and that which is not good: and so for all the rest.

Being, again, is a term which has various meanings, signifying sometimes the particular thing, sometimes quantity or quality or any other of the categories which have been already determined. Is the soul to be derived from all of these, or not? It cannot be: the general opinion is that there are no elements common to all the categories. Does the soul, then, consist of those elements alone which are the elements of substances? How then does it know each of the other categories? Or will they say that each summum genus has special elements and principles of its own, and that the soul is composed of these? Then soul will be at once quantity, quality and substance. But it is impossible from the elements of quantity to derive substance or anything but quantity. These, then, and others like them are the difficulties which confront those who derive soul from all the elements. There is a further inconsistency in maintaining that like is unaffected by like and yet at the same time that like perceives like and knows like by like. But they assume that perceiving is a sort of being acted upon or moved. And the same holds of thinking and knowing.

Of the many problems and difficulties involved in holding with Empedocles that each thing is known through corporeal elements and by reference to its like (what has just been said is evidence).—For, it would seem, whatever within the bodies of animals consists entirely of earth, such as bones, sinews, hair, perceives nothing at all,   [410b and consequently cannot perceive its like; as in consistency it should. Moreover, each one of the elemental principles will have a far larger share of ignorance than of intelligence; there being many things of which it will be ignorant and only one which it will know: in fact, it will be ignorant of all besides that one. It follows, for Empedocles at any rate, that God is quite the most unintelligent of beings. There is one of the elements, viz. Strife, which he, and he alone, will not know, while mortal things, being composed of all the elements, will know them all. And in general, seeing that everything is either an element or derived from one or more or all elements, why should not all things that exist have soul? For they must certainly know one thing or some things or all. It might further be asked what it is that gives them unity. For the elements, at all events, correspond to matter. That other principle, whatever it be, which holds them together, is supreme. Yet it is impossible that anything should be superior to the soul and overrule it; and still more impossible that anything should overrule intelligence. This, it may reasonably be held, has a natural priority and authority. Yet we are told that the elements are prior to all other things that exist.

And it is characteristic, alike of those who derive the soul from the elements on the ground of perception and knowledge, and of those who define it as the thing most capable of causing motion, that their assertions do not apply to soul in every form. For not all sentient beings can cause motion; some animals are seen to be stationary in one place.

And yet it is at all events a received view that this, namely, change of place, is the one form of motion which the soul imparts to the animal. Similarly with those who derive intelligence and the faculty of sense from the elements. For plants are found to live without any share in locomotion or sensation, and many animals to be destitute of thought. If we waive this point and assume intellect to be a part of the soul, and the faculty of sense likewise, even then their statements would not apply generally to all soul, nor to the whole of any one soul. The account given in the so-called Orphic poems is open to the same strictures. For the soul, it is there asserted, enters from the universe in the process of respiration, being borne upon the winds. Now it is impossible that this should be so with plants or even with some ani-   [411a mals, seeing that they do not all respire: a point which the upholders of this theory have overlooked. And if the soul is to be constructed out of the elements, there is no need to employ them all, the one of a pair of contraries being sufficient to discern both itself and its opposite. For by that which is straight we discern both the straight and the crooked, the carpenter's rule being the test of both. On the other hand that which is crooked is not a test of itself or of that which is straight.

There are some, too, who say that soul is interfused throughout the universe: which is perhaps why Thales supposed all things to be full of gods. But this view presents some difficulties. For why should the soul not produce an animal, when present in air or fire, and yet do so when present in the compounds of these elements: and that, too, though in the former case it is believed to be purer? One might also enquire why the soul present in air is purer and more immortal than soul in animals. Whichever of the two suppositions open to us we adopt is absurd and irrational. To speak of fire or air as an animal is very irrational; and on the other hand not to call them animals, if they contain soul, is absurd. But it would seem that the reason why they suppose soul to be in these elements is that the whole is homogeneous with its parts. So that they cannot help regarding universal soul as also homogeneous with the parts of it in animals, since it is through something of the surrounding element being cut off and enclosed in animals that the animals become endowed with soul. But if the air when split up remains homogeneous, and yet soul is divisible into non-homogeneous parts, it is clear that, although one part of soul may be present in the air, there is another part which is not. Either, then, soul must be homogeneous, or else it cannot be present in every part of the universe.

From what has been said it is evident that it is not because the soul is compounded of the elements that knowledge belongs to it, nor is it correct or true to say that the soul is moved. Knowledge, however, is an attribute of the soul, and so are perception, opinion, desire, wish and appetency generally; animal locomotion also is produced by the soul; and likewise growth, maturity and decay. Shall we then say that each of these belongs to the whole soul, that we think, that   [411b is, and perceive and are moved and in each of the other operations act and are acted upon with the whole soul, or that the different operations are to be assigned to different parts? And what of life itself? Does it reside in any single one or more or all of these parts? Or has it a cause entirely distinct? Now some say that the soul is divisible and that one part of it thinks, another desires. What is it then which holds the soul together, if naturally divisible? Assuredly it is not the body: on the contrary, the soul seems rather to hold the body together; at all events, when it has departed, the body disperses in air and rots away. If, then, the unity of soul is due to some other thing that other thing would be properly speaking, soul. We shall need, then, to repeat the enquiry respecting it also, whether it is one or manifold. For, if it has unity, why not attribute unity to the soul itself at the outset? If, however, it be divisible, then again reason will go on to ask what it is that holds it together, and so the enquiry will go on to infinity. It might also be asked what power each of the parts of the soul exercises in the body. For, if the entire soul holds together the whole body, then each of its parts ought properly to hold together some part of the body. But this seems impossible. For it is difficult even to conjecture what part the intellect will hold together or how it can hold any part together. It is found that plants, and among animals certain insects or annelida, live when divided, which implies that the soul in their segments is specifically, though not numerically, the same. At any rate, each of the two segments retains sentience and the power of locomotion for some time: that they do not continue to do so is not surprising, as they lack the organs requisite to maintain their nature. But none the less all the parts of the soul are contained in each of the two segments, and the two halves of the soul are homogeneous alike with one another and with the whole; a fact which implies that, while the parts of the soul are inseparable from one another, the soul as a whole is divisible. It would seem that the vital principle in plants also is a sort of soul. For this principle is the only one common to plants and animals; and, while it can be separated from the sensitive principle, no being which has sensation is without it.

Book · I I

So much for the theories of soul handed down by our   [ch. 1 412a predecessors. Let us, then, make a fresh start and try to determine what soul is and what will be its most comprehensive definition. Now there is one class of existent things which we call substance, including under the term, firstly, matter, which in itself is not this or that; secondly, shape or form, in virtue of which the term this or that is at once applied; thirdly, the whole made up of matter and form. Matter is identical with potentiality, form with actuality. And there are two meanings of actuality: knowledge illustrates the one, exercise of knowledge the other. Now bodies above all things are held to be substances, particularly such bodies as are the work of nature; for to these all the rest owe their origin. Of natural bodies some possess life and some do not: where by life we mean the power of self-nourishment and of independent growth and decay. Consequently every natural body possessed of life must be substance, and substance of the composite order. And since in fact we have here body with a certain attribute, namely, the possession of life, the body will not be the soul: for the body is not an attribute of a subject, it stands rather for a subject of attributes, that is, matter. It must follow, then, that soul is substance in the sense that it is the form of a natural body having in it the capacity of life. Such substance is actuality. The soul, therefore, is the actuality of the body above described. But the term 'actuality' is used in two senses; in the one it answers to knowledge, in the other to the exercise of knowledge. Clearly in this case it is analogous to knowledge: for sleep, as well as waking, implies the presence of soul; and, whilst waking is analogous to the exercise of knowledge, sleep is analogous to the possession of knowledge without its exercise; and in the same individual the possession of knowledge comes in order of time before its exercise. Hence soul is the first actuality of a natural body having in it the capacity of life. And a body which is possessed of organs answers to this description.—We may note that the parts of plants, as well as those of animals, are   [412b organs, though of a very simple sort: for instance, a leaf is the sheath of the pod and the pod of the fruit. The roots, again, are analogous to the mouths of animals, both serving to take in nourishment.—If, then, we have to make a general statement touching soul in all its forms, the soul will be the first actuality of a natural body furnished with organs. Hence there is no need to enquire whether soul and body are one, any more than whether the wax and the imprint are one; or, in general, whether the matter of a thing is the same with that of which it is the matter. For, of all the various meanings borne by the terms unity and being, actuality is the meaning which belongs to them by the fullest right.

It has now been stated in general terms what soul is, namely, substance as notion or form. And this is the quiddity of such and such a body. Suppose, for example, that any instrument, say, an axe, were a natural body, its axeity would be its substance, would in fact be its soul. If this were taken away, it would cease, except in an equivocal sense, to be an axe. But the axe is after all an axe. For it is not of a body of this kind that the soul is the quiddity, that is, the notion or form, but of a natural body of a particular sort, having in itself the origination of motion and rest.

Further, we must view our statement in the light of the parts of the body. For, if the eye were an animal, eyesight would be its soul, this being the substance as notion or form of the eye. The eye is the matter of eyesight, and in default of eyesight it is no longer an eye, except equivocally, like an eye in stone or in a picture. What has been said of the part must be understood to apply to the whole living body; for, as the sensation of a part of the body is to that part, so is sensation as a whole to the whole sentient body as such. By that which has in it the capacity of life is meant not the body which has lost its soul, but that which possesses it. Now the seed in animals, like the fruit in plants, is that which is potentially such and such a body. As, then, the cutting of the axe or the seeing of the eye is full actuality, so, too, is the waking state; while the soul is actuality in the same sense as eyesight   [413a and the capacity of the instrument. The body, on the other hand, is simply that which is potentially existent. But, just as in the one case the eye means the pupil in conjunction with the eyesight, so in the other soul and body together constitute the animal.

Now it needs no proof that the soul—or if it is divisible into parts, certain of its parts—cannot be separated from the body, for there are cases where the actuality belongs to the parts themselves. There is, however, no reason why some parts should not be separated, if they are not the actualities of any body whatever. Again, it is not clear whether the soul may not be the actuality of the body as the sailor is of the ship. This, then, may suffice for an outline or provisional sketch of soul.

But, as it is from the things which are naturally obscure,   [ch. 2 though more easily recognised by us, that we proceed to what is clear and, in the order of thought, more knowable, we must employ this method in trying to give a fresh account of soul. For it is not enough that the defining statement should set forth the fact, as most definitions do; it should also contain and present the cause: whereas in practice what is stated in the definition is usually no more than a conclusion. For example, what is quadrature? The construction of an equilateral rectangle equal in area to a given oblong. But such a definition expresses merely the conclusion. Whereas, if you say that quadrature is the discovery of a mean proportional, then you state the reason.

We take, then, as our starting-point for discussion that it is life which distinguishes the animate from the inanimate. But the term life

is used in various senses; and, if life is present in but a single one of
these senses, we speak of a thing as living. Thus there is intellect, sensation, motion from place to place and rest, the motion concerned with
nutrition and, further, decay and growth. Hence it is that all plants
are supposed to have life. For apparently they have within themselves
a faculty and principle whereby they grow and decay in opposite directions. For plants do not grow upwards without growing downwards;
they grow in both directions equally, in fact in all directions, as many
as are constantly nourished and therefore continue to live, so long
as they are capable of absorbing nutriment. This form of life can be
separated from the others, though in mortal creatures the others cannot
be separated from it. In the case of plants the fact is manifest: for
they have no other faculty of soul at all.

It is, then, in virtue of this principle that all living things   [413b
live, whether animals or plants. But it is sensation primarily which constitutes the animal. For, provided they have sensation, even those creatures which are devoid of movement and do not change their place are
called animals and are not merely said to be alive. Now the primary
sense in all animals is touch. But, as the nutritive faculty may exist
without touch or any form of sensation, so also touch may exist apart
from the other senses. By nutritive faculty we mean the part of the
soul in which even plants share. Animals, however, are found universally to have the sense of touch: why this is so in each of the two
cases will be stated hereafter.

For the present it may suffice to say that the soul is the origin
of the functions above enumerated and is determined by them, namely,
by capacities of nutrition, sensation, thought, and by motion. But
whether each one of these is a soul or part of a soul and, if a part,
whether it is only logically distinct or separable in space also is a question, the answer to which is in some cases not hard to see: other cases
present difficulties. For, just as in the case of plants some of them are
found to live when divided and separated from each other (which implies that the soul in each plant, though actually one, is potentially
several souls), so, too, when insects or annelida are cut up, we see the
same thing happen with other varieties of soul: I mean, each of the
segments has sensation and moves from place to place, and, if it has
sensation, it has also imagination and appetency. For, where there is
sensation, there is also pleasure and pain: and, where these are, desire
also must of necessity be present. But as regards intellect and the speculative faculty the case is not yet clear. It would seem, however, to be
a distinct species of soul, and it alone is capable of separation from the
body, as that which is eternal from that which is perishable. The remaining parts of the soul are, as the foregoing consideration shows, not

separable in the way that some allege them to be: at the same time it is clear that they are logically distinct. For the faculties of sensation and of opinion taken in the abstract are distinct, since to have sensation and to opine are distinct. And so it is likewise with each of the other faculties above mentioned. Again, while some animals possess all these functions, others have only some of them, others only one. It is this which will differentiate animal from animal. The reason why this is so   [414a must be investigated hereafter. The case is similar with the several senses: some animals have all of them, others some of them, others again only one, the most indispensable, that is, touch.

Now "that by which we live and have sensation" is a phrase with two meanings, answering to the two meanings of "that by which we know" (the latter phrase means, firstly, knowledge and, secondly, soul, by either of which we say we know). Similarly that by which we have health means either health itself or a certain part, if not the whole, of the body. Now of these knowledge and health are the shape and in some sort form, the notion and virtual activity, of that which is capable of receiving in the one case knowledge, in the other health: that is to say, it is in that which is acted upon or conditioned that the activity of the causal agencies would seem to take effect. Now the soul is that whereby primarily we live, perceive, and have understanding: therefore it will be a species of notion or form, not matter or substratum. Of the three meanings of substance mentioned above, form, matter and the whole made up of these two, matter is potentiality and form is actuality. And, since the whole made up of the two is endowed with soul, the body is not the actuality of soul, but soul the actuality of a particular body. Hence those are right who regard the soul as not independent of body and yet at the same time as not itself a species of body. It is not body, but something belonging to body, and therefore resides in body and, what is more, in such and such a body. Our predecessors were wrong in endeavouring to fit the soul into a body without further determination of the nature and qualities of that body: although we do not even find that of any two things taken at random the one will admit the other. And this result is what we might expect. For the actuality of each comes naturally to be developed in the potentiality of each thing: in other words, in the appropriate matter. From these considerations, then, it is manifest that soul is a certain actuality, a notion or form, of that which has the capacity to be endowed with soul.

Of the powers of soul above mentioned, namely, those of   [ch. 3 nutrition, appetency, sensation, locomotion and understanding, some living things, as we remarked, possess all, others some, others again only one. Plants possess the nutritive faculty only: other things along with this have sensation; and, if sensation, then also appetency: where under appetency we include desire, anger and wish. But all animals have at least one sense, touch: and, where sensation is found, there [414b is pleasure and pain, and that which causes pleasure and pain; and, where these are, there also is desire, desire being appetite for what is pleasurable. Again, they have a sensation concernd with nutriment, touch being such a sense. For it is by what is dry and moist, hot and cold, that all living things are nourished (and these qualities are perceived by touch, whereas the other sensibles are not, except incidentally): for sound, colour and odour contribute nothing to nutriment, while flavour is one of the tangible objects. Hunger again, and thirst are forms of desire, the one for what is hot or dry, the other for what is cold or moist. Flavour is, as it were, the seasoning of these. We will deal with these in detail hereafter: at present let it suffice to say that all animals which have the sense of touch are also endowed with appetency. Whether they have imagination is not clear: this, too, must be considered later. Some have in addition the power of locomotion. Others— that is to say, man and any other species like man or, possibly, superior to him—have also the thinking faculty and intellect.

From this it is clear that there is one definition of soul exactly as there is one definition of figure: for there is in the one case no figure excepting triangle, quadrilateral and the rest, nor is there in the other any species of soul apart from those above mentioned. Again, a definition might be constructed which should apply to all figures, but not specially to any species of figure. And similarly with the species of soul above enumerated. Hence it would be absurd here as elsewhere to seek a general definition which will not be properly a definition of anything in existence and will not be applicable to the particular irreducible species before us, to the neglect of the definition which is so applicable.

The types of soul resemble the series of figures. For, alike in figures and in things animate, the earlier form exists potentially in the later, as, for instance, the triangle potentially in the quadrilateral, and the nutritive faculty in that which has sensation. So that we must examine in each case separately, what is the soul of plant, of man or of beast. Why they are related in this order of succession remains to be considered. There is no sensitive faculty apart from the nutri- [415a tive: and yet the latter exists without the former in plants. Again, none of the other senses is found apart from touch; while touch is found apart from the others, many animals having neither sight nor hearing nor sense of smell. Also of those which possess sensation, some can move from place to place, others cannot. Lastly and most rarely, they have the reasoning faculty and thought. For those perishable creatures which possess reason are endowed with all the other species of soul, but not all those which possess each of the other faculties have reason. Indeed, some of them have not even imagination, while others live by imagination alone. As for the speculative intellect, it calls for a separate discussion. Meanwhile it is clear that an account of the several faculties is at the same time the most appropriate account of soul.

The enquirer who approaches this subject must ascertain   [ch. 4 what each of these faculties is before he proceeds to investigate the questions next in order and so forth. But if we are asked to state what each of these is; that is to say, what the cognitive, sensitive and nutritive faculties respectively are, we must begin by stating what the act of thinking is and what the act of sensation is. For activities and functions are logically prior to faculties. But, if so, and if a study of the correlative objects should have preceded, these objects will for the same reason have to be defined first: I mean, nutriment and the sensible and intelligible. Consequently we have first to treat of nutriment and of generation.

The nutritive soul belongs to other living things as well as man, being the first and most widely distributed faculty, in virtue of which all things possess life. Its functions are reproduction and assimilation of nutriment. For it is the most natural function in all living things, if perfect and not defective or spontaneously generated, to reproduce their species; animal producing animal and plant plant, in order that they may, so far as they can, share in the eternal and the divine. For it is that which all things yearn after, and that is the final   [415b cause of all their natural activity. Here final cause is an ambiguous term, which denotes either the purpose for which, or the person for whom, a thing is done. Since, then, individual things are incapable of sharing continuously in the eternal and the divine, because nothing in the world of perishables can abide numerically one and the same, they partake in the eternal and divine, each in the only way it can, some more, some less. That is to say, each persists, though not in itself, yet in a representative which is specifically, not numerically, one with it.

Now the soul is cause and origin of the living body. But cause and origin are terms used in various senses: accordingly soul is cause in the three senses of the word already determined. For the soul is the cause of animate bodies as being in itself the origin of motion, as final cause and as substance. Clearly it is so as substance, substance being the cause of all existence. And for living things existence means life, and it is the soul which is the cause and origin of life. Furthermore, actuality is the notion or form of that which has potential existence. Manifestly, too, the soul is final cause. For nature, like intelligence, acts for a purpose, and this purpose is for it an end. Such an end the soul is in animals, and this in the order of nature, for all the natural bodies are instruments of soul: and this is as true of the bodies of plants as of those of animals, shewing that all are means to the soul as end; where end has two senses, the purpose for which and the person for whom. Moreover, the soul is also the origin of motion from place to place, but not all living things have this power of locomotion. Qualitative change, also, and growth are due to soul. For sensation is supposed to be a sort of qualitative change, and nothing devoid of soul has sensation. The same holds of growth and decay. For nothing undergoes natural decay or growth except it be nourished, and nothing is nourished unless it shares in life.

Empedocles is mistaken in adding that in plants, in so far as they strike their roots downwards, growth takes place because the earth in them has a natural tendency in this direction and that, when they shoot upwards, it is because the fire in them has a similar tend-   [416a] ency upwards. He is wrong in his view of up and down. For up and down are not the same for all individuals as for the universe. On the contrary, the roots of plants correspond to the heads of animals, if we are to make identity and diversity of organs depend upon their functions. Besides, what is it that holds together the fire and the earth, tending, as they do, in opposite directions? For they will be rent asunder, unless there is something to prevent it: while, if there is, it is this which is the soul and the cause of growth and nourishment.

Some hold the nature of fire to be singly and solely the cause of nourishment and growth. For it would seem that fire is the only body or element which of itself is nourished and grows. Hence fire might be supposed to be the operative cause, both in plants and animals. Whereas, though it is in a sense a joint cause, it is not a cause absolutely: it is rather the soul which is so. For fire goes on growing to infinity, as long as there is fuel to be consumed, but in natural wholes there is always a limit or proportion which determines growth and size. But this belongs to the soul and not to fire, to form rather than to matter.

The nutritive faculty of the soul being the same as the reproductive, it is necessary first to give a definition of nutriment. For it is by the nutritive function that this faculty is separated off from the others. The common view is that contrary is nutriment to contrary; though not in every case, but wherever each of two contraries is not only generated by, but derives growth from, the other. For many things are derived from one another, but not all of them are quantities: thus the sick man becomes well. But it is found that even the contraries supposed to derive growth from each other are not fed by one another in the same way: while water serves to feed fire, fire is not nutriment to water. It would seem, then, that it is in the simple bodies above all that of two contraries one is nutriment and the other is nourished. Yet here is a difficulty. It is said by the one side that like is nourished by, as well as derives its growth from, like; while the others, again, as we explained, hold that contrary is nourished by contrary, on the ground that like cannot be affected by like, while food undergoes change and is digested. Now change is always in the direction of the opposite, or of the intermediate state. Further, nutriment is acted upon by that which it nourishes, and not the latter by the former: just as   [416b the carpenter is not affected by his material, but on the contrary the material by the carpenter. The carpenter merely passes to activity from inaction. But it makes a difference whether by nutriment we mean the final, or the primary, form of what is added. If both are nutriment, the one as undigested, the other as digested, it will be possible to use the term nutriment in conformity with both theories. For, in so far as it is undigested, contrary is nourished by contrary: and, in so far as it is digested, like by like. So that clearly both sides are in a manner partly right and partly wrong. But, since nothing is nourished unless it possesses life, that which is nourished must be the animate body as such: so that nutriment also is relative to the animate being which it nourishes: and this not incidentally merely.

There is, however, a difference between nutritivity and conductivity to growth. In so far as the animate thing is quantitative, what is taken promotes growth; in so far as it is a definite individual, what is taken nourishes. For the animate thing preserves its substance or essential nature and exists as long as it is nourished: and it causes the production, not of that which is nourished, but of another individual like it. Its essential nature already exists, and nothing generates itself, it only maintains its existence. Hence the above described principle of the soul is the power to preserve in existence that which possesses it in so far as it is a definite individual, while nutrition prepares it for activity. Therefore it cannot live when deprived of nutriment. There are, then, these three things, that which is nourished, that with which it is nourished, and that which nourishes it. The last of the three is the primary soul, that which is nourished is the body which contains the soul, that wherewith it is nourished is nutriment. As, however, it is right to name all things from the end they subserve, and the end here is reproduction of the species, the primary soul is that which is capable of reproducing the species. That with which the living thing is nourished may be understood in two senses, just as that with which one steers may mean the hand or the rudder; the former, the hand, both causing motion and being moved, the latter, the rudder, being simply moved. Now it is necessary that all food should be capable of digestion, and digestion is promoted by heat; this explains why every animate thing has warmth. This, then, is an outline of what nutriment is. It must be more clearly defined hereafter in the discussion devoted specially to it.

Now that these points have been determined, let us [ch. 5 proceed to a general discussion of all sensation. As above remarked, sensation consists in being moved and acted upon, for it is held to be a species of qualitative change. Some add that like is in fact acted upon by like. How far this is possible or impossible we have ex- [417a plained in the general discussion of action and passivity. The question arises why there is no sensation of the senses themselves: that is, why they produce no sensation apart from external sensibles, though the senses contain fire, earth and the other elements, which are the objects of sensation either in themselves or through their attributes. Evidently it follows that the faculty of sensible perception exists not in activity, but only in potentiality. Hence it must be hereas with the fuel which does not burn of and in itself without something to make it burn; otherwise it would kindle itself and would have no need of the fire which is actually existent. Now to have sensation has two meanings: we use the terms hearing and seeing of that which has the capacity to hear and see, even though it be at the time asleep, just as we do of that which already actually hears and sees. And therefore sensation, too, will have two meanings: it may mean either potential or actual sensation. Similarly with having sensation, whether potential or actual.

Let us then first proceed on the assumption that to be acted upon or moved is identical with active operation. For movement is in fact active operation of some sort, though incomplete, as we have elsewhere explained. But in every case things are acted upon and moved by an agent in actual operation. It follows that in one sense what is acted upon is acted upon by what is like it, in another sense by what is unlike it, as we have explained. That is to say, while being acted upon it is unlike, after it has been acted upon it is like the agent.

We must also draw a distinction in regard to the terms potentiality and actuality: at present we are using them without qualification. For instance, we may use the term wise, firstly, in the sense in which we might speak of man as wise, because man is one of the genus of beings which are wise and have wisdom; secondly, in the sense in which we at once call the man wise who has learnt, say, grammar. Now of these two men each possesses the capacity, but in a different sense: the one because the genus to which he belongs, that is to say, his matter, is potentially wise; the other because he is capable, if he chose, of applying the wisdom he has acquired, provided there is nothing external to hinder. Whereas he who is at the moment exercising his wisdom is in actuality and is wise in the proper sense of the term: for example, he knows the A before him. Thus the first two are both potentially wise:

the first becomes wise actually after he has undergone qualitative change through instruction and often after transition from the reverse condition; while in the latter case it is by another kind of transition that the man passes from the mere possession, without the use, of sensation or grammar to the use of it. [417b

To suffer or be acted upon, too is a term of more than one meaning. Sometimes it means a sort of destruction by the contrary, sometimes it is rather a preservation of what is potentially existent by what is actually existent and like it, so far as likeness holds of potentiality when compared with actuality. For it is by exercise of knowledge that the possessor of knowledge becomes such in actuality: and this either is no qualitative change (for the thing develops into its own nature and actuality), or else is qualitative change of a different sort. Hence it is not right to say that that which thinks undergoes change when it thinks, any more than that the builder undergoes change when he builds. That, then, which works the change from potential existence to actuality in a thinking and intelligent being should properly receive a different name and not be called instruction: while that which learns and is brought from potential to actual knowledge by that which is in actuality and capable of instructing should either not be said to suffer or be acted upon at all, or else two modes of change should be assumed, one to the negative states and the other to the normal habits and the true nature.

In the sensitive subject the first change is due to the parent: once generated it possesses sensation exactly in the same sense as we possess knowledge. And to have actual sensation corresponds to exercise of knowledge. There is this difference, however, that in the one case the causes of the activity are external: as, for instance, the objects of sight, hearing and the other senses. The reason is that actual sensation is always of particulars, while knowledge is of universals: and these universals are, in a manner, in the soul itself. Hence it is in our power to think whenever we please, but sensation is not in our power: for the presence of the sensible object is necessary. It is much the same with the sciences which deal with sensible objects; and for the same reason, namely, that sensibles are particulars and are external.

But we shall have a further opportunity of making this clear hereafter. For the present let us be content to have established that of the two meanings of potentiality, the one according to which a child might be called potentially a general, and the other according to which a man of full age might be so called, it is the latter which applies to the faculty of sense-perception. But as this distinction has no word [418a to mark it, although the fact and the nature of the distinction have been established, we are compelled to use the terms to suffer or be acted upon and to be qualitatively changed as if they were the proper terms. Now, as has been explained, the sensitive faculty is potentially such as the sensible object is in actuality. While it is being acted upon, it is not yet similar, but, when once it has been acted upon, it is assimilated and has the same character as the sensible object.

In considering each separate sense we must first treat of   [ch. 6 their objects. By the sensible object may be meant any one of three things, two of which we say are perceived in themselves or directly, while the third is perceived *per accidens* or indirectly. Of the first two the one is the special object of a particular sense, the other an object common to all the senses. By a special object of a particular sense I mean that which cannot be perceived by any other sense and in respect to which deception is impossible; for example, sight is of colour, hearing of sound and taste of flavour, while touch no doubt has for its object several varieties. But at any rate each single sense judges of its proper objects and is not deceived as to the fact that there is a colour or a sound; though as to what or where the coloured object is or what or where the object is which produces the sound, mistake is possible. Such then, are the special objects of the several senses. By common sensibles are meant motion, rest, number, figure, size: for such qualities are not the special objects of any single sense, but are common to all. For example, a particular motion can be perceived by touch as well as by sight. What is meant by the indirect object of sense may be illustrated if we suppose that the white thing before you is Diares' son. You perceive Diares' son, but indirectly, for that which you perceive is accessory to the whiteness. Hence you are not affected by the indirect sensible as such. Of the two classes of sensibles directly perceived it is the objects special to the different senses which are properly perceptible: and it is to these that the essential character of each sense is naturally adapted.

The object, then, of sight is the visible: what is visible is   [ch. 7 colour and something besides which can be described, though it has no name. What we mean will best be made clear as we proceed. The visible, then, is colour. Now colour is that with which what is visible in itself is overlaid: and, when I say in itself, I do not mean what is visible by its essence or form, but what is visible because it contains within itself the cause of visibility, namely, colour. But colour is universally capable of exciting change in the actually transparent, that   [418b is, in light; this being, in fact, the true nature of colour. Hence colour is not visible without light, but the colour of each object is always seen in light. And so we shall have first to explain what light is.

There is, then, we assume, something transparent; and by this I mean that which, though visible, is not properly speaking, visible in itself, but by reason of extrinsic colour. Air, water and many solid bodies answer to this description. For they are not transparent *quâ* air or *quâ* water, but because there is a certain natural attribute present in both of them which is present also in the eternal body on high. Light is the actuality of this transparent *quâ* transparent. But where the transparent is only potentially present, there darkness is actually. Light is a sort of colour in the transparent when made transparent in actuality by the agency of fire or something resembling the celestial body: for this body also has an attribute which is one and the same with that of fire. What the transparent is, and what light is, has now been stated; namely, that it is neither fire nor body generally nor an effluence from any body (for even then it would still be a sort of body), but the presence of fire or something fiery in the transparent. For it is impossible for two bodies to occupy the same space at the same time.

Light is held to be contrary to darkness. But darkness is absence from the transparent of the quality above described: so that plainly light is the presence of it. Thus Empedocles and others who propounded the same view are wrong when they represent light as moving in space and arriving at a given point of time between the earth and that which surrounds it without our perceiving its motion. For this contradicts not only the clear evidence of reason, but also the facts of observation: since, though a movement of light might elude observation within a short distance, that it should do so all the way from east to west is too much to assume.

It is that which is colourless which is receptive of colour, as it is that which is soundless which is receptive of sound. And the transparent is colourless, and so is the invisible or the dimly visible which is our idea of the dark. Such is the transparent medium, not indeed when it is in actuality, but when potentially transparent. For it is the same natural attribute which is at one time darkness and at another time light. It is not everything visible which is visible in light, but only   [419a the proper colour of each thing. Some things, indeed, are not seen in daylight, though they produce sensation in the dark: as, for example, the things of fiery and glittering appearance, for which there is no one distinguishing name, like fungus, horn, the heads, scales and eyes of fishes. But in no one of these cases is the proper colour seen. Why these objects are seen must be discussed elsewhere. At present this much is clear, that the object seen in light is colour, and this is why it is not seen without light. For the very quiddity of colour is, as we saw, just this, that it is capable of exciting change in the operantly transparent medium: and the activity of the transparent is light. There is clear evidence of this. If you lay the coloured object upon your eye, you will not see it. On the contrary, what the colour excites is the transparent medium, say, the air, and by this, which is continuous, the sense-organ is stimulated. For it was a mistake in Democritus to suppose that if the intervening space became a void, even an ant would be distinctly seen, supposing there were one in the sky. That is impossible. For sight takes place through an affection of the sensitive faculty. Now it cannot be affected by that which is seen, the colour itself: therefore it can only be by the intervening medium: hence the existence of some medium is necessary. But, if the intermediate space became a void, so far from being seen distinctly, an object would not be visible at all.

We have explained the reason why colour must be seen in light. Fire is visible both in light and in darkness: and necessarily so, for it is owing to fire that the transparent becomes transparent. The same argument holds for sound and odour. For no sound or scent produces sensation by contact with the sense-organ: it is the intervening medium which is excited by sound and odour and the respective sense-organs by the medium. But, when the body which emits the sound or odour is placed on the sense-organ itself, it will not produce any sensation. The same holds of touch and taste, although it appears to be otherwise. The reason for this will be seen hereafter. The medium for sounds is air, that for odour has no name. For there is assuredly a common quality in air and water, and this quality, which is present in both, stands to the body which emits odour in the same relation as the transparent to colour. For the animals that live in water also appear to have the sense of smell. But man and the other land-animals which   [419b breathe are unable to smell without inhaling breath. The reason for this, too, must be reserved for future explanation.

Let us now begin by determining the nature of sound   [ch. 8 and hearing. There are two sorts of sound, one a sound which is operant, the other potential sound. For some things we say have no sound, as sponge, wool; others, for example, bronze and all things solid and smooth, we say have sound, because they can emit sound, that is, they can produce actual sound between the sonorous body and the organ of hearing. When actual sound occurs it is always of something on something and in something, for it is a blow which produces it. Hence it is impossible that a sound should be produced by a single thing, for, as that which strikes is distinct from that which is struck, that which sounds sounds upon something. And a blow implies spatial motion. As we stated above, it is not concussion of any two things taken at random which constitutes sound. Wool, when struck, emits no sound at all, but bronze does, and so do all smooth and hollow things; bronze emits sound because it is smooth, while hollow things by reverberation produce a series of concussions after the first, that which is set in motion being unable to escape. Further, sound is heard in air and, though more faintly, in water. It is not the air or the water, however, which chiefly determine the production of sound: on the contrary, there must be solid bodies colliding with one another and with the air: and this happens when the air after being struck resists the impact and is not dispersed. Hence the air must be struck quickly and forcibly if it is to give forth sound; for the movement of the striker must be too rapid to allow the air time to disperse: just as would be necessary if one aimed a blow at a heap of sand or a sandwhirl, while it was in rapid motion onwards.

Echo is produced when the air is made to rebound backwards like a ball from some other air which has become a single mass owing to its being within a cavity which confines it and prevents its dispersion. It seems likely that echo is always produced, but is not always distinctly audible: since surely the same thing happens with sound as with light. For light is always being reflected; else light would not be everywhere, but outside the spot where the sun's rays fall there would be darkness. But it is not always reflected in the same way as it is from water or bronze or any other smooth surface; I mean, it does not always produce the shadow, by which we define light.

Void is rightly stated to be the indispensable condition of hearing. For the air is commonly believed to be a void, and it is the air which causes hearing, when being one and continuous it is set in motion. But, owing to its tendency to disperse, it gives out no sound unless that which is struck is smooth. In that case the air when struck   [420a is simultaneously reunited because of the unity of the surface; for a smooth body presents a single surface.

That, then, is resonant which is capable of exciting motion in a mass of air continuously one as far as the ear. There is air naturally attached to the ear. And because the ear is in air, when the external air is set in motion, the air within the ear moves. Hence it is not at every point that the animal hears, nor that the air passes through: for it is not at every point that the part which is to set itself in motion and to be animate has a supply of air. Of itself, then, the air is a soundless thing because it is easily broken up. But, whenever it is prevented from breaking up, its movement is sound. But the air within the ears has been lodged fast within walls to make it immoveable, in order that it may perceive exactly all the varieties of auditory movement. This is why we hear in water also, because the water does not pass right up to the air attached to the ear, nor even into the ear at all, because of its convolutions. Should this happen, hearing is destroyed, as it is by an injury to the membrane of the tympanum, and as sight is by an injury to the cornea. Further, we have evidence whether we hear or not, according as there is or is not always a ringing sound in the ears, as in a horn: for the air imprisoned there is always moving with a proper motion of its own. But sound is something of external origin and is not native to the ear. And this is why it is said that we hear by means of what is empty and resonant, because that by which we hear has air confined within it.

Does that which is struck emit the sound or that which strikes? Is it not rather both, but each in a different way? For sound is motion of that which is capable of being moved in the same manner as things rebound from smooth surfaces when struck sharply against them. Thus, as above remarked, it is not everything which, when struck or striking, emits sound: supposing, for instance, a pin were to strike against a pin, there would be no sound. The thing struck must be of even surface, so that the air may rebound and vibrate in one mass.

The varieties of resonant bodies are clearly distinguished by the sound they actually emit. For, as without light colours are not seen, so without sound we cannot distinguish high and low or acute and grave in pitch. These latter terms are used by analogy from tangible objects. For the acute, that is, the high, note moves the sense much in a little time, while the grave or low note moves it little in much time. Not that what is shrill is identically rapid, nor what is low is slow, but it is in the one case the rapidity, in the other the slowness, which makes the motion or sensation such as has been described. And it would seem that there is a certain analogy between the acute and grave to   [420b the ear and the acute and blunt to the touch. For that which is acute or pointed, as it were, stabs, while the blunt, as it were, thrusts, because the one excites motion in a short, the other in a long time, so that *per accidens* the one is quick, the other slow. Let this account of sound suffice.

Voice is a sound made by an animate being. No inanimate thing is vocal, though it may by analogy be said to be vocal, as in the case of the pipe, the lyre and all other inanimate things that have pitch and tune and articulation: for these qualities, it would seem, the voice also possesses. But many animals have no voice: that is to say, all bloodless animals and, among animals that have blood, fishes. And this is what we might expect, since sound is a movement of air. Those fishes which are said to possess voice, such as those in the Achelöus, merely make a noise with their gills or some other such part. Voice is sound made by an animal, and not by any part of its body indifferently. But, as in every case of sound there is something that strikes, something struck and a medium, which is air, it is reasonable that only creatures which inhale air should have voice. For here nature uses the air that is inhaled for two purposes, just as it uses the tongue for tasting and for speech, the former use, for tasting, being indispensable and therefore more

widely found, while expression of thought is a means to well-being.
Similarly nature uses the breath first as a necessary means to the maintenance of internal warmth (the reason for which shall be explained elsewhere) and, further, as a means of producing voice and so promoting
well-being. The organ of respiration is the larynx, and the part to which
this part is subservient is the lung: for it is this organ, namely, the lung,
which enables land animals to maintain a higher temperature than others. Respiration is also needed primarily for the region about the heart.
Hence, as we draw breath, the air enters: and so the impact upon the
windpipe, as it is called, of the air breathed is voice, the cause of the
impact being the soul which animates the vocal organs. For, as we said
before, it is not every sound made by an animal that is voice. Noise
can be produced even with the tongue or as in coughing but it is necessary for voice that the part which strikes should be animate and that
some mental image should be present. For voice is certainly a sound
which has significance and is not like a cough, the noise of air respired:
rather with this air the animal makes the air in the windpipe strike
against the windpipe. A proof of this is the fact that we cannot   [421a
speak while inhaling or exhaling breath, but only while we hold it in:
for anyone who holds his breath uses the breath so held to cause motion.
And it is evident why fishes are voiceless. It is because they have no
larynx. And they are without this part because they do not take in the
air nor breathe. Why this is so does not concern us here.

    Of smell and the object of smell it is less easy to speak   [ch. 9
definitely than of the senses above-mentioned: for the nature of odour
is by no means so clear as is the nature of sound or of colour. The reason
is that this sense in us is not exact, but inferior to that of many animals. In fact, man has a poor olfactory sense and perceives none of
the objects of smell unless they be painful or pleasant, which implies
that the organ is wanting in accuracy. It is reasonable to suppose that
animals with hard eyes perceive colour in the same vague way and do
not distinguish the varieties of colour except in so far as they do, or
do not, inspire fear. And this is the way in which mankind perceive
odours. For it would seem that, while there is an analogy to taste and
the varieties of flavour answer to the varieties of smell, our sense of
taste is more exact because it is a modification of touch and the sense
of touch is the most exact of man's senses. In the other senses man
is inferior to many of the animals, but in delicacy of touch he is far
superior to the rest. And to this he owes his superior intelligence. This
may be seen from the fact that it is this organ of sense and nothing
else which makes all the difference in the human race between the natural endowments of man and man. For hard-skinned men are dull of
intellect, while those who are soft-skinned are gifted.

As with flavours, so with odours: some are sweet, some bitter. (But in some objects smell and flavour correspond; for example, they have sweet odour and sweet flavour: in other things the opposite is the case.) Similarly, too, an odour may be pungent, irritant, acid or oily. But because, as we said above, odours are not as clearly defined as the corresponding flavours, it is from these latter that the odours have taken their names, in virtue of the resemblance in the things.   [421b Thus the odour of saffron and honey is sweet, while the odour of thyme and the like is pungent; and so in all the other cases. Again, smell corresponds to hearing and to each of the other senses in that, as hearing is of the audible and inaudible, and sight of the visible and invisible, so smell is of the odorous and inodorous. By inodorous may be meant either that which is wholly incapable of having odour or that which has a slight or faint odour. The term tasteless involves a similar ambiguity.

Further, smell also operates through a medium, namely, air or water. For water animals, too, whether they are, or are not, possessed of blood, seem to perceive odour as much as the creatures in the air: since some of them also come from a great distance to seek their food, guided by the scent.

Hence there is an obvious difficulty, if the process of smell is everywhere the same, and yet man smells when inhaling but does not smell when instead of inhaling he is exhaling or holding his breath, no matter whether the object be distant or near, or even if it be placed on the inside of the nostril. The inability to perceive what is placed immediately on the sense-organ man shares with all animals: what is peculiar to him is that he cannot smell without inhaling. This is made plain by experiment. Consequently bloodless animals, since they do not breathe, might be thought to have a distinct sense other than those commonly recognised. But, we reply, that is impossible, since it is odour which they perceive. For perception of odour, be it fragrant or noisome, constitutes smelling. Moreover, it is found that these bloodless animals are destroyed by the same powerful odours as man, such as asphalt, brimstone and the like. It follows then that they do smell, but not by inhaling breath.

It would seem, again, that in man the organ of this sense differs from that of the other animals, as his eyes differ from those of hard-eyed animals. Man's eyes have, in the eyelids, a sort of screen or sheath and without moving or opening them he cannot see: while the hard-eyed animals have nothing of the kind, but at once see whatever is taking place in the transparent medium. So, too, it seems, the organ of smell in some animals is unenclosed, just as in the eye, but in   [422a those which take in the air it has a curtain, which is removed in the process of inhaling, by dilatation of the veins and passages. And this is the reason why animals which breathe cannot smell in the water. For it is necessary for them to take in breath before smelling and this they cannot do in the water. Odour is included under that which is dry, as flavour under that which is moist, and the organ of smell is potentially dry also.

The object of taste is a species of tangible. And this is   [ch. 10 the reason why it is not perceived through a foreign body as medium: for touch employs no such medium either. The body, too, in which the flavour resides, the proper object of taste, has the moist, which is something tangible, for its matter or vehicle. Hence, even if we lived in water, we should still perceive anything sweet thrown into the water, but our perception would not have come through the medium, but by the admixture of sweetness with the fluid, as is the case with what we drink. But it is not in this way, namely, by admixture, that colour is perceived, nor yet by emanations. Nothing, then, corresponds to the medium; but to colour, which is the object of sight, corresponds the flavour, which is the object of taste. But nothing produces perception of flavour in the absence of moisture, but either actually or potentially the producing cause must have liquid in it: salt, for instance, for that is easily dissolved and acts as a dissolvent upon the tongue.

Again, sight is of the invisible as well as the visible (for darkness is invisible and this, too, sight discerns as well as light) and, further, of that which is exceedingly bright, which is likewise invisible, though in a different way from darkness. Similarly hearing has to do with noise and silence, the former being audible, the latter inaudible, and, further, with loud noise, to which it is related as vision is to brightness, a loud and a violent sound being in a manner just as inaudible as a faint sound. The term invisible, be it noted, is applied not only to that which is wholly impossible to see, which corresponds to other cases of the impossible, but also when a thing has imperfectly or not at all its natural properties, answering to the footless and the kernel-less. So, too, taste has for object not only that which can be tasted, but also the tasteless, by which we mean that which has little flavor or hardly any at all, or a flavour destructive of the taste. Now in flavour this distinction is supposed to start with the drinkable and the undrinkable. Both are tastes of a sort, but the latter is poor or destructive of the faculty of taste, while the former is naturally adapted to it. The drinkable is the common object of touch and of taste. But, since the object of taste is moist, the sense-organ which perceives it must be neither actually   [422b moist nor yet incapable of becoming moist. For taste is acted upon by the object of taste as such. The organ of taste, then, which needs to be moistened, must have the capacity of absorbing moisture without being dissolved, while at the same time it must not be actually moist. A proof of this is the fact that the tongue has no perception either when very dry or very moist. In the latter case the contact is with the moisture originally in the tongue, just as when a man first makes trial of a strong flavour and then tastes some other flavour; or as with the sick, to whom all things appear bitter because they perceive them with their tongue full of bitter moisture.

As with the colours, so with the species of flavour, there are, firstly, simple flavours, which are opposites, the sweet and the bitter; next to these on one side the succulent, on the other the salt; and, thirdly, intermediate between these, the pungent, the rough, the astringent and the acid. These seem to be practically all the varieties of flavour. Consequently, while the faculty of taste has potentially the qualities just described, the object of taste converts the potentiality into actuality.

The same account is to be given of touch and the tangi-   [ch. 11 ble. If touch is not a single sense but includes more senses than one, there must be a plurality of tangible objects also. It is a question whether touch is several senses or only one. What, moreover, is the sense-organ for the faculty of touch? Is it the flesh or what is analogous to this in creatures that have not flesh? or is flesh, on the contrary, the medium, while the primary sense-organ is something different, something internal? We may argue thus: every sense seems to deal with a single pair of opposites, sight with white and black, hearing with high and low pitch, taste with bitter and sweet; but under the tangible are included several pairs of opposites, hot and cold, dry and moist, hard and soft and the like. A partial solution of this difficulty lies in the consideration that the other senses also apprehend more than one pair of opposites. Thus in vocal sound there is not only high and low pitch, but also loudness and faintness, smoothness and roughness, and so on. In regard to colour also there are other similar varieties. But what the one thing is which is subordinated to touch as sound is to hearing is not clear.

But is the organ of sense internal or is the flesh the immediate organ? No inference can be drawn, seemingly, from the fact   [423a that the sensation occurs simultaneously with contact. For even under present conditions, if a sort of membrane were constructed and stretched over the flesh, this would immediately on contact transmit the sensation as before. And yet it is clear that the organ of sense is not in this membrane; although, if by growth it became united to the flesh, the sensation would be transmitted even more quickly. Hence it appears that the part of the body in question, that is, the flesh, is related to us as the air would be if it were united to us all round by natural growth. We should then have thought we were perceiving sound, colour and smell by one and the same instrument: in fact, sight, hearing and smell would have seemed to us in a manner to constitute a single sense. But as it is, owing to the media, by which the various motions are transmitted, being separated from us, the difference of the organs of these three senses is manifest. But in regard to touch this point is at present obscure.

In fact, the animate body cannot consist of air or water singly, it must be something solid. The only alternative is that it should be a compound of earth and of these elements, as flesh and what is analogous to flesh profess to be. Consequently the body must be the naturally cohering medium for the faculty of touch, through which the plurality of sensations is communicated. That they are a plurality is made clear by touch in the case of the tongue, for the tongue perceives all tangible objects, and that at the same part at which it perceives flavour. Now, if the rest of the flesh also had perception of flavour, taste and touch would have seemed to be one and the same sense: whereas they are really two, because their organs are not interchangeable.

Here a question arises. All body has depth, this being the third dimension, and, if between two bodies a third body is interposed, the two cannot touch one another. Now that which is fluid is not independent of body, nor is that which is wet: if it is not itself water, it must contain water. But when bodies touch one another in the water, since their exterior surfaces are not dry, there must be water between them, the water with which their extremities are flooded. If, then, all this be true, no one thing can possibly touch another in the water, nor yet in the air: for the air stands to the objects in the air as water to the things in water, but this fact we are more apt to overlook, just as aquatic animals fail to notice that the things which touch one another in the water have wet surfaces. The question then arises: is [423b] the mode of perception uniform for all objects or does it differ for different objects? According to the prevalent view, taste and touch operate by direct contact, while the other senses operate at a distance. But this view is incorrect. On the contrary, we perceive the hard and the soft also mediately, just as much as we do the resonant, the visible, the odorous. But the latter are perceived at a distance, the former close at hand: and this is why the fact escapes us, since we really perceive all objects through a medium, though in touch and taste we fail to notice this. And yet, as we mentioned above, even if we perceived all objects of touch through a membrane without being aware of its interference, we should be just in the same position as we are now with regard to objects in the water or in the air: for, as it is, we suppose that we are touching the objects themselves and that there is no intervening medium. But there is this difference between the tangible on the one hand and visible and resonant things on the other: the latter we perceive because the medium acts in a certain way upon us, while tangible objects we perceive not by any action upon us of the medium, but concurrently with it, like the man who is struck through his shield. It is not that the shield was first struck and then passed on the blow, but, as it happened, both were struck simultaneously. And, generally, it would seem that the flesh and the tongue are related to the true sense-organ as are air and water to the organs of sight, hearing and smell respectively. But neither in the one case nor in the other would sensation follow on contact with the sense-organ; for instance, if a body that is white were placed on the outer surface of the eye: which shows that the instrument that apprehends the tangible is within. We should then get the same result as in the case of the other senses. What is placed on the sense-organ we do not perceive: what is placed on the flesh we do perceive: therefore flesh is the medium for the faculty of touch.

It is, then, the distinctive qualities of body as body which are the objects of touch: I mean those qualities which determine the elements, hot or cold, dry or moist, of which we have previously given an account in our discussion of the elements. And their sense-organ, the tactile organ, that is, in which the sense called touch primarily resides, is the part which has potentially the qualities of the tangible object. For   [424a perceiving is a sort of suffering or being acted upon: so that when the object makes the organ in actuality like itself it does so because that organ is potentially like it. Hence it is that we do not perceive what is just as hot or cold, hard or soft, as we are, but only the excesses of these qualities: which implies that the sense is a kind of mean between the opposite extremes in the sensibles. This is why it passes judgment on the things of sense. For the mean is capable of judging, becoming to each extreme in turn its opposite. And, as that which is to perceive white and black must not be actually either, though potentially both, and similarly for the other senses also, so in the case of touch the organ must be neither hot nor cold. Further, sight is in a manner, as we saw, of the invisible as well as the visible, and in the same way the remaining senses deal with opposites. So, too, touch is of the tangible and the intangible: where by intangible is meant, first, that which has the distinguishing quality of things tangible in quite a faint degree, as is the case with the air; and, secondly, tangibles which are in excess, such as those which are positively destructive. Each of the senses, then, has now been described in outline.

In regard to all sense generally we must understand   [ch. 12 that sense is that which is receptive of sensible forms apart from their matter, as wax receives the imprint of the signet-ring apart from the iron or gold of which it is made: it takes the imprint which is of gold or bronze, but not *quâ* gold or bronze. And similarly sense as relative to each sensible is acted upon by that which possesses colour, flavour or sound, not in so far as each of those sensibles is called a particular thing, but in so far as it possesses a particular quality and in respect of its character or form. The primary sense-organ is that in which such a power resides, the power to receive sensible forms. Thus the organ is one and the same with the power, but logically distinct from it. For that which perceives must be an extended magnitude. Sensitivity, however, is not an extended magnitude, nor is the sense: they are rather a certain character or power of the organ. From this it is evident why excesses in the sensible objects destroy the sense-organs. For if the motion is too violent for the sense-organ, the character or form (and this, as we saw, constitutes the sense) is annulled, just as the harmony and the pitch of the lyre suffer by too violent jangling of the strings. It is evident, again, why plants have no sensation, although they have one part of soul and are in some degree affected by the things themselves which are tangible: for example, they become cold and hot. The reason is that they have in them no mean, no principle capable of   [424b receiving the forms of sensible objects without their matter, but on the contrary, when they are acted upon, the matter acts upon them as well. It might be asked whether what is unable to smell would be in any way acted upon by an odour, or that which is incapable of seeing by a colour, and so for the other sensibles. But, if the object of smell is odour, the effect it produces, if it produces an effect at all, is smelling. Therefore none of the things that are unable to smell can be acted upon by odour, and the same is true of the other senses: nor can things be acted upon when they have the power of sensation, except as they individually possess the particular sense required. This may also be shown as follows. Light and darkness do not act upon bodies at all; neither does sound nor odour: it is the things which possess them that act. Thus it is the air accompanying the thunderbolt which rives the timber. But, it may be said, things tangible and flavours do so act: else by what agency are inanimate things acted upon or changed? Shall we, then, conclude that the objects of the other senses likewise act directly? Is it not rather the case that not all body can be affected by smell and sound, and that the bodies which are so affected are indeterminate and shifting: for example, air? For odour in the air implies that the air has been acted upon in some way. What then is smelling, besides a sort of suffering or being acted upon? Or shall we say that the act of smelling implies sense-perception, whereas the air, after it has been acted upon, so far from perceiving, at once becomes itself perceptible to sense?

Book · I I I

That there is no other sense distinct from the five, by which I   [ch. 1
mean sight, hearing, smell, taste, touch, anyone may convince himself
on the following grounds. Let us assume that, as a matter of fact, we
have sensation of every sensible object for which touch is the appropriate sense, all qualities of the tangible, as such, being perceptible to us
through touch. Let us further assume that, when any sense is lacking to
us, an organ of sense must also be lacking; and further, that whatever
we perceive by actual contact is perceptible by touch, a sense which we
do possess, while whatever we perceive mediately and not by actual
contact is perceptible by means of the elements, namely, air and water.
And here are implied two cases. Suppose, first, we have perception by
one and the same medium of two several things, different in kind from
one another, then whoever possesses the appropriate sense-organ must
be percipient of both: as, for example, if the sense-organ consists of air
and air is also the medium of both sound and colour. Next suppose several media to transmit the same object, as both air and water   [425a
transmit colour, both being transparent, then he who possesses one of
these alone will perceive whatever is perceptible through both media.
Now, of the elements, air and water are the only two of which sense-
organs are composed. For the pupil of the eye is of water, and the ear
is of air, and the organ of smell is of one or the other, while fire, if
present anywhere, enters into all, since nothing can be sentient without
warmth. Earth, again, belongs to none of the sense-organs, or, at most,
is a constituent peculiar to touch. It follows, then, that outside water
and air there is no sense-organ. Now sense-organs composed of air and
water certain animals do, in fact, possess. We may infer, then, that all
the senses are possessed by those animals which are fully developed and
are not crippled: even the mole is found to have eyes beneath its skin.
And thus, unless there exists some unknown body or some property
different from any possessed by any of the bodies within our experience,
there can be no sixth sense which we lack.

Nor, again, can there be any special sense-organ for the common
sensibles, which we perceive incidentally by every sense; for example,
motion, rest, figure, magnitude, number, unity. For all of these we
perceive by motion. Thus it is by motion that we perceive magnitude,
and consequently figure, figure being one variety of magnitude; while
that which is at rest we perceive by the fact that it is not moved.
Number we perceive by the negation of continuity and by the
special sense-organs also: for each sensation has a single object.
Clearly, then, it is impossible that there should be a special sense for

any one of these; for example, motion: for in that case we should perceive them in the same way as we now perceive sweetness by sight (and this we do because we have a sense which perceives both, and by this we actually apprehend the two simultaneously when they occur in conjunction). Otherwise we should never have more than an incidental perception of them; as of Cleon's son we perceive not that he is Cleon's son, but that he is a white object, and the fact of his being Cleon's son is accessory to the whiteness. But of the common sensibles we have already a common perception, which is direct and not indirect, so that there cannot be a special sense for them. For, if there were, we should never perceive them otherwise than in the way in which we said we saw Cleon's son.

But the various senses incidentally perceive each other's proper objects, not as so many separate senses, but as forming a single sense, when there is concurrent perception relating to the same object; as,   [425b for instance, when we perceive that gall is bitter and yellow. For it is certainly not the part of any other sense to declare that both objects are one and the same. Hence you are sometimes deceived and, on observing something yellow, fancy it to be gall.

But, it might be asked, why have we several senses, instead of only one? I answer, it is in order that we may not be so likely to overlook the common attributes, such as motion, magnitude, number, which accompany the special sensibles. For, if sight had been our only sense and whiteness its object, we should have been more apt to overlook the common sensibles and to confuse all sensibles, because colour and magnitude, for instance, must always go together. As it is, the fact that the common attributes are found in the object of another sense also shows that they are severally distinct.

Inasmuch as we perceive that we see and hear, it must   [ch. 2 either be by sight or by some other sense that the percipient perceives that he sees. But, it may be urged, the same sense which perceives sight will also perceive the colour which is the object of sight. So that either there will be two senses to perceive the same thing or the one sense, sight, will perceive itself. Further, if the sense perceiving sight were really a distinct sense, either the series would go on to infinity or some one of the series of senses would perceive itself. Therefore it will be better to admit this of the first in the series. Here, however, there is a difficulty. Assuming that to perceive by sight is to see and that it is colour or that which possesses colour which is seen, it may be argued that, if you are to see that which sees, that which in the first instance sees, the primary visual organ, will actually have colour. Clearly, then, to perceive by sight does not always mean one and the same thing. For, even when we do not see, it is nevertheless by sight that we discern both darkness and light, though not in the same manner. Further, that which sees is in a manner coloured. For the sense-organ is in every case receptive of the sensible object without its matter. And this is why the sensations and images remain in the sense-organs even when the sensible objects are withdrawn.

Now the actuality of the sensible object is one and the same with that of the sense, though, taken in the abstract, sensible object and sense are not the same. I mean, for example, actual sound and actual hearing are the same: for it is possible to have hearing and yet not hear; again, that which is resonant is not always sounding. But when that which is capable of hearing operantly hears and that which is capable of sounding sounds, the actual hearing and the actual sound occur simultaneously, and we might, if we pleased, call them audition   [426a and resonance respectively. If, then, motion, action and passivity reside in that which is acted upon, then of necessity it is in the potentiality of hearing that there is actual sound and there is actual hearing. For the activity of agent and movent comes into play in the patient; and this is why that which causes motion need not itself be moved. The actuality of the resonant, then, is sound or resonance, and the actuality of that which can hear is hearing or audition, hearing and sound both having two meanings. The same account may be given of the other senses and their objects. For, just as acting and being acted upon are in the subject acted upon and not in the agent, so also the actuality of the sensible object and that of the sensitive faculty will be in the percipient subject. But in some cases both activities have a name; for example, resonance and audition: in other cases one or the other has no name. Thus, while the actuality of sight is called seeing, that of colour has no name; and, while the actuality of the taste-faculty is called tasting, that of the flavour has no name. Now, as the actuality of the object and that of the faculty of sense are one and the same, although taken in the abstract they are different, hearing and sound thus understood as operant must simultaneously cease to be or simultaneously continue in being, and so also with flavour and taste, and similarly with the other senses and their objects: but when they are understood as potentialities, there is no such necessity. On this point the earlier natural philosophers were in error, when they supposed that without seeing there was neither white nor black, and without tasting no flavour. Their statement is in one sense true, in another false. For the terms sensation and sensible thing are ambiguous. When they mean the actual sensation and the actual sensible thing, the statement holds good: when they mean potential sensation and potential sensible, this is not the case. But our predecessors used terms without distinguishing their various meanings.

If, then, concord consists in a species of vocal sound, and if vocal sound and hearing are in one aspect one and the same, (*though in another aspect not the same*), and if concord is a proportion, it follows that hearing must also be a species of proportion. And this is the reason why hearing is destroyed by either excess, whether of high pitch or of low. And similarly, in the case of flavours, excess destroys the taste, and   [426b in colours excessive brightness or darkness destroys the sight, and so with smell, whether the excessive odour be agreeable or pungent. All this implies that the sense is a proportion. Hence sensibles are, it is true, pleasurable when they are brought into the range of this proportion pure and unmixed; for example, the shrill, the sweet, the salt: in that case, I say, they are pleasurable. But, speaking generally, that in which ingredients are blended is pleasurable in a higher degree, accord more pleasurable to the ear than high pitch or low pitch alone, and to touch that which admits of being still further heated or cooled. The due proportion constitutes the sense, while objects in excess give pain or cause destruction.

Now each sense is concerned with its own sensible object, being resident in the organ, *quâ* sense-organ, and judges the specific differences of its own sensible object. Thus sight pronounces upon white and black, taste upon sweet and bitter, and so with the rest. But, since we compare white and sweet and each of the sensibles with each, what in fact is it by means of which we perceive the difference between them? It must be by sense, for they are sensibles. And thus it is clear that the flesh is not the ultimate organ of sense; for, if it were, it would be necessary that that which judges should judge by contact with the sensible object. Nor indeed can we with separate organs judge that sweet is different from white, but both objects must be clearly presented to some single faculty. For, if we could, then the mere fact of my perceiving one thing and your perceiving another would make it clear that the two things were different. But the single faculty is required to pronounce them different, for sweet and white are pronounced to be different. It is one and the same faculty, then, which so pronounces. Hence, as it pronounces, so it also thinks and perceives. Clearly, then, it is not possible with separate organs to pronounce judgment upon things which are separate: nor yet at separate times, as the following considerations show. For, as it is one single faculty which pronounces that good and bad are different, so when it judges "A is different from B" it also judges "B is different from A" (and in this case the "when" is not accidental; I mean, accidental in the sense in which I may now say "Such and such things are different" without saying that they are different now. On the contrary, it pronounces now and pronounces that A and B are different now). That which judges judges, then, instantaneously and hence as an inseparable unit in an inseparable time. But, again, it is impossible for the same thing, in so far as indivisible and affected in indivisible time, to be moved at the same instant with contrary motions. For, if the object be sweet, it moves sense or thought in such [427a a way, but what is bitter moves it in a contrary way, and what is white in a different way. Is, then, that which judges instantaneous in its judgment and numerically undivided and inseparable, although separated logically? Then it is in a certain sense that which is divided which perceives divided objects; in another sense it is *quâ* indivisible that the divided perceives them: that is to say, logically it is divisible, locally and numerically it is indivisible. Or is this impossible? For the same indivisible unity, though in potentiality each of two opposites, in the order of thought and being is not so, but in actual operation is divided: it is impossible that it should be at the same time both white and black, and hence impossible that it should receive at the same time the forms of white and black, if reception of the forms constitutes sensation and thought. Rather is the case parallel to that of the point, as some describe it, which is divisible in so far as it is regarded as one or two. Well then, in so far as the faculty which judges is indivisible, it is one and judges instantaneously; but, in so far as it is divisible, it is not one, for it uses the same point at the same time twice. So far as it treats the boundary-point as two, it passes judgment on two separate things with a faculty which in a manner is separated into two; so far as it treats the point as one, it passes judgment on one thing, and that instantaneously. So much, then, for the principle in virtue of which we call the animal capable of sensation.

There are two different characteristics by which the soul [ch. 3 is principally defined; firstly, motion from place to place and, secondly, thinking and judging and perceiving. Both thought and intelligence are commonly regarded as a kind of perception, since the soul in both of these judges and recognises something existent. The ancients, at any rate, identify intelligence and perception: thus, in the words of Empedocles: "Wisdom for mankind is increased according to that which is present to them": and again "Whence they have also continually a shifting succession of thoughts." Homer's meaning, too, is the same when he says: "Such is the mind of men." In fact, all of them conceive thought to be corporeal like sensation and hold that we understand, as well as perceive, like by like: as we explained at the outset of the discussion. They ought, however, at the same time to have discussed error, a state which is peculiarly characteristic of ani- [427b mal life and in which the soul continues the greater part of its time. It follows from their premises that either all presentations of the senses must be true, as some affirm, or contact with what is unlike must constitute error; this being the converse of the position that like is known by like. But, as the knowledge of contraries is one and the same, so, too, it would seem, is error with respect to contraries one and the same.

Now it is clear that perception and intelligence are not the same thing. For all animals share in the one, but only a few in the other. And when we come to thinking, which includes right thinking and wrong thinking, right thinking being intelligence, knowledge and true opinion, and wrong thinking the opposites of these, neither is this identical with perception. For perception of the objects of the special senses is always true and is found in all animals, while thinking may be false as well as true and is found in none which have not reason also. Imagination, in fact, is something different both from perception and from thought, and is never found by itself apart from perception, any more than is belief apart from imagination. Clearly thinking is not the same thing as believing. For the former is in our own power, whenever we please: for we can represent an object before our eyes, as do those who range things under mnemonic headings and picture them to themselves. But opining is not in our power, for the opinion that we hold must be either false or true. Moreover, when we are of opinion that something is terrible or alarming, we at once feel the corresponding emotion, and so, too, with what is reassuring. But when we are under the influence of imagination we are no more affected than if we saw in a picture the objects which inspire terror or confidence. There are also different forms even of belief; knowledge, opinion, intelligence and their opposites. But the difference between these species must be reserved for another discussion.

To turn to thought: since it is different from sense-perception and seems to include imagination on the one hand and conception on the other, we must determine the nature of imagination before we proceed to discuss conception. If, then, imagination is the fac-   [428a ulty in virtue of which we say that an image presents itself to us, and if we exclude the metaphorical use of the term, it is some one of the faculties or habits in virtue of which we judge, and judge truly or falsely. Such faculties or habits are sensation, opinion, knowledge, intellect. It is clearly not sensation, for the following reasons. Sensation is either a faculty like sight or an activity like seeing. But we may have an image even when neither the one nor the other is present: for example, the images in dreams. Again, sensation is always present, but not so imagination. Besides, the identity of the two in actuality would involve the possibility that all the brutes have imagination. But this apparently is not the case; for example, the ant, the bee and the grub do not possess it. Moreover, sensations are always true, but imaginings prove for the most part false. Further, it is not when we direct our energies closely to the sensible object, that we say that this object appears to us to be a man, but rather when we do not distinctly perceive it (*then the term true or false is applied*). And, as we said before, visions present themselves even if we have our eyes closed.

Neither, again, can imagination be ranked with the faculties, like knowledge or intellect, which always judge truly: it may also be false. It remains, then, to consider whether it be opinion, as opinion may be true or false. But opinion is attended by conviction, for it is impossible to hold opinions without being convinced of them: but no brute is ever convinced, though many have imagination. Further, every opinion implies conviction, conviction implies that we have been persuaded, and persuasion implies reason. Among brutes, however, though some have imagination, none have reason. It is evident, then, that imagination is neither opinion joined with sensation nor opinion through sensation, nor yet a complex of opinion and sensation, both on these grounds and because nothing else is the object of opinion but that which is the object of sensation: I mean, it is the complex of the opinion of white and the sensation of white, not surely of the opinion of good with the sensation of white, which alone could constitute imagination. To   [428b imagine, then, will be on this supposition to opine directly, not indirectly, that which we perceive. But there are false imaginings concerning things of which we hold at the same time a true conception. For example, the sun appears only a foot in diameter, but we are convinced that it is larger than the inhabited world: in this case, therefore, either, without any alteration in the thing and without any lapse of memory on our part or conversion by argument, we have abandoned the true opinion which we had about it; or else, if we still retain it, the same opinion must be both true and false. It could have proved false only in the event of the object having changed without our observing it. It is not, then, either one of the two, opinion and sensation, singly, or a combination of the two, which constitutes imagination.

Now when one thing is moved, something else can be moved by it. And imagination is thought to be a species of motion and not to arise apart from sensation, but only in sentient beings and with the objects of sense for its objects. Motion, again, may be produced by actual sensation, and such motion must resemble the sensation which caused it. From all this it follows that this particular motion cannot arise apart from sensation nor be found anywhere except in sentient beings: and in virtue of this motion it is possible for its possessor to do and experience many things: imagination, too, may be both true and false. The reasons for the last conclusion are as follows. Perception of the objects of the special senses is true, or subject to the minimum of error. Next comes the perception that they are attributes: and at this point error may come in. As to the whiteness of an object sense is never mistaken, but it may be mistaken as to whether the white object is this thing or something else. Thirdly, there is perception of the common attributes, that is, the concomitants of the things to which the special attributes belong: I mean, for example, motion and magnitude, which are attributes of sensibles. And it is concerning them that sense is most apt to be deceived. But the motion which is the result of actual sensation will be different according as it arises from one or other of these three kinds of perception. The first kind, so long as the sensation is present, is true: the other kinds may be false, whether the sensation is present or absent, and especially when the object perceived is a long way off. If then, imagination possesses no other characteristics than the aforesaid, and if it is what it has been described to be, imagination will be a motion   [429a generated by actual perception. And, since sight is the principal sense, imagination has derived even its name ($\phi \alpha \nu \tau \alpha \sigma i \alpha$)[5] from light ($\phi \acute{\alpha} o \varsigma$)[6], because without light one cannot see. Again, because imaginations remain in us and resemble the corresponding sensations, animals perform many actions under their influence; some, that is, the brutes, through not having intellect, and others, that is, men, because intellect is sometimes obscured by passion or disease or sleep. Let this account of the nature and cause of imagination suffice.

As to the part of the soul with which it knows and under-   [ch. 4 stands, whether such part be separable spatially, or not separable spatially, but only in thought, we have to consider what is its distinctive character and how thinking comes about. Now, if thinking is analogous to perceiving, it will consist in a being acted upon by the object of thought or in something else of this kind. This part of the soul, then, must be impassive, but receptive of the form and potentially like this form, though not identical with it: and, as the faculty of sense is to sensible objects, so must intellect be related to intelligible objects. The mind, then, since it thinks all things, must needs, in the words of Anaxagoras, be unmixed with any, if it is to rule, that is, to know. For by intruding its own form it hinders and obstructs that which is alien to it; hence it has no other nature than this, that it is a capacity. Thus, then, the part of the soul which we call intellect (and by intellect I mean that whereby the soul thinks and conceives) is nothing at all actually before it thinks. Hence, too, we cannot reasonably conceive it to be mixed with the body: for in that case it would acquire some particular quality, cold or heat, or would even have some organ, as the perceptive faculty has. But as a matter of fact it has none. Therefore it has

---

[5] $\phi \alpha \nu \tau \alpha \sigma i \alpha$ = imagination.
[6] $\phi \acute{\alpha} o s$ = light.

been well said that the soul is a place of forms or ideas: except that this is not true of the whole soul, but only of the soul which can think, and again that the forms are there not in actuality, but potentially. But that the impassivity of sense is different from that of intellect is clear if we look at the sense-organs and at sense. The sense loses its power to perceive, if the sensible object has been too intense: thus it can- [429b not hear sound after very loud noises, and after too powerful colours and odours it can neither see nor smell. But the intellect, when it has been thinking on an object of intense thought, is not less, but even more, able to think of inferior objects. For the perceptive faculty is not independent of body, whereas intellect is separable. But when the intellect has thus become everything in the sense in which one who actually is a scholar is said to be so (which happens so soon as he can exercise his power of himself), even then it is still in one sense but a capacity: not, however, a capacity in the same sense as before it learned or discovered. And, moreover, at this stage intellect is capable of thinking itself.

Now, since magnitude is not the same as the quiddity of magnitude, nor water the same as the quiddity of water (and so also of many other things, though not of all, the thing and its quiddity being in some cases the same), we judge the quiddity of flesh and flesh itself either with different instruments or with the same instrument in different relations. For flesh is never found apart from matter, but, like "snub-nosed," it is a particular form in a particular matter. It is, then, with the faculty of sense that we discriminate heat and cold and all those qualities of which flesh is a certain proportion. But it is with another faculty, either separate from sense, or related to it as the bent line when it is straightened out is related to its former self, that we discriminate the quiddity of flesh. Again, when we come to the abstractions of mathematics, the straight answers to the quality "snub-nosed," being never found apart from extension. But the straightness of that which is straight, always supposing that the straight is not the same as straightness, is something distinct: we may, for instance, assume the definition of straightness to be duality. It is, then, with another instrument or with the same instrument in another relation that we judge it. In general, therefore, to the separation of the things from their matter corresponds a difference in the operations of the intellect.

The question might arise: assuming that the mind is something simple and impassive and, in the words of Anaxagoras, has nothing in common with anything else, how will it think, if to think is to be acted upon? For it is in so far as two things have something in common that the one of them is supposed to act and the other to be acted upon. Again, can mind itself be its own object? For then either its other objects will have mind in them, if it is not through something else, but in itself, that mind is capable of being thought, and if to be so capable is everywhere specifically one and the same; or else the mind will have some ingredient in its composition which makes it, like the rest, an object of thought. Or shall we recall our old distinction between two meanings of the phrase "to be acted upon in virtue of a common element," and say that the mind is in a manner potentially all objects of thought, but is actually none of them until it thinks: potentially in the [430a same sense as in a tablet which has nothing actually written upon it the writing exists potentially? This is exactly the case with the mind. Moreover, the mind itself is included among the objects which can be thought. For where the objects are immaterial that which thinks and that which is thought are identical. Speculative knowledge and its object are identical. (We must, however, enquire why we do not think always.) On the other hand, in things containing matter each of the objects of thought is present potentially. Consequently material objects will not have mind in them, for the mind is the power of becoming such objects without their matter; whereas the mind will have the attribute of being its own object.

But since, as in the whole of nature, to something which [ch. 5 serves as matter for each kind (and this is potentially all the members of the kind) there corresponds something else which is the cause or agent because it makes them all, the two being related to one another as art to its material, of necessity these differences must be found also in the soul. And to the one intellect, which answers to this description because it becomes all things, corresponds the other because it makes all things, like a sort of definite quality such as light. For in a manner light, too, converts colours which are potential into actual colours. And it is this intellect which is separable and impassive and unmixed, being in its essential nature an activity. For that which acts is always superior to that which is acted upon, the cause or principle to the matter. Now actual knowledge is identical with the thing known, but potential knowledge is prior in time in the individual; and yet not universally prior in time. But this intellect has no intermittence in its thought. It is, however, only when separated that it is its true self, and this, its essential nature, alone is immortal and eternal. But we do not remember because this is impassive, while the intellect which can be affected is perishable and without this does not think at all.

The process of thinking indivisible wholes belongs to a [ch. 6 sphere from which falsehood is excluded. But where both truth and falsehood are possible there is already some combining of notions into one. As, in the words of Empedocles, "where sprang into being the neckless heads of many creatures," then afterwards Love put them together, so these notions, first separate, are combined; as, for instance, the motions incommensurable and diagonal. And, if the thinking refers to the past or to the future, the notion of time is included in the combination. Falsehood, in fact, never arises except when   [430b notions are combined. For, even if white be asserted to be not-white, not-white is brought into a combination. We may equally well call every statement a disjunction. But at any rate under truth and falsehood we include not only the assertion that Cleon is white, but also the assertion that he was or will be. And the unifying principle is in every case the mind.

Since, however, the term indivisible has two meanings, according as a whole is not potentially divisible or is actually undivided, there is nothing to hinder us from thinking an indivisible whole, when we think of a length (that being actually undivided), or from thinking it in an indivisible time. For the time is a divisible or indivisible unit in the same way as the length thought of. We cannot therefore state what the mind thinks in each half of the time. For, if the whole be undivided, the half has only potential existence. But, if the mind thinks each half separately, it simultaneously divides the time also. And in that case it is as if the parts were separate lengths. If, however, the mind conceives the length as made up of the two halves, then the time may be regarded as made up of corresponding halves.

Again, that which is not quantitatively but specifically an indivisible whole the mind thinks in an indivisible unit of time and by an indivisible mental act. *Per accidens*, however, such specific unity is divisible, though not in the same way as they, the act of thought and the time required for the act, are divisible, but in the same way as they are whole and indivisible. For in these specific unities also there is present a something indivisible, though certainly not separately existent, the same as that which constitutes the unity of both the time and the length. And, as with time and length, so in like manner with whatever is continuous. But the point and every division and whatever is an undivided whole in the same sense as the point is clearly explained by the analogy of privation. And the same explanation holds in all other cases. How, for instance, is evil apprehended, or black? In some fashion by its contrary. But that which apprehends must potentially be, and must contain within itself, the contrary which it apprehends. If, however, there be something which has no contrary (*some one of the causes*), then it is itself the content of its own knowledge, is in actuality and is separately existent.

Now every proposition, like an affirmative proposition, predicating something of something, is true or false. But with thought this is not always so. When its object is the What in the sense of the quiddity and there is no predication, thought is in every case true. But, as the perception by sight of the proper object of sight is infallibly true, whereas in the question whether the white object is a man or not, perception by sight is not always true, so is it with immaterial objects.

Now actual knowledge is identical with the thing [ch. 7 431a known. But potential knowledge is prior in time in the individual, and yet not universally prior even in time. For it is from something actually existent that all which comes into being is derived. And manifestly the sensible object simply brings the faculty of sense which was potential into active exercise: in this transition, in fact, the sense is not acted upon or qualitatively changed. Consequently this must be a different species of motion. For motion is, as we saw, an activity of that which is imperfect; but activity in the absolute sense, that is, activity of that which has reached perfection, is quite distinct.

Sensation, then, is analogous to simple assertion or simple apprehension by thought and, when the sensible thing is pleasant or painful, the pursuit or avoidance of it by the soul is a sort of affirmation or negation. In fact, to feel pleasure or pain is precisely to function with the sensitive mean, acting upon good or evil as such. It is in this that actual avoidance and actual appetition consist: nor is the appetitive faculty distinct from the faculty of avoidance, nor either from the sensitive faculty; though logically they are different. But to the thinking soul images serve as present sensations: and when it affirms or denies good or evil, it avoids or pursues (this is why the soul never thinks without an image). To give an illustration: the air impresses a certain quality on the pupil of the eye, and this in turn upon something else, and so also with the organ of hearing, while the last thing to be impressed is one and is a single mean, though with a plurality of distinct aspects.

What that is by which the soul judges that sweet is different from warm has been explained above, but must be restated here. It is a unity, but one in the same sense as a boundary point, and its object, the unity by analogy of these two sensibles or their numerical unity, is related to each of the two in turn as they, taken separately, are to each other. For what difference does it make whether we ask how we judge the sensibles that do not fall under the same genus, or the contraries which do, like white and black? Suppose, then, that as A, the white, is to B, the black, so C is to D (*that is, as those sensibles are to one another*). It follows, convertendo, that A is to C as B to D. If, then, C and D are attributes of a single subject, the relation between them, like that between A and B, will be that they are one and the same, though the aspects they present are distinct: and so, too, of their single subject. The same would hold, supposing A were the sweet and B the [431b white.

Thus it is the forms which the faculty of thought thinks in mental images. And, as in the region of sense the objects of pursuit and avoidance have been defined for it, so also outside sensation, when engaged with images, it is moved to action: as, for instance, you perceive a beacon and say "That is fire"; and then *(by the central sense)*, seeing it in motion, you recognise that it signals the approach of an enemy. But at other times under the influence of the images or thoughts in the soul you calculate as though you had the objects before your eyes and deliberate about the future in the light of the present. And when you pronounce, just as there in sensation you affirm the pleasant or the painful, here in thought you pursue or avoid: and so in action generally. And, further, what is unrelated to action, as truth and falsehood, is in the same class with the good and the evil. Yet in this, at any rate, they differ, that the former are absolute, the latter relative to some one concerned.

But the abstractions of mathematics, as they are called, the mind thinks as it might conceive the snub-nosed; *quâ* snub-nosed, it would not be conceived apart from flesh, whereas *quâ* hollow, if anyone ever had actually so conceived it, he would have conceived it without the flesh in which the hollowness resides. So, too, when we think of mathematical objects, we conceive them, though not in fact separate from matter, as though they were separate. And, speaking generally, mind in active operation is its objects *(when it thinks them)*. The question, whether it is possible for the mind to think anything which is unextended without being itself unextended, must for the present be postponed.

And now let us sum up what has been said concerning [ch. 8 the soul by repeating that in a manner the soul is all existent things. For they are all either objects of sensation or objects of thought; and knowledge and sensation are in a manner identical with their respective objects. How this is so requires to be explained. Knowledge and sensation, then, are subdivided to correspond to the things. Potential knowledge and sensation answer to things which are potential, actual knowledge and sensation to things which are actual, while the sensitive and cognitive faculties in the soul are potentially these objects; I mean, object of sensation and object of cognition respectively. It follows that the faculties must be identical, if not with the things themselves, then with their forms. The things themselves they are not, for it is not the stone which is in the soul, but the form of the stone. So that there is an analogy between the soul and the hand; for, [432a as the hand is the instrument of instruments, so the intellect is the form of forms and sensation the form of sensibles. But, since, apart from sensible magnitudes there is nothing, as it would seem, independently existent, it is in the sensible forms that the intelligible forms exist, both the abstractions of mathematics, as they are called, and all the qualities and attributes of sensible things. And for this reason, as without sensation a man would not learn or understand anything, so at the very time when he is actually thinking he must have an image before him. For mental images are like present sensations, except that they are immaterial. Imagination, however, is distinct from affirmation and negation, for it needs a combination of notions to constitute truth or falsehood. But, it may be asked, how will the simplest notions differ in character from mental images? I reply that neither these nor the rest of our notions are images, but that they cannot dispense with images.

The soul in animals has been defined in virtue of two   [ch. 9 faculties, not only by its capacity to judge, which is the function of thought and perception, but also by the local movement which it imparts to the animal. Assuming the nature of sensation and intellect to have been so far determined, we have now to consider what it is in the soul which initiates motion: whether it is some one part of the soul, which is either locally separable or logically distinct, or whether it is the whole soul: and again, if a separate part, whether it is a special part distinct from those usually recognised and from those enumerated above, or whether it coincides with some one of these. A question at once arises in what sense it is proper to speak of parts of the soul and how many there are. For in one sense there appear to be an infinite number of parts and not merely those which some distinguish, the reasoning, passionate and concupiscent parts, for which others substitute the rational and the irrational. For, if we examine the differences on which they base their divisions, we shall find that there are other parts separated by a greater distance than these; namely, the parts which we have just discussed, the nutritive, which belongs to plants as well as to all animals, and the sensitive, which cannot easily be classed either as rational or irrational. Imagination, again, is logically distinct   [432b from them all, while it is very difficult to say with which of the parts it is in fact identical or not identical, if we are to assume separate parts in the soul. Then besides these there is appetency, which would seem to be distinct both in concept and in capacity from all the foregoing. And surely it is absurd to split this up. For wish in the rational part corresponds to concupiscence and passion in the irrational. And, if we make a triple division of soul, there will be appetency in all three parts.

To come now to the question at present before us, what is it that imparts to the animal local movement? For as for the motion of growth and decay, which is found in all animals, it would seem that this must be originated by that part of soul which is found in all of them, the generative and nutritive part. Inspiration and expiration of breath, sleep and waking, subjects full of difficulty, call for subsequent enquiry. But to return to locomotion we must enquire what it is that imparts to the animal progressive motion. That it is not the nutritive faculty is clear. For this motion is always directed to an end and is attended either by imagination or by appetency. No animal, which is not either seeking or avoiding something, moves except under compulsion. Moreover, if it were the nutritive faculty, plants also would be capable of locomotion and thus would have some part instrumental in producing this form of motion. Similarly it is not the sensitive faculty, since there are many animals which have sensation and yet are throughout their lives stationary and motionless. If, then, nature does nothing in vain and, except in mutilated and imperfect specimens, omits nothing that is indispensable, while the animals we are considering are fully developed and not mutilated—as is shown by the fact that they propagate their kind and have a period of maturity and a period of decline,—it follows that, if locomotion was implied in sensation, they would have had the parts instrumental to progression. Nor, again, is it the reasoning faculty or what is called intellect that is the cause of motion. For the speculative intellect thinks nothing that is practical and makes no assertion about what is to be avoided or pursued, whereas motion always implies that we are avoiding or pursuing something. But, even if the mind has something of the kind before it, it does not forthwith prompt avoidance or pursuit. For example, it often thinks of something alarming or pleasant without prompting to fear; the only effect is a beating of the heart or, when the thought is pleasant, some other bodily movement.   [433a Besides, even if the intellect issues the order and the understanding bids us avoid or pursue something, still we are not thereby moved to act: on the contrary, action is determined by desire; in the case, for instance, of the incontinent man. And generally we see that, although a man possesses a knowledge of medicine, it does not follow that he practises; and this implies that there is something else apart from the knowledge which determines action in accordance with the knowledge. Nor, again, is it solely appetency on which this motion depends. The continent, though they feel desire, that is appetite, do not act as their desires prompt, but on the contrary obey reason.

The motive causes are apparently, at any rate, these   [ch. 10 two, either appetency or intelligence, if we regard imagination as one species of thinking. For men often act contrary to knowledge in obedience to their imaginings, while in the other animals there is no process of thinking or reasoning, but solely imagination. Both these, then, are causes of locomotion, intelligence and appetency. By intelligence we mean that which calculates the means to an end, that is, the practical intellect, which differs from the speculative intellect by the end at which it aims. Appetency, too, is directed to some end in every case: for that which is the end of desire is the starting point of the practical intellect, and the last stage in this process of thought is the starting point of action. Hence there is good reason for the view that these two are the causes of motion, appetency and practical thought. For it is the object of appetency which causes motion; and the reason why thought causes motion is that the object of appetency is the starting point of thought. Again, when imagination moves to action, it does not move to action apart from appetency. Thus there is one single moving cause, the appetitive faculty. For, had there been two, intelligence and appetency, which moved to action, still they would have done so in virtue of some character common to both. But, as a matter of fact, intellect is not found to cause motion apart from appetency. For rational wish is appetency; and, when anyone is moved in accordance with reason, he is also moved according to rational wish. But appetency may move a man in opposition to reason, for concupiscence is a species of appetency. While, however, intellect is always right, appetency and imagination may be right or wrong. Hence it is invariably the object of appetency which causes motion, but this object may be either the good or the apparent good. Not all good, however, but practical good: where by practical good we mean something which may not be good under all circumstances.

It is evident, then, that motion is due to the faculty of the soul corresponding to this object—I mean what is known as ap-   [433b petency. But those who divide the soul into parts, if they divide it according to its powers and separate these from one another, will find that such parts tend to become very numerous: nutritive, sensitive, intelligent, deliberative, with the further addition of an appetent part: for these differ more widely from one another than the concupiscence does from the passionate. Now desires arise which are contrary to one another, and this occurs whenever reason and the appetites are opposed, that is, in those animals which have a perception of time. For intelligence bids us resist because of the future, while appetite has regard only to the immediate present; for the pleasure of the moment appears absolutely pleasurable and absolutely good because we do not see the future. Therefore, while generically the moving cause will be one, namely, the faculty of appetency, as such, and ultimately the object of appetency (which, without being in motion itself, causes motion by the mere fact of being thought of or imagined), numerically there is a plurality of moving causes.

Now motion implies three things, first, that which causes motion, secondly, that whereby it causes motion, and again, thirdly, that which is moved; and of these that which causes motion is twofold, firstly, that which is itself unmoved and, secondly, that which both causes motion and is itself moved. The unmoved movent is the practical good, that which is moved and causes motion is the appetitive faculty (for the animal which is moved is moved in so far as it desires, and desire is a species of motion or activity) and, finally, the thing moved is the animal. But the instrument with which desire moves it, once reached, is a part of the body: hence it must be dealt with under the functions common to body and soul. For the present, it may be enough to say summarily that we find that which causes motion by means of organs at the point where beginning and end coincide; as, for instance, they do in the hinge-joint, for there the convex and the concave are respectively the end and the beginning, with the result that the latter is at rest, while the former moves, convex and concave being logically distinct, but locally inseparable. For all animals move by pushing and pulling, and accordingly there must be in them a fixed point, like the centre in a circle, and from this the motion must begin. Thus, then, in general terms, as already stated, the animal is capable of moving itself just in so far as it is appetitive: and it cannot be appetitive without imagination. Now imagination may be rational or it may be imagination of sense. Of the latter the other animals also have a share.

We must also consider what is the moving cause in those [ch. 11 imperfect animals which have only the sense of touch. 434a Is it possible that they should have imagination and desire, or is it not? It is evident that they feel pleasure and pain: and, if they have these, then of necessity they must also feel desire. But how can they have imagination? Shall we say that, as their movements are vague and indeterminate, so though they have these faculties, they have them in a vague and indeterminate form? The imagination of sense, then, as we have said, is found in the other animals also, but deliberative imagination in those alone which have reason.—For the task of deciding whether to do this or that already implies reasoning. And the pursuit of the greater good necessarily implies some single standard of measurement. Hence we have the power of constructing a single image out of a number of images.—And the reason why the lower animals are thought not to have opinion is that they do not possess that form of imagination which comes from inference, while the latter implies the former. And so appetency does not imply the deliberative faculty. But sometimes it overpowers rational wish and moves to action; at other times the latter, rational wish, overpowers the former, appetency. Thus one appetency prevails over another appetency, like one sphere over another sphere, in the case where incontinence has supervened. But by nature the upper sphere always has the predominance and is a moving cause, so that the motion is actually the resultant of three orbits.

The cognitive faculty, however, is not subject to motion, but is at rest. The major premiss is universal, whether judgment or proposition, while the minor has to do with a particular fact: for, while the former asserts that such and such a person ought to do such and such an act, the latter asserts that a particular act is one of the sort and that I am such a person. Now it is the latter judgment which at once moves to action, not the universal. Or shall we say that it is both together, but the one is akin to the unmoved movent, the other is not?

Every living thing, then, must have the nutritive soul   [ch. 12 and in fact has a soul from its birth till its death. For what has been born must necessarily grow, reach maturity and decline, and for these processes nutriment is indispensable. It follows, then, of necessity that the nutritive faculty is present in all things that grow and decay. But sensation is not necessarily present in all living things. For wherever the body is uncompounded there can be no sense of touch (*yet without this sense animal existence is impossible*): nor, again, in those living things which are incapable of receiving forms apart from matter. But the animal must of necessity possess sensation, if nature makes nothing in vain: for everything in nature subserves an end or else will be an accessory of things which subserve an end. Now every living body having the power of progression and yet lacking sensation would be destroyed and never reach full development, which is its natural func-   [434b tion. For how in such a case is it to obtain nutriment? Motionless animals, it is true, have for nutriment that from which they have been developed. But a body, not stationary, but produced by generation, cannot possibly have a soul and an intelligence capable of judging without also having sensation. (*Neither can it, if it be not generated*). For why should it have the one without the other? Presumably for the advantage either of the soul or of the body. But neither of these alternatives is, in fact, admissible. For the soul will be no better able to think, and the body will be no better off, for the absence of sensation. We conclude, then, that no body that is not stationary has soul without having sensation.

But, further, the body, assuming that it has sensation, must be either simple or composite. But it cannot be simple, for then it would not have touch, and this sense is indispensable. This is clear from the following considerations. The animal is an animate body. Now body is always tangible and it is that which is perceptible by touch which is tangible: from which it follows that the body of the animal must have tactile sensation, if the animal is to survive. For the other senses, that is to say, smell, sight, hearing, have media of sensation, but a being which has no sensation will be unable when it comes into contact with things to avoid some and seize others. And if this is so, it will be impossible for the animal to survive. This is why taste is a kind of touch, for taste is of nutriment and nutriment is body which is tangible; whereas sound, colour and smell afford no nourishment and promote neither growth nor decay. So that taste also must be a kind of touch, because it is a sensation of that which is tangible and nutritive. These two senses, then, are necessary to the animal, and it is plain that without touch no animal can exist.

But the other senses are means to well-being, and are necessary, not to any and every species of animal, but only to certain species, as, for example, those capable of locomotion. For, if the animal capable of locomotion is to survive, it must have sensation, not only when in contact with anything, but also at a distance from it. And this will be secured if it can perceive through a medium, the medium being capable of being acted upon and set in motion by the sensible object, and the animal itself by the medium. Now that which causes motion from place to place produces a change operating within certain limits, and that which propels causes the thing propelled to propel in turn, the movement being transmitted through something intermediate. The first in the series initiates motion and propels without being itself propelled, while the last is simply propelled without propelling; the numerous middle terms of the series both propel and are propelled. So it is also with quali- [435a] tative change, except that what is subject to this change remains in the same place. Suppose we were to dip something into wax, the movement in the wax would extend just so far down as we had dipped the object, whereas in the like case a stone is not moved at all, while water is disturbed to a great distance and air is disturbed to the farthest extent possible and acts and is acted upon as long as it remains unbroken. And, to revert to the reflection of light, that is why, instead of holding that the visual ray leaving the eye is reflected, it would be better to say that the air is acted upon by the shape and colour, so long as it is one and unbroken. This is the case over any smooth surface: and accordingly the air acts on the organ of sight in turn, just as if the impress on the wax had penetrated right through to the other side.

It is evident that the body of an animal cannot be [ch. 13] uncompounded; I mean, it cannot consist entirely of fire, for instance, or of air. And animal, unless it has touch, can have no other sense, the animate body being always, as we have remarked, capable of tactile sensation. Now the other elements, with the exception of earth, would make sense-organs: but it is always indirectly and through media that such organs effect sensation. Touch, however, acts by direct contact with objects: hence its name. The other sense-organs, it is true, also perceive by contact, but it is by indirect contact: touch alone, it would seem, perceives directly in and through itself. Thus, then, no one of the three elements referred to can constitute the body of the animal. Nor indeed can it be of earth. For touch is a sort of mean between all tangible qualities, and its organ is receptive not only of all the distinctive qualities of earth, but also of heat and cold and all other tangible qualities. And this is why we do not perceive anything with our bones and our hair and such parts of us, namely, because they are of earth. And for the same reason plants, too, have no sensation,   [435b because they are composed of earth. Without touch, however, there can be no other sense; and the organ of this sense does not consist of earth nor of any other single element.

Thus it is evident that this is the only sense the loss of which necessarily involves the death of the animal. For it is not possible for anything that is not an animal to have this sense, nor is it necessary for anything that is an animal to have any other sense besides this. And this explains another fact. The other sensibles—I mean, colour, sound, odour— do not by their excess destroy the animal, but only the corresponding sense-organs: except incidentally, as when concurrently with the sound some thrust or blow is given, or when objects of sight or smell move something else which destroys by contact. Flavour, again, destroys only in so far as it is at the same time tactile. Tangible qualities, on the other hand, as heat, cold and hardness, if in excess, are fatal to the living animal. For excess of any sensible object is fatal to the organ, and so consequently excess of the tangible object is fatal to touch. And it is by this sense that the life of the animal is defined, touch having been proved to be indispensable to the existence of an animal. Hence excess in tangible qualities destroys not only the sense-organ, but also the animal itself. For touch is the one sense that the animal cannot do without. The other senses which it possesses are, as we have said, the means, not to its being, but to its well-being. Thus the animal has sight to see with, because it lives in air or water or, speaking generally, in a transparent medium. It has taste on account of what is pleasant and painful, to the end that it may perceive what is pleasant in food and feel desire and be impelled to movement. It has hearing in order that information may be conveyed to it, and a tongue, that in its turn it may convey information to its fellow.

THE

METAPHYSICS

Book · I

All men naturally desire knowledge. An indication of this   [ch. **1** 980a
is our esteem for the senses; for apart from their use we esteem them for
their own sake, and most of all the sense of sight. Not only with a
view to action, but even when no action is contemplated, we prefer
sight, generally speaking, to all the other senses. The reason of this is
that of all the senses sight best helps us to know things, and reveals many
distinctions.

Now animals are by nature born with the power of sensation, and
from this some acquire the faculty of memory, whereas others do not.
Accordingly the former are more intelligent and capable of   [980b
learning than those which cannot remember. Such as cannot hear sounds
(as the bee, and any other similar type of creature) are intelligent, but
cannot learn; those only are capable of learning which possess this sense
in addition to the faculty of memory.

Thus the other animals live by impressions and memories, and
have but a small share of experience; but the human race lives also
by art and reasoning. It is from memory that men acquire experience,
because the numerous memories of the same thing eventually produce
the effect of a single experience. Experience seems very similar   [981a
to science and art, but actually it is through experience that men acquire
science and art; for as Polus rightly says, "experience produces art, but
inexperience chance." Art is produced when from many notions of
experience a single universal judgement is formed with regard to like
objects. To have a judgement that when Callias was suffering from this

or that disease this or that benefited him, and similarly with Socrates and various other individuals, is a matter of experience; but to judge that it benefits all persons of a certain type, considered as a class, who suffer from this or that disease (*e.g.* the phlegmatic or bilious when suffering from burning fever) is a matter of art.

It would seem that for practical purposes experience is in no way inferior to art; indeed we see men of experience succeeding more than those who have theory without experience. The reason of this is that experience is knowledge of particulars, but art of universals; and actions and the effects produced are all concerned with the particular. For it is not man that the physician cures, except incidentally, but Callias or Socrates or some other person similarly named, who is incidentally a man as well. So if a man has theory without experience, and knows the universal, but does not know the particular contained in it, he will often fail in his treatment; for it is the particular that must be treated. Nevertheless we consider that knowledge and proficiency belong to art rather than to experience, and we assume that artists are wiser than men of mere experience (which implies that in all cases wisdom depends rather upon knowledge); and this is because the former know the cause, whereas the latter do not. For the experienced know the fact, but not the wherefore; but the artists know the wherefore and the cause. For the same reason we consider that the master craftsmen in every profession are more estimable and know more and are wiser than the [981b artisans, because they know the reasons of the things which are done; but we think that the artisans, like certain inanimate objects, do things, but without knowing what they are doing (as, for instance, fire burns); only whereas inanimate objects perform all their actions in virtue of a certain natural quality, artisans perform theirs through habit. Thus the master craftsmen are superior in wisdom, not because they can do things, but because they possess a theory and know the causes.

In general the sign of knowledge or ignorance is the ability to teach, and for this reason we hold that art rather than experience is scientific knowledge; for the artists can teach, but the others cannot. Further, we do not consider any of the senses to be Wisdom. They are indeed our chief sources of knowledge about particulars, but they do not tell us the reason for anything, as for example why fire is hot, but only that it *is* hot.

It is therefore probable that at first the inventor of any art which went further than the ordinary sensations was admired by his fellow-men, not merely because some of his inventions were useful, but as being a wise and superior person. And as more and more arts were discovered, some relating to the necessities and some to the pastimes of life, the inventors of the latter were always considered wiser than those of the former, because their branches of knowledge did not aim at utility. Hence when all the discoveries of this kind were fully developed, the sciences which relate neither to pleasure nor yet to the necessities of life were invented, and first in those places where men had leisure. Thus the mathematical sciences originated in the neighbourhood of Egypt, because there the priestly class was allowed leisure.

The difference between art and science and the other kindred mental activities has been stated in the *Ethics*; the reason for our present discussion is that it is generally assumed that what is called Wisdom is concerned with the primary causes and principles, so that, as has been already stated, the man of experience is held to be wiser than the mere possessors of any power of sensation, the artist than the man of experience, the master craftsman than the artisan; and the speculative sciences to be more learned than the productive.   [982a Thus it is clear that Wisdom is knowledge of certain principles and causes.

Since we are investigating this kind of knowledge, we   [ch. 2 must consider what these causes and principles are whose knowledge is Wisdom. Perhaps it will be clearer if we take the opinions which we hold about the wise man. We consider first, then, that the wise man knows all things, so far as it is possible, without having knowledge of every one of them individually; next, that the wise man is he who can comprehend difficult things, such as are not easy for human comprehension (for sense-perception, being common to all, is easy, and has nothing to do with Wisdom); and further that in every branch of knowledge a man is wiser in proportion as he is more accurately informed and better able to expound the causes. Again among the sciences we consider that science which is desirable in itself and for the sake of knowledge is more nearly Wisdom than that which is desirable for its results, and that the superior is more nearly Wisdom than the subsidiary; for the wise man should give orders, not receive them; nor should he obey others, but the less wise should obey him.

Such in kind and in number are the opinions which we hold with regard to Wisdom and the wise. Of the qualities there described the knowledge of everything must necessarily belong to him who in the highest degree possesses knowledge of the universal, because he knows in a sense all the particulars which it comprises. These things, viz. the most universal, are perhaps the hardest for man to grasp, because they are furthest removed from the senses. Again, the most exact of the sciences are those which are most concerned with the first principles; for those which are based on fewer principles are more exact than those which include additional principles; *e.g.*, arithmetic is more exact than geometry. Moreover, the science which investigates causes is more instructive than one which does not, for it is those who tell us the causes of any particular thing who instruct us. Moreover, knowledge and understanding which are desirable for their own sake are most attainable in the knowledge of that which is most knowable. For the man who desires knowledge for its own sake will most desire the most perfect knowledge, and this is the knowledge of the most knowable, and the things which are most knowable are first principles and   [982b causes; for it is through these and from these that other things come to be known, and not these through the particulars which fall under them. And that science is supreme, and superior to the subsidiary, which knows for what end each action is to be done; *i.e.* the Good in each particular case, and in general the highest Good in the whole of nature.

Thus as a result of all the above considerations the term which we are investigating falls under the same science, which must speculate about first principles and causes; for the Good, *i.e.* the *end*, is one of the causes.

That it is not a productive science is clear from a consideration of the first philosophers. It is through wonder that men now begin and originally began to philosophize; wondering in the first place at obvious perplexities, and then by gradual progression raising questions about the greater matters too, *e.g.* about the changes of the moon and of the sun, about the stars and about the origin of the universe. Now he who wonders and is perplexed feels that he is ignorant (thus the myth-lover is in a sense a philosopher, since myths are composed of wonders); therefore if it was to escape ignorance that men studied philosophy, it is obvious that they pursued science for the sake of knowledge, and not for any practical utility. The actual course of events bears witness to this; for speculation of this kind began with a view to recreation and pastime, at a time when practically all the necessities of life were already supplied. Clearly then it is for no extrinsic advantage that we seek this knowledge; for just as we call a man independent who exists for himself and not for another, so we call this the only independent science, since it alone exists for itself.

For this reason its acquisition might justly be supposed to be beyond human power, since in many respects human nature is servile; in which case, as Simonides says, "God alone can have this privilege," and man should only seek the knowledge which is within his reach. Indeed if the poets are right and the Deity is by nature jealous, it is probable that in this case He would be particularly jealous,   [983a and all those who excel in knowledge unfortunate. But it is impossible for the Deity to be jealous (indeed, as the proverb says, "poets tell many a lie"), nor must we suppose that any other form of knowledge is more precious than this; for what is most divine is most precious. Now there are two ways only in which it can be devine. A science is divine if it is peculiarly the possession of God, or if it is concerned with divine matters. And this science alone fulfils both these conditions; for (*a*) all believe that God is one of the causes and a kind of principle, and (*b*) God is the sole or chief possessor of this sort of knowledge. Accordingly, although all other sciences are more necessary than this, none is more excellent.

The acquisition of this knowledge, however, must in a sense result in something which is the reverse of the outlook with which we first approached the inquiry. All begin, as we have said, by wondering that things should be as they are, *e.g.* with regard to marionettes, or the solstices, or the incommensurability of the diagonal of a square; because it seems wonderful to everyone who has not yet perceived the cause that a thing should not be measurable by the smallest unit. But we must end with the contrary and (according to the proverb) the better view, as men do even in these cases when they understand them; for a geometrician would wonder at nothing so much as if the diagonal were to become measurable.

Thus we have stated what is the nature of the science which we are seeking, and what is the object which our search and our whole investigation must attain.

It is clear that we must obtain knowledge of the primary   [ch. 3 causes, because it is when we think that we understand its primary cause that we claim to know each particular thing. Now there are four recognized kinds of cause. Of these we hold that one is the essence or essential nature of the thing (since the "reason why" of a thing is ultimately reducible to its formula, and the ultimate "reason why" is a cause and principle); another is the matter or substrate; the third is the source of motion; and the fourth is the cause which is opposite to this, namely the purpose or "good"; for this is the end of every generative or motive process. We have investigated these sufficiently in   [983b the *Physics*, however, let us avail ourselves of the evidence of those who have before us approached the investigation of reality and philosophized about Truth. For clearly they too recognize certain principles and causes, and so it will be of some assistance to our present inquiry if we study their teaching; because we shall either discover some other kind of cause, or have more confidence in those which we have just described.

Most of the earliest philosophers conceived only of material principles as underlying all things. That of which all things consist, from which they first come and into which on their destruction they are ultimately resolved, of which the essence persists although modified by its affections—this, they say, is an element and principle of existing things. Hence they believe that nothing is either generated or destroyed, since this kind of primary entity always persists. Similarly we do not say that Socrates comes into being *absolutely* when he becomes handsome or cultured, nor that he is destroyed when he loses these qualities; because the substrate, Socrates himself, persists. In the same way nothing else is generated or destroyed; for there is some one entity (or more than one) which always persists and from which all other things are generated. All are not agreed, however, as to the number and character of these principles. Thales, the founder of this school of philosophy, says the permanent entity is water (which is why he also propounded that the earth floats on water). Presumably he derived this assumption from seeing that the nutriment of everything is moist, and that heat itself is generated from moisture and depends upon it for its existence (and that from which a thing is generated is always its first principle). He derived his assumption, then, from this; and also from the fact that the seeds of everything have a moist nature, whereas water is the first principle of the nature of moist things.

There are some who think that the men of very ancient times, long before the present era, who first speculated about the gods, also held this same opinion about the primary entity. For they represented Oceanus and Tethys to be the parents of creation, and the oath of the gods to be by water—Styx, as they call it. Now what is most ancient is most revered, and what is most revered is what we swear by.   [984a Whether this view of the primary entity is really ancient and time-honoured may perhaps be considered uncertain; however, it is said that this was Thales' opinion concerning the first cause. (I say nothing of Hippo, because no one would presume to include him in this company, in view of the paltriness of his intelligence.)

Anaximenes and Diogenes held that air is prior to water, and is of all corporeal elements most truly the first principle. Hippasus of Metapontum and Heraclitus of Ephesus hold this of fire; and Empedocles—adding earth as a fourth to those already mentioned—takes all four. These, he says, always persist, and are only generated in respect of multitude and paucity, according as they are combined into unity or differentiated out of unity.

Anaxagoras of Clazomenae—prior to Empedocles in point of age, but posterior in his activities—says that the first principles are infinite in number. For he says that as a general rule all things which are, like fire and water, homoeomerous, are generated and destroyed in this sense only, by combination and differentiation; otherwise they are neither generated nor destroyed, but persist eternally.

From this account it might be supposed that the only cause is of the kind called "material." But as men proceeded in this way, the very circumstances of the case led them on and compelled them to seek further; because if it is really true that all generation and destruction is out of some one entity or even more than one, *why* does this happen, and what is the cause? It is surely not the substrate itself which causes itself to change. I mean, *e.g.*, that neither wood nor bronze is responsible for changing itself; wood does not make a bed, nor bronze a statue, but something else is the cause of the change. Now to investigate this is to investigate the second type of cause: the *source of motion*, as we should say.

Those who were the very first to take up this inquiry, and who maintained that the substrate is one thing, had no misgivings on the subject; but some of those who regard it as one thing, being baffled, as it were, by the inquiry, say that that one thing (and indeed the whole physical world) is immovable in respect not only of generation and destruction (this was a primitive belief and was generally admitted) but of all other change. This belief is peculiar to them.

None of those who maintained that the universe is a   [984b unity achieved any conception of this type of cause, except perhaps Parmenides; and him only in so far as he admits, in a sense, not one cause only but two. But those who recognize more than one entity, *e.g.* hot and cold, or fire and earth, are better able to give a systematic explanation, because they avail themselves of fire as being of a kinetic nature, and of water, earth, etc., as being the opposite.

After these thinkers and the discovery of these causes, since they were insufficient to account for the generation of the actual world, men were again compelled (as we have said) by truth itself to investigate the next first principle. For presumably it is unnatural that either fire or earth or any other such element should cause existing things to be or become well and beautifully disposed; or indeed that those thinkers should hold such a view. Nor again was it satisfactory to commit so important a matter to spontaneity and chance. Hence when someone said that there is Mind in nature, just as in animals, and that this is the cause of all order and arrangement, he seemed like a sane man in contrast with the haphazard statements of his predecessors. We know definitely that Anaxagoras adopted this view; but Hermotimus of Clazomenae is credited with having stated it earlier. Those thinkers, then, who held this view assumed a principle in things which is the cause of beauty, and the sort of cause by which motion is communicated to things.

*   *   *

Book · I V

There is a science which studies Being *qua* Being, and   [ch. **1** 1003a
the properties inherent in it in virtue of its own nature. This science is
not the same as any of the so-called particular sciences, for none of
the others contemplates Being generally *qua* Being; they divide off
some portion of it and study the attribute of this portion, as do for
example the mathematical sciences. But since it is for the first principles
and the most ultimate causes that we are searching, clearly they must
belong to something in virtue of its own nature. Hence if these principles were investigated by those also who investigated the elements of
existing things, the elements must be elements of Being not incidentally,
but *qua* Being. Therefore it is of Being *qua* Being that we too must
grasp the first causes.

The term "being" is used in various senses, but with refer-   [ch. **2**
ence to one central idea and one definite characteristic, and not as merely
a common epithet. Thus as the term "healthy" always relates to health
(either as preserving it or as producing it or as indicating it or as
receptive of it), and as "medical" relates to the art of medi-   [1003b
cine (either as possessing it or as naturally adapted for it or as being a
function of medicine)—and we shall find other terms used similarly
to these—so "being" is used in various senses, but always with reference
to one principle. For some things are said to "be" because they are
substances; others because they are modifications of substance; others
because they are a process towards substance, or destructions or priva-
tions or qualities of substance, or productive or generative of substance
or of terms relating to substance, or negations of certain of these terms
or of substance. (Hence we even say that not-being *is* not-being.) And
so, just as there is one science of all healthy things, so it is true of
everything else. For it is not only in the case of terms which express
one common notion that the investigation belongs to one science, but
also in the case of terms which relate to one particular characteristic;
for the latter too, in a sense, express one common notion. Clearly
then the study of things which *are*, *qua* being, also belongs to one
science. Now in every case knowledge is principally concerned with
that which is primary, *i.e.* that upon which all other things depend,
and from which they get their names. If, then, substance is this primary
thing, it is of substances that the philosopher must grasp the first
principles and causes.

Now of every single class of things, as there is one perception, so
there is one science: *e.g.*, grammar, which is one science, studies all
articulate sounds. Hence the study of all the species of Being *qua*

Being belongs to a science which is generically one, and the study of the several species of Being belongs to the specific parts of that science.

Now if Being and Unity are the same, *i.e.* a single nature, in the sense that they are associated as principle and cause are, and not as being denoted by the same definition (although it makes no difference but rather helps our argument if we understand them in the same sense), since "one man" and "man" and "existent man" and "man" are the same thing, *i.e.* the duplication in the statement "he is a man and an *existent* man" gives no fresh meaning (clearly the concepts of humanity and existence are not dissociated in respect of either coming to be or ceasing to be), and similarly in the case of the term "one," so that obviously the additional term in these phrases has the same significance, and Unity is nothing distinct from Being; and further if the substance of each thing is one in no accidental sense, and similarly is of its very nature something which *is*—then there are just as many species of Being as of Unity. And to study the essence of these species (I mean, *e.g.*, the study of Same and Other and all the other similar concepts—roughly speaking all the "contraries" are reducible to this first principle; but we may consider that they have been suf-   [1004a ficiently studied in the "Selection of Contraries") is the province of a science which is generically one.

And there are just as many divisions of philosophy as there are kinds of substance; so that there must be among them a First Philosophy and one which follows upon it. For Being and Unity at once entail genera, and so the sciences will correspond to these genera. The term "philosopher" is like the term "mathematician" in its uses; for mathematics too has divisions,—there is a primary and a secondary science, and others successively, in the realm of mathematics.

*   *   *

Thus clearly it pertains to one science to give an account both of these concepts and of substance (this was one of the questions raised in the "Difficulties"), and it is the function of the philosopher to be able to study all subjects. If this is not so, who is it who will   [1004b investigate whether "Socrates" and "Socrates seated" are the same thing; or whether one thing has one contrary, or what the contrary is, or how many meanings it has? and similarly with all other such questions. Thus since these are the essential modifications of Unity *qua* Unity and of Being *qua* Being, and not *qua* numbers or lines or fire, clearly it pertains to that science to discover both the essence and the attributes of these concepts. And those who investigate them err, not in being unphilosophical, but because the substance, of which they have no real knowledge, is prior. For just as number *qua* number has its peculiar modifications, *e.g.* oddness and evenness, commensurability and equality, excess and defect, and these things are inherent in numbers both considered independently and in relation to other numbers; and as similarly other peculiar modifications are inherent in the solid and the immovable and the moving and the weightless and that which has weight; so Being *qua* Being has certain peculiar modifications, and it is about these that it is the philosopher's function to discover the truth. And here is evidence of this fact. Dialecticians and sophists wear the same appearance as the philosopher, for sophistry is Wisdom in appearance only, and dialecticians discuss all subjects, and Being is a subject common to them all; but clearly they discuss these concepts because they appertain to philosophy. For sophistry and dialectic are concerned with the same class of subjects as philosophy, but philosophy differs from the former in the nature of its capability and from the latter in its outlook on life. Dialectic treats as an exercise what philosophy tries to understand, and sophistry seems to be philosophy, but is not.

Further, the second column of contraries is privative, and everything is reducible to Being and Not-being, and Unity and Plurality; *e.g.* Rest falls under Unity and Motion under Plurality. And nearly everyone agrees that substance and existing things are composed of contraries; at any rate all speak of the first principles as contraries—some as Odd and Even some as Hot and Cold, some as Limit and Unlimited, some as Love and Strife. And it is apparent that all other things also are reducible to Unity and Plurality (we may as-   [1005a sume this reduction); and the principles adduced by other thinkers fall entirely under these as genera. It is clear, then, from these considerations also, that it pertains to a single science to study Being *qua* Being; for all things are either contraries or derived from contraries, and the first principles of the contraries are Unity and Plurality. And these belong to one science, whether they have reference to one common notion or not. Probably the truth is that they have not; but nevertheless even if the term "one" is used in various senses, the others will be related to the primary sense (and similarly with the contraries)—even if Being or Unity is not a universal and the same in all cases, or is not separable from particulars (as it presumably is not; the unity is in some cases one of reference and in others one of succession). For this very reason it is not the function of the geometrician to inquire what is Contrariety or Completeness or Being or Unity or Identity or Otherness, but to proceed from the assumption of them.

Clearly, then, it pertains to one science to study Being *qua* Being, and the attributes inherent in it *qua* Being; and the same science investigates, besides the concepts mentioned above, Priority and Posteriority, Genus and Species, Whole and Part, and all other such concepts.

We must pronounce whether it pertains to the same   [ch. 3 science to study both the so-called axioms in mathematics and sub- stance, or to different sciences. It is obvious that the investigation of these axioms too pertains to one science, namely the science of the philosopher; for they apply to all existing things, and not to a particular class separate and distinct from the rest. Moreover all thinkers employ them—because they are axioms of Being *qua* Being, and every genus possesses Being—but employ them only in so far as their purposes require; *i.e.*, so far as the genus extends about which they are carrying out their proofs. Hence since these axioms apply to all things *qua* Being (for this is what is common to them), it is the function of him who studies Being *qua* Being to investigate them as well. For this reason no one who is pursuing a particular inquiry—neither a geometrician nor an arithmetician—attempts to state whether they are true or false; but some of the physicists did so, quite naturally; for they alone professed to investigate nature as a whole, and Being. But inasmuch as there is a more ultimate type of thinker than the natural philosopher (for nature is only a genus of Being), the investigation of these axioms too will belong to the universal thinker who studies the primary   [1005b reality. Natural philosophy is a kind of Wisdom, but not the primary kind. As for the attempts of some of those who discuss how the truth should be received, they are due to lack of training in logic; for they should understand these things before they approach their task, and not investigate while they are still learning. Clearly then it is the function of the philosopher, *i.e.* the student of the whole of reality in its essential nature, to investigate also the principles of syllogistic reasoning. And it is proper for him who best understands each class of subject to be able to state the most certain principles of that subject; so that he who understands the modes of Being *qua* Being should be able to state the most certain principles of all things. Now this person is the philosopher, and the most certain principle of all is that about which one cannot be mistaken; for such a principle must be both the most familiar (for it is about the unfamiliar that errors are always made), and not based on hypothesis. For the principle which the student of any form of Being must grasp is no hypothesis; and that which a man must know if he knows anything he must bring with him to his task.

Clearly, then, it is a principle of this kind that is the most certain of all principles. Let us next state *what* this principle is. "It is impossible for the same attribute at once to belong and not to belong to the same thing and in the same relation"; and we must add any further qualifications that may be necessary to meet logical objections. This is the most certain of all principles, since it possesses the required definition; for it is impossible for anyone to suppose that the same thing is and is not, as some imagine that Heraclitus says—for what a man says does not necessarily represent what he believes. And if it is impossible for contrary attributes to belong at the same time to the same subject (the usual qualifications must be added to this premiss also), and an opinion which contradicts another is contrary to it, then clearly it is impossible for the same man to suppose at the same time that the same thing is and is not; for the man who made this error would entertain two contrary opinions at the same time. Hence all men who are demonstrating anything refer back to this as an ultimate belief; for it is by nature the starting-point of all the other axioms as well.

* * *

Thus in the first place it is obvious that this at any   [ch. 4 1006a rate is true: that the term "to be" or "not to be" has a definite meaning; so that not everything can be "so and not so." Again, if "man" has one meaning, let this be "two-footed animal." By "has one meaning" I mean this: if X means "man," then if anything is a man, its humanity will consist in being X. And it makes no difference even if it be said that "man" has several meanings, provided that they are limited in number; for one could assign a different name to each formula. For   [1006b instance, it might be said that "man" has not one meaning but several, one of which has the formula "two-footed animal," and there might be many other formulae as well, if they were limited in number; for a particular name could be assigned to each formula. If on the other hand it be said that "man" has an infinite number of meanings, obviously there can be no discourse; for not to have one meaning is to have no meaning, and if words have no meaning there is an end of discourse with others, and even, strictly speaking, with oneself; because it is impossible to think of anything if we do not think of one thing; and even if this were possible, one name might be assigned to that of which we think. Now let this name, as we said at the beginning, have a meaning; and let it have *one* meaning. Now it is impossible that "being man" should have the same meaning as "not being man," that is, if "man" is not merely predicable of one subject but has one meaning (for we do not identify "having one meaning" with "being predicable of one subject," since in this case "cultured" and "white" and "man" would have one meaning, and so all things would be one; for they would all have the same meaning). And it will be impossible for the same thing to be and not to be, except by equivocation, as *e.g.* one whom we call "man" others might call "not-man"; but the problem is whether the same thing can at once be and not be "man," not in *name*, but in *fact*. If "man" and "not-man" have not different meanings, clearly "not being a man" will mean nothing different from "being a man"; and so "being a man" will be "not being a man"; they will be one. For "to be one" means, as in the case of "garment" and "coat," that the formula is one. And if "being man" and "being not-man" are to be one, they will have the same meaning; but it has been proved above that they have different meanings. If then anything can be truly said to be "man," it must be "two-footed animal"; for this is what "man" was intended to mean. And if this is necessarily so, it is impossible that at the same time the same thing should *not* be "two-footed animal." For "to be necessarily so" means this: that it is impossible not to be so. Thus it cannot be true to say at the same time that the same thing is and is not man. And the same argument holds also in the case of not being man; because "being man" and "being not-man" have dif-   [1007a] ferent meanings if "being white" and "being man" have different meanings (for the opposition is much stronger in the former case so as to produce different meanings). And if we are told that "white" too means one and the same thing, we shall say again just what we said before, that in that case all things, and not merely the opposites, will be one. But if this is impossible, what we have stated follows; that is, if our opponent answers our question; but if when asked the simple question he includes in his answer the negations, he is not answering our question. There is nothing to prevent the same thing from being "man" and "white" and a multitude of other things; but nevertheless when asked whether it is true to say that X is man, or not, one should return an answer that means one thing, and not add that X is white and large. It is indeed impossible to enumerate all the infinity of accidents; and so let him enumerate either all or none. Similarly therefore, even if the same thing is ten thousand times "man" and "not-man," one should not include in one's answer to the question whether it is "man" that it is at the same time also "not-man," unless one is also bound to include in one's answer all the other accidental things that the subject is or is not. And if one does this, he is not arguing properly.

In general those who talk like this do away with substance and essence, for they are compelled to assert that all things are accidents, and that there is no such thing as "being essentially man" or "animal." For if there is to be such a thing as "being essentially man," this will not be "being not-man" nor "not-being man" (and yet these are negations of it); for it was intended to have one meaning, *i.e.* the substance of something. But to denote a substance means that the essence is that and nothing else; and if for it "being essentially man" is the same as either "being essentially not-man" or "essentially not-being man," the essence will be something else. Thus they are compelled to say that nothing can have such a definition as this, but that all things are accidental; for this is the distinction between substance and accident: "white" is an accident of "man," because although he is white, he is not white in essence. And since the accidental always implies a predication about some subject, if all statements are accidental, there will be nothing primary about which they are made; so the predication must [1007b] proceed to infinity. But this is impossible, for not even more than two accidents can be combined in predication. An accident cannot be an accident of an accident unless both are accidents of the same thing. I mean, e.g., that "white" is "cultured" and "cultured" "white" merely because both are accidents of a man. But it is not in this sense—that both terms are accidents of something else—that Socrates is cultured. Therefore since some accidents are predicated in the latter and some in the former sense, such as are predicated in the way that "white" is of Socrates cannot be an infinite series in the upper direction; e.g. there cannot be another accident of "white Socrates," for the sum of these predications does not make a single statement. Nor can "white" have a further accident, such as "cultured"; for the former is no more an accident of the latter than vice versa; and besides we have distinguished that although some predicates are accidental in this sense, others are accidental in the sense that "cultured" is to Socrates; and whereas in the former case the accident is an accident of an accident, it is not so in the latter; and thus not all predications will be of accidents. Therefore even so there will be something which denotes substance. And if this is so, we have proved that contradictory statements cannot be predicated at the same time.

Again, if all contradictory predications of the same subject at the same time are true, clearly all things will be one. For if it is equally possible either to affirm or deny anything of anything, the same thing will be a trireme and a wall and a man; which is what necessarily follows for those who hold the theory of Protagoras. For if anyone thinks that a man is not a trireme, he is clearly not a trireme; and so he also is a trireme if the contradictory statement is true. And the result is the dictum of Anaxagoras, "all things mixed together"; so that nothing truly exists. It seems, then, that they are speaking of the Indeterminate; and while they think that they are speaking of what exists, they are really speaking of what does not; for the Indeterminate is that which exists potentially but not actually. But indeed they must admit the affirmation or negation of any predicate of any subject, for it is absurd that in the case of each term its own negation should be true, and the negation of some other term which is not true of it should not be true. I mean, e.g., that if it is true to say that a man is not a man, it is obviously also true to say that he is or is not a trireme. Then if the affirmation is true, so must the negation be true; but if the affirmation is not true the negation will be even truer than the negation of the orig- [1008a inal term itself. Therefore if the latter negation is true, the negation of "trireme" will also be true; and if this is true, the affirmation will be true too.

And not only does this follow for those who hold this theory, but also that it is not necessary either to affirm or to deny a statement. For if it is true that X is both man and not-man, clearly he will be neither man nor not-man; for to the two statements there correspond two negations, and if the former is taken as a single statement compounded out of two, the latter is also a single statement and opposite to it.

Again, either this applies to all terms, and the same thing is both white and not-white, and existent and non-existent, and similarly with all other assertions and negations; or it does not apply to all, but only to some and not to others. And if it does not apply to all, the exceptions will be admitted; but if it does apply to all, again either (a) the negation will be true wherever the affirmation is true, and the affirmation will be true wherever the negation is true or (b) the negation will be true wherever the assertion is true, but the assertion will not always be true where the negation is true. And in the latter case there will be something which definitely is not, and this will be a certain belief; and if that it is not is certain and knowable, the opposite assertion will be still more knowable. But if what is denied can be equally truly asserted, it must be either true or false to state the predicates separately and say, e.g., that a thing is white, and again that it is not-white. And if it is not-true to state them separately, our opponent does not say what he professes to say, and nothing exists; and how can that which does not exist speak or walk? And again all things will be one, as we said before, and the same thing will be "man" and "God" and "trireme" and the negations of these terms. For if it is equally possible to assert or deny anything of anything, one thing will not differ from another; for if anything does differ, it will be true and unique. And similarly even if it is possible to make a true statement while separating the predicates, what we have stated follows. Moreover it follows that all statements would be true and all false; and that our opponent himself admits that what he says is false. Besides, it is obvious that discussion with him is pointless, because he makes no real statement. For he says neither "yes" nor "no," but "yes and no"; and again he denies both of these and says "neither yes nor no"; otherwise there would be already some definite statement.

Again, if when the assertion is true the negation is false, and when the latter is true the affirmation is false, it will be impossible to assert and deny with truth the same thing at the same time.   [1008b But perhaps it will be said that this is the point at issue.

Again, is the man wrong who supposes that a thing is so or not so, and he who supposes both right? If he is right, what is the meaning of saying that "such is the nature of reality"? And if he is not right, but is more right than the holder of the first view, reality will at once have a definite nature, and this will be true, and not at the same time not-true. And if all men are equally right and wrong, an exponent of this view can neither speak nor mean anything, since at the same time he says both "yes" and "no." And if he forms no judgement, but "thinks" and "thinks not" indifferently, what difference will there be between him and the vegetables?

Hence it is quite evident that no one, either of those who profess this theory or of any other school, is really in this position. Otherwise, why does a man walk to Megara and not stay at home, when he thinks he ought to make the journey? Why does he not walk early one morning into a well or ravine, if he comes to it, instead of clearly guarding against doing so, thus showing that he does *not* think that it is equally good and not good to fall in? Obviously then he judges that the one course is better and the other worse. And if this is so, he must judge that one thing is man and another not man, and that one thing is sweet and another not sweet. For when, thinking that it is desirable to drink water and see a man, he goes to look for them, he does not look for and judge all things indifferently; and yet he should, if the same thing were equally man and not-man. But as we have said, there is no one who does not evidently avoid some things and not others. Hence, as it seems, all men form unqualified judgements, if not about all things, at least about what is better or worse. And if they do this by guesswork and without knowledge, they should be all the more eager for truth; just as a sick man should be more eager for health than a healthy man; for indeed the man who guesses, as contrasted with him who knows, is not in a healthy relation to the truth.

Again, however much things may be "so and not so," yet differences of degree are inherent in the nature of things. For we should not say that 2 and 3 are equally even; nor are he who thinks that 4 is 5, and he who thinks it is 1000, equally wrong: hence if they are not equally wrong, the one is clearly less wrong, and so more right. If then that which has more the nature of something is nearer to that   [1009a something, there will be some truth to which the more true is nearer. And even if there is not, still there is now something more certain and true, and we shall be freed from the undiluted doctrine which precludes any mental determination.

* * *

Nor indeed can there be any intermediate   [ch. 7 1011b between contrary statements, but of one thing we must either assert or deny one thing, whatever it may be. This will be plain if we first define truth and falsehood. To say that what is is not, or that what is not is, is false; but to say that what is is, and what is not is not, is true; and therefore also he who says that a thing is or is not will say either what is true or what is false. But neither what is nor what is not is said not to be *or* to be. Further, an intermediate between contraries will be intermediate either as grey is between black and white, or as "neither man nor horse" is between man and horse. If in the latter sense, it cannot change (for change is from not-good to good, or from good to not-good); but in fact it is clearly always changing; for change can only be into the opposite and the intermediate. And if it is a true intermediate, in this case too there would be a kind of change into white not from not-white; but in fact this is not seen. Further, the understanding either affirms or denies every object of understanding or thought (as is clear   [1012a from the definition) whenever it is right or wrong. When, in asserting or denying, it combines the predicates in one way, it is right; when in the other, it is wrong.

Again, unless it is maintained merely for argument's sake, the intermediate must exist beside all contrary terms; so that one will say what is neither true nor false. And it will exist beside what is and what is not; so that there will be a form of change beside generation and destruction.

Again, there will also be an intermediate in all classes in which the negation of a term implies the contrary assertion; *e.g.*, among numbers there will be a number which is neither odd nor not-odd. But this is impossible, as is clear from the definition.

Again, there will be an infinite progression, and existing things will be not only half as many again, but even more. For again it will be possible to deny the intermediate in reference both to its assertion and to its negation, and the result will be something; for its essence is something distinct.

Again, when a man is asked whether a thing is white and says "no," he has denied nothing except that it is (white), and its not-being (white) is a negation.

Now this view has occurred to certain people in just the same way as other paradoxes have also occurred; for when they cannot find a way out from eristic arguments, they submit to the argument and admit that the conclusion is true. Some, then, hold the theory for this kind of reason, and others because they require an explanation for everything. In dealing with all such persons the starting-point is from definition; and definition results from the necessity of their meaning something; because the formula, which their term implies, will be a definition. The doctrine of Heraclitus, which says that everything is and is not, seems to make all things true; and that of Anaxagoras seems to imply an intermediate in contradiction, so that all things are false; for when things are mixed, the mixture is neither good nor not-good; and so no statement is true.

It is obvious from this analysis that the one-sided and   [ch. 8 sweeping statements which some people make cannot be substantially true—some maintaining that nothing is true (for they say that there is no reason why the same rule should not apply to everything as applies to the commensurability of the diagonal of a square), and some that everything is true. These theories are almost the same as that of Heraclitus. For the theory which says that all things are true and all false also makes each of these statements separately; so that if   [1012b they are impossible in combination they are also impossible individually. And again obviously there are contrary statements which cannot be true at the same time. Nor can they all be false, although from what we have said this might seem more possible. But in opposing all such theories we must demand, as was said in our discussion above, not that something should be or not be, but some significant statement; and so we must argue from a definition, having first grasped what "falsehood" or "truth" means. And if to assert what is true is nothing else than to deny what is false, everything cannot be false; for one part of the contradiction must be true. Further, if everything must be either asserted or denied, both parts cannot be false; for one and only one part of the contradiction is false. Indeed, the consequence follows which is notorious in the case of all such theories, that they destroy themselves; for he who says that everything is true makes the opposite theory true too, and therefore his own untrue (for the opposite theory says that his is not true); and he who says that everything is false makes himself a liar. And if they make exceptions, the one that the opposite theory alone is not true, and the other that his own theory alone is not false, it follows none the less that they postulate an infinite number of true and false statements. For the statement that the true statement is true is also true; and this will go on to infinity.

Nor, as is obvious, are those right who say that all things are at rest; nor those who say that all things are in motion. For if all things are at rest, the same things will always be true and false, whereas "this state of affairs" is obviously subject to change; for the speaker himself once did not exist, and again he will not exist. And if all things are in motion, nothing will be true, so everything will be false; but this has been proved to be impossible. Again, it must be that which *is* that changes, for change is from something into something. And further, neither is it true that all things are at rest or in motion sometimes, but nothing continuously; for there is something which always moves that which is moved, and the "prime mover" is itself unmoved.

Book · V I

It is the principles and causes of the *things which are*   [ch. 1 1025b that we are seeking; and clearly of the things which are *qua* being. There is a cause of health and physical fitness; and mathematics has principles and elements and causes; and in general every intellectual science or science which involves intellect deals with causes and principles, more or less exactly or simply considered. But all these sciences single out some existent thing or class, and concern themselves with that; not with Being unqualified, nor *qua* Being, nor do they give any account of the essence; but starting from it, some making it clear to perception, and others assuming it as a hypothesis, they demonstrate, more or less cogently, the essential attributes of the class with which they are dealing. Hence obviously there is no demonstration of substance or essence from this method of approach, but some other means of exhibiting it. And similarly they say nothing as to whether the class of objects with which they are concerned exists or not; because the demonstration of its essence and that of its existence belong to the same intellectual process. And since physical science also happens to deal with a genus of Being (for it deals with the sort of substance which contains in itself the principle of motion and rest), obviously it is neither a practical nor a productive science. For in the case of things produced the principle of motion (either mind or art or some kind of potency) is in the producer; and in the case of things done the will is the agent—for the thing done and the thing willed are the same. Thus if every intellectual activity is either practical or productive or speculative, physics will be a speculative science; but speculative about that kind of Being which can be moved, and about formulated substance for the most part only *qua* inseparable from matter. But we must not fail to observe *how* the essence and the formula exist, since without this our inquiry is ineffectual.

Now of things defined, *i.e.* of essences, some apply in the sense

that "snub" does, and some in the sense that "concave" does. The difference is that "snub" is a combination of form with matter; because
"the snub" is a concave *nose*, whereas concavity is independent of
sensible matter. Now if all physical terms are used in the same sense
as "snub"—*e.g.* nose, eye, face, flesh, bone, and in general   [1026a
animal; leaf, root, bark, and in general vegetable (for not one of these
has a definition without motion; the definition invariably includes
matter)—it is clear how we should look for and define the essence
in physical things, and why it is the province of the physicist to study
even some aspects of the soul, so far as it is not independent of matter.

It is obvious, then, from these considerations, that physics is a
form of speculative science. And mathematics is also speculative; but
it is not clear at present whether its objects are immutable and separable
from matter; it is clear, however, that some branches of mathematics
study their objects *qua* immutable and *qua* separable from matter.
Obviously it is the province of a speculative science to discover whether
a thing is eternal and immutable and separable from matter; not, however, of physics (since physics deals with mutable objects) nor of mathematics, but of a science prior to both. For physics deals with things
which exist separately but are not immutable; and some branches of
mathematics deal with things which are immutable, but presumably
not separable, but present in matter; but the primary science treats of
things which are both separable and immutable. Now all causes must
be eternal, but these especially; since they are the causes of what is
visible of things divine. Hence there will be three speculative philosophies: mathematics, physics, and theology—since it is obvious that if
the divine is present anywhere, it is present in this kind of entity; and
also the most honourable science must deal with the most honourable
class of subject.

*   *   *

But since the simple term "being" is used in various   [ch. 2
senses, of which we saw that one was *accidental*, and another *true*
(not-being being used in the sense of "false"); and since besides
these there are the categories, *e.g.* the "what," quality, quantity, place,
time, and any other similar meanings; and further besides all   [1026b
these the *potential* and *actual*: since the term "being" has various
senses, it must first be said of what "is" accidentally, that there can be
no speculation about it. This is shown by the fact that no science,
whether practical, productive or speculative, concerns itself with it. The
man who produces a house does not produce all the attributes which
are accidental to the house in its construction; for they are infinite in
number. There is no reason why the house so produced should not

be agreeable to some, injurious to others, and beneficial to others, and different perhaps from every other existing thing; but the act of building is productive of none of these results. In the same way the geometrician does not study the accidental attributes of his figures, nor whether a triangle is different from a triangle the sum of whose angles is equal to two right angles. And this accords with what we should reasonably expect, because "accident" is only, as it were, a sort of name.

*   *   *

Since, then, there are among existing things some which are invariable and of necessity (not necessity in the sense of compulsion, but that by which we mean that it cannot be otherwise), and some which are not necessarily so, nor always, but usually: this is the principle and this the cause of the accidental. For whatever is neither always nor usually so, we call an accident. E.g., if in the dog-days we have storm and cold, we call it an accident; but not if we have stifling and intense heat, because the latter always or usually comes at this time, but not the former. It is accidental for a man to be white (since this is neither always nor usually so), but it is not accidental for him to be an animal. It is by accident that a builder restores to   [1027a health, because it is not a builder but a doctor who naturally does this; but the builder happened accidentally to be a doctor. A confectioner, aiming at producing enjoyment, may produce something health-giving; but not in virtue of his confectioner's art. Hence, we say, it was accidental; and he produces it in a sense, but not in an unqualified sense. For there are potencies which produce other things, but there is no art or determinate potency of accidents, since the cause of things which exist or come to be by accident is also accidental. Hence, since not everything is or comes to be of necessity and always, but most things happen usually, the accidental must exist. E.g., the white man is neither always nor usually cultured; but since this sometimes happens, it must be regarded as accidental. Otherwise, everything must be regarded as of necessity. Therefore the cause of the accidental is the matter, which admits of variation from the usual.

We must take this as our starting-point: Is everything either "always" or "usually"? This is surely impossible. Then besides these alternatives there is something else: the fortuitous and accidental. But again, are things *usually* so, but nothing *always*, or are there things which are eternal? These questions must be inquired into later; but it is clear that there is no science of the accidental—because all scientific knowledge is of that which is *always* or *usually* so. How else indeed can one learn it or teach it to another? For a fact must be defined by being so always or usually; *e.g.*, honey-water is usually beneficial in case of fever. But science will not be able to state the exception to the rule: when it is not beneficial—*e.g.* at the new moon; because that which happens at the new moon also happens either always or usually; but the accidental is contrary to this. We have now explained the nature and cause of the accidental, and that there is no science of it.

It is obvious that there are principles and causes which   [ch. 3 are generable and destructible apart from the actual processes of generation and destruction; for if this is not true, everything will be of necessity: that is, if there must necessarily be some cause, other than accidental, of that which is generated and destroyed. Will A be, or not? Yes, if B happens; otherwise not. And B will happen if C does. It is clear that in this way, as time is continually subtracted from a limited period, we shall come to the present. Accordingly So-and-so   [1027b will die by disease or violence if he goes out; and this if he gets thirsty; and this if something else happens; and thus we shall come to what is the case now, or to something which has already happened. E.g. "if he is thirsty"; this will happen if he is eating pungent food, and this is either the case or not. Thus of necessity he will either die or not die. And similarly if one jumps over to the past, the principle is the same; for this—I mean that which has just happened—is already present in something. Everything, then, which is to be, will be of necessity; *e.g.*, he who is alive must die—for some stage of the process has been reached already; *e.g.*, the contraries are present in the same body —but whether by disease or violence is not yet determined; it depends upon whether so-and-so happens. Clearly, then, the series goes back to some starting-point, which does not go back to something else. This, therefore, will be the starting-point of the fortuitous, and nothing else is the cause of its generation. But to what sort of starting-point and cause this process of tracing back leads, whether to a material or final or moving cause, is a question for careful consideration.

Book · VII

The term "being" has several senses, which we have clas-   [ch. 1 1028a sified in our discussion of the number of senses in which terms are used. It denotes first the *"what"* of a thing, *i.e.* the individuality; and then the quality or quantity or any other such category. Now of all these senses which "being" has, the primary sense is clearly the "what," which denotes the *substance* (because when we describe the quality of a particular thing we say that it is "good" or "bad," and not "five feet high" or "a man"; but when we describe *what* it is, we say not that it is "white" or "hot" or "five feet high," but that it is "a man" or "a god"), and all other things are said to "be" because they are either quantities or qualities or affections or some other such thing.

Hence one might raise the question whether the terms "to walk" and "to be well" and "to sit" signify each of these things as "being," or not; and similarly in the case of any other such terms; for not one of them by nature has an independent existence or can be separated from its substance. Rather, if anything it is the *thing* which walks or sits or is well that is existent. The reason why these things are more truly existent is because their subject is something definite; *i.e.* the substance and the individual, which is clearly implied in a designation of this kind, since apart from it we cannot speak of "the good" or "the sitting." Clearly then it is by reason of the substance that each of the things referred to exists. Hence that which *is* primarily, not in a qualified sense but absolutely, will be substance.

Now "primary" has several meanings; but nevertheless substance is primary in all senses, both in definition and in knowledge and in time. For none of the other categories can exist separately, but substance alone; and it is primary also in definition, because in the formula of each thing the formula of substance must be inherent; and we assume that we know each particular thing most truly when we know *what* "man" or "fire" is—rather than its quality or quantity or [1028b position; because we know each of these points too when we know *what* the quantity or quality is. Indeed, the question which was raised long ago, is still and always will be, and which always baffles us—"What is Being?"—is in other words "What is substance?" Some say that it is one; others, more than one; some, finite; others, infinite. And so for us too our chief and primary and practically our only concern is to investigate the nature of "being" in the sense of substance.

Substance is thought to be present most obviously in [ch. 2 bodies. Hence we call animals and plants and their parts substances, and also natural bodies, such as fire, water, earth, etc., and all things which are parts of these or composed of these, either of parts of them or of their totality; *e.g.* the visible universe and its parts, the stars and moon and sun. We must consider whether (*a*) these are the only substances, or (*b*) these and some others, or (*c*) some of these, or (*d*) some of these and some others, or (*e*) none of these, but certain others. Some hold that the bounds of body—*i.e.* the surface, line, point and unit—are substances, and in a truer sense than body or the solid. Again, some believe that there is nothing of this kind besides sensible things, while others believe in eternal entities more numerous and more real than sensible things. Thus Plato posited the Forms and the objects of mathematics as two kinds of substance, and as a third the substance of sensible bodies; and Speusippus assumed still more kinds of substances, starting with "the One," and positing principles for each kind: one for numbers, another for magnitudes, and then another for the soul. In this way he multiplies the kinds of substance. Some again hold that the Forms and numbers have the same nature, and that other things—lines and planes—are dependent upon them; and so on back to the substance of the visible universe and sensible things. We must consider, then, with regard to these matters, which of the views expressed is right and which wrong; and what things are substances; and whether there are any substances besides the sensible substances, or not; and how sensible substances exist; and whether there is any separable substance (and if so, why and how) or no substance besides the sensible ones. We must first give a rough sketch of what substance is.

The term "substance" is used, if not in more, at least in   [ch. 3 four principal cases; for both the essence and the universal and the genus are held to be the substance of the particular, and fourthly the substrate. The substrate is that of which the rest are predicated, while it is not itself predicated of anything else. Hence we must   [1029a first determine its nature, for the primary substrate is considered to be in the truest sense substance.

Now in one sense we call the *matter* the substrate; in another, the *shape*; and in a third, the combination of the two. By matter I mean, for instance, bronze; by shape, the arrangement of the form; and by the combination of the two, the concrete thing: the statue. Thus if the form is prior to the matter and more truly existent, by the same argument it will also be prior to the combination.

We have now stated in outline the nature of substance—that it is not that which is predicated of a subject, but that of which the other things are predicated. But we must not merely define it so, for it is not enough. Not only is the statement itself obscure, but also it makes matter substance; for if matter is not substance, it is beyond our power to say what else is. For when everything else is removed, clearly nothing but matter remains; because all the other things are affections, products and potencies of bodies, and length, breadth and depth are kinds of quantity, and not substances. For quantity is not a substance; rather the substance is that to which these affections primarily belong. But when we take away length and breadth and depth we can see nothing remaining, unless it be the something bounded by them; so that on this view matter must appear to be the only substance. By matter I mean that which in itself is neither a particular thing nor a quantity nor designated by any of the categories which define Being. For there is something of which each of these is predicated, whose being is different from that of each one of the categories; because all other things are predicated of substance, but this is predicated of matter. Thus the ultimate substrate is in itself neither a particular thing nor a quantity nor anything else. Nor indeed is it the negations of these; for the negations too will only apply to it accidentally.

If we hold this view, it follows that matter is substance. But this is impossible; for it is accepted that separability and individuality belong especially to substance. Hence it would seem that the form and the combination of form and matter are more truly substance than matter is. The substance, then, which consists of both—I mean of matter and form—may be dismissed, since it is posterior and obvious. Matter too is in a sense evident. We must consider the third type, for this is the most perplexing.

Now it is agreed that some sensible things are substances, and so we should begin our inquiry in connexion with these.

It is convenient to advance to the more intelligi-   [ch. 4 1029b ble; for learning is always acquired in this way, by advancing through what is less intelligible by nature to what is more so. And just as in actions it is our task to start from the good of the individual and make absolute good good for the individual, so it is our task to start from what is more intelligible to oneself and make what is by nature intelligible intelligible to oneself. Now that which is intelligible and primary to individuals is often but slightly intelligible, and contains but little reality; but nevertheless, starting from that which is imperfectly intelligible but intelligible to oneself, we must try to understand the absolutely intelligible; advancing, as we have said, by means of these very things which are intelligible to us.

Since we distinguished at the beginning the number of ways in which substance is defined, and since one of these appeared to be essence, we must investigate this. First, let us make certain linguistic statements about it.

The essence of each thing is that which it is said to be *per se*. "To be you" is not "to be cultured," because you are not of your own nature cultured. Your essence, then, is that which you are said to be of your own nature. But not even all of this is the essence; for the essence is not that which is said to be *per se* in the sense that whiteness is said to belong to a surface, because "being a surface" is not "being white." Nor is the essence the combination of both, "being a white surface." Why? Because the word itself is repeated. Hence the formula of the essence of each thing is that which defines the term but does not contain it. Thus if "being a white surface" is the same as "being a smooth surface," "white" and "smooth" are one and the same.

But since in the other categories too there are compounds with substance (because there is a substrate for each category, *e.g.* quality, quantity, time, place and motion), we must inquire whether there is a formula of the essence of each one of them; whether these compounds, *e.g.* "white man," also have an essence. Let the compound be denoted by X. What is the essence of X?

"But this is not even a *per se* expression." We reply that there are two ways in which a definition can be not *per se* true of its subject: (*a*) by an addition, and (*b*) by an omission. In one case the definition is not *per se* true because the term which is being defined is combined with something else; as if, *e.g.*, in defining whiteness one were to state the definition of a white man. In the other, because something else (which is not in the definition) is combined with the subject; as if, *e.g.*, X were to denote "white man," and X were defined as "white." "White man" is white, but its essence is not "to be white."   [1030a But is "to be X" an essence at all? Surely not. The essence is an individual type; but when a subject has something distinct from it predicated of it, it is not an individual type. *E.g.*, "white man" is not an individual type; that is, assuming that individuality belongs only to substances. Hence essence belongs to all things the account of which is a definition. We have a definition, not if the name and the account signify the same (for then all accounts would be definitions; because any account can have a name, so that even "the *Iliad*" will be a definition), but if the account is of something primary. Such are all statements which do not involve the predication of one thing of another. Hence essence will belong to nothing except species of a genus, but to these only; for in these the predicate is not considered to be related to the subject by participation or affection, nor as an accident. But of everything else as well, if it has a name, there will be a formula of *what it means*—that X belongs to Y; or instead of a simple formula one more exact—but no definition, nor essence.

Or perhaps "definition," like the "what," has more than one sense. For the "what" in one sense means the substance and the individual, and in another each one of the categories: quantity, quality, etc. Just as "is" applies to everything, although not in the same way, but primarily to one thing and secondarily to others; so "what it is" applies in an unqualified sense to substance, and to other things in a qualified sense. For we might ask also what quality "is," so that quality also is a "what it is"; not however without qualification, but just as in the case of not-being some say by a verbal quibble that not-being "is"— not in an unqualified sense, but "is" not-being—so too with quality.

Now although we must also consider how we should express ourselves in each particular case, it is still more important to consider what the facts are. Hence now, since the language which we are using is clear, similarly essence also will belong primarily and simply to sub-stance, and secondarily to other things as well; just as the "what it is" is not essence simply, but the essence of a quality or quantity. For it must be either by equivocation that we say that these things *are*, or by adding and subtracting qualifications, as we say that the unknowable is known; since the truth is that we use the terms neither equivocally nor in the same sense, but just as we use the term "medical" in *rela-tion* to one and the same thing; but not *of* one and the   [1030b same thing, nor yet equivocally. The term "medical" is applied to a body and a function and an instrument, neither equivocally nor in one sense, but in relation to one thing.

However, in whichever way one chooses to speak of these things, it matters nothing; but this point is clear: that the primary and un-qualified definition, and the essence, belong to substances. It is true that they belong equally to other things too, but not *primarily*. For if we assume this, it does not necessarily follow that there is a defini-tion of anything which means the same as any formula; it must mean the same as a particular kind of formula, *i.e.* the formula of one thing —one not by continuity, like the *Iliad*, or things which are arbitrarily combined, but in one of the proper senses of "one." And "one" has the same variety of senses as "being." "Being" means sometimes the individual thing, sometimes the quantity, sometimes the quality. Hence even "white man" will have a formula and definition; but in a different sense from the definition of "whiteness" and "substance."

The question arises: If one denies that a formula involv-   [ch. 5 ing an added determinant is a definition, how can there be a definition of terms which are not simple but coupled? Because they can only be explained by adding a determinant. I mean, *e.g.*, there is "nose" and "concavity" and "snubness," the term compounded of the two, because the one is present in the other. Neither "concavity" nor "snubness" is an accidental, but a *per se* affection of the nose. Nor are they attributes in the sense that "white" is of Callias or a man, because Callias is white and is by accident a man; but in the sense that "male" is an attribute of animal, and equality of quantity, and all other attributes which we say belong *per se*. That is, all things which involve the formula or name of the subject of the affection, and cannot be explained apart from it. Thus "white" can be explained apart from "man," but not "female" apart from "animal." Thus either these terms have no essence or definition, or else they have it in a different sense, as we have said.

But there is also another difficulty about them. If "snub nose" is the same as "concave nose," "snub" will be the same as "concave." But if not, since it is impossible to speak of "snub" apart from the thing of which it is a *per se* affection (because "snub" means a concavity in the nose), either it is impossible to call the nose snub, or it will be a tautology, "concave-nose nose" because "snub nose" will equal "concave-nose nose." Hence it is absurd that such terms as these should have an essence. Otherwise there will be an infinite regression; for in "snub-nose nose" there will be yet another nose.

Clearly, then, there is definition of substance alone. If   [1031a there were definition of the other categories also, it would have to involve an added determinant, as in the case of the qualitative; and of the odd, for this cannot be defined apart from number; nor can "female" apart from "animal." By "involving an added determinant" I mean descriptions which involve a tautology, as in the above examples. Now if this is true, there will be no definition of compound expressions either; *e.g.*, "odd number." We fail to realize this because our terms are not used accurately. If on the other hand there are definitions of these too, either they are defined in a different way, or, as we have said, "definition" and "essence" must be used in more than one sense; thus in one sense there will be no definition of anything, and nothing will have an essence, except substances; and in another those other things will have a definition and essence. It is obvious, then, that the definition is the formula of the essence, and that the essence belongs either *only* to substances, or especially and primarily and simply.

We must inquire whether the essence is the same as the   [ch. 6 particular thing, or different. This is useful for our inquiry about substance; because a particular thing is considered to be nothing other than its own substance, and the essence is called the substance of the thing. In accidental predications, indeed, the thing itself would seem to be different from its essence; *e.g.*, "white man" is different from "essence of white man." If it were the same, "essence of man" and "essence of white man" would be the same. For "man" and "white man" are the same, they say, and therefore "essence of white man" is the same as "essence of man." But perhaps it is not necessarily true that the essence of accidental combinations is the same as that of the simple terms; because the extremes of the syllogism are not identical with the middle term in the same way. Perhaps it might be thought to follow that the accidental extremes are identical; *e.g.* "essence of white" and "essence of cultured"; but this is not admitted.

But in *per se* expressions, is the thing necessarily the same as its essence, *e.g.*, if there are substances which have no other substances or entities prior to them, such as some hold the Ideas to be? For if the Ideal Good is to be different from the essence of good, and the Ideal Animal and Being from the essence of animal and being,   [1031b there will be other substances and entities and Ideas besides the ones which they describe; and prior to them, if essence is substance. And if they are separate from each other, there will be no knowledge of the Ideas, and the essences will not exist (by "being separate" I mean if neither the essence of good is present in the Ideal Good, nor "being good" in the essence of good); for it is when we know the essence of it that we have knowledge of a thing. And it is the same with other essences as with the essence of good; so that if the essence of good is not good, neither will the essence of being "be," nor the essence of one be one. Either all essences exist alike, or none of them; and so if not even the essence of being "is," neither will any other essence exist. Again that to which "essentially good" does not apply cannot be good. Hence "the good" must be one with the essence of good, "the beautiful" with the essence of beauty, and so with all terms which are not dependent upon something else, but self-subsistent and primary. For it is enough if this is so, even if they are not Forms; or perhaps rather even if they are. (At the same time it is clear also that if the Ideas are such as some hold, the substrate will not be substance; for the Ideas must be substances, but not involving a substrate, because if they did involve one they would exist in virtue of its participation in them.)

That each individual thing is one and the same with its essence, and not merely accidentally so, is apparent, not only from the foregoing considerations, but because to have knowledge of the individual is to have knowledge of its essence; so that by setting out examples it is evident that both must be identical. But as for the accidental term, e.g. "cultured" or "white," since it has two meanings, it is not true to say that the term itself is the same as its essence; for both the accidental term and that of which it is an accident are "white," so that in one sense the essence and the term itself are the same, and in another they are not, because the essence is not the same as "the man" or "the white man," but it is the same as the affection.

The absurdity (of separating a thing from its essence) will be apparent also if one supplies a name for each essence; for then there will be another essence besides the original one, e.g. the essence of "horse" will have a further essence. Yet why should not some things be identified with their essence from the outset, if essence is substance? Indeed not only are the thing and its essence one, but their formula is the same, as is clear from what we have just stated; for it [1032a is not by accident that the essence of "one," and "the one," are one. Moreover, if they are different, there will be an infinite series; for the essence of "one" and "the one" will both exist; so that in that case too the same principle will apply. Clearly, then, in the case of primary and self-subsistent terms, the individual thing and its essence are one and the same.

It is obvious that the sophistical objections to this thesis are met in the same way as the question whether Socrates is the same as the essence of Socrates; for there is no difference either in the grounds for asking the question or in the means of meeting it successfully. We have now explained in what sense the essence is, and in what sense it is not, the same as the individual thing.

Of things which are generated, some are generated natu-   [ch. 7 rally, others artificially, and others spontaneously; but everything which is generated is generated by something and from something and becomes something. When I say "becomes something" I mean in any of the categories; it may come to be either a particular thing or of some quantity or quality or in some place.

Natural generation is the generation of things whose generation is by nature. That from which they are generated is what we call matter; that by which, is something which exists naturally; and that which they become is a man or a plant or something else of this kind, which we call substance in the highest degree. All things which are generated naturally or artificially have matter; for it is possible for each one of them both to be and not to be, and this possibility is the matter in each individual thing. And in general both that from which and that in accordance with which they are generated, is nature; for the thing generated, e.g. plant or animal, has a nature. And that by which they are generated is the so-called "formal" nature, which has the same form as the thing generated (although it is in something else); for man begets man.

Such is the generation of things which are naturally generated; the other kinds of generation are called productions. All productions proceed from either art or potency or thought. Some of them are also generated spontaneously and by chance in much the same way as things which are naturally generated; for sometimes even in the sphere of nature the same things are generated both from seed and without it. We shall consider cases of this kind later.

Things are generated artificially whose form is contained in the soul (by "form" I mean the essence of each thing, and its   [1032b primary substance); for even contraries have in a sense the same form. For the substance of the privation is the opposite substance; e.g., health is the substance of disease; for disease is the absence of health, and health is the formula and knowledge in the soul. Now the healthy subject is produced as the result of this reasoning: since health is so-and-so, if the subject is to be healthy, it must have such-and-such a quality, *e.g.* homogeneity; and if so, it must have heat. And the physician continues reasoning until he arrives at what he himself finally can do; then the process from this point onwards, *i.e.* the process towards health, is called "production." Therefore it follows in a sense that health comes from health and a house from a house; that which has matter from that which has not (for the art of medicine or of building is the *form* of health or the house). By substance without matter I mean the essence.

In generations and motions part of the process is called cogitation, and part production—that which proceeds from the starting-point and the form is cogitation, and that which proceeds from the conclusion of the cogitation is production. Each of the other intermediate measures is carried out in the same way. I mean, *e.g.*, that if A is to be healthy, his physical condition will have to be made uniform. What, then, does being made uniform entail? So-and-so; and this will be achieved if he is made hot. What does this entail? So-and-so; now this is potentially present, and the thing is now in his power.

The thing which produces, and from which the process of recovering health begins, is the form in the soul, if the process is artificial; if spontaneous, it is whatever is the starting-point of the production for the artificial producer; as in medical treatment the starting-point is, perhaps, the heating of the patient; and this the doctor produces by friction. Heat in the body, then, is either a part of health, or is followed (directly or through several intermediaries) by something similar which is a part of health. This is the ultimate thing, namely that produces, and in this sense is a part of, health—or of the house (in the form of stones) or of other things. Therefore, as we say, generation would be impossible if nothing were already existent. It is clear, then, that some part must necessarily pre-exist; because the matter is a part, since it is matter which pre-exists in the [1033a] product and becomes something. But then is matter part of the formula? Well, we define bronze circles in both ways; we describe the matter as bronze, and the form as such-and-such a shape; and this shape is the proximate genus in which the circle is placed. The bronze circle, then, has its matter in its formula. Now as for that from which, as matter, things are generated, some things when they are generated are called not "so-and-so," but "made of so-and-so"; *e.g.*, a statue is not called stone, but made of stone. But the man who becomes healthy is not called after that from which he becomes healthy. This is because the generation proceeds from the privation and the substrate, which we call matter (*e.g.*, both "the man" and "the invalid" become healthy), but it is more properly said to proceed from the privation; *e.g.*, a man becomes healthy from being an invalid rather than from being a man. Hence a healthy person is not called an invalid, but a man, and a healthy man. But where the privation is obscure and has no name—e.g. in bronze the privation of any given shape, or in bricks and wood the privation of the shape of a house—the generation is considered to proceed from these materials, as in the former case from the invalid. Hence just as in the former case the subject is not called that from which it is generated, so in this case the statue is not called wood, but is called by a verbal change not wood, but wooden; not bronze, but made of bronze; not stone, but made of stone; and the house is called not bricks, but made of bricks. For if we consider the matter carefully, we should not even say without qualification that a statue is generated from wood, or a house from bricks; because that from which a thing is generated should not persist, but be changed. This, then, is why we speak in this way.

Now since that which is generated is generated *by* some-   [ch. 8 thing (by which I mean the starting-point of the process of generation), and *from* something (by which let us understand not the privation but the matter; for we have already distinguished the meanings of these), and *becomes* something (*i.e.* a sphere or circle or whatever else it may be); just as the craftsman does not produce the substrate, *i.e.* the bronze, so neither does he produce the sphere; except accidentally, inasmuch as the bronze sphere is a sphere, and he makes the former. For to make an individual thing is to make it out of the substrate in the fullest sense. I mean that to make the bronze round is not to make the round or the sphere, but something else; *i.e.* to produce this form in another medium. For if we make the form, we must make it out of something else; for this has been assumed. E.g., we   [1033b make a bronze sphere; we do this in the sense that from A, *i.e.* bronze, we make B, *i.e.* a sphere. If, then, we make the spherical form itself, clearly we shall have to make it in the same way; and the processes of generation will continue to infinity.

It is therefore obvious that the form (or whatever we should call the shape in the sensible thing) is not generated—generation does not apply to it—nor is the essence generated; for this is that which is induced in something else either by art or by nature or by potency. But we do cause a bronze sphere to be, for we produce it from bronze and a sphere; we induce the form into this particular matter, and the result is a bronze sphere. But if the essence of sphere in general is generated, something must be generated from something; for that which is generated will always have to be divisible, and be partly one thing and partly another; I mean partly matter and partly form. If then a sphere is the figure whose circumference is everywhere equidistant from the centre, part of this will be the medium in which that which we produce will be contained, and part will be in that medium; and the whole will be the thing generated, as in the case of the bronze sphere. It is obvious, then, from what we have said, that the thing in the sense of form or essence is not generated, whereas the concrete whole which is called after it is generated; and that in everything that is generated matter is present, and one part is matter and the other form.

Is there then some sphere besides the particular spheres, or some house besides the bricks? Surely no individual thing would ever have been generated if form had existed thus independently. Form means "of such a kind"; it is not a definite individual, but we produce or generate from the individual something "of such a kind"; and when it is generated it is an individual "of such a kind." The whole individual, Callias or Socrates, corresponds to "this bronze sphere," but "man" and "animal" correspond to bronze sphere in general.

Obviously therefore the cause which consists of the Forms (in the sense in which some speak of them, assuming that there are certain entities besides particulars), in respect at least of generation and destruction, is useless; nor, for this reason at any rate, should they be regarded as self-subsistent substances. Indeed in some cases it is even obvious that that which generates is of the same kind as that which is generated—not however identical with it, nor numerically one with it, but formally one—*e.g.* in natural productions (for man begets man), unless something happens contrary to nature, as when a horse sires a mule. And even these cases are similar; for that which would be common to both horse and ass, the genus immediately above them, has no name; but it would probably be both, just as the mule   [1034a is both.

Thus obviously there is no need to set up a form as a pattern (for we should have looked for Forms in these cases especially, since living things are in a special sense substances); the thing which generates is sufficient to produce, and to be the cause of the form in the matter. The completed whole, such-and-such a form induced in this flesh and these bones, is Callias or Socrates. And it is different from that which generated it, because the matter is different; but identical in form, because the form is indivisible.

The question might be raised why some things are gen-   [ch. 9 erated both artificially and spontaneously—*e.g.* health—and others not; *e.g.* a house. The reason is that in some cases the matter—which is the starting-point of the process in the production and generation of artificial things, and in which some part of the result is already existent—is such that it can initiate its own motion, and in other cases it is not; and of the former kind some can initiate motion in a particular way, and some cannot. For many things can move themselves, but not in a particular way, *e.g.* so as to dance. It is impossible, then, for any things whose matter is of this kind (*e.g.* stones) to be moved in *this* particular way except by something else; but in *that* particular way it is possible. And it is so with fire. For this reason some things cannot exist apart from the possessor of the art, and others can; because the motion can be initiated by those things which do not indeed possess the art, but can themselves be moved either by other things which do not possess the art, or by the motion from the part of the product which pre-exists in them.

It is clear also from what we have said that in a sense all artificial things are generated either from something which bears the same name (as is the case with natural objects) or from a part of themselves which bears the same name as themselves (*e.g.* a house from a house, inasmuch as it is generated by mind; for the art is the form), or from something which contains some part; that is if the generation is not accidental; for the direct and independent cause of the production is a part of the product. Heat in the motion produces heat in the body; and either this is health or a part of health, or a part of health or health accompanies it. And this is why heat is said to produce health, because it produces that of which health is a concomitant and consequence. Therefore as essence is the starting-point of everything in syllogisms (because syllogisms start from the "what" of a thing), so too generation proceeds from it.

And it is the same with natural formations as it is with the products of art. For the seed produces just as do those things which function by art. It contains the form potentially, and that from which the seed comes has in some sense the same name as the prod-   [1034b uct (for we must not expect that all should have the same name in the sense that "man" is produced by "man"—since woman is also produced by man); unless the product is a freak. This is why a mule is not produced by a mule.

Those natural objects which are produced, like artificial objects, spontaneously, are those whose matter can also initiate for itself that motion which the seed initiates. Those whose matter cannot do this cannot be generated otherwise than by their proper parents.

It is not only with reference to substance that our argument shows that the form is not generated; the same argument is common in its application to all the primary divisions, *i.e.* quantity, quality and the other categories. For just as the bronze sphere is generated, but not the sphere nor the bronze; and as in the case of bronze, if it is generated the form and matter are not (because they must always pre-exist), so it is too with the "what" and the quality and quantity and the other categories similarly; for it is not the quality that is generated, but the wood of that quality; nor is it the size, but the wood or animal of that size. But a peculiarity of substance may be gathered from this: that some other substance must pre-exist in actuality which produces it; *e.g.* an animal, if an animal is being generated; but a quality or quantity need not pre-exist otherwise than potentially.

Since a definition is a formula, and every formula has parts; and since the formula is related to the thing in the same way as the part of the formula to the part of the thing, the question now arises: Must the formula of the parts be contained in the formula of the whole, or not? It seems clear that it is so in some cases, but not in others. The formula of the circle does not include that of the segments, but the formula of the syllable includes that of the letters. And yet the circle is divisible into its segments in just the same way as the syllable into its letters. [ch. 10

Again, if the parts are prior to the whole, and the acute angle is part of the right angle, and the finger part of the animal, the acute angle will be prior to the right angle, and the finger to the man. But it is considered that the latter are prior; for in the formula the parts are explained from them; and the wholes are prior also in virtue of their ability to exist independently. The truth probably is that "part" has several meanings, one of which is "that which measures in respect of quantity." However, let us dismiss this question and consider of what, in the sense of parts, substance consists.

If then matter, form, and the combination of the two are distinct, and if both matter and form and their combination are substance, there is one sense in which even matter may be called "part" of a thing; and another in which it is not, but the only parts are those elements of which the formula of the form consists. *E.g.*, flesh is not a part of concavity, because flesh is the matter in which concavity is induced; but it is a part of snubness. And bronze is part of the statue as a concrete whole, but not of the statue in the sense of form. We may speak of the form (or the thing as having a form) as an individual thing, but we may never so speak of that which is material by itself. This is why the formula of the circle does not contain that of the segments, whereas the formula of the syllable does contain that of the letters; for the letters are parts of the formula of the form; they are not matter; but the segments are parts in the sense of matter in which the form is induced. They approximate, however, more closely to the form than does the bronze when roundness is engendered in bronze. But there is a sense in which not even all the letters will be contained in the formula of the syllable; *e.g.* particular letters on wax or sounds in the air; for these too are part of the syllable in the sense that they [1035a are its sensible matter. For even if the line is divided and resolved into its halves, or if the man is resolved into bones and muscles and flesh, it does not follow that they are composed of these as parts of their essence, but as their matter; and these are parts of the concrete whole, but not of the form, or that to which the formula refers. Hence they are not in the formulae. Accordingly in some cases the formula will include the formula of such parts as the above, but in others it need not necessarily contain their formula, unless it is the formula of the concrete object. It is for this reason that some things are composed of parts in the sense of principles into which they can be resolved, while others are not. All things which are concrete combinations of form and matter (e.g. "the snub" or the bronze circle) can be resolved into form and matter, and the matter is a part of them; but such as are not concrete combinations with matter, but are without matter—whose formulae refer to the form only—cannot be resolved; either not at all, or at least not in this way. Thus these material components are principles and parts of the concrete objects, but they are neither parts nor principles of the form. For this reason the clay statue can be resolved into clay, and the sphere into bronze, and Callias into flesh and bones, and the circle too into segments, because it is something which is combined with matter. For we use the same name for the abso-   [1035b] lute circle and for the particular circle, since there is no special name for the particular circles.

We have now stated the truth; nevertheless let us recapitulate and state it more clearly. All constituents which are parts of the formula, and into which the formula can be divided, are prior to their wholes— either all or some of them. But the formula of the right angle is not divisible into the formula of an acute angle, but *vice versa*; since in defining the acute angle we use the right angle, because "the acute angle is less than a right angle." It is the same with the circle and the semicircle; for the semicircle is defined by means of the circle. And the finger is defined by means of the whole body; for a finger is a particular kind of part of a man. Thus such parts as are material, and into which the whole is resolved as into matter, are posterior to the whole; but such as are parts in the sense of parts of the formula and of the essence as expressed in the formula, are prior; either all or some of them. And since the soul of animals (which is the substance of the living creature) is their substance in accordance with the formula, and the form and essence of that particular kind of body (at least each part, if it is to be properly defined, will not be defined apart from its function; and this will not belong to it apart from perception); therefore the parts of the soul are prior, either all or some of them, to the concrete animal; and similarly in other individual cases. But the body and its parts are posterior to this substance, and it is not the substance, but the concrete whole, which is resolved into these parts as into matter. Therefore in one sense these parts are prior to the concrete whole, and in another not; for they cannot exist in separation. A finger cannot in every state be a part of a living animal; for the dead finger has only the name in common with the living one. Some parts are contemporary with the whole: such as are indispensable and in which the formula and the essence are primarily present; e.g. the heart or perhaps the brain, for it does not matter which of them is of this nature. But "man" and "horse" and terms which are applied in this way to individuals, but universally, are not substance, but a kind of concrete whole composed of *this* particular formula and *this* particular matter regarded as universal. But individually Socrates is already composed of ultimate matter; and similarly in all other cases.

A part, then, may be part of the form (by form I mean essence), or of the concrete whole composed of form and matter, or of the matter itself. But only the parts of the form are parts of the formula, and the formula refers to the universal; for "circle" is the same as "es-   [1036a] sence of circle," and "soul" the same as "essence of soul." But when we come to the concrete thing, e.g. *this* circle—which is a particular individual, either sensible or intelligible (by intelligible circles I mean those of mathematics, and by sensible those which are of bronze or wood)—of these individuals there is no definition; we apprehend them by intelligence or perception; and when they have passed from the sphere of actuality it is uncertain whether they exist or not, but they are always spoken of and apprehended by the universal formula. But the matter is in itself unknowable. Some matter is sensible and some intelligible; sensible, such as bronze and wood and all movable matter; intelligible, that which is present in sensible things not *qua* sensible, e.g. the objects of mathematics.

We have now discussed the case of the whole and part, and of prior and posterior. But we must answer the question, when we are asked which is prior—the right angle and circle and animal, or that into which they are resolved and of which they are composed, i.e. their parts—by saying that neither is *absolutely* prior. For if the soul also *is* the animal or living thing, or the soul of the individual *is* the individual, and "being a circle" *is* the circle, and "being a right angle" or the essence of the right angle *is* the right angle, then we must admit that the whole in one sense is posterior to the part in one sense: e.g. to the parts in the formula and the parts of a particular right angle (since both the material right angle of bronze and the right angle included by individual lines are posterior to their parts), but the immaterial angle is posterior to the parts in the formula, but prior to the parts in the individual. We must not give an unqualified answer. And if the soul is not the animal but something else, even so we must say that some wholes are prior and some are not, as has been stated.

The question naturally presents itself, what sort of parts　　[ch. 11 belong to the form and what sort belong not to it but to the concrete object. Yet if this is not plain it is impossible to define the particular; because the definition refers to the universal and the form. Therefore if it is not clear what kind of parts are material and what kind are not, the formula of the thing will not be clear either. In the case of things which can be seen to be induced in specifically different materials, as, e.g., a circle is in bronze and stone and wood, it seems clear that these things, the bronze and the stone, are in no sense part of the essential substance of the circle, because it is separable from them. As for things which are not visibly separable, there is no reason　　[1036b why the same should not apply to them; e.g., if all the circles that had ever been seen were bronze; for the bronze would be none the less no part of the form, but it is difficult to separate it in thought. For example, the form of "man" is always manifested in flesh and bones and elements of this kind; then are these actually parts of the form and formula, or are they not so, but matter, though since the form is not induced in other materials, we cannot separate it? Now since this seems to be possible, but it is not clear *when*, some thinkers are doubtful even in the case of the circle and the triangle, considering that it is not proper to define them by lines and continuous space, but that all these are to the circle or triangle as flesh or bone is to man, and bronze or stone to the statue; and they reduce everything to numbers, and say that the formula of "line" is the formula of 2. And of the exponents of the Forms, some make 2 the Ideal line, and some the form of the line; for they say that in some cases the form and that of which it is the form, *e.g.* 2 and the form of 2, are the same; but in the case of "line" this is no longer so. It follows, then, that there is one form of many things whose form is clearly different (a consequence which confronted the Pythagoreans too), and that it is possible to make one supreme Form of everything, and not to regard the rest as forms. In this way, however, all things would be one.

Now we have stated that the question of definitions involves some difficulty, and have shown why this is so. Hence to reduce everything in this way and to dispose of the matter is going too far; for some things are presumably a particular form in particular matter, or particular things in a particular state. And the analogy in the case of the living thing which the younger Socrates used to state is not a good one; for it leads one away from the truth, and makes one suppose that it is possible for a man to exist without his parts, as a circle does without the bronze. But the case is not similar; for the animal is sensible and cannot be defined without motion, and hence not unless its parts are in some definite condition; for it is not the hand in *any* condition that is a part of a man, but only when it can perform its function, and so has life in it. Without life in it it is not a part.

And with respect to mathematical objects, why are the formulae of the parts not parts of the formulae of the whole; *e.g.*, why are the formulae of the semicircles not parts of the formula of the circle? for they are not sensible. Probably this makes no difference; because there will be matter even of some things which are not sensible. In- [1037a] deed there will be matter in some sense in everything which is not essence or form considered independently, but a particular thing. Thus the semicircles will be parts not of the universal circle but of the particular circles, as we said before—for some matter is sensible, and some intelligible. It is clear also that the soul is the primary substance, and the body matter; and "man" or "animal" is the combination of both taken universally. And "Socrates" or "Coriscus" has a double sense, that is if the soul too can be called Socrates (for by Socrates some mean the soul and some the concrete person); but if Socrates means simply *this* soul and *this* body, the individual is composed similarly to the universal.

Whether there is some other material component of these substances besides their matter, and whether we should look for some further substance in them, such as numbers or something of that kind, must be considered later. It is with a view to this that we are trying to determine the nature of sensible substances, since in a sense the study of sensible substances belongs to physics or secondary philosophy; for the physicist must know not only about the matter, but also about the substance according to the formula; this is even more essential. And in the case of definitions, in what sense the elements in the formula are parts of the definition, and why the definition is one formula (for the thing is clearly one, but in virtue of what is it one, seeing that it has parts?); this must be considered later.

We have stated, then, in a general account which covers all cases, what essence is, and how it is independent; and why the formula of the essence of some things contains the parts of the thing defined, while that of others does not; and we have shown that the material parts of a thing cannot be present in the formula of the substance (since they are not even parts of the substance in that sense, but of the concrete substance; and of this in one sense there is a formula, and in another sense there is not. There is no formula involving the matter, for this is indeterminate; but there is a formula in accordance with the primary substance, *e.g.*, in the case of a man, the formula of the soul; because the substance is the indwelling form, of which and of the matter the so-called concrete substance is composed. *E.g.*, concavity is such a form, since from this and "nose" is derived "snub nose" and "snubness"—for "nose" will be present twice over in these expressions); but in the concrete substance, *e.g.* snub nose or Callias, matter will be present too. We have stated also that the essence and the individual are in some cases the same, as in the case of the primary substances; *e.g.*   [1037b crookedness and "essence of crookedness," if this is primary. By primary I mean that which does not imply the presence of something in something else as a material substrate. But such things as are material or are compounded with matter are not the same as their essence; not even if they are accidentally one, *e.g.* Socrates and "cultured"; for these are only accidentally the same.

Now let us first deal with definition, in so far as it has   [ch. 12 not been dealt with in the *Analytics*; for the problem stated there has a bearing upon our discussion of substance. The problem I mean is this: what constitutes the unity of the thing of which we say that the formula is a definition? *E.g.*, in the case of man, "two-footed animal"; for let us take this as the formula of "man." Why, then, is this a unity and not a plurality, "animal" and "two-footed"? For in the case of "man" and "white" we have a plurality when the latter does not refer to the former, but a unity when it does refer to it, and the subject, "man," has an attribute; for then they become a unity and we have "the white man." But in the case before us one term does not partake of the other; the genus is not considered to partake of its differentiae, for then the same thing would be partaking simultaneously of contraries, since the differentiae by which the genus is distinguished are contrary. And even if it does partake of them, the same argument applies, since the differentiae are many; *e.g.* terrestrial, two-footed, wingless. Why is it that these are a unity and not a plurality? Not because they are present in one genus, for in that case all the differentiae of the genus will form a unity. But all the elements in the definition must form a unity, because the definition is a kind of formula which is one and defines substance, so that it must be a formula of one particular thing; because the substance denotes one thing and an individual, as we say.

We must first examine definitions which are reached by the process of division. For there is nothing else in the definition but the primary genus and the differentiae; the other genera consist of the primary genus together with the differentiae which are taken with it. *E.g.*, the primary genus is "animal"; the next below it, "two-footed animal"; and again, "two-footed wingless animal"; and similarly also if the   [1038a expression contains more terms still. In general it does not matter whether it contains many or few terms, nor, therefore, whether it contains few or two. Of the two one is differentia and the other genus; *e.g.*, in "two-footed animal" "animal" is genus, and the other term differentia. If, then, the genus absolutely does not exist apart from the species which it includes, or if it exists, but only as matter (for speech is genus and matter, and the differentiae make the species, *i.e.* the letters, out of it), obviously the definition is the formula composed of the differentiae.

But further we must also divide by the differentia of the differentia. *E.g.*, "having feet" is a differentia of "animal"; then in turn we must discover the differentia of "animal having feet" *qua* "having feet." Accordingly we should not say that of "that which has feet" one kind is winged and another wingless (that is if we are to speak correctly; if we say this it will be through incapability), but only that one kind is cloven-footed and another not; because these are differentiae of "foot," since cloven-footedness is a kind of footedness. And thus we tend always to progress until we come to the species which contain no differentiae. At this point there will be just as many species of foot as there are differentiae, and the kinds of animals having feet will be equal in number to the differentiae. Then, if this is so, obviously the ultimate differentia will be the substance and definition of the thing, since we need not state the same things more than once in definitions, because this is superfluous. However, it does happen; for when we say "footed two-footed animal" we have simply said "animal having feet, having two feet." And if we divide this by its proper division, we shall be stating the same thing several times, as many times as there are differentiae.

If, then, we keep on taking a differentia of a differentia, one of them, the last, will be the form and the substance. But if we proceed with reference to accidental qualities—*e.g.* if we divide "that which has feet" into white and black—there will be as many differentiae as there are divisions. It is therefore obvious that the definition is the formula derived from the differentiae, and strictly speaking from the last of them. This will be clear if we change the order of such definitions, *e.g.* that of man, saying "two-footed footed animal"; for "footed" is superfluous when we have already said "two-footed." But there is no question of order in the substance; for how are we to think of one part as posterior and the other prior?

With regard, then, to definitions by division, let this suffice as a preliminary statement of their nature.

Since the subject of our inquiry is substance, let   [ch. **13** 1038b us return to it. Just as the substrate and the essence and the combination of these are called substance, so too is the universal. With two of these we have already dealt, *i.e.* with the essence and the substrate; of the latter we have said that it underlies in two senses—either being an individual thing (as the animal underlies its attributes), or as matter underlies the actuality. The universal also is thought by some to be in the truest sense a cause and a principle. Let us therefore proceed to discuss this question too; for it seems impossible that any universal term can be substance.

First, the substance of an individual is the substance which is peculiar to it and belongs to nothing else; whereas the universal is common; for by universal we mean that which by nature appertains to several things. Of what particular, then, will the universal be the substance? Either of all or of none. But it cannot be the substance of all; while, if it is to be the substance of one, the rest also will be that one; because things whose substance is one have also one essence and are themselves one.

Again, substance means that which is not predicated of a subject, whereas the universal is always predicated of some subject.

But perhaps although the universal cannot be substance in the sense that essence is, it can be present in the essence, as "animal" can be present in "man" and "horse." Then clearly there is in some sense a formula of the universal. It makes no difference even if there is not a formula of everything that is in the substance; for the universal will be none the less the substance of something; e.g., "man" will be the substance of the man in whom it is present. Thus the same thing will happen again; e.g. "animal" will be the substance of that in which it is present as peculiar to it.

Again, it is impossible and absurd that the individual or substance, if it is composed of anything, should be composed not of substances nor of the individual, but of a quality; for then non-substance or quality will be prior to substance or the individual. Which is impossible; for neither in formula nor in time nor in generation can the affections of substance be prior to the substance, since then they would be separable.

Again, a substance will be present in "Socrates," who is a substance; so that it will be the substance of two things. And in general it follows that if "man" and all terms used in this way are substance, none of the elements in the formula is the substance of anything, nor can it exist apart from the species or in anything else; I mean, e.g., that neither "animal" nor any other element of the formula can exist apart from the particular species.

If we look at the question from this standpoint it is obvious that no universal attribute is substance; and it is also clear from the fact that none of the common predicates means "so-and-so," but [1039a

"such-and-such." Otherwise amongst many other awkward consequences we have the "third man."

Again, it is clear in this way too. Substance cannot consist of substances actually present in it; for that which is actually two can never
be actually one, whereas if it is potentially two it can be one. *E.g.,* the
double consists of two halves—that is, potentially; for the actualization
separates the halves. Thus if substance is one, it cannot consist of substances present in it even in this sense, as Democritus rightly observes;
he says that it is impossible for two to come from one, or one from two,
because he identifies substance with the atoms. Clearly then the same
will also hold good in the case of number (assuming that number is a
composition of units, as it is said to be by some); because either 2 is
not 1, or there is not *actually* a unit in it.

The consequence involves a difficulty; for if no substance can consist of universals, because they mean "of such a kind," and not a particular thing; and if no substance can be actually composed of
substances, every substance will be incomposite, and so there will be
no formula of any substance. But in point of fact it is universally held,
and has been previously stated, that substance is the only or chief subject of definition; but on this showing there is no definition even of
substance. Then there can be no definition of anything; or rather in a
sense there can, and in a sense cannot. What this means will be clearer
from what follows later.

From these same considerations it is clear also what   [ch. 14
consequence follows for those who maintain that the Forms are substances and separable, and who at the same time make the species consist of the genus and the differentiae. If there are Forms, and if "animal"
is present in the man and the horse, it is either numerically one and
the same with them, or not. (In formula they are clearly one; for in
each case the speaker will enunciate the same formula.) If, then, there
is in some sense an Absolute Man, who is an individual and exists separately, then the constituents, *e.g.* "animal" and "two-footed," must have
an individual meaning and be separable and substances. Hence there
must be an Absolute Animal too.

(i)   Then if the "animal" which is in the horse and the man is
one and the same, as you are one and the same with yourself, how can
the one which in things that exist separately be one, and why   [1039b
should not this "animal" also be separated from itself? Again, if it is
to partake of "two-footed" and of "many-footed," an impossibility follows; for contrary attributes will belong to it although it is one and
individual. But if it does not, in what sense is it that one calls an
animal "two-footed" or "terrestrial"? Perhaps the terms are "com-

bined" and "in contact" or "mixed." But all these expressions are
absurd.

(ii) "But there is a different 'animal' in each species " Then there
will be practically an infinity of things of which "animal" is the substance, since it is not in an accidental sense that "man" is derived from
"animal." Again, the Absolute Animal will be a plurality. For (*a*) the
"animal" in each species will be the substance of that species, since
the species is called after it and no other thing. Otherwise "man" would
be derived from that other thing, which would be the genus of "man."
(*b*) Further, all the constituents of "man" will be Ideas. Then, since
nothing can be the Idea of one thing and the substance of another
(for this is impossible), each and every "animal" in the various species
will be the Absolute Animal.

Further, from what will these Forms be derived, and how can they
be derived from the Absolute Animal? Or how can "the animal," whose
very essence is "animal," exist apart from the Absolute Animal? And
further, in the case of sensible things both these and still more absurd
consequences follow. If, then, these consequences are impossible, clearly
there are not Forms of sensible things in the sense in which some hold
that there are.

Since substance is of two kinds, the concrete thing and   [ch. 15
the formula (I mean that one kind of substance is the formula in combination with the matter, and the other is the formula in its full sense),
substances in the former sense admit of destruction, for they also admit
of generation. But the formula does not admit of destruction in the
sense that it is ever *being* destroyed, since neither does it so admit of
generation (for the essence of house is not generated, but only the essence of *this* house); formulae *are*, and *are not*, independently of generation and destruction; for it has been shown that no one either
generates or creates them. For this reason also there is no definition or
demonstration of particular sensible substances, because they contain
matter whose nature is such that it can both exist and not exist. Hence
all the individual instances of them are perishable. If, then, the demonstration and definition of necessary truths requires scientific knowledge,
and if, just as knowledge cannot be sometimes knowledge and sometimes ignorance (it is opinion that is of this nature), so too demonstration and definition cannot vary (it is opinion that is concerned with
that which can be otherwise than it is)—then clearly there   [1040a
can be neither definition nor demonstration of individual sensible substances. For (*a*) things which perish are obscure to those who have
knowledge of them when they are removed from the sphere of their
perception, and (*b*) even though their formulae are preserved in the

soul, there will no longer be either definition or demonstration of them. Therefore in cases relating to definition, when we are trying to define any individual, we must not fail to realize that our definition may always be upset; because it is impossible to define these things.

Nor, indeed, can any Idea be defined; for the Idea is an individual, as they say, and separable; and the formula must consist of words, and the man who is defining must not coin a word, because it would not be comprehensible. But the words which are in use are common to all the things which they denote; and so they must necessarily apply to something else as well. E.g., if a man were to define you, he would say that you are an animal which is lean or white or has some other attribute which will apply to something else as well. And if it should be said that there is no reason why all the attributes separately should not belong to several things, and yet in combination belong to this alone, we must reply, (i.) that they also belong to both the elements; e.g., "two-footed animal" belongs both to "animal" and to "two-footed" (and in the case of eternal elements this is even necessarily so; since they are prior to the compound, and parts of it. Indeed they are also separable, if the term "man" is separable—for either neither can be separable, or both are so. If neither, the genus will not exist apart from the species, or if it is so to exist, so will the differentia); (ii.) that "animal" and "two-footed" are prior in being to "two-footed animal," and that which is prior to something else is not destroyed together with it.

Again, if the Ideas are composed of Ideas (for constituents are less composite than that which they compose), still the elements of which the Idea is composed (e.g. "animal" and "two-footed") will have to be predicated of many particulars. Otherwise, how can they be known? For there would be an Idea which cannot be predicated of more than one thing. But this is not considered possible; every Idea is thought to admit of participation.

Thus, as we have said, the impossibility of defining individuals is hard to realize when we are dealing with eternal entities, especially in the case of such as are unique, e.g. the sun and moon. For people go wrong not only by including in the definition attributes on whose removal it will still be sun—e.g., "that which goes round the earth," or "night-hidden" (for they suppose that if it stops or becomes visible it will no longer be sun; but it is absurd that this should be so, since "the sun" denotes a definite substance)—they also mention attributes which may apply to something else; e.g., if another thing with those attributes comes into being, clearly it will be a sun. The formula, [1040b then, is general; but the sun was supposed to be an individual, like Cleon or Socrates. Why does not one of the exponents of the Ideas produce a definition of them? If they were to try, it would become obvious that what we have just said is true.

It is obvious that even of those things which are thought [ch. 16 to be substances the majority are potentialities; both the parts of living things (for none of them has a separate substantial existence; and when they are separated, although they still exist, they exist as matter), and earth, fire and air; for none of these is one *thing*—they are a mere aggregate before they are digested and some one thing is generated from them. It might be supposed very reasonably that the parts of living things and the corresponding parts of their vital principle are both, *i.e.* exist both actually and potentially, because they contain principles of motion derived from something in their joints; and hence some animals live even when they are divided. Nevertheless it is only potentially that all of them will exist when they are one and continuous by nature and not by force or concretion; for this sort of thing is malformation.

And since "unity" has the same variety of senses as "being," and the substance of Unity is one, and things whose substance is numerically one are numerically one, evidently neither Unity nor Being can be the substance of things, just as neither "being an element" or "principle" can be the substance; but we ask what the principle is so that we may refer to something more intelligible. Now of these concepts Being and Unity are more nearly substance than are principle, element and cause; but not even the former are quite substance, since nothing else that is common is substance; for substance belongs to nothing except itself and that which contains it and of which it is the substance. Again, Unity cannot exist in many places at the same time, but that which is common is present in many things at the same time. Hence it is clear that no universal exists in separation apart from its particulars. The exponents of the Forms are partly right in their account when they make the Forms separate; that is, if the Forms are substances, but they are also partly wrong, since by "Form" they mean the "one-over-many." The reason for this is that they cannot explain what are the imperishable substances of this kind which exist besides particular sensible substances; so they make them the same in kind as perishable things (for these we know); *i.e.*, they make "Ideal Man" and "Ideal Horse," adding the word "Ideal" to the names of sensible things. However, I presume that even if we had never seen the stars, none the less there would [1041a be eternal substances besides those which we knew; and so in the present case even if we cannot apprehend what they are, still there must be eternal substances of some kind.

It is clear, then, both that no universal term is substance and that no substance is composed of substances.

As for what and what sort of thing we mean by sub-   [ch. 17
stance, let us explain this by making, as it were, another fresh start.
Perhaps in this way we shall also obtain some light upon that kind of
substance which exists in separation from sensible substances. Since,
then, substance is a kind of principle and cause, we had better pursue
our inquiry from this point.

Now when we ask why a thing is, it is always in the sense "why
does A belong to B?" To ask why the cultured man is a cultured man
is to ask either, as we have said, why the man is cultured, or something else. Now to ask why a thing is itself is no question; because
when we ask the reason of a thing the fact must first be evident; *e.g.*,
that the moon suffers eclipse; and "because it is itself" is the one explanation and reason which applies to all questions such as "why is
man man?" or "why is the cultured person cultured?" (unless one were
to say that each thing is indivisible from itself, and that this is what
"being one" really means); but this, besides being a general answer, is
a summary one. We may, however, ask why a man is an animal of such-
and-such a kind. It is clear, then, that we are not asking why he who is
a man is a man; therefore we are asking why A, which is predicated of
B, belongs to B. (The fact that A does belong to B must be evident,
for if this is not so, the question is pointless.) E.g., "Why does it thun-
der?" means "why is a noise produced in the clouds?" for the true form
of the question is one thing predicated in this way of another. Or again,
"why are these things, *e.g.* bricks and stones, a house?" Clearly then we
are inquiring for the cause (*i.e.*, to speak abstractly, the essence); which
is in the case of some things, *e.g.* house or bed, the *end*, and in others
the prime mover—for this also is a cause. We look for the latter kind of
cause in the case of generation and destruction, but for the former
also in the case of existence.

What we are now looking for is most obscure when one term is not
predicated of another; *e.g.* when we inquire what man is; be-   [1041b
cause the expression is a simple one not analysed into subject and attributes. We must make the question articulate before we ask it; otherwise we get something which shares the nature of a pointless and of a
definite question. Now since we must know that the fact actually exists,
it is surely clear that the question is "why is the *matter* so-and-so?" *e.g.*
"why are these materials a house?" Because the essence of house is present in them. And this matter, or the body containing this particular
form, is man. Thus what we are seeking is the cause (*i.e.* the form)
in virtue of which the matter is a definite thing; and this is the substance
of the thing.

Clearly then in the case of simple entities inquiry and explanation
are impossible; in such cases there is a different mode of inquiry.

Now since that which is composed of something in such a way that the whole is a unity; not as an aggregate is a unity, but as a syllable is —the syllable is not the letters, nor is BA the same as B and A; nor is flesh fire and earth; because after dissolution the compounds, *e.g.* flesh or the syllable, no longer exist; but the letters exist, and so do fire and earth. Therefore the syllable is some particular thing; not merely the letters, vowel and consonant, but something else besides. And flesh is not merely fire and earth, or hot and cold, but something else besides. Since then this something else must be either an element or composed of elements, (*a*) if it is an element, the same argument applies again; for flesh will be composed of *this* and fire and earth, and again of another element, so that there will be an infinite regression. And (*b*) if it is composed of elements, clearly it is composed not of one (otherwise it will itself be that element) but of several; so that we shall use the same argument in this case as about the flesh or the syllable. It would seem, however, that this "something else" is something that is not an element, but is the cause that *this* matter is flesh and *that* matter a syllable, and similarly in other cases. And this is the substance of each thing, for it is the primary cause of its existence. And since, although some things are not substances, all substances are constituted in accordance with and by nature, substance would seem to be this "nature," which is not an element but a principle. An element is that which is present as matter in a thing, and into which the thing is divided; *e.g.*, A and B are the elements of the syllable.

Book · V I I I

We must now draw our conclusions from what has   [ch. 1 1042a been said, and after summing up the result, bring our inquiry to a close. We have said that the objects of our inquiry are the causes and principles and elements of substances. Now some substances are agreed upon by all; but about others certain thinkers have stated individual theories. Those about which there is agreement are natural substances: *e.g.* fire, earth, water, air and all the other simple bodies; next, plants and their parts, and animals and the parts of animals; and finally the sensible universe and its parts; and certain thinkers individually include as substances the Forms and the objects of mathematics. And arguments show that there are yet other substances: the essence and the substrate. Again, from another point of view, the genus is more nearly substance than the species, and the universal than the particulars; and there is a close connexion between the universal and genus and the Ideas, for they are thought to be substance on the same grounds. And since the essence is substance, and definition is the formula of the essence, we have therefore systematically examined definition and essential predication. And since the definition is a formula, and the formula has parts, we have been compelled to investigate "parts," and to discover what things are parts of the substance, and what are not; and whether the parts of the substance are also parts of the definition. Further, then, neither the universal nor the genus is substance. As for the Ideas and the objects of mathematics (for some say that these exist apart from sensible substances) we must consider them later. But now let us proceed to discuss those substances which are generally accepted as such.

Now these are the sensible substances, and all sensible substances contain matter. And the substrate is substance; in one sense matter (by matter I mean that which is not actually, but is potentially, an individual thing); and in another the formula and the specific shape (which is an individual thing and is theoretically separable); and thirdly there is the combination of the two, which alone admits of generation and destruction, and is separable in an unqualified sense—for of substances in the sense of formula some are separable and some are not.

That matter is also substance is evident; for in all opposite processes of change there is something that underlies those processes; *e.g.*, if the change is of *place*, that which is now in one place and subsequently in another; and if the change is of *magnitude*, that which is now of such-and-such a size, and subsequently smaller or greater; and if the change is of *quality*, that which is now healthy and subsequently diseased. Similarly, if the change is in respect of *being*, there is something   [1042b which is now in course of generation, and subsequently in course of destruction, and which is the underlying substrate, now as *this* individual thing, and subsequently as deprived of its individuality. In this last process of change the others are involved, but in either one or two of the others it is not involved; for it does not necessarily follow that if a thing contains matter that admits of change of place, it also contains matter that is generable and destructible. The difference between absolute and qualified generation has been explained in the *Physics*.

Since substance in the sense of substrate or matter is ad-   [ch. **2** mittedly substance, and this is potential substance, it remains to explain the nature of the actual substance of sensible things. Now Democritus apparently assumes three differences in substance; for he says that the underlying body is one and the same in material, but differs in figure, *i.e.* shape; or inclination, *i.e.* position; or intercontact, *i.e.* arrangement. But evidently there are many differences; *e.g.* some things are defined by the way in which their materials are combined, as, for example, things which are unified by mixture, as honey-water; or by ligature, as a faggot; or by glue, as a book; or by clamping, as a chest; or by more than one of these methods. Other things are defined by their position, *e.g.* threshold and lintel (for these differ in being situated in a particular way); and others by place (or direction), *e.g.* the winds; others by time, *e.g.* dinner and breakfast; and others by the attributes peculiar to sensible things, *e.g.* hardness and softness, density and rarity, dryness and humidity. Some are distinguished by some of these differences, and others by all of them; and in general some by excess and some by defect.

Hence it is clear that "is" has the same number of senses; for a thing "is" a threshold because it is situated in a particular way, and "to be a threshold" means to be situated in this particular way; and "to be ice" means to be condensed in this particular way. Some things have their being defined in all these ways: by being partly mixed, partly blended, partly bound, partly condensed, and partly subjected to all the other different processes; as, for example, a hand or a foot. We must therefore comprehend the various kinds of differences—for these will be principles of being—*i.e.* the differences in degree, or in density and rarity, and in other such modifications; for they are all instances of excess and defect. And if anything differs in shape or in smoothness or roughness, all these are differences in straightness and curvature. For some things mixture will constitute being, and the opposite   [1043a state not-being.

From this it is evident that if substance is the cause of the existence of each thing, we must look among these "differences" for the cause of the being of each thing. No one of them, nor the combination of any two of them, is substance, but nevertheless each one of them contains something analogous to substance. And just as in the case of substances that which is predicated of the matter is the actuality itself, so in the other kinds of definition it is the nearest approximation to actuality. E.g., if we have to define a threshold, we shall call it "a piece of wood or stone placed in such-and-such a way"; and we shall define a house as "bricks and timber arranged in such-and-such a way"; or again in some cases there is the final cause as well. And if we are defining ice, we shall describe it as "water congealed or condensed in such-and-such a way"; and a harmony is "such-and-such a combination of high and low"; and similarly in the other cases.

From this it is evident that the actuality or formula is different in the case of different matter; for in some cases it is a combination, in others a mixture, and in others some other of the modes which we have described. Hence in defining the nature of a house, those who describe it as stones, bricks and wood, describe the potential house, since these things are its matter; those who describe it as "a receptacle for containing goods and bodies," or something else to the same effect, describe its actuality; but those who combine these two definitions describe the third kind of substance, that which is composed of matter and form. For it would seem that the formula which involves the differentiae is that of the form and the actuality, while that which involves the constituent parts is rather that of the matter. The same is true of the kind of definitions which Archytas used to accept; for they are definitions of the combined matter and form. E.g., what is "windlessness?" Stillness in a large extent of air; for the air is the matter, and the stillness is the actuality and substance. What is a calm? Levelness of sea. The sea is the material substrate, and the levelness is the actuality or form.

From the foregoing account it is clear what sensible substance is, and in what sense it exists; either as matter, or as form and actuality, or thirdly as the combination of the two.

We must not fail to realize that sometimes it is doubtful [ch. 3 whether a name denotes the composite substance or the actuality and the form—e.g. whether "house" denotes the composite thing, "a covering made of bricks and stones arranged in such-and-such a way," or the actuality and form, "a covering"; and whether "line" means "duality in length" or "duality"; and whether "animal" means "a soul in a body" or "a soul"; for the soul is the substance and actuality of some body. The term "animal" would be applicable to both cases; not as being defined by one formula, but as relating to one concept. These distinctions are of importance from another point of view, but unimportant for the investigation of sensible substance; because the essence be- [1043b longs to the form and the actualization. Soul and essence of soul are the same, but man and essence of man are not, unless the soul is also to be called man; and although this is so in one sense, it is not so in another.

It appears, then, upon inquiry into the matter, that a syllable is not derived from the phonetic elements plus combination, nor is a house bricks plus combination. And this is true; for the combination or mixture is not derived from the things of which it is a combination or mixture, nor, similarly, is any other of the "differences." E.g., if the threshold is defined by its position, the position is not derived from the threshold, but rather vice versa. Nor, indeed, is man "animal" plus "two-footed"; there must be something which exists besides these, if they are matter; but it is neither an element nor derived from an element, but the substance; and those who offer the definition given above are omitting this and describing the matter. If, then, this something else is the cause of a man's being, and this is his substance, they will not be stating his actual substance.

Now the substance must be either eternal or perishable without ever being in process of perishing, and generated without ever being in process of generation. It has been clearly demonstrated elsewhere that no one generates or creates the form; it is the individual thing that is created, and the compound that is generated. But whether the substances of perishable things are separable or not is not yet at all clear; only it is clear that this is impossible in some cases, *i.e.* in the case of all things which cannot exist apart from the particular instances; *e.g.* house or implement. Probably, then, neither these things themselves, nor anything else which is not naturally composed, are substances; for their nature is the only substance which one can assume in the case of perishable things. Hence the difficulty which perplexed the followers of Antisthenes and others similarly unlearned has a certain application; I mean the difficulty that it is impossible to define *what* a thing is (for the definition, they say, is a lengthy formula), but it is possible actually to teach others what a thing *is like*; *e.g.*, we cannot say *what* silver is, but we can say that it is like tin. Hence there can be definition and formula of one kind of substance, *i.e.* the composite, whether it is sensible or intelligible; but not of its primary constituents, since the defining formula denotes something predicated of something, and this must be partly of the nature of matter and partly of the nature of form.

It is also obvious that, if numbers are in any sense substances, they are such in this sense, and not, as some describe them, aggregates of units. For (*a*) the definition is a kind of number, since it is divisible, and divisible into indivisible parts (for formulae are not infinite); and number is of this nature. And (*b*) just as when any element which composes the number is subtracted or added, it is no longer the same number but a different one, however small the subtraction or ad-   [1044a dition is; so neither the definition nor the essence will continue to exist if something is subtracted from or added to it. And (*c*) a number must be something in virtue of which it is a unity (whereas our opponents cannot say what makes it one); that is, if it is a unity. For either it is not a unity but a kind of aggregate, or if it is a unity, we must explain what makes a unity out of a plurality. And the definition is a unity; but similarly they cannot explain the definition either. This is a natural consequence, for the same reason applies to both, and substance is a unity in the way which we have explained, and not as some thinkers say: *e.g.* because it is a kind of unit or point; but each substance is a kind of actuality and nature. Also (*d*) just as a number does not admit of variation in degree, so neither does substance in the sense of form; if any substance does admit of this, it is substance in combination with matter.

Let this suffice as a detailed account of the generation and destruction of so-called substances, in what sense they are possible and in what sense they are not; and of the reference of things to number.

As regards material substance, we must not fail to realize   [ch. 4 that even if all things are derived from the same primary cause, or from the same things as primary causes; *i.e.* even if all things that are generated have the same matter for their first principle, nevertheless each thing has some matter peculiar to it; *e.g.*, "the sweet" or "the viscous" is the proximate matter of mucus, and "the bitter" or some such thing is that of bile—although probably mucus and bile are derived from the same ultimate matter. The result is that there is more than one matter of the same thing, when one thing is the matter of the other; *e.g.*, mucus is derived from "the viscous"; and from "the sweet," if "the viscous" is derived from "the sweet"; and from bile, by the analysis of bile into its ultimate matter. For there are two senses in which X comes from Y; either because X will be found further on than Y in the process of development, or because X is produced when Y is analysed into its original constituents. And different things can be generated by the moving cause when the matter is one and the same, *e.g.* a chest and a bed from wood. But some different things must necessarily have different matter; *e.g.*, a saw cannot be generated from wood, nor does this lie in the power of the moving cause, for it cannot make a saw of wool or wood.

If, then, it is possible to make the same thing from different matter, clearly the art, *i.e.* the moving principle, is the same; for if both the matter and the mover are different, so too is the product.

So whenever we inquire what the cause is, since there are causes in several senses, we must state all the possible causes. E.g., what is the material cause of a man? The menses. What is the moving cause? The semen. What is the formal cause? The essence. What is the final cause? The end. (But perhaps both the latter are the same.) We [1044b] must, however, state the most proximate causes. What is the matter? Not fire or earth, but the matter proper to man.

Thus as regards generable natural substances we must proceed in this manner, if we are to proceed correctly; that is, if the causes are these and of this number, and it is necessary to know the causes. But in the case of substances which though natural are eternal the principle is different. For presumably some of them have no matter, or no matter of this kind, but only such as is spatially mobile. Moreover, things which exist by nature but are not substances have no matter; their substrate is their substance. E.g., what is the cause of an eclipse; what is its matter? It has none; it is the moon which is affected. What is the moving cause which destroys the light? The earth. There is probably no final cause. The formal cause is the formula; but this is obscure unless it includes the efficient cause. E.g., what is an eclipse? A privation of light; and if we add "caused by the earth's intervention," this is the definition which includes the (efficient) cause. In the case of sleep it is not clear what it is that is proximately affected. Is it the animal? Yes; but in respect of what, and of what proximately? The heart, or some other part.

Again, by what is it affected? Again, what is the affection which affects
that part, and not the whole animal? A particular kind of immobility?
Yes; but in virtue of what affection of the proximate subject is it this?

Since some things both are and are not, without being   [ch. 5
liable to generation and destruction—*e.g.* points, if they exist at all; and
in general the forms and shapes of things (because white does not come
to be, but the wood becomes white, since everything which comes into
being comes from something and becomes something)—not all the contraries can be generated from each other. White is not generated from
black in the same way as a white man is generated from a black man;
nor does everything contain matter, but only such things as admit of
generation and transformation into each other. And such things as, without undergoing a process of change, both are and are not, have no
matter.

There is a difficulty in the question how the matter of the individual
is related to the contraries. *E.g.,* if the body is potentially healthy, and
the contrary of health is disease, is the body potentially both healthy
and diseased? And is water potentially wine and vinegar? Probably in
the one case it is the matter in respect of the positive state and form,
and in the other case in respect of privation and degeneration which
is contrary to its proper nature.

There is also a difficulty as to why wine is not the matter of vinegar, nor potentially vinegar (though vinegar comes from it), and why
the living man is not potentially dead. In point of fact they are not;
their degeneration is accidental, and the actual matter of the   [1045a
living body becomes by degeneration the potentiality and matter of the
dead body, and water the matter of vinegar; for the one becomes the
other just as day becomes night. All things which change reciprocally in
this way must return into the matter; *e.g.,* if a living thing is generated
from a dead one, it must first become the matter, and then a living
thing; and vinegar must first become water, and then wine.

With regard to the difficulty which we have described in   [ch. 6
connexion with definitions and numbers, what is the cause of the unification? In all things which have a plurality of parts, and which are not
a total aggregate but a whole of some sort distinct from the parts, there
is some *cause*; inasmuch as even in bodies sometimes contact is the cause
of their unity, and sometimes viscosity or some other such quality. But
a definition is *one* account, not by connexion, like the *Iliad*, but because it is a definition of one thing.

What is it, then, that makes "man" one thing, and why does it
make him one thing and not many, *e.g.* "animal" and "two-footed," especially if, as some say, there is an Idea of "animal" and an Idea of
"two-footed"? Why are not these Ideas "man," and why should not

man exist by participation, not in any "man," but in two Ideas, those of "animal" and "two-footed"? And in general "man" will be not one, but two things—"animal" and "two-footed." Evidently if we proceed in this way, as it is usual to define and explain, it will be impossible to answer and solve the difficulty. But if, as we maintain, man is part matter and part form—the matter being potentially, and the form actually man—, the point which we are investigating will no longer seem to be a difficulty. For this difficulty is just the same as we should have if the definition of X were "round bronze"; for this name would give a clue to the formula, so that the question becomes "what is the cause of the unification of 'round' and 'bronze'?" The difficulty is no longer apparent, because the one is matter and the other form. What then is it (apart from the active cause) which causes that which exists potentially to exist actually in things which admit of generation? There *is* no other cause of the potential sphere's being an actual sphere; this was the essence of each.

Some matter is intelligible and some sensible, and part of the formula is always matter and part actuality; *e.g.*, the circle is a plane figure. But such things as have no matter, neither intelligible nor sensible, are *ipso facto* each one of them essentially something one;   [1045b just as they are essentially something existent: an individual substance, a quality, or a quantity. Hence neither "existent" nor "one" is present in their definitions. And their essence is *ipso facto* something one, just as it is something existent. Hence also there is no other cause of the unity of any of these things, or of their existence; for each one of them is "one" and "existent" not because it is contained in the genus "being" or "unity," nor because these genera exist separately apart from their particulars, but *ipso facto*.

It is because of this difficulty that some thinkers speak of "participation," and raise the question of what is the cause of participation, and what participation means; and others speak of "communion"; *e.g.,* Lycophron says that knowledge is a communion of the soul with "knowing"; and others call life a combination or connexion of soul with body. The same argument, however, applies in every case; for "being healthy" will be the "communion" or "connexion" or "combination" of soul and health; and "being a bronze triangle" a "combination" of bronze and triangle; and "being white" a "combination" of surface and whiteness. The reason for this is that people look for a unifying formula, and a difference, between potentiality and actuality. But, as we have said, the proximate matter and the shape are one and the same; the one existing potentially, and the other actually. Therefore to ask the cause of their unity is like asking the cause of unity in general; for each individual thing is one, and the potential and the actual are in a sense one. Thus there is no cause other than whatever initiates the development from potentiality to actuality. And such things as have no matter are all, without qualification, essential unities.

Book · I X

We have now dealt with Being in the primary sense, to which   [ch. 1 all the other categories of being are related; *i.e.* substance. For it is from the concept of substance that all the other modes of being take their meaning; both quantity and quality and all other such terms; for they will all involve the concept of substance, as we stated it in the beginning of our discussion. And since the senses of being are analysable not only into substance or quality or quantity, but also in accordance with potentiality and actuality and function, let us also gain a clear understanding about potentiality and actuality; and first about potentiality in the sense which is most proper to the word, but not most   [1046a useful for our present purpose—for potentiality and actuality extend beyond the sphere of terms which only refer to motion. When we have discussed this sense of potentiality we will, in the course of our definitions of actuality, explain the others also.

We have made it plain elsewhere that "potentiality" and "can" have several senses. All senses which are merely equivocal may be dismissed; for some are used by analogy, as in geometry, and we call things possible or impossible because they "are" or "are not" in some particular way. But the potentialities which conform to the same type are all principles, and derive their meaning from one primary sense of potency, which is the source of change in some other thing, or in the same thing *qua* other.

One kind of potentiality is the power of being affected; the principle in the patient itself which initiates a passive change in it by the action of some other thing, or of itself *qua* other. Another is a positive state of impassivity in respect of deterioration or destruction by something else or by itself *qua* something else; *i.e.* by a transformatory principle—for all these definitions contain the formula of the primary sense of potentiality. Again, all these potentialities are so called either because they merely act or are acted upon in a particular way, or because they do so *well*. Hence in their formulae also the formulae of potentiality in the senses previously described are present in some degree.

Clearly, then, in one sense the potentiality for acting and being acted upon is one (for a thing is "capable" both because it itself possesses the power of being acted upon, and also because something else has the power of being acted upon by it); and in another sense it is not; for it is partly in the patient (for it is because it contains a certain principle, and because even the matter is a kind of principle, that the patient is acted upon; *i.e.*, one thing is acted upon by another: oily stuff is inflammable, and stuff which yields in a certain way is breakable, and similarly in other cases)—and partly in the agent; *e.g.* heat and the art of building: the former in that which produces heat, and the latter in that which builds. Hence in so far as it is a natural unity, nothing is acted upon by itself; because it is one, and not a separate thing. "Incapacity" and "the incapable" is the privation contrary to "capacity" in this sense; so that every "capacity" has a contrary incapacity for producing the same result in respect of the same subject.

Privation has several senses—it is applied (i.) to anything which does not possess a certain attribute; (ii.) to that which would naturally possess it, but does not; either (*a*) in general, or (*b*) when it would naturally possess it; and either (1) in a particular way, *e.g.* entirely, or (2) in any way at all. And in some cases if things which would naturally possess some attribute lack it as the result of constraint, we say that they are "deprived."

Since some of these principles are inherent in inanimate   [ch. 2
things, and others in animate things and in the soul and in   [1046b
the rational part of the soul, it is clear that some of the potencies also will be irrational and some rational. Hence all arts, *i.e.* the productive sciences, are potencies; because they are principles of change in another thing, or in the artist himself *qua* other.

Every rational potency admits equally of contrary results, but irrational potencies admit of one result only. E.g., heat can only produce heat, but medical science can produce disease and health. The reason of this is that science is a rational account, and the same account explains both the thing and its privation, though not in the same way; and in one sense it applies to both, and in another sense rather to the actual fact. Therefore such sciences must treat of contraries—essentially of the one, and non-essentially of the other; for the rational account also applies essentially to the one, but to the other in a kind of accidental way, since it is by negation and removal that it throws light on the contrary. For the contrary is the primary privation, and this is the removal of that to which it is contrary. And since contrary attributes cannot be induced in the same subject, and science is a potency which depends upon the possession of a rational formula, and the soul contains a principle of motion, it follows that whereas "the salutary" can only produce health, and "the calefactory" only heat, and "the frigorific" only cold, the scientific man can produce both contrary results. For the rational account includes both, though not in the same way; and it is in the soul, which contains a principle of motion, and will therefore, by means of the same principle, set both processes in motion, by linking them with the same rational account. Hence things which have a rational potency produce results contrary to those of things whose potency is irrational; for the results of the former are included under one principle, the rational account. It is evident also that whereas the power of merely producing (or suffering) a given effect is implied in the power of producing that effect *well*, the contrary is not always true; for that which produces an effect well must also produce it, but that which merely produces a given effect does not necessarily produce it well.

There are some, *e.g.* the Megaric school, who say that a   [ch. 3 thing only has potency when it functions, and that when it is not functioning it has no potency. *E.g.*, they say that a man who is not building cannot build, but only the man who is building, and at the moment when he is building; and similarly in the other cases. It is not difficult to see the absurd consequences of this theory. Obviously a man will not be a builder unless he is building, because "to be a builder" is "to be capable of building"; and the same will be true of the other arts. If, therefore, it is impossible to possess these arts without learning them at some time and having grasped them, and impossible not to possess them without having lost them at some time (through forgetful-   [1047a ness or some affection or the lapse of time; not, of course, through the destruction of the object of the art, because it exists always), when the artist ceases to practise his art, he will not possess it; and if he immediately starts building again, how will he have re-acquired the art?

The same is true of inanimate things. Neither the cold nor the hot nor the sweet nor in general any sensible thing will exist unless we are perceiving it (and so the result will be that they are affirming Protagoras' theory). Indeed, nothing will have the faculty of sensation unless it is perceiving, *i.e.* actually employing the faculty. If, then, that is blind which has not sight, though it would naturally have it, and when it would naturally have it, and while it still exists, the same people will be blind many times a day; and deaf too.

Further, if that which is deprived of its potency is incapable, that which is not happening will be incapable of happening; and he who says that that which is incapable of happening *is* or *will be*, will be in error, for this is what "incapable" meant. Thus these theories do away with both motion and generation; for that which is standing will always stand, and that which is sitting will always sit; because if it is sitting it will not get up, since it is impossible that anything which is incapable of getting up should get up. Since, then, we cannot maintain this, obviously potentiality and actuality are different. But these theories make potentiality and actuality identical; hence it is no small thing that they are trying to abolish.

Thus it is possible that a thing may be capable of being and yet not be, and capable of not being and yet be; and similarly in the other categories that which is capable of walking may not walk, and that which is capable of not walking may walk. A thing is capable of doing something if there is nothing impossible in its having the actuality of that of which it is said to have the potentiality. I mean, *e.g.*, that if a thing is capable of sitting and is not prevented from sitting, there is nothing impossible in its actually sitting; and similarly if it is capable of being moved or moving or standing or making to stand or being or becoming or not being or not becoming.

The term "actuality," with its implication of "complete reality," has been extended from motions, to which it properly belongs, to other things; for it is agreed that actuality is properly motion. Hence people do not invest non-existent things with motion, although they do invest them with certain other predicates. *E.g.*, they say that non-existent things are conceivable and desirable, but not that they are in motion. This is because, although these things do not exist actually, they will exist actually; for some non-existent things exist potentially;   [1047b yet they do not exist, because they do not exist in complete reality.

Now if, as we have said, that is possible which does not   [ch. 4 involve an impossibility, obviously it cannot be true to say that so-and-so is possible, but will not be; this view entirely loses sight of the instances of impossibility. I mean, suppose that someone—*i.e.* the sort of man who does not take the impossible into account—were to say that it is possible to measure the diagonal of a square, but that it will not be measured, because there is nothing to prevent a thing which is capable of being or coming to be from neither being nor being likely ever to be. But from our premises this necessarily follows: that if we are to assume that which is not, but is possible, to be or to have come to be, nothing impossible must be involved. But in this case something impossible will take place; for the measuring of the diagonal is impossible.

The false is of course not the same as the impossible; for although it is false that you are now standing, it is not impossible. At the same time it is also clear that if B must be real if A is, then if it is possible for A to be real, it must also be possible for B to be real; for even if B is not necessarily possible, there is nothing to prevent its being possible. Let A, then, be possible. Then when A was possible, if A was assumed to be real, nothing impossible was involved; but B was necessarily real too. But *ex hypothesi* B was impossible. Let B be impossible. Then if B is impossible, A must also be impossible. But A was by definition possible. Therefore so is B.

If therefore, A is possible, B will also be possible; that is if their

relation was such that if A is real, B must be real. Then if, A and B
being thus related, B is not possible on this condition, A and B will not
be related as we assumed; and if when A is possible B is necessarily
possible, then if A is real B must be real too. For to say that B must
be possible if A is possible means that if A is real at the time when and
in the way in which it was assumed that it was possible for it to be
real, then B must be real at that time and in that way.

Since all potencies are either innate, like the senses, or   [ch. 5
acquired by practice, like flute-playing, or by study, as in the arts, some
—such as are acquired by practice or a rational formula—we can only
possess when we have first exercised them; in the case of others which
are not of this kind and which imply passivity, this is not necessary.

Since anything which is possible is something possible at some
time and in some way, and with any other qualifications   [1048a
which are necessarily included in the definition; and since some things
can set up processes rationally and have rational potencies, while others
are irrational and have irrational potencies; and since the former class can
only belong to a living thing, whereas the latter can belong both to
living and to inanimate things: it follows that as for potencies of the
latter kind, when the agent and the patient meet in accordance with
the potency in question, the one must act and the other be acted
upon; but in the former kind of potency this is not necessary, for
whereas each single potency of the latter kind is productive of a single effect, those of the former kind are productive of contrary effects,
so that one potency will produce at the same time contrary effects. But
this is impossible. Therefore there must be some other deciding factor,
by which I mean *desire* or *conscious choice*. For whichever of two things
an animal desires decisively it will do, when it is in circumstances appropriate to the potency and meets with that which admits of being
acted upon. Therefore everything which is rationally capable, when it
desires something of which it has the capability, and in the circumstances in which it has the capability, must do that thing. Now it has
the capability when that which admits of being acted upon is present
and is in a certain state; otherwise it will not be able to act. (To add
the qualification "if nothing external prevents it" is no longer necessary;
because the agent has the capability in so far as it is a capability of acting; and this is not in all, but in certain circumstances, in which external
hindrances will be excluded; for they are precluded by some of the
positive qualifications in the definition.) Hence even if it wishes or desires to do two things or contrary things simultaneously, it will not do
them, for it has not the capability to do them under these conditions,
nor has it the capability of doing things simultaneously, since it will only

do the things to which the capability applies and under the appropriate conditions.

Since we have now dealt with the kind of potency which   [ch. 6 is related to motion, let us now discuss actuality; what it is, and what its qualities are. For as we continue our analysis it will also become clear with regard to the potential that we apply the name not only to that whose nature it is to move or be moved by something else, either without qualification or in some definite way, but also in other senses; and it is on this account that in the course of our inquiry we have discussed these as well.

"Actuality" means the presence of the thing, not in the sense which we mean by "potentially." We say that a thing is present potentially as Hermes is present in the wood, or the half-line in the whole, because it can be separated from it; and as we call even a man who is not studying "a scholar" if he is capable of studying. That which is present in the opposite sense to this is present actually. What we mean can be plainly seen in the particular cases by induction; we need not seek a definition for every term, but must comprehend the analogy: that as that which is actually building is to that which is capable of   [1048b building, so is that which is awake to that which is asleep; and that which is seeing to that which has the eyes shut, but has the power of sight; and that which is differentiated out of matter to the matter; and the finished article to the raw material. Let actuality be defined by one member of this antithesis, and the potential by the other.

But things are not all said to exist actually in the same sense, but only by analogy—as A is in B or to B, so is C in or to D; for the relation is either that of motion to potentiality, or that of substance to some particular matter.

Infinity and void and other concepts of this kind are said to "be" potentially or actually in a different sense from the majority of existing things, e.g. that which sees, or walks, or is seen. For in these latter cases the predication may sometimes be truly made without qualification, since "that which is seen" is so called sometimes because it is seen and sometimes because it is capable of being seen; but the Infinite does not exist potentially in the sense that it will ever exist separately in actuality; it is separable only in knowledge. For the fact that the process of division never ceases makes this actuality exist potentially, but not separately.

Since no action which has a limit is an end, but only a means to the end, as, e.g., the process of thinning; and since the parts of the body themselves, when one is thinning them, are in motion in the sense that they are not already that which it is the object of the motion to make them, this process is not an action, or at least not a complete one, since it is not an end; it is the process which includes the end that is an action. E.g., at the same time we see and have seen, understand and have understood, think and have thought; but we cannot at the same time learn and have learnt, or become healthy and be healthy. We are living well and have lived well, we are happy and have been happy, at the same time; otherwise the process would have had to cease at some time, like the thinning-process; but it has not ceased at the present moment: we both are living and have lived.

Now of these processes we should call the one type motions, and the other actualizations. Every motion is incomplete—the processes of thinning, learning, walking, building—these are motions, and incomplete at that. For it is not the same thing which at the same time is walking and has walked, or is building and has built, or is becoming and has become, or is being moved and has been moved, but two different things; and that which is causing motion is different from that which has caused motion. But the same thing at the same time is seeing and has seen, is thinking and has thought. The latter kind of process, then, is what I mean by actualization, and the former what I mean by motion.

What the actual is, then, and what it is like, may be regarded as demonstrated from these and similar considerations.

We must, however, distinguish when a particular thing   [ch. 7 exists potentially, and when it does not; for it does not so exist at any and every time. E.g., is earth potentially a man? No, but   [1049a rather when it has already become semen, and perhaps not even then; just as not *everything* can be healed by medicine, or even by chance, but there is some definite kind of thing which is capable of it, and this is that which is potentially healthy.

The definition of that which as a result of thought comes, from existing potentially, to exist actually, is that, when it has been willed, if no external influence hinders it, it comes to pass; and the condition in the case of the patient, *i.e.* in the person who is being healed, is that nothing in him should hinder the process. Similarly a house exists potentially if there is nothing in X, the matter, to prevent it from becoming a house, *i.e.*, if there is nothing which must be added or removed or changed; then X is potentially a house; and similarly in all other cases where the generative principle is external. And in all cases where the generative principle is contained in the thing itself, one thing is potentially another when, if nothing external hinders, it will of itself become the other. E.g., the semen is not yet potentially a man; for it must further undergo a change in some other medium. But when, by its own generative principle, it has already come to have the necessary attributes, in this state it is now potentially a man, whereas in the former state it has need of another principle; just as earth is not yet potentially a statue, because it must undergo a change before it becomes bronze.

It seems that what we are describing is not a particular thing, but a definite material; e.g., a box is not wood, but wooden material, and wood is not earth, but earthen material; and earth also is an illustration of our point if it is similarly not some other thing, but a definite material—it is always the latter term in this series which is, in the fullest sense, potentially something else. E.g., a box is not earth, nor earthen, but wooden; for it is this that is potentially a box, and this is the matter of the box—that is, wooden material in general is the matter of "box" in general, whereas the matter of a particular box is a particular piece of wood.

If there is some primary stuff, which is not further called the material of some other thing, this is primary matter. E.g., if earth is "made of air," and air is not fire, but "made of fire," then fire is primary matter, not being an individual thing. For the subject or substrate is distinguishable into two kinds by either being or not being an individual thing. Take for example as the subject of the attributes "man," or "body" or "soul," and as an attribute "cultured" or "white." Now the subject, when culture is induced in it, is called not "culture" but "cultured," and the man is called not whiteness but white; nor is he called "ambulation" or "motion," but "walking" or "moving"; just as we said that things are of a definite material. Thus where "subject" has this sense, the ultimate substrate is substance; but where it has not this sense, and the predicate is a form or individuality, the ultimate substrate is matter or material substance. It is quite proper that both matter and attributes should be described by a derivative predicate, since [1049b they are both indefinite.

Thus it has now been stated when a thing should be said to exist potentially, and when it should not.

Now since we have distinguished the several senses of [ch. 8 priority, it is obvious that actuality is prior to potentiality. By potentiality I mean not that which we have defined as "a principle of change which is in something other than the thing changed, or in that same thing qua other," but in general any principle of motion or of rest; for nature also is in the same genus as potentiality, because it is a principle of motion, although not in some other thing, but in the thing itself qua itself. To every potentiality of this kind actuality is prior, both in formula and in substance; in time it is sometimes prior and sometimes not.

That actuality is prior in formula is evident; for it is because it can be actualized that the potential, in the primary sense, is potential,

I mean, *e.g.*, that the potentially constructive is that which can construct, the potentially seeing that which can see, and the potentially visible that which can be seen. The same principle holds in all other cases too, so that the formula and knowledge of the actual must precede the knowledge of the potential.

In time it is prior in this sense: the actual is prior to the potential with which it is formally identical, but not to that with which it is identical numerically. What I mean is this: that the matter and the seed and the thing which is capable of seeing, which are potentially a man and corn and seeing, but are not yet so actually, are prior in time to the individual man and corn and seeing subject which already exist in actuality. But prior in time to these potential entities are other actual entities from which the former are generated; for the actually existent is always generated from the potentially existent *by* something which is actually existent—*e.g.*, man by man, cultured by cultured—there is always some prime mover; and that which initiates motion exists already in actuality.

We have said in our discussion of substance that everything which is generated is generated from something and by something; and by something formally identical with itself. Hence it seems impossible that a man can be a builder if he has never built, or a harpist if he has never played a harp; because he who learns to play the harp learns by playing it, and similarly in all other cases. This was the origin of the sophists' quibble that a man who does not know a given science will be doing that which is the object of that science, because the learner does not know the science. But since something of that which is being generated is already generated, and something of that which is being moved as a whole is already moved (this is demonstrated in our discussion on Motion), presumably the learner too must   [1050a possess something of the science. At any rate from this argument it is clear that actuality is prior to potentiality in this sense too, *i.e.* in respect of generation and time.

But it is also prior in substantiality; (*a*) because things which are posterior in generation are prior in form and substantiality; *e.g.*, adult is prior to child, and man to semen, because the one already possesses the form, but the other does not; and (*b*) because everything which is generated moves towards a principle, *i.e.* its *end*. For the object of a thing is its principle; and generation has as its object the *end*. And the actuality is the end, and it is for the sake of this that the potentiality is acquired; for animals do not see in order that they may have sight, but have sight in order that they may see. Similarly men possess the art of building in order that they may build, and the power of speculation that they may speculate; they do not speculate in order that they may have the power of speculation—except those who are learning by practice; and they do not really speculate, but only in a limited sense, or about a subject about which they have no desire to speculate.

Further, matter exists potentially, because it may attain to the form; but when it exists actually, it is then *in* the form. The same applies in all other cases, including those where the end is motion. Hence, just as teachers think that they have achieved their end when they have exhibited their pupil performing, so it is with nature. For if this is not so, it will be another case of "Pauson's Hermes"; it will be impossible to say whether the knowledge is *in* the pupil or outside him, as in the case of the Hermes. For the activity is the end, and the actuality is the activity; hence the term "actuality" is derived from "activity," and tends to have the meaning of "complete reality."

Now whereas in some cases the ultimate thing is the use of the faculty, as, *e.g.*, in the case of sight seeing is the ultimate thing, and sight produces nothing else besides this; but in other cases something is produced, *e.g.* the art of building produces not only the act of building but a house; nevertheless in the one case the use of the faculty is the end, and in the other it is more truly the end than is the potentiality. For the act of building resides in the thing built; *i.e.*, it comes to be and exists simultaneously with the house.

Thus in all cases where the result is something other than the exercise of the faculty, the actuality resides in the thing produced; *e.g.* the act of building in the thing built, the act of weaving in the thing woven, and so on; and in general the motion resides in the thing moved. But where there is no other result besides the actualization, the actualization resides in the subject; *e.g.* seeing in the seer, and speculation in the speculator, and life in the soul (and hence also happi- [1050b ness, since happiness is a particular kind of life). Evidently, therefore, substance or form is actuality. Thus it is obvious by this argument that actuality is prior in substantiality to potentiality; and that in point of time, as we have said, one actuality presupposes another right back to that of the prime mover in each case.

It is also prior in a deeper sense; because that which is eternal is prior in substantiality to that which is perishable, and nothing eternal is potential. The argument is as follows. Every potentiality is at the same time a potentiality for the opposite. For whereas that which is incapable of happening cannot happen to anything, everything which is capable may fail to be actualized. Therefore that which is capable of being may both be and not be. Therefore the same thing is capable both of being and of not being. But that which is capable of not being may possibly not be; and that which may possibly not be is perishable; either absolutely, or in the particular sense in which it is said that it may possibly not be; that is, in respect either of place or of quantity or of quality. "Absolutely" means in respect of substance. Hence nothing which is absolutely imperishable is absolutely potential (although there is no reason why it should not be potential in some particular respect; *e.g.* of quality or place); therefore all imperishable things are actual. Nor can anything which is of necessity be potential; and yet these things are primary, for if they did not exist, nothing would exist. Nor can motion be potential, if there is any eternal motion. Nor, if there is anything eternally in motion, is it potentially in motion (except in respect of some starting-point or destination), and there is no reason why the matter of such a thing should not exist. Hence the sun and stars and the whole visible heaven are always active, and there is no fear that they will ever stop—a fear which the writers on physics entertain. Nor do the heavenly bodies tire in their activity; for motion does not imply for them, as it does for perishable things, the potentiality for the opposite, which makes the continuity of the motion distressing; this results when the substance is matter and potentiality, not actuality.

Imperishable things are resembled in this respect by things which are always undergoing transformation, such as earth and fire; for the latter too are always active, since they have their motion independently and in themselves. Other potentialities, according to the distinctions already made, all admit of the opposite result; for that which is capable of causing motion in a certain way can also cause it not in that way; that is if it acts rationally. The same irrational potentialties can only produce opposite results by their presence or absence.

Thus if there are any entities or substances such as the dialecticians describe the Ideas to be, there must be something which has much more knowledge than absolute knowledge, and much more mobility than motion; for they will be in a truer sense actualities, whereas [1051a] knowledge and motion will be their potentialities. Thus it is obvious that actuality is prior both to potentiality and to every principle of change.

That a good actuality is both better and more estimable [ch. 9] than a good potentiality will be obvious from the following arguments. Everything of which we speak as capable is alike capable of contrary results; *e.g.*, that which we call capable of being well is alike capable of being ill, and has both potentialities at once; for the same potentiality admits of health and disease, or of rest and motion, or of building and of pulling down, or of being built and of falling down. Thus the capacity for two contraries can belong to a thing at the same time, but the contraries cannot belong at the same time; *i.e.*, the actualities, *e.g.* health and disease, cannot belong to a thing at the same time. Therefore one of them must be the good; but the potentiality may equally well be both or neither. Therefore the actuality is better.

Also in the case of evils the end or actuality must be worse than the potentiality; for that which is capable is capable alike of both contraries.

Clearly, then, evil does not exist apart from *things*; for evil is by nature posterior to potentiality. Nor is there in things which are original and eternal any evil or error, or anything which has been destroyed—for destruction is an evil.

Geometrical constructions, too, are discovered by an actualization, because it is by dividing that we discover them. If the division were already done, they would be obvious; but as it is the division is only there potentially. Why is the sum of the interior angles of a triangle equal to two right angles? Because the angles about one point (in a straight line) are equal to two right angles. If the line parallel to the side had been already drawn, the answer would have been obvious at sight. Why is the angle in a semicircle always a right angle? If three lines are equal, the two forming the base, and the one set upright from the middle of the base, the answer is obvious to one who knows the former proposition. Thus it is evident that the potential constructions are discovered by being actualized. The reason for this is that the actualization is an act of thinking. Thus potentiality comes from actuality (and therefore it is by constructive action that we acquire knowledge). (But this is true only in the abstract), for the individual actuality is posterior in generation to its potentiality.

The terms "being" and "not-being" are used not only   [ch. 10 with reference to the types of predication, and to the potentiality or actuality, or non-potentiality and non-actuality, of these   [1051b types, but also (in the strictest sense) to denote truth and falsity. This depends, in the case of the objects, upon their being united or divided; so that he who thinks that what is divided is divided, or that what is united is united, is right; while he whose thought is contrary to the real condition of the objects is in error. Then *when* do what we call truth and falsity exist or not exist? We must consider what we mean by these terms.

It is not because we are right in thinking that you are white that you are white; it is because you are white that we are right in saying so. Now if whereas some things are always united and cannot be divided, and others are always divided and cannot be united, others again admit of both contrary states, then "to be" is to be united, *i.e.* a unity; and "not to be" is to be not united, but a plurality. Therefore as regards the class of things which admit of both contrary states, the same opinion or the same statement comes to be false and true, and it is possible at one time to be right and at another wrong; but as regards things which cannot be otherwise the same opinion is not sometimes true and sometimes false, but the same opinions are always true or always false.

But with regard to incomposite things, what is being or not-being, and truth or falsity? Such a thing is not composite, so as to be when it is united and not to be when it is divided, like the proposition that "the wood is white," or "the diagonal is incommensurable"; nor will truth and falsity apply in the same way to these cases as to the previous ones. In point of fact, just as truth is not the same in these cases, so neither is being. Truth and falsity are as follows: contact and assertion are truth (for assertion is not the same as affirmation), and ignorance is non-contact. I say ignorance, because it is impossible to be deceived with respect to what a thing is, except accidentally; and the same applies to incomposite substances, for it is impossible to be deceived about them. And they all exist actually, not potentially; otherwise they would be generated and destroyed; but as it is, Being itself is not generated (nor destroyed); if it were, it would be generated out of something. With respect, then, to all things which are essences and actual, there is no question of being mistaken, but only of thinking or not thinking them. Inquiry as to *what* they are takes the form of inquiring whether they are of such-and-such a nature or not.

As for being in the sense of truth, and not-being in the sense of falsity, a unity is true if the terms are combined, and if they are not combined it is false. Again, if the unity exists, it exists in a particular way, and if it does not exist in that way, it does not exist [1052a at all. Truth means to think these objects, and there is no falsity or deception, but only ignorance—not, however, ignorance such as blindness is; for blindness is like a total absence of the power of thinking. And it is obvious that with regard to immovable things also, if one assumes that there are immovable things, there is no deception in respect of time. *E.g.*, if we suppose that the triangle is immutable, we shall not suppose that it sometimes contains two right angles and sometimes does not, for this would imply that it changes; but we may suppose that one thing has a certain property and another has not; *e.g.*, that no even number is a prime, or that some are primes and others are not. But about a single number we cannot be mistaken even in this way, for we can no longer suppose that one instance is of such a nature, and another not, but whether we are right or wrong, the fact is always the same.

Book · XII

Since we have seen that there are three kinds   [ch. 6 1071b
of substance, two of which are natural and one immutable, we must
now discuss the last named and show that there must be some substance
which is eternal and immutable. Substances are the primary reality, and
if they are all perishable, everything is perishable. But motion cannot be
either generated or destroyed, for it always existed; nor can time, because there can be no priority or posteriority if there is no time. Hence
as time is continuous, so too is motion; for time is either identical with
motion or an affection of it. But there is no continuous motion except that which is spatial, and of spatial motion only that which is
circular.

But even if we are to suppose that there is something which is
kinetic and productive although it does not actually move or produce,
there will not necessarily be motion; for that which has a potentiality
may not actualize it. Thus it will not help matters if we posit eternal
substances, as do the exponents of the Forms, unless there is in them
some principle which can cause change. And even this is not enough,
nor is it enough if there is another substance besides the Forms; for unless it actually functions there will not be motion. And it will still not
be enough even if it does function, if its essence is potentiality; for there
will not be eternal motion, since that which exists potentially may not
exist. Therefore there must be a principle of this kind whose essence is
actuality. Furthermore these substances must be immaterial; for they
must be eternal if anything is. Therefore they are actuality.

There is a difficulty, however; for it seems that everything which
actually functions has a potentiality, whereas not everything which has a
potentiality actually functions; so that potentiality is prior. But if this
is so, there need be no reality; for everything may be capable of existing,
but not yet existent. Yet if we accept the statements of the cosmologists
who generate everything from Night, or the doctrine of the physicists
that "all things were together," we have the same impossibility; for how
can there be motion if there is no actual cause? Wood will not move
itself—carpentry must act upon it; nor will the menses or the earth
move themselves—the seeds must act upon the earth, and the semen on
the menses. Hence some, e.g. Leucippus and Plato, posit an eternal
actuality, for they say that there is always motion; but why there is,
and what it is, they do not say; nor, if it moves in this or that particular
way, what the cause is. For nothing is moved at haphazard, but in every
case there must be some reason present; as in point of fact things are
moved in one way by nature, and in another by force or mind or some

other agent. And further, what kind of motion is primary? For this is an extremely important point. Again, Plato at least cannot even explain what it is that he sometimes thinks to be the source of mo-   [1072a tion, *i.e.*, that which moves itself; for according to him the soul is posterior to motion and coeval with the sensible universe. Now to suppose that potentiality is prior to actuality is in one sense right and in another wrong; we have explained the distinction. But that actuality is prior is testified by Anaxagoras (since mind is actuality), and by Empedocles with his theory of Love and Strife, and by those who hold that motion is eternal, *e.g.* Leucippus.

Therefore Chaos or Night did not endure for an unlimited time, but the same things have always existed, either passing through a cycle or in accordance with some other principle—that is, if actuality is prior to potentiality. Now if there is a regular cycle, there must be something which remains always active in the same way; but if there is to be generation and destruction, there must be something else which is always active in two different ways. Therefore this must be active in one way independently, and in the other in virtue of something else, *i.e.* either of some third active principle or of the first. It must, then, be in virtue of the first; for this is in turn the cause both of the third and of the second. Therefore the first is preferable, since it was the cause of perpetual regular motion, and something else was the cause of variety; and obviously both together make up the cause of perpetual variety. Now this is just what actually characterizes motions; therefore why need we seek any further principles?

Since (*a*) this is a possible explanation, and (*b*) if it   [ch. 7 is not true, we shall have to regard everything as coming from "Night" and "all things together" and "not-being," these difficulties may be considered to be solved. There is something which is eternally moved with an unceasing motion, and that circular motion. This is evident not merely in theory, but in fact. Therefore the "ultimate heaven" must be eternal. Then there is also something which moves it. And since that which is moved while it moves is intermediate, there is something which moves without being moved; something eternal which is both substance and actuality.

Now it moves in the following manner. The object of desire and the object of thought move without being moved. The primary objects of desire and thought are the same. For it is the apparent good that is the object of appetite, and the real good that is the object of the rational will. Desire is the result of opinion rather than opinion that of desire; it is the act of thinking that is the starting-point. Now thought is moved by the intelligible, and one of the series of contraries is essentially intelligible. In this series substance stands first, and of substance that which is simple and exists actually. (The one and the simple are not the same; for one signifies a measure, whereas "simple" means that the subject itself is in a certain state.) But the Good, and that which is in itself desirable, are also in the same series; and that which is first in a class is always best or analogous to the best.

That the final cause may apply to immovable things is [1072b] shown by the distinction of its meanings. For the final cause is not only "the good *for something*," but also "the good which is *the end of some action*." In the latter sense it applies to immovable things, although in the former it does not; and it causes motion as being an object of love, whereas all other things cause motion because they are themselves in motion. Now if a thing is moved, it can be otherwise than it is. Therefore if the actuality of "the heaven" is primary locomotion, then in so far as "the heaven" is moved, in this respect at least it is possible for it to be otherwise; *i.e.* in respect of place, even if not of substantiality. But since there is something—X—which moves while being itself unmoved, existing actually, X cannot be otherwise in any respect. For the primary kind of change is locomotion and of locomotion circular locomotion; and this is the motion which X induces. Thus X is necessarily existent; and *qua* necessary it is good, and is in this sense a first principle. For the necessary has all these meanings: that which is by constraint because it is contrary to impulse; and that without which excellence is impossible; and that which cannot be otherwise, but is absolutely necessary.

Such, then, is the first principle upon which depend the sensible universe and the world of nature. And its life is like the best which we temporarily enjoy. It must be in that state always (which for us is impossible), since its actuality is also pleasure. (And for this reason waking, sensation and thinking are most pleasant, and hopes and memories are pleasant because of them.) Now thinking in itself is concerned with that which is in itself best, and thinking in the highest sense with that which is in the highest sense best. And thought thinks itself through participation in the object of thought; for it becomes an object of thought by the act of apprehension and thinking, so that thought and the object of thought are the same, because that which is receptive of the object of thought, *i.e.* essence, is thought. And it actually functions when it possesses this object. Hence it is actuality rather than potentiality that is held to be the divine possession of rational thought, and its active contemplation is that which is most pleasant and best. If, then, the happiness which God always enjoys is as great as that which we enjoy sometimes, it is marvellous; and if it is greater, this is still more marvellous. Nevertheless it is so. Moreover, life belongs to God. For the actuality of thought is life, and God is that actuality; and the essential actuality of God is life most good and eternal. We hold, then, that God is a living being, eternal, most good; and therefore life and a continuous eternal existence belong to God; for that is what God is.

Those who suppose, as do the Pythagoreans and Speusippus, that perfect beauty and goodness do not exist in the beginning (on the ground that whereas the first beginnings of plants and animals are causes, it is in the products of these that beauty and perfection are found) are mistaken in their views. For seed comes from prior creatures which are perfect, and that which is first is not the seed but the perfect creature. E.g., one might say that prior to the seed is the man   [1073a —not he who is produced from the seed, but another man from whom the seed comes.

Thus it is evident from the foregoing account that there is some substance which is eternal and immovable and separate from sensible things; and it has also been shown that this substance can have no magnitude, but is impartible and indivisible (for it causes motion for infinite time, and nothing finite has an infinite potentiality; and therefore since every magnitude is either finite or infinite, it cannot have finite magnitude, and it cannot have infinite magnitude because there is no such thing at all); and moreover that it is impassive and unalterable; for all the other kinds of motion are posterior to spatial motion. Thus it is clear why this substance has these attributes.

*   *   *

The subject of Mind involves certain dif-   [ch. 9 1074b line 15 ficulties. Mind is held to be of all phenomena the most supernatural; but the question of how we must regard it if it is to be of this nature involves certain difficulties. If Mind thinks nothing, where is its dignity? It is in just the same state as a man who is asleep. If it thinks, but something else determines its thinking, then since that which is its essence is not thinking but potentiality, it cannot be the best reality; because it derives its excellence from the act of thinking. Again, whether its essence is thought or thinking, what does it think? It must think either itself or something else; and if something else, then it must think either the same thing always, or different things at different times. Then does it make any difference, or not, whether it thinks that which is good or thinks at random? Surely it would be absurd for it to think about some subjects. Clearly, then, it thinks that which is most divine and estimable, and does not change; for the change would be for the worse, and anything of this kind would immediately imply some sort of motion. Therefore if Mind is not thinking but a potentiality, (a) it is reasonable to suppose that the continuity of its thinking is laborious; (b) clearly there must be something else which is more excellent than Mind; *i.e.* the object of thought; for both thought and the act of thinking will belong even to the thinker of the worst thoughts. Therefore if this is to be avoided (as it is, since it is better not to see some things than to see them), thinking cannot be the supreme good. Therefore Mind thinks itself, if it is that which is best; and its thinking is a thinking of thinking.

Yet it seems that knowledge and perception and opinion and understanding are always of something else, and only incidentally of themselves. And further, if to think is not the same as to be thought, in respect of which does goodness belong to thought? for the act of thinking and the object of thought have not the same essence. The answer is that in some cases the knowledge is the object. In   [1075a the productive sciences, if we disregard the matter, the substance, *i.e.* the essence, is the object; but in the speculative sciences the formula or the act of thinking is the object. Therefore since thought and the object of thought are not different in the case of things which contain no matter, they will be the same, and the act of thinking will be one with the object of thought.

There still remains the question whether the object of thought is composite; for if so, thought would change in passing from one part of the whole to another. The answer is that everything which contains no matter is indivisible. Just as the human mind, or rather the mind of composite beings, is in a certain space of time (for it does not possess the good at this or at that moment, but in the course of a certain whole period it attains to the supreme good, which is other than itself), so is absolute self-thought throughout all eternity.

*   *   *

NICOMACHEAN
ETHICS

Book · I

Every art and every investigation, and likewise every   [ch. 1 1094a
practical pursuit or undertaking, seems to aim at some good: hence it
has been well said that the Good is That at which all things aim. (It is
true that a certain variety is to be observed among the ends at which
the arts and sciences aim: in some cases the activity of practicing the art
is itself the end, whereas in others the end is some product over and
above the mere exercise of the art; and in the arts whose ends are
certain things beside the practice of the arts themselves, these products
are essentially superior in value to the activities.) But as there are
numerous pursuits and arts and sciences, it follows that their ends are
correspondingly numerous: for instance, the end of the science of
medicine is health, that of the art of shipbuilding a vessel, that of
strategy victory, that of domestic economy wealth. Now in cases where
several such pursuits are subordinate to some single faculty—as bridle-
making and the other trades concerned with horses' harness are subordinate to horsemanship, and this and every other military pursuit to the
science of strategy, and similarly other arts to different arts again—in all
these cases, I say, the ends of the master arts are things more to be
desired than all those of the arts subordinate to them; since the latter
ends are only pursued for the sake of the former. (And it makes no
difference whether the ends of the pursuits are the activities themselves
or some other thing beside these, as in the case of the sciences
mentioned.)

If therefore among the ends at which our actions aim   [ch. 2

there be one which we wish for its own sake, while we wish the others only for the sake of this, and if we do not choose everything for the sake of something else (which would obviously result in a process *ad infinitum*, so that all desire would be futile and vain), it is clear that this one ultimate End must be the Good, and indeed the Supreme Good. Will not then a knowledge of this Supreme Good be also of great practical importance for the conduct of life? Will it not better enable us to attain what is fitting, like archers having a target to aim at? If this be so, we ought to make an attempt to determine at all events in outline what exactly this Supreme Good is, and of which of the theoretical or practical sciences it is the object.

Now it would be agreed that it must be the object of the most authoritative of the sciences—some science which is pre-eminently a master-craft. But such is manifestly the science of Politics; for it is this that ordains which of the sciences are to exist in states, and   [1094b what branches of knowledge the different classes of the citizens are to learn, and up to what point; and we observe that even the most highly esteemed of the faculties, such as strategy, domestic economy, oratory, are subordinate to the political science. Inasmuch then as the rest of the sciences are employed by this one, and as it moreover lays down laws as to what people shall do and what things they shall refrain from doing, the end of this science must include the ends of all the others. Therefore, the Good of man must be the end of the science of Politics. For even though it be the case that the Good is the same for the individual and for the state, nevertheless, the good of the state is manifestly a greater and more perfect good, both to attain and to preserve. To secure the good of one person only is better than nothing; but to secure the good of a nation or a state is a nobler and more divine achievement.

This then being its aim, our investigation is in a sense the study of Politics.

Now our treatment of this science will be adequate, if it   [ch. 3 achieves that amount of precision which belongs to its subject matter. The same exactness must not be expected in all departments of philosophy alike, any more than in all the products of the arts and crafts. The subjects studied by political science are Moral Nobility and Justice; but these conceptions involve much difference of opinion and uncertainty, so that they are sometimes believed to be mere conventions and to have no real existence in the nature of things. And a similar uncertainty surrounds the conception of the Good, because it frequently occurs that good things have harmful consequences: people have before now been ruined by wealth, and in other cases courage has cost men their lives. We must therefore be content if, in dealing with subjects and starting from premises thus uncertain, we succeed in presenting a broad outline of the truth: when our subjects and our premises are merely generalities, it is enough if we arrive at generally valid conclusions. Accordingly we may ask the student also to accept the various views we put forward in the same spirit; for it is the mark of an educated mind to expect that amount of exactness in each kind which the nature of the particular subject admits. It is equally unreasonable to accept merely probable conclusions from a mathematician and to demand strict demonstration from an orator.

Again, each man judges correctly those matters with which he is acquainted; it is of these that he is a competent critic. To criticize a particular subject, therefore, a man must have been trained   [1095a in that subject: to be a good critic generally, he must have had an all-round education. Hence the young are not fit to be students of Political Science. For they have no experience of life and conduct, and it is these that supply the premises and subject matter of this branch of philosophy. And moreover they are led by their feelings; so that they will study the subject to no purpose or advantage, since the end of this science is not knowledge but action. And it makes no difference whether they are young in years or immature in character: the defect is not a question of time, it is because their life and its various aims are guided by feeling; for to such persons their knowledge is of no use, any more than it is to persons of defective self-restraint. But Moral Science may be of great value to those who guide their desires and actions by principle.

Let so much suffice by way of introduction as to the student of the subject, the spirit in which our conclusions are to be received, and the object that we set before us.

To resume, inasmuch as all studies and undertakings are   [ch. 4 directed to the attainment of some good, let us discuss what it is that we pronounce to be the aim of Politics, that is, what is the highest of all the goods that action can achieve. As far as the name goes, we may almost say that the great majority of mankind are agreed about this; for both the multitude and persons of refinement speak of it as Happiness, and conceive 'the good life' or 'doing well' to be the same thing as 'being happy.' But what constitutes happiness is a matter of dispute; and the popular account of it is not the same as that given by the philosophers. Ordinary people identify it with some obvious and visible good, such as pleasure or wealth or honour—some say one thing and some another, indeed very often the same man says different things at different times: when he falls sick he thinks health is happiness, when he is poor, wealth. At other times, feeling conscious of their own ignorance, men admire those who propound something grand and above their heads; and it has been held by some thinkers that beside the many good things we have mentioned, there exists another Good, that is good in itself, and stands to all those goods as the cause of their being good.

Now perhaps it would be a somewhat fruitless task to review all the different opinions that are held. It will suffice to examine those that are most widely prevalent, or that seem to have some argument in their favour.

And we must not overlook the distinction between arguments that start from first principles and those that lead to first principles. It was a good practice of Plato to raise this question, and to enquire whether the right procedure was to start from or to lead up to the first principles, as in a race-course one may run from the judges to the far end of the track or reversely. Now no doubt it is proper to start from   [1095b the known. But 'the known' has two meanings—'what is known to us,' which is one thing, and 'what is knowable in itself,' which is another. Perhaps then for us at all events it is proper to start from what is known to us. This is why in order to be a competent student of the Right and Just, and in short of the topics of Politics in general, the pupil is bound to have been well trained in his habits. For the starting-point or first principle is the fact that a thing is so; if this be satisfactorily ascertained, there will be no need also to know the reason why it is so. And the man of good moral training knows first principles already, or can easily acquire them. As for the person who neither knows nor can learn, let him hear the words of Hesiod:

> Best is the man who can himself advise;
> He too is good who hearkens to the wise;
> But who, himself being witless, will not heed
> Another's wisdom, is worthless indeed.

But let us continue from the point where we digressed.   [ch. 5 To judge from men's lives, the more or less reasoned conceptions of the Good or Happiness that seem to prevail among them are the following. On the one hand the generality of men and the most vulgar identify the Good with pleasure, and accordingly are content with the Life of Enjoyment—for there are three specially prominent Lives, the one just mentioned, the Life of Politics, and thirdly, the Life of Contemplation. The generality of mankind then show themselves to be utterly slavish, by preferring what is only a life for cattle; but they get a hearing for their view as reasonable because many persons of high position share the feelings of Sardanapallus.

Men of refinement, on the other hand, and men of action think that the Good is honour—for this may be said to be the end of the

Life of Politics. But honour after all seems too superficial to be the Good for which we are seeking; since it appears to depend on those who confer it more than on him upon whom it is conferred, whereas we instinctively feel that the Good must be something proper to its possessor and not easy to be taken away from him. Moreover men's motive in pursuing honour seems to be to assure themselves of their own merit; at least they seek to be honoured by men of judgement and by people who know them, that is, they desire to be honoured on the ground of virtue. It is clear therefore that in the opinion at all events of men of action, virtue is a greater good than honour; and one might perhaps accordingly suppose that virtue rather than honour is the end of the Political Life. But even virtue proves on examination to be too incomplete to be the End; since it appears possible to possess it while you are asleep, or without putting it into practice throughout the whole of your life; and also for the virtuous man to suffer the   [1096a greatest misery and misfortune—though no one would pronounce a man living a life of misery to be happy, unless for the sake of maintaining a paradox. But we need not pursue this subject, since it has been sufficiently treated in the ordinary discussions.

The third type of life is the Life of Contemplation, which we shall consider in the sequel.

The Life of Money-making is a constrained kind of life, and clearly wealth is not the Good we are in search of, for it is only good as being useful, a means to something else. On this score indeed one might conceive the ends before mentioned to have a better claim, for they are approved for their own sakes. But even they do not really seem to be the Supreme Good; however, many arguments have been laid down in regard to them, so we may dismiss them.

But perhaps it is desirable that we should examine the   [ch. 6 notion of a Universal Good, and review the difficulties that it involves, although such an enquiry goes against the grain because of our friendship for the authors of the Theory of Ideas. Still perhaps it would appear desirable, and indeed it would seem to be obligatory, especially for a philosopher, to sacrifice even one's closest personal ties in defence of the truth. Both are dear to us, yet 'tis our duty to prefer the truth.

The originators of this theory, then, used not to postulate Ideas of groups of things in which they posited an order of priority and posteriority (for which reason they did not construct an Idea of numbers in general). But Good is predicated alike in the Categories of Substance, of Quality, and of Relation; yet the Absolute, or Substance, is prior in nature to the Relative, which seems to be a sort of offshoot or 'accident' of Substance; so that there cannot be a common Idea corresponding to the absolutely good and the relatively good.

Again, the word 'good' is used in as many senses as the word 'is'; for we may predicate good in the Category of Substance, for instance of God or intelligence; in that of Quality—the excellences; in that of Quantity—moderate in amount; in that of Relation—useful; in that of Time—a favourable opportunity; in that of Place—a suitable 'habitat'; and so on. So clearly good cannot be a single and universal general notion; if it were, it would not be predicable in all the Categories, but only in one.

Again, things that come under a single Idea must be objects of a single science; hence there ought to be a single science dealing with all good things. But as a matter of fact there are a number of sciences even for the goods in one Category: for example, opportunity, for opportunity in war comes under the science of strategy, in disease under that of medicine; and the due amount in diet comes under medicine, in bodily exercise under gymnastics.

One might also raise the question what precisely they mean by their expression 'the Ideal so-and-so,' seeing that one and the same definition of man applies both to 'the Ideal man' and to 'man,' for in   [1096b so far as both are man, there will be no difference between them; and if so, no more will there be any difference between 'the Ideal Good' and 'Good' in so far as both are good. Nor yet will the Ideal Good be any more good because it is eternal, seeing that a white thing that lasts a long time is no whiter than one that lasts only a day.

The Pythagoreans seem to give a more probable doctrine on the subject of the Good when they place Unity in their column of goods; and indeed Speusippus appears to have followed them. But this subject must be left for another discussion.

We can descry an objection that may be raised against our arguments on the ground that the theory in question was not intended to apply to every sort of good, and that only things pursued and accepted for their own sake are pronounced good as belonging to a single species, while things productive or preservative of these in any way, or preventive of their opposites, are said to be good as a means to these, and in a different sense. Clearly then the term 'goods' would have two meanings, (1) things good in themselves and (2) things good as a means to these; let us then separate things good in themselves from things useful as means, and consider whether the former are called good because they fall under a single Idea. But what sort of things is one to class as good in themselves? Are they not those things which are sought after even without any accessory advantage, such as wisdom, sight, and certain pleasures and honours? for even if we also pursue these things as means to something else, still one would class them among things good in themselves. Or is there nothing else good in itself except the Idea? If so, the species

will be of no use. If on the contrary the class of things good in themselves includes these objects, the same notion of good ought to be
manifested in all of them, just as the same notion of white is manifested
in snow and in white paint. But as a matter of fact the notions of
honour and wisdom and pleasure, as being good, are different and
distinct. Therefore, good is not a general term corresponding to a single
Idea.

But in what sense then are different things called good? For they
do not seem to be a case of things that bear the same name merely by
chance. Possibly things are called good in virtue of being derived from
one good; or because they all contribute to one good. Or perhaps it is
rather by way of a proportion: that is, as sight is good in the body, so
intelligence is good in the soul, and similarly another thing in something else.

Perhaps however this question must be dismissed for the present,
since a detailed investigation of it belongs more properly to another
branch of philosophy. And likewise with the Idea of the Good; for even
if the goodness predicated of various things in common really is a unity
or something existing separately and absolute, it clearly will not be
practicable or attainable by man; but the Good which we are now
seeking is a good within human reach.

But possibly someone may think that to know the Ideal Good may
be desirable as an aid to achieving those goods which are practicable and
attainable: having the Ideal Good as a pattern we shall more   [1097a
easily know what things are good for us, and knowing them, obtain
them. Now it is true that this argument has a certain plausibility; but it
does not seem to square with the actual procedure of the sciences. For
these all aim at some good, and seek to make up their deficiencies, but
they do not trouble about a knowledge of the Ideal Good. Yet if it were
so potent an aid, it is improbable that all the professors of the arts and
sciences should not know it, nor even seek to discover it. Moreover, it is
not easy to see *how* knowing that same Ideal Good will help a weaver
or carpenter in the practice of his own craft, or how anybody will be a
better physician or general for having contemplated the absolute Idea.
In fact it does not appear that the physician studies even health in the
abstract; he studies the health of the human being—or rather of some
particular human being, for it is individuals that he has to cure.

Let us here conclude our discussion of this subject.

We may now return to the Good which is the object of   [ch. 7
our search, and try to find out what exactly it can be. For good appears
to be one thing in one pursuit or art and another in another: it is
different in medicine from what it is in strategy, and so on with the
rest of the arts. What definition of the Good then will hold true in all

the arts? Perhaps we may define it as that for the sake of which everything else is done. This applies to something different in each different
art—to health in the case of medicine, to victory in that of strategy, to a
house in architecture, and to something else in each of the other arts;
but in every pursuit or undertaking it describes the end of that pursuit or
undertaking, since in all of them it is for the sake of the end that
everything else is done. Hence if there be something which is the end
of all the things done by human action, this will be the practicable
Good—or if there be several such ends, the sum of these will be the
Good. Thus by changing its ground the argument has reached the
same result as before. We must attempt however to render this still more
precise.

Now there do appear to be several ends at which our actions aim;
but as we choose some of them—for instance wealth, or flutes, and
instruments generally—as a means to something else, it is clear that not
all of them are final ends; whereas the Supreme Good seems to be
something final. Consequently if there be some one thing which alone
is a final end, this thing—or if there be several final ends, the one among
them which is the most final—will be the Good which we are seeking.
In speaking of degrees of finality, we mean that a thing pursued as an
end in itself is more final than one pursued as a means to something
else, and that a thing never chosen as a means to anything else is more
final than things chosen both as ends in themselves and as means to
that thing; and accordingly a thing chosen always as an end and never
as a means we call absolutely final. Now happiness above all else appears
to be absolutely final in this sense, since we always choose it   [1097b
for its own sake and never as a means to something else; whereas
honour, pleasure, intelligence, and excellence in its various forms, we
choose indeed for their own sakes (since we should be glad to have each
of them although no extraneous advantage resulted from it), but we
also choose them for the sake of happiness, in the belief that they will
be a means to our securing it. But no one chooses happiness for the
sake of honour, pleasure, etc., nor as a means to anything whatever
other than itself.

The same conclusion also appears to follow from a consideration of
the self-sufficiency of happiness—for it is felt that the final good must
be a thing sufficient in itself. The term self-sufficient, however, we
employ with reference not to oneself alone, living a life of isolation,
but also to one's parents and children and wife, and one's friends and
fellow citizens in general, since man is by nature a social being. On the
other hand a limit has to be assumed in these relationships; for if the
list be extended to one's ancestors and descendants and to the friends of
one's friends, it will go on *ad infinitum*. But this is a point that must be

considered later on; we take a self-sufficient thing to mean a thing which merely standing by itself alone renders life desirable and lacking in nothing, and such a thing we deem happiness to be. Moreover, we think happiness the most desirable of all good things without being itself reckoned as one among the rest; for if it were so reckoned, it is clear that we should consider it more desirable when even the smallest of other good things were combined with it, since this addition would result in a larger total of good, and of two goods the greater is always the more desirable.

Happiness, therefore, being found to be something final and self-sufficient, is the End at which all actions aim.

To say however that the Supreme Good is happiness will probably appear a truism; we still require a more explicit account of what constitutes happiness. Perhaps then we may arrive at this by ascertaining what is man's function. For the goodness or efficiency of a flute-player or sculptor or craftsman of any sort, and in general of anybody who has some function or business to perform, is thought to reside in that function; and similarly it may be held that the good of man resides in the function of man, if he has a function.

Are we then to suppose that, while the carpenter and the shoe-maker have definite functions or businesses belonging to them, man as such has none, and is not designed by nature to fulfil any function? Must we not rather assume that, just as the eye, the hand, the foot and each of the various members of the body manifestly has a certain function of its own, so a human being also has a certain function over and above all the functions of his particular members? What then precisely can this function be? The mere act of living appears to be shared even by plants, whereas we are looking for the function peculiar to man; we must therefore set aside the vital activity of nu-　[1098a] trition and growth. Next in the scale will come some form of sentient life; but this too appears to be shared by horses, oxen, and animals generally. There remains therefore what may be called the practical life of the rational part of man. (This part has two divisions, one rational as obedient to principle, the other as possessing principle and exercising intelligence). Rational life again has two meanings; let us assume that we are here concerned with the active exercise of the rational faculty, since this seems to be the more proper sense of the term. If then the function of man is the active exercise of the soul's faculties in conformity with rational principle, or at all events not in dissociation from rational principle, and if we acknowledge the function of an individual and of a good individual of the same class (for instance, a harper and a good harper, and so generally with all classes) to be generically the same, the qualification of the latter's superiority in excellence being added to the function in his case (I mean that if the function of a harper is to play the harp, that of a good harper is to play the harp well): if this is so, and if we declare that the function of man is a certain form of life, and define that form of life as the exercise of the soul's faculties and activities in association with rational principle, and say that the function of a good man is to perform these activities well and rightly, and if a function is well performed when it is performed in accordance with its own proper excellence—from these premises it follows that the Good of man is the active exercise of his soul's faculties in conformity with excellence or virtue, or if there be several human excellences or virtues, in conformity with the best and most perfect among them. Moreover this activity must occupy a complete lifetime; for one swallow does not make spring, nor does one fine day; and similarly one day or a brief period of happiness does not make a man supremely blessed and happy.

Let this account then serve to describe the Good in outline—for no doubt the proper procedure is to begin by making a rough sketch, and to fill it in afterwards. If a work has been well laid down in outline, to carry it on and complete it in detail may be supposed to be within the capacity of anybody; and in this working out of details Time seems to be a good inventor or at all events coadjutor. This indeed is how advances in the arts have actually come about, since anyone can fill in the gaps. Also the warning given above must not be forgotten; we must not look for equal exactness in all departments of study, but only such as belongs to the subject matter of each, and in such a degree as is appropriate to the particular line of enquiry. A carpenter and a geometrician both seek after a right angle, but in different ways; the former is content with that approximation to it which satisfies the purpose of his work; the latter, being a student of truth, looks for its essence or essential attributes. We should therefore proceed in the same manner in other subjects also, and not allow side issues to outweigh the main task in hand.

Nor again must we in all matters alike demand an explanation of the reason why things are what they are; in some cases it is [1098b] enough if the fact that they are so is satisfactorily established. This is the case with first principles; and the fact is the primary thing—it *is* a first principle. And principles are studied—some by induction, others by perception, others by some form of habituation, and also others otherwise; so we must endeavour to arrive at the principles of each kind in their natural manner, and must also be careful to define them correctly, since they are of great importance for the subsequent course of the enquiry. The beginning is admittedly more than half of the whole, and throws light at once on many of the questions under investigation.

*   *   *

But inasmuch as happiness is a certain activity of soul   [ch. **13** in conformity with perfect goodness, it is necessary to examine the nature of goodness. For this will probably assist us in our investigation of the nature of happiness. Also, the true statesman seems to be one who has made a special study of goodness, since his aim is to make the citizens good and law-abiding men—witness the lawgivers of Crete and Sparta, and the other great legislators of history; but if the study of goodness falls within the province of Political Science, it is clear that in investigating goodness we shall be keeping to the plan which we adopted at the outset.

Now the goodness that we have to consider is clearly human goodness, since the good or happiness which we set out to seek was human good and human happiness. But human goodness means in our view excellence of soul, not excellence of body; also our definition of happiness is an activity of the soul. Now if this is so, clearly it behoves the statesman to have some acquaintance with psychology, just as the physician who is to heal the eye or the other parts of the body must know their anatomy. Indeed a foundation of science is even more requisite for the statesman, inasmuch as politics is a higher and more honourable art than medicine; but physicians of the better class devote much attention to the study of the human body. The student of politics therefore as well as the psychologist must study the nature of the soul, though he will do so as an aid to politics, and only so far as is requisite for the objects of enquiry that he has in view: to pursue the subject in further detail would doubtless be more laborious than is necessary for his purpose.

Now on the subject of psychology some of the teaching current in extraneous discourses is satisfactory, and may be adopted here: namely that the soul consists of two parts, one irrational and the other capable of reason. (Whether these two parts are really distinct in the sense that the parts of the body or of any other divisible whole are distinct, or whether though distinguishable in thought as two they are inseparable in reality, like the convex and concave sides of a curve, is a question of no importance for the matter in hand.) Of the irrational part of the soul again one division appears to be common to all living things, and of a vegetative nature: I refer to the part that causes nutrition and growth; for we must assume that a vital faculty of this nature exists in all things that assimilate nourishment, including embryos—the [1102b] same faculty being present also in the fully-developed organism (this is more reasonable than to assume a different nutritive faculty in the latter). The excellence of this faculty therefore appears to be common to all animate things and not peculiar to man; for it is believed that this faculty or part of the soul is most active during sleep, but when they are asleep you cannot tell a good man from a bad one (whence the saying that for half their lives there is no difference between the happy and the miserable). This is a natural result of the fact that sleep is a cessation of the soul from the activities on which its goodness or bad- ness depends—except that in some small degree certain of the sense- impressions may reach the soul during sleep, and consequently the dreams of the good are better than those of ordinary men. We need not however pursue this subject further, but may omit from consideration the nutritive part of the soul, since it exhibits no specifically human excellence.

But there also appears to be another element in the soul, which, though irrational, yet in a manner participates in rational principle. In self-restrained and unrestrained people we approve their principle, or the rational part of their souls, because it urges them in the right way and exhorts them to the best course; but their nature seems also to contain another element beside that of rational principle, which com- bats and resists that principle. Exactly the same thing may take place in the soul as occurs with the body in a case of paralysis: when the patient wills to move his limbs to the right they swerve to the left; and similarly in unrestrained persons their impulses run counter to their prin- ciple. But whereas in the body we see the erratic member, in the case of the soul we do not see it; nevertheless it cannot be doubted that in the soul also there is an element beside that of principle, which opposes and runs counter to principle (though in what sense the two are distinct does not concern us here). But this second element also seems, as we said, to participate in rational principle; at least in the self-restrained man it obeys the behest of principle—and no doubt in the temperate and brave man it is still more amenable, for all parts of his nature are in harmony with principle.

Thus we see that the irrational part, as well as the soul as a whole, is double. One division of it, the vegetative, does not share in rational principle at all; the other, the seat of the appetites and of desire in general, does in a sense participate in principle, as being amenable and obedient to it (in the sense in fact in which we speak of 'paying heed' to one's father and friends, not in the sense of the term 'rational' in mathematics). And that principle can in a manner appeal to the

irrational part, is indicated by our practice of admonishing   [1103a
delinquents, and by our employment of rebuke and exhortation generally.

If on the other hand it be more correct to speak of the appetitive
part of the soul also as rational, in that case it is the rational part which,
as well as the whole soul, is divided into two, the one division having
rational principle in the proper sense and in itself, the other obedient to
it as a child to its father.

Now virtue also is differentiated in correspondence with this division of the soul. Some forms of virtue are called intellectual virtues,
others moral virtues: Wisdom or intelligence and Prudence are intellectual, Liberality and Temperance are moral virtues. When describing
a man's moral character we do not say that he is wise or intelligent, but
gentle or temperate; but a wise man also is praised for his disposition,
and praiseworthy dispositions we term virtues.

Book · II

Virtue being, as we have seen, of two kinds, intellectual and   [ch. 1
moral, intellectual virtue is for the most part both produced and increased by instruction, and therefore requires experience and time;
whereas moral or ethical virtue is the product of habit (*ethos*), and has
indeed derived its name, with a slight variation of form, from that
word. And therefore it is clear that none of the moral virtues is
engendered in us by nature, for no natural property can be altered by
habit. For instance, it is the nature of a stone to move downwards, and
it cannot be trained to move upwards, even though you should try to
train it to do so by throwing it up into the air ten thousand times; nor
can fire be trained to move downwards, nor can anything else that
naturally behaves in one way be trained into a habit of behaving in
another way. The virtues therefore are engendered in us neither by
nature nor yet in violation of nature; nature gives us the capacity to
receive them, and this capacity is brought to maturity by habit.

Moreover, the faculties given us by nature are bestowed on us first
in a potential form; we exhibit their actual exercise afterwards. This is
clearly so with our senses: we did not acquire the faculty of sight or
hearing by repeatedly seeing or repeatedly listening, but the other way
about—because we had the senses we began to use them, we did not get
them by using them. The virtues on the other hand we acquire by first
having actually practiced them, just as we do the arts. We learn an art or
craft by doing the things that we shall have to do when we have learnt
it: for instance, men become builders by building houses, harpers by

playing on the harp. Similarly we become just by doing just   [1103b
acts, temperate by doing temperate acts, brave by doing brave acts. This
truth is attested by the experience of states: lawgivers make the citizens good by training them in habits of right action—this is the aim of
all legislation, and if it fails to do this it is a failure; this is what
distinguishes a good form of constitution from a bad one. Again, the actions from or through which any virtue is produced are the same as those
through which it also is destroyed—just as in the case with skill in the
arts, for both the good harpers and the bad ones are produced by harp-
ing, and similarly with builders and all the other craftsmen: as you will
become a good builder from building well, so you will become a bad one
from building badly. Were this not so, there would be no need for
teachers of the arts, but everybody would be born a good or bad craftsman as the case might be. The same then is true of the virtues. It is by
taking part in transactions with our fellowmen that some of us become
just and others unjust; by acting in dangerous situations and forming a
habit of fear or of confidence we become courageous or cowardly. And
the same holds good of our dispositions with regard to the appetites,
and anger; some men become temperate and gentle, other profligate and
irascible, by actually comporting themselves in one way or the other in
relation to those passions. In a word, our moral dispositions are
formed as a result of the corresponding activities. Hence it is incumbent
on us to control the character of our activities, since on the quality of
these depends the quality of our dispositions. It is therefore not of small
moment whether we are trained from childhood in one set of habits or
another; on the contrary it is of very great, or rather of supreme, importance.

As then our present study, unlike the other branches of   [ch. 2
philosophy, has a practical aim (for we are not investigating the nature
of virtue for the sake of knowing what it is, but in order that we may
become good, without which result our investigation would be of no
use), we have consequently to carry our enquiry into the region of
conduct, and to ask how we are to act rightly; since our actions, as we
have said, determine the quality of our dispositions.

Now the formula 'to act in conformity with right principle' is
common ground, and may be assumed as the basis of our discussion.
(We shall speak about this formula later, and consider both the definition of right principle and its relation to the other virtues.)

But let it be granted to begin with that the whole theory   [1104a
of conduct is bound to be an outline only and not an exact system, in
accordance with the rule we laid down at the beginning, that philosophical theories must only be required to correspond to their subject matter;
and matters of conduct and expediency have nothing fixed or invariable

about them, any more than have matters of health. And if this is true of the general theory of ethics, still less is exact precision possible in dealing with particular cases of conduct; for these come under no science or professional tradition, but the agents themselves have to consider what is suited to the circumstances on each occasion, just as is the case with the art of medicine or of navigation. But although the discussion now proceeding is thus necessarily inexact, we must do our best to help it out.

First of all then we have to observe, that moral qualities are so constituted as to be destroyed by excess and by deficiency—as we see is the case with bodily strength and health (for one is forced to explain what is invisible by means of visible illustrations). Strength is destroyed both by excessive and by deficient exercises, and similarly health is destroyed both by too much and by too little food and drink; while they are produced, increased and preserved by suitable quantities. The same therefore is true of Temperance, Courage, and the other virtues. The man who runs away from everything in fear and never endures anything becomes a coward; the man who fears nothing whatsoever but encounters everything becomes rash. Similarly he that indulges in every pleasure and refrains from none turns out a profligate, and he that shuns all pleasure, as boorish persons do, becomes what may be called insensible. Thus Temperance and Courage are destroyed by excess and deficiency, and preserved by the observance of the mean.

But not only are the virtues both generated and fostered on the one hand, and destroyed on the other, from and by the same actions, but they will also find their full exercise in the same actions. This is clearly the case with the other more visible qualities, such as bodily strength: for strength is produced by taking much food and undergoing much exertion, while also it is the strong man who will be able to eat most food and endure most exertion. The same holds good with the virtues. We become temperate by abstaining from pleasures, and at the same time we are best able to abstain from pleasures when we have become temperate. And so with Courage: we become brave by train-   [1104b] ing ourselves to despise and endure terrors, and we shall be best able to endure terrors when we have become brave.

An index of our dispositions is afforded by the pleasure   [ch. 3 or pain that accompanies our actions. A man is temperate if he abstains from bodily pleasures and finds this abstinence itself enjoyable, profligate if he feels it irksome; he is brave if he faces danger with pleasure or at all events without pain, cowardly if he does so with pain.

In fact pleasures and pains are the things with which moral virtue is concerned.

For (1) pleasure causes us to do base actions and pain causes us to abstain from doing noble actions. Hence the importance, as Plato points out, of having been definitely trained from childhood to like and dislike the proper things; this is what good education means.

(2) Again, if the virtues have to do with actions and feelings, and every feeling and every action is attended with pleasure or pain, this too shows that virtue has to do with pleasure and pain.

(3) Another indication is the fact that pain is the medium of punishment; for punishment is a sort of medicine, and it is the nature of medicine to work by means of opposites.

(4) Again, as we said before, every formed disposition of the soul realizes its full nature in relation to and in dealing with that class of objects by which it is its nature to be corrupted or improved. But men are corrupted through pleasures and pains, that is, either by pursuing and avoiding the wrong pleasures and pains, or by pursuing and avoiding them at the wrong time, or in the wrong manner, or in one of the other wrong ways under which errors of conduct can be logically classified. This is why some thinkers define the virtues as states of impassivity or tranquillity, though they make a mistake in using these terms absolutely, without adding 'in the right (or wrong) manner' and 'at the right (or wrong) time' and the other qualifications.

We assume therefore that moral virtue is the quality of acting in the best way in relation to pleasures and pains, and that vice is the opposite.

But the following considerations also will give us further light on the same point.

(5) There are three things that are the motives of choice and three that are the motives of avoidance; namely, the noble, the expedient, and the pleasant, and their opposites, the base, the harmful, and the painful. Now in respect of all these the good man is likely to go right and the bad to go wrong, but especially in respect of pleasure; for pleasure is common to man with the lower animals, and also it is a concomitant of all the objects of choice, since both the noble and the expedient appear to us pleasant.

(6) Again, the susceptibility to pleasure has grown up   [1105a with all of us from the cradle. Hence this feeling is hard to eradicate, being engrained in the fabric of our lives.

(7) Again, pleasure and pain are also the standards by which we all, in a greater or less degree, regulate our actions. On this account therefore pleasure and pain are necessarily our main concern, since to feel pleasure and pain rightly or wrongly has a great effect on conduct.

(8) And again, it is harder to fight against pleasure than against anger (hard as that is, as Heracleitus says); but virtue, like art, is constantly dealing with what is harder, since the harder the task the better is success. For this reason also therefore pleasure and pain are

necessarily the main concern both of virtue and of political science, since he who comports himself towards them rightly will be good, and he who does so wrongly, bad.

We may then take it as established that virtue has to do with pleasures and pains, that the actions which produce it are those which increase it, and also, if differently performed, destroy it, and that the actions from which it was produced are also those in which it is exercised.

*   *   *

We have next to consider the formal definition of virtue.   [ch. 5

A state of the soul is either (1) an emotion, (2) a capacity, or (3) a disposition; virtue therefore must be one of these three things. By the emotions, I mean desire, anger, fear, confidence, envy, joy, friendship, hatred, longing, jealousy, pity; and generally those states of consciousness which are accompanied by pleasure or pain. The capacities are the faculties in virtue of which we can be said to be liable to the emotions, for example, capable of feeling anger or pain or pity. The dispositions are the formed states of character in virtue of which we are well or ill disposed in respect of the emotions; for instance, we have a bad disposition in regard to anger if we are disposed to get angry too violently or not violently enough, a good disposition if we habitually feel a moderate amount of anger; and similarly in respect of the other emotions.

Now the virtues and vices are not emotions because we are not pronounced good or bad according to our emotions, but we are according to our virtues and vices; nor are we either praised or blamed for our emotions—a man is not praised for being frightened or angry, nor is he blamed for being angry merely, but for being angry in a certain way—but we are praised or blamed for our virtues and vices.   [1106a Again, we are not angry or afraid from choice, but the virtues are certain modes of choice, or at all events involve choice. Moreover, we are said to be 'moved' by the emotions, whereas in respect of the virtues and vices we are not said to be 'moved' but to be 'disposed' in a certain way.

And the same considerations also prove that the virtues and vices are not capacities; since we are not pronounced good or bad, praised or blamed, merely by reason of our capacity for emotion. Again, we possess certain capacities by nature, but we are not born good or bad by nature: of this however we spoke before.

If then the virtues are neither emotions nor capacities, it remains that they are dispositions.

Thus we have stated what virtue is generically.

But it is not enough merely to define virtue generically   [ch. 6
as a disposition; we must also say what species of disposition it is. It
must then be premised that all excellence has a twofold effect on the
thing to which it belongs: it not only renders the thing itself good,
but it also causes it to perform its function well. For example, the effect of excellence in the eye is that the eye is good *and* functions well;
since having good eyes means having good sight. Similarly excellence
in a horse makes it a good horse, and also good at galloping, at carrying
its rider, and at facing the enemy. If therefore this is true of all things,
excellence or virtue in a man will be the disposition which renders him
a good man and also which will cause him to perform his function
well. We have already indicated what this means; but it will throw more
light on the subject if we consider what constitutes the specific nature
of virtue.

Now of everything that is continuous and divisible, it is possible to
take the larger part, or the smaller part, or an equal part, and these parts
may be larger, smaller, and equal either with respect to the thing itself
or relatively to us; the equal part being a mean between excess and
deficiency. By the mean of the thing I denote a point equally distant
from either extreme, which is one and the same for everybody; by the
mean relative to us, that amount which is neither too much nor too
little, and this is not one and the same for everybody. For example,
let 10 be many and 2 few; then one takes the mean with respect to the
thing if one takes 6; since $6 - 2 = 10 - 6$, and this is the mean according to arithmetical proportion. But we cannot arrive by this method at
the mean relative to us. Suppose that 10 lb. of food is   [1106b
a large ration for anybody and 2 lb. a small one: it does not follow that
a trainer will prescribe 6 lb., for perhaps even this will be a large ration, or a small one, for the particular athlete who is to receive it; it is
a small ration for a Milo, but a large one for a man just beginning to
go in for athletics. And similarly with the amount of running or wrestling exercise to be taken. In the same way then an expert in any art
avoids excess and deficiency, and seeks and adopts the mean—the mean,
that is, not of the thing but relative to us. If therefore the way in which
every art or science performs its work well is by looking to the mean
and applying that as a standard to its productions (hence the common
remark about a perfect work of art, that you could not take from it nor
add to it—meaning that excess and deficiency destroy perfection, while
adherence to the mean preserves it)—if then, as we say, good craftsmen
look to the mean as they work, and if virtue, like nature, is more accurate and better than any form of art, it will follow that virtue has
the quality of hitting the mean. I refer to moral virtue, for this is concerned with emotions and actions, in which one can have excess or

deficiency or a due mean. For example, one can be frightened or bold, feel desire or anger or pity, and experience pleasure and pain in general, either too much or too little, and in both cases wrongly; whereas to feel these feelings at the right time, on the right occasion, towards the right people, for the right purpose and in the right manner, is to feel the best amount of them, which is the mean amount—and the best amount is of course the mark of virtue. And similarly there can be excess, deficiency, and the due mean in actions. Now feelings and actions are the objects with which virtue is concerned; and in feelings and actions excess and deficiency are errors, while the mean amount is praised, and constitutes success; and to be praised and to be successful are both marks of virtue. Virtue, therefore, is a mean state in the sense that it is able to hit the mean. Again, error is multiform (for evil is a form of the unlimited, as in the old Pythagorean imagery, and good of the limited), whereas success is possible in one way only (which is why it is easy to fail and difficult to succeed—easy to miss the target and difficult to hit it); so this is another reason why excess and deficiency are a mark of vice, and observance of the mean a mark of virtue:

Goodness is simple, badness manifold.

Virtue then is a settled disposition of the mind determining the choice of actions and emotions, consisting essentially in the   [1107a observance of the mean relative to us, this being determined by principle, that is, as the prudent man would determine it.

And it is a mean state between two vices, one of excess and one of defect. Furthermore, it is a mean state in that whereas the vices either fall short of or exceed what is right in feelings and in actions, virtue ascertains and adopts the mean. Hence while in respect of its substance and the definition that states what it really is in essence virtue is the observance of the mean, in point of excellence and rightness it is an extreme.

Not every action or emotion however admits of the observance of a due mean. Indeed the very names of some directly imply evil, for instance malice, shamelessness, envy, and, of actions, adultery, theft, murder. All these and similar actions and feelings are blamed as being bad in themselves; it is not the excess or deficiency of them that we blame. It is impossible therefore ever to go right in regard to them— one must always be wrong; nor does right or wrong in their case depend on the circumstances, for instance, whether one commits adultery with the right woman, at the right time, and in the right manner; the mere commission of any of them is wrong. One might as well suppose there could be a due mean and excess and deficiency in acts of injustice or cowardice or profligacy, which would imply that one could have a medium amount of excess and of deficiency, an excessive amount of excess and a deficient amount of deficiency. But just as there can be no excess or deficiency in temperance and justice, because the mean is in a sense an extreme, so there can be no observance of the mean nor excess nor deficiency in the corresponding vicious acts mentioned above, but however they are committed, they are wrong; since, to put it in general terms, there is no such thing as observing a mean in excess or deficiency, nor as exceeding or falling short in the observance of a mean.

We must not however rest content with stating this gen-   [ch. 7 eral definition, but must show that it applies to the particular virtues. In practical philosophy, although universal principles have a wider application, those covering a particular part of the field possess a higher degree of truth; because conduct deals with particular facts, and our theories are bound to accord with these.

Let us then take the particular virtues from the diagram.

The observance of the mean in fear and confidence is   [1107b Courage. The man that exceeds in fearlessness is not designated by any special name (and this is the case with many of the virtues and vices); he that exceeds in confidence is Rash; he that exceeds in fear and is deficient in confidence is Cowardly. In respect of pleasures and pains—not all of them, and to a less degree in respect of pains—the observance of the mean is Temperance, the excess Profligacy. Men deficient in the enjoyment of pleasures scarcely occur, and hence this character also has not been assigned a name, but we may call it Insensible. In regard to giving and getting money, the observance of the mean is Liberality; the excess and deficiency are Prodigality and Meanness, but the prodigal man and the mean man exceed and fall short in opposite ways to one another: the prodigal exceeds in giving and is deficient in getting, whereas the mean man exceeds in getting and is deficient in giving. For the present then we describe these qualities in outline and summarily, which is enough for the purpose in hand; but they will be more accurately defined later.

There are also other dispositions in relation to money, namely, the mode of observing the mean called Magnificence (the magnificent man being different from the liberal, as the former deals with large amounts and the latter with small ones), the excess called Tastelessness or Vulgarity, and the defect called Paltriness. These are not the same as Liberality and the vices corresponding to it; but the way in which they differ will be discussed later.

In respect of honour and dishonour, the observance of the mean is Greatness of Soul, the excess a sort of Vanity, as it may be called, and the deficiency, Smallness of Soul. And just as we said that Liberality is related to Magnificence, differing from it in being concerned with small amounts of money, so there is a certain quality related to Greatness of Soul, which is concerned with great honours, while this quality itself is concerned with small honours; for it is possible to aspire to minor honours in the right way, or more than is right, or less. He who exceeds in these aspirations is called ambitious, he who is deficient, unambitious; but the middle character has no name, and the dispositions of these persons are also unnamed, except that that of the ambitious man is called Ambitiousness. Consequently the extreme characters put in a claim to the middle position, and in fact we ourselves sometimes call the middle person ambitious and sometimes unambitious: we sometimes praise a man for being ambitious, sometimes for being unambitious. Why we do so shall be discussed later; for   [1108a the present let us classify the remaining virtues and vices on the lines which we have laid down.

In respect of anger also we have excess, deficiency, and the observance of the mean. These states are virtually without names, but as we call a person of the middle character gentle, let us name the observance of the mean Gentleness, while of the extremes, he that exceeds may be styled irascible and his vice Irascibility, and he that is deficient, spiritless, and the deficiency Spiritlessness.

There are also three other modes of observing a mean which bear some resemblance to each other, and yet are different; all have to do with intercourse in conversation and action, but they differ in that one is concerned with truthfulness of speech and behaviour, and the other with pleasantness, in its two divisions of pleasantness in social amusement and pleasantness in the general affairs of life. We must then discuss these qualities also, in order the better to discern that in all things the observance of the mean is to be praised, while the extremes are neither right nor praiseworthy, but reprehensible. Most of these qualities also are unnamed, but in these as in the other cases we must attempt to coin names for them ourselves, for the sake of clearness and so that our meaning may be easily followed.

In respect of truth then, the middle character may be called truthful, and the observance of the mean Truthfulness; pretence in the form of exaggeration is Boastfulness, and its possessor a boaster; in the form of understatement, Self-depreciation, and its possessor the self-depreciator.

In respect of pleasantness in social amusement, the middle character is witty and the middle disposition Wittiness; the excess is Buffoonery and its possessor a buffoon; the deficient man may be called boorish, and his disposition Boorishness. In respect of general pleasantness in life, the man who is pleasant in the proper manner is friendly, and the observance of the mean is Friendliness; he that exceeds, if from no interested motive, is obsequious, if for his own advantage, a flatterer; he that is deficient, and unpleasant in all the affairs of life, may be called quarrelsome and surly.

There are also modes of observing a mean in the sphere of and in relation to the emotions. For in these also one man is spoken of as moderate and another as excessive—for example the bashful man whose modesty takes alarm at everything; while he that is deficient in shame, or abashed at nothing whatsoever, is shameless, and the man of middle character modest. For though Modesty is not a virtue, it is praised, and so is the modest man.

Again, Righteous Indignation is the observance of a [1108b mean between Envy and Malice, and these qualities are concerned with pain and pleasure felt at the fortunes of one's neighbours. The righteously indignant man is pained by undeserved good fortune; the jealous man exceeds him and is pained by all the good fortune of others; while the malicious man so far falls short of being pained that he actually feels pleasure.

These qualities however it will be time to discuss in another place. After them we will treat Justice, distinguishing its two kinds—for it has more than one sense—and showing in what way each is a mode of observing the mean. [And we will deal similarly with the logical virtues.]

There are then three dispositions—two vices, one of ex- [ch. 8 cess and one of defect, and one virtue which is the observance of the mean; and each of them is in a certain way opposed to both the others. For the extreme states are the opposite both of the middle state and of each other, and the middle state is the opposite of both extremes; since just as the equal is greater in comparison with the less and less in comparison with the greater, so the middle states of character are in excess as compared with the defective states and defective as compared with the excessive states, whether in the case of feelings or of actions. For instance, a brave man appears rash in contrast with a coward and cowardly in contrast with a rash man; similarly a temperate man appears profligate in contrast with a man insensible to pleasure and pain, but insensible in contrast with a profligate; and a liberal man seems prodigal in contrast with a mean man, mean in contrast with one who is prodigal. Hence either extreme character tries to push the middle character towards the other extreme; a coward calls a brave man rash and a rash man calls him a coward, and correspondingly in other cases.

But while all three dispositions are thus opposed to one another, the greatest degree of contrariety exists between the two extremes. For the extremes are farther apart from each other than from the mean, just as great is farther from small and small from great than either from equal. Again some extremes show a certain likeness to the mean—for instance, Rashness resembles Courage, Prodigality Liberality, whereas the extremes display the greatest unlikeness to one another. But it is things farthest apart from each other that logicians define as contraries, so that the farther apart things are the more contrary they are.

And in some cases the defect, in others the excess, is   [1109a more opposed to the mean; for example Cowardice, which is a vice of deficiency, is more opposed to Courage than is Rashness, which is a vice of excess; but Profligacy, or excess of feeling, is more opposed to Temperance than is Insensibility, or lack of feeling. This results from either of two causes. One of these arises from the thing itself; owing to one extreme being nearer to the mean and resembling it more, we count not this but rather the contrary extreme as the opposite of the mean; for example, because Rashness seems to resemble Courage more than Cowardice does, and to be nearer to it, we reckon Cowardice rather than Rashness as the contrary of Courage; for those extremes which are more remote from the mean are thought to be more contrary to it. This then is one cause, arising out of the thing itself. The other cause has its origin in us: those things appear more contrary to the mean to which we are ourselves more inclined by our nature. For example, we are of ourselves more inclined to pleasure, which is why we are prone to Profligacy [more than to Propriety]. We therefore rather call those things the contrary of the mean, into which we are more inclined to lapse; and hence Profligacy, the excess, is more particularly the contrary of Temperance.

Book · I I I

Virtue however is concerned with emotions and actions, and   [ch. 1 it is only voluntary actions for which praise and blame are given; those that are involuntary are condoned, and sometimes even pitied. Hence it seems to be necessary for the student of ethics to define the difference between the Voluntary and the Involuntary; and this will also be of service to the legislator in assigning rewards and punishments.

It is then generally held that actions are involuntary when done (a) under compulsion or (b) through ignorance; and that   [1110a (a) an act is compulsory when its origin is from without, being of such a nature that the agent, who is really passive, contributes nothing to it: for example, when he is carried somewhere by stress of weather, or by people who have him in their power. But there is some doubt about actions done through fear of a worse alternative, or for some noble object—as for instance if a tyrant having a man's parents and children in his power commands him to do something base, when if he complies their lives will be spared but if he refuses they will be put to death. It is open to question whether such actions are voluntary or involuntary. A somewhat similar case is when cargo is jettisoned in a storm; apart from circumstances, no one voluntarily throws away his property, but to save his own life and that of his shipmates any sane man would do so. Acts of this kind, then, are 'mixed' or composite; but they approximate rather to the voluntary class. For at the actual time when they are done they are chosen or willed; and the end or motive of an act varies with the occasion, so that the terms 'voluntary' and 'involuntary' should be used with reference to the time of action; now the actual deed in the cases in question is done voluntarily, for the origin of the movement of the parts of the body instrumental to the act lies in the agent; and when the origin of an action is in oneself, it is in one's own power to do it or not. Such acts therefore are voluntary, though perhaps involuntary apart from circumstances—for no one would choose to do any such action in and for itself.

Sometimes indeed men are actually praised for deeds of this 'mixed' class, namely when they submit to some disgrace or pain as the price of some great and noble object; though if they do so without any such motive they are blamed, since it is contemptible to submit to a great disgrace with no advantage or only a trifling one in view. In some cases again, such submission though not praised is condoned, when a man does something wrong through fear of penalties that impose too great a strain on human nature, and that no one could endure. Yet there seem to be some acts which a man cannot be compelled to do, and rather than do them he ought to submit to the most terrible death: for instance, we think it ridiculous that Alcmaeon in Euripides' play is compelled by certain threats to murder his mother! But it is sometimes difficult to decide how far we ought to go in choosing to do a given act rather than suffer a given penalty, or in enduring a given penalty rather than commit a given action; and it is still more difficult to abide by our decision when made, since in most of such dilemmas the penalty threatened is painful and the deed forced upon us dishonourable, which is why praise and blame are bestowed according as we do or do not yield to such compulsion.

What kind of actions then are to be called 'compulsory'? [1110b] Used without qualification, perhaps this term applies to any case where the cause of the action lies in things outside the agent, and when the agent contributes nothing. But when actions intrinsically involuntary are yet in given circumstances deliberately chosen in preference to a given alternative, and when their origin lies in the agent, these actions are to be pronounced intrinsically involuntary but voluntary in the circumstances, and in preference to the alternative. They approximate however rather to the voluntary class, since conduct consists of particular things done, and the particular things done in the cases in question are voluntary. But it is not easy to lay down rules for deciding which of two alternatives is to be chosen, for particular cases differ widely.

To apply the term 'compulsory' to acts done for the sake of pleasure or for noble objects, on the plea that these exercise constraint on us from without, is to make every action compulsory. For (1) pleasure and nobility between them supply the motives of all actions whatsoever. Also (2) to act under compulsion and unwillingly is painful, but actions done for their pleasantness or nobility are done with pleasure. And (3) it is absurd to blame external things, instead of blaming ourselves for falling an easy prey to their attractions; or to take the credit of our noble deeds to ourselves, while putting the blame for our disgraceful ones upon the temptations of pleasure. It appears therefore that an act is compulsory when its origin is from outside, the person compelled contributing nothing to it.

(b) An act done through ignorance is in every case not voluntary, but it is involuntary only when it causes the agent pain and regret: since a man who has acted through ignorance and feels no compunction at all for what he has done, cannot indeed be said to have acted voluntarily, as he was not aware of his action, yet cannot be said to have acted involuntarily, as he is not sorry for it. Acts done through ignorance therefore fall into two classes: if the agent regrets the act, we think that he has acted involuntarily; if he does not regret it, to mark the distinction we may call him a 'non-voluntary' agent—for as the case is different it is better to give it a special name. Acting *through* ignorance however seems to be different from acting *in* ignorance; for when a man is drunk or in a rage, his actions are not thought to be done through ignorance but owing to one or other of the conditions mentioned, though he does act without knowing, and *in* ignorance. Now it is true that all wicked men are ignorant of what they ought to do and refrain from doing, and that this error is the cause of injustice and of vice in general. But the term 'involuntary' does not really apply to an action when the agent is ignorant of his true interests. The ignorance that makes an act blameworthy is not ignorance displayed in moral choice (that sort of ignorance constitutes vice)—that is to say, it is not general ignorance (because that is held to be blameworthy), but particular ignorance, ignorance of the circumstances of the act and of the things affected by it; for in this case the act is pitied   [1111a and forgiven, because he who acts in ignorance of any of these circumstances is an involuntary agent.

Perhaps then it will be as well to specify the nature and number of these circumstances. They are (1) the agent, (2) the act, (3) the thing that is affected by or is the sphere of the act; and sometimes also (4) the instrument, for instance, a tool with which the act is done, (5) the effect, for instance, saving a man's life, and (6) the manner, for instance, gently or violently.

Now no one, unless mad, could be ignorant of all these circumstances together; nor yet, obviously, of (1) the agent—for a man must know who he is himself. But a man may be ignorant of (2) what he is doing, as for instance when people say 'it slipped out while they were speaking,' or 'they were not aware that the matter was a secret,' as Aeschylus said of the Mysteries; or that 'they let it off when they only meant to show how it worked' as the prisoner pleaded in the catapult case. Again (3) a person might mistake his son for an enemy, as Merope does; or (4) mistake a sharp spear for one with a button on it, or a heavy stone for a pumice-stone; or (5) one might kill a man by giving him medicine with the intention of saving his life; or (6) in loose wrestling hit him a blow when meaning only to grip his hand. Ignorance therefore being possible in respect of all these circumstances of the act, one who has acted in ignorance of any of them is held to have acted involuntarily, and especially so if ignorant of the most important of them; and the most important of the circumstances seem to be the nature of the act itself and the effect it will produce.

Such then is the nature of the ignorance that justifies our speaking of an act as involuntary, given the further condition that the agent feels sorrow and regret for having committed it.

An involuntary action being one done under compulsion or through ignorance, a voluntary act would seem to be an act of which the origin lies in the agent, who knows the particular circumstances in which he is acting. For it is probably a mistake to say that acts caused by anger or by desire are involuntary. In the first place, (1) this will debar us from speaking of any of the lower animals as acting voluntarily, or children either. Then (2) are none of our actions that are caused by desire or anger voluntary, or are the noble ones voluntary and the base involuntary? Surely this is an absurd distinction when one person is the author of both. Yet perhaps it is strange to speak of acts aiming at things which it is right to aim at as involuntary; and it is right to feel anger at some things, and also to feel desire for some things, for instance health, knowledge. Also (3) we think that involuntary actions are painful and actions that gratify desire pleasant. And again (4) what difference is there in respect of their involuntary character between wrong acts committed deliberately and wrong acts done in anger? Both are to be avoided; and also we think that the irra-   [1111b tional feelings are just as much a part of human nature as the reason, so that the actions done from anger or desire also belong to the human being who does them. It is therefore strange to class these actions as involuntary.

Having defined voluntary and involuntary action, we [ch. 2 next have to examine the nature of Choice. For this appears to be intimately connected with virtue, and to afford a surer test of character than do our actions.

Choice is manifestly a voluntary act. But the two terms are not synonymous, the latter being the wider. Children and the lower animals as well as men are capable of voluntary action, but not of choice. Also sudden acts may be termed voluntary, but they cannot be said to be done by choice.

Some identify Choice with (1) Desire, or (2) Passion, or (3) Wish, or (4) some form of Opinion. These views however appear to be mistaken.

(1) The irrational animals do not exercise choice, but they do feel desire, and also passion. Also a man of defective self-restraint acts from desire but not from choice; and on the contrary a self-restrained man acts from choice and not from desire. Again, desire can run counter to choice, but not desire to desire. And desire has regard to an object as pleasant or painful, choice has not.

(2) Still less is choice the same as passion. Acts done from passion seem very far from being done of deliberate choice.

(3) Again, choice is certainly not a wish, though they appear closely akin. Choice cannot have for its object impossibilities: if a man were to say he chose something impossible he would be thought a fool; but we can wish for things that are impossible, for instance immortality. Also we may wish for what cannot be secured by our own agency, for instance, that a particular actor or athlete may win; but no one chooses what does not rest with himself, but only what he thinks can be attained by his own act. Again, we wish rather for ends than for means, but choose the means to our end; for example, we wish to be healthy, but choose things to make us healthy; we wish to be happy, and that is the word we use in this connexion, but it would not be proper to say that we choose to be happy; since, speaking generally, choice seems to be concerned with things within our own control.

(4) Nor yet again can it be opinion. It seems that anything may be matter of opinion—we form opinions about what is eternal, or impossible, just as much as about what is within our power. Also we distinguish opinion by its truth or falsehood, not by its being good or bad, but choice is distinguished rather as being good or bad. Probably therefore nobody actually identifies choice with opinion in gen- [1112a eral. But neither is it the same as some particular opinion. For it is our

choice of good or evil that determines our character, not our opinion about good or evil. And we choose to take or avoid some good or evil thing, but we opine what a thing is, or for whom it is advantageous, or how it is so: we do not exactly form an opinion to take or avoid a thing. Also we praise a choice rather for choosing the right thing, but an opinion for opining in the right way. And we choose only things that we absolutely know to be good, we opine things we do not quite certainly know to be true. Nor do the same persons appear to excel both at choosing and at forming opinions: some people seem to form opinions better, but yet to choose the wrong things from wickedness. That choice is preceded or accompanied by the formation of an opinion is immaterial, for that is not the point we are considering, but whether choice is the same thing as some form of opinion.

What then are the genus and differentia of Choice, inasmuch as it is not any of the things above mentioned? It manifestly belongs to the genus voluntary action; but not every voluntary act is chosen. Perhaps we may define it as voluntary action preceded by deliberation, since choice involves reasoning and some process of thought. Indeed previous deliberation seems to be implied by the very term *proaireton*, which denotes something *chosen before* other things.

As for Deliberation, do people deliberate about every-   [ch. 3 thing—are all things possible objects of deliberation—, or are there some things about which deliberation is impossible? The term 'object of deliberation' presumably must not be taken to include things about which a fool or a madman might deliberate, but to mean what a sensible person would deliberate about.

Well then, nobody deliberates about things eternal, such as the order of the universe, or the incommensurability of the diagonal and the side of a square. Nor yet about things that change but follow a regular process, whether from necessity or by nature or through some other cause: such phenomena for instance as the solstices and the sunrise. Nor about irregular occurrences, such as droughts and rains. Nor about the results of chance, such as finding a hidden treasure. The reason why we do not deliberate about these things is that none of them can be effected by our agency. We deliberate about things that are in our control and are attainable by action (which are in fact the only things that still remain to be considered; for Nature, Necessity, and Chance, with the addition of Intelligence and human agency generally, exhaust the generally accepted list of causes). But we do not deliberate about all human affairs without exception either: for example, no Lacedaemonian deliberates about the best form of government for Scythia; but any particular set of men deliberates about the things attainable by their own actions. Also there is no room for deliberation   [1112b about matters fully ascertained and completely formulated as sciences; such for instance as orthography, for we have no uncertainty as to how a word ought to be spelt. We deliberate about things in which our agency operates but does not always produce the same results; for instance about questions of medicine and of business; and we deliberate about navigation more than about athletic training, because it has been less completely reduced to a science; and similarly with other pursuits also. And we deliberate more about the arts than about the sciences, because we are more uncertain about them.

Deliberation then is employed in matters which, though subject to rules that generally hold good, are uncertain in their issue; or where the issue is indeterminate, and where, when the matter is important, we take others into our deliberations, distrusting our own capacity to decide.

And we deliberate not about ends, but about means. A doctor does not deliberate whether he is to cure his patient, nor an orator whether he is to convince his audience, nor a statesman whether he is to secure good government, nor does anyone else debate about the end of his profession or calling; they take some end for granted, and consider how and by what means it can be achieved. If they find that there are several means of achieving it, they proceed to consider which of these will attain it most easily and best. If there is only one means by which it can be accomplished, they ask how it is to be accomplished by that means, and by what means that means can itself be achieved, until they reach the first link in the chain of causes, which is the last in the order of discovery. (For when deliberating one seems in the procedure described to be pursuing an investigation or analysis that resembles the analysis of a figure in geometry—indeed it appears that though not all investigation is deliberation, for example, mathematical investigation is not, yet all deliberation is investigation—and the last step in the analysis seems to be the first step in the execution of the design.) Then, if they have come up against an impossibility, they abandon the project —for instance, if it requires money and money cannot be procured; but if on the other hand it proves to be something possible, they begin to act. By possible, I mean able to be performed by our agency—things we do through the agency of our friends counting in a sense as done by ourselves, since the origin of their action is in us.

(In practising an art) the question is at one moment what tools to use, and at another how to use them; and similarly in other spheres, we have to consider sometimes what means to employ, and sometimes how exactly any given means are to be employed.

It appears therefore, as has been said, that a man is the origin of his actions, and that the province of deliberation is to discover actions within one's own power to perform; and all our actions aim at ends other than themselves. It follows that we do not deliberate about ends, but about means. Nor yet do we deliberate about particular facts, for instance, Is this object a loaf? or, Is this loaf properly baked?   [1113a for these are matters of direct perception. Deliberation must stop at the particular fact, or it will embark on a process *ad infinitum*.

The object of deliberation and the object of choice are the same, except that when a thing is chosen it has already been determined, since it is the thing already selected as the result of our deliberation that is chosen. For a man stops enquiring how he shall act as soon as he has carried back the origin of action to himself, and to the dominant part of himself, for it is this part that chooses. This may be illustrated by the ancient constitutions represented in Homer: the kings used to proclaim to the people the measures they had chosen to adopt.

As then the object of choice is something within our power which after deliberation we desire, Choice will be a deliberate desire of things in our power; for we first deliberate, then select, and finally fix our desire according to the result of our deliberation.

Let this serve as a description in outline of Choice, and of the nature of its objects, and the fact that it deals with means to ends.

Wishes, on the contrary, as was said above, are for ends.   [ch. 4 But while some hold that what is wished for is the good, others think it is what appears to be good. Those however who say that what is wished for is the really good, are faced by the conclusion, that what a man who chooses his end wrongly wishes for is not really wished for at all; since if it is to be wished for, it must on their showing be good, whereas in the case assumed it may so happen that the man wishes for something bad. And those on the other hand who say that what appears good is wished for, are forced to admit that there is no such thing as that which is by nature wished for, but that what each man thinks to be good is wished for in his case; yet different, and it may be opposite, things appear good to different people.

If therefore neither of these views is satisfactory, perhaps we should say that what is wished for in the true and unqualified sense is the good, but that what appears good to each person is wished for by him; and accordingly that the good man wishes for what is truly wished for, the bad man for anything as it may happen (just as in the case of our bodies, a man of sound constitution finds really healthy food best for his health, but some other diet may be healthy for one who is delicate; and so with things bitter and sweet, hot, heavy, etc.). For the good man judges everything correctly; what things truly are, that they seem to him to be, in every department—for special things are noble and pleasant corresponding to each type of character, and perhaps what chiefly distinguishes the good man is that he sees the truth in each kind, being himself as it were the standard and measure of the noble and pleasant. It appears to be pleasure that misleads the mass of mankind; for it seems to them to be a good, though it is not, so they choose   [1113b what is pleasant as good and shun pain as evil.

If then whereas we wish for our end, the means to our   [ch. 5 end are matters of deliberation and choice, it follows that actions dealing with these means are done by choice, and voluntary. But the activities in which the virtues are exercised deal with means. Therefore virtue also depends on ourselves. And so also does vice. For where we are free to act we are also free to refrain from acting, and where we are able to say No we are also able to say Yes; if therefore we are responsible for doing a thing when to do it is right, we are also responsible for for not doing it when not to do it is wrong, and if we are responsible for rightly not doing a thing, we are also responsible for wrongly doing it. But if it is in our power to do and to refrain from doing right and wrong, and if, as we saw, being good or bad is doing right or wrong, it consequently depends on us whether we are virtuous or vicious. To say that

None would be vile, and none would not be blest

seems to be half false, though half true: it is true that no one is unwilling to be blessed, but not true that wickedness is involuntary; or else we must contradict what we just now asserted, and say that man is not the originator and begetter of his actions as he is of his children. But if it is manifest that a man is the author of his own actions, and if we are unable to trace our conduct back to any other origins than those within ourselves, then actions of which the origins are within us, themselves depend upon us, and are voluntary.

This conclusion seems to be attested both by men's behaviour in private life and by the practice of lawgivers; for they punish and exact redress from those who do evil (except when it is done under compulsion, or through ignorance for which the agent himself is not responsible), and honour those who do noble deeds, in order to encourage the one sort and to repress the other; but nobody tries to encourage us to do things that do not depend upon ourselves and are not voluntary, since it is no good our being persuaded not to feel heat or pain or hunger or the like, because we shall feel them all the same.

Indeed the fact that an offence was committed in ignorance is itself made a ground for punishment, in cases where the offender is held to be responsible for his ignorance; for instance, the penalty is doubled if the offender was drunk, because the origin of the offence was in the man himself, as he might have avoided getting drunk, which was

the cause of his not knowing what he was doing. Also men are punished
for offences committed through ignorance of some provision of the law
which they ought to have known, and might have known [1114a
without difficulty; and so in other cases where ignorance is held to be
due to negligence, on the ground that the offender need not have been
ignorant, as he could have taken the trouble to ascertain the facts.

It may be objected that perhaps he is not the sort of man to take
the trouble. Well, but men are themselves responsible for having become
careless through living carelessly, as they are for being unjust or profligate if they do wrong or pass their time in drinking and dissipation.
They acquire a particular quality by constantly acting in a particular
way. This is shown by the way in which men train themselves for some
contest or pursuit: they practice continually. Therefore only an utterly
senseless person can fail to know that our characters are the result of
our conduct; but if a man knowingly acts in a way that will result in
his becoming unjust, he must be said to be voluntarily unjust.

Again, though it is unreasonable to say that a man who acts un-
justly or dissolutely does not wish to be unjust or dissolute, nevertheless
this by no means implies that he can stop being unjust and become
just merely by wishing to do so; any more than a sick man can get well
by wishing, although it may be the case that his illness is voluntary,
in the sense of being due to intemperate living and neglect of the doctors' advice. At the outset then, it is true, he might have avoided the
illness, but once he has let himself go he can do so no longer. When
you have thrown a stone, you cannot afterwards bring it back again,
but nevertheless you are responsible for having taken up the stone and
flung it, for the origin of the act was within you. Similarly the unjust
and profligate might at the outset have avoided becoming so, and
therefore they are so voluntarily, although when they have become
unjust and profligate it is no longer open to them not to be so.

And not only are vices of the soul voluntary, but in some cases
bodily defects are so as well, and we blame them accordingly. Though
no one blames a man for being born ugly, we censure uncomeliness
that is due to neglecting exercise and the care of the person. And so
with infirmities and mutilations: though nobody would reproach, but
rather pity, a person blind from birth, or owing to disease or accident,
yet all would blame one who had lost his sight from tippling or de-
bauchery. We see then that bodily defects for which we are ourselves
responsible are blamed, while those for which we are not responsible
are not. This being so, it follows that we are responsible for blameworthy
moral defects also.

But suppose somebody says: "All men seek what seems to them
good, but they are not responsible for its seeming good: each man's

conception of his end is determined by his character, what-   [1114b]
ever that may be. Although therefore, on the hypothesis that each man
is in a sense responsible for his moral disposition, he will in a sense be
responsible for his conception of the good, if on the contrary this hypothesis be untrue, no man is responsible for his own wrongdoing. He
does wrong through ignorance of the right end, thinking that wrongdoing will procure him his greatest Good; and his aim at his end is
not of his own choosing. A man needs to be born with moral vision,
so to speak, whereby to discern correctly and choose what is truly good.
A man of good natural disposition is a man well endowed by nature
in this respect; for if a thing is the greatest and noblest of gifts, and is
something which cannot be acquired or learnt from another, but which
a man will possess in such form as it has been bestowed on him at birth,
a good and noble natural endowment in this respect will constitute a
good disposition in the full and true meaning of the term."

Now if this theory be true, how will virtue be voluntary any more
than vice? Both for the good man and the bad man alike, their view
of their end is determined in the same manner, by nature or however
it may be; and all their actions of whatever sort are guided by reference
to their end as thus determined. Whether then a man's view of his end,
whatever it may be, is not given by nature but is partly due to himself,
or whether, although his end is determined by nature, yet virtue is voluntary because the good man's actions to gain his end are voluntary,
in either case vice will be just as much voluntary as virtue; for the bad
man equally with the good possesses spontaneity in his actions, even
if not in his choice of an end. If then, as is said, our virtues are voluntary (and in fact we are in a sense ourselves partly the cause of our
moral dispositions, and it is our having a certain character that makes
us set up an end of a certain kind), it follows that our vices are voluntary also; they are voluntary in the same manner as our virtues.

We have then now discussed in outline the virtues in general, having indicated their genus [namely, that it is a mean, and a disposition],
and having shown that they render us apt to do the same actions as
those by which they are produced, and to do them in the way in which
right reason may enjoin; and that they depend on ourselves and are
voluntary.

But our dispositions are not voluntary in the same way as are our
actions. Our actions we can control from beginning to end, and we
are conscious of them at each stage. With our dispositions on the other
hand, though we can control their beginnings, each separate   [1115a]
addition to them is imperceptible, as is the case with the growth of a
disease; though they are voluntary in that we were free to employ our
capacities in the one way or the other.

But to resume, let us now discuss the virtues severally, defining the nature of each, the class of objects to which it is related, and the way in which it is related to them. In so doing we shall also make it clear how many virtues there are.

Let us first take Courage. We have already seen that   [ch. 6 Courage is the observance of the mean in respect of fear and confidence. Now it is clear that the things we fear are fearful things, which means, broadly speaking, evil things; so that fear is sometimes defined as the anticipation of evil. It is true then that we fear all evil things, for example, disgrace, poverty, disease, lack of friends, death; but it is not thought that Courage is related to all these things, for there are some evils which it is right and noble to fear and base not to fear, for instance, disgrace. One who fears disgrace is an honourable man, with a due sense of shame; one who does not fear it is shameless: though some people apply the term courageous to such a man by analogy, because he bears some resemblance to the courageous man in that the courageous man also is a fearless person.

Again, it is no doubt right not to fear poverty, or disease, or in general any evil not caused by vice and not due to ourselves. But one who is fearless in regard to these things is not courageous either (although the term is applied to him, too, by analogy); since some men who are cowards in war are liberal with money, and face loss of fortune boldly.

Nor yet is a man cowardly if he fears insult to his wife and children, or envy, or the like; nor courageous if he shows a bold face when about to undergo a flogging.

What then are the fearful things in respect of which Courage is displayed? I suppose those which are the greatest, since there is no one more brave in enduring danger than the courageous man. Now the most terrible thing of all is death; for it is the end, and when a man is dead, nothing, we think, either good or evil can befall him any more. But even death, we should hold, does not in all circumstances give an opportunity for Courage: for instance, we do not call a man courageous for facing death by drowning or disease. What form of death then is a test of Courage? Presumably that which is the noblest. Now the noblest form of death is death in battle, for it is encountered in the midst of the greatest and most noble of dangers. And this conclusion is borne out by the principle on which public honours are bestowed in republics and under monarchies.

The courageous man, therefore, in the proper sense of the term, will be he who fearlessly confronts a noble death, or some sudden peril that threatens death; and the perils of war answer this description most fully. Not that the courageous man is not also fearless in a   [1115b storm at sea (as also in illness), though not in the same way as sailors are fearless, for he thinks there is no hope of safety, and to die by drowning is revolting to him, whereas sailors keep up heart because of their experience. Also Courage is shown in dangers where a man can defend himself by valour or die nobly, but neither is possible in disasters like shipwreck.

Now although the same things are not fearful to every-   [ch. 7 body, there are some terrors which we pronounce beyond human endurance, and these of course are fearful to everyone in his senses. And the terrors that man can endure differ in magnitude and degree; as also do the situations inspiring confidence. But the courageous man is proof against fear so far as man may be. Hence although he will sometimes fear even terrors not beyond man's endurance, he will do so in the right way, and he will endure them as principle dictates, for the sake of what is noble; for that is the end at which virtue aims. On the other hand it is possible to fear such terrors too much, and too little; and also to fear things that are not fearful as if they were fearful. Error arises either from fearing what one ought not to fear, or from fearing in the wrong manner, or at the wrong time, or the like; and similarly with regard to occasions for confidence.

The courageous man then is he that endures or fears the right things and for the right purpose and in the right manner and at the right time, and who shows confidence in a similar way. (For the courageous man feels and acts as the circumstances merit, and as principle may dictate. And every activity aims at the end that corresponds to the disposition of which it is the manifestation. So it is therefore with the activity of the courageous man: his courage is noble; therefore its end is nobility, for a thing is defined by its end; therefore the courageous man endures the terrors and dares the deeds that manifest courage, for the sake of that which is noble.)

Of the characters that run to excess, on the other hand, he who exceeds in fearlessness has no name (this, as we remarked before, is the case with many qualities), but we should call a man mad, or else insensitive to pain, if he feared nothing, 'earthquake nor billows,' as they say of the Kelts; he who exceeds in confidence [in the face of fearful things] is rash. The rash man is generally thought to be an impostor, who pretends to courage which he does not possess; at least, he wishes to appear to feel towards fearful things as the courageous man actually does feel, and therefore he imitates him in the things in which he can. Hence most rash men really are cowards at heart, for they make a bold show in situations that inspire confidence, but do not endure terrors.

He that exceeds in fear is a coward, for he fears the wrong things, and in the wrong manner, and so on with the rest of the list.   [1116a

He is also deficient in confidence; but his excessive fear in face of pain is more apparent. The coward is therefore a despondent person, being afraid of everything; but the courageous man is just the opposite, for confidence belongs to a sanguine temperament.

The coward, the rash man, and the courageous man are therefore concerned with the same objects, but are differently disposed towards them: the two former exceed and fall short, the last keeps the mean and the right disposition. The rash, moreover, are impetuous, and though eager before the danger comes they hang back at the critical moment; whereas the courageous are keen at the time of action but calm beforehand.

As has been said then, Courage is the observance of the mean in relation to things that inspire confidence or fear, in the circumstances stated; and it is confident and endures because it is noble to do so or base not to do so. But to seek death in order to escape from poverty, or the pangs of love, or from pain or sorrow, is not the act of a courageous man, but rather of a coward; for it is weakness to fly from troubles, and the suicide does not endure death because it is noble to do so, but to escape evil.

Such is the nature of Courage; but the name is also ap-   [ch. 8
plied to five divergent types of character.

(1) First, as most closely resembling true Courage, comes the citizen's courage. Citizen troops appear to endure dangers because of the legal penalties and the reproach attaching to cowardice, and the honours awarded to bravery; hence those races appear to be the bravest among which cowards are degraded and brave men held in honour. It is this citizen courage which inspires the heroes portrayed by Homer, like Diomede and Hector:

> *Polydamas will be the first to flout me;*

and Diomede says

> *Hector will make his boast at Troy hereafter:*
> *"By me was Tydeus' son . . ."*

This type of courage most closely resembles the one described before, because it is prompted by a virtue, namely the sense of shame, and by the desire for something noble, namely honour, and the wish to avoid the disgrace of being reproached.

The courage of troops forced into battle by their officers may be classed as of the same type, though they are inferior inasmuch as their motive is not a sense of shame but fear, and the desire to avoid not disgrace but pain. Their masters compel them to be brave, after Hector's fashion:

Let me see any skulking off the field—
He shall not save his carcase from the dogs!

The same is done by commanders who draw up their troops in front
of them and beat them if they give ground, or who form   [1116b
them in line with a trench or some other obstacle in the rear; all these
are using compulsion. A man ought not to be brave because he is
compelled to be, but because courage is noble.

(2) Again, experience of some particular form of danger is taken
for a sort of Courage; hence arose Socrates' notion that Courage is
Knowledge. This type of bravery is displayed by various people in various circumstances, and particularly in war by professional soldiers. For
war (as the saying is) is full of false alarms, a fact which these men
have had most opportunity of observing; thus they appear courageous
owing to others' ignorance of the true situation. Also experience renders
them the most efficient in inflicting loss on the enemy without sustaining it themselves, as they are skilled in the use of arms, and equipped
with the best ones both for attack and defence. So that they are like
armed men fighting against unarmed, or trained athletes against ama-
teurs; for even in athletic contests it is not the bravest men who are
the best fighters, but those who are strongest and in the best training.
But professional soldiers prove cowards when the danger imposes too
great a strain, and when they are at a disadvantage in numbers and
equipment; for they are the first to run away, while citizen troops stand
their ground and die fighting, as happened in the battle at the temple
of Hermes. This is because citizens think it disgraceful to run away, and
prefer death to safety so procured; whereas professional soldiers were relying from the outset on superior strength, and when they discover they
are outnumbered they take to flight, fearing death more than disgrace.
But this is not true courage.

(3) Spirit or anger is also classed with Courage. Men emboldened
by anger, like wild beasts which rush upon the hunter that has wounded
them, are supposed to be courageous, because the courageous also are
high-spirited; for spirit is very impetuous in encountering danger. Hence
Homer writes, 'he put strength in their spirit,' and 'roused their might
and their spirit,' and 'bitter wrath up through his nostrils welled,' and
'his blood boiled'; for all such symptoms seem to indicate an excitement
and impulse of the spirit. Thus the real motive of courageous men is
the nobility of courage, although spirit operates in them as well; but
wild animals are emboldened by pain, for they turn to bay because
they are wounded, or frightened—since if they are in a forest or a swamp
they do not attack. Therefore they are not to be considered courageous
for rushing upon danger when spurred by pain and anger, and blind to

the dangers that await them; since on that reckoning even asses would be brave when they are hungry, for no blows will make them [1117a stop grazing! (And adulterers also are led to do many daring things by lust.)

But the form of courage that is inspired by spirit seems to be the most natural, and when reinforced by deliberate choice and purpose it appears to be true Courage. And human beings also feel pain when angry, and take pleasure in revenge. But those who fight for these motives, though valiant fighters, are not courageous; for the motive of their confidences is not honour, nor is it guided by principle, but it springs from feeling. However, they show some affinity to true Courage.

(4) Nor yet again is the boldness of the sanguine the same thing as Courage. The sanguine are confident in face of danger because they have won many victories over many foes before. They resemble the courageous, because both are confident, but whereas the courageous are confident for the reasons already explained, the sanguine are so because they think they are stronger than the enemy, and not likely to come to any harm. (A similar boldness is shown by those getting drunk, for this makes them sanguine for the time being.) When however things do not turn out as they expect, the merely sanguine run away, whereas the mark of the courageous man, as we have seen, is to endure things that are terrible to a human being and that seem so to him, because it is noble to do so and base not to do so. Hence it is thought a sign of still greater courage to be fearless and undismayed in sudden alarms than in dangers that were foreseen. Bravery in unforeseen danger springs more from character, as there is less time for preparation; one might resolve to face a danger one can foresee, from calculation and on principle, but only a fixed disposition of Courage will enable one to face sudden peril.

(5) Those who face danger in ignorance also appear courageous; and they come very near to those whose bravery rests on a sanguine temperament, though inferior to them inasmuch as they lack self-confidence, which the sanguine possess. Hence the sanguine stand firm for a time; whereas those who have been deceived as to the danger, if they learn or suspect the true state of affairs, take to flight, as the Argives did when they encountered the Lacedaemonians and thought they were Sicyonians.

We have now described the characteristics both of the courageous and of those who are thought to be courageous.

Courage is displayed with respect to confidence and fear, [ch. 9 but not with respect to both equally: it is more particularly displayed in regard to objects of fear; for one who is unperturbed in the presence of terrors and comports himself rightly towards these is courageous in a fuller sense than one who does so in situations that inspire confidence. In fact, as has been said, men are sometimes called courageous for enduring pain. Hence Courage itself is attended by pain; and it is justly praised, because it is harder to endure pain than to abstain from pleasure. Not but what it would appear that the end correspond-   [1117b ing to the virtue of Courage is really pleasant, only its pleasantness is obscured by the attendant circumstances. This is illustrated by the case of athletic contests: to boxers, for example, their end—the object they box for, the wreath and the honours of victory—is pleasant, but the blows they receive must hurt them, being men of flesh and blood, and also all the labour they undergo is painful; and these painful incidentals are so numerous that the final object, being a small thing, appears not to contain any pleasure at all. If then the same is true of Courage, the death or wounds that it may bring will be painful to the courageous man, and he will suffer them unwillingly; but he will endure them because it is noble to do so, or because it is base not to do so. And the more a man possesses all virtue, and the more happy he is, the more pain will death cause him; for to such a man life is worth most, and he stands to lose the greatest goods, and knows that this is so, and this must be painful. But he is none the less courageous on that account, perhaps indeed he is more so, because he prefers glory in war to the greatest prizes of life.

It is not true therefore of every virtue that its active exercise is essentially pleasant, save in so far as it attains its end.

No doubt it is possible that such men as these do not make the best professional soldiers, but men who are less courageous, and have nothing of value besides life to lose; for these face danger readily, and will barter their lives for trifling gains.

Let this suffice as an account of Courage: from what has been said it will not be difficult to form at all events a rough conception of its nature.

After Courage let us speak of Temperance; for these ap-   [ch. 10 pear to be the virtues of the irrational parts of the soul.

Now we have said that Temperance is the observance of the mean in relation to pleasures (for it is concerned only in a lesser degree and in a different way with pains); and Profligacy also is displayed in the same matters. Let us then now define the sort of pleasures to which these qualities are related.

Now we must make a distinction between pleasures of the body and pleasures of the soul. Take for instance ambition, or love of learning: the lover of honour or of learning takes pleasure in the thing he loves without his body being affected at all; the experience is purely mental. But we do not speak of men as either temperate or profligate in relation to the pleasures of ambition and of learning. Nor similarly can these terms be applied to the enjoyment of any of the other pleasures that are not bodily pleasures: those who love hearing marvellous tales and telling anecdotes, and who spend their days in trivial gossip, we call idle chatterers, but not profligates; nor do we call men profligate who feel excessive pain for the loss of fortune or friends.

Temperance therefore has to do with the pleasures of [1118a the body. But not with all even of these; for men who delight in the pleasures of the eye, in colours, forms and paintings, are not termed either temperate or profligate, although it would be held that these things also can be enjoyed in the right manner, or too much, or too little. Similarly with the objects of hearing: no one would term profligate those who take an excessive pleasure in music, or the theatre, nor temperate those who enjoy them as is right. Nor yet does Temperance apply to enjoyment of the sense of smell, unless accidentally; we do not call those who are fond of the scent of fruit or roses or incense profligate, though we may be inclined so to style those who love perfumes and the smell of savoury dishes, for the profligate take pleasure in these odours because they remind them of the objects of their desires. One may notice that other persons too like the smell of food when they are hungry; but to delight in things of this kind is a mark of the profligate, since they are the things on which the profligate's desires are set.

Nor do the lower animals derive any pleasure from these senses, except accidentally. Hounds do not take pleasure in scenting hares, but in eating them; the scent merely made them aware of the hare. The lion does not care about the lowing of the ox, but about devouring it, though the lowing tells him that the ox is near, and consequently he appears to take pleasure in the sound. Similarly he is not pleased by the sight of 'or stag or mountain goat,' but by the prospect of a meal.

Temperance and Profligacy are therefore concerned with those pleasures which man shares with the lower animals, and which consequently appear slavish and bestial. These are the pleasures of touch and taste. But even taste appears to play but a small part, if any, in Temperance. For taste is concerned with discriminating flavours, as is done by winetasters, and cooks preparing savoury dishes; but it is not exactly the flavours that give pleasure, or at all events not to the profligate: it is actually enjoying the object that is pleasant, and this is done solely through the sense of touch, alike in eating and drinking and in what are called the pleasures of sex. This is why a certain gourmand wished that his throat might be longer than a crane's, showing that his pleasure lay in the sensation of contact.

Hence the sense to which Profligacy is related is the [1118b most universal of the senses; and there appears to be good ground for the disrepute in which it is held, because it belongs to us not as human beings but as animals. Therefore it is bestial to revel in such pleasures, and to like them better than any others. We do not refer to the most refined of the pleasures of touch, such as the enjoyment of friction and warm baths in the gymnasia; the tactual pleasures of the profligate have to do with certain parts only, not with the whole of the body.

Desires seem to be of two kinds, one common to all men,   [ch. 11 the other peculiar to special peoples, and adventitious. For instance, the desire for food is natural, since everyone desires solid or liquid nourishment, and sometimes both, when in need of them; and also sexual intercourse, as Homer says, when young and lusty. But not everybody desires this or that particular sort of nourishment, any more than everyone desires the same particular portion of food; hence a taste for this or that sort of food seems to be an individual peculiarity. Not but what there is also something natural in such tastes; for different things are pleasant to different people, and there are some special delicacies which all men like better than ordinary food.

In the case of the natural desires, then, few men err, and in one way only, that of excess in quantity; for to eat or drink to repletion of ordinary food and drink is to exceed what is natural in amount, since the natural desire is only to satisfy one's wants. Hence people who overeat are called 'mad-bellies,' meaning that they fill that organ beyond the right measure; it is persons of especially slavish nature that are liable to this form of excess.

But in regard to the pleasures peculiar to particular people, many men err, and err in many ways. For when people are said to be 'very fond of' so-and-so, it is either because they like things that it is not right to like, or like them more than most people do, or like them in a wrong manner; and the profligate exceed in all these ways. For they like some things that are wrong, and indeed abominable, and any such things that it is right to like they like more than is right, and more than most people.

It is clear then that excess in relation to pleasures is Profligacy, and that it is blameworthy. As regards pains on the other hand, it is not with Temperance as it is with Courage: a man is not termed temperate for enduring pain and profligate for not enduring it, but profligate for feeling more pain than is right when he fails to get pleasures (in his case pleasure actually causing pain), and temperate for not feeling pain at the absence of pleasure [or at abstaining from it].

The profligate therefore desires all pleasures, or those   [1119a that are the most pleasant, and is led by his desire to pursue these in preference to everything else. He consequently feels pain not only when he fails to get them, but also from his desire for them, since desire is accompanied by pain; paradoxical though it seems that pain should be caused by pleasure.

Men erring on the side of deficiency as regards pleasures, and taking less than a proper amount of enjoyment in them, scarcely occur; such insensibility is not human. Indeed, even the lower animals discriminate in food, and like some kinds and not others; and if there be a creature that finds nothing pleasant, and sees no difference between one thing and another, it must be very far removed from humanity. As men of this type scarcely occur, we have no special name for them.

The temperate man keeps a middle course in these matters. He takes no pleasure at all in the things that the profligate enjoys most, on the contrary, he positively dislikes them; nor in general does he find pleasure in wrong things, nor excessive pleasure in anything of this sort; nor does he feel pain or desire when they are lacking, or only in a moderate degree, not more than is right, nor at the wrong time, *et cetera*. But such pleasures as conduce to health and fitness he will try to obtain in a moderate and right degree; as also other pleasures so far as they are not detrimental to health and fitness, and not ignoble, nor beyond his means. The man who exceeds these limits cares more for such pleasures than they are worth. Not so the temperate man; he only cares for them as right principle enjoins.

Profligacy seems to be more voluntary than Cowardice.   [ch. 12 For the former is caused by pleasure, the latter by pain, and pleasure is a thing we choose, pain a thing we avoid. Also pain makes us beside ourselves: it destroys the sufferer's nature; whereas pleasure has no such effect. Therefore Profligacy is the more voluntary vice. And consequently it is the more reprehensible; since moreover it is easier to train oneself to resist the temptations of pleasure, because these occur frequently in life, and to practice resistance to them involves no danger, whereas the reverse is the case with the objects of fear.

On the other hand, the possession of a cowardly character would seem to be more voluntary than particular manifestations of cowardice: for cowardliness in itself is not painful, but particular accesses of cowardice are so painful as to make a man beside himself, and cause him to throw away his arms or otherwise behave in an unseemly manner; so that cowardly actions actually seem to be done under compulsion. But with the profligate on the contrary the particular acts are voluntary, for they are done with desire and appetite, but the character in general is less so, since no one desires to be a profligate.

The word Profligacy or wantonness we also apply to the naughtiness of children, which has some resemblance to the licentious-   [1119b ness of adults. Which of the two takes its name from the other is of no importance for the present enquiry, but it would seem clear that the state which comes later in life must be named from the one which comes earlier. The metaphor appears apt enough, since it is that which desires what is disgraceful and whose appetites grow apace that needs chastisement or pruning, and this description applies in the fullest degree to desire, as it does to the child. For children, like profligates, live at the prompting of desire; and the appetite for pleasure is strongest in childhood, so that if it be not disciplined and made obedient to authority, it will make great headway. In an irrational being the appetite for pleasure is insatiable and undiscriminating, and the innate tendency is fostered by active gratification; indeed, if such gratification be great and intense it actually overpowers the reason. Hence our indulgences should be moderate and few, and never opposed to principle—this is what we mean by 'well-disciplined' and 'chastened'—; and the appetitive part of us should be ruled by principle, just as a boy should live in obedience to his tutor. Hence in the temperate man the appetitive element must be in harmony with principle. For (1) the aim of both Temperance and principle is that which is noble; and (2) the temperate man desires the right thing in the right way at the right time, which is what principle ordains.

Let this then be our account of Temperance.

Book · I V

Greatness of Soul, as the word itself implies, seems to be re-   [ch. 3 lated to great objects; let us first ascertain what sort of objects these are. It will make no difference whether we examine the   [1123b quality itself or the person that displays the quality.

Now a person is thought to be great-souled if he claims much and deserves much; he who claims much without deserving it is foolish, but no one of moral excellence is foolish or senseless. The great-souled man is then as we have described. He who deserves little and claims little is modest or temperate, but not great-souled, since to be great-souled involves greatness just as handsomeness involves size: small people may be neat and well-made, but not handsome. He that claims much but does not deserve much is vain; though not everybody who claims more than he deserves is vain. He that claims less than he deserves is small-souled, whether his deserts be great or only moderate, or even though he deserves little, if he claims still less. The most small-souled of all would seem to be the man who claims less than he deserves when his deserts are great; for what would he have done had he not deserved so much?

Though therefore in regard to the greatness of his claim the great-souled man is an extreme, by reason of its rightness he stands at the mean point, for he claims what he deserves; while the vain and the small-souled err by excess and defect respectively.

If then the great-souled man claims and is worthy of great things and most of all the greatest things, Greatness of Soul must be concerned with some one object especially. 'Worthy' is a term of relation: it denotes having a claim to goods external to oneself. Now the greatest external good we should assume to be the thing which we offer as a tribute to the gods, and which is most coveted by men of high station, and is the prize awarded for the noblest deeds; and such a thing is honour, for honour is clearly the greatest of external goods. Therefore the great-souled man is he who has the right disposition in relation to honours and disgraces. And even without argument it is evident that honour is the object with which the great-souled are concerned, since it is honour above all else which great men claim and deserve.

The small-souled man falls short both as judged by his own deserts and in comparison with the claim of the great-souled man; the vain man on the other hand exceeds as judged by his own standard, but does not however exceed the great-souled man.

And inasmuch as the great-souled man deserves most, he must be the best of men; for the better a man is the more he deserves, and he that is best deserves most. Therefore the truly great-souled man must be a good man. Indeed greatness in each of the virtues would seem to go with greatness of soul. For instance, one cannot imagine the great-souled man running at full speed when retreating in battle, nor acting dishonestly; since what motive for base conduct has a man to whom nothing is great? Considering all the virtues in turn, we shall feel it quite ridiculous to picture the great-souled man as other than a good man. Moreover, if he were bad, he would not be worthy of honour, since honour is the prize of virtue, and the tribute that we pay to the good. Greatness of Soul seems therefore to be as it were a　　[1124a crowning ornament of the virtues: it enhances their greatness, and it cannot exist without them. Hence it is hard to be truly great-souled, for greatness of soul is impossible without moral nobility.

Honour and dishonour then are the objects with which the great-souled man is especially concerned. Great honours accorded by persons of worth will afford him pleasure in a moderate degree: he will feel he is receiving only what belongs to him, or even less, for no honour can be adequate to the merits of perfect virtue, yet all the same he will deign to accept their honours, because they have no greater tribute to offer him.

Honour rendered by common people and on trivial grounds he will utterly despise, for this is not what he merits. He will also despise dishonour, for no dishonour can justly attach to him. The great-souled man then, as has been said, is especially concerned with honour; but he will also observe due measure in respect to wealth, power, and good and bad fortune in general, as they may befall him; he will not rejoice overmuch in prosperity, nor grieve overmuch at adversity. For he does not care much even about honour, which is the greatest of external goods (since power and wealth are desirable only for the honour they bring, at least their possessors wish to be honoured for their sake); he therefore to whom even honour is a small thing will be indifferent to other things as well. Hence great-souled men are thought to be haughty.

But it is thought that the gifts of fortune also conduce to greatness of soul; for the high-born and those who are powerful or wealthy are esteemed worthy of honour, because they are superior to their fellows, and that which is superior in something good is always held in higher honour; so that even these gifts of fortune make men more great-souled, because their possessors are honoured by some people. But in reality only the good man ought to be honoured, although he that has both virtue and fortune is esteemed still more worthy of honour; whereas those who possess the goods of fortune without virtue are not justified in claiming high worth, and cannot correctly be styled great-souled, since true worth and greatness of soul cannot exist without complete virtue. It is true that even those who merely possess the goods of fortune may be haughty and insolent; because without virtue it is not easy to bear good fortune becomingly, and such men, being unable to carry their prosperity, and thinking themselves superior to the rest   [1124b] of mankind, despise other people, although their own conduct is no better than another's. The fact is that they try to imitate the great-souled man without being really like him, and only copy him in what they can, reproducing his contempt for others but not his virtuous conduct. For the great-souled man is justified in despising other people —his estimates are correct; but most proud men have no good ground for their pride.

The great-souled man does not run into danger for trifling reasons, and is not a lover of danger, because there are few things he values; but he will face danger in a great cause, and when so doing will be ready to sacrifice his life, since he holds that life is not worth having at every price.

He is fond of conferring benefits, but ashamed to receive them, because the former is a mark of superiority and the latter of inferiority. He returns a service done to him with interest, since this will put the

original benefactor into his debt in turn, and make him the party benefited. The great-souled are thought to have a good memory for any
benefit they have conferred, but a bad memory for those which they
have received (since the recipient of a benefit is the inferior of his benefactor, whereas they desire to be superior); and to enjoy being reminded
of the former but to dislike being reminded of the latter: this is why
the poet makes Thetis not specify her services to Zeus; nor did the
Spartans treating with the Athenians recall the occasions when Sparta
had aided Athens, but those on which Athens had aided Sparta.

It is also characteristic of the great-souled man never to ask help
from others, or only with reluctance, but to render aid willingly; and
to be haughty towards men of position and fortune, but courteous towards those of moderate station, because it is difficult and distinguished to be superior to the great, but easy to outdo the lowly, and
to adopt a high manner with the former is not ill-bred, but it is vulgar
to lord it over humble people: it is like putting forth one's strength
against the weak. He will not compete for the common objects of ambition, or go where other people take the first place; and he will be idle
and slow to act, except when pursuing some high honour or achievement; and will not engage in many undertakings, but only in such as
are important and distinguished. He must be open both in love and
in hate, since concealment shows timidity; and care more for the truth
than for what people will think; and speak and act openly, since as
he despises other men he is outspoken and frank, except when speaking
with ironical self-depreciation, as he does to common people. He will
be incapable of living at the will of another, unless a friend,   [1125a
since to do so is slavish, and hence flatterers are always servile, and
humble people flatterers. He is not prone to admiration, since nothing is
great to him. He does not bear a grudge, for it is not a mark of greatness of soul to recall things against people, especially the wrongs they
have done you, but rather to overlook them. He is no gossip, for he will
not talk either about himself or about another, as he neither wants to
receive compliments nor to hear other people run down (nor is he lavish
of praise either); and so he is not given to speaking evil himself, even
of his enemies, except when he deliberately intends to give offence. In
troubles that cannot be avoided or trifling mishaps he will never cry
out or ask for help, since to do so would imply that he took them to
heart. He likes to own beautiful and useless things, rather than useful
things that bring in a return, since the former show his independence
more.

Other traits generally attributed to the great-souled man are a slow
gait, a deep voice, and a deliberate utterance; to speak in shrill tones

and walk fast denotes an excitable and nervous temperament, which does not belong to one who cares for few things and thinks nothing great.

Such then being the Great-souled man, the corresponding character on the side of deficiency is the Small-souled man, and on that of excess the Vain man. These also are not thought to be actually vicious, since they do no harm, but rather mistaken. The small-souled man deprives himself of the good things that he deserves; and his failure to claim good things makes it seem that he has something bad about him [and also that he does not know himself], for (people argue), if he deserved any good, he would try to obtain it. Not that such persons are considered foolish, but rather too retiring; yet this estimate of them is thought to make them still worse, for men's ambitions show what they are worth, and if they hold aloof from noble enterprises and pursuits, and forgo the good things of life, presumably they think they are not worthy of them.

The vain on the other hand are foolish persons, who are deficient in self-knowledge and expose their defect: they undertake honourable responsibilities of which they are not worthy, and then are found out. They are ostentatious in dress, manner and so on. They want people to know how well off they are, and talk about it, imagining that this will make them respected.

Smallness of Soul is more opposed than Vanity to Greatness of Soul, being both more prevalent and worse.

*   *   *

Book · V I

We have already said that it is right to choose the mean and   [ch. 1 to avoid excess and deficiency, and that the mean is prescribed by the right principle. Let us now analyse the latter notion.

In the case of each of the moral qualities or dispositions that have been discussed, as with all the other virtues also, there is a certain mark to aim at, on which the man who knows the principle involved fixes his gaze, and increases or relaxes the tension accordingly; there is a certain standard determining those modes of observing the mean which we define as lying between excess and defect, being in conformity with the right principle. This bare statement however, although true, is not at all enlightening. In all departments of human endeavour that have been reduced to a science, it is true to say that effort ought to be exerted and relaxed neither too much nor too little, but to the medium amount, and as the right principle decides. Yet a person knowing this truth will be no wiser than before: for example, he will not know what medicines to take merely from being told to take everything that medical science or a medical expert would prescribe. Hence with respect to the qualities of the soul also, it is not enough merely to have established the truth of the above formula; we also have to define exactly what the right principle is, and what is the standard that determines it.

Now we have divided the Virtues of the Soul into two groups, the Virtues of the Character and the Virtues of the Intellect.   [1139a The former, the Moral Virtues, we have already discussed. Our account of the latter must be prefaced by some remarks about psychology.

It has been said before that the soul has two parts, one rational and the other irrational. Let us now similarly divide the rational part, and let it be assumed that there are two rational faculties, one whereby we contemplate those things whose first principles are invariable, and one whereby we contemplate those things which admit of variation: since, on the assumption that knowledge is based on a likeness or affinity of some sort between subject and object, the parts of the soul adapted to the cognition of objects that are of different kinds must themselves differ in kind. These two rational faculties may be designated the Scientific Faculty and the Calculative Faculty respectively; since calculation is the same as deliberation, and deliberation is never exercised about things that are invariable, so that the Calculative Faculty is a separate part of the rational half of the soul.

We have therefore to ascertain what disposition of each of these faculties is the best, for that will be the special virtue of each.

But the virtue of a faculty is related to the special function which that faculty performs. Now there are three elements in the   [ch. 2 soul which control action and the attainment of truth: namely, Sensation, Intellect, and Desire.

Of these, Sensation never originates action, as is shown by the fact that animals have sensation but are not capable of action.

Pursuit and avoidance in the sphere of Desire correspond to affirmation and denial in the sphere of the Intellect. Hence inasmuch as moral virtue is a disposition of the mind in regard to choice, and choice is deliberate desire, it follows that, if the choice is to be good, both the principle must be true and the desire right, and that desire must pursue the same things as principle affirms. We are here speaking of practical thinking, and of the attainment of truth in regard to action; with speculative thought, which is not concerned with action or production, right and wrong functioning consist in the attainment of truth and falsehood respectively. The attainment of truth is indeed the function of every part of the intellect, but that of the practical intelligence is the attainment of truth corresponding to right desire.

Now the cause of action (the efficient, not the final cause) is choice, and the cause of choice is desire and reasoning directed to some end. Hence choice necessarily involves both intellect or thought and a certain disposition of character [for doing well and the reverse in the sphere of action necessarily involve thought and character].

Thought by itself however moves nothing, but only thought directed to an end, and dealing with action. This indeed is the   [1139b moving cause of productive activity also, since he who makes something always has some further end in view: the act of making is not an end in itself, it is only a means, and belongs to something else. Whereas a thing done is an end in itself: since doing well (welfare) is the End, and it is at this that desire aims.

Hence Choice may be called either thought related to desire or desire related to thought; and man, as an originator of action, is a union of desire and intellect.

(Choice is not concerned with anything that has happened already: for example, no one chooses to have sacked Troy; for neither does one deliberate about what has happened in the past, but about what still lies in the future and may happen or not; what has happened cannot be made not to have happened. Hence Agathon is right in saying

> *This only is denied even to God,*
> *The power to make what has been done undone.*)

The attainment of truth is then the function of both the intellectual parts of the soul. Therefore their respective virtues are those dispositions which will best quality them to attain truth.

Let us then discuss these virtues afresh, going more   [ch. 3 deeply into the matter.

Let it be assumed that there are five qualities through which the mind achieves truth in affirmation or denial, namely Art or technical skill, Scientific Knowledge, Prudence, Wisdom, and Intelligence. Conception and Opinion are capable of error.

The nature of Scientific Knowledge (employing the term in its exact sense and disregarding its analogous uses) may be made clear as follows. We all conceive that a thing which we know scientifically cannot vary; when a thing that can vary is beyond the range of our observation, we do not know whether it exists or not. An object of Scientific Knowledge, therefore, exists of necessity. It is therefore eternal, for everything existing of absolute necessity is eternal; and what is eternal does not come into existence or perish. Again, it is held that all Scientific Knowledge can be communicated by teaching, and that what is scientifically known must be learnt. But all teaching starts from facts previously known, as we state in the *Analytics*, since it proceeds either by way of induction, or else by way of deduction. Now induction supplies a first principle or universal, deduction works *from* universals; therefore there are first principles from which deduction starts, which cannot be proved by deduction; therefore they are reached by induction. Scientific Knowledge, therefore, is the quality whereby we demonstrate, with the further qualifications included in our definition of it in the *Analytics*, namely, that a man knows a thing scientifically when he possesses a conviction arrived at in a certain way, and when the first principles on which that conviction rests are known to him with certainty—for unless he is more certain of his first principles than of the conclusion drawn from them he will only possess the knowledge in question accidentally. Let this stand as our definition of Scientific Knowledge.

The class of things that admit of variation in-   [ch. 4 1140a
cludes both things made and actions done. But making is different from doing (a distinction we may accept from extraneous discourses). Hence the rational quality concerned with doing is different from the rational quality concerned with making. Nor is one of them a part of the other, for doing is not a form of making, nor making a form of doing. Now architectural skill, for instance, is an art, and it is also a rational quality concerned with making; nor is there any art which is not a rational quality concerned with making, nor any such quality which is not an art. It follows that an art is the same thing as a rational quality, concerned with making, that reasons truly. All Art deals with bringing something into existence; and to pursue an art means to study how to bring into existence a thing which may either exist or not, and the efficient cause of which lies in the maker and not in the thing made; for Art does not deal with things that exist or come into existence of necessity, or according to nature, since these have their efficient cause in themselves. But as doing and making are distinct, it follows that Art, being concerned with making, is not concerned with doing. And in a sense Art deals with the same objects as chance, as Agathon says:

Chance is beloved of Art, and Art of Chance.

Art, therefore, as has been said, is a rational quality, concerned with making, that reasons truly. Its opposite, Lack of Art, is a rational quality, concerned with making, that reasons falsely. Both deal with that which admits of variation.

We may arrive at a definition of Prudence by considering   [ch. 5
who are the persons whom we call prudent. Now it is held to be the mark of a prudent man to be able to deliberate well about what is good and advantageous for himself, not in some one department, for in-

stance what is good for his health or strength, but what is advantageous as a means to the good life in general. This is proved by the fact that we also speak of people as prudent or wise in some particular thing, when they calculate well with a view to attaining some particular end of value (other than those ends which are the object of an art); so that the prudent man in general will be the man who is good at deliberating in general.

But no one deliberates about things that cannot vary, nor about things not within his power to do. Hence inasmuch as scientific knowledge involves demonstration, whereas things whose fundamental principles are variable are not capable of demonstration, because everything about them is variable, and inasmuch as one cannot deliberate about things that are of necessity, it follows that Prudence is not the [1140b] same as Science. Nor can it be the same as Art. It is not Science, because matters of conduct admit of variation; and not Art, because doing and making are generically different, since making aims at an end distinct from the act of making, whereas in doing the end cannot be other than the act itself: doing well is in itself the end. It remains therefore that it is a truth-attaining rational quality, concerned with action in relation to things that are good and bad for human beings.

Hence men like Pericles are deemed prudent, because they possess a faculty of discerning what things are good for themselves and for mankind; and that is our conception of an expert in Domestic Economy or Political Science.

(This also accounts for the word Temperance, which signifies 'preserving prudence.' And Temperance does in fact preserve our belief as to our own good; for pleasure and pain do not destroy or pervert all beliefs, for instance, the belief that the three angles of a triangle are, or are not, together equal to two right angles, but only beliefs concerning action. The first principles of action are the end to which our acts are means; but a man corrupted by a love of pleasure or fear of pain, entirely fails to discern any first principle, and cannot see that he ought to choose and do everything as a means to this end, and for its sake; for vice tends to destroy the sense of principle.)

It therefore follows that Prudence is a truth-attaining rational quality, concerned with action in relation to the things that are good for human beings.

Moreover, we can speak of excellence in Art, but not of excellence in Prudence. Also in Art voluntary error is not so bad as involuntary, whereas in the sphere of Prudence it is worse, as it is in the sphere of the virtues. It is therefore clear that Prudence is an excellence or virtue, and not an Art.

Of the two parts of the soul possessed of reason, Prudence must be the virtue of one, namely, the part that forms opinions; for Opinion deals with that which can vary, and so does Prudence. But yet Prudence is not a rational quality merely, as is shown by the fact that a purely rational faculty can be forgotten, whereas a failure in Prudence is not a mere lapse of memory.

Scientific Knowledge is a mode of conception dealing   [ch. 6 with universals and things that are of necessity; and demonstrated truths and all scientific knowledge (since this involves reasoning) are derived from first principles. Consequently the first principles from which scientific truths are derived cannot themselves be reached by Science; nor yet are they apprehended by Art, nor by Prudence. To be matter of Scientific Knowledge a truth must be demonstrated by deduction from other truths; while Art and Prudence are concerned only   [1141a with things that admit of variation. Nor is Wisdom the knowledge of first principles either: for the philosopher has to arrive at some things by demonstration.

If then the qualities whereby we attain truth, and are never led into falsehood, whether about things invariable or things variable, are Scientific Knowledge, Prudence, Wisdom, and Intelligence, and if the quality which enables us to apprehend first principles cannot be any one among three of these, namely Scientific Knowledge, Prudence, and Wisdom, it remains that first principles must be apprehended by Intelligence.

The term Wisdom is employed in the arts to denote those   [ch. 7 men who are the most perfect masters of their art, for instance, it is applied to Pheidias as a sculptor and to Polycleitus as a statuary. In this use then Wisdom merely signifies artistic excellence. But we also think that some people are wise in general and not in one department, not 'wise in something else,' as Homer says in the *Margites:*

> *Neither a delver nor a ploughman him*
> *The Gods had made, nor wise in aught beside.*

Hence it is clear that Wisdom must be the most perfect of the modes of knowledge. The wise man therefore must not only know the conclusions that follow from his first principles, but also have a true conception of those principles themselves. Hence Wisdom must be a combination of Intelligence and Scientific Knowledge: it must be a consummated knowledge of the most exalted objects.

For it is absurd to think that Political Science or Prudence is the loftiest kind of knowledge, inasmuch as man is not the highest thing in the world. And as 'wholesome' and 'good' mean one thing for men and another for fishes, whereas 'white' and 'straight' mean the same thing always, so everybody would denote the same thing by 'wise,' but not by 'prudent'; for each kind of beings will describe as prudent, and will entrust itself to, one who can discern its own particular welfare; hence even some of the lower animals are said to be prudent, namely those which display a capacity for forethought as regards their own lives.

It is also clear that Wisdom cannot be the same thing as Political Science; for if we are to call knowledge of our own interests wisdom, there will be a number of different kinds of wisdom, one for each species: there cannot be a single such wisdom dealing with the good of all living things, any more than there is one art of medicine for all existing things. It may be argued that man is superior to the other animals, but this makes no difference: since there exist other things far more divine in their nature than man, for instance, to mention   [1141b the most visible, the things of which the celestial system is composed.

These considerations therefore show that Wisdom is both Scientific Knowledge and Intuitive Intelligence as regards the things of the most exalted nature. This is why people say that men like Anaxagoras and Thales 'may be wise but are not prudent,' when they see them display ignorance of their own interests; and while admitting them to possess a knowledge that is rare, marvellous, difficult and even superhuman, they yet declare this knowledge to be useless, because these sages do not seek to know the things that are good for human beings. Prudence on the other hand is concerned with the affairs of men, and with things that can be the object of deliberation. For we say that to deliberate well is the most characteristic function of the prudent man; but no one deliberates about things that cannot vary nor yet about variable things that are not a means to some end, and that end a good attainable by action; and a good deliberator in general is a man who can arrive by calculation at the best of the goods attainable by man.

Nor is Prudence a knowledge of general principles only: it must also take account of particular facts, since it is concerned with action, and action deals with particular things. This is why men who are ignorant of general principles are sometimes more successful in action than others who know them: for instance, if a man knows that light meat is easily digested and therefore wholesome, but does not know what kinds of meat are light, he will not be so likely to restore you to health as a man who merely knows that chicken is wholesome; and in other matters men of experience are more successful than theorists. And Prudence is concerned with action, so one requires both forms of it, or indeed knowledge of particular facts even more than knowledge of general principles. Here too however there must be some supreme directing faculty.

Prudence is indeed the same quality of mind as Political   [ch. 8

Science, though their essence is different. Of Prudence as regards the state, one kind, as supreme and directive, is called Legislative Science; the other, as dealing with particular occurrences, has the name, Political Science, that really belongs to both kinds. The latter is concerned with action and deliberation (for a parliamentary enactment is a thing to be done, being the last step in a deliberative process), and this is why it is only those persons who deal with particular facts who are spoken of as 'taking part in politics,' because it is only they who perform actions, like the workmen in an industry. Prudence also is commonly understood to mean especially that kind of wisdom which is concerned with oneself, the individual; and this is given the name, Prudence, which really belongs to all the kinds, while the others are distinguished as Domestic Economy, Legislature, and Political Science, the latter being subdivided into Deliberative Science and Judicial Science. Now knowledge of one's own interest will certainly be one kind of Prudence; though it is very different from the other kinds, and people   [1142a think that the man who knows and minds his own business is prudent, and that politicians are busybodies: thus Euripides writes—

> Would that be prudent? when I might have lived
> A quiet life, a cipher in the crowd,
> Sharing the common fortune . . .
> Restless, aspiring, busy men of action . . .

For people seek their own good, and suppose that it is right to do so. Hence this belief has caused the word 'prudent' to mean those who are wise in their own interest. Yet probably as a matter of fact a man cannot pursue his own welfare without Domestic Economy and even Politics. Moreover, even the proper conduct of one's own affairs is a difficult problem, and requires consideration.

A further proof of what has been said is, that although the young may be experts in geometry and mathematics and similar branches of knowledge, we do not consider that a young man can have Prudence. The reason is that Prudence includes a knowledge of particular facts, and this is derived from experience, which a young man does not possess; for experience is the fruit of years. (One might indeed further enquire why it is that, though a boy may be a mathematician, he cannot be a metaphysician or a natural philosopher. Perhaps the answer is that Mathematics deals with abstractions, whereas the first principles of Metaphysics and Natural Philosophy are derived from experience: the young can only repeat them without conviction of their truth, whereas the formal concepts of Mathematics are easily understood.) Again, in deliberation there is a double possibility of error: you may go wrong either in your general principle or in your particular fact: for instance, either in asserting that all heavy water is unwholesome, or that the particular water in question is heavy.

And it is clear that Prudence is not the same as Scientific Knowledge: for as has been said, it apprehends ultimate particular things, since the thing to be done is an ultimate particular thing.

Prudence then stands opposite to Intelligence; for Intelligence apprehends definitions, which cannot be proved by reasoning, while Prudence deals with the ultimate particular thing, which cannot be apprehended by Scientific Knowledge, but only by perception: not the perception of the special senses, but the sort of intuition whereby we perceive that the ultimate figure in mathematics is a triangle; for there, too, there will be a stop. But the term perception applies in a fuller sense to mathematical intuition than to Prudence; the practical intuition of the latter belongs to a different species.

*   *   *

Book · V I I I

Our next business after this will be to discuss Friend-   [ch. 1 1155a
ship. For friendship is a virtue, or involves virtue; and also it is one of the most indispensable requirements of life. For no one would choose to live without friends, but possessing all other good things. In fact rich men, rulers and potentates are thought especially to require friends, since what would be the good of their prosperity without an outlet for beneficence, which is displayed in its fullest and most praiseworthy form towards friends? and how could such prosperity be safeguarded and preserved without friends? for the greater it is, the greater is its insecurity. And in poverty or any other misfortune men think friends are their only resource. Friends are an aid to the young, to guard them from error; to the elderly, to tend them, and to supplement their failing powers of action; to those in the prime of life, to assist them in noble deeds—

When twain together go—

for two are better able both to plan and to execute. And the affection of parent for offspring and of offspring for parent seems to be a natural instinct, not only in man but also in birds and in most animals; as also is friendship between members of the same species; and this is especially strong in the human race; for which reason we praise those who love their fellow men. Even when travelling abroad one can observe that a natural affinity and friendship exist between man and man universally.

Moreover, friendship appears to be the bond of the state; and lawgivers seem to set more store by it than they do by justice, for to promote concord, which seems akin to friendship, is their chief aim, while faction, which is enmity, is what they are most anxious to banish. And if men are friends, there is no need of justice between them; whereas merely to be just is not enough—a feeling of friendship also is necessary. Indeed the highest form of justice seems to have an element of friendly feeling in it.

And friendship is not only indispensable as a means, it is also noble in itself. We praise those who love their friends, and it is counted a noble thing to have many friends; and some people think that a true friend must be a good man.

But there is much difference of opinion as to the nature of friendship. Some define it as a matter of similarity; they say that we love those who are like ourselves: whence the proverbs 'Like finds his like,' 'Birds of a feather flock together,' and so on. Others on the [1155b] contrary say that with men who are alike it is always a case of 'two of a trade.' Some try to find a more profound and scientific explanation of the nature of affection. Euripides writes that 'Earth yearneth for the rain' when dried up, 'And the majestic Heaven when filled with rain Yearneth to fall to Earth.' Heracleitus says, 'Opposition unites,' and 'The fairest harmony springs from difference,' and ' 'Tis strife that makes the world go on.' Others maintain the opposite view, notably Empedocles, who declares that 'Like seeks after like.'

Dismissing then these scientific speculations as not germane to our present enquiry, let us investigate the human aspect of the matter, and examine the questions that relate to man's character and emotions: for instance, whether all men are capable of friendship, or bad men cannot be friends; and whether there is only one sort of friendship or several. Those who hold that all friendship is of the same kind because friendship admits of degree, are relying on an insufficient proof, for things of different kinds also can differ in degree. But this has been discussed before.

Perhaps the answer to these questions will appear if we [ch. 2 ascertain what sort of things arouse liking or love. It seems that not everything is loved, but only what is lovable, and that this is either what is good, or pleasant, or useful. But useful may be taken to mean productive of some good or of pleasure, so that the class of things lovable as ends is reduced to the good and the pleasant. Then, do men like what is really good, or what is good for them? for sometimes the two may be at variance; and the same with what is pleasant. Now it appears that each person loves what is good for himself, and that while what is really good is lovable absolutely, what is good for a particular person is lovable for that person. Further, each person loves not what is really good for himself, but what appears to him to be so; however, this will not affect our argument, for 'lovable' will mean 'what appears lovable.'

There being then three motives of love, the term Friendship is not applied to love for inanimate objects, since here there is no return of affection, and also no wish for the good of the object—for instance, it would be ridiculous to wish well to a bottle of wine: at the most one wishes that it may keep well in order that one may have it oneself; whereas we are told that we ought to wish our friend well for his own sake. But persons who wish another good for his own sake, if the feeling is not reciprocated, are merely said to feel goodwill for him: only when mutual is such goodwill termed friendship. And perhaps we should also add the qualification that the feeling of goodwill must be known to its object. For a man often feels goodwill towards persons whom he has never seen, but whom he believes to be good or useful, and one of these persons may also entertain the same feeling towards   [1156a him. Here then we have a case of two people mutually well-disposed, whom nevertheless we cannot speak of as friends, because they are not aware of each other's regard. To be friends therefore, men must (1) feel goodwill for each other, that is, wish each other's good, and (2) be aware of each other's goodwill, and (3) the cause of their goodwill must be one of the lovable qualities mentioned above.

Now these qualities differ in kind; hence the affection or   [ch. 3 friendship they occasion may differ in kind also. There are accordingly three kinds of friendship, corresponding in number to the three lovable qualities; since a reciprocal affection, known to either party, can be based on each of the three, and when men love each other, they wish each other well in respect of the quality which is the ground of their friendship. Thus friends whose affection is based on utility do not love each other in themselves, but in so far as some benefit accrues to them from each other. And similarly with those whose friendship is based on pleasure: for instance, we enjoy the society of witty people not because of what they are in themselves, but because they are agreeable to us. Hence in a friendship based on utility or on pleasure men love their friend for their own good or their own pleasure, and not as being the person loved, but as useful or agreeable. And therefore these friendships are based on an accident, since the friend is not loved for being what he is, but as affording some benefit or pleasure as the case may be. Consequently friendships of this kind are easily broken off, in the event of the parties themselves changing, for if no longer pleasant or useful to each other, they cease to love each other. And utility is not a permanent quality; it differs at different times. Hence when the motive of the friendship has passed away, the friendship itself is dissolved, having existed merely as a means to that end.

Friendships of Utility seem to occur most frequently between the old, as in old age men do not pursue pleasure but profit; and between those persons in the prime of life and young people whose object in life is gain. Friends of this kind do not indeed frequent each other's company much, for in some cases they are not even pleasing to each other, and therefore have no use for friendly intercourse unless they are mutually profitable; since their pleasure in each other goes no further than their expectations of advantage.

With these friendships are classed family ties of hospitality with foreigners.

With the young on the other hand the motive of friendship appears to be pleasure, since the young guide their lives by emotion, and for the most part pursue what is pleasant to themselves, and the object of the moment. And the things that please them change as their age alters; hence they both form friendships and drop them quickly, since their affections alter with what gives them pleasure, and the tastes of youth change quickly. Also the young are prone to fall in love, as [1156b love is chiefly guided by emotion, and grounded on pleasure; hence they form attachments quickly and give them up quickly, often changing before the day is out.

The young do desire to pass their time in their friend's company, for that is how they get the enjoyment of their friendship.

The perfect form of friendship is that between the good, and those who resemble each other in virtue. For these friends wish each alike the other's good in respect of their goodness, and they are good in themselves; but it is those who wish the good of their friends for their friends' sake who are friends in the fullest sense, since they love each other for themselves and not accidentally. Hence the friendship of these lasts as long as they continue to be good; and virtue is a permanent quality. And each is good relatively to his friend as well as absolutely, since the good are both good absolutely and profitable to each other. And each is pleasant in both ways also, since good men are pleasant both absolutely and to each other; for everyone is pleased by his own actions, and therefore by actions that resemble his own, and the actions of all good men are the same or similar.—Such friendship is naturally permanent, since it combines in itself all the attributes that friends ought to possess. All affection is based on good or on pleasure, either absolute or relative to the person who feels it, and is prompted by similarity of some sort; but this friendship possesses all these attributes in the friends themselves, for they are alike, *et cetera*, in that way. Also the absolutely good is pleasant absolutely as well; but the absolutely good and pleasant are the chief objects of affection; therefore it is between good men that affection and friendship exist in their fullest and best form.

Such friendships are of course rare, because such men are few. Moreover they require time and intimacy: as the saying goes, you cannot get to know a man till you have consumed the proverbial amount of salt in his company; and so you cannot admit him to friendship or really be friends, before each has shown the other that he is worthy of friendship and has won his confidence. People who enter into friendly relations quickly have the wish to be friends, but cannot really be friends without being worthy of friendship, and also knowing each other to be so; the wish to be friends is a quick growth, but friendship is not.

This form of friendship is perfect both in point of dura-   [ch. 4 tion and of the other attributes of friendship; and in all respects either party receives from the other the same or similar benefits, as it is proper that friends should do.

Friendship based on pleasure has a similarity to friend-   [1157a ship based on virtue, for good men are pleasant to one another; and the same is true of friendship based on utility, for good men are useful to each other. In these cases also the friendship is most lasting when each friend derives the same benefit, for instance pleasure, from the other, and not only so, but derives it from the same thing, as in a friendship between two witty people, and not as in one between a lover and his beloved. These do not find their pleasure in the same things: the lover's pleasure is in gazing at his beloved, the loved one's pleasure is in receiving the attentions of the lover; and when the loved one's beauty fades, the friendship sometimes fades too, as the lover no longer finds pleasure in the sight of his beloved, and the loved one no longer receives the attentions of the lover; though on the other hand many do remain friends if as a result of their intimacy they have come to love each other's characters, both being alike in character. But when a pair of lovers exchange not pleasure for pleasure but pleasure for gain, the friendship is less intense and less lasting.

A friendship based on utility dissolves as soon as its profit ceases; for the friends did not love each other, but what they got out of each other.

*   *   *

Book · I X

*   *   *

The forms which friendly feeling for our neighbours   [ch. 4 1166a takes, and the marks by which the different forms of friendship are defined, seem to be derived from the feelings of regard which we entertain for ourselves. A friend is defined as (a) one who wishes, and promotes by action, the real or apparent good of another for that other's sake; or (b) one who wishes the existence and preservation of his friend for the friend's sake. (This is the feeling of mothers towards their children, and of former friends who have quarrelled.) Others say that a friend is (c) one who frequents another's society, and (d) who desires the same things as he does, or (e) one who shares his friend's joys and sorrows. (This too is very characteristic of mothers.) Friendship also is defined by one or other of these marks. But each of them is also found in a good man's feelings towards himself (and in those of all other men as well, in so far as they believe themselves to be good; but, as has been said, virtue and the virtuous man seem to be the standard in everything). For (d) the good man is of one mind with himself, and desires the same things with every part of his nature. Also (a) he wishes his own good, real as well as apparent, and seeks it by action (for it is a mark of a good man to exert himself actively for the good); and he does so for his own sake (for he does it on account of the intellectual part of himself, and this appears to be a man's real self). Also (b) he desires his own life and security, and especially that of his rational part. For existence is good for the virtuous man; and everyone wishes his own good: no one would choose to possess every good in the world on condition of becoming somebody else (for God possesses the good even as it is), but only while remaining himself, whatever he may be; and it would appear that the thinking part is the real self, or is so more than anything else. And (c) the good man desires his own company; for he enjoys being by himself, since he has agreeable memories of the past, and good hopes for the future, which are pleasant too; also his mind is stored with subjects for contemplation. And (e) he is keenly conscious of his own joys and sorrows; for the same things give him pleasure or pain at all times, and not different things at different times, since he is not apt to change his mind.

It is therefore because the good man has these various feelings towards himself, and because he feels towards his friend in the same way as towards himself (for a friend is another self), that friendship also is thought to consist in one or other of these feelings, and the possession of them is thought to be the test of a friend.

Whether a man can be said actually to feel friendship for himself is a question that may be dismissed for the present; though it may be held that he can do so in so far as he is a dual or composite being, and because very intense friendship resembles self-regard.   [1166b

As a matter of fact, the feelings of self-regard described appear to be found in most people, even though they are of inferior moral worth.

Perhaps men share them in so far as they have their own approval
and believe in their own virtue; since the utterly worthless and criminal
never possess them, or even have the appearance of doing so. Indeed it
may almost be said that no morally inferior persons possess them. For
(d) such persons are at variance with themselves, desiring one thing and
wishing another: this is the mark of the unrestrained, who choose what
is pleasant but harmful instead of what they themselves think to be
good. (a) Others again, out of cowardice and idleness, neglect to do
what they think best for their own interests. And (b) men who have
committed a number of crimes, and are hated for their wickedness, actually flee from life and make away with themselves. Also (c) bad men
constantly seek the society of others and shun their own company, because when they are by themselves they recall much that was unpleasant
in the past and anticipate the same in the future, whereas with other
people they can forget. Moreover they feel no affection for themselves,
because they have no lovable qualities. Hence (e) such men do not
enter into their own joys and sorrows, as there is civil war in their souls;
one part of their nature, owing to depravity, is pained by abstinence
from certain indulgences while another part is pleased by it; one part
pulls them one way and another the other, as if dragging them asunder.
Or if it be impossible to feel pain and pleasure at the same time, at all
events after indulging in pleasure they regret it a little later, and wish
they had never acquired a taste for such indulgences; since the bad are
always changing their minds.

Thus a bad man appears to be devoid even of affection for himself, because he has nothing lovable in his nature. If then such a state
of mind is utterly miserable, we should do our utmost to shun wickedness and try to be virtuous. That is the way both to be friends with
ourselves and to win the friendship of others.

*   *   *

The question is also raised whether one ought to love   [ch. 8
oneself or someone else most. We censure those who put themselves first,
and 'lover of self' is used as a term of reproach. And it is thought that
a bad man considers himself in all he does, and the more so the worse
he is—so it is a complaint against him for instance that 'he never does a
thing unless you make him'—whereas a good man acts from a sense of
what is noble, and the better he is the more he so acts, and he considers his friend's interest, disregarding his own.

But the facts do not accord with these theories; nor is this surprising. For we admit that one should love one's best friend   [1168b

most; but the best friend is he that, when he wishes a person's good, wishes it for that person's own sake, even though nobody will ever know of it. Now this condition is most fully realized in a man's regard for himself, as indeed are all the other attributes that make up the definition of a friend; for it has been said already that all the feelings that constitute friendship for others are an extension of regard for self. Moreover, all the proverbs agree with this; for example, 'Friends have one soul between them,' 'Friends' goods are common property,' 'Amity is equality,' 'The knee is nearer than the shin.' All of these sayings will apply most fully to oneself; for a man is his own best friend. Therefore he ought to love himself most.

So it is naturally debated which of these two views we ought to adopt, since each of them has some plausibility.

Now where there is a conflict of opinion the proper course is doubtless to get the two views clearly distinguished, and to define how far and in what way each of them is true. So probably the matter may become clear if we ascertain what meaning each side attaches to the term 'self-love.'

Those then who make it a term of reproach call men lovers of self when they assign to themselves the larger share of money, honours, or bodily pleasures; since these are the things which most men desire and set their hearts on as being the greatest goods, and which accordingly they compete with each other to obtain. Now those who take more than their share of these things are men who indulge their appetites, and generally their passions and the irrational part of their souls. But most men are of this kind. Accordingly the use of the term 'lover of self' as a reproach has arisen from the fact that self-love of the ordinary kind is bad. Hence self-love is rightly censured in those who are lovers of self in this sense. And that it is those who take too large a share of things of this sort whom most people usually mean when they speak of lovers of self, is clear enough. For if a man were always bent on outdoing everybody else in acting justly or temperately or in displaying any other of the virtues, and in general were always trying to secure for himself moral nobility, no one will charge him with love of self nor find any fault with him. Yet as a matter of fact such a man might be held to be a lover of self in an exceptional degree. At all events he takes for himself the things that are noblest and most truly good. Also it is the most dominant part of himself that he indulges and obeys in everything. But (a) as in the state it is the sovereign that is held in the fullest sense to *be* the state, and in any other composite whole it is the dominant part that is deemed especially to be that whole, so it is with man. He therefore who loves and indulges the dominant part of himself is a lover of self in the fullest degree. Again (b), the terms 'self-restrained' and 'unrestrained' denote being restrained or not by one's intellect, and thus imply that the intellect is the man himself. Also (c) it is our reasoned acts that are felt to be in the fullest sense *our own* acts, *vol-* [1169a *untary* acts. It is therefore clear that a man is or is chiefly the dominant part of himself, and that a good man values this part of himself most. Hence the good man will be a lover of self in the fullest degree, though in another sense than the lover of self so-called by way of reproach, from whom he differs as much as living by principle differs from living by passion, and aiming at what is noble from aiming at what seems expedient. Persons therefore who are exceptionally zealous in noble actions are universally approved and commended; and if all men vied with each other in moral nobility and strove to perform the noblest deeds, the common welfare would be fully realized, while individuals also could enjoy the greatest of goods, inasmuch as virtue is the greatest good.

Therefore the good man ought to be a lover of self, since he will then both benefit himself by acting nobly and aid his fellows; but the bad man ought not to be a lover of self, since he will follow his base passions, and so injure both himself and his neighbours. With the bad man therefore, what he does is not in accord with what he ought to do, but the good man does what he ought, since intelligence always chooses for itself that which is best, and the good man obeys his intelligence.

But it is also true that the virtuous man's conduct is often guided by the interests of his friends and of his country, and that he will if necessary lay down his life in their behalf. For he will surrender wealth and power and all the goods that men struggle to win, if he can secure nobility for himself; since he would prefer an hour of rapture to a long period of mild enjoyment, a year of noble life to many years of ordinary existence, one great and glorious exploit to many small successes. And this is doubtless the case with those who give their lives for others; thus they choose great nobility for themselves. Also the virtuous man is ready to forgo money if by that means his friends may gain more money; for thus, though his friend gets money, he himself achieves nobility, and so he assigns the greater good to his own share. And he behaves in the same manner as regards honours and offices also: all these things he will relinquish to his friend, for this is noble and praiseworthy for himself. He is naturally therefore thought to be virtuous, as he chooses moral nobility in preference to all other things. It may even happen that he will surrender to his friend the performance of some achievement, and that it may be nobler for him to be the cause of his friend's performing it than to perform it himself.

Therefore in all spheres of praiseworthy conduct it is manifest that the good man takes the larger share of moral nobility for [1169b himself. In this sense then, as we said above, it is right to be a lover of self, though self-love of the ordinary sort is wrong.

* * *

Book · X

* * *

Having now discussed the various kinds of Virtue, of Friend- [ch. 6 ship and of Pleasure, it remains for us to treat in outline of Happiness, inasmuch as we count this to be the End of human life. But it will shorten the discussion if we recapitulate what has been said already.

Now we stated that happiness is not a certain disposition of character; since if it were it might be possessed by a man who passed the whole of his life asleep, living the life of a vegetable, or by one who was plunged in the deepest misfortune. If then we reject this as [1176b unsatisfactory, and feel bound to class happiness rather as some form of activity, as has been said in the earlier part of this treatise, and if activities are of two kinds, some merely necessary means and desirable only for the sake of something else, others desirable in themselves, it is clear that happiness is to be classed among activities desirable in themselves, and not among those desirable as a means to something else; since happiness lacks nothing, and is self-sufficient.

But those activities are desirable in themselves which do not aim at any result beyond the mere exercise of the activity. Now this is felt to be the nature of actions in conformity with virtue; for to do noble and virtuous deeds is a thing desirable for its own sake.

But agreeable amusements also are desirable for their own sake; we do not pursue them as a means to something else, for as a matter of fact they are more often harmful than beneficial, causing men to neglect their health and their estates. Yet persons whom the world counts happy usually have recourse to such pastimes; and this is why adepts in such pastimes stand in high favour with princes, because they make themselves agreeable in supplying what their patrons desire, and what they want is amusement. So it is supposed that amusements are a component part of happiness, because princes and potentates devote their leisure to them.

But (i) perhaps princes and potentates are not good evidence. Virtue and intelligence, which are the sources of man's higher activities, do not depend on the possession of power; and if these persons, having no taste for pure and liberal pleasure, have recourse to the pleasures of the body, we must not on that account suppose that bodily pleasures are the more desirable. Children imagine that the things they themselves value are actually the best; it is not surprising therefore that, as children and grown men have different standards of value, so also should the worthless and the virtuous. Therefore, as has repeatedly been said, those things are actually valuable and pleasant which appear so to the good man; but each man thinks that activity most desirable which suits his particular disposition, and therefore the good man thinks virtuous activity most desirable. It follows therefore that happiness is not to be found in amusements.

(ii)   Indeed it would be strange that amusement should be our End—that we should toil and moil all our life long in order that we may amuse ourselves. For virtually every object we adopt is pursued as a means to something else, excepting happiness, which is an end in itself; to make amusement the object of our serious pursuits and our work seems foolish and childish to excess: Anacharsis's motto, Play in order that you may work, is felt to be the right rule. For amusement is a form of rest; but we need rest because we are not able to go on working without a break, and therefore it is not an end, since we take it as a means to further activity.

(iii)   And the life that conforms with virtue is thought   [1177a to be a happy life; but virtuous life involves serious purpose, and does not consist in amusement.

(iv)   Also we pronounce serious things to be superior to things that are funny and amusing; and the nobler a faculty or a person is, the more serious, we think, are their activities; therefore, the activity of the nobler faculty or person is itself superior, and therefore more productive of happiness.

(v)   Also anybody can enjoy the pleasures of the body, a slave no less than the noblest of mankind; but no one allows a slave any measure of happiness, any more than a life of his own. Therefore happiness does not consist in pastimes and amusements, but in activities in accordance with virtue, as has been said already.

But if happiness consists in activity in accordance with   [ch. 7 virtue, it is reasonable that it should be activity in accordance with the highest virtue; and this will be the virtue of the best part of us. Whether then this be the intellect, or whatever else it be that is thought to rule and lead us by nature, and to have cognizance of what is noble and divine, either as being itself also actually divine, or as being relatively the divinest part of us, it is the activity of this part of us in accordance with the virtue proper to it that will constitute perfect happiness; and it has been stated already that this activity is the activity of contemplation.

And that happiness consists in contemplation may be accepted as agreeing both with the results already reached and with the truth. For contemplation is at once the highest form of activity (since the intellect is the highest thing in us, and the objects with which the intellect deals are the highest things that can be known), and also it is the most continuous, for we can reflect more continuously than we can carry on any form of action. And again we suppose that happiness must contain an element of pleasure; now activity in accordance with wisdom is admittedly the most pleasant of the activities in accordance with virtue: at all events it is held that philosophy or the pursuit of wisdom contains pleasures of marvellous purity and permanence, and it is reasonable to suppose that the enjoyment of knowledge is a still pleasanter occupation than the pursuit of it. Also the activity of contemplation will be found to possess in the highest degree the quality that is termed self-sufficiency; for while it is true that the wise man equally with the just man and the rest requires the necessaries of life, yet, these being adequately supplied, whereas the just man needs other persons towards whom or with whose aid he may act justly, and so likewise do the temperate man and the brave man and the others, the wise man on the contrary can also contemplate by himself, and the more so the wiser he is; no doubt he will study better with the aid of fellow-workers, but still he is the most self-sufficient of men. Also the activity of con-   [1177b] templation may be held to be the only activity that is loved for its own sake: it produces no result beyond the actual act of contemplation, whereas from practical pursuits we look to secure some advantage, greater or smaller, beyond the action itself. Also happiness is thought to involve leisure; for we do business in order that we may have leisure, and carry on war in order that we may have peace. Now the practical virtues are exercised in politics or in warfare; but the pursuits of politics and war seem to be unleisured—those of war indeed entirely so, for no one desires to be at war for the sake of being at war, nor deliberately takes steps to cause a war: a man would be thought an utterly blood-thirsty character if he declared war on a friendly state for the sake of causing battles and massacres. But the activity of the politician also is unleisured, and aims at securing something beyond the mere participation in politics—positions of authority and honour, or, if the happiness of the politician himself and of his fellow-citizens, this happiness conceived as something distinct from political activity (indeed we are clearly investigating it as so distinct). If then among practical pursuits displaying the virtues, politics and war stand out pre-eminent in nobility and grandeur, and yet they are unleisured, and directed to some further end, not chosen for their own sakes: whereas the activity of the intellect is felt to excel in serious worth, consisting as it does in contemplation, and to aim at no end beyond itself, and also to contain a pleasure peculiar to itself, and therefore augmenting its activity: and if accordingly the attributes of this activity are found to be self-sufficiency, leisuredness, such freedom from fatigue as is possible for man, and all the other attributes of blessedness: it follows that it is the activity of the intellect that constitutes complete human happiness—provided it be granted a complete span of life, for nothing that belongs to happiness can be incomplete.

Such a life as this however will be higher than the human level: not in virtue of his humanity will a man achieve it, but in virtue of something within him that is divine; and by as much as this something is superior to his composite nature, by so much is its activity superior to the exercise of the other forms of virtue. If then the intellect is something divine in comparison with man, so is the life of the intellect divine in comparison with human life. Nor ought we to obey those who enjoin that a man should have man's thoughts and a mortal the thoughts of mortality, but we ought so far as possible to achieve immortality, and do all that man may to live in accordance with the highest thing in him; for though this be small in bulk, in power and value it far   [1178a surpasses all the rest.

It may even be held that this is the true self of each, inasmuch as it is the dominant and better part; and therefore it would be a strange thing if a man should choose to live not his own life but the life of some other than himself.

Moreover what was said before will apply here also: that which is best and most pleasant for each creature is that which is proper to the nature of each; accordingly the life of the intellect is the best and the pleasantest life for man, inasmuch as the intellect more than anything else is man; therefore this life will be the happiest.

The life of moral virtue, on the other hand, is happy only   [ch. 8 in a secondary degree. For the moral activities are purely human: Justice, I mean, Courage and the other virtues we display in our intercourse with our fellows, when we observe what is due to each in contracts and services and in our various actions, and in our emotions also; and all of these things seem to be purely human affairs. And some moral actions are thought to be the outcome of the physical constitution, and moral virtue is thought to have a close affinity in many respects with the passions. Moreover, Prudence is intimately connected with Moral Virtue, and this with Prudence, inasmuch as the first principles which Prudence employs are determined by the Moral Virtues, and the right standard for the Moral Virtues is determined by Prudence. But these being also connected with the passions are related to our composite nature; now the virtues of our composite nature are purely human; so therefore also is the life that manifests these virtues, and the happiness that belongs to it.

Whereas the happiness that belongs to the intellect is separate: so much may be said about it here, for a full discussion of the matter is beyond the scope of our present purpose. And such happiness would appear to need but little external equipment, or less than the happiness based on moral virtue. Both, it may be granted, require the mere necessaries of life, and that in an equal degree (though the politician does as a matter of fact take more trouble about bodily requirements and so forth than the philosopher); for in this respect there may be little difference between them. But for the purpose of their special activities their requirements will differ widely. The liberal man will need wealth in order to do liberal actions, and so indeed will the just man in order to discharge his obligations (since mere intentions are invisible, and even the unjust pretend to wish to act justly); and the brave man will need strength if he is to perform any action displaying his virtue; and the temperate man opportunity for indulgence: otherwise how can he, or the possessor of any other virtue, show that he is virtuous? It is disputed also whether purpose or performance is the more important factor in virtue, as it is alleged to depend on both; now the perfection of virtue will   [1178b] clearly consist in both; but the performance of virtuous actions requires much outward equipment, and the more so the greater and more noble the actions are. But the student, so far as the pursuit of his activity is concerned, needs no external apparatus: on the contrary, worldly goods may almost be said to be a hindrance to contemplation; though it is true that, being a man and living in the society of others, he chooses to engage in virtuous action, and so will need external goods to carry on his life as a human being.

The following considerations also will show that perfect happiness is some form of contemplative activity. The gods, as we conceive them, enjoy supreme felicity and happiness. But what sort of actions can we attribute to them? Just actions? but will it not seem ridiculous to think of them as making contracts, restoring deposits and the like? Then brave actions—enduring terrors and running risks for the nobility of so doing? Or liberal actions? but to whom will they give? Besides, it would be absurd to suppose that they actually have a coinage or currency of some sort! And temperate actions—what will these mean in their case? surely it would be derogatory to praise them for not having evil desires! If we go through the list we shall find that all forms of virtuous conduct seem trifling and unworthy of the gods. Yet nevertheless they have always been conceived as, at all events, living, and therefore living actively, for we cannot suppose they are always asleep like Endymion. But for a living being, if we eliminate action, and *a fortiori* creative action, what remains save contemplation? It follows that the activity of God, which is transcendent in blessedness, is the activity of contemplation; and therefore among human activities that which is most akin to the divine activity of contemplation will be the greatest source of happiness.

A further confirmation is that the lower animals cannot partake of happiness, because they are completely devoid of the contemplative activity. The whole of the life of the gods is blessed, and that of man is so in so far as it contains some likeness to the divine activity; but none of the other animals possess happiness, because they are entirely incapable of contemplation. Happiness therefore is co-extensive in its range with contemplation: the more a class of beings possesses the faculty of contemplation, the more it enjoys happiness, not as an accidental concomitant of contemplation but as inherent in it, since contemplation is valuable in itself. It follows that happiness is some form of contemplation.

But the philosopher being a man will also need external well-being, since man's nature is not self-sufficient for the activity of contemplation, but he must also have bodily health and a supply of food and other requirements. Yet if supreme blessedness is not possible with-   [1179a] out external goods, it must not be supposed that happiness will demand many or great possessions; for self-sufficiency does not depend on excessive abundance, nor does moral conduct, and it is possible to perform noble deeds even without being ruler of land and sea: one can do virtuous acts with quite moderate resources. This may be clearly observed in experience: private citizens do not seem to be less but more given to doing virtuous actions than princes and potentates. It is sufficient then if moderate resources are forthcoming; for a life of virtuous activity will be essentially a happy life.

Solon also doubtless gave a good description of happiness, when he said that in his opinion those men were happy who, being moderately equipped with external goods, had performed noble exploits and had lived temperately; for it is possible for a man of but moderate possessions to do what is right. Anaxagoras again does not seem to have conceived the happy man as rich or powerful, since he says that he would not be surprised if he were to appear a strange sort of person in the eyes of the many; for most men judge by externals, which are all that they can perceive. So our theories seem to be in agreement with the opinions of the wise.

Such arguments then carry some degree of conviction; but it is by the practical experience of life and conduct that the truth is really tested, since it is there that the final decision lies. We must therefore examine the conclusions we have advanced by bringing them to the test of the facts of life. If they are in harmony with the facts, we may accept them; if found to disagree, we must deem them mere theories.

And it seems likely that the man who pursues intellectual activity, and who cultivates his intellect and keeps that in the best condition, is also the man most beloved of the gods. For if, as is generally believed, the gods exercise some superintendence over human affairs, then it will be reasonable to suppose that they take pleasure in that part of man which is best and most akin to themselves, namely the intellect, and that they recompense with their favours those men who esteem and honour this most, because these care for the things dear to themselves, and act rightly and nobly. Now it is clear that all these attributes belong most of all to the wise man. He therefore is most beloved by the gods; and if so, he is naturally most happy. Here is another proof that the wise man is the happiest.

*   *   *

DESCARTES

INTRODUCTION TO

Descartes

BACKGROUND

The century preceding Descartes' appearance on the philosophic scene saw a successive series of waves of new thoughts and discoveries gradually undermine both the method and the world view of the Aristotelian-Thomistic philosophy, which had largely dominated the philosophic and scientific landscape since the thirteenth century.

As this book does not include any selections from the medieval philosophers, it is necessary to make a brief statement about the medieval world outlook as well as about the later thought which undermined it, in order that we may recognize the background out of which Descartes developed his philosophy.

The great achievement of St. Thomas Aquinas (1225–74) was to synthesize the Augustinian theological interpretation of Christian doctrine with Aristotelian naturalism and science into a new philosophic whole. According to Christian teaching the universe was created by God *ex nihilo* (distinct from the most common Greek view of God as a maker who organized an already quasi-existent matter or stuff). For Christianity, God is an absolutely transcendent being upon whom all other existence is unqualifiedly dependent and by whom all that exists is created. Indeed, St. Augustine (354–430) made this dependence on God so absolute that it has often proved difficult to understand and justify his account of freedom of the will.

It was further held that God made the world because He is good, and thus that the universe and all in it bear His stamp of goodness. He made it out of pure love and to glorify Himself. So too God made man out of the same love and spontaneous effulgence of His own goodness. The world is a temporal home for man in which everything exists for human beneficence. All that God has made is both good and beautiful. In this doctrine one can discern a teleological position which has some points of similarity with Aristotle, and also some considerable divergences from Aristotle's naturalistic teleology.

Man, having been given the gift of free will, in the persons of Adam and Eve, willfully ate of the fruit of the tree of knowledge of Good and Evil and thus brought sin and death into the human world. Banished from his earthly paradise, man was doomed to wander and to labor in anguish and grief for this original sin, until Jesus Christ, the son of God, redeemed him through His divine suffering. It is thus through divine love and grace that man is once more returned to God who created him.

This earthly frame is made for man and is the stage on which he works out the drama of his life. Although the City of the World is made for man, man has another destiny—namely, the City of God, wherein he may hope to live another eternal life after this human one. Admission to that heavenly city, however, is possible only through divine grace which forgives us our sins. He who dies in a state of mortal sin is doomed to eternal damnation in Hell. Thus salvation rests on divine grace, and wisdom on divine revelation, which is the highest source of knowledge and certainty.

It can readily be seen from this somewhat oversimplified picture that the primary focus of man's attention in the middle ages is directed to God and to the task of human salvation. It is also evident how, from this point of view, worldly knowledge and inquiry into nature must appear both comparatively trivial and vainglorious. They did to many theologians. Other theologians, however, defended rational knowledge and inquiry into nature on the grounds that God gave man the gift of reason so that he might use it in all things. This view prevailed in the end.

In another respect it was often held that all claims to knowledge on grounds other than revelation must be subordinate to revelation. Nonetheless, revelation, the writings of the Patristics [1], the teachings of St. Augustine, and the proclamations of the popes and ecumenical councils required interpretation and extensive commentary if they were to be understood. As a consequence, many subtle and difficult philosophical and theological questions were raised and examined with exquisite dialectical skill by the philosophers of the eleventh and twelfth centuries.

---

[1] The Fathers of the early Christian church.

During the twelfth century translations of the works of Aristotle began to appear in western Christiandom.[2] At first these writings were looked upon askance by ecclesiastical authorities for many reasons; probably the most important was the interpretation of Aristotle's *De Anima* by Averroes, an earlier Arabic philosopher, in which he denied the immortality of the individual human soul. St. Thomas Aquinas was later to argue both in his commentaries on the *De Anima* and in other works that this conclusion does not necessarily follow in Aristotle.

Although the study of Aristotle was discouraged, Albertus Magnus (1193 or 1206–80), teacher of St. Thomas Aquinas, traveled throughout Europe advocating the case for Aristotle as well as lecturing extensively on Aristotelian philosophy.

Despite interdictions and critical analysis of Aristotle, the study of his works continued, because he presented to the thirteenth century, which had little of scientific and naturalistic knowledge, an abundance of information and interpretations of nature, man, and society in a well-organized philosophical system.

The first task St. Thomas undertook to accomplish was to show that reason and revelation were parallel and independent ways of knowledge, neither subordinate to the other. Since God had given to man His revelation of what all men had to know for salvation and the faculty of reason as another distinct way of knowing, the goodness and wisdom of God was a sufficient guarantee that these two ways would prove in the end entirely consistent and compatible.[3]

The second major task of St. Thomas was to re-examine Christian theology, particularly as it was presented by St. Augustine, in such a way that he could restate its doctrines in a form consistent with Aristotelian philosophy. This he did with consummate skill. The result was a new philosophy which was neither purely Aristotelian nor Augustinian, but a unique position of his own. Even today this is a living and viable philosophy which has a quasi-official status among many thinkers.

By the end of the thirteenth century the philosophy of St. Thomas Aquinas had all but swept away other philosophical positions.

The fundamental category of Thomism was, as with Aristotle, *substance*. God was perfect infinite substance who created the universe *ex nihilo* (unlike Aristotle's conception of God). The four causes of Aristotle were invoked in all explanations, theological as well as philo-

---

[2] Only some of the logical works of Aristotle were known to the earlier Christian philosophers.

[3] The question of faith and reason was of concern to Descartes himself as well as it was to the philosophers of the middle ages. This will appear most evident from the *Dedication* of the *Meditations, To the Most Wise and Illustrious the Dean and Doctors of the Sacred Faculty of Theology in Paris*. See also the *Principles of Philosophy*.

sophical, in such a way that the supernatural teleology of Christian doctrine was combined with the naturalistic teleology of Aristotle.

The Aristotelian position about life and soul was fused with Christian doctrines of immortality and salvation. So too was the pragmatic ethics of Aristotle united with Christian morality. Most important of all for our present discussion, because it later will be the major point of scientific attack in the seventeenth century, the Aristotelian view of nature was encompassed within the Christian framework.

The conception that species are real and that there is a hierarchy of species fitted well into the medieval theological position. The lowest physical substances—earth, fire, air, and water—were held to be essentially different in kind and to be characterized by recognizable qualitative differences. Thus fire is hot, dry, and light and tends to move upward, when it can, to its natural place in the heavens; this teleological trait of fire was called "levity." Earth, on the other hand, is cold, dry, and heavy; hence gravity is the impulsion by which it tends to move downward as far as it can to the ground. Water is cold, wet, and relatively heavy, while air is warm, dry, and relatively light. An account of the movements of these bodies therefore required a topological explanation, because in order to know how and where a body would move, or if it would move at all, one had to know both the nature of the particular body and where it is located: for example, air surrounded by water tends to move upward, but air in fire moves downward. When bodies are either mixtures or compounds of the four elements, greater complexities necessarily ensue.

It is important to stress here that the sensible qualities which we perceive by sight, touch, and so on are truly attributed to things in themselves. They are not merely considered to be subjectively in the mind of the perceiver. When one says "fire is hot" the stress is on the *is*. Two difficulties required explanation: first, how do we become aware of the qualities or "take on the sensible forms of things without the matter" and, second, how can we account for conflicting perceptions such as the situation in which water is cool to one hand and warm to the other. Various explanations, with varying success, were offered to account for these difficulties and for various other illusions. We shall soon see how and why Galileo dismissed this *qualitative* physics and substituted for it a predominantly *quantitative* physics. But first to medieval astronomy.

To the Aristotelian notion of a finite but unbounded universe was added the astronomical theories and observations of Ptolemy. Aristotle had rejected the notion of a void or empty space, because he could not concede the possibility of an extended nothing; that is, he held that every attribute must inhere in a subject. Therefore, the universe must be finite as is the number of actual substances at any given time. Aristotle held that the earth is at the actual physical center of the cosmos, surrounded by successive layers of water, air, fire, ether, and the successive crystalline heavenly spheres. He argued that at the outer limit of the universe there is an eternally moving sphere, which forever turns upon itself and which gives motion to the various inner spheres between it and the earth. These spheres were not mathematical abstractions but physical entities carrying the stars, sun, planets, and moon in their various orbits.

Ptolemy (127–41 or 151 A.D.), the last great astronomer of the ancient world, worked out the mathematical calculations of this enormously complicated scheme. The most difficult problem presented to him was the apparent forward and backward movements of the planets. To account for these movements, he advanced the theory that they moved in small circles (epicycles) within the various spheres which circled the earth. Subsequent astronomers had to suppose additional epicycles to account for other astronomical phenomena.

Despite the conceptual and mathematical complications of this system, one must remember that it was an effective working astronomy, that it fitted in well with Christian doctrine, and that it confirmed the reliability of most ordinary sensory experience. New scientific instruments, calculations, and mathematical concepts were required before it could be successfully challenged.

Before Copernicus (1473–1543), Nicholas of Cusa (1401–64), and Bernadino Telesio (1508–88) made extensive and telling criticism of the Aristotelian conception of nature and cosmology. Nevertheless, it was only after the Copernican hypothesis was abundantly verified and the consequences of his hypothesis fully seen that the Aristotelian-Ptolemaic system, as formulated in the middle ages, was given its death blow.

The Copernican or heliocentric hypothesis is familiar and fairly simple to understand. It holds that the sun is the center of our planetary system, and that the earth is one planet among others circling the sun, whereas the moon is a satellite circling the earth. (Galileo's observation of the moons circling Jupiter tended to confirm this thesis by showing at least one other planet with moons in orbit). Copernicus also supposed that the earth rotates on its axis to account for the diurnal cycle of night and day, and that the sun, in turn, is comparatively at rest in relation to the so-called fixed stars.

Copernicus was not definitive about the paths of the planetary orbits, but he supposed them probably to be circular. It remained to Kepler (1571–1630) to discover finally the orbital paths of the various planets.

In some ways the assumptions and consequences of the Copernican hypothesis are more interesting and significant than the hypothesis itself.

Copernicus advanced his heliocentric theory in opposition to the Ptolemaic astronomy on two primary grounds, simplicity and relativity. He contended that one could eliminate the artificial complexity of the multiple cycles and epicycles of the Ptolemaic system by his own hypothesis, which presented a far simpler picture of heavenly movements. He made this assumption because of the evident methodological and mathematical simplicity of his hypothesis, and because he was convinced that nature itself always acts in the simplest way possible—a metaphysical assumption which he could hardly hope to prove.

The question of relativity is somewhat more difficult. Mathematicians had long known that from a strictly mathematical point of view it is possible to take any point as a place of reference for spatial measurement and to regard motion in relation to any assumed place of rest. It is quite another matter, however, to argue that in the existent universe place and motion are actually relative. Nonetheless, this is what Copernicus did. He supported his argument with the observation that one cannot perceive which of two bodies is at motion or at rest. Indeed, it is quite possible that both are in motion.

While reaction to the Copernican theory came quickly, the full effect of the consequences and the conflicts concerning it developed slowly. We can state but briefly some of them. On theological grounds it was argued that if the earth is not the physical center of the universe, doubt might be raised that man is the spiritual center of finite existence. This argument was, of course, irrelevant but it did carry a certain psychological weight. Although Copernicus did not commit himself on the finitude or infinitude of the universe, others, such as Giordano Bruno (1548–1600), did. If the earth or the sun may be assumed to be the center of the physical universe, then any other convenient place might equally be taken to be the center. Once certainty about the actual center of the universe was destroyed, the notion of an infinite universe became a plausible position. In the minds of some theologians this possibility challenged the infinity of God Himself. But, even apart from theology, the notion of infinite space and endless matter presented scientific and metaphysical problems enough. In any case, the new astronomy introduced the minimal requirement that the universe be conceived of as enormously larger than man had dared to dream previously.

Another important consequence of the new astronomy was that the qualitative distinction between heaven and earth disappeared as a viable hypothesis and the Aristotelian teleology no longer could be applied readily to the four elements. If the earth is but one of many planets, then there is a presumption that it is more nearly like them than not.

Might not an observer on another planet have as much reason to think our earth is fire as we do of the other planets?

Finally there is a strong suggestion that the indispensable key to understanding nature is mathematics with its concepts of quantity, measure, order, and number. Indeed, Kepler and others did proceed to advance such a view.

In spite of the fact that Kepler (1571–1630) did turn to a somewhat mystical Pythagorean-Platonic conception of the order and structure of physical existence—a view which was severely criticized by Galileo—he made a most important advance in astronomy. By employing the detailed astronomical observations of Tycho Brahe (1546–1601), he determined with considerable accuracy the paths of the orbiting planets. Only by a slow and tedious application of Tycho Brahe's mathematics and observations to one hypothetical orbit after another did he finally find the meeting place of observation, measurements, and hypotheses in the eliptical curve. It was at this moment that the new hypothesis was first firmly supported by observation, measurement, and prediction.

It was Galileo Galilei (1564–1642) who gave the most telling confirmation to the new astronomy. With his new telescope he saw the satellites around Jupiter and discovered other celestial phenomena, all of which tended to confirm the Copernican position.

Galileo's achievements, however, went far beyond anything which preceded him. From his earliest youth he set himself the task of making an exact mathematical study of the motions of bodies. He regarded the syllogistic logic of the schools as useless for making new discoveries, whereas on the contrary he was convinced that *mathematics* systematically and exactly applied to observations and experiments offered *the indispensable method of discovery in nature*. He conceded that our sensory experience presents us with a world to be explained, but he insisted that understanding can come only through a mathematical analysis. His series of experiments on accelerated motion, which were dramatized in the famous leaning tower of Pisa experiment, clearly illustrated his method and purpose. He demonstrated that all bodies, without regard to weight or other qualities, fall at the same rate of speed, at least in a vacuum, and that the rate of their acceleration can be exactly measured and predicted.

On the basis of this and other experiments, he went on to reject the qualitative and teleological explanations of the Aristotelians. He substituted "force" for the notion of "purpose," and replaced the concepts of "form" and "telos" with the notion of "law," which describes the *how* of change in precise quantitative terms. Increasingly he was convinced that all of nature could be described in terms of body in motion (locomotion) in space and time. This conviction led him to distinguish between primary and secondary qualities in nature in a way that was to have enormous consequences for subsequent philosophic inquiry. He maintained that the only qualities which actually exist in nature itself are number, figure, magnitude, position, and motion. Thus, sound can be described in terms of the measurement of the frequency of vibrations of a vibrating body. Similarly, heat is not a quality actually existing in nature; in actuality there is only a certain quantitatively measurable amount of movement in the particles which compose a given body.

On the other hand, the *secondary* qualities—such as color, sound, odor, flavor, hot, and cold—do not actually exist in nature itself. They are subjective effects produced in us when other bodies act upon our sense organs. At best they are no more than subjective signs of events occurring in nature (bodies in motion) and in no way resemble the events of which they are signs. Apart from our perceiving of them, he argued, these secondary qualities have no reality at all.

After nature was thus stripped of all the secondary qualities, the remainder, the primary qualities, readily lent themselves to a purely mathematical description and explanation. While this position worked exceedingly well for the purpose of the new physics, it introduced what Alfred North Whitehead in the twentieth century calls a "bifurcatoin of nature" which had devastating effects for the concept of man and for all extant theories of knowledge. In banishing the secondary qualities from nature itself and calling them subjective, Galileo did not thereby dispose of them altogether. *There* they remained manifest to all who have senses to perceive, and they could not be ruled utterly out of existence. If they could not exist in the physical world at all, then they had to be placed elsewhere—in the human mind. This presented philosophy with some all but insoluble problems as can be discovered upon reading Descartes, Berkeley, Hume, and Kant. Indeed, virtually all the philosophers of the seventeenth and eighteenth centuries and beyond addressed themselves to these questions—and to many others which we have not yet raised. None, however, offered solutions which were universally acceptable.

It has been necessary to present this brief account of the background of Descartes to make clear what were some of the problems to which Descartes addressed himself. We must hasten to add that many other philosophic and scientific problems influenced Descartes, but space has not allowed consideration of them here. An examination of some of the works in the secondary bibliography on Descartes will quickly acquaint the student with these issues.

LIFE

René Descartes was born into a noble French family on March 31, 1596. Although delicate in health, he early displayed a quick and inquiring mind. Given a most careful education at the Jesuit College of La Flèche, he was trained in scholastic philosophy and physics. He showed, however, a remarkable talent for mathematics and at a comparatively early age had mastered the entire field of mathematics as it was then known. Later he was to become one of the greatest mathematicians of the seventeenth century. After his departure from La Flèche, Descartes had a brief try at the social world of Paris. He soon became bored with this life and turned to seclusion, thought, and inquiry for two years.

Determined to study the "great book of the world," Descartes volunteered as a soldier under Maurice of Orange. Later he joined the army with the Elector of Bavaria. He reports that during the interval of winter quarters in 1619–20 he discovered the method which was later to shape the whole of his philosophy. Specifically he recalled with remarkable vividness that on the night of November 10, 1619, the angel of truth appeared to him and confirmed his growing conviction that mathematics was the incomparable instrument for the understanding of nature. Overwhelmed with enthusiasm, he prayed to the Virgin Mary for inspiration and guidance and vowed a pilgrimage to Loretto.

From 1621–5 he spent his time in study and travel. After this interval Descartes returned to Paris, where he continued his researches into mathematics and mechanics. In 1629 he moved to Holland in search of solitude and freedom to write and think. Certainly the climate of intellectual freedom was at that time greater in Holland than in France. Descartes remained in Holland until 1649, the year before his death. It was during this period in Holland that he wrote and published his most important works. At the same time he maintained a lively and extensive correspondence with many of the leading minds of the age and persistently requested that his friend Father Mersenne and others as well inform him of all the new work in science and mathematics that came to their attention.

In 1649 Descartes ventured to go to Sweden at the invitation of Queen Christina. Apparently the climate was too severe for his somewhat delicate constitution, for he became ill and died in Stockholm the following year, 1650.

PHILOSOPHY

Whenever in the course of history there is a major change in the scientific and philosophic outlook, there is an accompanying re-examination of the methods of inquiry. The seventeenth century saw every major philosopher engaged in an effort to reformulate and redefine the methods of philosophic and scientific inquiry and knowledge. Method and the subject matter of scientific thought are not two separable things; rather, they are inescapably bound together. Yet it is only when a new method has proved fertile as an instrument of inquiry that method is reflectively examined and explicitly formulated. Descartes was thoroughly familiar with the works of Copernicus, Kepler, Galileo, and others who had made new discoveries about nature. In comparison with their work he found the scholastic science which he had studied at La Flèche poor in content and fruitless in method.

To give a rounded picture of Decartes' thought, it may prove valuable to begin with a discussion of matters which are either briefly touched upon or not discussed at all in the *Meditations*—namely, Descartes' scientific and mathematical thought.

There is much evidence to show that Descartes was deeply committed to the new sciences and to a strictly mathematical understanding of nature at an early stage of his development. That mathematics and the new physics were among his deepest interests is amply attested to by his voluminous correspondence. In his conception of nature Descartes discarded without hesitation the Aristotelian notions of natural teleology, hierarchy of substances, and the reality of species. The physical universe he thought of as a vast machine, with all the particular bodies in it as machines which can be understood clearly and distinctly only in terms of mathematical expressions. He argued that there is but one matter throughout the universe and that the variety of bodies and their properties "may be reduced to the one, viz. that it (*body*) can be divided, or moved according to its parts. . . ." [4]

The title page of the *Discourse on Method* clearly shows that the aim of this work was to show the value of his method for scientific inquiry. It reads, "*Discours De La Méthode*, Pour bien conduire sa raison et chercher la vérité dans les sciences. Plus *La Dioptrique, Les Meteores*, et *La Geometrie*, qui sont des essais de cette Méthode." [5] The

---

[4] *Principles of Philosophy*, Part II, Principle XXIII. In *The Philosophical Works of Descartes*. Translated by Elizabeth S. Haldane and G. R. T. Ross (Second Edition: Cambridge: Cambridge University; 1931), Vol. I.

[5] "Discourse on the Method of rightly Conducting the Reason and Seeking for Truth in the Sciences. Plus the *Dioptrics*, the *Meteorology* and the *Geometry* which are illustrations on that method."

last of these works is the celebrated analytic geometry wherein Descartes demonstrated that any spatial relationship can be expressed in the form of an algebraic equation—thereby laying a firm basis for a mathematical physics and preparing the way for the calculus. The two other works, *La Dioptrique* and *Les Meteores*, illustrate Descartes' application of his mathematical techniques to the areas of optics and meteorology. In the first few pages of *Les Meteores* he discloses the bent of his mind when he writes:

> I suppose, firstly, that water, earth, air, and all other such bodies which surround us are composed of many small particles of diverse figures and sizes which are never so well arranged nor so exactly joined together that they remain for long intervals in contact with each other.[6]

On reading the three works which Descartes presents as applications of his method, the question arises of why he felt the need to discourse on his own existence, and the existence of God, and to try to demonstrate the existence of matter. The most plausible explanation lies in supposing that he believed it imperative to provide a metaphysical justification of a mechanical universe before he could freely and safely turn to develop his program for the new sciences.

To be sure, Descartes argued that God created matter and set it in motion. Indeed, he went further, to argue that as much activity of God was needed to maintain the continued existence of the world as to create it. Thus, although God was seen to be the first cause of the world, it was nonetheless nothing but a vast machine.

The essence of matter for Descartes was extension (three-dimensional), and its sole mode of action, locomotion. Obviously this meant that every relationship in matter and every motion allowed of mathematical description. Descartes rejected the actual existence of atoms in the literal sense of irreducible particles, because every body is potentially divisible in principle, and he regarded the notion of an empty space or void a self-contradictory absurdity. Nonetheless, when confronted with the proposition that matter is infinite, Descartes admitted only that it is indefinitely large. Even though Descartes held that the world is a *plenum* (full of matter), he argued that there is no impediment to the existence of motion. The latter he defines in a truly relativistic way: "it is the transference of one part of matter or one body from the vicinity of those bodies that are in immediate contact with it, and which we regard as in repose, into the vicinity of others."[7]

---

[6] My translation from *Oeuvres de Descartes*. Edited by Charles Adam and Paul Tannery (Paris: Leopold Cerf; 1896–1913), Vol. VI, p. 233.

[7] Part II, Principle XXV.

In an early work, *Le Monde*,[8] which Descartes decided not to publish when he heard of the ordeal of Galileo and the condemnation of the
Copernican theory by the College of the Inquisition in 1633, he argued
that place and motion must be taken to be relative. The definition of
motion in the *Principles of Philosophy*, when considered together with
the theories advanced in *Le Monde*, suggests that Descartes was looking
for firm ground on which he could support either the Ptolemaic or the
Copernican astronomy to be equally valid, depending on the frame of
reference assumed.

Descartes was, on one hand, bold in his general conceptions, and,
on the other, extremely hesitant about a specific commitment on the
Copernican astronomy out of fear of ecclesiastical condemnation. Nonetheless, it is evident that Descartes probably accepted the Copernican
hypothesis, for he argued for the relativity of motion on virtually the
same grounds that Copernicus advanced. Since absolute motion is not
observable, we can apply the following statement of Descartes to
heavenly movements: "That touching the things which our senses do
not perceive, it is sufficient to explain what the possibilities are about
the nature of their existence, though perhaps they are not what we
describe them to be. . . ."[9]

Descartes unfortunately weakened the force of his physical theories,
which were the first great comprehensive alternative to the still prevailing
medieval views, when he held to the view that the sum total of motion
in the world was constant. This weakness stems from the fact that he
had to explain all motion, or change of motion, in terms of a "push"
from behind. It was therefore left to Newton, who further developed
Galileo's notion of force, to give an adequate account of gravitation and
the movements of heavenly bodies.

Despite this failure, Descartes gave a most lucid account of the
general structure of a mathematical mechanical universe and deduced
many of the philosophical consequences which it entailed. He applied
his principles to such natural phenomena as light, sound, meteorology,
hydraulics, and to as many other phenomena as he could, including life.
The Aristotelian distinction between living and nonliving substances,
with the exception of mind, was obliterated. For Descartes a living
creature is no more than a complex machine. All the processes Aristotle
discusses in terms of the nutritive soul Descartes discusses in terms of
mechanics. He shows that the gross movements of the body can be
accounted for in terms of pushes, pulls, pulleys, and levers. Harvey's

---

[8] *Le Monde* was not published until 1670, twenty years after the death of
Descartes.
[9] Part IV, Principle CCIV.

account [1] of the circulation of the blood, published in 1628, was in brilliant conformity with Descartes' thesis, and Descartes made apt use of its explanation of the action of the heart and the circulation of the blood as an elaborate pump system; the same principles are applied by Descartes to muscular action and the nervous system. Indeed, in *The Passions of the Soul* [2] he speaks of animal spirits coursing along the nerves, but by "animal spirits" he means certain motions of body. The concept is only roughly similar to the notion of nervous impulses. Descartes thought of "animal spirits" as air or wind moving along hollow tubes in the nerves. The particular account was not important. What mattered is that he understood nervous activity in terms of body in motion.

From this account certain conclusions may be drawn. Animals are automatons, for they are nothing other than extremely complex machines. Since they have no minds, according to Descartes, they neither perceive nor are they conscious; consequently, Descartes also reduced Aristotle's conception of the sensitive soul, as far as animals are concerned, to part of the complex machinery of animal bodies. An extreme behaviorism is entirely consistent with Descartes' account of the animal world. Man, however, presented some difficulties.

If we momentarily set the mind aside, then the human body and its functions, although more complex than those of other bodies, are subject to the same mechanical explanations as all other bodies. Man, according to Descartes, is not merely another material body; he is essentially and primarily an immaterial, spiritual substance, different in kind from matter or body. However, this mind is temporarily attached in some mysterious way to a particular body. In the case of man, then, the sensitive soul of Aristotle is bifurcated: on the one side it is body in motion, merely physiological function; on the other hand it is mind, spiritual substance, thinking. Sensible qualities (the proper sensibles of Aristotle) are termed "confused ideas." Having stripped matter of all the secondary qualities, as did Galileo, Descartes placed them in the mind. Thus they in no way resemble the actual attributes of matter and are at best subjective signs of *events in nature* (certain movements of bodies).

Having destroyed the hierarchical and qualitative conception of substance, Descartes was confronted with a dualism of two radically distinct substances which have virtually nothing in common. Before considering mind, it is important that we discuss several difficult problems concerning the relation of body and mind. The first question is,

---

[1] Harvey, William (1578–1657) *Exercitatio anatoria de motie cordis et sanguinis.* (1628)

[2] Published in 1649; written in 1645–6.

How can body and mind be attached at all? Descartes suggested that the pineal gland of the brain is the point of contact—a suggestion for which he has been unfairly ridiculed. If we can conceive how body and mind can be attached at all, the place of connection is of minor importance.[3] Secondly, By what means does the body affect the mind if the sole mode of bodily action is motion? How does a body push or pull something which is not a body at all? How can the mind be conceived to produce any effect or influence on a body when they have nothing in common? Yet my mind appears to have some effect on my body. How is it possible that thinking, in any of its modes, can have an effect on my body? Moreover, even if my mind could do so, would not this action upset the laws of motion by either increasing or decreasing the sum total of motion in the world, or at least by changing the direction and motion of some body—for example, when I think and choose to speak? These are but some of the difficulties attending the dualism of Descartes.

It would be unfair to him to dwell unduly on the difficulties or to suggest that Descartes was not aware of them. Certainly he thought that somehow they could be overcome. The main consideration for Descartes was his conviction that the new sciences seemed to require some such solution. Moreover, it is part of his lasting merit that he foresaw so many of the consequences which the new physics entailed if it were taken as a real and literal description of the natural world. After Descartes every major philosopher set out to solve in one way or another the epistomological and metaphysical problems he raised. It is not at all clear that anyone has yet succeeded.

At the heart of all these questions there are epistomological and metaphysical considerations, to which we must now turn. Quite early in his career Descartes saw that if there were to be progress in the acquisition of new human knowledge, new methods were required. When he surveyed the opinions, theories, and doctrines which were competing for acceptance, he found uncertainty, doubt, and disagreement. Only in mathematics—notably in arithmetic and geometry—did all who understood the subject agree, and only where number and quantity could be applied—be it to men, to stars, to distances, or to size—did all consent. Descartes also noted that the certainties of mathematics were established by either intuition or deduction. In the *Rules for the Direction of the Mind* he writes:

> By intuition I understand, not the fluctuating testimony of the senses, nor the misleading judgment that proceeds from the blundering constructions of imagination, but the conception

---

[3] See *Passions of the Soul*. Part I, Articles XXX, XXXI.

which an unclouded and attentive mind gives us so readily and distinctly that we are wholly freed from doubt about that which we understand. Or, what comes to the same thing, intuition is the undoubting conception of an unclouded and attentive mind, and springs from the light of reason alone; it is more certain than deduction itself, in that it is simpler, though deduction, as we have noted above, cannot by us be erroneously conducted. Thus each individual can mentally have intuition of the fact that he exists, and that he thinks; that the triangle is bounded by three lines only, the sphere by a single superficies, and so on. Facts of such a kind are far more numerous than many people think, disdaining as they do to direct their attention upon such simple matters.[4]

By deduction Descartes means the pure illation by which the mind proceeds from one or more concepts through logical necessity to other certainties, as in a geometrical demonstration. The senses, for Descartes, are sources of information that provide no certainty. Too many illusions attest to this fact. Only mathematical and scientific reasoning can correct these errors. For example, the sensory experience should be compared with the scientific understanding of such matters as the straight stick that looks bent in water, the size, distance, and movement of the sun or moon, and countless other similar phenomena.

The traditional logic failed, Descartes believed, because it took the sensory world on its face value and was inadequate to lead on to new knowledge or to give an exact analysis of phenomena such as mathematics could. The central question which Descartes raises is this, Is the certainty of mathematics due to its peculiar content or to its method? He asserted that certainty is entirely due to the method of mathematics, and he set out to discover what that method is in the hope that it could be applied elsewhere.

In *The Rules for the Direction of the Mind* he writes:

Method consists entirely in the order and disposition of the objects towards which our mental vision must be directed if we would find out any truth. We shall comply with it exactly if we reduce involved and obscure propositions step by step to those that are simpler, and then starting with the intuitive apprehension of all those that are absolutely simple, attempt to ascend to the knowledge of all others by precisely similar steps.[5]

---

[4] Rule III. In *The Philosophic Works of Descartes*. Op. cit.
[5] Rule V. In *The Philosophic Works of Descartes*. Op. cit.

Again in the *Discourse on Method* he lays down four rules for arriving at certainty:

> The first of these was to accept nothing as true which I did not clearly recognise to be so: that is to say, carefully to avoid precipitation and prejudice in judgments, and to accept in them nothing more than what was presented to my mind so clearly and distinctly that I could have no occasion to doubt it.
>
> The second was to divide up each of the difficulties which I examined into as many parts as possible, and as seemed requisite in order that it might be resolved in the best manner possible.
>
> The third was to carry on my reflections in due order, commencing with objects that were the most simple and easy to understand, in order to rise little by little, or by degrees, to knowledge of the most complex, assuming an order, even if a fictitious one, among those which do not follow a natural sequence relatively to one another.
>
> The last was in all cases to make enumerations so complete and reviews so general that I should be certain of having omitted nothing.[6]

Three terms in this quotation require some brief explanation—"simple," "clear," and "distinct." By a simple idea Descartes means a logically simple idea—one which is neither deducible from other ideas nor a generalization from experience. It has been argued that there is no difference in meaning between "clear" and "distinct." I believe, however, Descartes means that a distinct idea is one which is set off distinctly from any other idea, much as we say that we can distinguish A from B. The relationship here is between two separate ideas. A clear idea is one in which all the internal relationships of the idea itself are manifest to the mind, particularly where the enunciation of the idea entails a number of terms—for example, "Two things equal to a third thing are equal to each other." The difference in meaning between "clear" and "distinct," then, may be termed one of internal and external relationships.

It is the foregoing method which underlies mathematics. Descartes believed that the application of this method to existence would afford as much certainty about the real nature and existence of mind, God, and matter as it assures of the formal knowledge and certainty of mathematics. Descartes' view that by the use of this method we can come to discover certain innate ideas in our own minds seems to some

---

[6] Part II.

extent to be derived from Plato. If so, the derivation is vague and uncertain. Nevertheless, innate ideas are not to be taken as already present in the mind, for Descartes writes, "Innate ideas proceed from the capacity of thought itself." [7] Innate ideas are implicitly in the mind: God implants in the nature and structure of the mind only the power of thought by which innate ideas can be made explicit to us.

The method of "systematic doubt" which Descartes employs is an application of the rules laid down in the *Discourse on Method*. It must always be remembered that his purpose is to arrive at certainty about existence. Descartes is not a sceptic, for scepticism is not so much a method as it is a conclusion that we cannot really know anything. Descartes, in contrast, is confident that being and reality are open to certainty and knowledge, if only we go about reaching for knowledge in the right way. Neither is the method of "systematic doubt" to be confused with practical doubt which, when it exists, makes us pause or hesitate before acting in the ordinary affairs of life. Underlying Descartes' method and metaphysics is the conviction that existence is intelligible and that, as Spinoza was later to put it, "the order and connection of ideas is the same as the order and connection of things." It is in this commitment that Descartes' rationalism lies, for if it be false, reason must be irrelevant to reality. Descartes understood his arguments which established the certainty of his own existence and the proofs for the existence of God and of matter to be firm substantiation of his rationalistic realism.

It is both unnecessary and undesirable to restate in this preface the arguments advanced in the *Meditations*. Nonetheless, a few brief comments on some problems and terms in Descartes' work may be of value to the student.

"Cogito ergo sum"; "Je pense donc je suis"; "I think therefore I exist." [8] This assertion, which startles with all the impact and ambiguity of the famous utterances of the Delphic oracle, has been one of the pivotal statements of modern philosophy. Volumes have been written about it—to explain it, to refute it, and to justify it. Descartes would have been astounded to discover how many burdens the *cogito* has been made to carry since he first enunciated it. It has been claimed and blamed as the cornerstone for various philosophical positions, such as solipcism, subjectivism, individualism, and numerous others. Even today philosophers as diverse as Gilbert Ryle [9] and Jean-Paul Sartre [1] have

---

[7] See also Descartes' reply to Hobbes in the *Objections and Replies*.

[8] In the remainder of this essay the single word *cogito* will be used to refer to the complete statement.

[9] Gilbert Ryle: *The Concept of Mind* (New York: Hutchinson; 1949).

[1] Jean-Paul Sartre. *Being and Nothingness*. (New York: Philosophical Library; 1956).

given their deepest attention to it. Whenever a philosophic statement is examined and re-examined, refuted, and rerefuted, the suspicion arises that the ghost has not been laid entirely to rest. Whatever the influence of the *cogito* on later minds in the history of Western thought may be, it seems reasonably safe to say that Descartes had other things in mind.

He was concerned to discover some knowledge of real existence which could not be doubted under any conceivable circumstances. The *cogito* represented for him his first piece of certainty about existence, for it cannot be doubted, he held, without absurdity and contradiction. This certainty was intuitive, for, however much we explore and analyze the *cogito*, once it is understood it cannot seriously be doubted. If this is sound, the *cogito* at once vindicated Descartes' method and established the possibility of that method being the key to additional real knowledge about existence, God, and nature. The singularity in thought is this: since the act of the mind is reflective, the *cogito* establishes, not my existence, but the *knowledge* of my existence. It is then the fulcrum point by which I can raise my mind to additional real knowledge. To say that I think and know that I think is to say that I am a thinking being at least; whatever else I may be is another matter. To say that I exist is, for Descartes, to say that I am a substance, and so a thinking substance.

In the *Principles of Philosophy* Descartes writes, "By substance, we can understand nothing else than a thing which so exists that it needs no other thing in order to exist." [2] It is evident that only God satisfies this definition. However, of created substances, it may be said that they need only God to exist. He also argues that substance cannot be discovered except by means of one of its attributes. Hence it is by *thinking* that we know that we exist, since any act of thinking is a *mode* of mind. Of mode Descartes writes, ". . . when we here speak of modes we mean nothing more than what elsewhere is termed *attribute* or *quality*. But when we consider substance as modified or diversified by them, I avail myself of the word *mode*. . . ." [3] Consequently, when he applies these concepts to the mind he writes,

> For all the modes of thinking that we observed in ourselves may be related to two general modes, the one of which consists in perception, or in the operation of the understanding, and the other in volition, or the operation of the will. Thus sense perception, imagining, and conceiving things that are purely intelligible, are just different methods of perceiving; but desiring, holding in aversion, affirming, denying, doubting, all these are the different modes of willing. [4]

[2] Part I, Principle LI.
[3] Part I, Principle LVI.
[4] Part I, Principle XXXII.

It should be added here that by *idea* Descartes means any object, simple or complex, clear and distinct or confused and vague, which is perceived by the mind or is the object of consciousness.

One thing should be quite clear: if matter really is as either Descartes, Galileo, or even later philosophers and physicists describe it, then that matter certainly cannot think. Perhaps this issue is clearly disclosed by several apparently contradictory statements of John Locke (1632–1704), who wrote:

> We have the ideas of *matter* and *thinking*, but possibly shall never be able to know whether any mere material being thinks or no; it being impossible for us, by the contemplation of our own ideas, without revelation, to discover whether Omnipotency has not given to some systems of matter, fitly disposed, a power to perceive and think, or else joined and fixed to matter, so disposed, a thinking immaterial substance: it being, in respect to our notions, not much more remote from our comprehension to conceive that God can, if he pleases, superadd to matter a faculty of thinking, than that he should superadd to it another substance with a faculty of thinking.[5]

Yet elsewhere he writes that matter certainly cannot think:

> It is as repugnant to the idea of senseless matter, that it should put into itself sense, perception, and knowledge, as it is repugnant to the idea of a triangle, that it should put into itself greater angles than two right ones.[6] . . . Matter, incogitative matter and motion, whatever changes it might produce of figure and bulk could never produce thought.[7]

One can readily eliminate the contradiction by noting that if matter is as it was conceived in the seventeenth century, then that stuff cannot think. Or, stated conversely, a matter that could think would be a very different kind of matter from the prevailing conceptions of matter in Descartes' century.

It remains but to say a few words about Descartes' arguments for the existence of God. It is uncalled for here to comment on the substance of these arguments. However, a brief account of the history of the "ontological argument" may be of some value. The argument was first clearly and fully stated by St. Anselm in the twelfth century, although it was suggested much earlier by St. Augustine. St. Anselm

---

[5] John Locke. *Essay Concerning Human Understanding.* Book IV, Ch. III, par. 6.

[6] Book IV, Ch. X, par. 5.

[7] Book IV, Ch. X, par. 10.

argues that since God is that than which nothing greater can be conceived, it necessarily follows that God must exist, for if He did not, a contradiction would arise—namely, that something greater could exist than that than which nothing greater can be conceived. The argument was instantly subjected to criticism by Gannilo, a monk of Mamoutiers. He stressed that being and thought are quite distinct, inasmuch as we can conceive of beings which do not exist. St. Thomas Aquinas further subjected the argument of St. Anselm to severe criticism. Descartes revised and restated it in the *Meditations,* and in one sense the first book of Spinoza's *Ethics* is a further refinement and development of the argument. In the main the British empirical philosophers—Locke, Berkeley, and Hume—either rejected it or avoided it.

Kant gave the severest blow to the ontological argument by arguing that existence adds nothing to the *perfection* or to the *idea* of a thing. Like Gannilo, he sets up a sharp distinction between being and thought. Hegel, however, holding to the unity of being and thought, was not only sympathetic to St. Anselm's argument; he revived it in a somewhat modified form—possibly a pantheistic one.

In recent years the argument has been set aside for the most part, even though it continues to haunt the imagination of philosophers. Nonetheless, in a recent article Professor Norman Malcolm [8] defended St. Anselm's ontological proof for the existence of God. Subsequently, a number of replies to Professor Malcolm's arguments appeared in the same journal.[9] Apparently this issue has not been laid to rest.

The serious student of philosophy will neither accept nor reject these arguments out of hand. Rather, he will use them for deeper insights into philosophical problems and issues. One thing, however, should be clear: in the main, philosophers in the tradition of rationalism and realism either accept the ontological argument as valid in some form or are at least sympathetic with it; on the other hand, philosophers in the empiricist and nominalistic traditions reject the argument altogether. The student will profit by trying to relate Descartes' arguments and conclusions to other philosophers whom he studies.

JAMES GORDON CLAPP

---

[8] "Anselm's Ontological Arguments." *The Philosophical Review,* Vol. LXIX (1960).

[9] Ibid., Vol. LXX (1961).

SELECTED BIBLIOGRAPHY

Works

Oeuvres Completes. Edited by Charles Adam and Paul Tannery. 13 vol. Paris: Leopold Cerf; 1896–1913.

The Philosophic Works of Descartes. Translated by Elizabeth S. Haldane and G. R. T. Ross. 2 vol. Second Edition. Cambridge: Cambridge University Press; 1931. (Also Dover Publishers, Inc., republication of the 1931 edition)

The Meditations and Selections from the Principles. Edited by John Veitch La Salle, Ill.: Open Court; 1948.

Commentaries

Balz, Albert G. A.: *Descartes and the Modern Mind.* New Haven: Yale University Press; 1952.

Beck, Leslie John: *The Method of Descartes, a Study of the Regulae.* Oxford: Clarendon; 1952.

Burtt, E. A.: *The Metaphysical Foundations of Modern Physical Science.* New York: Harcourt, Brace; 1927.

Gibson, Alexander Boyce: *The Philosophy of Descartes.* London: Methuen; 1932.

Gilson, Etienne: *The Unity of Philosophic Experience.* New York: Scribner; 1937.

Keeling, S. V.: *Descartes.* London: Ernest Benn; 1934.

Maritain, Jacques: *The Dream of Descartes.* New York: Philosophical Library; 1944.

Maritain, Jacques: *Three Reformers: Luther, Descartes, Rousseau.* New York: Sheed and Ward; 1929.

Smith, Norman Kemp: *New Studies in the Philosophy of Descartes.* London: Macmillan; 1952.

Spinoza, Benedictus de: *The Principles of Descartes' Philosophy.* Translated by Halbert Hains Britan. La Salle, Ill.: Open Court; 1905, reprinted 1943.

Vartanian, Aram: *Diderot and Descartes.* Princeton: Princeton University Press; 1953.

MEDITATIONS
ON FIRST PHILOSOPHY

PREFATORY NOTE
TO THE MEDITATIONS

The first edition of the 'Meditations' was published in Latin by
Michael Soly of Paris 'at the Sign of the Phoenix' in 1641 *cum
Privilegio et Approbatione Doctorum*. The Royal 'privilege' was indeed
given, but the 'approbation' seems to have been of a most indefinite
kind. The reason of the book being published in France and not in
Holland, where Descartes was living in a charming country house at
Endegeest near Leiden, was apparently his fear that the Dutch ministers
might in some way lay hold of it. His friend, Père Mersenne, took charge
of its publication in Paris and wrote to him about any difficulties that
occurred in the course of its progress through the press. The second
edition was however published at Amsterdam in 1642 by Louis Elzevir,
and this edition was accompanied by the now completed 'Objections
and Replies.' The edition from which the present translation is made
is the second just mentioned, and is that adopted by MM. Adam and
Tannery as the more correct, for reasons that they state in detail in the
preface to their edition. The work was translated into French by the
Duc de Luynes in 1642 and Descartes considered the translation so
excellent that he had it published some years later. Clerselier, to complete matters, had the 'Objections' also published in French with the

'Replies,' and this, like the other, was subject to Descartes' revision and correction. This revision renders the French edition specially valuable. Where it seems desirable an alternative reading from the French is given in square brackets.

E. S. H.

TO THE MOST WISE AND ILLUSTRIOUS
THE DEAN AND DOCTORS OF THE
SACRED FACULTY OF THEOLOGY IN PARIS

The motive which induces me to present to you this Treatise is so excellent, and, when you become acquainted with its design, I am convinced that you will also have so excellent a motive for taking it under your protection, that I feel that I cannot do better, in order to render it in some sort acceptable to you, than in a few words to state what I have set myself to do.

I have always considered that the two questions respecting God and the Soul were the chief of those that ought to be demonstrated by philosophical rather than theological argument. For although it is quite enough for us faithful ones to accept by means of faith the fact that the human soul does not perish with the body, and that God exists, it certainly does not seem possible ever to persuade infidels of any religion, indeed, we may almost say, of any moral virtue, unless, to begin with, we prove these two facts by means of the natural reason. And inasmuch as often in this life greater rewards are offered for vice than for virtue, few people would prefer the right to the useful, were they restrained neither by the fear of God nor the expectation of another life; and although it is absolutely true that we must believe that there is a God, because we are so taught in the Holy Scriptures, and, on the other hand, that we must believe the Holy Scriptures because they come from God (the reason of this is, that, faith being a gift of God, He who gives the grace to cause us to believe other things can likewise give it to cause us to believe that He exists), we nevertheless could not place this argument before infidels, who might accuse us of reasoning in a circle. And, in truth, I have noticed that you, along with all the theologians, did not only affirm that the existence of God may be proved by the natural reason, but also that it may be inferred from the Holy Scriptures, that knowledge about Him is much clearer than that which we have of many created things, and, as a matter of fact, is so easy to acquire, that those who have it not are culpable in their ignorance. This indeed appears from the Wisdom of Solomon, chapter xiii., where it is said 'Howbeit they are not to be excused; for if their understanding was so great that they could discern the world and the creatures, why did they not rather find out the Lord thereof?' and in Romans, chapter i., it is said that they are 'without excuse'; and again in the same place, by these words 'that which may be known of God is manifest in them,' it seems as though we were shown that all that which can be known of God may be made manifest by means which are not derived from anywhere but from ourselves, and from the simple consideration of the nature of our minds. Hence I thought it not beside my purpose to inquire how this is so, and how God may be more easily and certainly known than the things of the world.

And as regards the soul, although many have considered that it is not easy to know its nature, and some have even dared to say that human reasons have convinced us that it would perish with the body, and that faith alone could believe the contrary, nevertheless, inasmuch as the Lateran Council held under Leo X (in the eighth session) condemns these tenets, and as Leo expressly ordains Christian philosophers to refute their arguments and to employ all their powers in making known the truth, I have ventured in this treatise to undertake the same task.

More than that, I am aware that the principal reason which causes many impious persons not to desire to believe that there is a God, and that the human soul is distinct from the body, is that they declare that hitherto no one has been able to demonstrate these two facts; and although I am not of their opinion but, on the contrary, hold that the greater part of the reasons which have been brought forward concerning these two questions by so many great men are, when they are rightly understood, equal to so many demonstrations, and that it is almost impossible to invent new ones, it is yet in my opinion the case that nothing more useful can be accomplished in philosophy than once for all to seek with care for the best of these reasons, and to set them forth in so clear and exact a manner, that it will henceforth be evident to everybody that they are veritable demonstrations. And, finally, inasmuch as it was desired that I should undertake this task by many who were aware that I had cultivated a certain Method for the resolution of difficulties of every kind in the Sciences—a method which it is true is not novel, since there is nothing more ancient than the truth, but of which they were aware that I had made use successfully enough in other matters of difficulty—I have thought that it was my duty also to make trial of it in the present matter.

Now all that I could accomplish in the matter is contained in this Treatise. Not that I have here drawn together all the different reasons which might be brought forward to serve as proofs of this subject: for that never seemed to be necessary excepting when there was no one single proof that was certain. But I have treated the first and principal ones in such a manner that I can venture to bring them forward as very evident and very certain demonstrations. And more than that, I will say that these proofs are such that I do not think that there is any way open to the human mind by which it can ever succeed in discovering better. For the importance of the subject, and the glory of God to which all this relates, constrain me to speak here somewhat more freely of myself than is my habit. Nevertheless, whatever certainty and evidence I find in my reasons, I cannot persuade myself that all the world is capable of understanding them. Still, just as in Geometry there are many demonstrations that have been left to us by Archimedes, by Apollonius, by Pappus, and others, which are accepted by everyone as perfectly certain and evident (because they clearly contain nothing which, considered by itself, is not very easy to understand, and as all through that which follows has an exact connection with, and dependence on that which precedes), nevertheless, because they are somewhat lengthy, and demand a mind wholly devoted to their consideration, they are only taken in and understood by a very limited number of persons. Similarly, although I judge that those of which I here make use are equal to, or even surpass in certainty and evidence, the demonstrations of Geometry, I yet apprehend that they cannot be adequately understood by many, both because they are also a little lengthy and dependent the one on the other, and principally because they demand a mind wholly free of prejudices, and one which can be easily detached from the affairs of the senses. And, truth to say, there are not so many in the world who are fitted for metaphysical speculations as there are for those of Geometry. And more than that; there is still this difference, that in Geometry, since each one is persuaded that nothing must be advanced of which there is not a certain demonstration, those who are not entirely adepts more frequently err in approving what is false, in order to give the impression that they understand it, than in refuting the true. But the case is different in philosophy where everyone believes that all is problematical, and few give themselves to the search after truth; and the greater number, in their desire to acquire a reputation for boldness of thought, arrogantly combat the most important of truths.

That is why, whatever force there may be in my reasonings, seeing they belong to philosophy, I cannot hope that they will have much effect on the minds of men, unless you extend to them your protection. But the estimation in which your Company is universally held is so great, and the name of Sorbonne carries with it so much authority, that, next to the Sacred Councils, never has such deference been paid to the judgment of any Body, not only in what concerns the faith, but also in what regards human philosophy as well: everyone indeed believes that it is not possible to discover elsewhere more perspicacity and solidity, or more integrity and wisdom in pronouncing judgment. For this reason I have no doubt that if you deign to take the trouble in the first place of correcting this work (for being conscious not only of my infirmity, but also of my ignorance, I should not dare to state that it was free from errors), and then, after adding to it these things that are lacking to it, completing those which are imperfect, and yourselves taking the trouble to give a more ample explanation of those things which have need of it, or at least making me aware of the defects so that I may apply myself to remedy them—when this is done and when finally the reasonings by which I prove that there is a God, and that the human soul differs from the body, shall be carried to that point of perspicuity to which I am sure they can be carried in order that they may be esteemed as perfectly exact demonstrations, if you deign to authorise your approbation and to render public testimony to their truth and certainty, I do not doubt, I say, that henceforward all the errors and false opinions which have ever existed regarding these two questions will soon be effaced from the minds of men. For the truth itself will easily cause all men of mind and learning to subscribe to your judgment; and your authority will cause the atheists, who are usually more arrogant than learned or judicious, to rid themselves of their spirit of contradiction or lead them possibly themselves to defend the reasonings which they find being received as demonstrations by all persons of consideration, lest they appear not to understand them. And, finally, all others will easily yield to such a mass of evidence, and there will be none who dares to doubt the existence of God and the real and true distinction between the human soul and the body. It is for you now in your singular wisdom to judge of the importance of the establishment of such beliefs [you who see the disorders produced by the doubt of them] [1]. But it would not become me to say more in consideration of the cause of God and religion to those who have always been the most worthy supports of the Catholic Church.

---

[1] When it is thought desirable to insert additional readings from the French version this will be indicated by the use of square brackets.

PREFACE TO THE READER

I have already slightly touched on these two questions of God and the human soul in the Discourse on the Method of rightly conducting the Reason and seeking truth in the Sciences, published in French in the year 1637. Not that I had the design of treating these with any thoroughness, but only so to speak in passing, and in order to ascertain by the judgment of the readers how I should treat them later on. For these questions have always appeared to me to be of such importance that I judged it suitable to speak of them more than once; and the road which I follow in the explanation of them is so little trodden, and so far removed from the ordinary path, that I did not judge it to be expedient to set it forth at length in French and in a Discourse which might be read by everyone, in case the feebler minds should believe that it was permitted to them to attempt to follow the same path.

But, having in this Discourse on Method begged all those who have found in my writings somewhat deserving of censure to do me the favour of acquainting me with the grounds of it, nothing worthy of remark has been objected to in them beyond two matters: to these two I wish here to reply in a few words before undertaking their more detailed discussion.

The first objection is that it does not follow from the fact that the human mind reflecting on itself does not perceive itself to be other than a thing that thinks, that its nature or its essence consists only in its being a thing that thinks, in the sense that this word *only* excludes all other things which might also be supposed to pertain to the nature of the soul. To this objection I reply that it was not my intention in that place to exclude these in accordance with the order that looks to the truth of the matter (as to which I was not then dealing), but only in accordance with the order of my thought [perception]; thus my meaning was that so far as I was aware, I knew nothing clearly as belonging to my essence, excepting that I was a thing that thinks, or a thing that has in itself the faculty of thinking. But I shall show hereafter how from the fact that I know no other thing which pertains to my essence, it follows that there is no other thing which really does belong to it.

The second objection is that it does not follow from the fact that I have in myself the idea of something more perfect than I am, that this idea is more perfect than I, and much less that what is represented by this idea exists. But I reply that in this term *idea* there is here something equivocal, for it may either be taken materially, as an act of my understanding, and in this sense it cannot be said that it is more perfect than I; or it may be taken objectively, as the thing which is represented by this act, which, although we do not suppose it to exist outside of my understanding, may, none the less, be more perfect than I, because of its essence. And in following out this Treatise I shall show more fully how, from the sole fact that I have in myself the idea of a thing more perfect than myself, it follows that this thing truly exists.

In addition to these two objections I have also seen two fairly lengthy works on this subject, which, however, did not so much impugn my reasonings as my conclusions, and this by arguments drawn from the ordinary atheistic sources. But, because such arguments cannot make any impression on the minds of those who really understand my reasonings, and as the judgments of many are so feeble and irrational that they very often allow themselves to be persuaded by the opinions which they have first formed, however false and far removed from reason they may be, rather than by a true and solid but subsequently received refutation of these opinions, I do not desire to reply here to their criticisms in case of being first of all obliged to state them. I shall only say in general that all that is said by the atheist against the existence of God, always depends either on the fact that we ascribe to God affections which are human, or that we attribute so much strength and wisdom to our minds that we even have the presumption to desire to determine and understand that which God can and ought to do. In this way all that they allege will cause us no difficulty, provided only we remember that we must consider our minds as things which are finite and limited, and God as a Being who is incomprehensible and infinite.

Now that I have once for all recognised and acknowledged the opinions of men, I at once begin to treat of God and the human soul, and at the same time to treat of the whole of the First Philosophy, without however expecting any praise from the vulgar and without the hope that my book will have many readers. On the contrary, I should never advise anyone to read it excepting those who desire to meditate seriously with me, and who can detach their minds from affairs of sense, and deliver themselves entirely from every sort of prejudice. I know too well that such men exist in a very small number. But for those who, without caring to comprehend the order and connections of my reasonings, form their criticisms on detached portions arbitrarily selected, as is the custom with many, these, I say, will not obtain much profit from reading this Treatise. And although they perhaps in several parts find occasion of cavilling, they can for all their pains make no objection which is urgent or deserving of reply.

And inasmuch as I make no promise to others to satisfy them at once, and as I do not presume so much on my own powers as to believe myself capable of foreseeing all that can cause difficulty to anyone, I shall first of all set forth in these Meditations the very considerations by which I persuade myself that I have reached a certain and evident knowledge of the truth, in order to see if, by the same reasons which persuaded me, I can also persuade others. And, after that, I shall reply to the objections which have been made to me by persons of genius and learning to whom I have sent my Meditations for examination, before submitting them to the press. For they have made so many objections and these so different, that I venture to promise that it will be difficult for anyone to bring to mind criticisms of any consequence which have not been already touched upon. This is why I beg those who read these Meditations to form no judgment upon them unless they have given themselves the trouble to read all the objections as well as the replies which I have made to them [2].

SYNOPSIS OF THE SIX FOLLOWING MEDITATIONS

In the first Meditation I set forth the reasons for which we may, generally speaking, doubt about all things and especially about material things, at least so long as we have no other foundations for the sciences than those which we have hitherto possessed. But although the utility of a Doubt which is so general does not at first appear, it is at the same time very great, inasmuch as it delivers us from every kind of prejudice, and sets out for us a very simple way by which the mind may detach itself from the senses; and finally it makes it impossible for us ever to doubt those things which we have once discovered to be true.

In the second Meditation, mind, which making use of the liberty which pertains to it, takes for granted that all those things of whose existence it has the least doubt, are non-existent, recognises that it is however absolutely impossible that it does not itself exist. This point is likewise of the greatest moment, inasmuch as by this means a distinction is easily drawn between the things which pertain to mind—that is to say to the intellectual nature—and those which pertain to body.

But because it may be that some expect from me in this place a statement of the reasons establishing the immortality of the soul, I feel

---

[2] Between the *Præfatio ad Lectorem* and the *Synopsis*, the Paris Edition (1st Edition) interpolates an *Index* which is not found in the Amsterdam Edition (2nd Edition). Since Descartes did not reproduce it, he was doubtless not its author. Mersenne probably composed it himself, adjusting it to the paging of the first Edition [Note in Adam and Tannery's Edition].

that I should here make known to them that having aimed at writing nothing in all this Treatise of which I do not possess very exact demonstrations, I am obliged to follow a similar order to that made use of by the geometers, which is to begin by putting forward as premises all those things upon which the proposition that we seek depends, before coming to any conclusion regarding it. Now the first and principal matter which is requisite for thoroughly understanding the immortality of the soul is to form the clearest possible conception of it, and one which will be entirely distinct from all the conceptions which we may have of body; and in this Meditation this has been done. In addition to this it is requisite that we may be assured that all the things which we conceive clearly and distinctly are true in the very way in which we think them; and this could not be proved previously to the Fourth Meditation. Further we must have a distinct conception of corporeal nature, which is given partly in this Second, and partly in the Fifth and Sixth Meditations. And finally we should conclude from all this, that those things which we conceive clearly and distinctly as being diverse substances, as we regard mind and body to be, are really substances essentially distinct one from the other; and this is the conclusion of the Sixth Meditation. This is further confirmed in this same Meditation by the fact that we cannot conceive of body excepting in so far as it is divisible, while the mind cannot be conceived of excepting as indivisible. For we are not able to conceive of the half of a mind as we can do of the smallest of all bodies; so that we see that not only are their natures different but even in some respects contrary to one another. I have not however dealt further with this matter in this treatise, both because what I have said is sufficient to show clearly enough that the extinction of the mind does not follow from the corruption of the body, and also to give men the hope of another life after death, as also because the premises from which the immortality of the soul may be deduced depend on an elucidation of a complete system of Physics. This would mean to establish in the first place that all substances generally—that is to say all things which cannot exist without being created by God—are in their nature incorruptible, and that they can never cease to exist unless God, in denying to them his concurrence, reduce them to nought; and secondly that body, regarded generally, is a substance, which is the reason why it also cannot perish, but that the human body, inasmuch as it differs from other bodies, is composed only of a certain configuration of members and of other similar accidents, while the human mind is not similarly composed of any accidents, but is a pure substance. For although all the accidents of mind be changed, although, for instance, it think certain things, will others, perceive others, etc., despite all this it does not emerge from these changes another mind: the human body on the other hand becomes a different thing from the sole fact that the figure or form of any of its portions is found to be changed. From this it follows that the human body may indeed easily enough perish, but the mind [or soul of man (I make no distinction between them)] is owing to its nature immortal.

In the third Meditation it seems to me that I have explained at sufficient length the principal argument of which I make use in order to prove the existence of God. But none the less, because I did not wish in that place to make use of any comparisons derived from corporeal things, so as to withdraw as much as I could the minds of readers from the senses, there may perhaps have remained many obscurities which, however, will, I hope, be entirely removed by the Replies which I have made to the Objections which have been set before me. Amongst others there is, for example, this one, 'How the idea in us of a being supremely perfect possesses so much objective reality [that is to say participates by representation in so many degrees of being and perfection] that it necessarily proceeds from a cause which is absolutely perfect. This is illustrated in these Replies by the comparison of a very perfect machine, the idea of which is found in the mind of some work-man. For as the objective contrivance of this idea must have some cause, i.e. either the science of the workman or that of some other from whom he has received the idea, it is similarly impossible that the idea of God which is in us should not have God himself as its cause.

In the fourth Meditation it is shown that all these things which we very clearly and distinctly perceive are true, and at the same time it is explained in what the nature of error or falsity consists. This must of necessity be known both for the confirmation of the preceding truths and for the better comprehension of those that follow. (But it must meanwhile be remarked that I do not in any way there treat of sin—that is to say of the error which is committed in the pursuit of good and evil, but only of that which arises in the deciding between the true and the false. And I do not intend to speak of matters pertaining to the Faith or the conduct of life, but only of those which concern speculative truths, and which may be known by the sole aid of the light of nature.)

In the fifth Meditation corporeal nature generally is explained, and in addition to this the existence of God is demonstrated by a new proof in which there may possibly be certain difficulties also, but the solution of these will be seen in the Replies to the Objections. And further I show in what sense it is true to say that the certainty of geometrical demonstrations is itself dependent on the knowledge of God.

Finally in the Sixth I distinguish the action of the understanding[3]

---

[3] intellectio.

from that of the imagination [4]; *the marks by which this distinction is made are described. I here show that the mind of man is really distinct from the body, and at the same time that the two are so closely joined together that they form, so to speak, a single thing. All the errors which proceed from the senses are then surveyed, while the means of avoiding them are demonstrated, and finally all the reasons from which we may deduce the existence of material things are set forth. Not that I judge them to be very useful in establishing that which they prove, to wit, that there is in truth a world, that men possess bodies, and other such things which never have been doubted by anyone of sense; but because in considering these closely we come to see that they are neither so strong nor so evident as those arguments which lead us to the knowledge of our mind and of God; so that these last must be the most certain and most evident facts which can fall within the cognizance of the human mind. And this is the whole matter that I have tried to prove in these Meditations, for which reason I here omit to speak of many other questions with which I dealt incidentally in this discussion.*

MEDITATIONS ON THE FIRST PHILOSOPHY

IN WHICH THE EXISTENCE OF GOD

AND THE DISTINCTION BETWEEN

MIND AND BODY ARE DEMONSTRATED [5]

MEDITATION I · *Of the things which may be brought within the sphere of the doubtful.*

It is now some years since I detected how many were the false beliefs that I had from my earliest youth admitted as true, and how doubtful was everything I had since constructed on this basis; and from that time I was convinced that I must once for all seriously undertake to rid myself of all the opinions which I had formerly accepted, and commence to build anew from the foundation, if I wanted to establish any firm

---

[4] *imaginatio.*

[5] In place of this long title at the head of the page the first Edition had immediately after the Synopsis, and on the same page 7, simply 'First Meditation.' (Adam's Edition.)

and permanent structure in the sciences. But as this enterprise appeared to be a very great one, I waited until I had attained an age so mature that I could not hope that at any later date I should be better fitted to execute my design. This reason caused me to delay so long that I should feel that I was doing wrong were I to occupy in deliberation the time that yet remains to me for action. To-day, then, since very opportunely for the plan I have in view I have delivered my mind from every care [and am happily agitated by no passions] and since I have procured for myself an assured leisure in a peaceable retirement, I shall at last seriously and freely address myself to the general upheaval of all my former opinions.

Now for this object it is not necessary that I should show that all of these are false—I shall perhaps never arrive at this end. But inasmuch as reason already persuades me that I ought no less carefully to withhold my assent from matters which are not entirely certain and indubitable than from those which appear to me manifestly to be false, if I am able to find in each one some reason to doubt, this will suffice to justify my rejecting the whole. And for that end it will not be requisite that I should examine each in particular, which would be an endless undertaking; for owing to the fact that the destruction of the foundations of necessity brings with it the downfall of the rest of the edifice, I shall only in the first place attack those principles upon which all my former opinions rested.

All that up to the present time I have accepted as most true and certain I have learned either from the senses or through the senses; but it is sometimes proved to me that these senses are deceptive, and it is wiser not to trust entirely to any thing by which we have once been deceived.

But it may be that although the senses sometimes deceive us concerning things which are hardly perceptible, or very far away, there are yet many others to be met with as to which we cannot reasonably have any doubt, although we recognise them by their means. For example, there is the fact that I am here, seated by the fire, attired in a dressing gown, having this paper in my hands and other similar matters. And how could I deny that these hands and this body are mine, were it not perhaps that I compare myself to certain persons, devoid of sense, whose cerebella are so troubled and clouded by the violent vapours of black bile, that they constantly assure us that they think they are kings when they are really quite poor, or that they are clothed in purple when they are really without covering, or who imagine that they have an earthenware head or are nothing but pumpkins or are made of glass. But they are mad, and I should not be any the less insane were I to follow examples so extravagant.

At the same time I must remember that I am a man, and that consequently I am in the habit of sleeping, and in my dreams representing to myself the same things or sometimes even less probable things, than do those who are insane in their waking moments. How often has it happened to me that in the night I dreamt that I found myself in this particular place, that I was dressed and seated near the fire, whilst in reality I was lying undressed in bed! At this moment it does indeed seem to me that it is with eyes awake that I am looking at this paper; that this head which I move is not asleep, that it is deliberately and of set purpose that I extend my hand and perceive it; what happens in sleep does not appear so clear nor so distinct as does all this. But in thinking over this I remind myself that on many occasions I have in sleep been deceived by similar illusions, and in dwelling carefully on this reflection I see so manifestly that there are no certain indications by which we may clearly distinguish wakefulness from sleep that I am lost in astonishment. And my astonishment is such that it is almost capable of persuading me that I now dream.

Now let us assume that we are asleep and that all these particulars, e.g. that we open our eyes, shake our head, extend our hands, and so on, are but false delusions; and let us reflect that possibly neither our hands nor our whole body are such as they appear to us to be. At the same time we must at least confess that the things which are represented to us in sleep are like painted representations which can only have been formed as the counterparts of something real and true, and that in this way those general things at least, i.e. eyes, a head, hands, and a whole body, are not imaginary things, but things really existent. For, as a matter of fact, painters, even when they study with the greatest skill to represent sirens and satyrs by forms the most strange and extraordinary, cannot give them natures which are entirely new, but merely make a certain medley of the members of different animals; or if their imagination is extravagant enough to invent something so novel that nothing similar has ever before been seen, and that then their work represents a thing purely fictitious and absolutely false, it is certain all the same that the colours of which this is composed are necessarily real. And for the same reason, although these general things, to wit, [a body], eyes, a head, hands, and such like, may be imaginary, we are bound at the same time to confess that there are at least some other objects yet more simple and more universal, which are real and true; and of these just in the same way as with certain real colours, all these images of things which dwell in our thoughts, whether true and real or false and fantastic, are formed.

To such a class of things pertains corporeal nature in general, and its extension, the figure of extended things, their quantity or magnitude and number, as also the place in which they are, the time which measures their duration, and so on.

That is possibly why our reasoning is not unjust when we conclude from this that Physics, Astronomy, Medicine and all other sciences which have as their end the consideration of composite things, are very dubious and uncertain; but that Arithmetic, Geometry and other sciences of that kind which only treat of things that are very simple and very general, without taking great trouble to ascertain whether they are actually existent or not, contain some measure of certainty and an element of the indubitable. For whether I am awake or asleep, two and three together always form five, and the square can never have more than four sides, and it does not seem possible that truths so clear and apparent can be suspected of any falsity [or uncertainty].

Nevertheless I have long had fixed in my mind the belief that an all-powerful God existed by whom I have been created such as I am. But how do I know that He has not brought it to pass that there is no earth, no heaven, no extended body, no magnitude, no place, and that nevertheless [I possess the perceptions of all these things and that] they seem to me to exist just exactly as I now see them? And, besides, as I sometimes imagine that others deceive themselves in the things which they think they know best, how do I know that I am not deceived every time that I add two and three, or count the sides of a square, or judge of things yet simpler, if anything simpler can be imagined? But possibly God has not desired that I should be thus deceived, for He is said to be supremely good. If, however, it is contrary to His goodness to have made me such that I constantly deceive myself, it would also appear to be contrary to His goodness to permit me to be sometimes deceived, and nevertheless I cannot doubt that He does permit this.

There may indeed be those who would prefer to deny the existence of a God so powerful, rather than believe that all other things are uncertain. But let us not oppose them for the present, and grant that all that is here said of a God is a fable; nevertheless in whatever way they suppose that I have arrived at the state of being that I have reached— whether they attribute it to fate or to accident, or make out that it is by a continual succession of antecedents, or by some other method— since to err and deceive oneself is a defect, it is clear that the greater will be the probability of my being so imperfect as to deceive myself ever, as is the Author to whom they assign my origin the less powerful. To these reasons I have certainly nothing to reply, but at the end I feel constrained to confess that there is nothing in all that I formerly believed to be true, of which I cannot in some measure doubt, and that not merely through want of thought or through levity, but for reasons which are very powerful and maturely considered; so that henceforth I ought not the less carefully to refrain from giving credence to these opinions than to that which is manifestly false, if I desire to arrive at any certainty [in the sciences].

But it is not sufficient to have made these remarks, we must also be careful to keep them in mind. For these ancient and commonly held opinions still revert frequently to my mind, long and familiar custom having given them the right to occupy my mind against my inclination and rendered them almost masters of my belief; nor will I ever lose the habit of deferring to them or of placing my confidence in them, so long as I consider them as they really are, i.e. opinions in some measure doubtful, as I have just shown, and at the same time highly probable, so that there is much more reason to believe in than to deny them. That is why I consider that I shall not be acting amiss, if, taking of set purpose a contrary belief, I allow myself to be deceived, and for a certain time pretend that all these opinions are entirely false and im- aginary, until at last, having thus balanced my former prejudices with my latter [so that they cannot divert my opinions more to one side than to the other], my judgment will no longer be dominated by bad usage or turned away from the right knowledge of the truth. For I am assured that there can be neither peril nor error in this course, and that I cannot at present yield too much to distrust, since I am not considering the question of action, but only of knowledge.

I shall then suppose, not that God who is supremely good and the fountain of truth, but some evil genius not less powerful than deceitful, has employed his whole energies in deceiving me; I shall consider that the heavens, the earth, colours, figures, sound, and all other external things are nought but the illusions and dreams of which this genius has availed himself in order to lay traps for my credulity; I shall consider myself as having no hands, no eyes, no flesh, no blood, nor any senses, yet falsely believing myself to possess all these things; I shall remain obstinately attached to this idea, and if by this means it is not in my power to arrive at the knowledge of any truth, I may at least do what is in my power [i.e. suspend my judgment], and with firm purpose avoid giving credence to any false thing, or being imposed upon by this arch deceiver, however powerful and deceptive he may be. But this task is a laborious one, and insensibly a certain lassitude leads me into the course of my ordinary life. And just as a captive who in sleep enjoys an imaginary liberty, when he begins to suspect that his liberty is but a dream, fears to awaken, and conspires with these agree- able illusions that the deception may be prolonged, so insensibly of my own accord I fall back into my former opinions, and I dread awakening from this slumber, lest the laborious wakefulness which would follow the tranquillity of this repose should have to be spent not in daylight, but in the excessive darkness of the difficulties which have just been discussed.

Meditation II · *Of the Nature of the Human Mind; and that it is more easily known than the Body.*

The Meditation of yesterday filled my mind with so many doubts that it is no longer in my power to forget them. And yet I do not see in what manner I can resolve them; and, just as if I had all of a sudden fallen into very deep water, I am so disconcerted that I can neither make certain of setting my feet on the bottom, nor can I swim and so support myself on the surface. I shall nevertheless make an effort and follow anew the same path as that on which I yesterday entered, i.e. I shall proceed by setting aside all that in which the least doubt could be supposed to exist, just as if I had discovered that it was absolutely false; and I shall ever follow in this road until I have met with something which is certain, or at least, if I can do nothing else, until I have learned for certain that there is nothing in the world that is certain. Archimedes, in order that he might draw the terrestrial globe out of its place, and transport it elsewhere, demanded only that one point should be fixed and immoveable; in the same way I shall have the right to conceive high hopes if I am happy enough to discover one thing only which is certain and indubitable.

I suppose, then, that all the things that I see are false; I persuade myself that nothing has ever existed of all that my fallacious memory represents to me. I consider that I possess no senses; I imagine that body, figure, extension, movement and place are but the fictions of my mind. What, then, can be esteemed as true? Perhaps nothing at all, unless that there is nothing in the world that is certain.

But how can I know there is not something different from those things that I have just considered, of which one cannot have the slightest doubt? Is there not some God, or some other being by whatever name we call it, who puts these reflections into my mind? That is not necessary, for is it not possible that I am capable of producing them myself? I myself, am I not at least something? But I have already denied that I had senses and body. Yet I hesitate, for what follows from that? Am I so dependent on body and senses that I cannot exist without these? But I was persuaded that there was nothing in all the world, that there was no heaven, no earth, that there were no minds, nor any bodies: was I not then likewise persuaded that I did not exist? Not at all; of a surety I myself did exist since I persuaded myself of something [or merely because I thought of something]. But there is some deceiver or other, very powerful and very cunning, who ever employs his ingenuity in deceiving me. Then without doubt I exist also if he deceives me, and let him deceive me as much as he will, he can never cause me to be nothing so long as I think that I am something. So that after having reflected well and carefully examined all things, we must come to the definite conclusion that this proposition: I am, I exist, is necessarily true each time that I pronounce it, or that I mentally conceive it.

But I do not yet know clearly enough what I am, I who am certain that I am; and hence I must be careful to see that I do not imprudently take some other object in place of myself, and thus that I do not go astray in respect of this knowledge that I hold to be the most certain and most evident of all that I have formerly learned. That is why I shall now consider anew what I believed myself to be before I embarked upon these last reflections; and of my former opinions I shall withdraw all that might even in a small degree be invalidated by the reasons which I have just brought forward, in order that there may be nothing at all left beyond what is absolutely certain and indubitable.

What then did I formerly believe myself to be? Undoubtedly I believed myself to be a man. But what is a man? Shall I say a reasonable animal? Certainly not; for then I should have to inquire what an animal is, and what is reasonable; and thus from a single question I should insensibly fall into an infinitude of others more difficult; and I should not wish to waste the little time and leisure remaining to me in trying to unravel subtleties like these. But I shall rather stop here to consider the thoughts which of themselves spring up in my mind, and which were not inspired by anything beyond my own nature alone when I applied myself to the consideration of my being. In the first place, then, I considered myself as having a face, hands, arms, and all that system of members composed of bones and flesh as seen in a corpse which I designated by the name of body. In addition to this I considered that I was nourished, that I walked, that I felt, and that I thought, and I referred all these actions to the soul: but I did not stop to consider what the soul was, or if I did stop, I imagined that it was something extremely rare and subtle like a wind, a flame, or an ether, which was spread throughout my grosser parts. As to body I had no manner of doubt about its nature, but thought I had a very clear knowledge of it; and if I had desired to explain it according to the notions that I had then formed of it, I should have described it thus: By the body I understand all that which can be defined by a certain figure: something which can be confined in a certain place, and which can fill a given space in such a way that every other body will be excluded from it; which can be perceived either by touch, or by sight, or by hearing, or by taste, or by smell: which can be moved in many ways not, in truth, by itself, but by something which is foreign to it, by which it is touched [and from which it receives impressions]: for to have the power of self-movement, as also of feeling or of thinking, I did not consider to appertain to the nature of body: on the contrary, I was rather astonished to find that faculties similar to them existed in some bodies.

But what am I, now that I suppose that there is a certain genius which is extremely powerful, and, if I may say so, malicious, who employs all his powers in deceiving me? Can I affirm that I possess the least of all those things which I have just said pertain to the nature of body? I pause to consider, I revolve all these things in my mind, and I find none of which I can say that it pertains to me. It would be tedious to stop to enumerate them. Let us pass to the attributes of soul and see if there is any one which is in me? What of nutrition or walking [the first mentioned]? But if it is so that I have no body it is also true that I can neither walk nor take nourishment. Another attribute is sensation. But one cannot feel without body, and besides I have thought I perceived many things during sleep that I recognised in my waking moments as not having been experienced at all. What of thinking? I find here that thought is an attribute that belongs to me; it alone cannot be separated from me. I am, I exist, that is certain. But how often? Just when I think; for it might possibly be the case if I ceased entirely to think, that I should likewise cease altogether to exist. I do not now admit anything which is not necessarily true: to speak accurately I am not more than a thing which thinks, that is to say a mind or a soul, or an understanding, or a reason, which are terms whose significance was formerly unknown to me. I am, however, a real thing and really exist; but what thing? I have answered: a thing which thinks.

And what more? I shall exercise my imagination [in order to see if I am not something more]. I am not a collection of members which we call the human body: I am not a subtle air distributed through these members, I am not a wind, a fire, a vapour, a breath, nor anything at all which I can imagine or conceive; because I have assumed that all these were nothing. Without changing that supposition I find that I only leave myself certain of the fact that I am somewhat. But perhaps it is true that these same things which I supposed were non-existent because they are unknown to me, are really not different from the self which I know. I am not sure about this, I shall not dispute about it now; I can only give judgment on things that are known to me. I know that I exist, and I inquire what I am, I whom I know to exist. But it is very certain that the knowledge of my existence taken in its precise significance does not depend on things whose existence is not yet known to me; consequently it does not depend on those which I can feign in imagination. And indeed the very term *feign* in imagination [6] proves to me my error, for I really do this if I image myself a something, since to imagine is nothing else than to contemplate the figure or image of a corporeal thing. But I already know for certain that I am, and that it may be that all these images, and, speaking generally, all things that relate to the nature of body are nothing but dreams [and chimeras]. For this reason I see clearly that I have as little reason to say, 'I shall stimulate my imagination in order to know more distinctly what I am,' than if I were to say, 'I am now awake, and I perceive somewhat that is real and true: but because I do not yet perceive it distinctly enough, I shall go to sleep of express purpose, so that my dreams may represent the perception with greatest truth and evidence.' And, thus, I know for certain that nothing of all that I can understand by means of my imagination belongs to this knowledge which I have of myself, and that it is necessary to recall the mind from this mode of thought with the utmost diligence in order that it may be able to know its own nature with perfect distinctness.

But what then am I? A thing which thinks. What is a thing which thinks? It is a thing which doubts, understands, [conceives], affirms, denies, wills, refuses, which also imagines and feels.

Certainly it is no small matter if all these things pertain to my nature. But why should they not so pertain? Am I not that being who now doubts nearly everything, who nevertheless understands certain things, who affirms that one only is true, who denies all the others, who desires to know more, is averse from being deceived, who imagines many things, sometimes indeed despite his will, and who perceives many likewise, as by the intervention of the bodily organs? Is there nothing in all this which is as true as it is certain that I exist, even though I should always sleep and though he who has given me being employed all his ingenuity in deceiving me? Is there likewise any one of these attributes which can be distinguished from my thought, or which might be said to be separated from myself? For it is so evident of itself that it is I who doubts, who understands, and who desires, that there is no reason here to add anything to explain it. And I have certainly the power of imagining likewise; for although it may happen (as I formerly supposed) that none of the things which I imagine are true, neverthe-

---

[6] Or 'form an image' (effingo).

less this power of imagining does not cease to be really in use, and it forms part of my thought. Finally, I am the same who feels, that is to say, who perceives certain things, as by the organs of sense, since in truth I see light, I hear noise, I feel heat. But it will be said that these phenomena are false and that I am dreaming. Let it be so; still it is at least quite certain that it seems to me that I see light, that I hear noise and that I feel heat. That cannot be false; properly speaking it is what is in me called feeling[7]; and used in this precise sense that is no other thing than thinking.

From this time I begin to know what I am with a little more clearness and distinction than before; but nevertheless it still seems to me, and I cannot prevent myself from thinking, that corporeal things, whose images are framed by thought, which are tested by the senses, are much more distinctly known than that obscure part of me which does not come under the imagination. Although really it is very strange to say that I know and understand more distinctly these things whose existence seems to me dubious, which are unknown to me, and which do not belong to me, than others of the truth of which I am convinced, which are known to me and which pertain to my real nature, in a word, than myself. But I see clearly how the case stands: my mind loves to wander, and cannot yet suffer itself to be retained within the just limits of truth. Very good, let us once more give it the freest rein, so that, when afterwards we seize the proper occasion for pulling up, it may the more easily be regulated and controlled.

Let us begin by considering the commonest matters, those which we believe to be the most distinctly comprehended, to wit, the bodies which we touch and see; not indeed bodies in general, for these general ideas are usually a little more confused, but let us consider one body in particular. Let us take, for example, this piece of wax: it has been taken quite freshly from the hive, and it has not yet lost the sweetness of the honey which it contains; it still retains somewhat of the odour of the flowers from which it has been culled; its colour, its figure, its size are apparent; it is hard, cold, easily handled, and if you strike it with the finger, it will emit a sound. Finally all the things which are requisite to cause us distinctly to recognise a body, are met with in it. But notice that while I speak and approach the fire what remained of the taste is exhaled, the smell evaporates, the colour alters, the figure is destroyed, the size increases, it becomes liquid, it heats, scarcely can one handle it, and when one strikes it, no sound is emitted. Does the same wax remain after this change? We must confess that it remains; none would judge otherwise. What then did I know so distinctly in

---

[7] Sentire.

this piece of wax? It could certainly be nothing of all that the senses brought to my notice, since all these things which fall under taste, smell, sight, touch, and hearing, are found to be changed, and yet the same wax remains.

Perhaps it was what I now think, viz. that this wax was not that sweetness of honey, nor that agreeable scent of flowers, nor that particular whiteness, nor that figure, nor that sound, but simply a body which a little while before appeared to me as perceptible under these forms, and which is now perceptible under others. But what, precisely, is it that I imagine when I form such conceptions? Let us attentively consider this, and, abstracting from all that does not belong to the wax, let us see what remains. Certainly nothing remains excepting a certain extended thing which is flexible and movable. But what is the meaning of flexible and movable? Is it not that I imagine that this piece of wax being round is capable of becoming square and of passing from a square to a triangular figure? No, certainly it is not that, since I imagine it admits of an infinitude of similar changes, and I nevertheless do not know how to compass the infinitude by my imagination, and consequently this conception which I have of the wax is not brought about by the faculty of imagination. What now is this extension? Is it not also unknown? For it becomes greater when the wax is melted, greater when it is boiled, and greater still when the heat increases; and I should not conceive [clearly] according to truth what wax is, if I did not think that even this piece that we are considering is capable of receiving more variations in extension than I have ever imagined. We must then grant that I could not even understand through the imagination what this piece of wax is, and that it is my mind [8] alone which perceives it. I say this piece of wax in particular, for as to wax in general it is yet clearer. But what is this piece of wax which cannot be understood excepting by the [understanding or] mind? It is certainly the same that I see, touch, imagine, and finally it is the same which I have always believed it to be from the beginning. But what must particularly be observed is that its perception is neither an act of vision, nor of touch, nor of imagination, and has never been such although it may have appeared formerly to be so, but only an intuition [9] of the mind, which may be imperfect and confused as it was formerly, or clear and distinct as it is at present, according as my attention is more or less directed to the elements which are found in it, and of which it is composed.

Yet in the meantime I am greatly astonished when I consider [the great feebleness of mind] and its proneness to fall [insensibly]

---

[8] entendement F., mens L.
[9] inspectio.

into error; for although without giving expression to my thoughts I consider all this in my own mind, words often impede me and I am almost deceived by the terms of ordinary language. For we say that we see the same wax, if it is present, and not that we simply judge that it is the same from its having the same colour and figure. From this I should conclude that I knew the wax by means of vision and not simply by the intuition of the mind; unless by chance I remember that, when looking from a window and saying I see men who pass in the street, I really do not see them, but infer that what I see is men, just as I say that I see wax. And yet what do I see from the window but hats and coats which may cover automatic machines? Yet I judge these to be men. And similarly solely by the faculty of judgment which rests in my mind, I comprehend that which I believed I saw with my eyes.

A man who makes it his aim to raise his knowledge above the common should be ashamed to derive the occasion for doubting from the forms of speech invented by the vulgar; I prefer to pass on and consider whether I had a more evident and perfect conception of what the wax was when I first perceived it, and when I believed I knew it by means of the external senses or at least by the common sense [1] as it is called, that is to say by the imaginative faculty, or whether my present conception is clearer now that I have most carefully examined what it is, and in what way it can be known. It would certainly be absurd to doubt as to this. For what was there in this first perception which was distinct? What was there which might not as well have been perceived by any of the animals? But when I distinguish the wax from its external forms, and when, just as if I had taken from it its vestments, I consider it quite naked, it is certain that although some error may still be found in my judgment, I can nevertheless not perceive it thus without a human mind.

But finally what shall I say of this mind, that is, of myself, for up to this point I do not admit in myself anything but mind? What then, I who seem to perceive this piece of wax so distinctly, do I not know myself, not only with much more truth and certainty, but also with much more distinctness and clearness? For if I judge that the wax is or exists from the fact that I see it, it certainly follows much more clearly that I am or that I exist myself from the fact that I see it. For it may be that what I see is not really wax, it may also be that I do not possess eyes with which to see anything; but it cannot be that when I see, or (for I no longer take account of the distinction) when I think I see, that I myself who think am nought. So if I judge that the wax exists from the fact that I touch it, the same thing will follow, to wit, that

---

[1] sensus communis.

I am; and if I judge that my imagination, or some other cause, whatever it is, persuades me that the wax exists, I shall still conclude the same. And what I have here remarked of wax may be applied to all other things which are external to me [and which are met with outside of me]. And further, if the [notion or] perception of wax has seemed to me clearer and more distinct, not only after the sight or the touch, but also after many other causes have rendered it quite manifest to me, with how much more [evidence] and distinctness must it be said that I now know myself, since all the reasons which contribute to the knowledge of wax, or any other body whatever, are yet better proofs of the nature of my mind! And there are so many other things in the mind itself which may contribute to the elucidation of its nature, that those which depend on body such as these just mentioned, hardly merit being taken into account.

But finally here I am, having insensibly reverted to the point I desired, for, since it is now manifest to me that even bodies are not properly speaking known by the senses or by the faculty of imagination, but by the understanding only, and since they are not known from the fact that they are seen or touched, but only because they are understood, I see clearly that there is nothing which is easier for me to know than my mind. But because it is difficult to rid oneself so promptly of an opinion to which one was accustomed for so long, it will be well that I should halt a little at this point, so that by the length of my meditation I may more deeply imprint on my memory this new knowledge.

MEDITATION III · *Of God: that He exists.*

I shall now close my eyes, I shall stop my ears, I shall call away all my senses, I shall efface even from my thoughts all the images of corporeal things, or at least (for that is hardly possible) I shall esteem them as vain and false; and thus holding converse only with myself and considering my own nature, I shall try little by little to reach a better knowledge of and a more familiar acquaintanceship with myself. I am a thing that thinks, that is to say, that doubts, affirms, denies, that knows a few things, that is ignorant of many [that loves, that hates], that wills, that desires, that also imagines and perceives; for as I remarked before, although the things which I perceive and imagine are perhaps nothing at all apart from me and in themselves, I am nevertheless assured that these modes of thought that I call perceptions and imaginations, inasmuch only as they are modes of thought, certainly reside [and are met with] in me.

And in the little that I have just said, I think I have summed up all that I really know, or at least all that hitherto I was aware that I knew. In order to try to extend my knowledge further, I shall now look around more carefully and see whether I cannot still discover in myself some other things which I have not hitherto perceived. I am certain that I am a thing which thinks; but do I not then likewise know what is requisite to render me certain of a truth? Certainly in this first knowledge there is nothing that assures me of its truth, excepting the clear and distinct perception of that which I state, which would not indeed suffice to assure me that what I say is true, if it could ever happen that a thing which I conceived so clearly and distinctly could be false; and accordingly it seems to me that already I can establish as a general rule that all things which I perceive [2] very clearly and very distinctly are true.

At the same time I have before received and admitted many things to be very certain and manifest, which yet I afterwards recognised as being dubious. What then were these things? They were the earth, sky, stars and all other objects which I apprehended by means of the senses. But what did I clearly [and distinctly] perceive in them? Nothing more than that the ideas or thoughts of these things were presented to my mind. And not even now do I deny that these ideas are met with in me. But there was yet another thing which I affirmed, and which, owing to the habit which I had formed of believing it, I thought I perceived very clearly, although in truth I did not perceive it at all, to wit, that there were objects outside of me from which these ideas proceeded, and to which they were entirely similar. And it was in this that I erred, or, if perchance my judgment was correct, this was not due to any knowledge arising from my perception.

But when I took anything very simple and easy in the sphere of arithmetic or geometry into consideration, e.g. that two and three together made five, and other things of the sort, were not these present to my mind so clearly as to enable me to affirm that they were true? Certainly if I judged that since such matters could be doubted, this would not have been so for any other reason than that it came into my mind that perhaps a God might have endowed me with such a nature that I may have been deceived even concerning things which seemed to me most manifest. But every time that this preconceived opinion of the sovereign power of a God presents itself to my thought,

---

[2] Percipio, F. nous concevons.

I am constrained to confess that it is easy to Him, if He wishes it, to cause me to err, even in matters in which I believe myself to have the best evidence. And, on the other hand, always when I direct my attention to things which I believe myself to perceive very clearly, I am so persuaded of their truth that I let myself break out into words such as these: Let who will deceive me, He can never cause me to be nothing while I think that I am, or some day cause it to be true to say that I have never been, it being true now to say that I am, or that two and three make more or less than five, or any such thing in which I see a manifest contradiction. And, certainly, since I have no reason to believe that there is a God who is a deceiver, and as I have not yet satisfied myself that there is a God at all, the reason for doubt which depends on this opinion alone is very slight, and so to speak metaphysical. But in order to be able altogether to remove it, I must inquire whether there is a God as soon as the occasion presents itself; and if I find that there is a God, I must also inquire whether He may be a deceiver; for without a knowledge of these two truths I do not see that I can ever be certain of anything.

And in order that I may have an opportunity of inquiring into this in an orderly way [without interrupting the order of meditation which I have proposed to myself, and which is little by little to pass from the notions which I find first of all in my mind to those which I shall later on discover in it] it is requisite that I should here divide my thoughts into certain kinds, and that I should consider in which of these kinds there is, properly speaking, truth or error to be found. Of my thoughts some are, so to speak, images of the things, and to these alone is the title 'idea' properly applied; examples are my thought of a man or of a chimera, of heaven, of an angel, or [even] of God. But other thoughts possess other forms as well. For example in willing, fearing, approving, denying, though I always perceive something as the subject of the action of my mind [3], yet by this action I always add something else to the idea [4] which I have of that thing; and of the thoughts of this kind some are called volitions or affections, and others judgments.

Now as to what concerns ideas, if we consider them only in themselves and do not relate them to anything else beyond themselves, they cannot properly speaking be false; for whether I imagine a goat or a chimera, it is not less true that I imagine the one than the other. We must not fear likewise that falsity can enter into will and into affections, for although I may desire evil things, or even things that never existed, it is not the less true that I desire them. Thus there remains no more

---

[3] The French version is followed here as being more explicit. In it 'action de mon esprit' replaces 'mea cogitatio.'
[4] In the Latin version 'similitudinem.'

than the judgments which we make, in which I must take the greatest care not to deceive myself. But the principal error and the commonest which we may meet with in them, consists in my judging that the ideas which are in me are similar or conformable to the things which are outside me; for without doubt if I considered the ideas only as certain modes of my thoughts, without trying to relate them to anything beyond, they could scarcely give me material for error.

But among these ideas, some appear to me to be innate, some adventitious, and others to be formed [or invented] by myself; for, as I have the power of understanding what is called a thing, or a truth, or a thought, it appears to me that I hold this power from no other source than my own nature. But if I now hear some sound, if I see the sun, or feel heat, I have hitherto judged that these sensations proceeded from certain things that exist outside of me; and finally it appears to me that sirens, hippogryphs, and the like, are formed out of my own mind. But again I may possibly persuade myself that all these ideas are of the nature of those which I term adventitious, or else that they are all innate, or all fictitious: for I have not yet clearly discovered their true origin.

And my principal task in this place is to consider, in respect to those ideas which appear to me to proceed from certain objects that are outside me, what are the reasons which cause me to think them similar to these objects. It seems indeed in the first place that I am taught this lesson by nature; and, secondly, I experience in myself that these ideas do not depend on my will nor therefore on myself—for they often present themselves to my mind in spite of my will. Just now, for instance, whether I will or whether I do not will, I feel heat, and thus I persuade myself that this feeling, or at least this idea of heat, is produced in me by something which is different from me, i.e. by the heat of the fire near which I sit. And nothing seems to me more obvious than to judge that this object imprints its likeness rather than anything else upon me.

Now I must discover whether these proofs are sufficiently strong and convincing. When I say that I am so instructed by nature, I merely mean a certain spontaneous inclination which impels me to believe in this connection, and not a natural light which makes me recognise that it is true. But these two things are very different; for I cannot doubt that which the natural light causes me to believe to be true, as, for example, it has shown me that I am from the fact that I doubt, or other facts of the same kind. And I possess no other faculty whereby to distinguish truth from falsehood, which can teach me that what this light shows me to be true is not really true, and no other faculty that is equally trustworthy. But as far as [apparently] natural impulses are concerned, I have frequently remarked, when I had to make active choice between virtue and vice, that they often enough led me to the part that was worse; and this is why I do not see any reason for following them in what regards truth and error.

And as to the other reason, which is that these ideas must proceed from objects outside me, since they do not depend on my will, I do not find it any the more convincing. For just as these impulses of which I have spoken are found in me, notwithstanding that they do not always concur with my will, so perhaps there is in me some faculty fitted to produce these ideas without the assistance of any external things, even though it is not yet known by me; just as, apparently, they have hitherto always been found in me during sleep without the aid of any external objects.

And finally, though they did proceed from objects different from myself, it is not a necessary consequence that they should resemble these. On the contrary, I have noticed that in many cases there was a great difference between the object and its idea. I find, for example, two completely diverse ideas of the sun in my mind; the one derives its origin from the senses, and should be placed in the category of adventitious ideas; according to this idea the sun seems to be extremely small; but the other is derived from astronomical reasonings, i.e. is elicited from certain notions that are innate in me, or else it is formed by me in some other manner; in accordance with it the sun appears to be several times greater than the earth. These two ideas cannot, indeed, both resemble the same sun, and reason makes me believe that the one which seems to have originated directly from the sun itself, is the one which is most dissimilar to it.

All this causes me to believe that until the present time it has not been by a judgment that was certain [or premeditated], but only by a sort of blind impulse that I believed that things existed outside of, and different from me, which, by the organs of my senses, or by some other method whatever it might be, conveyed these ideas or images to me [and imprinted on me their similitudes].

But there is yet another method of inquiring whether any of the objects of which I have ideas within me exist outside of me. If ideas are only taken as certain modes of thought, I recognise amongst them no difference or inequality, and all appear to proceed from me in the same manner; but when we consider them as images, one representing one thing and the other another, it is clear that they are very different one from the other. There is no doubt that those which represent to me substances are something more, and contain so to speak more objective reality within them [that is to say, by representation participate in a higher degree of being or perfection] than those that simply

represent modes or accidents; and that idea again by which I understand a supreme God, eternal, infinite, [immutable], omniscient, omnipotent, and Creator of all things which are outside of Himself, has
certainly more objective reality in itself than those ideas by which finite
substances are represented.

Now it is manifest by the natural light that there must at least be
as much reality in the efficient and total cause as in its effect. For,
pray, whence can the effect derive its reality, if not from its cause? And
in what way can this cause communicate this reality to it, unless it
possessed it in itself? And from this it follows, not only that something
cannot proceed from nothing, but likewise that what is more perfect—
that is to say, which has more reality within itself—cannot proceed
from the less perfect. And this is not only evidently true of those effects
which possess actual or formal reality, but also of the ideas in which we
consider merely what is termed objective reality. To take an example,
the stone which has not yet existed not only cannot now commence
to be unless it has been produced by something which possesses within
itself, either formally or eminently, all that enters into the composition
of the stone [i.e. it must possess the same things or other more excellent things than those which exist in the stone] and heat can only
be produced in a subject in which it did not previously exist by a
cause that is of an order [degree or kind] at least as perfect as heat,
and so in all other cases. But further, the idea of heat, or of a stone,
cannot exist in me unless it has been placed within me by some cause
which possesses within it at least as much reality as that which I conceive to exist in the heat or the stone. For although this cause does not
transmit anything of its actual or formal reality to my idea, we must
not for that reason imagine that it is necessarily a less real cause; we
must remember that [since every idea is a work of the mind] its nature
is such that it demands of itself no other formal reality than that which
it borrows from my thought, of which it is only a mode [i.e. a manner
or way of thinking]. But in order that an idea should contain some one
certain objective reality rather than another, it must without doubt
derive it from some cause in which there is at least as much formal
reality as this idea contains of objective reality. For if we imagine that
something is found in an idea which is not found in the cause, it must
then have been derived from nought; but however imperfect may
be this mode of being by which a thing is objectively [or by representa-
tion] in the understanding by its idea, we cannot certainly say that this
mode of being is nothing, nor, consequently, that the idea derives its
origin from nothing.

Nor must I imagine that, since the reality that I consider in these
ideas is only objective, it is not essential that this reality should be

formally in the causes of my ideas, but that it is sufficient that it should be found objectively. For just as this mode of objective existence pertains to ideas by their proper nature, so does the mode of formal existence pertain to the causes of those ideas (this is at least true of the first and principal) by the nature peculiar to them. And although it may be the case that one idea gives birth to another idea, that cannot continue to be so indefinitely; for in the end we must reach an idea whose cause shall be so to speak an archetype, in which the whole reality [or perfection] which is so to speak objectively [or by representation] in these ideas is contained formally [and really]. Thus the light of nature causes me to know clearly that the ideas in me are like [pictures or] images which can, in truth, easily fall short of the perfection of the objects from which they have been derived, but which can never contain anything greater or more perfect.

And the longer and the more carefully that I investigate these matters, the more clearly and distinctly do I recognise their truth. But what am I to conclude from it all in the end? It is this, that if the objective reality of any one of my ideas is of such a nature as clearly to make me recognise that it is not in me either formally or eminently, and that consequently I cannot myself be the cause of it, it follows of necessity that I am not alone in the world, but that there is another being which exists, or which is the cause of this idea. On the other hand, had no such an idea existed in me, I should have had no sufficient argument to convince me of the existence of any being beyond myself; for I have made very careful investigation everywhere and up to the present time have been able to find no other ground.

But of my ideas, beyond that which represents me to myself, as to which there can here be no difficulty, there is another which represents a God, and there are others representing corporeal and inanimate things, others angels, others animals, and others again which represent to me men similar to myself.

As regards the ideas which represent to me other men or animals, or angels, I can however easily conceive that they might be formed by an admixture of the other ideas which I have of myself, of corporeal things, and of God, even although there were apart from me neither men nor animals, nor angels, in all the world.

And in regard to the ideas of corporeal objects, I do not recognise in them anything so great or so excellent that they might not have possibly proceeded from myself; for if I consider them more closely, and examine them individually, as I yesterday examined the idea of wax, I find that there is very little in them which I perceive clearly and distinctly. Magnitude or extension in length, breadth, or depth, I do so perceive; also figure which results from a termination of this

extension, the situation which bodies of different figure preserve in relation to one another, and movement or change of situation; to which
we may also add substance, duration and number. As to other things
such as light, colours, sounds, scents, tastes, heat, cold and the other
tactile qualities, they are thought by me with so much obscurity and
confusion that I do not even know if they are true or false, i.e. whether
the ideas which I form of these qualities are actually the ideas of real
objects or not [or whether they only represent chimeras which cannot
exist in fact]. For although I have before remarked that it is only in
judgments that falsity, properly speaking, or formal falsity, can be met
with, a certain material falsity may nevertheless be found in ideas, i.e.
when these ideas represent what is nothing as though it were something.
For example, the ideas which I have of cold and heat are so far from
clear and distinct that by their means I cannot tell whether cold is
merely a privation of heat, or heat a privation of cold, or whether both
are real qualities, or are not such. And inasmuch as [since ideas resemble images] there cannot be any ideas which do not appear to represent some things, if it is correct to say that cold is merely a privation
of heat, the idea which represents it to me as something real and positive will not be improperly termed false, and the same holds good of
other similar ideas.

To these it is certainly not necessary that I should attribute any
author other than myself. For if they are false, i.e. if they represent
things which do not exist, the light of nature shows me that they issue from nought, that is to say, that they are only in me in so far as
something is lacking to the perfection of my nature. But if they are
true, nevertheless because they exhibit so little reality to me that I cannot even clearly distinguish the thing represented from non-being, I
do not see any reason why they should not be produced by myself.

As to the clear and distinct idea which I have of corporeal things,
some of them seem as though I might have derived them from the idea
which I possess of myself, as those which I have of substance, duration,
number, and such like. For [even] when I think that a stone is a substance, or at least a thing capable of existing of itself, and that I am
a substance also, although I conceive that I am a thing that thinks and
not one that is extended, and that the stone on the other hand is an
extended thing which does not think, and that thus there is a notable
difference between the two conceptions—they seem, nevertheless, to
agree in this, that both represent substances. In the same way, when
I perceive that I now exist and further recollect that I have in former
times existed, and when I remember that I have various thoughts of
which I can recognise the number, I acquire ideas of duration and number which I can afterwards transfer to any object that I please. But

as to all the other qualities of which the ideas of corporeal things are composed, to wit, extension, figure, situation and motion, it is true that they are not formally in me, since I am only a thing that thinks; but because they are merely certain modes of substance [and so to speak the vestments under which corporeal substance appears to us] and because I myself am also a substance, it would seem that they might be contained in me eminently.

Hence there remains only the idea of God, concerning which we must consider whether it is something which cannot have proceeded from me myself. By the name God I understand a substance that is infinite [eternal, immutable], independent, all-knowing, all-powerful, and by which I myself and everything else, if anything else does exist, have been created. Now all these characteristics are such that the more diligently I attend to them, the less do they appear capable of proceeding from me alone; hence, from what has been already said, we must conclude that God necessarily exists.

For although the idea of substance is within me owing to the fact that I am substance, nevertheless I should not have the idea of an infinite substance—since I am finite—if it had not proceeded from some substance which was veritably infinite.

Nor should I imagine that I do not perceive the infinite by a true idea, but only by the negation of the finite, just as I perceive repose and darkness by the negation of movement and of light; for, on the contrary, I see that there is manifestly more reality in infinite substance than in finite, and therefore that in some way I have in me the notion of the infinite earlier than the finite—to wit, the notion of God before that of myself. For how would it be possible that I should know that I doubt and desire, that is to say, that something is lacking to me, and that I am not quite perfect, unless I had within me some idea of a Being more perfect than myself, in comparison with which I should recognise the deficiencies of my nature?

And we cannot say that this idea of God is perhaps materially false and that consequently I can derive it from nought [i.e. that possibly it exists in me because I am imperfect], as I have just said is the case with ideas of heat, cold and other such things; for, on the contrary, as this idea is very clear and distinct and contains within it more objective reality than any other, there can be none which is of itself more true, nor any in which there can be less suspicion of falsehood. The idea, I say, of this Being who is absolutely perfect and infinite, is entirely true; for although, perhaps, we can imagine that such a Being does not exist, we cannot nevertheless imagine that His idea represents nothing real to me, as I have said of the idea of cold. This idea is also very clear and distinct; since all that I conceive clearly and distinctly of the real and the true, and of what conveys some perfection, is in its entirety contained in this idea. And this does not cease to be true although I do not comprehend the infinite, or though in God there is an infinitude of things which I cannot comprehend, nor possibly even reach in any way by thought; for it is of the nature of the infinite that my nature, which is finite and limited, should not comprehend it; and it is sufficient that I should understand this, and that I should judge that all things which I clearly perceive and in which I know that there is some perfection, and possibly likewise an infinitude of properties of which I am ignorant, are in God formally or eminently, so that the idea which I have of Him may become the most true, most clear, and most distinct of all the ideas that are in my mind.

But possibly I am something more than I suppose myself to be, and perhaps all those perfections which I attribute to God are in some way potentially in me, although they do not yet disclose themselves, or issue in action. As a matter of fact I am already sensible that my knowledge increases [and perfects itself] little by little, and I see nothing which can prevent it from increasing more and more into infinitude; nor do I see, after it has thus been increased [or perfected], anything to prevent my being able to acquire by its means all the other perfections of the Divine nature; nor finally why the power I have of acquiring these perfections, if it really exists in me, shall not suffice to produce the ideas of them.

At the same time I recognise that this cannot be. For, in the first place, although it were true that every day my knowledge acquired new degrees of perfection, and that there were in my nature many things potentially which are not yet there actually, nevertheless these excellences do not pertain to [or make the smallest approach to] the idea which I have of God in whom there is nothing merely potential [but in whom all is present really and actually]; for it is an infallible token of imperfection in my knowledge that it increases little by little. And further, although my knowledge grows more and more, nevertheless I do not for that reason believe that it can ever be actually infinite, since it can never reach a point so high that it will be unable to attain to any greater increase. But I understand God to be actually infinite, so that He can add nothing to His supreme perfection. And finally I perceive that the objective being of an idea cannot be produced by a being that exists potentially only, which properly speaking is nothing, but only by a being which is formal or actual.

To speak the truth, I see nothing in all that I have just said which by the light of nature is not manifest to anyone who desires to think attentively on the subject; but when I slightly relax my attention, my mind, finding its vision somewhat obscured and so to speak blinded by the images of sensible objects, I do not easily recollect the reason why the idea that I possess of a being more perfect than I, must necessarily have been placed in me by a being which is really more perfect; and this is why I wish here to go on to inquire whether I, who have this idea, can exist if no such being exists.

And I ask, from whom do I then derive my existence? Perhaps from myself or from my parents, or from some other source less perfect than God; for we can imagine nothing more perfect than God, or even as perfect as He is.

But [were I independent of every other and] were I myself the author of my being, I should doubt nothing and I should desire nothing, and finally no perfection would be lacking to me; for I should have bestowed on myself every perfection of which I possessed any idea and should thus be God. And it must not be imagined that those things that are lacking to me are perhaps more difficult of attainment than those which I already possess; for, on the contrary, it is quite evident that it was a matter of much greater difficulty to bring to pass that I, that is to say, a thing or a substance that thinks, should emerge out of nothing, than it would be to attain to the knowledge of many things of which I am ignorant, and which are only the accidents of this thinking substance. But it is clear that if I had of myself possessed this greater perfection of which I have just spoken [that is to say, if I had been the author of my own existence], I should not at least have denied myself the things which are the more easy to acquire [to wit, many branches of knowledge of which my nature is destitute]; nor should I have deprived myself of any of the things contained in the idea which I form of God, because there are none of them which seem to me specially difficult to acquire: and if there were any that were more difficult to acquire, they would certainly appear to me to be such (supposing I myself were the origin of the other things which I possess) since I should discover in them that my powers were limited.

But though I assume that perhaps I have always existed just as I am at present, neither can I escape the force of this reasoning, and imagine that the conclusion to be drawn from this is, that I need not seek for any author of my existence. For all the course of my life may be divided into an infinite number of parts, none of which is in any way dependent on the other; and thus from the fact that I was in existence a short time ago it does not follow that I must be in existence now, unless some cause at this instant, so to speak, produces me anew, that is to say, conserves me. It is as a matter of fact perfectly clear and evident to all those who consider with attention the nature of time, that, in order to be conserved in each moment in which it endures, a substance has need of the same power and action as would be necessary to produce and create it anew, supposing it did not yet exist, so that the light of nature shows us clearly that the distinction between creation and conservation is solely a distinction of the reason.

All that I thus require here is that I should interrogate myself, if I wish to know whether I possess a power which is capable of bringing it to pass that I who now am shall still be in the future; for since I am nothing but a thinking thing, or at least since thus far it is only this portion of myself which is precisely in question at present, if such a power did reside in me, I should certainly be conscious of it. But I am conscious of nothing of the kind, and by this I know clearly that I depend on some being different from myself.

Possibly, however, this being on which I depend is not that which I call God, and I am created either by my parents or by some other cause less perfect than God. This cannot be, because, as I have just said, it is perfectly evident that there must be at least as much reality in the cause as in the effect; and thus since I am a thinking thing, and possess an idea of God within me, whatever in the end be the cause assigned to my existence, it must be allowed that it is likewise a thinking thing and that it possesses in itself the idea of all the perfections which I attribute to God. We may again inquire whether this cause derives its origin from itself or from some other thing. For if from itself, it follows by the reasons before brought forward, that this cause must itself be God; for since it possesses the virtue of self-existence, it must also without doubt have the power of actually possessing all the perfections of which it has the idea, that is, all those which I conceive as existing in God. But if it derives its existence from some other cause than itself, we shall again ask, for the same reason, whether this second cause exists by itself or through another, until from one step to another, we finally arrive at an ultimate cause, which will be God.

And it is perfectly manifest that in this there can be no regression into infinity, since what is in question is not so much the cause which formerly created me, as that which conserves me at the present time.

Nor can we suppose that several causes may have concurred in my production, and that from one I have received the idea of one of the perfections which I attribute to God, and from another the idea of some other, so that all these perfections indeed exist somewhere in the universe, but not as complete in one unity which is God. On the contrary, the unity, the simplicity or the inseparability of all things which are in God is one of the principal perfections which I conceive to be in Him. And certainly the idea of this unity of all Divine perfections cannot have been placed in me by any cause from which I have not likewise received the ideas of all the other perfections; for this cause could not make me able to comprehend them as joined together in an inseparable unity without having at the same time caused me in some measure to know what they are [and in some way to recognise each one of them].

Finally, so far as my parents [from whom it appears I have sprung] are concerned, although all that I have ever been able to believe of them were true, that does not make it follow that it is they who conserve me, nor are they even the authors of my being in any sense, in so far as I am a thinking being; since what they did was merely to implant certain dispositions in that matter in which the self—i.e. the mind, which alone I at present identify with myself—is by me deemed to exist. And thus there can be no difficulty in their regard, but we must of necessity conclude from the fact alone that I exist, or that the idea of a Being supremely perfect—that is of God—is in me, that the proof of God's existence is grounded on the highest evidence.

It only remains to me to examine into the manner in which I have acquired this idea from God; for I have not received it through the senses, and it is never presented to me unexpectedly, as is usual with the ideas of sensible things when these things present themselves, or seem to present themselves, to the external organs of my senses; nor is it likewise a fiction of my mind, for it is not in my power to take from or to add anything to it; and consequently the only alternative is that it is innate in me, just as the idea of myself is innate in me.

And one certainly ought not to find it strange that God, in creating me, placed this idea within me to be like the mark of the workman imprinted on his work; and it is likewise not essential that the mark shall be something different from the work itself. For from the sole fact that God created me it is most probable that in some way he has placed his image and similitude upon me, and that I perceive this similitude (in which the idea of God is contained) by means of the same faculty by which I perceive myself—that is to say, when I reflect on myself I not only know that I am something [imperfect], incomplete and dependent on another, which incessantly aspires after something which is better and greater than myself, but I also know that He on whom I depend possesses in Himself all the great things towards which I aspire [and the ideas of which I find within myself], and that not indefinitely or potentially alone, but really, actually and infinitely; and that thus He is God. And the whole strength of the argument which I have here made use of to prove the existence of God consists in this, that I recognise that it is not possible that my nature should be what it is, and indeed that I should have in myself the idea of a God, if God did not veritably exist—a God, I say, whose idea is in me, i.e. who possesses all those supreme perfections of which our mind may indeed have some idea but without understanding them all, who is liable to no errors or defect [and who has none of all those marks which denote imperfection]. From this it is manifest that He cannot be a deceiver, since the light of nature teaches us that fraud and deception necessarily proceed from some defect.

But before I examine this matter with more care, and pass on to the consideration of other truths which may be derived from it, it seems to me right to pause for a while in order to contemplate God Himself, to ponder at leisure His marvellous attributes, to consider, and admire, and adore, the beauty of this light so resplendent, at least as far as the strength of my mind, which is in some measure dazzled by the sight, will allow me to do so. For just as faith teaches us that the supreme felicity of the other life consists only in this contemplation of the Divine Majesty, so we continue to learn by experience that a similar meditation, though incomparably less perfect, causes us to enjoy the greatest satisfaction of which we are capable in this life.

MEDITATION IV · Of the True and the False.

I have been well accustomed these past days to detach my mind from my senses, and I have accurately observed that there are very few things that one knows with certainty respecting corporeal objects, that there are many more which are known to us respecting the human mind, and yet more still regarding God Himself; so that I shall now without any difficulty abstract my thoughts from the consideration of [sensible or] imaginable objects, and carry them to those which, being withdrawn from all contact with matter, are purely intelligible. And certainly the idea which I possess of the human mind inasmuch as it is a thinking thing, and not extended in length, width and depth, nor participating in anything pertaining to body, is incomparably more distinct than is the idea of any corporeal thing. And when I consider that I doubt, that is to say, that I am an incomplete and dependent being, the idea of a being that is complete and independent, that is of God, presents itself to my mind with so much distinctness and clearness —and from the fact alone that this idea is found in me, or that I who possess this idea exist, I conclude so certainly that God exists, and that my existence depends entirely on Him in every moment of my life— that I do not think that the human mind is capable of knowing anything with more evidence and certitude. And it seems to me that I now have before me a road which will lead us from the contemplation of the true God (in whom all the treasures of science and wisdom are contained) to the knowledge of the other objects of the universe.

For, first of all, I recognise it to be impossible that He should ever deceive me; for in all fraud and deception some imperfection is to be found, and although it may appear that the power of deception is a mark of subtility or power, yet the desire to deceive without doubt testifies to malice or feebleness, and accordingly cannot be found in God.

In the next place I experienced in myself a certain capacity for judging which I have doubtless received from God, like all the other things that I possess; and as He could not desire to deceive me, it is clear that He has not given me a faculty that will lead me to err if I use it aright.

And no doubt respecting this matter could remain, if it were not that the consequence would seem to follow that I can thus never be deceived; for if I hold all that I possess from God, and if He has not placed in me the capacity for error, it seems as though I could never fall into error. And it is true that when I think only of God [and direct my mind wholly to Him] [5], I discover [in myself] no cause of error, or falsity; yet directly afterwards, when recurring to myself, experience shows me that I am nevertheless subject to an infinitude of errors, as to which, when we come to investigate them more closely, I notice that not only is there a real and positive idea of God or of a Being of supreme perfection present to my mind, but also, so to speak, a certain negative idea of nothing, that is, of that which is infinitely removed from any kind of perfection; and that I am in a sense something intermediate between God and nought, i.e. placed in such a manner between the supreme Being and non-being, that there is in truth nothing in me that can lead to error in so far as a sovereign Being has formed me; but that, as I in some degree participate likewise in nought or in non-being, i.e. in so far as I am not myself the supreme Being, and as I find myself subject to an infinitude of imperfections, I ought not to be astonished if I should fall into error. Thus do I recognise that error, in so far as it is such, is not a real thing depending on God, but simply a defect; and therefore, in order to fall into it, that I have no need to possess a special faculty given me by God for this very purpose, but that I fall into error from the fact that the power given me by God for the purpose of distinguishing truth from error is not infinite.

Nevertheless this does not quite satisfy me; for error is not a pure negation [i.e. is not the simple defect or want of some perfection which ought not to be mine], but it is a lack of some knowledge which it seems that I ought to possess. And on considering the nature of God

---

[5] Not in the French version.

it does not appear to me possible that He should have given me a faculty which is not perfect of its kind, that is, which is wanting in some perfection due to it. For if it is true that the more skilful the artizan, the more perfect is the work of his hands, what can have been produced by this supreme Creator of all things that is not in all its parts perfect? And certainly there is no doubt that God could have created me so that I could never have been subject to error; it is also certain that He ever wills what is best; is it then better that I should be subject to err than that I should not?

In considering this more attentively, it occurs to me in the first place that I should not be astonished if my intelligence is not capable of comprehending why God acts as He does; and that there is thus no reason to doubt of His existence from the fact that I may perhaps find many other things besides this as to which I am able to understand neither for what reason nor how God has produced them. For, in the first place, knowing that my nature is extremely feeble and limited, and that the nature of God is on the contrary immense, incomprehensible, and infinite, I have no further difficulty in recognising that there is an infinitude of matters in His power, the causes of which transcend my knowledge; and this reason suffices to convince me that the species of cause termed final, finds no useful employment in physical [or natural] things; for it does not appear to me that I can without temerity seek to investigate the [inscrutable] ends of God.

It further occurs to me that we should not consider one single creature separately, when we inquire as to whether the works of God are perfect, but should regard all his creations together. For the same thing which might possibly seem very imperfect with some semblance of reason if regarded by itself, is found to be very perfect if regarded as part of the whole universe; and although, since I resolved to doubt all things, I as yet have only known certainly my own existence and that of God, nevertheless since I have recognised the infinite power of God, I cannot deny that He may have produced many other things, or at least that He has the power of producing them, so that I may obtain a place as a part of a great universe.

Whereupon, regarding myself more closely, and considering what are my errors (for they alone testify to there being any imperfection in me), I answer that they depend on a combination of two causes, to wit, on the faculty of knowledge that rests in me, and on the power of choice or of free will—that is to say, of the understanding and at the same time of the will. For by the understanding alone I [neither assert nor deny anything, but] apprehend [6] the ideas of things as to

---

[6] percipio.

which I can form a judgment. But no error is properly speaking found in it, provided the word error is taken in its proper signification; and though there is possibly an infinitude of things in the world of which I have no idea in my understanding, we cannot for all that say that it is deprived of these ideas [as we might say of something which is required by its nature], but simply it does not possess these; because in truth there is no reason to prove that God should have given me a greater faculty of knowledge than He has given me; and however skilful a workman I represent Him to be, I should not for all that consider that He was bound to have placed in each of His works all the perfections which He may have been able to place in some. I likewise cannot complain that God has not given me a free choice or a will which is sufficient, ample and perfect, since as a matter of fact I am conscious of a will so extended as to be subject to no limits. And what seems to me very remarkable in this regard is that of all the qualities which I possess there is no one so perfect and so comprehensive that I do not very clearly recognise that it might be yet greater and more perfect. For, to take an example, if I consider the faculty of comprehension which I possess, I find that it is of very small extent and extremely limited, and at the same time I find the idea of another faculty much more ample and even infinite, and seeing that I can form the idea of it, I recognise from this very fact that it pertains to the nature of God. If in the same way I examine the memory, the imagination, or some other faculty, I do not find any which is not small and circumscribed, while in God it is immense [or infinite]. It is free-will alone or liberty of choice which I find to be so great in me that I can conceive no other idea to be more great; it is indeed the case that it is for the most part this will that causes me to know that in some manner I bear the image and similitude of God. For although the power of will is incomparably greater in God than in me, both by reason of the knowledge and the power which, conjoined with it, render it stronger and more efficacious, and by reason of its object, inasmuch as in God it extends to a great many things; it nevertheless does not seem to me greater if I consider it formally and precisely in itself: for the faculty of will consists alone in our having the power of choosing to do a thing or choosing not to do it (that is, to affirm or deny, to pursue or to shun it), or rather it consists alone in the fact that in order to affirm or deny, pursue or shun those things placed before us by the understanding, we act so that we are unconscious that any outside force constrains us in doing so. For in order that I should be free it is not necessary that I should be indifferent as to the choice of one or the other of two contraries; but contrariwise the more I lean to the one—whether I recognise clearly that the reasons of the good and true are to be found in it, or whether God so disposes my inward thought—the more freely do I choose and embrace it. And undoubtedly both divine grace and natural knowledge, far from diminishing my liberty, rather increase it and strengthen it. Hence this indifference which I feel, when I am not swayed to one side rather than to the other by lack of reason, is the lowest grade of liberty, and rather evinces a lack or negation in knowledge than a perfection of will: for if I always recognised clearly what was true and good, I should never have trouble in deliberating as to what judgment or choice I should make, and then I should be entirely free without ever being indifferent.

From all this I recognise that the power of will which I have received from God is not of itself the source of my errors—for it is very ample and very perfect of its kind—any more than is the power of understanding; for since I understand nothing but by the power which God has given me for understanding, there is no doubt that all that I understand, I understand as I ought, and it is not possible that I err in this. Whence then come my errors? They come from the sole fact that since the will is much wider in its range and compass than the understanding, I do not restrain it within the same bounds, but extend it also to things which I do not understand: and as the will is of itself indifferent to these, it easily falls into error and sin, and chooses the evil for the good, or the false for the true.

For example, when I lately examined whether anything existed in the world, and found that from the very fact that I considered this question it followed very clearly that I myself existed, I could not prevent myself from believing that a thing I so clearly conceived was true: not that I found myself compelled to do so by some external cause, but simply because from great clearness in my mind there followed a great inclination of my will; and I believed this with so much the greater freedom or spontaneity as I possessed the less indifference towards it. Now, on the contrary, I not only know that I exist, inasmuch as I am a thinking thing, but a certain representation of corporeal nature is also presented to my mind; and it comes to pass that I doubt whether this thinking nature which is in me, or rather by which I am what I am, differs from this corporeal nature, or whether both are not simply the same thing; and I here suppose that I do not yet know any reason to persuade me to adopt the one belief rather than the other. From this it follows that I am entirely indifferent as to which of the two I affirm or deny, or even whether I abstain from forming any judgment in the matter.

And this indifference does not only extend to matters as to which the understanding has no knowledge, but also in general to all those which are not apprehended with perfect clearness at the moment when the will is deliberating upon them: for, however probable are the conjectures which render me disposed to form a judgment respecting anything, the simple knowledge that I have that those are conjectures alone and not certain and indubitable reasons, suffices to occasion me to judge the contrary. Of this I have had great experience of late when I set aside as false all that I had formerly held to be absolutely true, for the sole reason that I remarked that it might in some measure be doubted.

But if I abstain from giving my judgment on any thing when I do not perceive it with sufficient clearness and distinctness, it is plain that I act rightly and am not deceived. But if I determine to deny or affirm, I no longer make use as I should of my free will, and if I affirm what is not true, it is evident that I deceive myself; even though I judge according to truth, this comes about only by chance, and I do not escape the blame of misusing my freedom; for the light of nature teaches us that the knowledge of the understanding should always precede the determination of the will. And it is in the misuse of the free will that the privation which constitutes the characteristic nature of error is met with. Privation, I say, is found in the act, in so far as it proceeds from me, but it is not found in the faculty which I have received from God, nor even in the act in so far as it depends on Him.

For I have certainly no cause to complain that God has not given me an intelligence which is more powerful, or a natural light which is stronger than that which I have received from Him, since it is proper to the finite understanding not to comprehend a multitude of things, and it is proper to a created understanding to be finite; on the contrary, I have every reason to render thanks to God who owes me nothing and who has given me all the perfections I possess, and I should be far from charging Him with injustice, and with having deprived me of, or wrongfully withheld from me, these perfections which He has not bestowed upon me.

I have further no reason to complain that He has given me a will more ample than my understanding, for since the will consists only of one single element, and is so to speak indivisible, it appears that its nature is such that nothing can be abstracted from it [without destroying it]; and certainly the more comprehensive it is found to be, the more reason I have to render gratitude to the giver.

And, finally, I must also not complain that God concurs with me in forming the acts of the will, that is the judgment in which I go astray, because these acts are entirely true and good, inasmuch as they depend on God; and in a certain sense more perfection accrues to my nature from the fact that I can form them, than if I could not do so. As to the privation in which alone the formal reason of error or sin consists, it has no need of any concurrence from God, since it is not a thing [or an existence], and since it is not related to God as to a cause, but should be termed merely a negation [according to the significance given to these words in the Schools]. For in fact it is not an imperfection in God that He has given me the liberty to give or withhold my assent from certain things as to which He has not placed a clear and distinct knowledge in my understanding; but it is without doubt an imperfection in me not to make a good use of my freedom, and to give my judgment readily on matters which I only understand obscurely. I nevertheless perceive that God could easily have created me so that I never should err, although I still remained free, and endowed with a limited knowledge, viz. by giving to my understanding a clear and distinct intelligence of all things as to which I should ever have to deliberate; or simply by His engraving deeply in my memory the resolution never to form a judgment on anything without having a clear and distinct understanding of it, so that I could never forget it. And it is easy for me to understand that, in so far as I consider myself alone, and as if there were only myself in the world, I should have been much more perfect than I am, if God had created me so that I could never err. Nevertheless I cannot deny that in some sense it is a greater perfection in the whole universe that certain parts should not be exempt from error as others are than that all parts should be exactly similar. And I have no right to complain if God, having placed me in the world, has not called upon me to play a part that excels all others in distinction and perfection.

And further I have reason to be glad on the ground that if He has not given me the power of never going astray by the first means pointed out above, which depends on a clear and evident knowledge of all the things regarding which I can deliberate, He has at least left within my power the other means, which is firmly to adhere to the resolution never to give judgment on matters whose truth is not clearly known to me; for although I notice a certain weakness in my nature in that I cannot continually concentrate my mind on one single thought, I can yet, by attentive and frequently repeated meditation, impress it so forcibly on my memory that I shall never fail to recollect it whenever I have need of it, and thus acquire the habit of never going astray.

And inasmuch as it is in this that the greatest and principal perfection of man consists, it seems to me that I have not gained little by this day's Meditation, since I have discovered the source of falsity and error. And certainly there can be no other source than that which I have explained; for as often as I so restrain my will within the limits of my knowledge that it forms no judgment except on matters which are clearly and distinctly represented to it by the understanding, I can never be deceived; for every clear and distinct conception[7] is without doubt something, and hence cannot derive its origin from what is nought, but must of necessity have God as its author—God, I say, who being supremely perfect, cannot be the cause of any error; and consequently we must conclude that such a conception [or such a judgment] is true. Nor have I only learned to-day what I should avoid in order that I may not err, but also how I should act in order to arrive at a knowledge of the truth; for without doubt I shall arrive at this end if I devote my attention sufficiently to those things which I perfectly understand; and if I separate from these that which I only understand confusedly and with obscurity. To these I shall henceforth diligently give heed.

MEDITATION V · Of the essence of material things, and, again, of God, that He exists.

Many other matters respecting the attributes of God and my own nature or mind remain for consideration; but I shall possibly on another occasion resume the investigation of these. Now (after first noting what must be done or avoided, in order to arrive at a knowledge of the truth) my principal task is to endeavour to emerge from the state of doubt into which I have these last days fallen, and to see whether nothing certain can be known regarding material things.

But before examining whether any such objects as I conceive exist outside of me, I must consider the ideas of them in so far as they are in my thought, and see which of them are distinct and which confused.

In the first place, I am able distinctly to imagine that quantity which philosophers commonly call continuous, or the extension in length, breadth, or depth, that is in this quantity, or rather in the object to which it is attributed. Further, I can number in it many different parts, and attribute to each of its parts many sorts of size, figure, situation and local movement, and, finally, I can assign to each of these movements all degrees of duration.

And not only do I know these things with distinctness when I consider them in general, but, likewise [however little I apply my attention to the matter], I discover an infinitude of particulars respecting numbers, figures, movements, and other such things, whose truth is so

[7] perceptio.

manifest, and so well accords with my nature, that when I begin to discover them, it seems to me that I learn nothing new, or recollect what I formerly knew—that is to say, that I for the first time perceive things which were already present to my mind, although I had not as yet applied my mind to them.

And what I here find to be most important is that I discover in myself an infinitude of ideas of certain things which cannot be esteemed as pure negations, although they may possibly have no existence outside of my thought, and which are not framed by me, although it is within my power either to think or not to think them, but which possess natures which are true and immutable. For example, when I imagine a triangle, although there may nowhere in the world be such a figure outside my thought, or ever have been, there is nevertheless in this figure a certain determinate nature, form, or essence, which is immutable and eternal, which I have not invented, and which in no wise depends on my mind, as appears from the fact that diverse properties of that triangle can be demonstrated, viz. that its three angles are equal to two right angles, that the greatest side is subtended by the greatest angle, and the like, which now, whether I wish it or do not wish it, I recognise very clearly as pertaining to it, although I never thought of the matter at all when I imagined a triangle for the first time, and which therefore cannot be said to have been invented by me.

Nor does the objection hold good that possibly this idea of a triangle has reached my mind through the medium of my senses, since I have sometimes seen bodies triangular in shape; because I can form in my mind an infinitude of other figures regarding which we cannot have the least conception of their ever having been objects of sense, and I can nevertheless demonstrate various properties pertaining to their nature as well as to that of the triangle, and these must certainly all be true since I conceive them clearly. Hence they are something, and not pure negation; for it is perfectly clear that all that is true is something, and I have already fully demonstrated that all that I know clearly is true. And even although I had not demonstrated this, the nature of my mind is such that I could not prevent myself from holding them to be true so long as I conceive them clearly; and I recollect that even when I was still strongly attached to the objects of sense, I counted as the most certain those truths which I conceived clearly as regards figures, numbers, and the other matters which pertain to arithmetic and geometry, and, in general, to pure and abstract mathematics.

But now, if just because I can draw the idea of something from my thought, it follows that all which I know clearly and distinctly as pertaining to this object does really belong to it, may I not derive from this an argument demonstrating the existence of God? It is certain that

I no less find the idea of God, that is to say, the idea of a supremely perfect Being, in me, than that of any figure or number whatever it is; and I do not know any less clearly and distinctly that an [actual and] eternal existence pertains to this nature than I know that all that which I am able to demonstrate of some figure or number truly pertains to the nature of this figure or number, and therefore, although all that I concluded in the preceding Meditations were found to be false, the existence of God would pass with me as at least as certain as I have ever held the truths of mathematics (which concern only numbers and figures) to be.

This indeed is not at first manifest, since it would seem to present some appearance of being a sophism. For being accustomed in all other things to make a distinction between existence and essence, I easily persuade myself that the existence can be separated from the essence of God, and that we can thus conceive God as not actually existing. But, nevertheless, when I think of it with more attention, I clearly see that existence can no more be separated from the essence of God than can its having its three angles equal to two right angles be separated from the essence of a [rectilinear] triangle, or the idea of a mountain from the idea of a valley; and so there is not any less repugnance to our conceiving a God (that is, a Being supremely perfect) to whom existence is lacking (that is to say, to whom a certain perfection is lacking), than to conceive of a mountain which has no valley.

But although I cannot really conceive of a God without existence any more than a mountain without a valley, still from the fact that I conceive of a mountain with a valley, it does not follow that there is such a mountain in the world; similarly although I conceive of God as possessing existence, it would seem that it does not follow that there is a God which exists; for my thought does not impose any necessity upon things, and just as I may imagine a winged horse, although no horse with wings exists, so I could perhaps attribute existence to God, although no God existed.

But a sophism is concealed in this objection; for from the fact that I cannot conceive a mountain without a valley, it does not follow that there is any mountain or any valley in existence, but only that the mountain and the valley, whether they exist or do not exist, cannot in any way be separated one from the other. While from the fact that I cannot conceive God without existence, it follows that existence is inseparable from Him, and hence that He really exists; not that my thought can bring this to pass, or impose any necessity on things, but, on the contrary, because the necessity which lies in the thing itself, i.e. the necessity of the existence of God determines me to think in this way. For it is not within my power to think of God without existence (that is of a supremely perfect Being devoid of a supreme perfection) though it is in my power to imagine a horse either with wings or without wings.

And we must not here object that it is in truth necessary for me to assert that God exists after having presupposed that He possesses every sort of perfection, since existence is one of these, but that as a matter of fact my original supposition was not necessary, just as it is not necessary to consider that all quadrilateral figures can be inscribed in the circle; for supposing I thought this, I should be constrained to admit that the rhombus might be inscribed in the circle since it is a quadrilateral figure, which, however, is manifestly false. [We must not, I say, make any such allegations because] although it is not necessary that I should at any time entertain the notion of God, nevertheless whenever it happens that I think of a first and a sovereign Being, and, so to speak, derive the idea of Him from the storehouse of my mind, it is necessary that I should attribute to Him every sort of perfection, although I do not get so far as to enumerate them all, or to apply my mind to each one in particular. And this necessity suffices to make me conclude (after having recognised that existence is a perfection) that this first and sovereign Being really exists; just as though it is not necessary for me ever to imagine any triangle, yet, whenever I wish to consider a rectilinear figure composed only of three angles, it is absolutely essential that I should attribute to it all those properties which serve to bring about the conclusion that its three angles are not greater than two right angles, even although I may not then be considering this point in particular. But when I consider which figures are capable of being inscribed in the circle, it is in no wise necessary that I should think that all quadrilateral figures are of this number; on the contrary, I cannot even pretend that this is the case, so long as I do not desire to accept anything which I cannot conceive clearly and distinctly. And in consequence there is a great difference between the false suppositions such as this, and the true ideas born within me, the first and principal of which is that of God. For really I discern in many ways that this idea is not something factitious, and depending solely on my thought, but that it is the image of a true and immutable nature; first of all, because I cannot conceive anything but God himself to whose essence existence [necessarily] pertains; in the second place because it is not possible for me to conceive two or more Gods in this same position; and, granted that there is one such God who now exists, I see clearly that it is necessary that He should have existed from all eternity, and that He must exist eternally; and finally, because I know an infinitude of other properties in God, none of which I can either diminish or change.

For the rest, whatever proof or argument I avail myself of, we must always return to the point that it is only those things which we conceive clearly and distinctly that have the power of persuading me entirely. And although amongst the matters which I conceive of in this way, some indeed are manifestly obvious to all, while others only manifest themselves to those who consider them closely and examine them attentively; still, after they have once been discovered, the latter are not esteemed as any less certain than the former. For example, in the case of every right-angled triangle, although it does not so manifestly appear that the square of the base is equal to the squares of the two other sides as that this base is opposite to the greatest angle; still, when this has once been apprehended, we are just as certain of its truth as of the truth of the other. And as regards God, if my mind were not preoccupied with prejudices, and if my thought did not find itself on all hands diverted by the continual pressure of sensible things, there would be nothing which I could know more immediately and more easily than Him. For is there anything more manifest than that there is a God, that is to say, a Supreme Being, to whose essence alone existence pertains [8]?

And although for a firm grasp of this truth I have need of a strenuous application of mind, at present I not only feel myself to be as assured of it as of all that I hold as most certain, but I also remark that the certainty of all other things depends on it so absolutely, that without this knowledge it is impossible ever to know anything perfectly.

For although I am of such a nature that as long as [9] I understand anything very clearly and distinctly, I am naturally impelled to believe it to be true, yet because I am also of such a nature that I cannot have my mind constantly fixed on the same object in order to perceive it clearly, and as I often recollect having formed a past judgment without at the same time properly recollecting the reasons that led me to make it, it may happen meanwhile that other reasons present themselves to me, which would easily cause me to change my opinion, if I were ignorant of the facts of the existence of God, and thus I should have no true and certain knowledge, but only vague and vacillating opinions. Thus, for example, when I consider the nature of a [rectilinear] triangle, I who have some little knowledge of the principles of geometry recognise quite clearly that the three angles are equal to two right angles, and it is not possible for me not to believe this so long as I apply my mind to its demonstration; but so soon as I abstain from attending to the proof, although I still recollect having clearly comprehended it, it may easily occur that I come to doubt its truth, if I am ignorant of there being a God. For I can persuade myself of having been so con-

---

[8] 'In the idea of whom alone necessary or eternal existence is comprised.' French version.

[9] 'From the moment that.' French version.

stituted by nature that I can easily deceive myself even in those matters which I believe myself to apprehend with the greatest evidence and certainty, especially when I recollect that I have frequently judged matters to be true and certain which other reasons have afterwards impelled me to judge to be altogether false.

But after I have recognised that there is a God—because at the same time I have also recognised that all things depend upon Him, and that He is not a deceiver, and from that have inferred that what I perceive clearly and distinctly cannot fail to be true—although I no longer pay attention to the reasons for which I have judged this to be true, provided that I recollect having clearly and distinctly perceived it no contrary reason can be brought forward which could ever cause me to doubt of its truth; and thus I have a true and certain knowledge of it. And this same knowledge extends likewise to all other things which I recollect having formerly demonstrated, such as the truths of geometry and the like; for what can be alleged against them to cause me to place them in doubt? Will it be said that my nature is such as to cause me to be frequently deceived? But I already know that I cannot be deceived in the judgment whose grounds I know clearly. Will it be said that I formerly held many things to be true and certain which I have afterwards recognised to be false? But I had not had any clear and distinct knowledge of these things, and not as yet knowing the rule whereby I assure myself of the truth, I had been impelled to give my assent from reasons which I have since recognised to be less strong than I had at the time imagined them to be. What further objection can then be raised? That possibly I am dreaming (an objection I myself made a little while ago), or that all the thoughts which I now have are no more true than the phantasies of my dreams? But even though I slept the case would be the same, for all that is clearly present to my mind is absolutely true.

And so I very clearly recognise that the certainty and truth of all knowledge depends alone on the knowledge of the true God, in so much that, before I knew Him, I could not have a perfect knowledge of any other thing. And now that I know Him I have the means of acquiring a perfect knowledge of an infinitude of things, not only of those which relate to God Himself and other intellectual matters, but also of those which pertain to corporeal nature in so far as it is the object of pure mathematics [which have no concern with whether it exists or not].

MEDITATION VI · *Of the Existence of Material Things, and of the real distinction between the Soul and Body of Man.*

Nothing further now remains but to inquire whether material things exist. And certainly I at least know that these may exist in so far as they are considered as the objects of pure mathematics, since in this aspect I perceive them clearly and distinctly. For there is no doubt that God possesses the power to produce everything that I am capable of perceiving with distinctness, and I have never deemed that anything was impossible for Him, unless I found a contradiction in attempting to conceive it clearly. Further, the faculty of imagination which I possess, and of which, experience tells me, I make use when I apply myself to the consideration of material things, is capable of persuading me of their existence; for when I attentively consider what imagination is, I find that it is nothing but a certain application of the faculty of knowledge to the body which is immediately present to it, and which therefore exists.

And to render this quite clear, I remark in the first place the difference that exists between the imagination and pure intellection [or conception [1]]. For example, when I imagine a triangle, I do not conceive it only as a figure comprehended by three lines, but I also apprehend [2] these three lines as present by the power and inward vision of my mind [3], and this is what I call imagining. But if I desire to think of a chiliagon, I certainly conceive truly that it is a figure composed of a thousand sides, just as easily as I conceive of a triangle that it is a figure of three sides only; but I cannot in any way imagine the thousand sides of a chiliagon [as I do the three sides of a triangle], nor do I, so to speak, regard them as present [with the eyes of my mind]. And although in accordance with the habit I have formed of always employing the aid of my imagination when I think of corporeal things, it may happen that in imagining a chiliagon I confusedly represent to myself some figure, yet it is very evident that this figure is not a chiliagon, since it in no way differs from that which I represent to myself when I think of a myriagon or any other many-sided figure; nor does it serve my purpose in discovering the properties which go to form the distinction between a chiliagon and other polygons. But if the question turns upon a penta-

---

[1] 'Conception,' French version. 'intellectionem,' Latin version.
[2] intueor.
[3] acie mentis.

gon, it is quite true that I can conceive its figure as well as that of a chiliagon without the help of my imagination; but I can also imagine it by applying the attention of my mind to each of its five sides, and at the same time to the space which they enclose. And thus I clearly recognise that I have need of a particular effort of mind in order to effect the act of imagination, such as I do not require in order to understand, and this particular effort of mind clearly manifests the difference which exists between imagination and pure intellection [4].

I remark besides that this power of imagination which is in one, inasmuch as it differs from the power of understanding, is in no wise a necessary element in my nature, or in [my essence, that is to say, in] the essence of my mind; for although I did not possess it I should doubtless ever remain the same as I now am, from which it appears that we might conclude that it depends on something which differs from me. And I easily conceive that if some body exists with which my mind is conjoined and united in such a way that it can apply itself to consider it when it pleases, it may be that by this means it can imagine corporeal objects; so that this mode of thinking differs from pure intellection only inasmuch as mind in its intellectual activity in some manner turns on itself, and considers some of the ideas which it possesses in itself; while in imagining it turns towards the body, and there beholds in it something conformable to the idea which it has either conceived of itself or perceived by the senses. I easily understand, I say, that the imagination could be thus constituted if it is true that body exists; and because I can discover no other convenient mode of explaining it, I conjecture with probability that body does exist; but this is only with probability, and although I examine all things with care, I nevertheless do not find that from this distinct idea of corporeal nature, which I have in my imagination, I can derive any argument from which there will necessarily be deduced the existence of body.

But I am in the habit of imagining many other things besides this corporeal nature which is the object of pure mathematics, to wit, the colours, sounds, scents, pain, and other such things, although less distinctly. And inasmuch as I perceive these things much better through the senses, by the medium of which, and by the memory, they seem to have reached my imagination, I believe that, in order to examine them more conveniently, it is right that I should at the same time investigate the nature of sense perception, and that I should see if from the ideas which I apprehend by this mode of thought, which I call feeling, I cannot derive some certain proof of the existence of corporeal objects.

And first of all I shall recall to my memory those matters which I

---

[4] intellectionem.

hitherto held to be true, as having perceived them through the senses, and the foundations on which my belief has rested; in the next place I shall examine the reasons which have since obliged me to place them in doubt; in the last place I shall consider which of them I must now believe.

First of all, then, I perceived that I had a head, hands, feet, and all other members of which this body—which I considered as a part, or possibly even as the whole, of myself—is composed. Further I was sensible that this body was placed amidst many others, from which it was capable of being affected in many different ways, beneficial and hurtful, and I remarked that a certain feeling of pleasure accompanied those that were beneficial, and pain those which were harmful. And in addition to this pleasure and pain, I also experienced hunger, thirst, and other similar appetites, as also certain corporeal inclinations towards joy, sadness, anger, and other similar passions. And outside myself, in addition to extension, figure, and motions of bodies, I remarked in them hardness, heat, and all other tactile qualities, and, further, light and colour, and scents and sounds, the variety of which gave me the means of distinguishing the sky, the earth, the sea, and generally all the other bodies, one from the other. And certainly, considering the ideas of all these qualities which presented themselves to my mind, and which alone I perceived properly or immediately, it was not without reason that I believed myself to perceive objects quite different from my thought, to wit, bodies from which those ideas proceeded; for I found by experience that these ideas presented themselves to me without my consent being requisite, so that I could not perceive any object, however desirous I might be, unless it were present to the organs of sense; and it was not in my power not to perceive it, when it was present. And because the ideas which I received through the senses were much more lively, more clear, and even, in their own way, more distinct than any of those which I could of myself frame in meditation, or than those I found impressed on my memory, it appeared as though they could not have proceeded from my mind, so that they must necessarily have been produced in me by some other things. And having no knowledge of those objects excepting the knowledge which the ideas themselves gave me, nothing was more likely to occur to my mind than that the objects were similar to the ideas which were caused. And because I likewise remembered that I had formerly made use of my senses rather than my reason, and recognised that the ideas which I formed of myself were not so distinct as those which I perceived through the senses, and that they were most frequently even composed of portions of these last, I persuaded myself easily that I had no idea in my mind which had not formerly come to me through the senses. Now was it without some reason that I be-

lieved that this body (which by a certain special right I call my own)
belonged to me more properly and more strictly than any other; for in
fact I could never be separated from it as from other bodies; I experienced in it and on account of it all my appetites and affections, and
finally I was touched by the feeling of pain and the titillation of pleasure
in its parts, and not in the parts of other bodies which were separated
from it. But when I inquired, why, from some, I know not what, painful sensation, there follows sadness of mind, and from the pleasurable
sensation there arises joy, or why this mysterious pinching of the stomach which I call hunger causes me to desire to eat, and dryness of throat
causes a desire to drink, and so on, I could give no reason excepting
that nature taught me so; for there is certainly no affinity (that I at
least can understand) between the craving of the stomach and the desire to eat, any more than between the perception of whatever causes
pain and the thought of sadness which arises from this perception. And
in the same way it appeared to me that I had learned from nature all
the other judgments which I formed regarding the objects of my senses,
since I remarked that these judgments were formed in me before I had
the leisure to weigh and consider any reasons which might oblige me
to make them.

But afterwards many experiences little by little destroyed all the
faith which I had rested in my senses; for I from time to time observed that those towers which from afar appeared to me to be round,
more closely observed seemed square, and that colossal statues raised on
the summit of these towers, appeared as quite tiny statues when viewed
from the bottom; and so in an infinitude of other cases I found error
in judgments founded on the external senses. And not only in those
founded on the external senses, but even in those founded on the internal as well; for is there anything more intimate or more internal than
pain? And yet I have learned from some persons whose arms or legs
have been cut off, that they sometimes seemed to feel pain in the part
which had been amputated, which made me think that I could not be
quite certain that it was a certain member which pained me, even although I felt pain in it. And to those grounds of doubt I have lately
added two others, which are very general; the first is that I never have
believed myself to feel anything in waking moments which I cannot also
sometimes believe myself to feel when I sleep, and as I do not think
that these things which I seem to feel in sleep, proceed from objects
outside of me, I do not see any reason why I should have this belief
regarding objects which I seem to perceive while awake. The other was
that being still ignorant, or rather supposing myself to be ignorant, of
the author of my being, I saw nothing to prevent me from having been
so constituted by nature that I might be deceived even in matters which

seemed to me to be most certain. And as to the grounds on which I
was formerly persuaded of the truth of sensible objects, I had not
much trouble in replying to them. For since nature seemed to cause
me to lean towards many things from which reason repelled me, I did not
believe that I should trust much to the teachings of nature. And although the ideas which I receive by the senses do not depend on my
will, I did not think that one should for that reason conclude that they
proceeded from things different from myself, since possibly some faculty
might be discovered in me—though hitherto unknown to me—which
produced them.

But now that I begin to know myself better, and to discover more
clearly the author of my being, I do not in truth think that I should
rashly admit all the matters which the senses seem to teach us, but, on
the other hand, I do not think that I should doubt them all universally.

And first of all, because I know that all things which I apprehend
clearly and distinctly can be created by God as I apprehend them, it
suffices that I am able to apprehend one thing apart from another clearly
and distinctly in order to be certain that the one is different from the
other, since they may be made to exist in separation at least by the
omnipotence of God; and it does not signify by what power this separation is made in order to compel me to judge them to be different: and,
therefore, just because I know certainly that I exist, and that meanwhile I do not remark that any other thing necessarily pertains to my
nature or essence, excepting that I am a thinking thing, I rightly conclude that my essence consists solely in the fact that I am a thinking
thing [or a substance whose whole essence or nature is to think]. And
although possibly (or rather certainly, as I shall say in a moment) I possess a body with which I am very intimately conjoined, yet because,
on the one side, I have a clear and distinct idea of myself inasmuch as
I am only a thinking and unextended thing, and as, on the other, I
possess a distinct idea of body, inasmuch as it is only an extended and
unthinking thing, it is certain that this [that is to say, my soul by which
I am what I am], is entirely and absolutely distinct from my body, and
can exist without it.

I further find in myself faculties employing modes of thinking peculiar to themselves, to wit, the faculties of imagination and feeling,
without which I can easily conceive myself clearly and distinctly as a
complete being; while, on the other hand, they cannot be so conceived
apart from me, that is without an intelligent substance in which they
reside, for [in the notion we have of these faculties, or, to use the language of the Schools] in their formal concept, some kind of intellection
is comprised, from which I infer that they are distinct from me as its
modes are from a thing. I observe also in me some other faculties

such as that of change of position, the assumption of different figures and such like, which cannot be conceived, any more than can the preceding, apart from some substance to which they are attached, and consequently cannot exist without it; but it is very clear that these faculties, if it be true that they exist, must be attached to some corporeal or extended substance, and not to an intelligent substance, since in the clear and distinct conception of these there is some sort of extension found to be present, but no intellection at all. There is certainly further in me a certain passive faculty of perception, that is, of receiving and recognising the ideas of sensible things, but this would be useless to me [and I could in no way avail myself of it], if there were not either in me or in some other thing another active faculty capable of forming and producing these ideas. But this active faculty cannot exist in me [inasmuch as I am a thing that thinks] seeing that it does not presuppose thought, and also that those ideas are often produced in me without my contributing in any way to the same, and often even against my will; it is thus necessarily the case that the faculty resides in some substance different from me in which all the reality which is objectively in the ideas that are produced by this faculty is formally or eminently contained, as I remarked before. And this substance is either a body, that is, a corporeal nature in which there is contained formally [and really] all that which is objectively [and by representation] in those ideas, or it is God Himself, or some other creature more noble than body in which that same is contained eminently. But, since God is no deceiver, it is very manifest that He does not communicate to me these ideas immediately and by Himself, nor yet by the intervention of some creature in which their reality is not formally, but only eminently, contained. For since He has given me no faculty to recognise that this is the case, but, on the other hand, a very great inclination to believe [that they are sent to me or] that they are conveyed to me by corporeal objects, I do not see how He could be defended from the accusation of deceit if these ideas were produced by causes other than corporeal objects. Hence we must allow that corporeal things exist. However, they are perhaps not exactly what we perceive by the senses, since this comprehension by the senses is in many instances very obscure and confused; but we must at least admit that all things which I conceive in them clearly and distinctly, that is to say, all things which, speaking generally, are comprehended in the object of pure mathematics, are truly to be recognised as external objects.

As to other things, however, which are either particular only, as, for example, that the sun is of such and such a figure, etc., or which are less clearly and distinctly conceived, such as light, sound, pain and the like, it is certain that although they are very dubious and uncertain, yet on the sole ground that God is not a deceiver, and that consequently He has not permitted any falsity to exist in my opinion which He has not likewise given me the faculty of correcting, I may assuredly hope to conclude that I have within me the means of arriving at the truth even here. And first of all there is no doubt that in all things which nature teaches me there is some truth contained; for by nature, considered in general, I now understand no other thing than either God Himself or else the order and disposition which God has established in created things; and by my nature in particular I understand no other thing than the complexus of all the things which God has given me.

But there is nothing which this nature teaches me more expressly [nor more sensibly] than that I have a body which is adversely affected when I feel pain, which has need of food or drink when I experience the feelings of hunger and thirst, and so on; nor can I doubt there being some truth in all this.

Nature also teaches me by these sensations of pain, hunger, thirst, etc., that I am not only lodged in my body as a pilot in a vessel, but that I am very closely united to it, and so to speak so intermingled with it that I seem to compose with it one whole. For if that were not the case, when my body is hurt, I, who am merely a thinking thing, should not feel pain, for I should perceive this wound by the understanding only, just as the sailor perceives by sight when something is damaged in his vessel; and when my body has need of drink or food, I should clearly understand the fact without being warned of it by confused feelings of hunger and thirst. For all these sensations of hunger, thirst, pain, etc. are in truth none other than certain confused modes of thought which are produced by the union and apparent intermingling of mind and body.

Moreover, nature teaches me that many other bodies exist around mine, of which some are to be avoided, and others sought after. And certainly from the fact that I am sensible of different sorts of colours, sounds, scents, tastes, heat, hardness, etc., I very easily conclude that there are in the bodies from which all these diverse sense-perceptions proceed certain variations which answer to them, although possibly these are not really at all similar to them. And also from the fact that amongst these different sense-perceptions some are very agreeable to me and others disagreeable, it is quite certain that my body (or rather myself in my entirety, inasmuch as I am formed of body and soul) may receive different impressions agreeable and disagreeable from the other bodies which surround it.

But there are many other things which nature seems to have taught me, but which at the same time I have never really received from her, but which have been brought about in my mind by a certain habit which I have of forming inconsiderate judgments on things; and thus it may easily happen that these judgments contain some error. Take, for example, the opinion which I hold that all space in which there is nothing that affects [or makes an impression on] my senses is void; that in a body which is warm there is something entirely similar to the idea of heat which is in me; that in a white or green body there is the same whiteness or greenness that I perceive; that in a bitter or sweet body there is the same taste, and so on in other instances; that the stars, the towers, and all other distant bodies are of the same figure and size as they appear from far off to our eyes, etc. But in order that in this there should be nothing which I do not conceive distinctly, I should define exactly what I really understand when I say that I am taught somewhat by nature. For here I take nature in a more limited signification than when I term it the sum of all the things given me by God, since in this sum many things are comprehended which only pertain to mind (and to these I do not refer in speaking of nature) such as the notion which I have of the fact that what has once been done cannot ever be undone and an infinitude of such things which I know by the light of nature [without the help of the body]; and seeing that it comprehends many other matters besides which only pertain to body, and are no longer here contained under the name of nature, such as the quality of weight which it possesses and the like, with which I also do not deal; for in talking of nature I only treat of those things given by God to me as a being composed of mind and body. But the nature here described truly teaches me to flee from things which cause the sensation of pain, and seek after the things which communicate to me the sentiment of pleasure and so forth; but I do not see that beyond this it teaches me that from those diverse sense-perceptions we should ever form any conclusion regarding things outside of us, without having [carefully and maturely] mentally examined them beforehand. For it seems to me that it is mind alone, and not mind and body in conjunction, that is requisite to a knowledge of the truth in regard to such things. Thus, although a star makes no larger an impression on my eye than the flame of a little candle there is yet in me no real or positive propensity impelling me to believe that it is not greater than that flame; but I have judged it to be so from my earliest years, without any rational foundation. And although in approaching fire I feel heat, and in approaching it a little too near I even feel pain, there is at the same time no reason in this which could persuade me that there is in the fire something resembling this heat any more than there is in it something resembling the pain; all that I have any reason to believe from this is, that there is something in it, whatever it may be, which excites in me these sensations of heat or of pain. So also, although there are spaces in which I find nothing which excites my senses, I must not from that conclude that these spaces contain no body; for I see in this, as in other similar things, that I have been in the habit of perverting the order of nature, because these perceptions of sense having been placed within me by nature merely for the purpose of signifying to my mind what things are beneficial or hurtful to the composite whole of which it forms a part, and being up to that point sufficiently clear and distinct, I yet avail myself of them as though they were absolute rules by which I might immediately determine the essence of the bodies which are outside me, as to which, in fact, they can teach me nothing but what is most obscure and confused.

But I have already sufficiently considered how, notwithstanding the supreme goodness of God, falsity enters into the judgments I make. Only here a new difficulty is presented—one respecting those things the pursuit or avoidance of which is taught me by nature, and also respecting the internal sensations which I possess, and in which I seem to have sometimes detected error [and thus to be directly deceived by my own nature]. To take an example, the agreeable taste of some food in which poison has been intermingled may induce me to partake of the poison, and thus deceive me. It is true, at the same time, that in this case nature may be excused, for it only induces me to desire food in which I find a pleasant taste, and not to desire the poison which is unknown to it; and thus I can infer nothing from this fact, except that my nature is not omniscient, at which there is certainly no reason to be astonished, since man, being finite in nature, can only have knowledge the perfectness of which is limited.

But we not unfrequently deceive ourselves even in those things to which we are directly impelled by nature, as happens with those who when they are sick desire to drink or eat things hurtful to them. It will perhaps be said here that the cause of their deceptiveness is that their nature is corrupt, but that does not remove the difficulty, because a sick man is none the less truly God's creature than he who is in health; and it is therefore as repugnant to God's goodness for the one to have a deceitful nature as it is for the other. And as a clock composed of wheels and counter-weights no less exactly observes the laws of nature when it is badly made, and does not show the time properly, than when it entirely satisfies the wishes of its maker, and as, if I consider the body of a man as being a sort of machine so built up and composed of nerves, muscles, veins, blood and skin, that though there were no mind in it at all, it would not cease to have the same motions as at present, exception being made of those movements which are due to the direction of the will, and in consequence depend upon the mind [as opposed to those which operate by the disposition of its organs], I easily recognise that it would be as natural to this body, supposing it to be, for example, dropsical, to suffer the parchedness of the throat which usually signifies to the mind the feeling of thirst, and to be disposed by this parched feeling to move the nerves and other parts in the way requisite for drinking, and thus to augment its malady and do harm to itself, as it is natural to it, when it has no indisposition, to be impelled to drink for its good by a similar cause. And although, considering the use to which the clock has been destined by its maker, I may say that it deflects from the order of its nature when it does not indicate the hours correctly; and as, in the same way, considering the machine of the human body as having been formed by God in order to have in itself all the movements usually manifested there, I have reason for thinking that it does not follow the order of nature when, if the throat is dry, drinking does harm to the conservation of health, nevertheless I recognise at the same time that this last mode of explaining nature is very different from the other. For this is but a purely verbal characterisation depending entirely on my thought, which compares a sick man and a badly constructed clock with the idea which I have of a healthy man and a well made clock, and it is hence extrinsic to the things to which it is applied; but according to the other interpretation of the term nature I understand something which is truly found in things and which is therefore not without some truth.

But certainly although in regard to the dropsical body it is only so to speak to apply an extrinsic term when we say that its nature is corrupted, inasmuch as apart from the need to drink, the throat is parched; yet in regard to the composite whole, that is to say, to the mind or soul united to this body, it is not a purely verbal predicate, but a real error of nature, for it to have thirst when drinking would be hurtful to it. And thus it still remains to inquire how the goodness of God does not prevent the nature of man so regarded from being fallacious.

In order to begin this examination, then, I here say, in the first place, that there is a great difference between mind and body, inasmuch as body is by nature always divisible, and the mind is entirely indivisible. For, as a matter of fact, when I consider the mind, that is to say, myself inasmuch as I am only a thinking thing, I cannot distinguish in myself any parts, but apprehend myself to be clearly one and entire; and although the whole mind seems to be united to the whole body, yet if a foot, or an arm, or some other part, is separated from my body, I am aware that nothing has been taken away from my mind. And the faculties of willing, feeling, conceiving, etc. cannot be properly speaking said to be its parts, for it is one and the same mind which employs itself in willing and in feeling and understanding. But it is quite otherwise with corporeal or extended objects, for there is not one of these imaginable by me which my mind cannot easily divide into parts, and which consequently I do not recognise as being divisible; this would be sufficient to teach me that the mind or soul of man is entirely different from the body, if I had not already learned it from other sources.

I further notice that the mind does not receive the impressions from all parts of the body immediately, but only from the brain, or perhaps even from one of its smallest parts, to wit, from that in which the common sense [5] is said to reside, which, whenever it is disposed in the same particular way, conveys the same thing to the mind, although meanwhile the other portions of the body may be differently disposed, as is testified by innumerable experiments which it is unnecessary here to recount.

I notice, also, that the nature of body is such that none of its parts can be moved by another part a little way off which cannot also be moved in the same way by each one of the parts which are between the two, although this more remote part does not act at all. As, for example, in the cord ABCD [which is in tension] if we pull the last part D, the first part A will not be moved in any way differently from what would be the case if one of the intervening parts B or C were pulled, and the last part D were to remain unmoved. And in the same way, when I feel pain in my foot, my knowledge of physics teaches me that this sensation is communicated by means of nerves dispersed through the foot, which, being extended like cords from there to the brain, when they are contracted in the foot, at the same time contract the inmost portions of the brain which is their extremity and place of origin, and then excite a certain movement which nature has established in order to cause the mind to be affected by a sensation of pain represented as existing in the foot. But because these nerves must pass through the tibia, the thigh, the loins, the back and the neck, in order to reach from the leg to the brain, it may happen that although their extremities which are in the foot are not affected, but only certain ones of their intervening parts [which pass by the loins or the neck], this action will excite the same movement in the brain that might have been excited there by a hurt received in the foot, in consequence of which the mind will necessarily feel in the foot the same pain as if it had received a hurt. And the same holds good of all the other perceptions of our senses.

I notice finally that since each of the movements which are in the portion of the brain by which the mind is immediately affected brings about one particular sensation only, we cannot under the circumstances imagine anything more likely than that this movement, amongst all the sensations which it is capable of impressing on it, causes mind to be affected by that one which is best fitted and most generally useful for

---

[5] sensus communis.

the conservation of the human body when it is in health. But experience makes us aware that all the feelings with which nature inspires us are such as I have just spoken of; and there is therefore nothing in them which does not give testimony to the power and goodness of the God [who has produced them [6]]. Thus, for example, when the nerves which are in the feet are violently or more than usually moved, their movement, passing through the medulla of the spine [7] to the inmost parts of the brain, gives a sign to the mind which makes it feel somewhat, to wit, pain, as though in the foot, by which the mind is excited to do its utmost to remove the cause of the evil as dangerous and hurtful to the foot. It is true that God could have constituted the nature of man in such a way that this same movement in the brain would have conveyed something quite different to the mind; for example, it might have produced consciousness of itself either in so far as it is in the brain, or as it is in the foot, or as it is in some other place between the foot and the brain, or it might finally have produced consciousness of anything else whatsoever; but none of all this would have contributed so well to the conservation of the body. Similarly, when we desire to drink, a certain dryness of the throat is produced which moves its nerves, and by their means the internal portions of the brain; and this movement causes in the mind the sensation of thirst, because in this case there is nothing more useful to us than to become aware that we have need to drink for the conservation of our health; and the same holds good in other instances.

From this it is quite clear that, notwithstanding the supreme goodness of God, the nature of man, inasmuch as it is composed of mind and body, cannot be otherwise than sometimes a source of deception. For if there is any cause which excites, not in the foot but in some part of the nerves which are extended between the foot and the brain, or even in the brain itself, the same movement which usually is produced when the foot is detrimentally affected, pain will be experienced as though it were in the foot, and the sense will thus naturally be deceived; for since the same movement in the brain is capable of causing but one sensation in the mind, and this sensation is much more frequently excited by a cause which hurts the foot than by another existing in some other quarter, it is reasonable that it should convey to the mind pain in the foot rather than in any other part of the body. And although the parchedness of the throat does not always proceed, as it usually does, from the fact that drinking is necessary for the health of the body, but sometimes comes from quite a different cause, as is the case with dropsi-

---

[6] Latin version only.

[7] spini dorsae medullam.

cal patients, it is yet much better that it should mislead on this occasion than if, on the other hand, it were always to deceive us when the body is in good health; and so on in similar cases.

And certainly this consideration is of great service to me, not only in enabling me to recognise all the errors to which my nature is subject, but also in enabling me to avoid them or to correct them more easily. For knowing that all my senses more frequently indicate to me truth than falsehood respecting the things which concern that which is beneficial to the body, and being able almost always to avail myself of many of them in order to examine one particular thing, and, besides that, being able to make use of my memory in order to connect the present with the past, and of my understanding which already has discovered all the causes of my errors, I ought no longer to fear that falsity may be found in matters every day presented to me by my senses. And I ought to set aside all the doubts of these past days as hyperbolical and ridiculous, particularly that very common uncertainty respecting sleep, which I could not distinguish from the waking state; for at present I find a very notable difference between the two, inasmuch as our memory can never connect our dreams one with the other, or with the whole course of our lives, as it unites events which happen to us while we are awake. And, as a matter of fact, if someone, while I was awake, quite suddenly appeared to me and disappeared as fast as do the images which I see in sleep, so that I could not know from whence the form came nor whither it went, it would not be without reason that I should deem it a spectre or a phantom formed by my brain [and similar to those which I form in sleep], rather than a real man. But when I perceive things as to which I know distinctly both the place from which they proceed, and that in which they are, and the time at which they appeared to me; and when, without any interruption, I can connect the perceptions which I have of them with the whole course of my life, I am perfectly assured that these perceptions occur while I am waking and not during sleep. And I ought in no wise to doubt the truth of such matters, if, after having called up all my senses, my memory, and my understanding, to examine them, nothing is brought to evidence by any one of them which is repugnant to what is set forth by the others. For because God is in no wise a deceiver, it follows that I am not deceived in this. But because the exigencies of action often oblige us to make up our minds before having leisure to examine matters carefully, we must confess that the life of man is very frequently subject to error in respect to individual objects, and we must in the end acknowledge the infirmity of our nature.

BERKELEY

INTRODUCTION TO

Berkeley

One of the arresting things in the history of ideas is to see those ideas caught in the logic of their own movement. The tendency for this to happen is always there; but it takes a skillful strategist in dialectic to help the movement along, so that its intellectually revolutionary results appear inevitable. To refute any viewpoint in the simple sense is not too difficult; all that is necessary is to interpose obstacles and objections, which are usually in plentiful supply. The clash of ideas then becomes an endurance contest, with victory going to the one that tires last and least. But to let the opponent defeat himself, or to make it appear that he has done so by the built-in mechanisms of his own procedure, is a more artful achievement; and the results are sometimes permanent.

This latter is what happens, in the broad historical sense, in the case of George Berkeley.

Berkeley was born in the county of Kilkenny, Ireland, on March 12, 1685. His first schooling was at Kilkenny School, where twenty years earlier the Restoration playwright Congreve and the great Jonathan Swift had preceded him. He was enrolled in Trinity College, Dublin, in March, 1700. Trinity College in those days was to Ireland what the University of Paris was to medieval France: the nurture ground of early genius, the jousting field for theological and philosophical controversy—the two being then not always distinguishable—and the base of operations for sorties into new worlds of thought, opened up by the pioneers of the older generation: Locke, Newton, and their contemporaries.

In 1705, Berkeley and his friends in Dublin formed a society for the discussion of the "new philosophy," the novelties in question being those of the whole post-Cartesian movement that had begun to displace the lingering scholasticism in the British universities.[1] In the same year, the young Berkeley began his first philosophical writing—a series of jottings, inquiries, expostulations, and exclamatory rebuttals of the leading scientific and philosophical ideas of the time. The manuscript containing this material was published by Berkeley's first editor as the *Commonplace Book*.[2] The book is Berkeley's dialogue with himself on the fundamental issues which he was to attack in his major writings.

The *Commonplace Book* suggests that Berkeley's was one of those philosophical talents whose basic philosophical project is not the result of slow and painful discovery but is given at once, in the mind's first awakening. His problem is not to have the intuition but to explain it and prove it. The doubts come later, in the course of demonstration and application. These doubts never quite leave him; but, on the other hand, he never merely dismisses them.

In 1707, Berkeley was admitted to the M.A. degree at Trinity and to a fellowship at the College. Within three years, two of his fundamental writings appeared: the *Essay toward the New Theory of Vision* (1709) and the *Treatise Concerning the Principles of Human Knowledge* (1710). In the same year in which the *Essay* was published, Berkeley took holy orders, a normal prerequisite to academic preferment.

The *Three Dialogues between Hylas and Philonous* was published in 1713.

The technical core of all three works is the analysis of the phenomenon of vision as first proposed in the *Essay*. The *Treatise* and the *Dialogues* generalize that analysis and apply it to sense experience as a whole, so that in the latter works the problem of vision appears as merely one of the illustrative situations.

Berkeley's remaining philosophical writings—apart from some topical pamphleteering which the times occasionally provoked from him— are for the most part expansion, defense, and re-examination of the principal issues already precipitated in these three early works, written before the age of twenty-eight.

Apart from that literary and philosophical productivity, Berkeley's life follows the approximately normal course of an eighteenth-century English wit and bishop. He was of course, universally "beloved" by such men as Pope and Swift, and various others less well known. Pope

---

[1] Locke's *Essay Concerning the Human Understanding* had appeared in 1690, Newton's *Philosophiae naturalis principia mathematica* (*Mathematical Principles of Natural Philosophy*), in 1687. The works of the "occasionalist" Malebranche (1638–1715) were also in circulation at Trinity.

[2] A later edition has given to this work the title *Philosophical Commentaries*. But the earlier title still seems more appropriate to the genre which the book represents.

attributed to him "every virtue under heaven." He was also variously suspected and sometimes openly accused of being mad, which was an accusation freely traded at the time. He waited on the great and struggled for preferment. In due course he became a bishop. He spent nearly three reportedly happy years in Rhode Island, on his way to found a new college in the Bermudas, where he never arrived. Samuel Johnson, first president of King's College (later Columbia), and Jonathan Edwards, first president of New Jersey College (later Princeton), were among his American friends and callers. Berkeley died peacefully, in his episcopal residence of Cloyne, on January 14, 1753.

The English eighteenth century was by its own avowal an Age of Reason. Its tree of knowledge had two roots: the nominalist-empiricist root and the mechanist-materialist root. Of the two roots the former is the older in the British tradition, going all the way back to William of Occam in the early fourteenth century.

William of Occam's nominalism arises in criticism of and revolt against the medieval form of "realism," which asserted that universals are real—that is, have a status in existence, not only in discourse. The universals in question are such concepts as "humanity," "goodness," "redness," and the like. They are the scholastic heirs of the Platonic-Aristotelian forms and essences.

As against this, nominalism asserted that only particular things were "real," and that all other alleged "reals"—such as "man as such" or "goodness as such"—were but *names*.[3]

This position is dear both to Britons in philosophy and to common sense. It goes hand in hand with its twin point of view, empiricism. The latter is a larger and less exact term than nominalism. It, too, however, is notoriously associated with the British tradition, where the great names before Berkeley are Bacon, Hobbes, and Locke; and its impact on American philosophy, as in pragmatism, has been more emphatic than that of any other tradition.

Generally speaking, empiricism is associated with, (1) an attempt to get rid of preconceptions, in estimating the problems of philosophy; (2) the effort to *externalize* the view—to look without, at the world and its processes, at men in their behavior rather than in their thoughts, at things rather than at ideas; and if at ideas (as in Hobbes), then at ideas as if they were things, or at the side effects of ideas rather than at their causes; (3) putting greater premium on *control* (as in Bacon's eulogy of knowledge when it is power) than on plumbing the depths of understanding.

None of these orientations, or their variations, is peculiar to em-

---

[3] Hence the term "nominalism," from the Latin *nomen*, a name.

piricism in any local or period sense of that term, whether in Thomas Hobbes's seventeenth century or in John Dewey's twentieth. All of these attitudes or motivations may also be found in the philosophic enterprise of thinkers who stand outside the empirical tradition in its narrow sense: in Plato, for example, in his rejection of Parmenidean "idealism"; or in Descartes, in his insistence that "method" must issue in controls that are appropriate to science as well as in understanding appropriate to morals.

But when these attitudes congeal into a particular kind of strategy, steadfastly or stubbornly adhered to, and in particular when they combine with the nominalist conviction that only concrete particulars—whether thing, event, or situation; whether object of experience, or "experience" as the object itself—are *real*, then we have the characteristically British form of empiricism, and a source of fruitful controversy. To this tradition all British philosophers, one way or another, are heirs at law.

The philosophical trouble with this tradition—attractive, powerful, and beneficent as it has been in the hands of most empiricists—like the trouble with most traditions when they have hardened, lies in its dogmatic implications rather than in its uses as a method.

What, for example, is a particular, concrete "thing" that is said to exercise control, or serve as source or cause or limit of everything else, and be also the satisfaction to the nominalist quest to understand?

Is it the smallest, theoretically "touchable" thing which the Eleatic Stranger in Plato's *Sophist* was compelled to discard as the mark of real existence? Is it the material substance that Descartes found it feasible to doubt? Or the proximate matter in determinate form of Aristotle's analysis of nature?

Is it Locke's "simple idea," or immediate, uncompounded and irreducible sensation, which "the mind can neither make nor destroy"? Obviously this is the ultimate thing for Locke in a psychological sense. But what is ultimate in a psychological sense is not for Locke ultimate in the world. Because behind the "simple ideas" stand the things those ideas "resemble"—namely, the "primary qualities" of bodies and of the smallest particles of any body; and behind the "primary qualities" of "solidity, extension, figure, and mobility" stands that unknown but certain "something" which, because it "supports" all the "qualities" and/or the "ideas," is entitled to the name of *substance*. Even though we have "no clear or distinct idea" of it, still it has to be there.[4]

Is this the ultimate "thing" that the nominalist-empiricists are after? This question, pushed to its limit, becomes the question of whether

---

[4] Locke's *Essay*, Book II, Chapters 8, 9, and 23.

nominalist-empiricism rests in principle upon the metaphysics of materialism.

If we should classify "materialism" into types, we should have to distinguish at least four.[5]

1. The materialism of common sense—namely, the ordinary belief that external things *are* external, and are real.

2. Metaphysical materialism in the strict sense. Its prototype is the materialism of Lucretius in *Of the Nature of Things*, in the first century B.C. He is the philosophical heir of the "giants" in Plato's *Sophist*, and his answer to the question "What exists?" is the passionate affirmation that atomic matter in motion is the source of all other realities, including life and mind.

3. Ideological materialism, of which an example would be Marxism, sometimes called "dialectical" or "historical" materialism. Ideological materialism generally rests on metaphysical materialism, in one version or another of it, but is usually more concerned to employ the doctrine as an argument for social or political purposes, which could just as well be argued on other grounds, than it is to defend the "metaphysical" core of the ideology on philosophical grounds.

4. Scientific or methodological materialism, which uses matter and motion (or "mass" and "force") as the only factors capable of being measured, and therefore worthy of investigation. Beyond that it normally makes no metaphysical "hypotheses," but is content merely to describe, preferably in mathematical terms. The great English examples in the seventeenth century are the chemist Robert Boyle and the mathematical astronomer and cosmologist Isaac Newton. Neither one was a materialist in the metaphysical sense.

The materialism of common sense is noncontroversial and serves as a point of departure for any empiricism. The nominalism in the British tradition tends toward a "reduction" to the smallest particular, and therefore pulls toward metaphysical materialism, which does the same. But the empiricism in the British tradition tends to avoid this extreme as both too speculative and too dogmatic.

Ordinarily, British philosophy would have muddled through as usual, without trying to achieve a thoroughgoing consistency. What made the difference in the eighteenth century is the vast triumph of scientific or methodological materialism in the form of the mechanistic cosmology of Newton.

The Three Laws of Motion of Newton's *Principia* express the me-

---

[5] For a full discussion of the problem in its historical development, see F. A. Lange's classic work, *The History of Materialism*, translated by E. C. Thomas; 3rd ed., with an Introduction by Bertrand Russell; 3 vols. in 1 (New York: Humanities Press; 1950).

chanics of the universe in comprehensive form: (1) the law of inertia
and its corollary, the law of action and reaction; (2) the law of universal attraction, directly according to the product of the masses, and
inversely according to the square of the distances; and (3) the law of
the composition of forces. Without implying any answer to the question
of how it all started, the three universal mechanical principles are built
into the nature of matter as such.

Behind the mechanistic description of nature lies latent a metaphysical materialism in the emphasis on matter (or mass) as the subject-object of all describable relations. As the scope of the descriptive
laws widens, so does the implied scope of matter as the sole object of
scientific description.

There would be, inevitably, an attempt to extend these laws, grand
and all-embracing as they purport to be, to the field of mental motion,
or the mechanics of the mind. From such an attempt would come the
first scientific psychology of the new age, the associationist psychology
of David Hartley in England.[6]

This universal mechanism begins, finally, to invade the realm of
deity. The universal *laws* of that mechanism have become coextensive
with all of conceivable reality. Behind or above those laws there stands,
in the Newtonian type of deism, a Supreme Mathematical *Lawgiver*,
who has disposed and patterned out the Newtonian absolutes of Time,
Space, and Motion. But there is practically nothing, except a little internal resistance from remembered piety, to prevent that Supreme
Lawgiver from coinciding with or absorbing into His mechanical laws
and their framework of Absolutes. That is the tendency even among
some otherwise orthodox thinkers.[7] The philosophical religion known as
deism is, in the eighteenth century, a compromise with that tendency
and a stopping short of it.

What stops a philosophical deist from being an abstract kind of
pantheist, worshipping Time, Space, and Mathematical Motion? What
stops him is a quasi-philosophical attitude called skepticism.

For Descartes, skepticism was the initial phase of sound method
and, properly used, was an instrument of certainty. That is not the
meaning of the term that Berkeley has in mind or would accept.[8] For

---

[6] On the relation of Hartley and the French psychological materialists to the
ideological currents of the eighteenth century, see F. A. Lange, op. cit. First Book,
fourth section, chapters 1 and 2.

[7] See E. A. Burtt: *The Metaphysical Foundations of Modern Physical Science*,
rev. ed. (New York and London: Routledge, Kegan Paul, Ltd.; 1951); especially
Ch. V, on More and Barrow, the "Cambridge Platonists" of the seventeenth century;
also Chs. VI and VII, on Newton's wrestling with the problem.

[8] The run-down of the English usage of "scepticism" (to use the British spelling) through the eighteenth century, given in the *Oxford English Dictionary*, vol. IX,

Berkeley, skepticism is intellectual "refusal to follow through." As such, skepticism is the mask of improper method, and what lies behind it is really intellectual confusion.

The intellectual confusion that Berkeley aims to clarify is compounded, then, of nominalist-empiricism plus universal-mechanism plus a latent materialism which has already captured mind and threatens deity.

Berkeley's general purpose will be: to free scientific method from its materialist latencies, to free mind and religion from invasion by mechanism, and at the same time to free theism from its dependence on improper method, or "skepticism."

That general purpose will be advanced by a threefold operation: (1) The traditional *method* of nominalist-empiricism will be redirected and, in effect, reversed. (2) The essentially materialist causal premises underlying nominalist-empiricism will be re-examined.[9] This will result in a new orientation toward the subject-object relation, which will henceforth throw into overriding prominence the notion of the "subject," or the "agent" and his "activity," as the decisive rather than merely correlative feature of the world. (3) The empirical fact of the world's stability, or relative stability, must be reinterpreted so as to replace the account given by the mechanists. That account had been found to be inextricably bound up with materialism.

Let us briefly consider each of these operations in turn.

1. The "reductive method" is characteristic of materialism, and the same method is also the built-in tendency of nominalist-empiricism. It signifies just what the term implies—namely, the translation *downward* of things that are given (ordinary objects, persons, and the like), into smaller things, until a limit is reached.

---

pp. 201 f., suggests that, in addition to the usual meanings, it also had the meaning of "hypocritical speech." Thus, "Here he taketh occasion to examine Pyrrhonism or Scepticism professed by a set of men that speak otherwise than they think." Cited from *Phil. Trans.* VII 5081, 1672. The meaning seems to be akin to that of George Orwell's "Newspeak" in his novel 1984.

The rehabilitation of the term "skepticism" as a term of solid philosophical meaning remained to be accomplished by David Hume in his *Dialogues Concerning Natural Religion,* and in the "Defence of Scepticism" that Hume proposes on his own behalf and also puts into the mouth of Epicurus in the *Enquiries Concerning the Human Understanding and Concerning the Principles of Morals* (Oxford: at the Clarendon Press; 1902), Sections V, XI, and XII of the first Enquiry. The Humean meaning has been continued by Bertrand Russell, in "The Free Man's Worship" in *Essays in Mysticism and Logic* (London: George Allen and Unwin; 1932), and *The Will to Doubt* (New York: Philosophical Library; 1958); and, in a more epistemological sense, by George Santayana, in *Scepticism and Animal Faith* (New York: Charles Scribners; 1923).

[9] That these causal premises are essentially materialist is clearest in Hobbes, but the case is not fundamentally different in Locke. See Locke's *Essay,* Book II, Ch. 26.

The limit is imposed not by observation for nobody can "see" a Lucretian atom, or any other kind, but by theory. In other words, the limit is a "rational" one. The aim of understanding is to relate phenomena theoretically to those atomic limits.

There is a further guiding principle, one that also comes from the theory rather than from observation, and that is that the "further down" one gets, the nearer one is to what is really *real*. In other words, the *really* real is the limit of the reductive movement.

Berkeley reverses this, and ostensibly he is enabled to do so because he really starts with observation, or claims to, and follows what he considers to be the natural, or "common sense," course of observation.

As to that, Hume and Kant will in due course say that there is no built-in natural direction to "common sense" along the lines that Berkeley said there was. But this is merely a way of saying that "common sense" always carries with it its own native *theory*.

Let us call Berkeley's method here, for the sake of contrast, the "method of upward reduction."

Its starting point, again, harks back to Locke. In Locke's empiricism, the atom had been replaced by the "simple idea," or irreducible sensation immediately perceived—that is, *not* perceived by association or by inference.

There was an ambiguity in Locke as to whether the "primary qualities" (extension, figure, motion, solidity, and the like) are in the mind or in things. They seem to be in both, though not in the same way in both. There is no doubt, however, as to where the "secondary qualities" (warmth, odor, taste, color, and the like) are located: they are definitely in the mind, and not anywhere else; though they are "supported" by the "primary qualities," which latter are in turn supported by the "substance" of things.

It is Locke's indubitable location of the "secondary qualities" in the mind that facilitated Berkeley's task, for it made clear where the "reductive method" had to point if it was to be consistent. It had to point to the mind. If, as Berkeley will show, the distinction between the primary and the secondary qualities can be eliminated, the reductive method would then be pointing "upward," or away from that source outside the mind that Locke still assumed for the primary qualities.

Berkeley's "upward reduction" procedure is, then, almost naively simple: (a) Start as an uncompromising empiricist, with what is absolutely authenticated for experience. These are the objects of "immediate perception." Berkeley assumes these to be identical with the "secondary qualities." Locke, as a matter of fact, wavered considerably in his identification of the objects of "immediate perception," but Berkeley is forgiving Locke his indecision and getting down to empirical bedrock. The only thing one can be sure of, for example, is the feeling of warmth (and the like). Anything *behind* the warmth is *not* "immediately perceived." *To be,* in short, is *to be perceived.* (b) Reduce as many as possible of the so-called primary qualities (they are mostly matters allied to solidity and extension) *upward* to the secondary qualities, where they will wholly absorb. (c) Along with them will be found to go the geometric "abstractions"—that is, concepts of scientific mechanism such as "distance," "motion," "space," "infinite," and so forth. They either absorb "upward," like the primary qualities, or else are found to be quite empty of perceptual content to begin with, and therefore without value for philosophy.

All things are now concrete things. But what kind of concreteness can things have if they do not depend upon matter? Obviously, it must be an "immaterial" or "spiritual" concreteness.

The dialectic is both simple and ingenious, and has consistently been admired even by thinkers disposed to question its results.[1]

2. But the real significance of Berkeley's redirection of reductionist method lies much deeper than the technical ingenuity. What has really taken place is a radical shift in the point of view from "thingness" to "activity." In effect, Berkeley is saying: There are no "things"; there are only "actions" and the agents of "actions." This is no longer the "problem of knowledge" as it was thought to be; it is the problem of "orientation toward action."

That, it now appears, was Berkeley's root motivation from the beginning. What he wanted was a world of "activity." He cannot conceive or justify the possibility that, in a world in which activity is observed, the observed activity should be subordinate or inferior to anything else.[2] Can activity be conceived to spring from inactivity? Obviously not. Does activity need a material object (or "material cause") to act upon? No. Causative activity is its own excuse for being.

Thus the only causes are efficient causes. "How often must I repeat," says Philonous, in the Third Dialogue, "that I know or am conscious of my own being; and that I *myself* am not my ideas, but somewhat else, a thinking, active principle that perceives, knows, wills, and operates about ideas. I know that I, one and the same self, per-

---

[1] V. I. Lenin, for instance, a Marxist materialist, has considerable polemical anger for all "compromise" forms of "empiricist idealism" but speaks with unique respectfulness of Berkeley's philosophic clarity, candor, consistency, and the like. See *Materialism and Empirico-Criticism; critical comments on a reactionary philosophy* (New York: International Publishers; 1927); especially the introductory essay, "In Lieu of Introduction," pp. 13 ff.

[2] Cf. Plato's *Sophist,* 248, 249.

ceive both colours and sounds: that a colour cannot perceive a sound, nor a sound a colour; that I am therefore one individual principle, distinct from colour and sound; and, for the same reason, from all other sensible things and inert ideas." [3] The concrete efficient causes of anything are defined as "spirits."

At this point, Berkeley's dialectic began to raise more problems for itself than he was apparently able to solve. His attempts to deal with them have a somewhat half-hearted air and are delivered more in the spirit of devout assertion than of firm demonstration. Among such problems are: (a) The problem of "individuals": how and why are the "spirits" differentiated from each other? (b) The problem of communication between different, individual "spirits," or the problem of "other minds": how do we and they "know" each other, and since our knowledge of each other is not really "idea" but that vaguer thing that Berkeley calls "notion," what empirical warrant would there be for including "notion" within the perimeter of knowledge at all? The term "notion" remains an empirical makeshift. The problem here, which Berkeley was unable to resolve with methodological consistency, is the problem of the relation of self to the "other," whether in parity to oneself as spirit, or as the Supreme "wholly other" who is God. (c) To confront this last problem, the problem of the internal dialectic of the realm of spirits, Berkeley would have had to engage such systematic questions as those of monism vs. dualism, the "part" vs. the "whole," freedom vs. necessity. These problems could also have been treated as problems of conflicting, competing or interacting causes. Apparently disinclined to engage the question on so ultimate a scale, Berkeley prefers to introduce the methodologically exceptional term "notion," and he allows it to foreclose the question.[4]

The basic achievement as to the nature of "causal" or "productive" action remains, however, intact and does not stand or fall with Berkeley's incomplete and not wholly philosophical theory of "spirits."

What Berkeley has done, in effect, is to reassert the classic Platonic-Aristotelian view on the problem. True causality must be distinguishable from the realm of "effects." Causes and effects are not to be considered interchangeable, depending on the point of view, as in the Hobbesian position. Nor is their relation in the "causal series" reversi-

---

[3] Cf. Berkeley's *Principles*, sections 2,7,27,137,138,139, etc.

[4] A. A. Luce: *Berkeley and Malebranche* (London: Oxford University Press; 1934), pp. 107 ff., gives a more positive character to Berkeley's thoughts on "knowledge of other spirits" by finding those thoughts to be rooted in Malebranche's conception of knowing by "analogy." Malebranche calls this "conjecture," and considers it to be the reliable ground of a good deal of real knowledge.

ble. True causes have an absolute priority, independence, and distinctiveness in the world of phenomena. This is proved by the fact that there *are* phenomena, recognizable and differentiated. The recognition and differentiation imply the existence of a "principle" distinct from the series. The only thing that satisfies the requirements of such a "principle" is spirit. Spirit is never, as in materialism, an effect; it is always and only a cause.

This is the position of the *Three Dialogues*. The argument in *Theory of Vision* (as in the *Principles*) was to the same effect. Precisely *because* ordinary "vision" is a complex phenomenon, involving the sense of touch (that is, oculo-muscular action both directly and as a kind of translated adaptation from our actual touch encounter with the world) and the sense of sight; and precisely *because* there are some otherwise unsolvable discrepancies between the touch element in vision and the optical element; therefore we must assume that the coordinating agent is not the eye taken as a camera (for a camera does not coordinate), but an *agent* using *eye*, tactile senses, and judgment as a complex instrument of *action* in the world.

That agent is, of course, the only *cause* of vision (it is not light, or the object, or color that could be such a cause), and that agent, as we have seen, is "spirit."

As for such "abstractions" as "extension," "space," "distance," "length," and so forth, one does not "see" them at all; and since "to be is to be perceived," those abstractions do not exist. What is more, it is hard to see what purpose it would serve if they did exist.[5] "We may fairly conclude," says Berkeley, "that the proper objects of Vision constitute the Universal Language of Nature." [6]

The "objects" of any perceptual activity are merely the signs, symbols, or signals for creative response on the part of an agent. These perceived signals are what Berkeley means by the "Universal Language of Nature." Empiricism has come all the way home in a theory of language as *action signs*.

3. Accounting for the stability of the world gives Berkeley no trouble at all.

If the traditional "system of nature" as a system of material objects has now been supplanted by a language system, and this language system is a series of clues for action by agents, then all one needs to guarantee the stability and reliability of the language is one of two things:

---

[5] Berkeley makes frequent use at these stages of his argument of the favorite tool of nominalist dialectic, "Occam's razor," or the principle of parsimony: "do not multiply essences," or abstractions.

[6] *Theory of Vision*, 147. Cf., 143, 144.

either established usage or a Supreme Speaker, Agent, Producer, and Arbiter of the Language, always there and always having spoken it— namely, God.[7]

A mere evolutionary naturalist or empiricist, such as the "emergent evolutionists" or "evolutionary pragmatists" of our day, might be content with the former. A revisionist-occasionalist, or philosopher of Theistic Being, might be happy with the latter. Berkeley has both: customary usage and God who supports the custom.

The difficulties that are really there arise *after* the conclusion, and not before it, and they have to do, as we have seen, with the problems of the status of "individuals" and their relation to the individual called original or supreme.

But Berkeley has already said all that he is prepared to say, as philosopher, on these questions, and we cannot press him for more. He leaves the problems of the details of "stability" to others who will come after him. The semantic and linguistic theorists, culminating in Wittgenstein, will press into the question of the real stability of language systems and "language games"[8] and the meaning to be assigned to the view that language *is* the world. The theorists of physical relativity— philosophers or physicists or both—will press into the question of how discrepant "parameters" of time or space or motion, mass or energy, co-ordinate into stable world lines; they will sometimes argue that a straight line is "really" the *longest* distance between two points (neither of which exist); and they will, on the whole, support, while refining, Berkeley's interpretation of nature, while not necessarily accept-

---

[7] If one must, one may recall here Ronald Knox's limerick on Berkeley's theory, which has been quoted almost to death:

> There was a young man who said, "God
> Must think it exceedingly odd
> If he finds that this tree
> Continues to be
> When there's no one about in the Quad."

Reply

> "Dear Sir:
> Your astonishment's odd:
> I am always about in the Quad.
> And that's why the tree
> Will continue to be,
> Since observed by
> Yours faithfully,
> God."

[8] Ludwig Wittgenstein: *Tractatus logico-philosophicus*, with an Introduction by Bertrand Russell (London: K. Paul, Trench and Trubner; 1922); and *Philosophical Investigations* (New York: Macmillan; 1953). The various references to Berkeley in J. O. Urmson: *Philosophical Analysis: Its Development Between the Two World Wars* (Oxford: at the Clarendon Press; 1956) suggest the general significance of Berkeley's philosophy in the background of the analytic movement.

ing either his premises or more ultimate conclusions.[9] Intuitionists such as Bergson [1] and Gestalt psychologists will share Berkeley's view that a sense activity such as "vision" is not a cameralike inverted recording of the mysteries of projective geometry "in" the world but rather a creative *reading* and *making* of the world which it reads. Physiologists of the eye are still engaged with some of the detailed mechanics of the situation that Berkeley handled, perhaps, rather cavalierly. But a considerable body of both scientific and philosophic opinion remains obligated to him, above and beyond the details.

Was Berkeley an "idealist"?

The answer seems to be, "Of course." Was Plato, then, an "idealist"? Is the answer here equally, "Of course"? Consider the difference between the status of "ideas" in Plato, and their status in Berkeley: how in the one they are "above" experience, judging it, in a sense producing it or making it conform to standards of recognizability; how they have the properties of "deathlessness," and so on. Their properties are quite the opposite in Berkeley.[2] In fact, they have for him no properties at all, except to be produced, to be inert, to be existent only because there is a perceiver about, even if he is only God! It is obvious that this word "idealism" covers a multitude of epistemological and ontological sins.

It is difficult even to fit Berkeley within the category of Kant's "Fourth Paralogism" of Pure Reason, which he calls the "Paralogism of Ideality" and which may be read to contain a reference, however oblique, to Berkeley.[3] For that which Kant there takes as the earmark of "ideality"—namely, a "doubtfulness" as to the existence of an ex-

---

[9] Some introduction to the paradoxes of contemporary relativity theory and their relation to traditional philosophic and scientific ideas may be obtained from A. N. Whitehead: *Science and the Modern World* (New York: Macmillan; 1925), Chs. VII, VIII, and IX, or from Bertrand Russell: *An Outline of Philosophy* (London: George Allen and Unwin, Ltd.; 1927), Part II.

[1] Henri Bergson: *The Creative Mind* (New York: Philosophical Library; 1946), Lecture on "Philosophical Intuition," esp. pp. 134 ff.

[2] In his *Siris: A Chain of Philosophical Reflexions and Inquiries* (1744), Berkeley is, as might be expected, well aware of the special character of the "idea" in Plato. Thus, *Siris*, section 335: "In Plato's style, the term *idea* doth not merely signify an inert inactive object of the understanding, but is used as synonymous with αἴτιον and ἀρχή, cause and principle." But Berkeley does not develop the significance of this difference for the two kinds of "idealism," nor does he seem to be wholly aware of the development that has taken place in his own philosophical "style," from the nominalist-empiricism of the *Three Dialogues* to the neo-Platonism of *Siris*. Perhaps the fact that the greater part of *Siris* is given over to a general philosophy of nature inspired by the medicinal properties of tar-water has something to do with Berkeley's failure to pursue the question.

[3] Kant: *Critique of Pure Reason*. Translated by Norman Kemp Smith (London: Macmillan; 1958), Second Division, Book II, Chapter I, pp. 344 ff. Cf. pp. 89, 244.

ternal (material?) object—is precisely that about which Berkeley has no doubts whatsoever: it certainly does *not* exist. What Kant calls "ideality" Berkeley would call merely "skepticism."

The question we have raised, if it is merely a question of a proper label, has and deserves no answer. It is only worth raising if it suggests, as it is meant to, that in the history of ideas the meaning of a label stands always in question.

The particular label of "idealist" is one that Berkeley hardly uses. His own profession is that of "immaterialist" and critic of "abstractions." His criticism of abstractionism outlives his so-called idealism.

Henry M. Rosenthal

SELECTED BIBLIOGRAPHY

Works

The Works of George Berkeley, D. D., formerly Bishop of Cloyne, including his posthumous works. With prefaces, annotations, appendices, and an account of his life by Alexander Campbell Fraser. Oxford: The Clarendon Press; 1901.
Vol. I. Philosophical Works, 1705–21.
Vol. II. Philosophical Works, 1732–33.
Vol. III. Philosophical Works, 1734–52.
Vol. IV. Miscellaneous Works, 1707–50.
The Works of George Berkeley, Bishop of Cloyne. Edited by A. A. Luce and T. E. Jessop. 9 vols. London: Nelson; 1948–57.

About Berkeley

Johnston, G. A.: *The Development of Berkeley's Philosophy.* London: Macmillan; 1923.
Luce, A. A.: *Berkeley and Malebranche; A Study in the Origins of Berkeley's Thought.* London: Oxford University Press; 1934.
—————— *Berkeley's Immaterialism.* London and New York: Nelson; 1945.
Rand, B.: *Berkeley's American Sojourn.* Cambridge: Harvard University Press; 1932.
Sillem, E. A.: *George Berkeley and the Proofs for the Existence of God.* London, New York, and Toronto: Longmans, Green; 1957.
Warnock, G. J.: *Berkeley.* Harmondsworth: Penguin Books (Pelican Paperback); 1953.
Wild, John: *George Berkeley, A Study of His Life and Philosophy.* Cambridge: Harvard University Press; 1936.
Wisdom, J. O.: *The Unconscious Origin of Berkeley's Philosophy.* London: Hogarth Press; 1953.

Articles on Berkeley in

The Dictionary of National Biography. Vol. IV. New York: Oxford University Press; 1885.
The Encyclopaedia Britannica. Ninth Edition. Vol. III. London; 1887.

THREE DIALOGUES

BETWEEN HYLAS AND PHILONOUS, IN OPPOSITION TO SCEPTICS AND ATHEISTS

THE PREFACE[1]

Though it seems the general opinion of the world, no less than the design of nature and providence, that the end of speculation be Practice, or the improvement and regulation of our lives and actions; yet those who are most addicted to speculative studies, seem as generally of another mind. And, indeed, if we consider the pains that have been taken to perplex the plainest things—that distrust of the senses, those doubts and scruples, those abstractions and refinements that occur in the very entrance of the sciences; it will not seem strange that men of leisure and curiosity should lay themselves out in fruitless disquisitions, without descending to the practical parts of life, or informing themselves in the more necessary and important parts of knowledge.

---

[1] This Preface was omitted by the author in the edition of 1734.

Upon the common principles of philosophers, we are not assured of the existence of things from their being perceived. And we are taught to distinguish their real nature from that which falls under our senses. Hence arises Scepticism and Paradoxes. It is not enough that we see and feel, that we taste and smell a thing: its true nature, its absolute external entity, is still concealed. For, though it be the fiction of our own brain, we have made it inaccessible to all our faculties. Sense is fallacious, reason defective. We spend our lives in doubting of those things which other men evidently know, and believing those things which they laugh at and despise.

In order, therefore, to divert the busy mind of man from vain researches, it seemed necessary to inquire into the source of its perplexities; and, if possible, to lay down such Principles as, by an easy solution of them, together with their own native evidence, may at once recommend themselves for genuine to the mind, and rescue it from those endless pursuits it is engaged in. Which with a plain demonstration of the Immediate Providence of an all-seeing God, and the natural Immortality of the soul, should seem the readiest preparation, as well as the strongest motive, to the study and practice of virtue.

This design I proposed in the First Part of a treatise concerning *Principles of Human Knowledge*, published in the year 1710. But, before I proceed to publish the Second Part, I thought it requisite to treat more clearly and fully of certain Principles laid down in the First, and to place them in a new light. Which is the business of the following *Dialogues*.

In this treatise, which does not presuppose in the reader any knowledge of what was contained in the former, it has been my aim to introduce the notions I advance into the mind in the most easy and familiar manner; especially because they carry with them a great opposition to the prejudices of philosophers, which have so far prevailed against the common sense and natural notions of mankind.

If the principles which I here endeavour to propagate are admitted for true, the consequences which, I think, evidently flow from thence are, that Atheism and Scepticism will be utterly destroyed, many intricate points made plain, great difficulties solved, several useless parts of science retrenched, speculation referred to practice, and men reduced from paradoxes to common sense.

And, although it may, perhaps, seem an uneasy reflexion to some that, when they have taken a circuit through so many refined and unvulgar notions, they should at last come to think like other men; yet, methinks, this return to the simple dictates of nature, after having wandered through the wild mazes of philosophy, is not unpleasant. It is like coming home from a long voyage: a man reflects with pleasure on the many difficulties and perplexities he has passed through, sets his heart at ease, and enjoys himself with more satisfaction for the future.

As it was my intention to convince Sceptics and Infidels by reason, so it has been my endeavour strictly to observe the most rigid laws of reasoning. And, to an impartial reader, I hope it will be manifest that the sublime notion of a God, and the comfortable expectation of Immortality, do naturally arise from a close and methodical application of thought—whatever may be the result of that loose, rambling way, not altogether improperly termed Free-thinking, by certain libertines in thought, who can no more endure the restraints of logic than those of religion or government.

It will perhaps be objected to my design that, so far as it tends to ease the mind of difficult and useless inquiries, it can affect only a few speculative persons; but, if by their speculations rightly placed, the study of morality and the law of nature were brought more into fashion among men of parts and genius, the discouragements that draw to Scepticism removed, the measures of right and wrong accurately defined, and the principles of Natural Religion reduced into regular systems, as artfully disposed and clearly connected as those of some other sciences: there are grounds to think these effects would not only have a gradual influence in repairing the too much defaced sense of virtue in the world; but also, by showing that such parts of revelation as lie within the reach of human inquiry are most agreeable to right reason, would dispose all prudent, unprejudiced persons to a modest and wary treatment of those sacred mysteries which are above the comprehension of our faculties.

It remains that I desire the reader to withhold his censure of these *Dialogues* till he has read them through. Otherwise he may lay them aside, in a mistake of their design, or on account of difficulties or objections which he would find answered in the sequel. A treatise of this nature would require to be once read over coherently, in order to comprehend its design, the proofs, solution of difficulties, and the connexion and disposition of its parts. If it be thought to deserve a second reading, this, I imagine, will make the entire scheme very plain; especially if recourse be had to an Essay I wrote some years since upon *Vision*, and the Treatise concerning the *Principles of Human Knowledge*—wherein divers notions advanced in these *Dialogues* are farther pursued, or placed in different lights, and other points handled which naturally tend to confirm and illustrate them.

THE

FIRST DIALOGUE

Philonous. Good morning, *Hylas:* I did not expect to find you abroad so early.

Hylas. It is indeed something unusual; but my thoughts were so taken up with a subject I was discoursing of last night, that finding I could not sleep, I resolved to rise and take a turn in the garden.

Philonous. It happened well, to let you see what innocent and agreeable pleasures you lose every morning. Can there be a pleasanter time of the day, or a more delightful season of the year? That purple sky, those wild but sweet notes of birds, the fragrant bloom upon the trees and flowers, the gentle influence of the rising sun, these and a thousand nameless beauties of nature inspire the soul with secret transports; its faculties too being at this time fresh and lively, are fit for these meditations, which the solitude of a garden and tranquillity of the morning naturally dispose us to. But I am afraid I interrupt your thoughts: for you seemed very intent on something.

Hylas. It is true, I was, and shall be obliged to you if you will permit me to go on in the same vein; not that I would by any means deprive myself of your company, for my thoughts always flow more easily in conversation with a friend, than when I am alone: but my request is, that you would suffer me to impart my reflexions to you.

Philonous. With all my heart, it is what I should have requested myself if you had not prevented me.

Hylas. I was considering the old fate of those men who have in all ages, through an affectation of being distinguished from the vulgar, or some unaccountable turn of thought, pretended either to believe nothing at all, or to believe the most extravagant things in the world.

This however might be borne, if their paradoxes and scepticism did not draw after them some consequences of general disadvantage to mankind. But the mischief lieth here; that when men of less leisure see them who are supposed to have spent their whole time in the pursuits of knowledge professing an entire ignorance of all things, or advancing such notions as are repugnant to plain and commonly received principles, they will be tempted to entertain suspicions concerning the most important truths, which they had hitherto held sacred and unquestionable.

Philonous. I entirely agree with you, as to the ill tendency of the affected doubts of some philosophers, and fantastical conceits of others. I am even so far gone of late in this way of thinking, that I have quitted several of the sublime notions I had got in their schools for vulgar opinions. And I give it you on my word, since this revolt from metaphysical notions, to the plain dictates of nature and common sense, I find my understanding strangely enlightened, so that I can now easily comprehend a great many things which before were all mystery and riddle.

Hylas. I am glad to find there was nothing in the accounts I heard of you.

Philonous. Pray, what were those?

Hylas. You were represented in last night's conversation, as one who maintained the most extravagant opinion that ever entered into the mind of man, to wit, that there is no such thing as *material substance* in the world.

Philonous. That there is no such thing as what Philosophers call *material substance*, I am seriously persuaded: but, if I were made to see anything absurd or sceptical in this, I should then have the same reason to renounce this that I imagine I have now to reject the contrary opinion.

Hylas. What! can anything be more fantastical, more repugnant to common sense, or a more manifest piece of Scepticism, than to believe there is no such thing as *matter*?

Philonous. Softly, good Hylas. What if it should prove, that you, who hold there is, are, by virtue of that opinion, a greater sceptic, and maintain more paradoxes and repugnances to common sense, than I who believe no such thing?

Hylas. You may as soon persuade me, the part is greater than the whole, as that, in order to avoid absurdity and Scepticism, I should ever be obliged to give up my opinion in this point.

Philonous. Well then, are you content to admit that opinion for true, which, upon examination, shall appear most agreeable to common sense, and remote from Scepticism?

Hylas. With all my heart. Since you are for raising disputes about the plainest things in nature, I am content for once to hear what you have to say.

Philonous. Pray, *Hylas*, what do you mean by a *sceptic?*

Hylas. I mean what all men mean, one that doubts of everything.

Philonous. He then who entertains no doubt concerning some particular point, with regard to that point cannot be thought a sceptic.

Hylas. I agree with you.

Philonous. Whether doth doubting consist in embracing the affirmative or negative side of a question?

Hylas. In neither; for whoever understands English cannot but know that *doubting* signifies a suspense between both.

Philonous. He then that denieth any point, can no more be said to doubt of it, than he who affirmeth it with the same degree of assurance.

Hylas. True.

Philonous. And, consequently, for such his denial is no more to be esteemed a sceptic than the other.

Hylas. I acknowledge it.

Philonous. How cometh it to pass then, *Hylas*, that you pronounce me a *sceptic*, because I deny what you affirm, to wit, the existence of Matter? Since, for aught you can tell, I am as peremptory in my denial, as you in your affirmation.

Hylas. Hold, *Philonous*, I have been a little out in my definition; but every false step a man makes in discourse is not to be insisted on. I said indeed that a *sceptic* was one who doubted of everything; but I should have added, or who denies the reality and truth of things.

Philonous. What things? Do you mean the principles and theorems of sciences? But these you know are universal intellectual notions, and consequently independent of Matter; the denial therefore of this doth not imply the denying them.

Hylas. I grant it. But are there no other things? What think you of distrusting the senses, of denying the real existence of sensible things, or pretending to know nothing of them. Is not this sufficient to denominate a man a *sceptic?*

Philonous. Shall we therefore examine which of us it is that denies the reality of sensible things, or professes the greatest ignorance of them; since, if I take you rightly, he is to be esteemed the greatest *sceptic?*

Hylas. That is what I desire.

Philonous. What mean you by Sensible Things?

Hylas. Those things which are perceived by the senses. Can you imagine that I mean anything else?

Philonous. Pardon me, *Hylas,* if I am desirous clearly to apprehend your notions, since this may much shorten our inquiry. Suffer me then to ask you this farther question. Are those things only perceived by the senses which are perceived immediately? Or, may those things properly be said to be *sensible* which are perceived mediately, or not without the intervention of others?

Hylas. I do not sufficiently understand you.

Philonous. In reading a book, what I immediately perceive are the letters, but mediately, or by means of these, are suggested to my mind the notions of God, virtue, truth, &c. Now, that the letters are truly sensible things, or perceived by sense, there is no doubt: but I would know whether you take the things suggested by them to be so too.

Hylas. No, certainly; it were absurd to think God or *virtue* sensible things, though they may be signified and suggested to the mind by sensible marks, with which they have an arbitrary connexion.

Philonous. It seems then, that by *sensible things* you mean those only which can be perceived *immediately* by sense?

Hylas. Right.

Philonous. Doth it not follow from this, that though I see one part of the sky red, and another blue, and that my reason doth thence evidently conclude there must be some cause of that diversity of colours, yet that cause cannot be said to be a sensible thing, or perceived by the sense of seeing?

Hylas. It doth.

Philonous. In like manner, though I hear variety of sounds, yet I cannot be said to hear the causes of those sounds?

Hylas. You cannot.

Philonous. And when by my touch I perceive a thing to be hot and heavy, I cannot say, with any truth or propriety, that I feel the cause of its heat or weight?

Hylas. To prevent any more questions of this kind, I tell you once for all, that by *sensible things* I mean those only which are perceived by sense, and that in truth the senses perceive nothing which they do not perceive immediately: for they make no inferences. The deducing therefore of causes or occasions from effects and appearances, which alone are perceived by sense, entirely relates to reason.

Philonous. This point then is agreed between us—that *sensible things are those only which are immediately perceived by sense.* You will farther inform me, whether we immediately perceive by sight anything beside light, and colours, and figures; or by hearing, anything but sounds; by the palate, anything beside tastes; by the smell, beside odours; or by the touch, more than tangible qualities.

Hylas. We do not.

Philonous. It seems, therefore, that if you take away all sensible qualities, there remains nothing sensible?

Hylas. I grant it.

Philonous. Sensible things therefore are nothing else but so many sensible qualities, or combinations of sensible qualities?

Hylas. Nothing else.

Philonous. Heat is then a sensible thing?

Hylas. Certainly.

Philonous. Doth the reality of sensible things consist in being perceived? or, is it something distinct from their being perceived, and that bears no relation to the mind?

Hylas. To *exist* is one thing, and to be *perceived* is another.

Philonous. I speak with regard to sensible things only: and of these I ask, whether by their real existence you mean a subsistence exterior to the mind, and distinct from their being perceived?

Hylas. I mean a real absolute being, distinct from, and without any relation to their being perceived.

Philonous. Heat therefore, if it be allowed a real being, must exist without the mind?

Hylas. It must.

Philonous. Tell me, *Hylas,* is this real existence equally compatible to all degrees of heat, which we perceive; or is there any reason why we should attribute it to some, and deny it to others? and if there be, pray let me know that reason.

Hylas. Whatever degree of heat we perceive by sense, we may be sure the same exists in the object that occasions it.

Philonous. What! the greatest as well as the least?

Hylas. I tell you, the reason is plainly the same in respect of both: they are both perceived by sense; nay, the greater degree of heat is more sensibly perceived; and consequently, if there is any difference, we are more certain of its real existence than we can be of the reality of a lesser degree.

Philonous. But is not the most vehement and intense degree of heat a very great pain?

Hylas. No one can deny it.

Philonous. And is any unperceiving thing capable of pain or pleasure?

Hylas. No certainly.

Philonous. Is your material substance a senseless being, or a being endowed with sense and perception?

Hylas. It is senseless without doubt.

Philonous. It cannot therefore be the subject of pain?

Hylas. By no means.

Philonous. Nor consequently of the greatest heat perceived by sense, since you acknowledge this to be no small pain?

Hylas. I grant it.

Philonous. What shall we say then of your external object; is it a material Substance, or no?

Hylas. It is a material substance with the sensible qualities inhering in it.

Philonous. How then can a great heat exist in it, since you own it cannot in a material substance? I desire you would clear this point.

Hylas. Hold, *Philonous,* I fear I was out in yielding intense heat to be a pain. It should seem rather, that pain is something distinct from heat, and the consequence or effect of it.

Philonous. Upon putting your hand near the fire, do you perceive one simple uniform sensation, or two distinct sensations?

Hylas. But one simple sensation.

Philonous. Is not the heat immediately perceived?

Hylas. It is.

Philonous. And the pain?

Hylas. True.

Philonous. Seeing therefore they are both immediately perceived at the same time, and the fire affects you only with one simple, or un-compounded idea, it follows that this same simple idea is both the intense heat immediately perceived, and the pain; and, consequently, that the intense heat immediately perceived, is nothing distinct from a particular sort of pain.

Hylas. It seems so.

Philonous. Again, try in your thoughts, *Hylas,* if you can conceive a vehement sensation to be without pain or pleasure.

Hylas. I cannot.

Philonous. Or can you frame to yourself an idea of sensible pain or pleasure, in general, abstracted from every particular idea of heat, cold, tastes, smells? &c.

Hylas. I do not find that I can.

Philonous. Doth it not therefore follow, that sensible pain is nothing distinct from those sensations or ideas,—in an intense degree?

Hylas. It is undeniable; and, to speak the truth, I begin to suspect a very great heat cannot exist but in a mind perceiving it.

Philonous. What! are you then in that *sceptical* state of suspense, between affirming and denying?

Hylas. I think I may be positive in the point. A very violent and painful heat cannot exist without the mind.

Philonous. It hath not therefore, according to you, any real being?

Hylas. I own it.

Philonous. Is it therefore certain, that there is no body in nature really hot?

Hylas. I have not denied there is any real heat in bodies. I only say, there is no such thing as an intense real heat.

Philonous. But, did you not say before that all degrees of heat were equally real; or, if there was any difference, that the greater were more undoubtedly real than the lesser?

Hylas. True: but it was because I did not then consider the ground there is for distinguishing between them, which I now plainly see. And it is this:—because intense heat is nothing else but a particular kind of painful sensation; and pain cannot exist but in a perceiving being; it follows that no intense heat can really exist in an unperceiving corporeal substance. But this is no reason why we should deny heat in an inferior degree to exist in such a substance.

Philonous. But how shall we be able to discern those degrees of heat which exist only in the mind from those which exist without it?

Hylas. That is no difficult matter. You know the least pain cannot exist unperceived; whatever, therefore, degree of heat is a pain exists only in the mind. But, as for all other degrees of heat, nothing obliges us to think the same of them.

Philonous. I think you granted before that no unperceiving being was capable of pleasure, any more than of pain.

Hylas. I did.

Philonous. And is not warmth, or a more gentle degree of heat than what causes uneasiness, a pleasure?

Hylas. What then?

Philonous. Consequently, it cannot exist without the mind in an unperceiving substance, or body.

Hylas. So it seems.

Philonous. Since, therefore, as well those degrees of heat that are not painful, as those that are, can exist only in a thinking substance; may we not conclude that external bodies are absolutely incapable of any degree of heat whatsoever?

Hylas. On second thoughts, I do not think it is so evident that warmth is a pleasure, as that a great degree of heat is a pain.

Philonous. I do not pretend that warmth is as great as pleasure as heat is a pain. But, if you grant it to be even a small pleasure, it serves to make good my conclusion.

Hylas. I could rather call it an *indolence*. It seems to be nothing more than a privation of both pain and pleasure. And that such a quality or state as this may agree to an unthinking substance, I hope you will not deny.

Philonous. If you are resolved to maintain that warmth, or a gentle degree of heat, is no pleasure, I know not how to convince you otherwise, than by appealing to your own sense. But what think you of cold?

Hylas. The same that I do of heat. An intense degree of cold is a pain; for to feel a very great cold, is to perceive a great uneasiness: it cannot therefore exist without the mind; but a lesser degree of cold may, as well as a lesser degree of heat.

Philonous. Those bodies, therefore, upon whose application to our own, we perceive a moderate degree of heat, must be concluded to have a moderate degree of heat or warmth in them; and those, upon whose application we feel a like degree of cold, must be thought to have cold in them.

Hylas. They must.

Philonous. Can any doctrine be true that necessarily leads a man into an absurdity?

Hylas. Without doubt it cannot.

Philonous. Is it not an absurdity to think that the same thing should be at the same time both cold and warm?

Hylas. It is.

Philonous. Suppose now one of your hands hot, and the other cold, and that they are both at once put into the same vessel of water, in an intermediate state; will not the water seem cold to one hand, and warm to the other?

Hylas. It will.

Philonous. Ought we not therefore, by our principles, to conclude it is really both cold and warm at the same time, that is, according to your own concession, to believe an absurdity?

Hylas. I confess it seems so.

Philonous. Consequently, the principles themselves are false, since you have granted that no true principle leads to an absurdity.

Hylas. But, after all, can anything be more absurd than to say, *there is no heat in the fire?*

Philonous. To make the point still clearer; tell me whether, in two cases exactly alike, we ought not to make the same judgment?

Hylas. We ought.

Philonous. When a pin pricks your finger, doth it not rend and divide the fibres of your flesh?

Hylas. It doth.

Philonous. And when a coal burns your finger, doth it any more?

Hylas. It doth not.

Philonous. Since, therefore, you neither judge the sensation itself occasioned by the pin, nor anything like it to be in the pin; you should not, conformably to what you have now granted, judge the sensation occasioned by the fire, or anything like it, to be in the fire.

Hylas. Well, since it must be so, I am content to yield this point, and acknowledge that heat and cold are only sensations existing in our minds. But there still remain qualities enough to secure the reality of external things.

Philonous. But what will you say, *Hylas,* if it shall appear that the case is the same with regard to all other sensible qualities, and that they can no more be supposed to exist without the mind, than heat and cold?

Hylas. Then indeed you will have done something to the purpose; but that is what I despair of seeing proved.

Philonous. Let us examine them in order. What think you of *tastes* —do they exist without the mind, or no?

Hylas. Can any man in his senses doubt whether sugar is sweet, or wormwood bitter?

Philonous. Inform me, *Hylas.* Is a sweet taste a particular kind of pleasure or pleasant sensation, or is it not?

Hylas. It is.

Philonous. And is not bitterness some kind of uneasiness or pain?

Hylas. I grant it.

Philonous. If therefore sugar and wormwood are unthinking corporeal substances existing without the mind, how can sweetness and bitterness, that is, pleasure and pain, agree to them?

Hylas. Hold, *Philonous,* I now see what it was deluded me all this time. You asked whether heat and cold, sweetness and bitterness, were not particular sorts of pleasure and pain; to which I answered simply, that they were. Whereas I should have thus distinguished:—those qualities, as perceived by us, are pleasures or pains; but not as existing in the external objects. We must not therefore conclude absolutely, that there is no heat in the fire, or sweetness in the sugar, but only that heat or sweetness, as perceived by us, are not in the fire or sugar. What say you to this?

Philonous. I say it is nothing to the purpose. Our discourse proceeded altogether concerning sensible things, which you defined to be, *the things we immediately perceive by our senses.* Whatever other qualities, therefore, you speak of, as distinct from these, I know nothing of them, neither do they at all belong to the point in dispute. You may, indeed, pretend to have discovered certain qualities which you do not perceive, and assert those insensible qualities exist in fire and sugar. But what use can be made of this to your present purpose, I am at a loss to conceive. Tell me then once more, do you acknowledge that heat and cold, sweetness and bitterness (meaning those qualities which are perceived by the senses), do not exist without the mind?

Hylas. I see it is to no purpose to hold out, so I give up the cause as to those mentioned qualities. Though I profess it sounds oddly, to say that sugar is not sweet.

Philonous. But, for your farther satisfaction, take this along with you: that which at other times seems sweet, shall, to a distempered palate, appear bitter. And, nothing can be plainer than that divers persons perceive different tastes in the same food; since that which one man delights in, another abhors. And how could this be, if the taste was something really inherent in the food?

Hylas. I acknowledge I know not how.

Philonous. In the next place, *odours* are to be considered. And, with regard to these, I would fain know whether what has been said of tastes doth not exactly agree to them? Are they not so many pleasing or displeasing sensations?

Hylas. They are.

Philonous. Can you then conceive it possible that they should exist in an unperceiving thing?

Hylas. I cannot.

Philonous. Or, can you imagine that filth and ordure affect those brute animals that feed on them out of choice, with the same smells which we perceive in them?

Hylas. By no means.

Philonous. May we not therefore conclude of smells, as of the other forementioned qualities, that they cannot exist in any but a perceiving substance or mind.

Hylas. I think so.

Philonous. Then as to *sounds*, what must we think of them: are they accidents really inherent in external bodies, or not?

Hylas. That they inhere not in the sonorous bodies is plain from hence; because a bell struck in the exhausted receiver of an air-pump sends forth no sound. The air, therefore, must be thought the subject of sound.

Philonous. What reason is there for that, *Hylas?*

Hylas. Because, when any motion is raised in the air, we perceive a sound greater or lesser, according to the air's motion; but without some motion in the air, we never hear any sound at all.

Philonous. And granting that we never hear a sound but when some motion is produced in the air, yet I do not see how you can infer from thence, that the sound itself is in the air.

Hylas. It is this very motion in the external air that produces in the mind the sensation of *sound*. For, striking on the drum of the ear, it causeth a vibration, which by the auditory nerves being communicated to the brain, the soul is thereupon affected with the sensation called *sound*.

Philonous. What! is sound then a sensation?

Hylas. I tell you, as perceived by us, it is a particular sensation in the mind.

Philonous. And can any sensation exist without the mind?

Hylas. No, certainly.

Philonous. How then can sound, being a sensation, exist in the air, if by the *air* you mean a senseless substance existing without the mind?

Hylas. You must distinguish, *Philonous*, between sound as it is perceived by us, and as it is in itself; or (which is the same thing) between the sound we immediately perceive, and that which exists without us. The former, indeed, is a particular kind of sensation, but the latter is merely a vibrative or undulatory motion in the air.

Philonous. I thought I had already obviated that distinction, by the answer I gave when you were applying it in a like case before. But, to say no more of that, are you sure then that sound is really nothing but motion?

Hylas. I am.

Philonous. Whatever therefore agrees to real sound, may with truth be attributed to motion?

Hylas. It may.

Philonous. It is then good sense to speak of *motion* as of a thing that is *loud, sweet, acute, or grave*.

Hylas. I see you are resolved not to understand me. Is it not evident those accidents or modes belong only to sensible sound, or *sound* in the common acceptation of the word, but not to *sound* in the real and philosophic sense; which, as I just now told you, is nothing but a certain motion of the air?

Philonous. It seems then there are two sorts of sound—the one vulgar, or that which is heard, the other philosophical and real?

Hylas. Even so.

Philonous. And the latter consists in motion?

Hylas. I told you so before.

Philonous. Tell me, *Hylas*, to which of the senses, think you, the idea of motion belongs? to the hearing?

Hylas. No, certainly; but to the sight and touch.

Philonous. It should follow then, that, according to you, real sounds may possibly be *seen* or *felt*, but never *heard*.

Hylas. Look you, *Philonous*, you may, if you please, make a jest of my opinion, but that will not alter the truth of things. I own, indeed, the inferences you draw me into, sound something oddly; but common language, you know, is framed by, and for the use of the vulgar: we must not therefore wonder, if expressions adapted to exact philosophic notions seem uncouth and out of the way.

Philonous. Is it come to that? I assure you, I imagine myself to have gained no small point, since you make so light of departing from common phrases and opinions; it being a main part of our inquiry, to examine whose notions are widest of the common road, and most repugnant to the general sense of the world. But, can you think it no more than a philosophical paradox, to say that *real sounds are never heard,* and that the idea of them is obtained by some other sense? And is there nothing in this contrary to nature and the truth of things?

Hylas. To deal ingenuously, I do not like it. And, after the concessions already made, I had as well grant that sounds too have no real being without the mind.

Philonous. And I hope you will make no difficulty to acknowledge the same of *colours.*

Hylas. Pardon me: the case of colours is very different. Can anything be plainer than that we see them on the objects?

Philonous. The objects you speak of are, I suppose, corporeal Substances existing without the mind?

Hylas. They are.

Philonous. And have true and real colours inhering in them?

Hylas. Each visible object hath that colour which we see in it.

Philonous. How! is there anything visible but what we perceive by sight?

Hylas. There is not.

Philonous. And, do we perceive anything by sense which we do not perceive immediately?

Hylas. How often must I be obliged to repeat the same thing? I tell you, we do not.

Philonous. Have patience, good *Hylas;* and tell me once more, whether there is anything immediately perceived by the senses, except sensible qualities. I know you asserted there was not; but I would now be informed, whether you still persist in the same opinion.

Hylas. I do.

Philonous. Pray, is your corporeal substance either a sensible quality, or made up of sensible qualities?

Hylas. What a question that is! who ever thought it was?

Philonous. My reason for asking was, because in saying, *each visible object hath that colour which we see in it,* you make visible objects to be corporeal substances; which implies either that corporeal substances are sensible qualities, or else that there is something beside sensible qualities perceived by sight: but, as this point was formerly agreed between us, and is still maintained by you, it is a clear consequence, that your corporeal substance is nothing distinct from sensible qualities.

Hylas. You may draw as many absurd consequences as you please, and endeavour to perplex the plainest things; but you shall never persuade me out of my senses. I clearly understand my own meaning.

Philonous. I wish you would make me understand it too. But, since you are unwilling to have your notion of corporeal substance examined, I shall urge that point no farther. Only be pleased to let me know, whether the same colours which we see exist in external bodies, or some other.

Hylas. The very same.

Philonous. What! are then the beautiful red and purple we see on yonder clouds really in them? Or do you imagine they have in themselves any other form than that of a dark mist or vapour?

Hylas. I must own, *Philonous,* those colours are not really in the clouds as they seem to be at this distance. They are only apparent colours.

Philonous. Apparent call you them? how shall we distinguish these apparent colours from real?

Hylas. Very easily. Those are to be thought apparent which, appearing only at a distance, vanish upon a nearer approach.

Philonous. And those, I suppose, are to be thought real which are discovered by the most near and exact survey.

Hylas. Right.

Philonous. Is the nearest and exactest survey made by the help of a microscope, or by the naked eye?

Hylas. By a microscope, doubtless.

Philonous. But a microscope often discovers colours in an object different from those perceived by the unassisted sight. And, in case we had microscopes magnifying to any assigned degree, it is certain that no object whatsoever, viewed through them, would appear in the same colour which it exhibits to the naked eye.

Hylas. And what will you conclude from all this? You cannot argue that there are really and naturally no colours on objects: because by artificial managements they may be altered, or made to vanish.

Philonous. I think it may evidently be concluded from your own concessions, that all the colours we see with our naked eyes are only apparent as those on the clouds, since they vanish upon a more close and accurate inspection which is afforded us by a microscope. Then, as to what you say by way of prevention: I ask you whether the real and natural state of an object is better discovered by a very sharp and piercing sight, or by one which is less sharp?

Hylas. By the former without doubt.

Philonous. Is it not plain from *Dioptrics* that microscopes make the sight more penetrating, and represent objects as they would appear to the eye in case it were naturally endowed with a most exquisite sharpness?

Hylas. It is.

Philonous. Consequently the microscopical representation is to be thought that which best sets forth the real nature of the thing, or what it is in itself. The colours, therefore, by it perceived are more genuine and real than those perceived otherwise.

Hylas. I confess there is something in what you say.

Philonous. Besides, it is not only possible but manifest, that there actually are animals whose eyes are by nature framed to perceive those things which by reason of their minuteness escape our sight. What think you of those inconceivably small animals perceived by glasses? must we suppose they are all stark blind? Or, in case they see, can it be imagined their sight hath not the same use in preserving their bodies from injuries, which appears in that of all other animals? And if it hath, is it not evident they must see particles less than their own bodies, which will present them with a far different view in each object from that which strikes our senses? Even our own eyes do not always represent objects to us after the same manner. In the *jaundice* every one knows that all things seem yellow. Is it not therefore highly probable those animals in whose eyes we discern a very different texture from that of ours, and whose bodies abound with different humours, do not see the same colours in every object that we do? From all which, should it not seem to follow that all colours are equally apparent, and that none of those which we perceive are really inherent in any outward object?

Hylas. It should.

Philonous. The point will be past all doubt, if you consider that, in case colours were real properties or affections inherent in external bodies, they could admit of no alteration without some change wrought in the very bodies themselves: but, is it not evident from what hath been said that, upon the use of microscopes, upon a change happening in the humours of the eye, or a variation of distance, without any manner of real alteration in the thing itself, the colours of any object are either changed, or totally disappear? Nay, all other circumstances remaining the same, change but the situation of some objects, and they shall present different colours to the eye. The same thing happens upon viewing an object in various degrees of light. And what is more known than that the same bodies appear differently coloured by candlelight from what they do in the open day? Add to these the experiment of a prism which, separating the heterogeneous rays of light, alters the colour of any object, and will cause the whitest to appear of a deep blue or red to the naked eye. And now tell me whether you are still of opinion that every body hath its true real colour inhering in it; and, if you think it hath, I would fain know farther from you, what certain distance and position of the object, what peculiar texture and formation of the eye, what degree or kind of light is necessary for ascertaining that true colour, and distinguishing it from apparent ones.

Hylas. I own myself entirely satisfied, that they are all equally apparent, and that there is no such thing as colour really inhering in external bodies, but that it is altogether in the light. And what confirms me in this opinion is that in proportion to the light colours are still more or less vivid; and if there be no light, then are there no colours perceived. Besides, allowing there are colours on external objects, yet, how is it possible for us to perceive them? For no external body affects the mind, unless it acts first on our organs of sense. But the only action of bodies is motion; and motion cannot be communicated otherwise than by impulse. A distant object therefore cannot act on the eye, nor consequently make itself or its properties perceivable to the soul. Whence it plainly follows that it is immediately some contiguous substance, which, operating on the eye, occasions a perception of colours: and such is light.

Philonous. How! is light then a substance?

Hylas. I tell you, *Philonous*, external light is nothing but a thin fluid substance, whose minute particles being agitated with a brisk motion, and in various manners reflected from the different surfaces of outward objects to the eyes, communicate different motions to the optic nerves; which, being propagated to the brain, cause therein various impressions; and these are attended with the sensations of red, blue, yellow, &c.

Philonous. It seems then the light doth no more than shake the optic nerves.

Hylas. Nothing else.

Philonous. And, consequent to each particular motion of the nerves, the mind is affected with a sensation, which is some particular colour.

Hylas. Right.

Philonous. And these sensations have no existence without the mind.

Hylas. They have not.

Philonous. How then do you affirm that colours are in the light; since by *light* you understand a corporeal substance external to the mind?

Hylas. Light and colours, as immediately perceived by us, I grant cannot exist without the mind. But, in themselves they are only the motions and configurations of certain insensible particles of matter.

Philonous. Colours, then, in the vulgar sense, or taken for the immediate objects of sight, cannot agree to any but a perceiving substance.

Hylas. That is what I say.

Philonous. Well then, since you give up the point as to those sensible qualities which are alone thought colours by all mankind beside, you may hold what you please with regard to those invisible ones of the philosophers. It is not my business to dispute about them; only I would advise you to bethink yourself, whether, considering the inquiry we are upon, it be prudent for you to affirm—*the red and blue which we see are not real colours, but certain unknown motions and figures, which no man ever did or can see, are truly so.* Are not these shocking notions, and are not they subject to as many ridiculous inferences, as those you were obliged to renounce before in the case of sounds?

Hylas. I frankly own, *Philonous,* that it is in vain to stand out any longer. Colours, sounds, tastes, in a word all those termed *secondary qualities,* have certainly no existence without the mind. But, by this acknowledgement I must not be supposed to derogate anything from the reality of Matter or external objects; seeing it is no more than several philosophers maintain, who nevertheless are the farthest imaginable from denying Matter. For the clearer understanding of this, you must know sensible qualities are by philosophers divided into *primary* and *secondary.* The former are Extension, Figure, Solidity, Gravity, Motion, and Rest. And these they hold exist really in bodies. The latter are those above enumerated; or, briefly, all sensible qualities beside the Primary, which they assert are only so many sensations or ideas existing nowhere but in the mind. But all this, I doubt not, you are apprised of. For my part, I have been a long time sensible there was such an opinion current among philosophers, but was never thoroughly convinced of its truth until now.

Philonous. You are still then of opinion that *extension* and *figures* are inherent in external unthinking substances?

Hylas. I am.

Philonous. But what if the same arguments which are brought against Secondary Qualities will hold good against these also?

Hylas. Why then I shall be obliged to think, they too exist only in the mind.

Philonous. Is it your opinion the very figure and extension which you perceive by sense exist in the outward object or material substance?

Hylas. It is.

Philonous. Have all other animals as good grounds to think the same of the figure and extension which they see and feel?

Hylas. Without doubt, if they have any thought at all.

Philonous. Answer me, *Hylas.* Think you the senses were bestowed upon all animals for their preservation and well-being in life? or were they given to men alone for this end?

Hylas. I make no question but they have the same use in all other animals.

Philonous. If so, is it not necessary they should be enabled by them to perceive their own limbs, and those bodies which are capable of harming them?

Hylas. Certainly.

Philonous. A mite therefore must be supposed to see his own foot, and things equal or even less than it, as bodies of some considerable dimension; though at the same time they appear to you scarce discernible, or at best as so many visible points?

Hylas. I cannot deny it.

Philonous. And to creatures less than the mite they will seem yet larger?

Hylas. They will.

Philonous. Insomuch that what you can hardly discern will to another extremely minute animal appear as some huge mountain?

Hylas. All this I grant.

Philonous. Can one and the same thing be at the same time in itself of different dimensions?

Hylas. That were absurd to imagine.

Philonous. But, from what you have laid down it follows that both the extension by you perceived, and that perceived by the mite itself, as likewise all those perceived by lesser animals, are each of them the true extension of the mite's foot; that is to say, by your own principles you are led into an absurdity.

Hylas. There seems to be some difficulty in the point.

Philonous. Again, have you not acknowledged that no real inherent property of any object can be changed without some change in the thing itself?

Hylas. I have.

Philonous. But, as we approach to or recede from an object, the visible extension varies, being at one distance ten or a hundred times greater than at another. Doth it not therefore follow from hence likewise that it is not really inherent in the object?

Hylas. I own I am at a loss what to think.

Philonous. Your judgment will soon be determined, if you will venture to think as freely concerning this quality as you have done concerning the rest. Was it not admitted as a good argument, that neither heat nor cold was in the water, because it seemed warm to one hand and cold to the other?

Hylas. It was.

Philonous. Is it not the very same reasoning to conclude there is no extension or figure in an object, because to one eye it shall seem little, smooth, and round, when at the same time it appears to the other, great, uneven, and angular?

Hylas. The very same. But does this latter fact ever happen?

Philonous. You may at any time make the experiment, by looking with one eye bare, and with the other through a microscope.

Hylas. I know not how to maintain it, and yet I am loath to give up *extension*, I see so many odd consequences following upon such a concession.

Philonous. Odd, say you? After the concessions already made, I hope you will stick at nothing for its oddness.[1] But, on the other hand, should it not seem very odd, if the general reasoning which includes all other sensible qualities did not also include extension? If it be allowed that no idea nor anything like an idea can exist in an unperceiving substance, then surely it follows that no figure or mode of extension, which we can either perceive or imagine, or have any idea of, can be really inherent in Matter; not to mention the peculiar difficulty there must be in conceiving a material substance, prior to and distinct from extension, to be the *substratum* of extension. Be the sensible quality what it will— figure, or sound, or colour; it seems alike impossible it should subsist in that which doth not perceive it.

Hylas. I give up the point for the present, reserving still a right to retract my opinion, in case I shall hereafter discover any false step in my progress to it.

Philonous. That is a right you cannot be denied. Figures and extension being despatched, we proceed next to *motion*. Can a real motion in any external body be at the same time both very swift and very slow?

Hylas. It cannot.

Philonous. Is not the motion of a body swift in a reciprocal proportion to the time it takes up in describing any given space? Thus a body that describes a mile in an hour moves three times faster than it would in case it described only a mile in three hours.

Hylas. I agree with you.

Philonous. And is not time measured by the succession of ideas in our minds?

---

[1] The remainder of the present paragraph was not contained in the first and second editions.

Hylas. It is.

Philonous. And is it not possible ideas should succeed one another twice as fast in your mind as they do in mine, or in that of some spirit of another kind?

Hylas. I own it.

Philonous. Consequently, the same body may to another seem to perform its motion over any space in half the time that it doth to you. And the same reasoning will hold as to any other proportion: that is to say, according to your principles (since the motions perceived are both really in the object) it is possible one and the same body shall be really moved the same way at once, both very swift and very slow. How is this consistent either with common sense, or with what you just now granted?

Hylas. I have nothing to say to it.

Philonous. Then as for *solidity*; either you do not mean any sensible quality by that word, and so it is beside our inquiry: or if you do, it must be either hardness or resistance. But both the one and the other are plainly relative to our senses: it being evident that what seems hard to one animal may appear soft to another, who hath greater force and firmness of limbs. Nor is it less plain that the resistance I feel is not in the body.

Hylas. I own the very sensation of resistance, which is all you immediately perceive, is not in the *body*, but the cause of that sensation is.

Philonous. But the causes of our sensations are not things immediately perceived, and therefore not sensible. This point I thought had been already determined.

Hylas. I own it was; but you will pardon me if I seem a little embarrassed: I know not how to quit my old notions.

Philonous. To help you out, do but consider that if *extension* be once acknowledged to have no existence without the mind, the same must necessarily be granted of motion, solidity, and gravity—since they all evidently suppose extension. It is therefore superfluous to inquire particularly concerning each of them. In denying extension, you have denied them all to have any real existence.

Hylas. I wonder, *Philonous*, if what you say be true, why those philosophers who deny the Secondary Qualities any real existence, should yet attribute it to the Primary. If there is no difference between them, how can this be accounted for?

Philonous. It is not my business to account for every opinion of the philosophers. But, among other reasons which may be assigned for this, it seems probable that pleasure and pain being rather annexed to the former than the latter may be one. Heat and cold, tastes and smells, have something more vividly pleasing or disagreeable than the ideas of extension, figure, and motion affect us with. And, it being too visibly absurd to hold that pain or pleasure can be in an unperceiving Substance, men are more easily weaned from believing the external existence of the Secondary than the Primary Qualities. You will be satisfied there is something in this, if you recollect the difference you made between an intense and more moderate degree of heat; allowing the one a real existence, while you denied it to the other. But, after all, there is no rational ground for that distinction; for, surely an indifferent sensation is as truly *a sensation* as one more pleasing or painful; and consequently should not any more than they be supposed to exist in an unthinking subject.

Hylas. It is just come into my head, *Philonous*, that I have somewhere heard of a distinction between absolute and sensible extension. Now, though it be acknowledged that *great* and *small*, consisting merely in the relation which other extended beings have to the parts of our own bodies, do not really inhere in the Substances themselves; yet nothing obliges us to hold the same with regard to *absolute extension*, which is something abstracted from *great* and *small*, from this or that particular magnitude or figure. So likewise as to motion; *swift* and *slow* are altogether relative to the succession of ideas in our own minds. But, it doth not follow, because those modifications of motion exist not without the mind, that therefore absolute motion abstracted from them doth not.

Philonous. Pray what is it that distinguishes one motion, or one part of extension, from another? Is it not something sensible, as some degree of swiftness or slowness, some certain magnitude or figure peculiar to each?

Hylas. I think so.

Philonous. These qualities, therefore, stripped of all sensible properties, are without all specific and numerical differences, as the schools call them.

Hylas. They are.

Philonous. That is to say, they are extension in general, and motion in general.

Hylas. Let it be so.

Philonous. But it is a universally received maxim that *Everything which exists is particular*. How then can motion in general, or extension in general, exist in any corporeal Substance?

Hylas. I will take time to solve your difficulty.

Philonous. But I think the point may be speedily decided. Without doubt you can tell whether you are able to frame this or that idea. Now I am content to put our dispute on this issue. If you can frame in your thoughts a distinct abstract idea of motion or extension; divested of all those sensible modes, as swift and slow, great and small, round and square, and the like, which are acknowledged to exist only in the mind, I will then yield the point you contend for. But, if you cannot, it will be unreasonable on your side to insist any longer upon what you have no notion of.

Hylas. To confess ingenuously, I cannot.

Philonous. Can you even separate the ideas of extension and motion from the ideas of all those qualities which they who make the distinction term *secondary?*

Hylas. What! is it not an easy matter to consider extension and motion by themselves, abstracted from all other sensible qualities? Pray how do the mathematicians treat of them?

Philonous. I acknowledge, *Hylas,* it is not difficult to form general propositions and reasonings about those qualities, without mentioning any other; and, in this sense, to consider or treat of them abstractedly. But, how doth it follow that, because I can pronounce the word *motion* by itself, I can form the idea of it in my mind exclusive of body? Or, because theorems may be made of extension and figures, without any mention of *great* or *small,* or any other sensible mode or quality, that therefore it is possible such an abstract idea of extension, without any particular size or figure, or sensible quality, should be distinctly formed, and apprehended by the mind? Mathematicians treat of quantity, without regarding what other sensible qualities it is attended with, as being altogether indifferent to their demonstrations. But, when laying aside the words, they contemplate the bare ideas, I believe you will find, they are not the pure abstracted ideas of extension.

Hylas. But what say you to *pure intellect?* May not abstracted idea be framed by that faculty?

Philonous. Since I cannot frame abstract ideas at all, it is plain I cannot frame them by the help of *pure intellect;* whatsoever faculty you understand by those words. Besides, not to inquire into the nature of pure intellect and its spiritual objects, as *virtue, reason, God,* or the like, thus much seems manifest, that sensible things are only to be perceived by sense, or represented by the imagination. Figures, therefore, and extension, being originally perceived by sense, do not belong to pure intellect: but, for your farther satisfaction, try if you can frame the idea of any figure, abstracted from all particularities of size, or even from other sensible qualities.

Hylas. Let me think a little—I do not find that I can.

Philonous. And can you think it possible that should really exist in nature which implies a repugnancy in its conception?

Hylas. By no means.

Philonous. Since therefore it is impossible even for the mind to disunite the ideas of extension and motion from all other sensible qualities, doth it not follow, that where the one exist there necessarily the other exist likewise?

Hylas. It should seem so.

Philonous. Consequently, the very same arguments which you admitted as conclusive against the Secondary Qualities are, without any farther application of force, against the Primary too. Besides, if you will trust your senses, is it not plain all sensible qualities coexist, or to them appear as being in the same place? Do they ever represent a motion, or figure, as being diversted of all other visible and tangible qualities?

Hylas. You need say no more on this head. I am free to own, if there be no secret error or oversight in our proceedings hitherto, that all sensible qualities are alike to be denied existence without the mind. But, my fear is that I have been too liberal in my former concessions, or overlooked some fallacy or other. In short, I did not take time to think.

Philonous. For that matter, *Hylas*, you may take what time you please in reviewing the progress of our inquiry. You are at liberty to recover any slips you might have made, or offer whatever you have omitted which makes for your first opinion.

Hylas. One great oversight I take to be this—that I did not sufficiently distinguish the *object* from the *sensation*. Now, though this latter may not exist without the mind, yet it will not thence follow that the former cannot.

Philonous. What object do you mean? The object of the senses?

Hylas. The same.

Philonous. It is then immediately perceived?

Hylas. Right.

Philonous. Make me to understand the difference between what is immediately perceived, and a sensation.

Hylas. The sensation I take to be an act of the mind perceiving; besides which, there is something perceived; and this I call the *object*. For example, there is red and yellow on that tulip. But then the act of perceiving those colours is in me only, and not in the tulip.

Philonous. What tulip do you speak of? Is it that which you see?

Hylas. The same.

Philonous. And what do you see beside colour, figure, and extension?

Hylas. Nothing.

Philonous. What you would say then is that the red and yellow are coexistent with the extension; is it not?

Hylas. That is not all; I would say they have a real existence without the mind, in some unthinking substance.

Philonous. That the colours are really in the tulip which I see is manifest. Neither can it be denied that this tulip may exist independent of your mind or mine; but, that any immediate object of the senses—that is, any idea, or combination of ideas—should exist in an unthinking substance, or exterior to all minds, is in itself an evident contradiction. Nor can I imagine how this follows from what you said just now, to wit, that the red and yellow were on the tulip *you saw*, since you do not pretend to *see* that unthinking substance.

Hylas. You have an artful way, *Philonous*, of diverting our inquiry from the subject.

Philonous. I see you have no mind to be pressed that way. To return then to your distinction between *sensation* and *object*; if I take you right, you distinguish in every perception two things, the one an action of the mind, the other not.

Hylas. True.

Philonous. And this action cannot exist in, or belong to, any unthinking thing; but, whatever beside is implied in a perception may?

Hylas. That is my meaning.

Philonous. So that if there was a perception without any act of the mind, it were possible such a perception should exist in an unthinking substance?

Hylas. I grant it. But it is impossible there should be such a perception.

Philonous. When is the mind said to be active?

Hylas. When it produces, puts an end to, or changes, anything.

Philonous. Can the mind produce, discontinue, or change anything, but by an act of the will?

Hylas. It cannot.

Philonous. The mind therefore is to be accounted *active* in its perceptions so far forth as *volition* is included in them?

Hylas. It is.

Philonous. In plucking this flower I am active; because I do it by the motion of my hand, which was consequent upon my volition; so likewise in applying it to my nose. But is either of these smelling?

Hylas. No.

Philonous. I act too in drawing the air through my nose; because my breathing so rather than otherwise is the effect of my volition. But neither can this be called *smelling*: for, if it were, I should smell every time I breathed in that manner?

Hylas. True.

Philonous. Smelling then is somewhat consequent to all this?

Hylas. It is.

Philonous. But I do not find my will concerned any farther. Whatever more there is—as that I perceive such a particular smell, or any smell at all—this is independent of my will, and therein I am altogether passive. Do you find it otherwise with you, *Hylas?*

Hylas. No, the very same.

Philonous. Then, as to seeing, is it not in your power to open your eyes, or keep them shut; to turn them this or that way?

Hylas. Without doubt.

Philonous. But, doth it in like manner depend on your will that in looking on this flower you perceive *white* rather than any other colour? Or, directing your open eyes towards yonder part of the heaven, can you avoid seeing the sun? Or is light or darkness the effect of your volition?

Hylas. No certainly.

Philonous. You are then in these respects altogether passive?

Hylas. I am.

Philonous. Tell me now, whether *seeing* consists in perceiving light and colours, or in opening and turning the eyes?

Hylas. Without doubt, in the former.

Philonous. Since therefore you are in the very perception of light and colours altogether passive, what is become of that action you were speaking of as an ingredient in every sensation? And, doth it not follow from your own concessions, that the perception of light and colours, including no action in it may exist in an unperceiving substance? And is not this a plain contradiction?

Hylas. I know not what to think of it.

Philonous. Besides, since you distinguish the *active* and *passive* in every perception, you must do it in that of pain. But how is it possible that pain, be it as little active as you please, should exist in an unperceiving substance? In short, do but consider the point, and then confess ingenuously, whether light and colours, tastes, sounds, &c., are not all equally passions or sensations in the soul. You may indeed call them *external objects,* and give them in words what subsistence you please. But, examine your own thoughts, and then tell me whether it be not as I say?

Hylas. I acknowledge, *Philonous,* that, upon a fair observation of what passes in my mind, I can discover nothing else but that I am a thinking being, affected with variety of sensations; neither is it possible to conceive how a sensation should exist in an unperceiving substance. But then, on the other hand, when I look on sensible things in a different view, considering them as so many modes and qualities, I find it necessary to suppose a material substratum, without which they cannot be conceived to exist.

Philonous. Material substratum call you it? Pray, by which of your senses came you acquainted with that being?

Hylas. It is not itself sensible; its modes and qualities only being perceived by the senses.

Philonous. I presume then it was by reflection and reason you obtained the idea of it?

Hylas. I do not pretend to any proper positive idea of it. However, I conclude it exists, because qualities cannot be conceived to exist without a support.

Philonous. It seems then you have only a relative notion of it, or that you conceive it not otherwise than by conceiving the relation it bears to sensible qualities?

Hylas. Right.

Philonous. Be pleased therefore to let me know wherein that relation consists.

Hylas. Is it not sufficiently expressed in the term *substratum* or *substance?*

Philonous. If so, the word *substratum* should import that it is spread under the sensible qualities or accidents?

Hylas. True.

Philonous. And consequently under extension?

Hylas. I own it.

Philonous. It is therefore somewhat in its own nature entirely distinct from extension?

Hylas. I tell you, extension is only a mode, and Matter is something that supports modes. And is it not evident the thing supported is different from the thing supporting?

Philonous. So that something distinct from, and exclusive of, extension is supposed to be the *substratum* of extension?

Hylas. Just so.

Philonous. Answer me, *Hylas.* Can a thing be spread without extension? or is not the idea of extension necessarily included in *spreading?*

Hylas. It is.

Philonous. Whatsoever therefore you suppose spread under anything must have in itself an extension distinct from the extension of that thing under which it is spread?

Hylas. It must.

Philonous. Consequently, every corporeal substance being the *substratum* of extension must have in itself another extension, by which it is qualified to be a *substratum,* and so on to infinity? And I ask whether this be not absurd in itself, and repugnant to what you granted just now, to wit, that the *substratum* was something distinct from and exclusive of extension?

Hylas. Aye, but, *Philonous,* you take me wrong. I do not mean that Matter is *spread* in a gross literal sense under extension. The word *substratum* is used only to express in general the same thing with *substance*.

Philonous. Well then, let us examine the relation implied in the term *substance*. Is it not that it stands under accidents?

Hylas. The very same.

Philonous. But, that one thing may stand under or support another, must it not be extended?

Hylas. It must.

Philonous. Is not therefore this supposition liable to the same absurdity with the former?

Hylas. You still take things in a strict literal sense; that is not fair, *Philonous.*

Philonous. I am not for imposing any sense on your words: you are at liberty to explain them as you please. Only, I beseech you, make me understand something by them. You tell me Matter supports or stands under accidents. How! is it as your legs support your body?

Hylas. No; that is the literal sense.

Philonous. Pray let me know any sense, literal or not literal, that you understand it in. . . . How long must I wait for an answer, *Hylas?*

Hylas. I declare I know not what to say. I once thought I understood well enough what was meant by Matter's supporting accidents. But now, the more I think on it the less can I comprehend it; in short I find that I know nothing of it.

Philonous. It seems then you have no idea at all, neither relative nor positive, of Matter; you know neither what it is in itself, nor what relation it bears to accidents?

Hylas. I acknowledge it.

Philonous. And yet you asserted that you could not conceive how qualities or accidents should really exist, without conceiving at the same time a material support of them?

Hylas. I did.

Philonous. That is to say, when you conceive the real existence of qualities, you do withal conceive something which you cannot conceive?

Hylas. It was wrong I own. But still I fear there is some fallacy or other. Pray what think you of this? It is just come into my head that the ground of all our mistake lies in your treating of each quality by itself. Now, I grant that each quality cannot singly subsist without the mind. Colour cannot without extension, neither can figure without some other sensible quality. But, as the several qualities united or blended together form entire sensible things, nothing hinders why such things may not be supposed to exist without the mind.

Philonous. Either, *Hylas,* you are jesting, or have a very bad memory. Though indeed we went through all the qualities by name one after another; yet my arguments, or rather your concessions, nowhere tended to prove that the Secondary Qualities did not subsist each alone by itself; but, that they were not *at all* without the mind. Indeed, in treating of figure and motion we concluded they could not exist without the mind, because it was impossible even in thought to separate them from all secondary qualities, so as to conceive them existing by themselves. But then this was not the only argument made use of upon that occasion. But (to pass by all that hath been hitherto said, and reckon it for nothing, if you will have it so) I am content to put the whole upon this issue. If you can conceive it possible for any mixture or combination of qualities, or any sensible object whatever, to exist without the mind, then I will grant it actually to be so.

Hylas. If it comes to that the point will soon be decided. What more easy than to conceive a tree or house existing by itself, independent of, and unperceived by, any mind whatsoever? I do at this present time conceive them existing after that manner.

Philonous. How say you, *Hylas*, can you see a thing which is at the same time unseen?

Hylas. No, that were a contradiction.

Philonous. Is it not as great a contradiction to talk of *conceiving* a thing which is *unconceived*?

Hylas. It is.

Philonous. The tree or house therefore which you think of is conceived by you?

Hylas. How should it be otherwise?

Philonous. And what is conceived is surely in the mind?

Hylas. Without question, that which is conceived is in the mind.

Philonous. How then came you to say, you conceived a house or tree existing independent and out of all minds whatsoever?

Hylas. That was I own an oversight; but stay, let me consider what led me into it.—It is a pleasant mistake enough. As I was thinking of a tree in a solitary place where no one was present to see it, methought that was to conceive a tree as existing unperceived or unthought of— not considering that I myself conceived it all the while. But now I plainly see that all I can do is to frame ideas in my own mind. I may indeed conceive in my own thoughts the idea of a tree, or a house, or a mountain, but that is all. And this is far from proving that I can conceive them *existing out of the minds of all Spirits.*

Philonous. You acknowledge then that you cannot possibly conceive how any one corporeal sensible thing should exist otherwise than in a mind?

Hylas. I do.

Philonous. And yet you will earnestly contend for the truth of that which you cannot so much as conceive?

Hylas. I profess I know not what to think; but still there are some scruples remain with me. Is it not certain I *see* things at a distance? Do we not perceive the stars and moon, for example, to be a great way off? Is not this, I say, manifest to the senses?

Philonous. Do you not in a dream too perceive those or the like objects?

Hylas. I do.

Philonous. And have they not then the same appearance of being distant?

Hylas. They have.

Philonous. But you do not thence conclude the apparitions in a dream to be without the mind?

Hylas. By no means.

Philonous. You ought not therefore to conclude that sensible objects are without the mind, from their appearance or manner wherein they are perceived.

Hylas. I acknowledge it. But doth not my sense deceive me in those cases?

Philonous. By no means. The idea or thing which you immediately perceive, neither sense nor reason informs you that it actually exists without the mind. By sense you only know that you are affected with such certain sensations of light and colours, &c. And these you will not say are without the mind.

Hylas. True: but, beside all that, do you not think the sight suggests something of *outness* or *distance?*

Philonous. Upon approaching a distant object, do the visible size and figure change perpetually, or do they appear the same at all distances?

Hylas. They are in a continual change.

Philonous. Sight therefore doth not suggest or any way inform you that the visible object you immediately perceive exists at a distance [2] or will be perceived when you advance farther onward; there being a continued series of visible objects succeeding each other during the whole time of your approach.

Hylas. It doth not; but still I know, upon seeing an object, what object I shall perceive after having passed over a certain distance: no matter whether it be exactly the same or no: there is still something of distance suggested in the case.

---

[2] See the "Essay towards a New Theory of Vision," and its "Vindication."— Author, 1734.

Philonous. Good *Hylas,* do but reflect a little on the point, and then tell me whether there be any more in it than this:—From the ideas you actually perceive by sight, you have by experience learned to collect what other ideas you will (according to the standing order of nature) be affected with, after such a certain succession of time and motion.

Hylas. Upon the whole, I take it to be nothing else.

Philonous. Now, is it not plain that if we suppose a man born blind was on a sudden made to see, he could at first have no experience of what may be suggested by sight?

Hylas. It is.

Philonous. He would not then, according to you, have any notion of distance annexed to the things he saw; but would take them for a new set of sensations existing only in his mind?

Hylas. It is undeniable.

Philonous. But, to make it still more plain: is not *distance* a line turned endwise to the eye?

Hylas. It is.

Philonous. And can a line so situated be perceived by sight?

Hylas. It cannot.

Philonous. Doth it not therefore follow that distance is not properly and immediately perceived by sight?

Hylas. It should seem so.

Philonous. Again, is it your opinion that colours are at a distance?

Hylas. It must be acknowledged they are only in the mind.

Philonous. But do not colours appear to the eye as coexisting in the same place with extension and figures?

Hylas. They do.

Philonous. How can you then conclude from sight that figures exist without, when you acknowledge colours do not; the sensible appearance being the very same with regard to both?

Hylas. I know not what to answer.

Philonous. But, allowing that distance was truly and immediately perceived by the mind, yet it would not thence follow it existed out of the mind. For, whatever is immediately perceived is an idea: and can any *idea* exist out of the mind?

Hylas. To suppose that were absurd: but, inform me, *Philonous,* can we perceive or know nothing beside our ideas?

Philonous. As for the rational deducing of causes from effects, that is beside our inquiry. And, by the senses you can best tell whether you perceive anything which is not immediately perceived. And I ask you, whether the things immediately perceived are other than your own sensations or ideas? You have indeed more than once, in the course of this conversation, declared yourself on those points; but you seem, by this last question, to have departed from what you then thought.

Hylas. To speak the truth, *Philonous*, I think there are two kinds of objects:—the one perceived immediately, which are likewise called *ideas*; the other are real things or external objects, perceived by the mediation of ideas, which are their images and representations. Now, I own ideas do not exist without the mind; but the latter sort of objects do. I am sorry I did not think of this distinction sooner; it would probably have cut short your discourse.

Philonous. Are those external objects perceived by sense, or by some other faculty?

Hylas. They are perceived by sense.

Philonous. How! is there anything perceived by sense which is not immediately perceived?

Hylas. Yes, *Philonous*, in some sort there is. For example, when I look on a picture or statue of Julius Cæsar, I may be said after a manner to perceive him (though not immediately) by my senses.

Philonous. It seems then you will have our ideas, which alone are immediately perceived, to be pictures of external things: and that these also are perceived by sense, inasmuch as they have a conformity or resemblance to our ideas?

Hylas. That is my meaning.

Philonous. And, in the same way that Julius Cæsar, in himself invisible, is nevertheless perceived by sight; real things, in themselves imperceptible, are perceived by sense.

Hylas. In the very same.

Philonous. Tell me, *Hylas*, when you behold the picture of Julius Cæsar, do you see with your eyes any more than some colours and figures, with a certain symmetry and composition of the whole?

Hylas. Nothing else.

Philonous. And would not a man who had never known anything of Julius Cæsar see as much?

Hylas. He would.

Philonous. Consequently he hath his sight, and the use of it, in as perfect a degree as you?

Hylas. I agree with you.

Philonous. Whence comes it then that your thoughts are directed to the Roman emperor, and his are not? This cannot proceed from the sensations or ideas of sense by you then perceived; since you acknowledge you have no advantage over him in that respect. It should seem therefore to proceed from reason and memory: should it not?

Hylas. It should.

Philonous. Consequently, it will not follow from that instance that anything is perceived by sense which is not immediately perceived. Though I grant we may, in one acceptation, be said to perceive sensible things mediately by sense—that is, when, from a frequently perceived connexion, the immediate perception of ideas by one sense suggest to the mind others, perhaps belonging to another sense, which are wont to be connected with them. For instance, when I hear a coach drive along the streets, immediately I perceive only the sound; but, from the experience I have had that such a sound is connected with a coach, I am said to hear the coach. It is nevertheless evident that, in truth and strictness, nothing can be *heard* but *sound*; and the coach is not then properly perceived by sense, but suggested from experience. So likewise when we are said to see a red-hot bar of iron; the solidity and heat of the iron are not the objects of sight, but suggested to the imagination by the colour and figure which are properly perceived by that sense. In short, those things alone are actually and strictly perceived by any sense, which would have been perceived in case that same sense had then been first conferred on us. As for other things, it is plain they are only suggested to the mind by experience, grounded on former perceptions. But, to return to your comparison of Cæsar's picture, it is plain, if you keep to that, you must hold the real things or archetypes of our ideas are not perceived by sense, but by some internal faculty of the soul, as reason or memory. I would therefore fain know what arguments you can draw from reason for the existence of what you call *real things* or *material objects*. Or, whether you remember to have seen them formerly as they are in themselves; or, if you have heard or read of any one that did.

Hylas. I see, *Philonous*, you are disposed to raillery; but that will never convince me.

Philonous. My aim is only to learn from you the way to come at the knowledge of *material beings*. Whatever we perceive is perceived immediately or mediately: by sense; or by reason and reflection. But, as you have excluded sense, pray shew me what reason you have to believe their existence; or what *medium* you can possibly make use of to prove it, either to mine or your own understanding.

Hylas. To deal ingenuously, *Philonous*, now I consider the point, I do not find I can give you any good reason for it. But, thus much seems pretty plain, that it is at least possible such things may really exist. And, as long as there is no absurdity in supposing them, I am resolved to believe as I did, till you bring good reasons to the contrary.

Philonous. What! is it come to this, that you only believe the existence of material objects, and that your belief is founded barely on the possibility of its being true? Then you will have me bring reasons against it: though another would think it reasonable the proof should lie on him who holds the affirmative. And, after all, this very point which you are now resolved to maintain, without any reason, is in effect what you have more than once during this discourse seen good reason to give up. But, to pass over all this; if I understand you rightly, you say our ideas do not exist without the mind; but that they are copies, images, or representations, of certain originals that do?

Hylas. You take me right.

Philonous. They are then like external things?

Hylas. They are.

Philonous. Have those things a stable and permanent nature, independent of our senses; or are they in a perpetual change, upon our producing any motions in our bodies, suspending, exerting, or altering, our faculties or organs of sense?

Hylas. Real things, it is plain, have a fixed and real nature, which remains the same notwithstanding any change in our senses, or in the posture and motion of our bodies; which indeed may affect the ideas in our minds, but it were absurd to think they had the same effect on things existing without the mind.

Philonous. How then is it possible that things perpetually fleeting and variable as our ideas should be copies or images of anything fixed and constant? Or, in other words, since all sensible qualities, as size, figure, colour, &c., that is, our ideas, are continually changing upon every alteration in the distance, medium, or instruments of sensation; how can any determinate material objects be properly represented or painted forth by several distinct things, each of which is so different from and unlike the rest? Or, if you say it resembles some one only of our ideas, how shall we be able to distinguish the true copy from all the false ones?

Hylas. I profess, *Philonous*, I am at a loss. I know not what to say to this.

Philonous. But neither is this all. Which are material objects in themselves—perceptible or imperceptible?

Hylas. Properly and immediately nothing can be perceived but ideas. All material things, therefore, are in themselves insensible, and to be perceived only by our ideas.

Philonous. Ideas then are sensible, and their archetypes or originals insensible?

Hylas. Right.

Philonous. But how can that which is sensible be like that which is insensible? Can a real thing, in itself *invisible*, be like a *colour*; or a real thing, which is not *audible*, be like a *sound*? In a word, can anything be like a sensation or idea, but another sensation or idea?

Hylas. I must own, I think not.

Philonous. Is it possible there should be any doubt on the point? Do you not perfectly know your own ideas?

Hylas. I know them perfectly; since what I do not perceive or know can be no part of my idea.

Philonous. Consider, therefore, and examine them, and then tell me if there be anything in them which can exist without the mind? or if you can conceive anything like them existing without the mind?

Hylas. Upon inquiry, I find it is impossible for me to conceive or understand how anything but an idea can be like an idea. And it is most evident that *no idea can exist without the mind.*

Philonous. You are therefore, by our principles, forced to deny the reality of sensible things; since you made it to consist in an absolute existence exterior to the mind. That is to say, you are a downright sceptic. So I have gained my point, which was to shew your principles led to Scepticism.

Hylas. For the present I am, if not entirely convinced, at least silenced.

Philonous. I would fain know what more you would require in order to a perfect conviction. Have you not had the liberty of explaining yourself all manner of ways? Were any little slips in discourse laid hold and insisted on? Or were you not allowed to retract or reinforce anything you had offered, as best served your purpose? Hath not everything you could say been heard and examined with all the fairness imaginable? In a word, have you not in every point been convinced out of your own mouth? and, if you can at present discover any flaw in any of your former concessions, or think of any remaining subterfuge, any new distinction, colour, or comment whatsoever, why do you not produce it?

Hylas. A little patience, *Philonous.* I am at present so amazed to see myself ensnared, and as it were imprisoned in the labyrinths you have drawn me into, that on the sudden it cannot be expected I should find my way out. You must give me time to look about me and recollect myself.

Philonous. Hark; is not this the college bell?

Hylas. It rings for prayers.

Philonous. We will go in then, if you please, and meet here again to-morrow morning. In the meantime, you may employ your thoughts on this morning's discourse, and try if you can find any fallacy in it, or invent any new means to extricate yourself.

Hylas. Agreed.

THE
SECOND
DIALOGUE

Hylas. I beg your pardon, *Philonous*, for not meeting you sooner. All this morning my head was so filled with our late conversation that I had not leisure to think of the time of the day, or indeed of anything else.

Philonous. I am glad you were so intent upon it, in hopes if there were any mistakes in your concessions, or fallacies in my reasonings from them, you will now discover them to me.

Hylas. I assure you I have done nothing ever since I saw you but search after mistakes and fallacies, and, with that view, have minutely examined the whole series of yesterday's discourse: but all in vain, for the notions it led me into, upon review, appear still more clear and evident; and, the more I consider them, the more irresistibly do they force my assent.

Philonous. And is not this, think you, a sign that they are genuine, that they proceed from nature, and are conformable to right reason? Truth and beauty are in this alike, that the strictest survey sets them both off to advantage; while the false lustre of error and disguise cannot endure being reviewed, or too nearly inspected.

Hylas. I own there is a great deal in what you say. Nor can any one be more entirely satisfied of the truth of those odd consequences, so long as I have in view the reasonings that lead to them. But, when these are out of my thoughts, there seems, on the other hand, something so satisfactory, so natural and intelligible, in the modern way of explaining things that, I profess, I know not how to reject it.

Philonous. I know not what way you mean.

Hylas. I mean the way of accounting for our sensations or ideas.

Philonous. How is that?

Hylas. It is supposed the soul makes her residence in some part of the brain, from which the nerves take their rise, and are thence extended to all parts of the body; and that outward objects, by the different impressions they make on the organs of sense, communicate certain vibrative motions to the nerves; and these being filled with spirits propagate them to the brain or seat of the soul, which, according to the various impressions or traces thereby made in the brain, is variously affected with ideas.

Philonous. And call you this an explication of the manner whereby we are affected with ideas?

Hylas. Why not, *Philonous*; have you anything to object against it?

Philonous. I would first know whether I rightly understand your hypothesis. You make certain traces in the brain to be the causes or occasions of our ideas. Pray tell me whether by the *brain* you mean any sensible thing.

Hylas. What else think you I could mean?

Philinous. Sensible things are all immediately perceivable; and those things which are immediately perceivable are ideas; and these exist only in the mind. Thus much you have, if I mistake not, long since agreed to.

Hylas. I do not deny it.

Philonous. The brain therefore you speak of, being a sensible thing, exists only in the mind. Now, I would fain know whether you think it reasonable to suppose that one idea or thing existing in the mind occasions all other ideas. And, if you think so, pray how do you account for the origin of that primary idea or brain itself?

Hylas. I do not explain the origin of our ideas by that brain which is perceivable to sense, this being itself only a combination of sensible ideas, but by another which I imagine.

Philonous. But are not things imagined as truly *in the mind* as things perceived?

Hylas. I must confess they are.

Philonous. It comes, therefore, to the same thing; and you have been all this while accounting for ideas by certain motions or impressions of the brain, that is, by some alterations in an idea, whether sensible or imaginable it matters not.

Hylas. I begin to suspect my hypothesis.

Philonous. Besides spirits, all that we know or conceive are our own ideas. When, therefore, you say all ideas are occasioned by impressions in the brain, do you conceive this brain or no? If you do, then you talk of ideas imprinted in an idea causing that same idea, which is absurd. If you do not conceive it, you talk unintelligibly, instead of forming a reasonable hypothesis.

Hylas. I now clearly see it was a mere dream. There is nothing in it.

Philonous. You need not be much concerned at it; for after all, this way of explaining things, as you called it, could never have satisfied any reasonable man. What connexion is there between a motion in the nerves, and the sensations of sound or colour in the mind? Or how is it possible these should be the effect of that?

Hylas. But I could never think it had so little in it as now it seems to have.

Philonous. Well then, are you at length satisfied that no sensible things have a real existence; and that you are in truth an arrant *sceptic?*

Hylas. It is too plain to be denied.

Philonous. Look! are not the fields covered with a delightful verdure? Is there not something in the woods and groves, in the rivers and clear springs, that sooths, that delights, that transports the soul? At the prospect of the wide and deep ocean, or some huge mountain whose top is lost in the clouds, or of an old gloomy forest, are not our minds filled with a pleasing horror? Even in rocks and deserts is there not an agreeable wildness? How sincere a pleasure is it to behold the natural beauties of the earth! To preserve and renew our relish for them, is not the veil of night alternately drawn over her face, and doth she not change her dress with the seasons? How aptly are the elements disposed! What variety and use in the meanest productions of nature! What delicacy, what beauty, what contrivance, in animal and vegetable bodies! How exquisitely are all things suited, as well to their particular ends, as to constitute opposite parts of the whole! And, while they mutually aid and support, do they not also set off and illustrate each other? Raise now your thoughts from this ball of earth to all those glorious luminaries that adorn the high arch of heaven. The motion and situation of the planets, are they not admirable for use and order? Were those (miscalled *erratic*) globes ever known to stray, in their repeated journeys through the pathless void? Do they not measure areas round the sun ever proportioned to the times? So fixed, so immutable are the laws by which the unseen Author of nature actuates the universe. How vivid and radiant is the lustre of the fixed stars! How magnificent and rich that negligent profusion with which they appear to be scattered throughout the whole azure vault! Yet, if you take the telescope, it brings into your sight a new host of stars that escape the naked eye. Here they seem contiguous and minute, but to a nearer view immense orbs of light at various distances, far sunk in the abyss of space. Now you must call imagination to your aid. The feeble narrow sense cannot descry innumerable worlds revolving round the central fires; and in those worlds the energy of an all-perfect Mind displayed in endless forms. But, neither sense nor imagination are big enough to comprehend the boundless extent, with all its glittering furniture. Though the labouring mind exert and strain each power to its utmost reach, there still stands out ungrasped a surplusage immeasurable. Yet all the vast bodies that compose this mighty frame, how distant and remote soever, are by some secret mechanism, some divine art and force, linked in a mutual dependence and intercourse with each other, even with this earth, which was almost slipt from my thoughts and lost in the crowd of worlds. Is not the whole system immense, beautiful, glorious beyond expression and beyond thought! What treatment, then, do those philosophers deserve, who would deprive these noble and delightful scenes of all reality? How should those Principles be entertained that lead us to think all the visible beauty of the creation a false imaginary glare? To be plain, can you expect this Scepticism of yours will not be thought extravagantly absurd by all men of sense?

Hylas. Other men may think as they please; but for your part you have nothing to reproach me with. My comfort is, you are as much a sceptic as I am.

Philonous. There, *Hylas,* I must beg leave to differ from you.

Hylas. What! have you all along agreed to the premises, and do you now deny the conclusion, and leave me to maintain those paradoxes by myself which you led me into? This surely is not fair.

Philonous. I deny that I agreed with you in those notions that led to Scepticism. You indeed said the *reality* of sensible things consisted in an *absolute existence* out of the minds of spirits, or distinct from their being perceived. And, pursuant to this notion of reality, you are obliged to deny sensible things any real existence: that is, according to your own definition, you profess yourself a sceptic. But I neither said nor thought the reality of sensible things was to be defined after that manner. To me it is evident, for the reasons you allow of, that sensible things cannot exist otherwise than in a mind or spirit. Whence I conclude, not that they have no real existence, but that, seeing they depend not on my thought, and have an existence distinct from being perceived by me, *there must be some other mind wherein they exist.* As sure, therefore, as the sensible world really exists, so sure is there an infinite omnipresent Spirit, who contains and supports it.

Hylas. What! this is no more than I and all Christians hold; nay, and all others too who believe there is a God, and that He knows and comprehends all things.

Philonous. Aye, but here lies the difference. Men commonly believe that all things are known or perceived by God, because they believe the being of a God; whereas I, on the other side, immediately and necessarily conclude the being of a God, because all sensible things must be perceived by him.

Hylas. But so long as we all believe the same thing, what matter is it how we come by that belief?

Philonous. But neither do we agree in the same opinion. For philosophers, though they acknowledge all corporeal beings to be perceived by God, yet they attribute to them an absolute subsistence distinct from their being perceived by any mind whatever, which I do not. Besides, is there no difference between saying, *There is a God, therefore He perceives all things,* and saying, *Sensible things do really exist; and, if they really exist, they are necessarily perceived by an infinite mind: therefore there is an infinite mind, or God?* This furnishes you with a direct and immediate demonstration, from a most evident principle, of the *being of a God.* Divines and philosophers had proved beyond all controversy, from the beauty and usefulness of the several parts of the creation, that it was the workmanship of God. But that—setting aside all help of astronomy and natural philosophy, all contemplation of the contrivance, order and adjustment of things—an infinite mind should be necessarily inferred from the bare *existence* of the sensible world, is an advatage to them only who have made this easy reflexion, that the sensible world is that which we perceive by our several senses; and that nothing is perceived by the senses beside ideas; and that no idea or archetype of an idea can exist otherwise than in a mind. You may now, without any laborious search into the sciences, without any subtlety of reason, or tedious length of discourse, oppose and baffle the most strenuous advocate for Atheism; those miserable refuges, whether in an eternal succession of unthinking causes and effects, or in a fortuitous concourse of atoms; those wild imaginations of Vanini, Hobbes, and Spinoza: in a word, the whole system of Atheism, is it not entirely overthrown, by this single reflexion on the repugnancy included in supposing the whole, or any part, even the most rude and shapeless, of the visible world, to exist without a mind? Let any one of those abettors of impiety but look into his own thoughts, and there try if he can conceive how so much as a rock, a desert, a chaos, or confused jumble of atoms; how anything at all, either sensible or imaginable, can exist independent of a mind, and he need go no farther to be convinced of his folly. Can anything be fairer than to put a dispute on such an issue, and leave it to a man himself to see if he can conceive, even in thought, what he holds to be true in fact, and from a notional to allow it a real existence?

Hylas. It cannot be denied there is something highly serviceable to religion in what you advance. But do you not think it looks very like a notion entertained by some eminent moderns, of *seeing all things in God?*

Philonous. I would gladly know that opinion: pray explain it to me.

Hylas. They conceive that the soul, being immaterial, is incapable of being united with material things, so as to perceive them in themselves; but that she perceives them by her union with the substance of God, which, being spiritual, is therefore purely intelligible, or capable of being the immediate object of a spirit's thought. Besides, the Divine essence contains in it perfections correspondent to each created being; and which are, for that reason, proper to exhibit or represent them to the mind.

Philonous. I do not understand how our ideas, which are things altogether passive and inert, can be the essence, or any part (or like any part) of the essence or substance of God, who is an impassive, indivisible, purely active being. Many more difficulties and objections there are which occur at first view against this hypothesis; but I shall only add that it is liable to all the absurdities of the common hypothesis, in making a created world exist otherwise than in the mind of a Spirit. Beside all which it hath this peculiar to itself; that it makes that material world serve to no purpose. And, if it pass for a good argument against other hypotheses in the sciences that they suppose nature or the Divine wisdom to make something in vain, or do that by tedious roundabout methods which might have been performed in a much more easy and compendious way, what shall we think of that hypothesis which supposes the whole world made in vain?

Hylas. But what say you, are not you too of opinion that we see all things in God? If I mistake not, what you advance comes near it.

Philonous. [Few men think, yet all have opinions. Hence men's opinions are superficial and confused. It is nothing strange that tenets, which in themselves are ever so different should nevertheless be confounded with each other by those who do not consider them attentively. I shall not therefore be surprised if some men imagine that I run into the enthusiasm of Malebranche; though in truth I am very remote from it. He builds on the most abstract general ideas, which I entirely disclaim. He asserts an absolute external world, which I deny. He maintains that we are deceived by our senses, and know not the real natures or the true forms and figures of extended beings; of all which I hold the direct contrary. So that upon the whole there are no principles more fundamentally opposite than his and mine. It must be owned that,] ¹

---

¹ What precedes in this paragraph did not appear in the first and second editions.

I entirely agree with what the holy Scripture saith, "That in God we live and move and have our being." But that we see things in His essence, after the manner above set forth, I am far from believing. Take here in brief my meaning.—It is evident that the things I perceive are my own ideas, and that no idea can exist unless it be in a mind. Nor is it less plain that these ideas or things by me perceived, either themselves or their archetypes, exist independently of my mind; since I know myself not to be their author, it being out of my power to determine at pleasure what particular ideas I shall be affected with upon opening my eyes or ears. They must therefore exist in some other mind, whose will it is they should be exhibited to me. The things, I say, immediately perceived are ideas or sensations, call them which you will. But how can any idea or sensation exist in, or be produced by, anything but a mind or spirit? This indeed is inconceivable; and to assert that which is inconceivable is to talk nonsense: is it not?

Hylas. Without doubt.

Philonous. But, on the other hand, it is very conceivable that they should exist in and be produced by a Spirit; since this is no more than I daily experience in myself, inasmuch as I perceive numberless ideas; and, by an act of my will, can form a great variety of them, and raise them up in my imagination: though, it must be confessed, these creatures of the fancy are not altogether so distinct, so strong, vivid, and permanent, as those perceived by my senses, which latter are called *real things*. From all which I conclude, *there is a Mind which affects me every moment with all the sensible impressions I perceive*. And, from the variety, order, and manner of these, I conclude the Author of them to be *wise, powerful, and good, beyond comprehension*. Mark it well; I do not say, I see things by perceiving that which represents them in the intelligible Substance of God. This I do not understand; but I say, the things by me perceived are known by the understanding, and produced by the will of an infinite Spirit. And is not all this most plain and evident? Is there any more in it than what a little observation of our own minds, and that which passeth in them, not only enableth us to conceive, but also obligeth us to acknowledge?

Hylas. I think I understand you very clearly; and own the proof you give of a Deity seems no less evident than surprising. But, allowing that God is the supreme and universal Cause of all things, yet, may there not be still a third nature besides Spirits and Ideas? May we not admit a subordinate and limited cause of our ideas? In a word, may there not for all that be *Matter?*

Philonous. How often must I inculcate the same thing? You allow the things immediately perceived by sense to exist nowhere without the mind; but there is nothing perceived by sense which is not perceived immediately: therefore there is nothing sensible that exists without the mind. The Matter, therefore, which you still insist on is something intelligible, I suppose; something that may be discovered by reason, and not by sense.

Hylas. You are in the right.

Philonous. Pray let me know what reasoning your belief of Matter is grounded on; and what this Matter is in your present sense of it.

Hylas. I find myself affected with various ideas, whereof I know I am not the cause; neither are they the cause of themselves, or of one another, or capable of subsisting by themselves, as being altogether inactive, fleeting, dependent beings. They have therefore some cause distinct from me and them: of which I pretend to know no more than that it is *the cause of my ideas*. And this thing, whatever it be, I call Matter.

Philonous. Tell me, *Hylas*, hath every one a liberty to change the current proper signification attached to a common name in any language? For example, suppose a traveller should tell you that in a certain country men pass unhurt through the fire; and, upon explaining himself, you found he meant by the word *fire* that which others call *water:* or, if he should assert that there are trees that walk upon two legs, meaning men by the term *trees*. Would you think this reasonable?

Hylas. No, I should think it very absurd. Common custom is the standard of propriety in language. And for any man to affect speaking improperly is to pervert the use of speech, and can never serve to a better purpose than to protract and multiply disputes where there is no difference in opinion.

Philonous. And doth not *Matter*, in the common current acceptation of the word, signify an extended, solid, moveable, unthinking, inactive Substance?

Hylas. It doth.

Philonous. And, hath it not been made evident that no such substance can possibly exist? And, though it should be allowed to exist, yet how can that which is *inactive* be a *cause*; or that which is *unthinking* be a *cause of thought?* You may, indeed, if you please, annex to the word *Matter* a contrary meaning to what is vulgarly received; and tell me you understand by it an unextended, thinking, active being, which is the cause of our ideas. But what else is this than to play with words, and run into that very fault you just now condemned with so much reason? I do by no means find fault with your reasoning, in that you collect a cause from the *phenomena:* but I deny that the cause deducible by reason can properly be termed Matter.

Hylas. There is indeed something in what you say. But I am afraid you do not thoroughly comprehend my meaning. I would by no means be thought to deny that God, or an infinite Spirit, is the Supreme Cause of all things. All I contend for is, that, subordinate to the Supreme Agent, there is a cause of a limited and inferior nature, which concurs in the production of our ideas, not by any act of will or spiritual efficiency, but by that kind of action which belongs to Matter, viz., *motion*.

Philonous. I find you are at every turn relapsing into your old exploded conceit, of a moveable, and consequently an extended, substance existing without the mind. What! have you already forgotten you were convinced, or are you willing I should repeat what has been said on that head? In truth this is not fair dealing in you, still to suppose the being of that which you have so often acknowledged to have no being. But, not to insist farther on what has been so largely handled, I ask whether all your ideas are not perfectly passive and inert, including nothing of action in them.

Hylas. They are.

Philonous. And are sensible qualities anything else but ideas?

Hylas. How often have I acknowledged that they are not.

Philonous. But is not motion a sensible quality?

Hylas. It is.

Philonous. Consequently it is no action?

Hylas. I agree with you. And indeed it is very plain that when I stir my finger it remains passive; but my will which produced the motion is active.

Philonous. Now, I desire to know, in the first place, whether, motion being allowed to be no action, you can conceive any action besides volition: and, in the second place, whether to say something and conceive nothing be not to talk nonsense: and, lastly, whether, having considered the premises, you do not perceive that to suppose any efficient or active cause of our ideas, other than *Spirit*, is highly absurd and unreasonable?

Hylas. I give up the point entirely. But, though Matter may not be a cause, yet what hinders its being an *instrument* subservient to the supreme Agent in the production of our ideas?

Philonous. An instrument say you; pray what may be the figure, springs, wheels, and motions, of that instrument?

Hylas. Those I pretend to determine nothing of, both the substance and its qualities being entirely unknown to me.

Philonous. What! You are then of opinion it is made up of unknown parts, that it hath unknown motions, and an unknown shape?

Hylas. I do not believe that it hath any figure or motion at all, being already convinced, that no sensible qualities can exist in an unperceiving substance.

Philonous. But what notion is it possible to frame of an instrument void of all sensible qualities, even extension itself?

Hylas. I do not pretend to have any notion of it.

Philonous. And what reason have you to think this unknown, this inconceivable Somewhat doth exist? Is it that you imagine God cannot act as well without it; or that you find by experience the use of some such thing, when you form ideas in your own mind?

Hylas. You are always teasing me for reasons of my belief. Pray what reasons have you not to believe it?

Philonous. It is to me a sufficient reason not to believe the existence of anything, if I see no reason for believing it. But, not to insist on reasons for believing, you will not so much as let me know what it is you would have me believe; since you say you have no manner of notion of it. After all, let me entreat you to consider whether it be like a philosopher, or even like a man of common sense, to pretend to believe you know not what, and you know not why.

Hylas. Hold, *Philonous.* When I tell you matter is an *instrument,* I do not mean altogether nothing. It is true, I know not the particular kind of instrument; but, however, I have some notion of *instrument in general,* which I apply to it.

Philonous. But what if it should prove that there is something, even in the most general notion of *instrument,* as taken in a distinct sense from *cause,* which makes the use of it inconsistent with the Divine attributes?

Hylas. Make that appear and I shall give up the point.

Philonous. What mean you by the general nature or notion of *instrument?*

Hylas. That which is common to all particular instruments composeth the general notion.

Philonous. Is it not common to all instruments, that they are applied to the doing those things only which cannot be performed by the mere act of our wills? Thus, for instance, I never use an instrument to move my finger, because it is done by a volition. But I should use one if I were to remove part of a rock, or tear up a tree by the roots. Are you of the same mind? Or, can you shew any example where an instrument is made use of in producing an effect immediately depending on the will of the agent?

Hylas. I own I cannot.

Philonous. How therefore can you suppose that an all-perfect Spirit, on whose will all things have an absolute and immediate dependence, should need an instrument in his operations, or, not needing it, make use of it? Thus, it seems to me that you are obliged to own the use of a lifeless inactive instrument to be incompatible with the infinite perfection of God; that is, by your own confession, to give up the point.

Hylas. It doth not readily occur what I can answer you.

Philonous. But, methinks you should be ready to own the truth, when it hath been fairly proved to you. We indeed, who are beings of finite powers, are forced to make use of instruments. And the use of an instrument sheweth the agent to be limited by rules of another's prescription, and that he cannot obtain his end but in such a way, and by such conditions. Whence it seems a clear consequence, that the supreme unlimited Agent useth no tool or instrument at all. The will of an Omnipotent Spirit is no sooner exerted than executed, without the application of means—which, if they are employed by inferior agents, it is not upon account of any real efficacy that is in them, or necessary aptitude to produce any effect, but merely in compliance with the laws of nature, or those conditions prescribed to them by the First Cause, who is Himself above all limitation or prescription whatsoever.

Hylas. I will no longer maintain that Matter is an instrument. However, I would not be understood to give up its existence neither; since, notwithstanding what hath been said, it may still be an *occasion*.

Philonous. How many shapes is your Matter to take? Or, how often must it be proved not to exist, before you are content to part with it? But, to say no more of this (though by all the laws of disputation I may justly blame you for so frequently changing the signification of the principal term) I would fain know what you mean by affirming that matter is an occasion, having already denied it to be a cause. And, when you have shewn in what sense you understand *occasion*, pray, in the next place, be pleased to shew me what reason induceth you to believe there is such an occasion of our ideas?

Hylas. As to the first point: by *occasion* I mean an inactive unthinking being, at the presence whereof God excites ideas in our minds.

Philonous. And what may be the nature of that inactive unthinking being?

Hylas. I know nothing of its nature.

Philonous. Proceed then to the second point, and assign some reason why we should allow an existence to this inactive, unthinking, unknown thing.

Hylas. When we see ideas produced in our minds after an orderly and constant manner, it is natural to think they have some fixed and regular occasions, at the presence of which they are excited.

Philonous. You acknowledge then God alone to be the cause of our ideas, and that He causes them at the presence of those occasions.

Hylas. That is my opinion.

Philonous. Those things which you say are present to God, without doubt He perceives.

Hylas. Certainly; otherwise they could not be to Him an occasion of acting.

Philonous. Not to insist now on your making sense of this hypothesis, or answering all the puzzling questions and difficulties it is liable to: I only ask whether the order and regularity observable in the series of our ideas, or the course of nature, be not sufficiently accounted for by the wisdom and power of God; and whether it doth not derogate from those attributes, to suppose He is influenced, directed, or put in mind, when and what He is to act, by an unthinking substance? And, lastly, whether, in case I granted all you contend for, it would make anything to your purpose, it not being easy to conceive how the external or absolute existence of an unthinking substance, distinct from its being perceived, can be inferred from my allowing that there are certain things perceived by the mind of God, which are to Him the occasion of producing ideas in us?

Hylas. I am perfectly at a loss what to think, this notion of *occasion* seeming now altogether as groundless as the rest.

Philonous. Do you not at length perceive that in all these different acceptations of *Matter*, you have been only supposing you know not what, for no manner of reason, and to no kind of use?

Hylas. I freely own myself less fond of my notions since they have been so accurately examined. But still, methinks, I have some confused perception that there is such a thing as *Matter*.

Philonous. Either you perceive the being of Matter immediately, or mediately. If immediately, pray inform me by which of the senses you perceive it. If mediately, let me know by what reasoning it is inferred from those things which you perceive immediately. So much for the perception. Then for the Matter itself, I ask whether it is object, *substratum*, cause, instrument, or occasion? You have already pleaded for each of these, shifting your notions, and making Matter to appear sometimes in one shape, then in another. And what you have offered hath been disapproved and rejected by yourself. If you have anything new to advance I would gladly hear it.

Hylas. I think I have already offered all I had to say on those heads. I am at a loss what more to urge.

Philonous. And yet you are loath to part with your old prejudice. But, to make you quit it more easily, I desire that, beside what has been hitherto suggested, you will farther consider whether, upon supposition that Matter exists, you can possibly conceive how you should be affected by it? Or, supposing it did not exist, whether it be not evident you might for all that be affected with the same ideas you now are, and consequently have the very same reasons to believe its existence that you now can have?

Hylas. I acknowledge it is possible we might perceive all things just as we do now, though there was no Matter in the world; neither can I conceive, if there be Matter, how it should produce any idea in our minds. And, I do farther grant you have entirely satisfied me that it is impossible there should be such a thing as Matter in any of the foregoing acceptations. But still I cannot help supposing that there is *Matter* in some sense or other. What that is I do not indeed pretend to determine.

Philonous. I do not expect you should define exactly the nature of that unknown being. Only be pleased to tell me whether it is a Substance—and if so, whether you can suppose a substance without accidents; or, in case you suppose it to have accidents or qualities, I desire you will let me know what those qualities are, at least what is meant by Matter's supporting them?

Hylas. We have already argued on those points. I have no more to say to them. But, to prevent any farther questions, let me tell you I at present understand by *Matter* neither substance nor accident, thinking nor extended being, neither cause, instrument, nor occasion, but something entirely unknown, distinct from all these.

Philonous. It seems then you include in your present notion of Matter nothing but the general abstract idea of *entity*.

Hylas. Nothing else, save only that I superadd to this general idea the negation of all those particular things, qualities, or ideas, that I perceive, imagine, or in anywise apprehend.

Philonous. Pray where do you suppose this unknown Matter to exist?

Hylas. Oh *Philonous!* now you think you have entangled me; for, if I say it exists in place then you will infer that it exists in the mind, since it is agreed that place or extension exists only in the mind: but I am not ashamed to own my ignorance. I know not where it exists; only I am sure it exists not in place. There is a negative answer for you. And you must expect no other to all the questions you put for the future about Matter.

Philonous. Since you will not tell me where it exists, be pleased to inform me after what manner you suppose it to exist, or what you mean by its *existence?*

Hylas. It neither thinks nor acts, neither perceives nor is perceived.

Philonous. But what is there positive in your abstracted notion of its existence?

Hylas. Upon a nice observation, I do not find I have any positive notion or meaning at all. I tell you again, I am not ashamed to own my ignorance. I know not what is meant by its *existence*, or how it exists.

Philonous. Continue, good *Hylas*, to act the same ingenuous part, and tell me sincerely whether you can frame a distinct idea of Entity in general, prescinded from and exclusive of all thinking and corporeal beings, all particular things whatsoever.

Hylas. Hold, let me think a little—I profess, *Philonous*, I do not find that I can. At first glance, methought I had some dilute and airy notion of pure Entity in abstract; but, upon closer attention, it hath quite vanished out of sight. The more I think on it, the more am I confirmed in my prudent resolution of giving none but negative answers, and not pretending to the least degree of any positive knowledge or conception of Matter, its *where*, its *how*, its *entity*, or anything belonging to it.

Philonous. When, therefore, you speak of the existence of Matter, you have not any notion in your mind?

Hylas. None at all.

Philonous. Pray tell me if the case stands not thus:—at first, from a belief of material substance, you would have it that the immediate objects existed without the mind; then that they are archetypes; then causes; next instruments; then occasions: lastly, *something in general*, which being interpreted proves *nothing*. So Matter comes to nothing. What think you, *Hylas*, is not this a fair summary of your whole proceeding?

Hylas. Be that as it will, yet I still insist upon it, that our not being able to conceive a thing is no argument against its existence.

Philonous. That from a cause, effect, operation, sign, or other circumstance there may reasonably be inferred the existence of a thing not immediately perceived; and that it were absurd for any man to argue against the existence of that thing, from his having no direct and positive notion of it, I freely own. But, where there is nothing of all this; where neither reason nor revelation induces us to believe the existence of a thing; where we have not even a relative notion of it; where an abstraction is made from perceiving and being perceived, from Spirit and idea: lastly, where there is not so much as the most inadequate or faint idea pretended to: I will not indeed thence conclude against the reality of any notion, or existence of anything; but my inference shall be, that you mean nothing at all; that you employ words to no manner of purpose, without any design or signification whatsoever. And I leave it to you to consider how mere jargon should be treated.

Hylas. To deal frankly with you, *Philonous*, your arguments seem in themselves unanswerable; but they have not so great an effect on me as to produce that entire conviction, that hearty acquiescence, which attends demonstration. I find myself still relapsing into an obscure surmise of I know not what, *matter.*

Philonous. But, are you not sensible, *Hylas,* that two things must concur to take away all scruple, and work a plenary assent in the mind? Let a visible object be set in never so clear a light, yet, if there is any imperfection in the sight, or if the eye is not directed towards it, it will not be distinctly seen. And, though a demonstration be never so well grounded and fairly proposed, yet, if there is withal a stain of prejudice, or a wrong bias on the understanding, can it be expected on a sudden to perceive clearly and adhere firmly to the truth? No, there is need of time and pains: the attention must be awakened and detained by a frequent repetition of the same thing placed oft in the same, oft in different lights. I have said it already, and find I must still repeat and inculcate, that it is an unaccountable licence you take, in pretending to maintain you know not what, for you know not what reason, to you know not what purpose. Can this be paralleled in any art or science, any sect or profession of men? Or is there anything so barefacedly groundless and unreasonable to be met with even in the lowest of common conversation? But, perhaps you will still say, Matter may exist; though at the same time you neither know what is meant by *Matter,* or by its *existence.* This indeed is surprising, and the more so because it is altogether voluntary, you not being led to it by any one reason; for I challenge you to shew me that thing in nature which needs matter to explain or account for it.

Hylas. The reality of things cannot be maintained without supposing the existence of Matter. And is not this, think you, a good reason why I should be earnest in its defence?

Philonous. The reality of things! What things, sensible or intelligible?

Hylas. Sensible things.

Philonous. My glove, for example?

Hylas. That or any other thing perceived by the senses.

Philonous. But to fix on some particular thing; is it not a sufficient evidence to me of the existence of this *glove,* that I see it, and feel it, and wear it? Or, if this will not do, how is it possible I should be assured of the reality of this thing, which I actually see in this place, by supposing that some unknown thing, which I never did or can see, exists after an unknown manner, in an unknown place, or in no place at all? How can the supposed reality of that which is intangible be a proof that anything tangible really exists? Or, of that which is invisible, that any visible thing, or, in general of anything which is imperceptible, that a perceptible exists? Do but explain this and I shall think nothing too hard for you.

Hylas. Upon the whole, I am content to own the existence of Matter is highly improbable; but the direct and absolute impossibility of it does not appear to me.

Philonous. But, granting Matter to be possible, yet, upon that account merely, it can have no more claim to existence than a golden mountain or a centaur.

Hylas. I acknowledge it; but still you do not deny it is possible; and that which is possible, for aught you know, may actually exist.

Philonous. I deny it to be possible; and have, if I mistake not, evidently proved, from your own concessions, that it is not. In the common sense of the word *Matter*, is there any more implied than an extended, solid, figured, moveable substance existing without the mind? And have not you acknowledged, over and over, that you have seen evident reason for denying the possibility of such a substance?

Hylas. True, but that is only one sense of the term *Matter*.

Philonous. But, is it not the only proper genuine received sense? and, if Matter in such a sense be proved impossible, may it not be thought with good grounds absolutely impossible? Else how could anything be proved impossible? Or, indeed, how could there be any proof at all one way or other, to a man who takes the liberty to unsettle and change the common signification of words?

Hylas. I thought philosophers might be allowed to speak more accurately than the vulgar, and were not always confined to the common acceptation of a term.

Philonous. But this now mentioned is the common received sense among philosophers themselves. But, not to insist on that, have you not been allowed to take Matter in what sense you pleased? And have you not used this privilege in the utmost extent, sometimes entirely changing, at others leaving out or putting into the definition of it whatever, for the present, best served your design, contrary to all the known rules of reason and logic? And hath not this shifting, unfair method of yours spun out our dispute to an unnecessary length; Matter having been particularly examined, and by your own confession refuted in each of those senses? And can any more be required to prove the absolute impossibility of a thing, than the proving it impossible in every particular sense that either you or any one else understands it in?

Hylas. But I am not so thoroughly satisfied that you have proved the impossibility of matter, in the last most obscure abstracted and indefinite sense.

Philonous. When is a thing shewn to be impossible?

Hylas. When a repugnancy is demonstrated between the ideas comprehended in its definition.

Philonous. But where there are no ideas, there no repugnancy can be demonstrated between ideas?

Hylas. I agree with you.

Philonous. Now, in that which you call the obscure indefinite sense of the word *Matter*, it is plain, by your own confession, there was included no idea at all, no sense except an unknown sense, which is the same thing as none. You are not, therefore, to expect I should prove a repugnancy between ideas, where there are no ideas: or the impossibility of Matter taken in an *unknown* sense, that is, no sense at all. My business was only to shew you meant *nothing*; and this you were brought to own. So that, in all your various senses, you have been shewed either to mean nothing at all, or, if anything, an absurdity. And if this be not sufficient to prove the impossibility of a thing, I desire you will let me know what is.

Hylas. I acknowledge you have proved that Matter is impossible; nor do I see what more can be said in defence of it. But, at the same time that I give up this, I suspect all my other notions. For surely none could be more seemingly evident than this once was: and yet it now seems as false and absurd as ever it did true before. But I think we have discussed the point sufficiently for the present. The remaining part of the day I would willingly spend in running over in my thoughts the several heads of this morning's conversation, and to-morrow shall be glad to meet you here again about the same time.

Philonous. I will not fail to attend you.

THE
THIRD DIALOGUE

Philonous. Tell me, *Hylas*, what are the fruits of yesterday's meditation? Hath it confirmed you in the same mind you were in at parting?
or have you since seen cause to change your opinion?

Hylas. Truly my opinion is that all our opinions are alike vain and
uncertain. What we approve to-day, we condemn to-morrow. We keep a
stir about knowledge, and spend our lives in the pursuit of it, when,
alas! we know nothing all the while: nor do I think it possible for us
ever to know anything in this life. Our faculties are too narrow and too
few. Nature certainly never intended us for speculation.

Philonous. What! say you we can know nothing, *Hylas?*

Hylas. There is not that single thing in the world whereof we can
know the real nature, or what it is in itself.

Philonous. Will you tell me I do not really know what fire or
water is?

Hylas. You may indeed know that fire appears hot, and water fluid;
but this is no more than knowing what sensations are produced in your
own mind, upon the application of fire and water to your organs of
sense. Their internal constitution, their true and real nature, you are
utterly in the dark as to *that.*

Philonous. Do I not know this to be a real stone that I stand on,
and that which I see before my eyes to be a real tree?

Hylas. Know? No, it is impossible you or any man alive should
know it. All you know is, that you have such a certain idea or appearance
in your own mind. But what is this to the real tree or stone? I tell you
that colour, figure, and hardness, which you perceive, are not the real
natures of those things, or in the least like them. The same may be said

of all other real things or corporeal substances which compose the world. They have none of them anything of themselves, like those sensible qualities by us perceived. We should not therefore pretend to affirm or know anything of them, as they are in their own nature.

Philonous. But surely, *Hylas,* I can distinguish gold, for example, from iron: and how could this be, if I knew not what either truly was?

Hylas. Believe me, *Philonous,* you can only distinguish between your own ideas. That yellowness, that weight, and other sensible qualities, think you they are really in the gold? They are only relative to the senses and have no absolute existence in nature. And in pretending to distinguish the species of real things, by the appearances in your mind, you may perhaps act as wisely as he that should conclude two men were of a different species, because their clothes were not of the same colour.

Philonous. It seems, then, we are altogether put off with the appearances of things, and those false ones too. The very meat I eat, and the cloth I wear, have nothing in them like what I see and feel.

Hylas. Even so.

Philonous. But is it not strange the whole world should be thus imposed on, and so foolish as to believe their senses? And yet I know not how it is, but men eat, and drink, and sleep, and perform all the offices of life, as comfortably and conveniently as if they really knew the things they are conversant about.

Hylas. They do so: but you know ordinary practice does not require a nicety of speculative knowledge. Hence the vulgar retain their mistakes, and for all that make a shift to bustle through the affairs of life. But philosophers know better things.

Philonous. You mean, they know that they *know nothing.*

Hylas. That is the very top and perfection of human knowledge.

Philonous. But are you all this while in earnest, *Hylas*; and are you seriously persuaded that you know nothing real in the world? Suppose you are going to write, would you not call for pen, ink, and paper, like another man; and do you not know what it is you call for?

Hylas. How often must I tell you, that I know not the real nature of any one thing in the universe? I may indeed upon occasion make use of pen, ink, and paper. But, what any one of them is in its own true nature, I declare positively I know not. And the same is true with regard to every other corporeal thing. And, what is more, we are not only ignorant of the true and real nature of things, but even of their existence. It cannot be denied that we perceive such certain appearances or ideas; but it cannot be concluded from thence that bodies really exist. Nay, now I think on it, I must, agreeably to my former concessions, farther declare that it is impossible any real corporeal thing should exist in nature.

Philonous. You amaze me. Was ever anything more wild and extravagant than the notions you now maintain: and is it not evident you are led into all these extravagances by the belief of *material substance?* This makes you dream of those unknown natures in everything. It is this occasions your distinguishing between the reality and sensible appearances of things. It is to this you are indebted for being ignorant of what everybody else knows perfectly well. Nor is this all: you are not only ignorant of the true nature of everything, but you know not whether any thing really exists, or whether there are any true natures at all; forasmuch as you attribute to your material beings an absolute or external existence, wherein you suppose their reality consists. And, as you are forced in the end to acknowledge such an existence means either a direct repugnancy, or nothing at all, it follows that you are obliged to pull down your own hypothesis of material Substance, and positively to deny the real existence of any part of the universe. And so you are plunged into the deepest and most deplorable *Scepticism* that ever man was. Tell me, *Hylas*, is it not as I say?

Hylas. I agree with you. *Material substance* was no more than an hypothesis, and a false and groundless one too. I will no longer spend my breath in defence of it. But, whatever hypothesis you advance, or whatsoever scheme of things you introduce in its stead, I doubt not it will appear every whit as false: let me but be allowed to question you upon it. That is, suffer me to serve you in your own kind, and I warrant it shall conduct you through as many perplexities and contradictions, to the very same state of Scepticism that I myself am in at present.

Philonous. I assure you, *Hylas*, I do not pretend to frame any hypothesis at all. I am of a vulgar cast, simple enough to believe my senses, and leave things as I find them. To be plain, it is my opinion that the real things are those very things I see and feel, and perceive by my senses. These I know, and, finding they answer all the necessities and purposes of life, have no reason to be solicitous about any other unknown beings. A piece of sensible bread, for instance, would stay my stomach better than ten thousand times as much of that insensible, unintelligible, real bread you speak of. It is likewise my opinion that colours and other sensible qualities are on the objects. I cannot for my life help thinking that snow is white, and fire hot. You indeed, who by *snow* and *fire* mean certain external, unperceived, unperceiving substances, are in the right to deny whiteness or heat to be affections inherent in them. But I, who understand by those words the things I see and feel, am obliged to think like other folks. And, as I am no sceptic with regard to the nature of things, so neither am I as to their existence. That a thing should be really perceived by my senses, and at the same time not really exist, is to me a plain contradiction; since I cannot prescind or abstract, even in thought, the existence of a sensible thing from its being perceived. Wood, stones, fire, water, flesh, iron, and the like things, which I name and discourse of, are things that I know. And I should not have known them but that I perceived them by my senses; and things perceived by the senses are immediately perceived; and things immediately perceived are ideas; and ideas cannot exist without the mind; their existence therefore consists in being perceived; when, therefore, they are actually perceived there can be no doubt of their existence. Away then with all that Scepticism, all those ridiculous philosophical doubts. What a jest is it for a philosopher to question the existence of sensible things, till he hath it proved to him from the veracity of God; or to pretend our knowledge in this point falls short of intuition or demonstration! I might as well doubt of my own being, as of the being of those things I actually see and feel.

Hylas. Not so fast, *Philonous:* you say you cannot conceive how sensible things should exist without the mind. Do you not?

Philonous. I do.

Hylas. Supposing you were annihilated, cannot you conceive it possible that things perceivable by sense may still exist?

Philonous. I can; but then it must be in another mind. When I deny sensible things an existence out of the mind, I do not mean my mind in particular, but all minds. Now, it is plain they have an existence exterior to my mind; since I find them by experience to be independent of it. There is therefore some other mind wherein they exist, during the intervals between the times of my perceiving them: as likewise they did before my birth, and would do after my supposed annihilation. And, as the same is true with regards to all other finite created spirits, it necessarily follows there is an *omnipresent eternal Mind*, which knows and comprehends all things, and exhibits them to our view in such a manner, and according to such rules, as He Himself hath ordained, and are by us termed the *laws of nature*.

Hylas. Answer me, *Philonous.* Are all our ideas perfectly inert beings? Or have they any agency included in them?

Philonous. They are altogether passive and inert.

Hylas. And is not God an agent, a being purely active?

Philonous. I acknowledge it.

Hylas. No idea therefore can be like unto, or represent the nature of God?

Philonous. It cannot.

Hylas. Since therefore you have no idea of the mind of God, how can you conceive it possible that things should exist in His mind? Or, if you can conceive the mind of God, without having an idea of it, why may not I be allowed to conceive the existence of Matter, notwithstanding I have no idea of it?

Philonous. As to your first qustion: I own I have properly no *idea,* either of God or any other spirit; for these being active, cannot be represented by things perfectly inert, as our ideas are. I do nevertheless know that I, who am a spirit or thinking substance, exist as certainly as I know my ideas exist. Farther, I know what I mean by the terms *I* and *myself;* and I know this immediately or intuitively, though I do not perceive it as I perceive a triangle, a colour, or a sound. The Mind, Spirit, or Soul is that indivisible unextended thing which thinks, acts, and perceives. I say *indivisible,* because unextended; and *unextended,* because extended, figured, moveable things are ideas; and that which perceives ideas, which thinks and wills, is plainly itself no idea, nor like an idea. Ideas are things inactive, and perceived. And Spirits a sort of beings altogether different from them. I do not therefore say my soul is an idea, or like an idea. However, taking the word *idea* in a large sense, my soul may be said to furnish me with an idea, that is, an image or likeness of God, though indeed extremely inadequate. For, all the notion I have of God is obtained by reflecting on my own soul, heightening its powers, and removing its imperfections. I have, therefore, though not an inactive idea, yet in *myself* some sort of an active thinking image of the Deity. And, though I perceive Him not by sense, yet I have a notion of Him, or know Him by reflexion and reasoning. My own mind and my own ideas I have an immediate knowledge of; and, by the help of these, do mediately apprehend the possibility of the existence of other spirits and ideas. Farther, from my own being, and from the dependency I find in myself and my ideas, I do, by an act of reason, necessarily infer the existence of a God, and of all created things in the mind of God. So much for your first question. For the second: I suppose by this time you can answer it yourself. For you neither perceive Matter objectively, as you do an inactive being or idea; nor know it, as you do yourself, by a reflex act; neither do you mediately apprehend it by similitude of the one or the other; nor yet collect it by reasoning from that which you know immediately. All which makes the case of *Matter* widely different from that of the *Deity.*[1]

Hylas. You say your own soul supplies you with some sort of an idea or image of God. But, at the same time, you acknowledge you have, properly speaking, no *idea* of your own soul. You even affirm that spirits are a sort of beings altogether different from ideas. Consequently that

---

[1] The four following paragraphs were not contained in the first and second editions.

no idea can be like a spirit. We have therefore no idea of any spirit. You admit nevertheless that there is spiritual Substance, although you have no idea of it; while you deny there can be such a thing as material Substance, because you have no notion or idea of it. Is this fair dealing? To act consistently, you must either admit Matter or reject Spirit. What say you to this?

Philonous. I say, in the first place, that I do not deny the existence of material substance, merely because I have no notion of it, but because the notion of it is inconsistent; or, in other words, because it is repugnant that there should be a notion of it. Many things, for aught I know, may exist, whereof neither I nor any other man hath or can have any idea or notion whatsoever. But then those things must be possible, that is, nothing inconsistent must be included in their definition. I say, secondly, that, although we believe things to exist which we do not perceive, yet we may not believe that any particular thing exists, without some reason for such belief: but I have no reason for believing the existence of Matter. I have no immediate intuition thereof: neither can I immediately from my sensations, ideas, notions, actions, or passions, infer an unthinking, unperceiving, inactive Substance, either by probable deduction, or necessary consequence. Whereas the being of my Self, that is, my own soul, mind, or thinking principle, I evidently know by reflexion. You will forgive me if I repeat the same things in answer to the same objections. In the very notion or definition of *material Substance*, there is included a manifest repugnance and inconsistency. But this cannot be said of the notion of Spirit. That ideas should exist in what doth not perceive, or be produced by what doth not act, is repugnant. But, it is no repugnancy to say that a perceiving thing should be the subject of ideas, or an active thing the cause of them. It is granted we have neither an immediate evidence nor a demonstrative knowledge of the existence of other finite spirits; but it will not thence follow that such spirits are on a foot with material substances: if to suppose the one be inconsistent, and it be not inconsistent to suppose the other; if the one can be inferred by no argument, and there is a probability for the other; if we see signs and effects indicating distinct finite agents like ourselves, and see no sign or symptom whatever that leads to a rational belief of Matter. I say, lastly, that I have a notion of Spirit, though I have not, strictly speaking, an idea of it. I do not perceive it as an idea, or by means of an idea, but know it by reflexion.

Hylas. Notwithstanding all you have said, to me it seems that, according to your own way of thinking, and in consequence of your own principles, it should follow that *you* are only a system of floating ideas, without any substance to support them. Words are not to be used without a meaning. And, as there is no more meaning in *spiritual Substance* than in *material Substance,* the one is to be exploded as well as the other.

Philonous. How often must I repeat, that I know or am conscious of my own being; and that *I myself* am not my ideas, but somewhat else, a thinking, active principle that perceives, knows, wills, and operates about ideas. I know that I, one and the same self, perceive both colours and sounds: that a colour cannot perceive a sound, nor a sound a colour: that I am therefore one individual principle, distinct from colour and sound; and, for the same reason, from all other sensible things and inert ideas. But, I am not in like manner conscious either of the existence or essence of Matter. On the contrary, I know that nothing inconsistent can exist, and that the existence of Matter implies an inconsistency. Farther, I know what I mean when I affirm that there is a spiritual sub-stance or support of ideas, that is, that a spirit knows and perceives ideas. But, I do not know what is meant when it is said that an unperceiving substance hath inherent in it and supports either ideas or the arche-types of ideas. There is therefore upon the whole no parity of case be-tween Spirit and Matter.

Hylas. I own myself satisfied in this point. But, do you in earnest think the real existence of sensible things consists in their being actually perceived? If so; how comes it that all mankind distinguish between them? Ask the first man you meet, and he shall tell you, *to be perceived* is one thing, and *to exist* is another.

Philonous. I am content, *Hylas,* to appeal to the common sense of the world for the truth of my notion. Ask the gardener why he thinks yonder cherry-tree exists in the garden, and he shall tell you, because he sees and feels it; in a word, because he perceives it by his senses. Ask him why he thinks an orange-tree not to be there, and he shall tell you, because he does not perceive it. What he perceives by sense, that he terms a real being, and saith it *is* or *exists*; but, that which is not perceivable, the same, he saith, hath no being.

Hylas. Yes, *Philonous,* I grant the existence of a sensible thing con-sists in being perceivable, but not in being actually perceived.

Philonous. And what is perceivable but an idea? And can an idea exist without being actually perceived? These are points long since agreed between us.

Hylas. But, be your opinion never so true, yet surely you will not deny it is shocking, and contrary to the common sense of men. Ask the fellow whether yonder tree hath an existence out of his mind: what an-swer think you he would make?

Philonous. The same that I should myself, to wit, that it doth exist out of his mind. But then to a Christian it cannot surely be shocking to say, the real tree, existing without his mind, is truly known and comprehended by (that is, *exists in*) the infinite mind of God. Probably he may not at first glance be aware of the direct and immediate proof there is of this; inasmuch as the very being of a tree, or any other sensible thing, implies a mind wherein it is. But the point itself he cannot deny. The question between the Materialists and me is not, whether things have a *real* existence out of the mind of this or that person, but, whether thay have an *absolute* existence, distinct from being perceived by God, and exterior to all minds. This indeed some heathens and philosophers have affirmed, but whoever entertains notions of the Deity suitable to the Holy Scriptures will be of another opinion.

Hylas. But, according to your notions, what difference is there between real things, and chimeras formed by the imagination, or the visions of a dream, since they are all equally in the mind?

Philonous. The ideas formed by the imagination are faint and indistinct; they have, besides, an entire dependence on the will. But the ideas perceived by sense, that is, real things, are more vivid and clear; and, being imprinted on the mind by a spirit distinct from us, have not the like dependence on our will. There is therefore no danger of confounding these with the foregoing: and there is as little of confounding them with the visions of a dream, which are dim, irregular, and confused. And, though they should happen to be never so lively and natural, yet, by their not being connected, and of a piece with the preceding and subsequent transactions of our lives, they might easily be distinguished from realities. In short, by whatever method you distinguish *things* from *chimeras* on your scheme, the same, it is evident, will hold also upon mine. For, it must be, I presume, by some perceived difference; and I am not for depriving you of any one thing that you perceive.

Hylas. But still, *Philonous*, you hold, there is nothing in the world but spirits and ideas. And this, you must needs acknowledge, sounds very oddly.

Philonous. I own the word *idea*, not being commonly used for *thing*, sounds something out of the way. My reason for using it was, because a necessary relation to the mind is understood to be implied by that term; and it is now commonly used by philosophers to denote the immediate objects of the understanding. But, however oddly the proposition may sound in words, yet it includes nothing so very strange or shocking in its sense; which in effect amounts to no more than this, to wit, that there are only things perceiving, and things perceived; or that every unthinking being is necessarily, and from the very nature of its existence, perceived by some mind; if not by a finite created mind, yet certainly by the infinite mind of God, in whom "we live, and move, and have our being." Is this as strange as to say, the sensible qualities are not on the objects: or that we cannot be sure of the existence of things, or know anything of their real natures, though we both see and feel them, and perceive them by all our senses?

Hylas. And, in consequence of this, must we not think there are no such things as physical or corporeal causes; but that a Spirit is the immediate cause of all the phenomena in nature? Can there be anything more extravagant than this?

Philonous. Yes, it is infinitely more extravagant to say a thing which is inert operates on the mind, and which is unperceiving, is the cause of our perceptions, without any regard either to consistency, or the old known axiom, *Nothing can give to another that which it hath not itself.*[2] Besides, that which to you, I know not for what reason, seems so extravagant is no more than the Holy Scriptures assert in a hundred places. In them God is represented as the sole and immediate Author of all those effects which some heathens and philosophers are wont to ascribe to Nature, Matter, Fate, or the like unthinking principle. This is so much the constant language of Scripture that it were needless to confirm it by citations.

Hylas. You are not aware, *Philonous,* that, in making God the immediate Author of all the motions in nature, you make Him the Author of murder, sacrilege, adultery, and the like heinous sins.

Philonous. In answer to that, I observe, first, that the imputation of guilt is the same, whether a person commits an action with or without an instrument. In case therefore you suppose God to act by the mediation of an instrument, or occasion, called *Matter,* you as truly make Him the author of sin as I, who think Him the immediate agent in all those operations vulgarly ascribed to Nature. I farther observe that sin or moral turpitude doth not consist in the outward physical action or motion, but in the internal deviation of the will from the laws of reason and religion. This is plain, in that the killing an enemy in a battle, or putting a criminal legally to death, is not thought sinful; though the outward act be the very same with that in the case of murder. Since, therefore, sin doth not consist in the physical action, the making God an immediate cause of all such actions is not making Him the Author of sin. Lastly, I have nowhere said that God is the only agent who produces all the motions in bodies. It is true I have denied there are any other agents besides spirits; but this is very consistent with allowing to thinking rational beings, in the production of motions, the use of limited powers, ultimately indeed derived from God, but immediately under the direction of their own wills, which is sufficient to entitle them to all the guilt of their actions.

---

[2] The words of this sentence from "without" to the end were omitted from the last edition.

Hylas. But the denying Matter, *Philonous*, or corporeal Substance; there is the point. You can never persuade me that this is not repugnant to the universal sense of mankind. Were our dispute to be determined by most voices, I am confident you would give up the point, without gathering the votes.

Philonous. I wish both our opinions were fairly stated and submitted to the judgment of men who had plain common sense, without the prejudices of a learned education. Let me be represented as one who trusts his senses, who thinks he knows the things he sees and feels, and entertains no doubts of their existence; and you fairly set forth with all your doubts, your paradoxes, and your scepticism about you, and I shall willingly acquiesce in the determination of any indifferent person. That there is no substance wherein ideas can exist beside spirit is to me evident. And that the objects immediately perceived are ideas, is on all hands agreed. And that sensible qualities are objects immediately perceived no one can deny. It is therefore evident there can be no *substratum* of those qualities but spirit; in which they exist, not by way of mode or property, but as a thing perceived in that which perceives it. I deny therefore that there is any unthinking *substratum* of the objects of sense, and in that acceptation that there is any material substance. But if by *material substance* is meant only sensible body, that which is seen and felt (and the unphilosophical part of the world, I dare say, mean no more), then I am more certain of matter's existence than you or any other philosopher pretend to be. If there be anything which makes the generality of mankind averse from the notions I espouse, it is a misapprehension that I deny the reality of sensible things: but, as it is you who are guilty of that and not I, it follows that in truth their aversion is against your notions and not mine. I do therefore assert that I am as certain as of my own being, that there are bodies or corporeal substances (meaning the things I perceive by my senses); and that, granting this, the bulk of mankind will take no thought about, nor think themselves at all concerned in the fate of those unknown natures and philosophical quiddities which some men are so fond of.

Hylas. What say you to this? Since, according to you, men judge of the reality of things by their senses, how can a man be mistaken in thinking the moon a plain lucid surface, about a foot in diameter; or a square tower, seen at a distance, round; or an oar, with one end in the water, crooked?

Philonous. He is not mistaken with regard to the ideas he actually perceives, but in the inferences he makes from his present perceptions Thus, in the case of the oar, what he immediately perceives by sight is certainly crooked; and so far he is in the right. But, if he thence conclude that upon taking the oar out of the water he shall perceive the same crookedness; or that it would affect his touch as crooked things are wont to do: in that he is mistaken. In like manner, if he shall conclude from what he perceives in one station, that, in case he advances towards the moon or tower, he should still be affected with the like ideas, he is mistaken. But his mistake lies not in what he perceives immediately and at present (it being a manifest contradiction to suppose he should err in respect of that), but in the wrong judgment he makes concerning the ideas he apprehends to be connected with those immediately perceived: or, concerning the ideas that, from what he perceives at present, he imagines would be perceived in other circumstances. The case is the same with regard to the Copernican system. We do not here perceive any motion of the earth: but it were erroneous thence to conclude, that, in case we were placed at as great a distance from that as we are now from the other planets, we should not then perceive its motion.

Hylas. I understand you; and must needs own you say things plausible enough: but, give me leave to put you in mind of one thing. Pray, *Philonous,* were you not formerly as positive that Matter existed, as you are now that it does not?

Philonous. I was. But here lies the difference. Before my positiveness was founded, without examination, upon prejudice; but now, after inquiry, upon evidence.

Hylas. After all, it seems our dispute is rather about words than things. We agree in the thing, but differ in the name. That we are affected with ideas from without is evident; and it is no less evident that there must be (I will not say archetypes, but) powers without the mind, corresponding to those ideas. And, as these powers cannot subsist by themselves, there is some subject of them necessarily to be admitted, which I call *Matter,* and you call *Spirit.* This is all the difference.

Philonous. Pray, *Hylas,* is that powerful being, or subject of powers, extended?

Hylas. It hath not extension; but it hath the power to raise in you the idea of extension.

Philonous. It is therefore itself unextended?

Hylas. I grant it.

Philonous. Is it not also active?

Hylas. Without doubt: otherwise, how could we attribute powers to it?

Philonous. Now let me ask you two questions: *First,* whether it be agreeable to the usage either of philosophers or others to give the name *Matter* to an unextended active being? And, *Secondly,* whether it be not ridiculously absurd to misapply names contrary to the common use of language?

Hylas. Well then, let it not be called Matter, since you will have it so, but some *third nature* distinct from Matter and Spirit. For what reason is there why you should call it Spirit? Does not the notion of spirit imply that it is thinking, as well as active and unextended?

Philonous. My reason is this: because I have a mind to have some notion of meaning in what I say: but I have no notion of any action distinct from volition, neither can I conceive volition to be anywhere but in a spirit; therefore, when I speak of an active being, I am obliged to mean a spirit. Beside, what can be plainer than that a thing which hath no ideas in itself cannot impart them to me; and, if it hath ideas, surely it must be a spirit. To make you comprehend the point still more clearly if it be possible: I assert as well as you that, since we are affected from without, we must allow powers to be without, in a being distinct from ourselves. So far we are agreed. But then we differ as to the kind of this powerful being. I will have it to be spirit, you Matter, or I know not what (I may add too, you know not what) third nature. Thus, I prove it to be spirit. From the effects I see produced I conclude there are actions; and, because actions, volitions; and, because there are volitions, there must be a will. Again, the things I perceive must have an existence, they or their archetypes, out of my mind: but, being ideas, neither they nor their archetypes can exist otherwise than in an understanding; there is therefore an understanding. But will and understanding constitute in the strictest sense a mind or spirit. The powerful cause, therefore, of my ideas is in strict propriety of speech a *spirit*.

Hylas. And now I warrant you think you have made the point very clear, little suspecting that what you advance leads directly to a contradiction. Is it not an absurdity to imagine any imperfection in God?

Philonous. Without a doubt.

Hylas. To suffer pain is an imperfection?

Philonous. It is.

Hylas. Are we not sometimes affected with pain and uneasiness by some other being?

Philonous. We are.

Hylas. And have you not said that being is a spirit, and is not that spirit God?

Philonous. I grant it.

Hylas. But you have asserted that whatever ideas we perceive from without are in the mind which affects us. The ideas, therefore, of pain and uneasiness are in God; or, in other words, God suffers pain: that is to say, there is an imperfection in the Divine nature, which, you acknowledge, was absurd. So you are caught in a plain contradiction.

Philonous. That God knows or understands all things, and that He knows, among other things, what pain is, even every sort of painful sensation, and what it is for His creatures to suffer pain, I make no question. But, that God, though He knows and sometimes causes painful sensations in us, can Himself suffer pain, I positively deny. We, who are limited and dependent spirits, are liable to impressions of sense, the effects of an external agent, which, being produced against our wills, are sometimes painful and uneasy. But God, whom no external being can affect, who perceives nothing by sense as we do, whose will is absolute and independent, causing all things, and liable to be thwarted or resisted by nothing; it is evident, such a Being as this can suffer nothing, nor be affected with any painful sensation, or indeed any sensation at all. We are chained to a body, that is to say, our perceptions are connected with corporeal motions. By the law of our nature, we are affected upon every alteration in the nervous parts of our sensible body; which sensible body, rightly considered, is nothing but a complexion of such qualities or ideas as have no existence distinct from being perceived by a mind: so that this connexion of sensations with corporeal motions means no more than a correspondence in the order of nature between two sets of ideas, or things immediately perceivable. But God is a pure spirit, disengaged from all such sympathy or natural ties. No corporeal motions are attended with the sensations of pain or pleasure in His mind. To know everything knowable is certainly a perfection; but to endure, or suffer, or feel anything by sense, is an imperfection. The former, I say, agrees to God, but not the latter. God knows or hath ideas; but His ideas are not conveyed to Him by sense, as ours are. Your not distinguishing, where there is so manifest a difference, makes you fancy you see an absurdity where there is none.

Hylas. But, all this while you have not considered that the quantity of Matter hath been demonstrated to be proportioned to the gravity of bodies. And what can withstand demonstration?

Philonous. Let me see how you demonstrate that point.

Hylas. I lay it down for a principle that the moments or quantities of motion in bodies are in a direct compounded reason of the velocities and quantities of Matter contained in them. Hence, where the velocities are equal, it follows the moments are directly as the quantity of Matter in each. But it is found by experience that all bodies (bating the small inequalities, arising from the resistance of the air) descend with an equal velocity; the motion therefore of descending bodies, and consequently their gravity, which is the cause or principle of that motion, is proportional to the quantity of Matter; which was to be demonstrated.

Philonous. You lay it down as a self-evident principle that the quantity of motion in any body is proportional to the velocity and

Matter taken together; and this is made use of to prove a proposition from whence the existence of *Matter* is inferred. Pray is not this arguing in a circle?

Hylas. In the premise I only mean that the motion is proportional to the velocity, jointly with the extension and solidity.

Philonous. But, allowing this to be true, yet it will not thence follow that gravity is proportional to *Matter*, in your philosophic sense of the word; except you take it for granted that unknown *substratum*, or whatever else you call it, is proportional to those sensible qualities; which to suppose is plainly begging the question. That there is magnitude and solidity, or resistance, perceived by sense, I readily grant; as likewise, that gravity may be proportional to those qualities I will not dispute. But that either these qualities as perceived by us, or the powers producing them, do exist in a *material substratum;*—this is what I deny and you indeed affirm, but, notwithstanding your demonstration, have not yet proved.

Hylas. I shall insist no longer on that point. Do you think, however, you shall persuade me the natural philosophers have been dreaming all this while? Pray what becomes of all their hypotheses and explications of the phenomena, which suppose the existence of Matter?

Philonous. What mean you, *Hylas*, by the *phenomena?*

Hylas. I mean the appearances which I perceive by my senses.

Philonous. And the appearance perceived by sense, are they not ideas?

Hylas. I have told you so a hundred times.

Philonous. Therefore, to explain the phenomena is to shew how we come to be affected with ideas, in that manner and order wherein they are imprinted on our senses. Is it not?

Hylas. It is.

Philonous. Now, if you can prove that any philosopher hath explained the production of any one idea in our minds by the help of *Matter*, I shall for ever acquiesce, and look on all that hath been said against it as nothing; but, if you cannot, it is vain to urge the explication of phenomena. That a Being endowed with knowledge and will should produce or exhibit ideas is easily understood. But, that a Being which is utterly destitute of these faculties should be able to produce ideas, or in any sort to affect an intelligence, this I can never understand. This I say, though we had some positive conception of Matter, though we knew its qualities, and could comprehend its existence, would yet be so far from explaining things, that it is itself the most inexplicable thing in the world. And yet, for all this, it will not follow that philosophers have been doing nothing; for, by observing and reasoning upon the connexion of ideas, they discover the laws and methods of nature, which is a part of knowledge both useful and entertaining.

Hylas. After all, can it be supposed God would deceive all mankind? Do you imagine He would have induced the whole world to believe the being of Matter, if there was no such thing?

Philonous. That every epidemical opinion arising from prejudice, or passion, or thoughtlessness may be imputed to God, as the Author of it, I believe you will not affirm. Whatsoever opinion we father on Him, it must be either because He has discovered it to us by supernatural revelation; or because it is so evident to our natural faculties, which were framed and given us by God, that it is impossible we should withhold our assent from it. But where is the revelation? or where is the evidence that extorts the belief of Matter? Nay, how does it appear, that Matter, taken for something distinct from what we perceive by our senses, is thought to exist by all mankind; or, indeed, by any except a few philosophers, who do not know what they would be at? Your question supposes these points are clear; and, when you have cleared them, I shall think myself obliged to give you another answer. In the meantime let it suffice that I tell you, I do not suppose God has deceived mankind at all.

Hylas. But the novelty, *Philonous,* the novelty! There lies the danger. New notions should always be discountenanced; they unsettle men's minds, and nobody knows where they will end.

Philonous. Why the rejecting a notion that hath no foundation, either in sense, or in reason, or in Divine authority, should be thought to unsettle the belief of such opinions as are grounded on all or any of these, I cannot imagine. That innovations in government and religion are dangerous, and ought to be discountenanced, I freely own. But, is there the like reason why they should be discouraged in philosophy? The making anything known which was unknown before is an innovation in knowledge: and, if all such innovations had been forbidden, men would [not] [3] have made a notable progress in the arts and sciences. But it is none of my business to plead for novelties and paradoxes. That the qualities we perceive are not on the objects: that we must not believe our senses: that we know nothing of the real nature of things, and can never be assured even of their existence: that real colours and sounds are nothing but certain unknown figures and motions: that motions are in themselves neither swift nor slow: that there are in bodies absolute extensions, without any particular magnitude, or figure: that a thing stupid, thoughtless, and inactive, operates on a

---

[3] The meaning requires the word "not." Its omission from Berkeley's text is evidently a typographical error.

spirit: that the least particle of a body contains innumerable extended parts:—these are the novelties, these are the strange notions which shock the genuine uncorrupted judgment of all mankind; and being once admitted, embarass the mind with endless doubts and difficulties. And it is against these and the like innovations I endeavour to vindicate Common Sense. It is true, in doing this, I may perhaps be obliged to use some *ambages*, and ways of speech not common. But, if my notions are once thoroughly understood, that which is most singular in them will, in effect, be found to amount to no more than this:—that it is absolutely impossible, and a plain contradiction, to suppose any unthinking being should exist without being perceived by a mind. And, if this notion be singular, it is a shame it should be so at this time of day, and in a Christian country.

Hylas. As for the difficulties other opinions may be liable to, those are out of the question. It is your business to defend your own opinion. Can anything be plainer than that you are for changing all things into ideas? You, I say, who are not ashamed to charge me with *scepticism.* This is so plain, there is no denying it.

Philonous. You mistake me. I am not for changing things into ideas, but rather ideas into things; since those immediate objects of perception, which, according to you, are only appearances of things, I take to be the real things themselves.

Hylas. Things! you may pretend what you please; but it is certain you leave us nothing but the empty forms of things, the outside only which strikes the senses.

Philonous. What you call the empty forms and outside of things seem to me the very things themselves. Nor are they empty or incomplete, otherwise than upon your supposition that Matter is an essential part of all corporeal things. We both, therefore, agree in this, that we perceive only sensible forms: but herein we differ, you will have them to be empty appearances, I real beings. In short, you do not trust your senses, I do.

Hylas. You say you believe your senses; and seem to applaud yourself that in this you agree with the vulgar. According to you, therefore, the true nature of a thing is discovered by the senses. If so, whence comes that disagreement? Why, is not the same figure, and other sensible qualities, perceived all manner of ways? And why should we use a microscope the better to discover the true nature of a body, if it were discoverable to the naked eye?

Philonous. Strictly speaking, *Hylas,* we do not see the same object that we feel; neither is the same object perceived by the microscope which was by the naked eye. But, in case every variation was thought sufficient to constitute a new kind or individual, the endless number or confusion of names would render language impracticable. Therefore, to avoid this as well as other inconveniences which are obvious upon a little thought, men combine together several ideas, apprehended by divers senses, or by the same sense at different times, or in different circumstances, but observed, however, to have some connexion in nature, either with respect to coexistence or succession; all which they refer to one name, and consider as one thing. Hence, it follows that when I examine by my other senses a thing I have seen, it is not in order to understand better the same object which I had perceived by sight, the object of one sense not being perceived by the other senses. And, when I look through a microscope, it is not that I may perceive more clearly what I perceived already with my bare eyes; the object perceived by the glass being quite different from the former. But, in both cases, my aim is only to know what ideas are connected together; and the more a man knows of the connexion of ideas, the more he is said to know of the nature of things. What, therefore, if our ideas are variable; what if our senses are not in all circumstances affected with the same appearances? It will not thence follow they are not to be trusted, or that they are inconsistent either with themselves or anything else; except it be with your preconceived notion of (I know not what) one single, unchanged, unperceivable, real nature, marked by each name: which prejudice seems to have taken its rise from not rightly understanding the common language of men, speaking of several distinct ideas as united into one thing by the mind. And, indeed, there is cause to suspect several erroneous conceits of the philosophers are owing to the same original: while they began to build their schemes not so much on notions as words, which were framed by the vulgar, merely for conveniency and dispatch in the common actions of life, without any regard to speculation.

Hylas. Methinks I apprehend your meaning.

Philonous. It is your opinion the ideas we perceive by our senses are not real things, but images or copies of them. Our knowledge, therefore, is no farther real than as our ideas are the true representations of those originals. But, as these supposed originals are in themselves unknown, it is impossible to know how far our ideas resemble them; or whether they resemble them at all. We cannot, therefore, be sure we have any real knowledge. Farther, as our ideas are perpetually varied, without any change in the supposed real things, it necessarily follows they cannot all be true copies of them: or, if some are and others are not, it is impossible to distinguish the former from the latter. And this plunges us yet deeper in uncertainty. Again, when we consider the point, we cannot conceive how any idea, or anything like an idea, should have an absolute existence out of a mind: nor consequently, according to you, how there should be any real thing in nature. The result of all which is that we are thrown into the most hopeless and abandoned Scepticism. Now, give me leave to ask you, First, Whether your referring ideas to certain absolutely existing unperceived substances, as their originals, be not the source of all this Scepticism? Secondly, whether you are informed, either by sense or reason, of the existence of those unknown originals? And, in case you are not, whether it be not absurd to suppose them? Thirdly, Whether, upon inquiry, you find there is anything distinctly conceived or meant by the *absolute or external existence of unperceiving substances*? Lastly, Whether, the premises considered, it be not the wisest way to follow nature, trust your senses, and, laying aside all anxious thought about unknown natures or substances, admit with the vulgar those for real things which are perceived by the senses?

Hylas. For the present, I have no inclination to the answering part. I would much rather see how you can get over what follows. Pray are not the objects perceived by the senses of one, likewise perceivable to others present? If there were a hundred more here, they would all see the garden, the trees, and flowers, as I see them. But they are not in the same manner affected with the ideas I frame in my imagination. Does not this make a difference between the former sort of objects and the latter?

Philonous. I grant it does. Nor have I ever denied a difference between the objects of sense and those of imagination. But what would you infer from thence? You cannot say that sensible objects exist unperceived, because they are perceived by many.

Hylas. I own I can make nothing of that objection: but it hath led me into another. Is it not your opinion that by our senses we perceive only the ideas existing in our minds?

Philonous. It is.

Hylas. But the same idea which is in my mind cannot be in yours, or in any other mind. Doth it not therefore follow, from your principles, that no two can see the same thing? And is not this highly absurd?

Philonous. If the term *same* be taken in the vulgar acceptation, it is certain (and not at all repugnant to the principles I maintain) that different persons may perceive the same thing; or the same thing or idea exist in different minds. Words are of arbitrary imposition; and, since men are used to apply the word *same* where no distinction or variety is perceived, and I do not pretend to alter their perceptions, it follows that, as men have said before, *several saw the same thing*, so they may, upon like occasions, still continue to use the same phrase, without any deviation either from propriety of language, or the truth of things. But, if the term *same* be used in the acceptation of philosophers, who pretend to an abstracted notion of identity, then, according to their sundry definitions of this notion (for it is not yet agreed wherein that philosophic identity consists), it may or may not be possible for divers persons to perceive the same thing. But whether philosophers shall think fit to call a thing the *same* or no, is, I conceive, of small importance. Let us suppose several men together, all endued with the same faculties, and consequently affected in like sort by their senses, and who had yet never known the use of language; they would without question, agree in their perceptions. Though perhaps, when they came to the use of speech, some regarding the uniformness of what was perceived, might call it the *same* thing: others, especially regarding the diversity of persons who perceived, might choose the denomination of *different* things. But who sees not that all the dispute is about a word? to wit, whether what is perceived by different persons may yet have the term *same* applied to it? Or, suppose a house, whose walls or outward shell remaining unaltered, the chambers are all pulled down, and new ones built in their place; and that you should call this the *same*, and I should say it was not the *same* house:—would we not, for all this, perfectly agree in our thoughts of the house, considered in itself? And would not all the difference consist in a sound? If you should say, We differ in our notions; for that you superadded to your idea of the house the simple abstracted idea of identity, whereas I did not; I would tell you, I know not what you mean by the *abstracted idea of identity*; and should desire you to look into your own thoughts, and be sure you understood yourself.—Why so silent, *Hylas?* Are you not yet satisfied men may dispute about identity and diversity, without any real difference in their thoughts and opinions, abstracted from names? Take this farther reflexion with you—that whether Matter be allowed to exist or no, the case is exactly the same as to the point in hand. For, the Materialists themselves acknowledge what we immediately perceive by our senses to be our own ideas. Your difficulty, therefore, that no two see the same thing, makes equally against the Materialists and me.

Hylas. But they suppose an external archetype, to which referring their several ideas they may truly be said to perceive the same thing.

Philonous. And (not to mention your having discarded those archetypes) so may you suppose an external archetype on my principles; *external*, I mean, to your own mind; though indeed it must be supposed to exist in that mind which comprehends all things; but then, this serves all the ends of *identity*, as well as if it existed out of a mind. And I am sure you yourself will not say it is less intelligible.

Hylas. You have indeed clearly satisfied me, either that there is no difficulty at bottom in this point; or, if there be, that it makes equally against both opinions.

Philonous. But that which makes equally against two contradictory opinions can be a proof against neither.

Hylas. I acknowledge it. But, after all, *Philonous,* when I consider the substance of what you advance against *Scepticism,* it amounts to no more than this:—We are sure that we really see, hear, feel; in a word, that we are affected with sensible impressions.

Philonous. And how are we concerned any farther? I see this *cherry,* I feel it, I taste it: and I am sure *nothing* cannot be seen, or felt, or tasted: it is therefore *real.* Take away the sensations of softness, moisture, redness, tartness, and you take away the *cherry.* Since it is not a being distinct from sensations; a *cherry,* I say, is nothing but a congeries of sensible impressions, or ideas perceived by various senses: which ideas are united into one thing (or have one name given them) by the mind; because they are observed to attend each other. Thus, when the palate is affected with such a particular taste, the sight is affected with a red colour, the touch with roundness, softness, &c. Hence, when I see, and feel, and taste, in sundry certain manners, I am sure the *cherry* exists, or is real; its reality being in my opinion nothing abstracted from those sensations. But if, by the word *cherry,* you mean an unknown nature, distinct from all those sensible qualities, and by its *existence* something distinct from its being perceived; then, indeed, I own, neither you or I, nor any one else, can be sure it exists.

Hylas. But, what would you say, *Philonous,* if I should bring the very same reasons against the existence of sensible things in a mind, which you have offered against their existing in a material *substratum?*

Philonous. When I see your reasons, you shall hear what I have to say to them.

Hylas. Is the mind extended or unextended?

Philonous. Unextended, without doubt.

Hylas. Do you say the things you perceive are in your mind?

Philonous. They are.

Hylas. Again, have I not heard you speak of sensible impressions?

Philonous. I believe you may.

Hylas. Explain to me now, O *Philonous!* how is it possible there should be room for all those trees and houses to exist in your mind. Can extended things be contained in that which is unextended? Or, are we to imagine impressions made on a thing void of all solidity? You cannot say objects are in your mind, as books in your study: or that things are imprinted on it, as the figure of a seal upon wax. In what sense, therefore, are we to understand those expressions? Explain me this if you can:

and I shall then be able to answer all those queries you formerly put to me about my *substratum*.

Philonous. Look you, *Hylas*, when I speak of objects as existing in the mind, or imprinted on the senses, I would not be understood in the gross literal sense—as when bodies are said to exist in a place, or a seal to make an impression upon wax. My meaning is only that the mind comprehends or perceives them; and that it is affected from without, or by some being distinct from itself. This is my explication of your difficulty; and how it can serve to make your tenet of an unperceiving material *substratum* intelligible, I would fain know.

Hylas. Nay, if that be all, I confess I do not see what use can be made of it. But are you not guilty of some abuse of language in this?

Philonous. None at all. It is no more than common custom, which you know is the rule of language, hath authorised: nothing being more usual, than for philosophers to speak of the immediate objects of the understanding as things existing in the mind. Nor is there anything in this but what is conformable to the general analogy of language; most part of the mental operations being signified by words borrowed from sensible things; as is plain in the terms *comprehend, reflect, discourse, &c.*, which, being applied to the mind, must not be taken in their gross original sense.

Hylas. You have, I own, satisfied me in this point. But there still remains one great difficulty, which I know not how you will get over. And, indeed, it is of such importance that if you could solve all others, without being able to find a solution for this, you must never expect to make me a proselyte to your principles.

Philonous. Let me know this mighty difficulty.

Hylas. The Scripture account of the creation is what appears to me utterly irreconcilable with your notions. Moses tells us of a creation: a creation of what? of ideas? No certainly, but of things, of real things, solid corporeal substances. Bring your principles to agree with this, and I shall perhaps agree with you.

Philonous. Moses mentions the sun, moon, and stars, earth and sea, plants and animals. That all these do really exist, and were in the beginning created by God, I make no question. If by *ideas* you mean fictions and fancies of the mind, then these are no ideas. If by *ideas* you mean immediate objects of the understanding, or sensible things which cannot exist unperceived, or out of a mind, then these things are ideas. But whether you do or do not call them *ideas*, it matters little. The difference is only about a name. And, whether that name be retained or rejected, the sense, the truth, and reality of things continues the same. In common talk, the objects of our senses are not termed *ideas* but *things*.

Call them so still—provided you do not attribute to them any absolute external existence—and I shall never quarrel with you for a word. The creation, therefore, I allow to have been a creation of things, of *real* things. Neither is this in the least inconsistent with my principles, as is evident from what I have now said; and would have been evident to you without this, if you had not forgotten what had been so often said before. But as for solid corporeal substances, I desire you to shew where Moses makes any mention of them; and, if they should be mentioned by him, or any other inspired writer, it would still be incumbent on you to shew those words were not taken in the vulgar acceptation, for things falling under our senses, but in the philosophic acceptation, for Matter, or an unknown quiddity, with an absolute existence. When you have proved these points, then (and not till then) may you bring the authority of Moses into our dispute.

Hylas. It is in vain to dispute about a point so clear. I am content to refer it to your own conscience. Are you not satisfied there is some peculiar repugnancy between the Mosaic account of the creation and your notions?

Philonous. If all possible sense which can be put on the first chapter of Genesis may be conceived as consistently with my principles as any other, then it has no peculiar repugnancy with them. But there is no sense you may not as well conceive, believing as I do. Since, besides spirits, all you conceive are ideas; and the existence of these I do not deny. Neither do you pretend they exist without the mind.

Hylas. Pray let me see any sense you can understand it in.

Philonous. Why, I imagine that if I had been present at the creation, I should have seen things produced into being—that is become perceptible—in the order perscribed by the sacred historian. I ever before believed the Mosaic account of the creation, and now find no alteration in my manner of believing it. When things are said to begin or end their existence, we do not mean this with regard to God, but His creatures. All objects are eternally known by God, or, which is the same thing, have an eternal existence in His mind: but when things, before imperceptible to creatures, are, by a decree of God, perceptible to them, then are they said to begin a relative existence, with respect to created minds. Upon reading therefore the Mosaic account of the creation, I understand that the several parts of the world became gradually perceivable to finite spirits, endowed with proper faculties; so that, whoever such were present, they were in truth perceived by them. This is the literal obvious sense suggested to me by the words of the Holy Scripture: in which is included no mention or no thought, either of *substratum*, instrument, occasion, or absolute existence. And, upon inquiry, I doubt not it will be found that most plain honest men, who believe the creation, never think of those things any more than I. What metaphysical sense you may understand it in, you only can tell.

Hylas. But, *Philonous,* you do not seem to be aware that you allow created things, in the beginning, only a relative, and consequently hypothetical being: that is to say, upon supposition there were men to perceive them, without which they have no actuality of absolute existence wherein creation might terminate. Is it not, therefore, according to you, plainly impossible the creation of any inanimate creatures should precede that of man? And is not this directly contrary to the Mosaic account?

Philonous. In answer to that, I say, first, created beings might begin to exist in the mind of other created intelligences beside men. You will not therefore be able to prove any contradiction between Moses and my notions, unless you first shew there was no other order of finite created spirits in being before man. I say farther, in case we conceive the creation, as we should at this time a parcel of plants or vegetables of all sorts produced, by an invisible power, in a desert where nobody was present —that this way of explaining or conceiving it is consistent with my principles, since they deprive you of nothing, either sensible or imaginable; that it exactly suits with the common, natural, and undebauched notions of mankind; that it manifests the dependence of all things on God; and consequently hath all the good effect or influence, which it is possible that important article of our faith should have in making men humble, thankful, and resigned to their Creator. I say, moreover, that, in this naked conception of things, divested of words, there will not be found any notion of what you call the *actuality of absolute existence.* You may indeed raise a dust with those terms, and so lengthen our dispute to no purpose. But I entreat you calmly to look into your own thoughts, and then tell me if they are not a useless and unintelligible jargon.

Hylas. I own I have no very clear notion annexed to them. But what say you to this? Do you not make the existence of sensible things consist in their being in a mind? And were not all things eternally in the mind of God? Did they not therefore exist from all eternity, according to you? And how could that which was eternal be created in time? Can anything be clearer or better connected than this?

Philonous. And are not you too of opinion, that God knew all things from eternity?

Hylas. I am.

Philonous. Consequently they always had a being in the Divine intellect.

Hylas. This I acknowledge.

Philonous. By your own confession, therefore, nothing is new, or begins to be, in respect of the mind of God. So we are agreed in that point.

Hylas. What shall we make then of the creation?

Philonous. May we not understand it to have been entirely in respect of finite spirits; so that things, with regard to us, may properly be said to begin their existence, or be created, when God decreed they should become perceptible to intelligent creatures, in that order and manner which He then established, and we now call the laws of nature? You may call this a *relative*, or *hypothetical existence* if you please. But so long as it supplies us with the most natural, obvious, and literal sense of the Mosaic history of the creation; so long as it answers all the religious ends of that great article; in a word, so long as you can assign no other sense or meaning in its stead; why should we reject this? Is it to comply with a ridiculous sceptical humour of making everything nonsense and unintelligible? I am sure you cannot say it is for the glory of God. For, allowing it to be a thing possible and conceivable that the corporeal world should have an absolute existence extrinsical to the mind of God, as well as to the minds of all created spirits; yet how could this set forth either the immensity or omniscience of the Deity, or the necessary and immediate dependence of all things on Him? Nay, would it not rather seem to derogate from those attributes?

Hylas. Well, but as to this decree of God's, for making things perceptible, what say you, *Philonous*, is it not plain, God did either execute that decree from all eternity, or at some certain time began to will what He had not actually willed before, but only designed to will? If the former, then there could be no creation or beginning of existence in finite things. If the latter, then we must acknowledge something new to befall the Deity; which implies a sort of change: and all change argues imperfection.

Philonous. Pray consider what you are doing. Is it not evident this objection concludes equally against a creation in any sense; nay, against every other act of the Deity, discoverable by the light of nature? None of which can we conceive, otherwise than as performed in time, and having a beginning. God is a Being of transcendent and unlimited perfections: His Nature, therefore, is incomprehensible to finite spirits. It is not, therefore, to be expected, that any man, whether *Materialist* or *Immaterialist*, should have exactly just notions of the Deity, His attributes, and ways of operation. If then you would infer anything against me, your difficulty must not be drawn from the inadequateness of our conceptions of the Divine nature, which is unavoidable on any scheme, but from the denial of Matter, of which there is not one word, directly or indirectly, in what you have now objected.

Hylas. I must acknowledge the difficulties you are concerned to clear are such only as arise from the nonexistence of Matter, and are peculiar to that notion. So far you are in the right. But I cannot by any means bring myself to think there is no such peculiar repugnancy between the creation and your opinion: though indeed where to fix it, I do not distinctly know.

Philonous. What would you have? Do I not acknowledge a twofold state of things, the one ectypal or natural, the other archetypal and eternal? The former was created in time; the latter existed from everlasting in the mind of God. Is not this agreeable to the common notions of divines? Or is any more than this necessary in order to conceive the creation? But you suspect some peculiar repugnancy, though you know not where it lies. To take away all possibility of scruple in the case, do but consider this one point. Either you are not able to conceive the creation on any hypothesis whatsoever; and, if so, there is no ground for dislike or complaint against any particular opinion on that score: or you are able to conceive it; and, if so, why not on my principles, since thereby nothing conceivable is taken away? You have all along been allowed the full scope of sense, imagination, and reason. Whatever, therefore, you could before apprehend, either immediately or mediately by your senses, or by ratiocination from your senses; whatever you could perceive, imagine, or understand, remains still with you. If, therefore, the notion you have of the creation by other principles be intelligible, you have it still upon mine; if it be not intelligible, I conceive it to be no notion at all; and so there is no loss of it. And indeed it seems to me very plain that the supposition of Matter, that is a thing perfectly unknown and inconceivable, cannot serve to make us conceive anything. And, I hope it need not be proved to you that if the existence of Matter doth not make the creation conceivable, the creation's being without it inconceivable can be no objection against its nonexistence.

Hylas. I confess, *Philonous*, you have almost satisfied me in this point of the creation.

Philonous. I would fain know why you are not quite satisfied. You tell me indeed of a repugnancy between the Mosaic history and Immaterialism: but you know not where it lies. Is this reasonable, *Hylas*? Can you expect I should solve a difficulty without knowing what it is? But, to pass by all that, would not a man think you were assured there is no repugnancy between the received notions of Materialists and the inspired writings?

Hylas. And so I am.

Philonous. Ought the historical part of Scripture to be understood in a plain obvious sense, or in a sense which is metaphysical and out of the way?

Hylas. In the plain sense, doubtless.

Philonous. When Moses speaks of herbs, earth, water, &c., as having been created by God; think you not the sensible things commonly signified by those words are suggested to every unphilosophical reader?

Hylas. I cannot help thinking so.

Philonous. And are not all ideas, or things perceived by sense, to be denied a real existence by the doctrine of the Materialist?

Hylas. This I have already acknowledged.

Philonous. The creation, therefore, according to them, was not the creation of things sensible, which have only a relative being, but of certain unknown natures, which have an absolute being, wherein creation might terminate?

Hylas. True.

Philonous. Is it not therefore evident the assertors of Matter destroy the plain obvious sense of Moses, with which their notions are utterly inconsistent; and instead of it obtrude on us I know not what, something equally unintelligible to themselves and me?

Hylas. I cannot contradict you.

Philonous. Moses tells us of a creation. A creation of what? of unknown quiddities, of occasions, or *substratum?* No, certainly; but of things obvious to the senses. You must first reconcile this with your notions, if you expect I should be reconciled to them.

Hylas. I see you can assault me with my own weapons.

Philonous. Then as to *absolute existence;* was there ever known a more jejune notion than that? Something it is so abstracted and unintelligible that you have frankly owned you could not conceive it, much less explain anything by it. But, allowing Matter to exist, and the notion of absolute existence to be as clear as light, yet, was this ever known to make the creation more credible? Nay, hath it not furnished the atheists and infidels of all ages with the most plausible arguments against a creation? That a corporeal substance, which hath an absolute existence without the minds of spirits, should be produced out of nothing, by the mere will of a Spirit, hath been looked upon as a thing so contrary to all reason, so impossible and absurd, that not only the most celebrated among the ancients, but even divers modern and Christian philosophers have thought Matter co-eternal with the Deity. Lay these things together, and then judge you whether Materialism disposes men to believe the creation of things.

Hylas. I own, *Philonous,* I think it does not. This of the *creation* is the last objection I can think of; and I must needs own it hath been sufficiently answered as well as the rest. Nothing now remains to be overcome but a sort of unaccountable backwardness that I find in myself towards your notions.

Philonous. When a man is swayed, he knows not why, to one side of the question, can this, think you, be anything else but the effect of prejudice, which never fails to attend old and rooted notions? And indeed in this respect I cannot deny the belief of Matter to have very much the advantage over the contrary opinion, with men of a learned education.

Hylas. I confess it seems to be as you say.

Philonous. As a balance, therefore, to this weight of prejudice, let us throw into the scale the great advantages that arise from the belief of Immaterialism, both in regard to religion and human learning. The being of a God, and incorruptibility of the soul, those great articles of religion, are they not proved with the clearest and most immediate evidence? When I say the being of a *God*, I do not mean an obscure general cause of things, whereof we have no conception, but *God*, in the strict and proper sense of the word; a Being whose spirituality, omnipresence, providence, omniscience, infinite power and goodness, are as conspicuous as the existence of sensible things, of which (notwithstanding the fallacious pretences and affected scruples of Sceptics) there is no more reason to doubt than of our own being. Then, with relation to human sciences: in Natural Philosophy, what intricacies, what obscurities, what contradictions hath the belief of Matter led men into! To say nothing of the numberless disputes about its extent, continuity, homogeneity, gravity, divisibility, &c.—do they not pretend to explain all things by bodies operating on bodies, according to the laws of motion? and yet, are they able to comprehend how one body should move another? Nay, admitting there was no difficulty in reconciling the notion of an inert being with a cause, or in conceiving how an accident might pass from one body to another; yet, by all their strained thoughts and extravagant suppositions, have they been able to reach the mechanical production of any one animal or vegetable body? Can they account, by the laws of motion, for sounds, tastes, smells, or colours, or for the regular course of things? Have they accounted, by physical principles, for the aptitude and contrivance even of the most inconsiderable parts of the universe? But laying aside Matter and corporeal causes, and admitting only the efficiency of an All-perfect Mind, are not all the effects of nature easy and intelligible? If the *phenomena* are nothing else but *ideas*; God is a *spirit*, but Matter an unintelligent, unperceiving being. If they demonstrate an unlimited power in their cause; God is active and omnipotent, but Matter an inert mass. If the order, regularity, and usefulness of them can never be sufficiently admired; God is infinitely wise and provident, but Matter destitute of all contrivance and design. These surely are great advantages in *physics*. Not to mention that the apprehension of a distant Deity naturally disposes men to a negligence of their moral actions, which they would be more cautious of, in case they thought him immediately present, and acting on their minds, without the interposition of Matter, or unthinking second causes. Then in *metaphysics:* what difficulties concerning entity in abstract, substantial forms, hylarchic principles, plastic natures, substance and accident, principle of individuation, possibility of Matter's thinking, origin of ideas, the manner how two independent substances so widely different as *Spirit* and *Matter*, should mutually operate on each other? what difficulties, I say, and endless disquisitions, concerning these and innumerable other the like points, do we escape, by supposing only Spirits and ideas? Even the *mathematics* themselves, if we take away the absolute existence of extended things, become much more clear and easy; the most shocking paradoxes and intricate speculations in those sciences depending on the infinite divisibility of finite extension, which depends on that supposition.—But what need is there to insist on the particular sciences? Is not that opposition to all science whatsoever, that frenzy of the ancient and modern Sceptics, built on the same foundation? Or can you produce so much as one argument against the reality of corporeal things or in behalf of that avowed utter ignorance of their natures, which doth not suppose their reality to consist in an external absolute existence? Upon this supposition, indeed, the objections from the change of colours in a pigeon's neck, or the appearance of the broken oar in the water, must be allowed to have weight. But these and the like objections vanish, if we do not maintain the being of absolute external originals, but place the reality of things in ideas, fleeting indeed, and changeable; however, not changed at random, but according to the fixed order of nature. For, herein consists that constancy and truth of things which secures all the concerns of life, and distinguishes that which is real from the irregular visions of the fancy.

Hylas. I agree to all you have now said, and must own that nothing can incline me to embrace your opinion more than the advantages I see it is attended with. I am by nature lazy; and this would be a mighty abridgment in knowledge. What doubts, what hypotheses, what labyrinths of amusement, what fields of disputation, what an ocean of false learning may be avoided by that single notion of *Immaterialism!*

Philonous. After all, is there anything farther remaining to be done? You may remember you promised to embrace that opinion which upon examination should appear most agreeable to Common Sense and remote from Scepticism. This, by your own confession, is that which denies Matter, or the absolute existence of corporeal things. Nor is this all; the same notion has been proved several ways, viewed in different lights, pursued in its consequences, and all objections against it cleared. Can there be a greater evidence of its truth? or is it possible it should have all the marks of a true opinion and yet be false?

Hylas. I own myself entirely satisfied for the present in all respects. But, what security can I have that I shall still continue the same full assent to your opinion, and that no unthought-of objection or difficulty will occur hereafter?

Philonous. Pray, *Hylas,* do you in other cases, when a point is once evidently proved, withhold your consent on account of objections or difficulties it may be liable to? Are the difficulties that attend the doctrine of incommensurable quantities, of the angle of contact, of the asymptotes to curves, or the like, sufficient to make you hold out against mathematical demonstration? Or will you disbelieve the Providence of God, because there may be some particular things which you know not how to reconcile with it? If there are difficulties attending *Immaterialism,* there are at the same time direct and evident proofs of it. But for the existence of Matter there is not one proof, and far more numerous and insurmountable objections lie against it. But where are those mighty difficulties you insist on? Alas! you know not where or what they are; something which may possibly occur hereafter. If this be a sufficient pretence for withholding your full assent, you should never yield it to any proposition, how free soever from exceptions, how clearly and solidly soever demonstrated.

Hylas. You have satisfied me, *Philonous.*

Philonous. But, to arm you against all future objections, do but consider, that which bears equally hard on two contradictory opinions can be proof against neither. Whenever, therefore, any difficulty occurs, try if you can find a solution for it on the hypothesis of the *Materialists.* Be not deceived by words; but sound your own thoughts. And in case you cannot conceive it easier by the help of *Materialism,* it is plain it can be no objection against *Immaterialism.* Had you proceeded all along by this rule, you would probably have spared yourself abundance of trouble in objecting; since of all your difficulties I challenge you to shew one that is explained by Matter: nay, which is not more unintelligible with than without that supposition, and consequently makes rather *against* than *for* it. You should consider, in each particular, whether the difficulty arises from the *non-existence of Matter.* If it doth not, you might as well argue from the infinite divisibility of extension against the Divine prescience, as from such a difficulty against *Immaterialism.* And yet, upon recollection, I believe you will find this to have been often if not always the case. You should likewise take heed not to argue on a *petitio principii.* One is apt to say, the unknown substances ought to be esteemed real things, rather than the ideas in our minds:

and who can tell but the unthinking external substance may concur as a cause or instrument in the productions of our ideas? But, is not this proceeding on a supposition that there are such external substances? And to suppose this, is it not begging the question? But, above all things, you should beware of imposing on yourself by that vulgar sophism which is called *ignoratio elenchi*. You talked often as if you thought I maintained the non-existence of Sensible Things: whereas in truth no one can be more thoroughly assured of their existence than I am: and it is you who doubt; I should have said, positively deny it. Everything that is seen, felt, heard, or any way perceived by the senses, is, on the principles I embrace, a real being, but not on yours. Remember, the Matter you contend for is an unknown somewhat (if indeed it may be termed *somewhat*), which is quite stripped of all sensible qualities, and can neither be perceived by sense, nor apprehended by the mind. Remember, I say, that it is not any object which is hard or soft, hot or cold, blue or white, round or square, &c.;—for all these things I affirm do exist. Though indeed I deny they have an existence distinct from being perceived; or that they exist out of all minds whatsoever. Think on these points; let them be attentively considered and still kept in view. Otherwise you will not comprehend the state of the question; without which your objections will always be wide of the mark, and instead of mine, may possibly be directed (as more than once they have been) against your own notions.

Hylas. I must needs own, *Philonous*, nothing seems to have kept me from agreeing with you more than this same *mistaking the question*. In denying Matter, at first glimpse I am tempted to imagine you deny the things we see and feel: but, upon reflexion, find there is no ground for it. What think you, therefore, of retaining the name *Matter*, and applying it to *sensible things*? This may be done without any change in your sentiments: and, believe me, it would be a means of reconciling them to some persons who may be more shocked at an innovation in words than in opinion.

Philonous. With all my heart: retain the word *Matter*, and apply it to the objects of sense, if you please; provided you do not attribute to them any subsistence distinct from their being perceived. I shall never quarrel with you for an expression. *Matter*, or *material substance*, are terms introduced by philosophers; and, as used by them, imply a sort of independency, or a subsistence distinct from being perceived by a mind: but are never used by common people; or, if ever, it is to signify the immediate objects of sense. One would think, therefore, so long as the names of all particular things, with the terms *sensible, substance, body, stuff*, and the like, are retained, the word *Matter* should be never missed in common talk. And in philosophical discourses it seems the best way to leave it quite out: since there is not, perhaps, any one thing that hath more favoured and strengthened the depraved bent of the mind towards Atheism than the use of that general confused term.

Hylas. Well but, *Philonous*, since I am content to give up the notion of an unthinking substance exterior to the mind, I think you ought not to deny me the privilege of using the word *Matter* as I please, and annexing it to a collection of sensible qualities subsisting only in the mind. I freely own there is no other substance, in a strict sense, than *Spirit*. But I have been so long accustomed to the term *Matter* that I know not how to part with it. To say, there is no *Matter* in the World, is still shocking to me. Whereas to say There is no *Matter*, if by that term be meant an unthinking substance existing without the mind; but if by *Matter* is meant some sensible thing, whose existence consists in being perceived, then there is *Matter*:—this distinction gives it quite another turn; and men will come into your notions with small difficulty, when they are proposed in that manner. For, after all, the controversy about *Matter* in the strict acceptation of it, lies together between you and the philosophers: whose principles, I acknowledge, are not near so natural, or so agreeable to the common sense of mankind, and Holy Scripture, as yours. There is nothing we either desire or shun but as it makes, or is apprehended to make, some part of our happiness or misery. But what hath happiness or misery, joy or grief, pleasure or pain, to do with Absolute Existence; or with unknown entities, abstracted from all relation to us? It is evident, things regard us only as they are pleasing or displeasing: and they can please or displease only so far forth as they are perceived. Farther, therefore, we are not concerned; and thus far you leave things as you found them. Yet still there is something new in this doctrine. It is plain, I do not now think with the philosophers, nor yet altogether with the vulgar. I would know how the case stands in that respect; precisely, what you have added to, or altered in my former notions.

Philonous. I do not pretend to be a setter-up of new notions. My endeavours tend only to unite and place in a clearer light that truth which was before shared between the vulgar and the philosophers:—the former being of opinion, that *those things they immediately perceive are the real things*; and the latter, that *the things immediately perceived are ideas which exist only in the mind*. Which two notions put together, do, in effect, constitute the substance of what I advance.

Hylas. I have been a long time distrusting my senses; methought I saw things by a dim light and through false glasses. Now the glasses are removed and a new light breaks in upon my understanding. I am clearly convinced that I see things in their native forms, and am no longer in pain about their *unknown natures* or *absolute existence*. This is the state I find myself in at present; though, indeed, the course that brought me to it I do not yet thoroughly comprehend. You set out upon the same principles that Academics, Cartesians, and the like sects usually do, and for a long time it looked as if you were advancing their Philosophical Scepticism; but, in the end, your conclusions are directly opposite to theirs.

Philonous. You see, *Hylas,* the water of yonder fountain, how it is forced upwards, in a round column, to a certain height; at which it breaks, and falls back into the basin from whence it rose: its ascent as well as descent proceeding from the same uniform law or principle of *gravitation.* Just so, the same principles which, at first view, lead to Scepticism, pursued to a certain point, bring men back to Common Sense.

HUME

INTRODUCTION TO

Hume

LIFE

It may seem paradoxical to hear that David Hume is the most influential philosopher England has produced, since he is not commonly thought of as the most popular. The philosophic writings of Francis Bacon, John Locke, or John Stuart Mill might ordinarily be thought of as more influential, for they have had a greater impact on intellectual and social life independent of strictly philosophic concerns. But Hume's influence has been very much deeper and broader within the history of philosophy proper.

The period of his life—from 1711 to 1776—parallels the heyday of rationalist Enlightenment on the Continent, but the vigor, the depth, and the importance of his thinking were directed *against* the *intellectual optimism* of the rationalists. Optimism, in this sense, refers to both the expectation of finding philosophic laws to explain all of nature rationally and the expectation that reason alone would be able to improve all aspects of human behavior. His works have subsequently stimulated a notable variety of thinkers, from his personal friend Adam Smith, to writers and movements as diverse as Immanuel Kant, the American pragmatists, Santayana, British analysts of language, and the logical-empiricists of our century.

A sketch of David Hume's life shows him to have been a man of the world as well as an intellectual explorer. He was a man of good character, born into a family of the landed gentry in Scotland. In his early twenties, well tempered, well educated, and ambitious, he went to France, where he spent three years writing A *Treatise On Human*

Nature, the book he hoped would make his fame. But it was difficult for him to get it published, and when it did appear in 1738, it went unnoticed. For an ambitious intellectual of somewhat different temperament, this experience of seeing his youthful masterpiece "fall dead-born from the press" (Hume's phrase) might have resulted in a collapse of some sort; Hume consciously and deliberately avoided this possibility by engaging himself in other, more practical, pursuits.

He immersed himself successively in law, trade, travel, and diplomacy. He was for a time a paid companion of a mad nobleman and then private secretary to a general during an expedition against France. This same general, subsequently a British ambassador, took him to the courts of Vienna, Turin, and Paris. In the meantime, Hume published two volumes of essays on political and ethical subjects and radically revised the unfortunately received *Treatise.* These new works, in which he restated the positions more fully developed in the *Treatise,* were published as *An Enquiry Concerning Human Understanding* (1748) and *An Enquiry Concerning The Principles Of Morals* (1751). For a short while thereafter, he was the librarian of the Advocates' Library in Edinburgh, where he began his impressive *History Of England.* By the mid-1750's, his work had become well known on the Continent and, when he returned to France in 1763, he enjoyed the intellectual and social success that, since early childhood, he had associated with the idea of being "a writer." He frequented some of the most distinguished literary *salons* of the century and had a love affair with the Comtesse de Bouffleurs, a woman universally admired for her beauty. After three years in France, he returned to find his fame as considerable in Britain as it was in France; and in his last years, spent in Edinburgh, he maintained his reputation as a man of good company and good sense, kindly, witty, mellow, and wise.

In the history of philosophy, David Hume stands out as the honest "simpleton" in the story of the Emperor's new clothes. He embarrassed the heirs to a century of rationalist thought by saying, "But the Emperor is naked!" He looked steadily and openly at eighteenth-century rationalism and declared, "But it is *not* rational!"

During a given intellectual period, the degree of "unity" of thought or interest is constituted by the fact that certain philosophers are "in conversation" with each other. This arises out of a willingness to examine a set of common problems, to proceed from a set of common principles, and to examine various implications that may follow from those principles. An historical movement away from such a "unity" begins when another thinker raises new problems or challenges some of the *accepted principles* themselves. Hume's position is that of a doubting Thomas, whose adherence to the concern for an experimental method and *intelligible proof* brought him to the point of reformulating and challenging the most important concepts of rationalism.

After a hundred years, the revolution that Descartes initiated in speculative thought had been carried to its exhaustive conclusion by a variety of extraordinary minds bent on pursuing the implications of Descartes's position. Hume's analysis of rationalism cleared the ground for a new, and possibly more "scientific," formulation of philosophic issues to be cultivated in the following century.

THEORY OF KNOWLEDGE

The century following Galileo and then Descartes saw the specialized development of the physical and natural sciences—such as the elaboration in the sixteenth and seventeenth centuries of mathematics, astronomy, and physics, and the gradual development in the eighteenth century of botany, biology, and chemistry. Philosophers cognizant of these developments in the discrete or positive sciences tried to relate such sciences to each other in an over-all conception of human knowledge—epistemology. Hume cultivated a disposition of mind focused on the question, What *certainty* can we have for the most general of our ideas concerning knowledge? In this, he follows his three most important predecessors in England—Hobbes, Locke, and Berkeley—all of whom share a common concern with the basic conditions for any discipline of thought (any particular science) that can qualify as knowledge. In this pursuit, Hume is the heir to the British tradition of *empirical psychology* as the basis for philosophy.

One way of characterizing the difference between Continental rationalism and British empiricism is to point out that the English writers conceived *physics* to be their "model science," whereas on the Continent the Galileo-Descartes-Spinoza tradition conceived of *mathematics* as the "model science." The difference of emphasis meant that for the rationalists sensory perceptions are untrustworthy and lead to confusion; the "abstractions" of mathematics alone yield certainty. Therefore, induction from empirical evidence is not as important as searching for the invariable abstract elements of a given subject matter. And the rationalists pursued these by application of the methods of mathematics. By contrast, the British empiricists emphasized the origin of ideas in just such impressions.

Hume begins with the essential assumption that all ideas are derived from experience (a posteriori—that is, "after the facts") and can never be intellectually justified unless they are grounded in experience (that is, never a priori, or independent of experience). Hume argues that there is a radical distinction between our immediate perceptions and the memory of any perception; and that what we call "ideas" are our recollections of perceptions. He distinguishes the two by the different degrees of intensity or liveliness between them. For example, the sensory impression of being cold is more "intense" than the recollected impression of having been cold; thought, thereby, is described as "mirroring" our perceptions. But all perceptions are divisible into two kinds, depending on their source. We may have *impressions* of either (1) "outward" experiences or sentiments such as hearing, smelling, seeing, or (2) "inward" sentiments, such as our emotions, feeling, willing. Strictly speaking, then, every simple idea is a copy of a simple impression. Simple ideas may then be compounded into complex ideas.

This leads to the following two significant points for Hume. One is that, to examine the meaningfulness of an idea is to ask the following question, from what impression of experience (outward or inward) is the idea supposed to be derived? If no such impression or combination of impressions is found, then the idea cannot be said to be either true or false; it becomes, rather, meaningless or nonsense. A second point of development for Hume has to do with the problem of *relations* among ideas. He conceives that the creative power of the mind consists only in the ways in which ideas are organized, arranged, or associated with each other. He analyzes these possible arrangements as "compounding, transposing, augmenting, and diminishing the materials offered us by the senses and experience." The various arrangements that the mind makes of our ideas follow certain patterns. These are (1) resemblance, (2) contiguity, and (3) cause and effect. That is to say, the associations of our ideas are brought about by (1) their similarity to each other, (2) their associations in space, and (3) their associations in time (succession; before and after). However, Hume points out that these three patterns have *no rational necessity*. They are neither self-evident nor demonstrable. They can be explained only as "natural" relations—in effect, only as habits or patterns of thought to which the mind is accustomed. Therefore, our most general or most abstract concepts (those making possible the rational solution of more specific problems) are themselves not rational (not based on empirical evidence or on formal analysis) but only "psychological" or conditioned.

This aspect of Hume's thought is not only consistent with the experimental method of British empiricism but maintains the tradition of nominalism [1] concerning abstract ideas. Hume carried Berkeley's

---

[1] See the introduction to the material on George Berkeley.

method of analysis one step further; finding no more justification of "mental or spiritual" substance than Berkeley had for physical substance, Hume confined it to the class of meaningless words.

The two chief arguments for substance in the seventeenth century were (1) every attribute must inhere in a subject, and (2) without substance, no one thing could *cause* another. Berkeley retained *both* of these arguments in favor of mind or spirit even while he showed we could eliminate "matter" as substance. Hume took Berkeley's arguments against *inherence in matter* and turned them on *inherence in mind*. Berkeley was aware of his weakness and fell back on *cause*. Only when Hume had demolished all the arguments for *efficacious cause* could he dispose of spiritual as well as mental substance in the sense of seventeenth- and eighteenth-century philosophy—that is, a *substratum*, a something *behind* the scene, mental and physical.

Hume analyzed the idea of causality in the following way. What we experience is succession—events occur in time, one after the other, and we come to *associate* them with respect to "before" and "after." But we do *not* experience any *necessary* connection between events, in perception, in action, or in thought. What have given rise to the idea that cause exists in nature are the repeated perceptions of two or more events which occur in conjunction and in the same relation of before and after —for example, first gray clouds, then rain; first a wound, then pain; first a fire, then warmth. Because of repeated perceptions of similar sequences, the human mind has developed the habit of expecting the future to be like the past. But, Hume argues, a principle expressing this anticipation (called "the uniformity of nature") has no rational justification. If every impression is a distinct individual fact and it is impossible to deduce one impression from another, then there can be no necessary connection between impressions; therefore, still less can there be any assertion made about "necessary connection" (causality) *in nature*.

In summation, Hume attacks the pretensions to metaphysical certainty expressed by philosophers of natural science and mathematics. The Cartesian attitude of mind assumes that what is essential in nature is of the character of a machine that can best be analyzed by the methods of mathematics. It also assumes that mathematical knowledge, being demonstrative (proceeding from more general premises to more particular conclusions), offers the only possible certainty and truth. It would then follow that as each science approximates the methods of mathematics, it achieves higher degrees of certainty.

In contrast to this view, Hume distinguished the *natural sciences* from *mathematics*. First, the natural sciences are concerned with "matters of fact"—knowledge of events in space and time, relations among

sense data—but they can never offer certainty, because such generalizations are continually open to being altered on the basis of new impressions. Therefore, theories developed concerning natural science can
never give us "truth" but only *degrees of probability*. The natural
sciences can never be demonstrative, since they are always inductive. On
the other hand, "pure" mathematics is concerned with agreement or
disagreement of names, not with matters of fact. That is to say, mathematics can be universal and its deductions necessary, but mathematics
can give us no information concerning the world of nature.

If we perceive a patch of color, we may divide it to perceive a
smaller patch. Eventually we reach a limit which is the smallest perceptible object. Similarly with time, we reach the smallest perceptible
duration in the succession of our ideas and impressions. These least or
smallest perceptible objects Hume terms *"minimum sensibles."* [2] He
concludes that space and time as experienced are not infinite either by
addition or division. In contrast to our sensory experience of space and
time, the mathematician's conceptions of them are fictions and artificial
constructions made by the mathematician. For example, two straight
lines may be said to "cross at but a *single* point," but the mathematician
and the empiricist understand this statement differently. A mathematical point is without dimension. One can, therefore, have no experience
or impression of it—or, for that matter, of lines without thickness. All
the lines we can perceive have some actual thickness. From a mathematical point of view too such (sensible) lines which cross must touch
each other at more than one (mathematical) point. If, however, we
mean by "point" the place where two visible lines cross, then the (empirical) point is not without dimension. Hume argues that no such
purely mathematical line exists apart from the abstractions invented by
mathematicians. For Hume, therefore, our experience of space and time
are made up of a mosaic of minimal impressions, whereas the ideal
objects of mathematics do not exist in heaven, nature, or some realm of
Platonic Ideas. They are the constructions, fictions, and inventions of
abstract thought.

We can have certainty of knowledge only when the subject matter
makes no pretension of giving us information about matters of fact. All
sciences that interpret matters of fact can give us only probability.
Therefore *no knowledge* of "ultimate reality" is possible.

---

[2] We get our ideas of space and time from perceptual experience. Hume writes,
"As 'tis from the disposition of visible and tangible objects we receive the idea of
space, so from the succession of ideas and impressions we form the idea of time, nor
is it possible for time alone ever to make its appearance, or to be taken notice of by
the mind." A *Treatise on Human Nature*—Book I, Part II, Section II, p. 35. Selby-
Bigge edition, Oxford.

These conclusions of Hume's do not, however, lead him into a purely subjective attitude or a social indifference. They arise from the determined effort to be as rigorously "experimental" as possible, and they are in keeping with his position that *the conditions for usefulness are not to be confused with the conditions for intellectual certainty.* This leads us into an analysis of Hume's theories concerned with social life and purposes, and the following selection consisting of the entire *Dialogues Concerning Natural Religion.*

MORALITY AND RELIGION

In almost every respect, Hume was in advance of his age. Eighteenth-century Continental rationalism was permeated with the assumptions taken from the philosophic and scientific writings of the followers of Galileo and Descartes: (1) that the universe has a rational structure, (2) that the mind is capable of understanding these "laws," and (3) that the will is capable of acting on knowledge of them. These attitudes united thought and action in the over-all belief that individual and social life could be not only understood, but also could be lived, *rationally.* The challenge that Hume threw down to this optimism was not grasped by his contemporaries; it remained for the following generation to begin to grapple with his criticism. It is the romanticists of the first half of the nineteenth century who had to reckon with the irrefragable *conflict* between ideas that Hume was able to keep in *balance*—namely, the opposition between reason and experience.

For Hume, all three assumptions of rationalist optimism are illusions. He is too thoroughgoing a skeptic to find any intellectual justification for them. However, his refusal to conceive of experience as rational does not hurl him into despair. Individual and social life may not be rational in themselves, but it is necessary to discover how they function and to pursue the questions of how to make the best of them intellectually. Hume believed that socially conditioned *feeling* was completely adequate for achieving the ends we experience as daily life. It never occurs to Hume to doubt the value of satisfying the ends of ordinary daily life, or to abdicate the responsibility of attempting to improve them.

The practical conditions for improvement of social life—both in respect to individual morality and to political organization—were seen throughout the seventeenth and eighteenth centuries (that is, up through the French Revolution) as a rational pursuit in relation to the inherited morality and political theory derived from Christianity. There-fore, the philosophers of the period expended considerable energy of thought in the analysis of religion. No one, however, through the course of that period, separated philosophy and "natural religion" as Hume did. For Hume, just as there is no possibility for a metaphysics of objec-tive reality, so a rationally justified (a philosophically defensible) reli-gion is not possible.

"Natural religion" is a concept developed by philosophers of the Enlightenment to characterize the possibility of a rational belief in cer-tain tenets of religion abstracted from the "elaborations" of particular religions. These were especially concerned with the idea of God as the origin of the universe and the creator of its rational laws. While Euro-pean philosophers were cognizant of Mohammedanism and Judaism, and somewhat more remotely introduced to Buddhism and Confucian-ism, it goes without saying that the almost exclusive object of their criticism was the form of Christianity that each one had been most familiar with since his own childhood. The deism that the majority of eighteenth-century philosophers adopted for themselves could be char-acterized as the selection of those religious principles that they con-ceived to be scientifically (rationally) defensible. It was Hume's ac-complishment, in the following *Dialogues*, however, to present his analysis of religion as one that under no circumstances could be be-lieved in on grounds of rational demonstration. From the standpoint of his principles and method of analysis, not one of the tenets of "natural religion" is capable of being established by reason.

While the inferences for morality from historically developed or revealed religions cannot yield rational conditions for morality, this did not mean for Hume that morality is neither possible nor important. On the contrary, beginning with the assumption of its practical value for individual and social life, Hume concerned himself with the possibility of understanding religion "in its own terms." The consequence is Hume's moral theory that stands in opposition to rationalistic ethics. For the Enlightenment it appeared sufficient to use Reason (with a capital R) as a new authority to replace the authoritative structure of church religion in answer to the questions of whether or why one should "be good." In his various analyses, Hume argues, for example, that it cannot be the function of reason to judge our conflicts or values; nor can the ends or goals or purposes of human actions be accounted for by reason in the sense that principles are used in natural sciences or maxims employed in the mathematical sciences. Essential here is the idea that, just as reality is not in itself rational, for Hume reality in it-self also cannot be mistaken to have the qualities or characteristics of morality. The only possible basis for the choice of a goal, or the evaluation of means toward achieving a goal, is *experience*, not reason. In effect, a metaphysics of morals was as impossible for Hume as a metaphysics of nature. But thinking about moral life with the standards of experimental rational thought—in the manner that Galileo might consider a physical object and its behavior—Hume established the possibility of a descriptive, rather than a normative, ethic—that is to say, a basis on which to employ the empirical method in ethics, without mistaking the powers of philosophy as being able to make rational judgments about the *values* of human behavior.

The conditions for judgments of praise or blame in morality, then, are seen as essentially subjective and individual. This immediately leads one to imagine Hume's theory might result in as great a variety of moral evaluations as there are people. But further examination of the facts shows that there are sufficient similarities within groups of people and sufficient distinguishing features among kinds of pleasures, so that moral goodness is distinguished from other kinds of virtues by (1) a pleasure resulting from consideration of character or motive and (2) a disinterested approbation. "Disinterest" is a word meaning *objective awareness*, such as one who does *not* have a *vested* interest should be able to appreciate. It is not to be mistaken for "uninterest," which, on the contrary, means simply a complete *absence* of interest and appreciation. Primarily, then, after arguing against criticisms of "subjectivism," Hume sees in moral goodness not something external, objective, or eternal, but the disinterested approbation, a *feeling*, that arises under certain habitual circumstances and gains significance out of the facts of the social worlds in which people find themselves.

The idea of a "state of nature," such as Rousseau and others appealed to in their effort to consider what is essential to human psychology, is not one that appealed to British empiricists. It did, however, drive them to arguing that, for human life as we know it, *society*—social groups, social life, in effect—*is the state of nature* for the only facts which can be called human life. A person is either socially civilized or he can be characterized only as animal and *ipso facto* not as a human being. The greatest consequence of social life is that it operates through the character of the various relationships set up among people in a group so as to mitigate subjective selfishness and to cultivate feelings of sympathy. Therefore the basis of morality is emotional and affective and arises out of social conditioning—all of which may have its desirable and admirable effects for the harmonious development of practical life—although none of it can be seen to be rational (or to be justified on any grounds other than its usefulness).

Recognizing that for Hume the attack on misconceptions concerning morality does not make morality impossible, we may turn to the

Dialogues Concerning Natural Religion. Given Hume's principles, it is not possible for him to acknowledge any validity in the ontological argument for the existence of God (since all demonstrative knowledge examines only the consequence of names, such as in the mathematical sciences). Likewise, no form of the causal proof is acceptable for the existence of God (since the concept of cause itself is not intellectually legitimate in Hume's thought). But neither of these foregoing arguments was the "favored" one used by the deists of the Enlightenment. Rather, they were primarily appealed to by the "argument from design."

This refers to the use of the analogy that either the universe of nature is *like* a work of art and that God is therefore *like* the artist-creator, or that the universe is like a machine and God is like the inventor-designer. The analysis in *Dialogues Concerning Natural Religion* is a relentlessly consistent examination of deist arguments. The core of Hume's criticism rests on his insistence for the highest rational standard of evidence. Arguments *from analogy* cannot survive rigorous critical examination. They are analyzed from numerous points of view which necessarily raise to the foreground such questions as why it should be concluded that there is but one God rather than several. Cannot the universe, with equal justification, be compared with an *organism* as with a *machine?* If that is equally plausible, then, a designer would not be necessary; but we might conclude otherwise that the origin of the universe is "to be ascribed to generation or vegetation . . ." If the universe resembles an animal or a vegetable more than it does a clock or a weaving machine, why does it require a conscious mind as its source? Even more strongly, why should we make the inference, *if* there were such a conscious mind, that it have moral characteristics? If it is impossible to justify inferences concerning *one* cause, and one having intelligence, how much less warranted are assumptions about the cause being either all powerful or all good.

Hume's attitudes are ultimately characterized by his belief that all social and natural *orders* are empirical facts. Experience shows considerable regularity in the behavior of nature, as well as in the behavior of human beings in social groups. Knowledge of such experienced regularity is all that a reasonable man requires for organizing a sensible life for himself. But as for trying to make a rational system of thought adequate to grasping "the universe as a whole," while there is the appeal to feeling (the immediate aesthetic satisfaction) in analogies, there is no evidence from such an attitude to justify any of the elaborate conclusions and fanciful inferences drawn by mythmakers in the service of particular religions.

Thus, again ahead of his time, Hume eliminates the "rationality" for "natural religion" and the deism fashionable in the eighteenth century. He introduces through his interpretation of both ethics and religion the seeds for a vast development of subsequent thought—relativistic in tone and historical in method. In general, the philosophy of the Enlightenment is devoid of historical consciousness, an understanding focused upon developments through time; it was fascinated by the "absolute" or "pure" conceptions of what was either timeless or always valid. This fascination it shared with the originators of modern science. But in his writings about matters of social significance David Hume showed that questions concerning the origin of religion must be separated from speculative philosophy. Thereby he lays the groundwork for a sociology of knowledge in accordance with empirical principles. This method of intellectual examination, using the perspectives of psychology and the *history* of civilizations, proved to be one of the most fruitful stimulations to the speculations of romanticists during the first half of the nineteenth century.

In any case, the over-all effect of Hume's thought gives rise to more than one possible development. It is true that one may respond to this intellectual "house cleaning" by admitting the limitations of the powers of reason and 1) taking refuge in some sort of nonrational authority, whether it be religious, political, or psychological. Or one might 2) willingly accept life in a world "without rational certainty" as long as practical satisfactions are adequate. Without the latter it may well be that philosophical despair is vastly compounded by practical despair. However, over and above these alternatives is the possibility that 3) something is wrong with the premises from which Hume started, and, however reasonable they may appear to begin with, it might be more useful to abandon them in the effort to discover a more rationally satisfactory basis for philosophy. This last possibility is the one that Immanuel Kant chose to pursue. And we shall turn to his efforts in the next section.

MORRIS PHILIPSON

SELECTED BIBLIOGRAPHY

Hume's Works and Letters

A *Treatise on Human Nature* (1738)
Essays, Moral and Political (Vol. I: 1741; Vol. II: 1742)
An *Enquiry Concerning Human Understanding* (1748) (Includes Hume's *Autobiography* etc., La Salle, Ill. The Open Court Publishing Company, 1927)

Political Discourse (1752)
History of England (1754–62)
Four Dissertations: (1757)
   (1) Natural History of Religion
   (2) Of the Passions
   (3) Of Tragedy
   (4) Of the Standard of Taste
Dialogues Concerning Natural Religion (1779) (latest edition, edited by H. D. Aiken, New York, Hafner Publishing Company, 1948)

The *Treatise* and the *Enquiries* are available in standard editions published by the Oxford University Press. Selections from Hume's other writings are to be found in such volumes as:

   New Letters, edited by Klibansky and Mosner, Oxford, Clarendon Press (1954) *Hume's Theory of Politics*, edited by Watkins (Nelson) *Hume's Moral and Political Philosophy*, edited by Aiken (Hafner) *Hume's Political Essays*, edited by Hendel (Liberal Arts) *Selections*, edited by Hendel (Scribner's) *Natural History of Religion*, edited by Root (Stanford)

Works on Hume

Basson, A.: *David Hume*. Harmondsworth: Penguin Books (Pelican Philosophy Series); 1958.

Church, R. W.: *Hume's Theory of the Understanding*. London: Allen & Unwin; 1935.

Hendel, C. W.: *Studies in the Philosophy of David Hume*. Princeton: Princeton University Press; 1925.

Kuypers, M. S.: *Studies in the Eighteenth Century Background of Hume's Empiricism*. Minneapolis: The University of Minnesota Press; 1930.

Laing, B. M.: *David Hume*. London: Benn; 1932.

Laird, J.: *Hume's Philosophy of Human Nature*. London: Methuen; 1932.

Mossner, E. C.: *The Life of David Hume*. Austin: University of Texas Press; 1954.

Smith, N. K.: *The Philosophy of David Hume: A Critical Study of its Origins and Central Doctrines*. London: Macmillan; 1949.

Taylor, A. E.: *David Hume and the Miraculous*. Cambridge: Cambridge University Press; 1927.

DIALOGUES

CONCERNING NATURAL

RELIGION

❧❧❧❧❧❦❦❦

PAMPHILUS TO HERMIPPUS

It has been remarked, my Hermippus, that, though the ancient philosophers conveyed most of their instruction in the form of dialogue, this method of composition has been little practised in later ages, and has seldom succeeded in the hands of those who have attempted it. Accurate and regular argument, indeed, such as is now expected of philosophical inquirers, naturally throws a man into the methodical and didactic manner, where he can immediately, without preparation, explain the point at which he aims; and thence proceed, without interruption, to deduce the proofs on which it is established. To deliver a *system* in conversation scarcely appears natural; and, while the dialogue writer desires, by departing from the direct style of composition, to give a freer air to his performance, and avoid the appearance of *author* and *reader*, he is apt to run into a worse inconvenience and convey the image of *pedagogue* and *pupil*. Or, if he carries on the dispute in the natural spirit of good company, by throwing in a variety of topics and preserving a proper balance among the speakers, he often loses so much time in preparations and transitions that the reader will scarcely think himself compensated, by all the graces of dialogue, for the order, brevity, and precision, which are sacrificed to them.

There are some subjects, however, to which dialogue-writing is peculiarly adapted, and where it is still preferable to the direct and simple method of composition.

Any point of doctrine which is so *obvious* that it scarcely admits of dispute, but at the same time so *important* that it cannot be too often inculcated, seems to require some such method of handling it; where the novelty of the manner may compensate the triteness of the subject; where the vivacity of conversation may enforce the precept; and where the variety of lights, presented by various personages and characters, may appear neither tedious nor redundant.

Any question of philosophy, on the other hand, which is so *obscure* and *uncertain* that human reason can reach no fixed determination with regard to it—if it should be treated at all—seems to lead us naturally into the style of dialogue and conversation. Reasonable men may be allowed to differ where no one can reasonably be positive. Opposite sentiments, even without any decision, afford an agreeable amusement; and if the subject be curious and interesting, the book carries us, in a manner, into company and unites the two greatest and purest pleasures of human life—study and society.

Happily, these circumstances are all to be found in the subject of *natural religion*. What truth so obvious, so certain, as the being of a God, which the most ignorant ages have acknowledged, for which the most refined geniuses have ambitiously striven to produce new proofs and arguments? What truth so important as this, which is the ground of all our hopes, the surest foundation of morality, the firmest support of society, and the only principle which ought never to be a moment absent from our thoughts and meditations? But, in treating of this obvious and important truth, what obscure questions occur concerning the nature of that Divine Being, his attributes, his decrees, his plan of providence? These have been always subjected to the disputations of men; concerning these human reason has not reached any certain determination. But these are topics so interesting that we cannot restrain our restless inquiry with regard to them, though nothing but doubt, uncertainty, and contradiction have as yet been the result of our most accurate researches.

This I had lately occasion to observe, while I passed, as usual, part of the summer season with Cleanthes, and was present at those conversations of his with Philo and Demea, of which I gave you lately some imperfect account. Your curiosity, you then told me, was so excited that I must, of necessity, enter into a more exact detail of their reasonings, and display those various systems which they advanced with regard to so delicate a subject as that of natural religion. The remarkable contrast in their characters still further raised your expectations, while you opposed the accurate philosophical turn of Cleanthes to the careless scepticism of Philo, or compared either of their dispositions with the rigid inflexible orthodoxy of Demea. My youth rendered me a mere auditor of their disputes; and that curiosity, natural to the early season of life, has so deeply imprinted in my memory the whole chain and connexion of their arguments that, I hope, I shall not omit or confound any considerable part of them in the recital.

Part · I

After I joined the company whom I found sitting in Cleanthes' library, Demea paid Cleanthes some compliments on the great care which he took of my education, and on his unwearied perseverance and constancy in all his friendships. The father of Pamphilus, said he, was your intimate friend; the son is your pupil, and may indeed be regarded as your adopted son were we to judge by the pains which you bestow in conveying to him every useful branch of literature and science. You are no more wanting, I am persuaded, in prudence than in industry. I shall, therefore, communicate to you a maxim which I have observed with regard to my own children, that I may learn how far it agrees with your practice. The method I follow in their education is founded on the saying of an ancient, "That students of philosophy ought first to learn logics, then ethics, next physics, last of all the nature of the gods." [1] This science of natural theology, according to him, being the most profound and abstruse of any, required the maturest judgment in its students; and none but a mind enriched with all the other sciences can safely be entrusted with it.

Are you so late, says Philo, in teaching your children the principles of religion? Is there no danger of their neglecting or rejecting altogether those opinions of which they have heard so little during the whole course of their education? It is only as a science, replied Demea, subjected to human reasoning and disputation, that I postpone the study of natural theology. To season their minds with early piety is my chief care; and by continual precept and instruction and, I hope, too, by example, I imprint deeply on their tender minds an habitual reverence for all the principles of religion. While they pass through every other science, I still remark the uncertainty of each part; the eternal disputations of men; the obscurity of all philosophy; and the strange, ridiculous conclusions which some of the greatest geniuses have derived from the principles of mere human reason. Having thus tamed their mind to a proper submission and self-diffidence, I have no longer any scruple of opening to them the greatest mysteries of religion, nor apprehend any danger from that

---

[1] Chrysippus *apud* Plut., *De repug. Stoicorum.*

assuming arrogance of philosophy, which may lead them to reject the most established doctrines and opinions.

Your precaution, says Philo, of seasoning your children's minds early with piety is certainly very reasonable, and no more than is requisite in this profane and irreligious age. But what I chiefly admire in your plan of education is your method of drawing advantage from the very principles of philosophy and learning which, by inspiring pride and self-sufficiency, have commonly, in all ages, been found so destructive to the principles of religion. The vulgar, indeed, we may remark, who are unacquainted with science and profound inquiry, observing the endless disputes of the learned, have commonly a thorough contempt for philosophy, and rivet themselves the faster, by that means, in the great points of theology which have been taught them. Those who enter a little into study and inquiry, finding many appearances of evidence in doctrines the newest and most extraordinary, think nothing too difficult for human reason and, presumptuously breaking through all fences, profane the inmost sanctuaries of the temple. But Cleanthes will, I hope, agree with me that, after we have abandoned ignorance, the surest remedy, there is still one expedient left to prevent this profane liberty. Let Demea's principles be improved and cultivated; let us become thoroughly sensible of the weakness, blindness, and narrow limits of human reason; let us duly consider its uncertainty and endless contrarieties, even in subjects of common life and practice; let the errors and deceits of our very senses be set before us; the insuperable difficulties which attend first principles in all systems; the contradictions which adhere to the very ideas of matter, cause and effect, extension, space, time, motion, and, in a word, quantity of all kinds, the object of the only science that can fairly pretend to any certainty or evidence—when these topics are displayed in their full light, as they are by some philosophers and almost all divines, who can retain such confidence in this frail faculty of reason as to pay any regard to its determinations in points so sublime, so abstruse, so remote from common life and experience? When the coherence of the parts of a stone, or even that composition of parts which renders it extended; when these familiar objects, I say, are so inexplicable, and contain circumstances so repugnant and contradictory, with what assurance can we decide concerning the origin of worlds or trace their history from eternity to eternity?

While Philo pronounced these words, I could observe a smile in the countenance both of Demea and Cleanthes. That of Demea seemed to imply an unreserved satisfaction in the doctrines delivered; but in Cleanthes' features I could distinguish an air of finesse, as if he perceived some raillery of artificial malice in the reasonings of Philo.

You propose then, Philo, said Cleanthes, to erect religious faith on philosophical scepticism; and you think that, if certainty or evidence be expelled from every other subject of inquiry, it will all retire to these theological doctrines, and there acquire a superior force and authority. Whether your scepticism be as absolute and sincere as you pretend, we shall learn by and by, when the company breaks up; we shall then see whether you go out at the door or the window, and whether you really doubt if your body has gravity or can be injured by its fall, according to popular opinion derived from our fallacious senses and more fallacious experience. And this consideration, Demea, may, I think, fairly serve to abate our ill-will to this humorous sect of the sceptics. If they be thoroughly in earnest, they will not long trouble the world with their doubts, cavils, and disputes; if they be only in jest, they are, perhaps, bad railers, but can never be very dangerous, either to the state, to philosophy, or to religion.

In reality, Philo, continued he, it seems certain that, though a man, in a flush of humour, after intense reflection on the many contradictions and imperfections of human reason, may entirely renounce all belief and opinion, it is impossible for him to persevere in this total scepticism or make it appear in his conduct for a few hours. External objects press in upon him; passions solicit him; his philosophical melancholy dissipates; and even the utmost violence upon his own temper will not be able, during any time, to preserve the poor appearance of scepticism. And for what reason impose on himself such a violence? This is a point in which it will be impossible for him ever to satisfy himself, consistently with his sceptical principles. So that, upon the whole, nothing could be more ridiculous than the principles of the ancient Pyrrhonians if, in reality, they endeavoured, as is pretended, to extend throughout the same scepticism which they had learned from the declamations of their schools, and which they ought to have confined to them.

In this view, there appears a great resemblance between the sects of the Stoics and Pyrrhonians, though perpetual antagonists; and both of them seem founded on this erroneous maxim that what a man can perform sometimes, and in some dispositions, he can perform always and in every disposition. When the mind, by Stoical reflections, is elevated into a sublime enthusiasm of virtue and strongly smit with any *species* of honour or public good, the utmost bodily pain and sufferings will not prevail over such a high sense of duty; and it is possible, perhaps, by its means, even to smile and exult in the midst of tortures. If this sometimes may be the case in fact and reality, much more may a philosopher, in his school or even in his closet, work himself up to such an enthusiasm and support, in imagination, the acutest pain or most calamitous event which he can possibly conceive. But how shall he support this enthusiasm itself? The bent of his mind relaxes and cannot be recalled at pleasure; avocations lead him astray; misfortunes attack him unawares; and the *philosopher* sinks, by degrees, into the *plebeian*.

I allow of your comparison between the Stoics and Sceptics, replied Philo. But you may observe, at the same time, that though the mind cannot, in Stoicism, support the highest flights of philosophy, yet, even when it sinks lower, it still retains somewhat of its former disposition; and the effects of the Stoic's reasoning will appear in his conduct in common life, and through the whole tenor of his actions. The ancient schools, particularly that of Zeno, produced examples of virtue and constancy which seem astonishing to present times.

> *Vain Wisdom all and false Philosophy.*
> *Yet with a pleasing sorcery could charm*
> *Pain, for a while, or anguish; and excite*
> *Fallacious Hope, or arm the obdurate breast*
> *With stubborn Patience, as with triple steel.*[2]

In like manner, if a man has accustomed himself to sceptical considerations on the uncertainty and narrow limits of reason, he will not entirely forget them when he turns his reflection on other subjects; but in all his philosophical principles and reasoning, I dare not say in his common conduct, he will be found different from those who either never formed any opinions in the case or have entertained sentiments more favourable to human reason.

To whatever length any one may push his speculative principles of scepticism, he must act, I own, and live, and converse, like other men; and for this conduct he is not obliged to give any other reason than the absolute necessity he lies under of so doing. If he ever carries his speculations farther than this necessity constrains him, and philosophizes either on natural or moral subjects, he is allured by a certain pleasure and satisfaction which he finds in employing himself after that manner. He considers, besides, that everyone, even in common life, is constrained to have more or less of this philosophy; that from our earliest infancy we make continual advances in forming more general principles of conduct and reasoning; that the larger experience we acquire, and the stronger reason we are endued with, we always render our principles the more general and comprehensive; and that what we call *philosophy* is nothing but a more regular and methodical operation of the same kind. To philosophize on such subjects is nothing essentially different from reasoning on common life, and we may only expect greater stability, if not greater truth, from our philosophy on account of its exacter and more scrupulous method of proceeding.

---

[2] [Milton, *Paradise Lost*, Bk. II.]

But when we look beyond human affairs and the properties of the surrounding bodies; when we carry our speculations into the two eternities, before and after the present state of things: into the creation and formation of the universe, the existence and properties of spirits, the powers and operations of one universal Spirit existing without beginning and without end, omnipotent, omniscient, immutable, infinite, and incomprehensible—we must be far removed from the smallest tendency to scepticism not to be apprehensive that we have here got quite beyond the reach of our faculties. So long as we confine our speculations to trade, or morals, or politics, or criticism, we make appeals, every moment, to common sense and experience, which strengthen our philosophical conclusions and remove, at least in part, the suspicion which we so justly entertain with regard to every reasoning that is very subtle and refined. But, in theological reasonings, we have not this advantage; while at the same time we are employed upon objects which, we must be sensible, are too large for our grasp and, of all others, require most to be familiarized to our apprehension. We are like foreigners in a strange country to whom everything must seem suspicious, and who are in danger every moment of transgressing against the laws and customs of the people with whom they live and converse. We know not how far we ought to trust our vulgar methods of reasoning in such a subject, since, even in common life, and in that province which is peculiarly appropriated to them, we cannot account for them and are entirely guided by a kind of instinct or necessity in employing them.

All sceptics pretend that, if reason be considered in an abstract view, it furnishes invincible arguments against itself, and that we could never retain any conviction or assurance, on any subject, were not the sceptical reasonings so refined and subtle that they are not able to counterpoise the more solid and more natural arguments derived from the senses and experience. But it is evident, whenever our arguments lose this advantage and run wide of common life, that the most refined scepticism comes to be upon a footing with them, and is able to oppose and counterbalance them. The one has no more weight than the other. The mind must remain in suspense between them; and it is that very suspense or balance which is the triumph of scepticism.

But I observe, says Cleanthes, with regard to you, Philo, and all speculative sceptics that your doctrine and practice are as much at variance in the most abstruse points of theory as in the conduct of common life. Wherever evidence discovers itself, you adhere to it, notwithstanding your pretended scepticism; and I can observe, too, some of your sect to be as decisive as those who make greater professions of certainty and assurance. In reality, would not a man be ridiculous who pretended to reject Newton's explication of the wonderful phenomenon of the rainbow because that explication gives a minute anatomy of the rays of light—a subject, forsooth, too refined for human comprehension? And what would you say to one who, having nothing particular to object to the arguments of Copernicus and Galileo for the motion of the earth, should withhold his assent on that general principle that these subjects were too magnificent and remote to be explained by the narrow and fallacious reason of mankind?

There is indeed a kind of brutish and ignorant scepticism, as you well observed, which gives the vulgar a general prejudice against what they do not easily understand, and makes them reject every principle which requires elaborate reasoning to prove and establish it. This species of scepticism is fatal to knowledge, not to religion; since we find that those who make greatest profession of it give often their assent, not only to the great truths of theism and natural theology, but even to the most absurd tenets which a traditional superstition has recommended to them. They firmly believe in witches, though they will not believe nor attend to the most simple proposition of Euclid. But the refined and philosophical sceptics fall into an inconsistency of an opposite nature. They push their researches into the most abstruse corners of science, and their assent attends them in every step, proportioned to the evidence which they meet with. They are even obliged to acknowledge that the most abstruse and remote objects are those which are best explained by philosophy. Light is in reality anatomized; the true system of the heavenly bodies is discovered and ascertained. But the nourishment of bodies by food is still an inexplicable mystery; the cohesion of the parts of matter is still incomprehensible. These spectics, therefore, are obliged, in every question, to consider each particular evidence apart, and proportion their assent to the precise degree of evidence which occurs. This is their practice in all natural, mathematical, moral, and political science. And why not the same, I ask, in the theological and religious? Why must conclusions of this nature be alone rejected on the general presumption of the insufficiency of human reason, without any particular discussion of the evidence? Is not such an unequal conduct a plain proof of prejudice and passion?

Our senses, you say, are fallacious; our understanding erroneous; our ideas, even of the most familiar objects—extension, duration, motion—full of absurdities and contradictions. You defy me to solve the difficulties or reconcile the repugnancies which you discover in them. I have not capacity for so great an undertaking; I have not leisure for it. I perceive it to be superfluous. Your own conduct, in every circumstance, refutes your principles, and shows the firmest reliance on all the received maxims of science, morals, prudence, and behaviour.

I shall never assent to so harsh an opinion as that of a celebrated writer,[3] who says that the Sceptics are not a sect of philosophers: they are only a sect of liars. I may, however, affirm (I hope without offence) that they are a sect of jesters or railers. But for my part, whenever I find myself disposed to mirth and amusement, I shall certainly choose my entertainment of a less perplexing and abstruse nature. A comedy, a novel, or, at most, a history seems a more natural recreation than such metaphysical subtilties and abstractions.

In vain would the sceptic make a distinction between science and common life, or between one science and another. The arguments employed in all, if just, are of a similar nature and contain the same force and evidence. Or if there be any difference among them, the advantage lies entirely on the side of theology and natural religion. Many principles of mechanics are founded on very abstruse reasoning, yet no man who has any pretensions to science, even no speculative sceptic, pretends to entertain the least doubt with regard to them. The Copernican system contains the most surprising paradox, and the most contrary to our natural conceptions, to appearances, and to our very senses, yet even monks and inquisitors are now constrained to withdraw their opposition to it. And shall Philo, a man of so liberal a genius and extensive knowledge, entertain any general undistinguished scruples with regard to the religious hypothesis, which is founded on the simplest and most obvious arguments and, unless it meets with artificial obstacles, has such easy access and admission into the mind of man?

And here we may observe, continued he, turning himself towards Demea, a pretty curious circumstance in the history of the sciences. After the union of philosophy with the popular religion, upon the first establishment of Christianity, nothing was more usual, among all religious teachers, than declamations against reason, against the senses, against every principle derived merely from human research and inquiry. All the topics of the ancient Academics were adopted by the Fathers, and thence propagated for several ages in every school and pulpit throughout Christendom. The Reformers embraced the same principles of reasoning or rather declamation; and all panegyrics on the excellence of faith were sure to be interlarded with some severe strokes of satire against natural reason. A celebrated prelate, too,[4] of the Romish communion, a man of the most extensive learning, who wrote a demonstration of Christianity, has also composed a treatise which contains all the cavils of the boldest and most determined Pyrrhonism. Locke seems to have been the first Christian who ventured openly to assert that *faith* was nothing but a species of *reason;* that religion was only a branch of

---

[3] *L'art de penser* [Antoine (the great) Arnauld and others: *La Logique ou l'art de penser* (*Port-Royal Logic*), 1662.]

[4] Mons. Huet.

philosophy; and that a chain of arguments, similar to that which established any truth in morals, politics, or physics, was always employed in discovering all the principles of theology, natural and revealed. The ill use which Bayle and other libertines made of the philosophical scepticism of the Fathers and first Reformers still further propagated the judicious sentiment of Mr. Locke. And it is now in a manner avowed, by all pretenders to reasoning and philosophy, that *atheist* and *sceptic* are almost synonymous. And as it is certain that no man is in earnest when he professes the latter principle, I would fain hope that there are as few who seriously maintain the former.

Don't you remember, said Philo, the excellent saying of Lord Bacon on this head? That a little philosophy, replied Cleanthes, makes a man an Atheist; a great deal converts him to religion. That is a very judicious remark, too, said Philo. But what I have in my eye is another passage, where, having mentioned David's fool, who said in his heart there is no God, this great philosopher observes that the atheists nowadays have a double share of folly, for they are not contented to say in their hearts there is no God, but they also utter that impiety with their lips, and are thereby guilty of multiplied indiscretion and imprudence. Such people, though they were ever so much in earnest, cannot, methinks, be very formidable.

But though you should rank me in this class of fools, I cannot forbear communicating a remark that occurs to me, from the history of the religious and irreligious scepticism with which you have entertained us. It appears to me that there are strong symptoms of priestcraft in the whole progress of this affair. During ignorant ages, such as those which followed the dissolution of the ancient schools, the priests perceived that atheism, deism, or heresy of any kind, could only proceed from the presumptuous questioning of received opinions, and from a belief that human reason was equal to everything. Education had then a mighty influence over the minds of men, and was almost equal in force to those suggestions of the senses and common understanding by which the most determined sceptic must allow himself to be governed. But at present, when the influence of education is much diminished and men, from a more open commerce of the world, have learned to compare the popular principles of different nations and ages, our sagacious divines have changed their whole system of philosophy and talk the language of Stoics, Platonists, and Peripatetics, not that of Pyrrhonians and Academics. If we distrust human reason we have now no other principle to lead us into religion. Thus sceptics in one age, dogmatists in another—whichever system best suits the purpose of these reverend gentlemen in giving them an ascendant over mankind—they are sure to make it their favourite principle and established tenet.

It is very natural, said Cleanthes, for men to embrace those principles by which they find they can best defend their doctrines, nor need we have any recourse to priestcraft to account for so reasonable an expedient. And surely nothing can afford a stronger presumption that any set of principles are true and ought to be embraced than to observe that they tend to the confirmation of true religion, and serve to confound the cavils of atheists, libertines, and free-thinkers of all denominations.

Part · I I

I must own, Cleanthes, said Demea, that nothing can more surprise me than the light in which you have all along put this argument. By the whole tenor of your discourse, one would imagine that you were maintaining the Being of a God against the cavils of atheists and infidels, and were necessitated to become a champion for that fundamental principle of all religion. But this, I hope, is not by any means a question among us. No man, no man at least of common sense, I am persuaded, ever entertained a serious doubt with regard to a truth so certain and self-evident. The question is not concerning the *being* but the *nature* of GOD. This I affirm, from the infirmities of human understanding, to be altogether incomprehensible and unknown to us. The essence of that supreme Mind, his attributes, the manner of his existence, the very nature of his duration—these and every particular which regards so divine a Being are mysterious to men. Finite, weak, and blind creatures, we ought to humble ourselves in his august presence, and, conscious of our frailties, adore in silence his infinite perfections which eye hath not seen, ear hath not heard, neither hath it entered into the heart of man to conceive. They are covered in a deep cloud from human curiosity; it is profaneness to attempt penetrating through these sacred obscurities, and, next to the impiety of denying his existence, is the temerity of prying into his nature and essence, decrees and attributes.

But lest you should think that my *piety* has here got the better of my *philosophy*, I shall support my opinion, if it needs any support, by a very great authority. I might cite all the divines, almost from the foundation of Christianity, who have ever treated of this or any other theological subject; but I shall confine myself, at present, to one equally celebrated for piety and philosophy. It is Father Malebranche who, I remember, thus expresses himself.[1] "One ought not so much," says he, "to call God a spirit in order to express positively what he is, as in order to signify that he is not matter. He is a Being infinitely perfect—of this

---

[1] *Recherche de la Vérité*, liv. 3, cap. 9.

we cannot doubt. But in the same manner as we ought not to imagine, even supposing him corporeal, that he is clothed with a human body, as the anthropomorphites asserted, under colour that that figure was the most perfect of any, so neither ought we to imagine that the spirit of God has human ideas or bears any resemblance to our spirit, under colour that we know nothing more perfect than a human mind. We ought rather to believe that as he comprehends the perfections of matter without being material . . . he comprehends also the perfections of created spirits without being spirit, in the manner we conceive spirit: that his true name is *He that is,* or, in other words, Being without restriction, All Being, the Being infinite and universal."

After so great an authority, Demea, replied Philo, as that which you have produced, and a thousand more which you might produce, it would appear ridiculous in me to add my sentiment or express my approbation of your doctrine. But surely, where reasonable men treat these subjects, the question can never be concerning the *being* but only the *nature* of the Deity. The former truth, as you well observe, is unquestionable and self-evident. Nothing exists without a cause; and the original cause of this universe (whatever it be) we call God, and piously ascribe to him every species of perfection. Whoever scruples this fundamental truth deserves every punishment which can be inflicted among philosophers, to wit, the greatest ridicule, contempt, and disapprobation. But as all perfection is entirely relative, we ought never to imagine that we comprehend the attributes of this divine Being, or to suppose that his perfections have any analogy or likeness to the perfections of a human creature. Wisdom, thought, design, knowledge—these we justly ascribe to him because these words are honourable among men, and we have no other language or other conceptions by which we can express our adoration of him. But let us beware lest we think that our ideas anywise correspond to his perfections, or that his attributes have any resemblance to these qualities among men. He is infinitely superior to our limited view and comprehension, and is more the object of worship in the temple than of disputation in the schools.

In reality, Cleanthes, continued he, there is no need of having recourse to that affected scepticism so displeasing to you in order to come at this determination. Our ideas reach no farther than our experience. We have no experience of divine attributes and operations. I need not conclude my syllogism, you can draw the inference yourself. And it is a pleasure to me (and I hope to you, too) that just reasoning and sound piety here concur in the same conclusion, and both of them establish the adorably mysterious and incomprehensible nature of the Supreme Being.

Not to lose any time in circumlocutions, said Cleanthes, addressing himself to Demea, much less in replying to the pious declamations of Philo, I shall briefly explain how I conceive this matter. Look round the world, contemplate the whole and every part of it: you will find it to be nothing but one great machine, subdivided into an infinite number of lesser machines, which again admit of subdivisions to a degree beyond what human senses and faculties can trace and explain. All these various machines, and even their most minute parts, are adjusted to each other with an accuracy which ravishes into admiration all men who have ever contemplated them. The curious adapting of means to ends, throughout all nature, resembles exactly, though it much exceeds, the productions of human contrivance—of human design, thought, wisdom, and intelligence. Since therefore the effects resemble each other, we are led to infer, by all the rules of analogy, that the causes also resemble, and that the Author of nature is somewhat similar to the mind of man, though possessed of much larger faculties, proportioned to the grandeur of the work which he has executed. By this argument *a posteriori*, and by this argument alone, do we prove at once the existence of a Deity and his similarity to human mind and intelligence.

I shall be so free, Cleanthes, said Demea, as to tell you that from the beginning I could not approve of your conclusion concerning the similarity of the Deity to men, still less can I approve of the mediums by which you endeavour to establish it. What! No demonstration of the Being of God! No abstract arguments! No proofs *a priori!* Are these which have hitherto been so much insisted on by philosophers all fallacy, all sophism? Can we reach no farther in this subject than experience and probability? I will not say that this is betraying the cause of a Deity; but surely, by this affected candour, you give advantages to atheists which they never could obtain by the mere dint of argument and reasoning.

What I chiefly scruple in this subject, said Philo, is not so much that all religious arguments are by Cleanthes reduced to experience, as that they appear not to be even the most certain and irrefragable of that inferior kind. That a stone will fall, that fire will burn, that the earth has solidity, we have observed a thousand and a thousand times; and when any new instance of this nature is presented, we draw without hesitation the accustomed inference. The exact similarity of the cases gives us a perfect assurance of a similar event, and a stronger evidence is never desired nor sought after. But wherever you depart, in the least, from the similarity of the cases, you diminish proportionably the evidence, and may at last bring it to a very weak *analogy*, which is confessedly liable to error and uncertainty. After having experienced the circulation of the blood in human creatures, we make no doubt that it takes place in Titius and Maevius; but from its circulation in frogs and fishes it is only a presumption, though a strong one, from analogy that it takes place in men and other animals. The analogical reasoning is much weaker when we infer the circulation of the sap in vegetables from our experience that the blood circulates in animals; and those who hastily followed that imperfect analogy are found, by more accurate experiments, to have been mistaken.

If we see a house, Cleanthes, we conclude, with the greatest certainty, that it had an architect or builder because this is precisely that species of effect which we have experienced to proceed from that species of cause. But surely you will not affirm that the universe bears such a resemblance to a house that we can with the same certainty infer a similar cause, or that the analogy is here entire and perfect. The dissimilitude is so striking that the utmost you can here pretend to is a guess, a conjecture, a presumption concerning a similar cause; and how that pretension will be received in the world, I leave you to consider.

It would surely be very ill received, replied Cleanthes; and I should be deservedly blamed and detested did I allow that the proofs of a Deity amounted to no more than a guess or conjecture. But is the whole adjustment of means to ends in a house and in the universe so slight a resemblance? the economy of final causes? the order, proportion, and arrangement of every part? Steps of a stair are plainly contrived that human legs may use them in mounting; and this inference is certain and infallible. Human legs are also contrived for walking and mounting; and this inference, I allow, is not altogether so certain because of the dissimilarity which you remark; but does it, therefore, deserve the name only of presumption or conjecture?

Good God! cried Demea, interrupting him, where are we? Zealous defenders of religion allow that the proofs of a Deity fall short of perfect evidence! And you, Philo, on whose assistance I depended in proving the adorable mysteriousness of the Divine Nature, do you assent to all these extravagant opinions of Cleanthes? For what other name can I give them? or, why spare my censure when such principles are advanced, supported by such an authority, before so young a man as Pamphilus?

You seem not to apprehend, replied Philo, that I argue with Cleanthes in his own way, and, by showing him the dangerous consequences of his tenets, hope at last to reduce him to our opinion. But what sticks most with you, I observe, is the representation which Cleanthes has made of the argument a posteriori; and, finding that that argument is likely to escape your hold and vanish into air, you think it so disguised that you can scarcely believe it to be set in its true light. Now, however much I may dissent, in other respects, from the dangerous principle of Cleanthes, I must allow that he has fairly represented that argument, and I shall endeavour so to state the matter to you that you will entertain no further scruples with regard to it.

Were a man to abstract from everything which he knows or has seen, he would be altogether incapable, merely from his own ideas, to determine what kind of scene the universe must be, or to give the preference to one state or situation of things above another. For as nothing which he clearly conceives could be esteemed impossible or implying a contradiction, every chimera of his fancy would be upon an equal footing; nor could he assign any just reason why he adheres to one idea or system, and rejects the others which are equally possible.

Again, after he opens his eyes and contemplates the world as it really is, it would be impossible for him at first to assign the cause of any one event, much less of the whole of things, or of the universe. He might set his fancy a rambling, and she might bring him in an infinite variety of reports and representations. These would all be possible, but, being all equally possible, he would never of himself give a satisfactory account for his preferring one of them to the rest. Experience alone can point out to him the true cause of any phenomenon.

Now, according to this method of reasoning, Demea, it follows (and is, indeed, tacitly allowed by Cleanthes himself) that order, arrangement, or the adjustment of final causes, is not of itself any proof of design, but only so far as it has been experienced to proceed from that principle. For aught we can know *a priori*, matter may contain the source or spring of order originally within itself, as well as mind does; and there is no more difficulty in conceiving that the several elements, from an internal unknown cause, may fall into the most exquisite arrangement, than to conceive that their ideas, in the great universal mind, from a like internal unknown cause, fall into that arrangement. The equal possibility of both these suppositions is allowed. But, by experience, we find (according to Cleanthes) that there is a difference between them. Throw several pieces of steel together, without shape or form, they will never arrange themselves so as to compose a watch. Stone and mortar and wood, without an architect, never erect a house. But the ideas in a human mind, we see, by an unknown, inexplicable economy, arrange themselves so as to form the plan of a watch or house. Experience, therefore, proves that there is an original principle of order in mind, not in matter. From similar effects we infer similar causes. The adjustment of means to ends is alike in the universe, as in a machine of human contrivance. The causes, therefore, must be resembling.

I was from the beginning scandalized, I must own, with this resemblance which is asserted between the Deity and human creatures, and must conceive it to imply such a degradation of the Supreme Being as no sound theist could endure. With your assistance, therefore, Demea, I shall endeavour to defend what you justly call the adorable mysteriousness of the Divine Nature, and shall refute this reasoning of

Cleanthes, provided he allows that I have made a fair representation of it.

When Cleanthes had assented, Philo, after a short pause, proceeded in the following manner.

That all inferences, Cleanthes, concerning fact are founded on experience, and that all experimental reasonings are founded on the supposition that similar causes prove similar effects, and similar effects similar causes, I shall not at present much dispute with you. But observe, I entreat you, with what extreme caution all just reasoners proceed in the transferring of experiments to similar cases. Unless the cases be exactly similar, they repose no perfect confidence in applying their past observation to any particular phenomenon. Every alteration of circumstances occasions a doubt concerning the event; and it requires new experiments to prove certainly that the new circumstances are of no moment or importance. A change in bulk, situation, arrangement, age, disposition of the air, or surrounding bodies—any of these particulars may be attended with the most unexpected consequences. And unless the objects be quite familiar to us, it is the highest temerity to expect with assurance, after any of these changes, an event similar to that which before fell under our observation. The slow and deliberate steps of philosophers here, if anywhere, are distinguished from the precipitate march of the vulgar, who, hurried on by the smallest similitude, are incapable of all discernment or consideration.

But can you think, Cleanthes, that your usual phlegm and philosophy have been preserved in so wide a step as you have taken when you compared to the universe houses, ships, furniture, machines, and, from their similarity in some circumstances, inferred a similarity in their causes? Thought, design, intelligence, such as we discover in men and other animals, is no more than one of the springs and principles of the universe, as well as heat or cold, attraction or repulsion, and a hundred others which fall under daily observation. It is an active cause by which some particular parts of nature, we find, produce alterations on other parts. But can a conclusion, with any propriety, be transferred from parts to the whole? Does not the great disproportion bar all comparison and inference? From observing the growth of a hair, can we learn anything concerning the generation of a man? Would the manner of a leaf's blowing, even though perfectly known, afford us any instruction concerning the vegetation of a tree?

But allowing that we were to take the *operations* of one part of nature upon another for the foundation of our judgment concerning the *origin* of the whole (which never can be admitted), yet why select so minute, so weak, so bounded a principle as the reason and design of animals is found to be upon this planet? What peculiar privilege has this little agitation of the brain which we call *thought*, that we must thus make it the model of the whole universe? Our partiality in our own favour does indeed present it on all occasions, but sound philosophy ought carefully to guard against so natural an illusion.

So far from admitting, continued Philo, that the operations of a part can afford us any just conclusion concerning the origin of the whole, I will not allow any one part to form a rule for another part if the latter be very remote from the former. Is there any reasonable ground to conclude that the inhabitants of other planets possess thought, intelligence, reason, or anything similar to these faculties in men? When nature has so extremely diversified her manner of operation in this small globe, can we imagine that she incessantly copies herself throughout so immense a universe? And if thought, as we may well suppose, be confined merely to this narrow corner and has even there so limited a sphere of action, with what propriety can we assign it for the original cause of all things? The narrow views of a peasant who makes his domestic economy the rule for the government of kingdoms is in comparison a pardonable sophism.

But were we ever so much assured that a thought and reason resembling the human were to be found throughout the whole universe, and were its activity elsewhere vastly greater and more commanding than it appears in this globe, yet I cannot see why the operations of a world constituted, arranged, adjusted, can with any propriety be extended to a world which is in its embryo state, and is advancing towards that constitution and arrangement. By observation we know somewhat of the economy, action, and nourishment of a finished animal, but we must transfer with great caution that observation to the growth of a fœtus in the womb, and still more to the formation of an animalcule in the loins of its male parent. Nature, we find, even from our limited experience, possesses an infinite number of springs and principles which incessantly discover themselves on every change of her position and situation. And what new and unknown principles would actuate her in so new and unknown a situation as that of the formation of a universe, we cannot, without the utmost temerity, pretend to determine.

A very small part of this great system, during a very short time, is very imperfectly discovered to us; and do we thence pronounce decisively concerning the origin of the whole?

Admirable conclusion! Stone, wood, brick, iron, brass, have not, at this time, in this minute globe of earth, an order or arrangement without human art and contrivance; therefore, the universe could not originally attain its order and arrangement without something similar to human art. But is a part of nature a rule for another part very wide of the former? Is it a rule for the whole? Is a very small part a rule for the universe? Is nature in one situation a certain rule for nature in another situation vastly different from the former?

And can you blame me, Cleanthes, if I here imitate the prudent reserve of Simonides, who, according to the noted story, being asked by Hiero, *What God was?* desired a day to think of it, and then two days more; and after that manner continually prolonged the term, without ever bringing in his definition or description? Could you even blame me if I had answered, at first, *that I did not know*, and was sensible that this subject lay vastly beyond the reach of my faculties? You might cry out sceptic and rallier, as much as you pleased; but, having found in so many other subjects much more familiar the imperfections and even contradictions of human reason, I never should expect any success from its feeble conjectures in a subject so sublime and so remote from the sphere of our observation. When two *species* of objects have always been observed to be conjoined together, I can *infer*, by custom, the existence of one wherever I *see* the existence of the other; and this I call an argument from experience. But how this argument can have place where the objects, as in the present case, are single, individual, without parallel or specific resemblance, may be difficult to explain. And will any man tell me with a serious countenance that an orderly universe must arise from some thought and art like the human because we have experience of it? To ascertain this reasoning it were requisite that we had experience of the origin of worlds; and it is not sufficient, surely, that we have seen ships and cities arise from human art and contrivance.

Philo was proceeding in this vehement manner, somewhat between jest and earnest, as it appeared to me, when he observed some signs of impatience in Cleanthes, and then immediately stopped short. What I had to suggest, said Cleanthes, is only that you would not abuse terms, or make use of popular expressions to subvert philosophical reasonings. You know that the vulgar often distinguish reason from experience, even where the question relates only to matter of fact and existence, though it is found, where that *reason* is properly analyzed, that it is nothing but a species of experience. To prove by experience the origin of the universe from mind is not more contrary to common speech than to prove the motion of the earth from the same principle. And a caviller might raise all the same objections to the Copernican system which you have urged against my reasonings. Have you other earths, might he say, which you have seen to move? Have . . .

Yes! cried Philo, interrupting him, we have other earths. Is not the moon another earth, which we see to turn round its centre? Is not Venus another earth, where we observe the same phenomenon? Are not the revolutions of the sun also a confirmation, from analogy, or the same theory? All the planets, are they not earths which revolve about the sun? Are not the satellites moons which move round Jupiter and Saturn, and along with these primary planets round the sun? These analogies and resemblances, with others which I have not mentioned, are the sole proofs of the Copernican system; and to you it belongs to consider whether you have any analogies of the same kind to support your theory.

In reality, Cleanthes, continued he, the modern system of astronomy is now so much received by all inquirers, and has become so essential a part even of our earliest education, that we are not commonly very scrupulous in examining the reasons upon which it is founded. It is now become a matter of mere curiosity to study the first writers on that subject who had the full force of prejudice to encounter, and were obliged to turn their arguments on every side in order to render them popular and convincing. But if we peruse Galileo's famous *Dialogues*[2] concerning the system of the world, we shall find that that great genius, one of the sublimest that ever existed, first bent all his endeavours to prove that there was no foundation for the distinction commonly made between elementary and celestial substances. The schools, proceeding from the illusions of sense, had carried this distinction very far; and had established the latter substances to be ingenerable, incorruptible, unalterable, impassible; and had assigned all the opposite qualities to the former. But Galileo, beginning with the moon, proved its similarity in every particular to the earth: its convex figure, its natural darkness when not illuminated, its density, its distinction into solid and liquid, the variations of its phases, the mutual illuminations of the earth and moon, their mutual eclipses, the inequalities of the lunar surface, etc. After many instances of this kind, with regard to all the planets, men plainly saw that these bodies became proper objects of experience, and that the similarity of their nature enabled us to extend the same arguments and phenomena from one to the other.

In this cautious proceeding of the astronomers you may read your own condemnation, Cleanthes, or rather may see that the subject in which you are engaged exceeds all human reason and inquiry. Can you pretend to show any such similarity between the fabric of a house and the generation of a universe? Have you ever seen nature in any such situation as resembles the first arrangement of the elements? Have worlds ever been formed under your eye, and have you had leisure to observe the whole progress of the phenomenon, from the first appearance of order to its final consummation? If you have, then cite your experience and deliver your theory.

---

[2] [*Dialogo dei due Massimi Sistemi del Mondo* (1632).]

Part · I I I

How the most absurd argument, replied Cleanthes, in the hands of a man of ingenuity and invention, may acquire an air of probability! Are you not aware, Philo, that it became necessary for Copernicus and his first disciples to prove the similarity of the terrestrial and celestial matter because several philosophers, blinded by old systems and supported by some sensible appearances, had denied this similarity? But that it is by no means necessary that theists should prove the similarity of the works of *nature* to those of *art* because this similarity is self-evident and undeniable? The same matter, a like form; what more is requisite to show an analogy between their causes, and to ascertain the origin of all things from a divine purpose and intention? Your objections, I must freely tell you, are no better than the abstruse cavils of those philosophers who denied motion, and ought to be refuted in the same manner—by illustrations, examples, and instances rather than by serious argument and philosophy.

Suppose, therefore, that an articulate voice were heard in the clouds, much louder and more melodious than any which human art could ever reach; suppose that this voice were extended in the same instant over all nations and spoke to each nation in its own language and dialect; suppose that the words delivered not only contain a just sense and meaning, but convey some instruction altogether worthy of a benevolent Being superior to mankind—could you possibly hesitate a moment concerning the cause of this voice, and must you not instantly ascribe it to some design or purpose? Yet I cannot see but all the same objections (if they merit that appellation) which lie against the system of theism may also be produced against this inference.

Might you not say that all conclusions concerning fact were founded on experience; that, when we hear an articulate voice in the dark and thence infer a man, it is only the resemblance of the effects which leads us to conclude that there is a like resemblance in the cause; but that this extraordinary voice, by its loudness, extent, and flexibility to all languages, bears so little analogy to any human voice that we have no reason to suppose any analogy in their causes; and, consequently, that a rational, wise, coherent speech proceeded, you know not whence, from some accidental whistling of the winds, not from any divine reason or intelligence? You see clearly your own objections in these cavils, and I hope too you see clearly that they cannot possibly have more force in the one case than in the other.

But to bring the case still nearer the present one of the universe, I shall make two suppositions which imply not any absurdity or impossibility. Suppose that there is a natural, universal, invariable language, common to every individual of human race, and that books are natural productions which perpetuate themselves in the same manner with animals and vegetables, by descent and propagation. Several expressions of our passions contain a universal language: all brute animals have a natural speech, which, however limited, is very intelligible to their own species. And as there are infinitely fewer parts and less contrivance in the finest composition of eloquence than in the coarsest organized body, the propagation of an *Iliad* or *Æneid* is an easier supposition than that of any plant or animal.

Suppose, therefore, that you enter into your library thus peopled by natural volumes containing the most refined reason and most exquisite beauty; could you possibly open one of them and doubt that its original cause bore the strongest analogy to mind and intelligence? When it reasons and discourses; when it expostulates, argues, and enforces its views and topics; when it applies sometimes to the pure intellect, sometimes to the affections; when it collects, disposes, and adorns every consideration suited to the subject; could you persist in asserting that all this, at the bottom, had really no meaning, and that the first formation of this volume in the loins of its original parent proceeded not from thought and design? Your obstinacy, I know, reaches not that degree of firmness; even your sceptical play and wantonness would be abashed at so glaring an absurdity.

But if there be any difference, Philo, between this supposed case and the real one of the universe, it is all to the advantage of the latter. The anatomy of an animal affords many stronger instances of design then the perusal of Livy or Tacitus; and any objection which you start in the former case, by carrying me back to so unusual and extraordinary a scene as the first formation of worlds, the same objection has place on the supposition of our vegetating library. Choose, then, your party, Philo, without ambiguity or evasion; assert either that a rational volume is no proof of a rational cause or admit of a similar cause to all the works of nature.

Let me here observe, too, continued Cleanthes, that this religious argument, instead of being weakened by that scepticism so much affected by you, rather acquires force from it and becomes more firm and undisputed. To exclude all argument or reasoning of every kind is either affectation or madness. The declared profession of every reasonable sceptic is only to reject abstruse, remote, and refined arguments; to adhere to common sense and the plain instincts of nature; and to assent, wherever any reasons strike him with so full a force that he cannot, without the greatest violence, prevent it. Now the arguments for natural religion are plainly of this kind; and nothing but the most perverse, obstinate metaphysics can reject them. Consider, anatomize the eye, survey its structure and contrivance, and tell me, from your own feeling, if the idea of a contriver does not immediately flow in upon you with a force like that of sensation. The most obvious conclusion, surely, is in favour of design; and it requires time, reflection, and study, to summon up those frivolous though abstruse objections which can support infidelity. Who can behold the male and female of each species, the correspondence of their parts and instincts, their passions and whole course of life before and after generation, but must be sensible that the propagation of the species is intended by nature? Millions and millions of such instances present themselves through every part of the universe, and no language can convey a more intelligible irresistible meaning than the curious adjustment of final causes. To what degree, therefore, of blind dogmatism must one have attained to reject such natural and such convincing arguments?

Some beauties in writing we may meet with which seem contrary to rules, and which gain the affections and animate the imagination in opposition to all the precepts of criticism and to the authority of the established masters of art. And if the argument for theism be, as you pretend, contradictory to the principles of logic, its universal, its irresistible influence proves clearly that there may be arguments of a like irregular nature. Whatever cavils may be urged, an orderly world, as well as a coherent, articulate speech, will still be received as an incontestable proof of design and intention.

It sometimes happens, I own, that the religious arguments have not their due influence on an ignorant savage and barbarian, not because they are obscure and difficult, but because he never asks himself any question with regard to them. Whence arises the curious structure of an animal? From the copulation of its parents. And these whence? From *their* parents? A few removes set the objects at such a distance that to him they are lost in darkness and confusion; nor is he actuated by any curiosity to trace them farther. But this is neither dogmatism nor scepticism, but stupidity: a state of mind very different from your sifting, inquisitive disposition, my ingenious friend. You can trace causes from effects; you can compare the most distant and remote objects; and your greatest errors proceed not from barrenness of thought and invention, but from too luxuriant a fertility which suppresses your natural good sense by a profusion of unnecessary scruples and objections.

Here I could observe, Hermippus, that Philo was a little embarrassed and confounded; but, while he hesitated in delivering an answer, luckily for him, Demea broke in upon the discourse and saved his countenance.

Your instance, Cleanthes, said he, drawn from books and language, being familiar, has, I confess, so much more force on that account; but is there not some danger, too, in this very circumstance, and may it not render us presumptuous, by making us imagine we comprehend the Deity and have some adequate idea of his nature and attributes? When I read a volume, I enter into the mind and intention of the author; I become him, in a manner, for the instant, and have an immediate feeling and conception of those ideas which revolved in his imagination while employed in that composition. But so near an approach we never surely can make to the Deity. His ways are not our ways. His attributes are perfect but incomprehensible. And this volume of nature contains a great and inexplicable riddle, more than any intelligible discourse or reasoning.

The ancient Platonists, you know, were the most religious and devout of all the pagan philosophers, yet many of them, particularly Plotinus, expressly declare that intellect or understanding is not to be ascribed to the Deity, and that our most perfect worship of him consists, not in acts of veneration, reverence, gratitude, or love, but in a certain mysterious self-annihilation or total extinction of all our faculties. These ideas are, perhaps, too far stretched, but still it must be acknowledged that, by representing the Deity as so intelligible and comprehensible, and so similar to a human mind, we are guilty of the grossest and most narrow partiality, and make ourselves the model of the whole universe.

All the *sentiments* of the human mind, gratitude, resentment, love, friendship, approbation, blame, pity, emulation, envy, have a plain reference to the state and situation of man, and are calculated for preserving the existence and promoting the activity of such a being in such circumstances. It seems, therefore, unreasonable to transfer such sentiments to a supreme existence or to suppose him actuated by them; and the phenomena, besides, of the universe will not support us in such a theory. All our *ideas* derived from the senses are confessedly false and illusive, and cannot therefore be supposed to have place in a supreme intelligence. And as the ideas of internal sentiment, added to those of the external senses, compose the whole furniture of human understanding, we may conclude that none of the *materials* of thought are in any respect similar in the human and in the divine intelligence. Now, as to the *manner* of thinking, how can we make any comparison between them or suppose them anywise resembling? Our thought is fluctuating, uncertain, fleeting, successive, and compounded; and were we to remove these circumstances, we absolutely annihilate its essence, and it would in such a case be an abuse of terms to apply to it the name of thought or reason. At least, if it appear more pious and respectful (as it really is) still to retain these terms when we mention the Supreme Being, we ought to acknowledge that their meaning, in that case, is totally incomprehensible, and that the infirmities of our nature do not permit us to reach any ideas which in the least correspond to the ineffable sublimity of the Divine attributes.

Part · I V

It seems strange to me, said Cleanthes, that you, Demea, who are so sincere in the cause of religion, should still maintain the mysterious, incomprehensible nature of the Deity, and should insist so strenuously that he has no manner of likeness or resemblance to human creatures. The Deity, I can readily allow, possesses many powers and attributes of which we can have no comprehension; but, if our ideas, so far as they go, be not just and adequate and correspondent to his real nature, I know not what there is in this subject worth insisting on. Is the name, without any meaning, of such mighty importance? Or how do you mystics, who maintain the absolute incomprehensibility of the Deity, differ from sceptics or atheists, who assert that the first cause of all is unknown and unintelligible? Their temerity must be very great if, after rejecting the production by a mind—I mean a mind resembling the human (for I know of no other)—they pretend to assign, with certainty, any other specific intelligible cause; and their conscience must be very scrupulous, indeed, if they refuse to call the universal unknown cause a God or Deity, and to bestow on him as many sublime eulogies and unmeaning epithets as you shall please to require of them.

Who could imagine, replied Demea, that Cleanthes, the calm philosophical Cleanthes, would attempt to refute his antagonists by affixing a nickname to them, and, like the common bigots and inquisitors of the age, have recourse to invective and declamation instead of reasoning? Or does he not perceive that these topics are easily retorted, and that *anthropomorphite* is an appellation as invidious, and implies as dangerous consequences, as the epithet of *mystic* with which he has honoured us? In reality, Cleanthes, consider what it is you assert when you represent the Deity as similar to a human mind and understanding. What is the soul of man? A composition of various faculties, passions, sentiments, ideas—united, indeed, into one self or person, but still distinct from each other. When it reasons, the ideas which are the parts of its discourse arrange themselves in a certain form or order which is not preserved entire for a moment, but immediately gives place to another arrangement. New opinions, new passions, new affections, new feelings arise which continually diversify the mental scene and produce in it the greatest variety and most rapid succession imaginable. How is this compatible with that perfect immutability and simplicity which all true theists ascribe to the Deity? By the same act, say they, he sees past, present, and future; his love and hatred, his mercy and justice, are one individual operation; he is entire in every point of space, and complete in every instant of duration. No succession, no change, no acquisition, no diminution. What he is implies not in it any shadow of distinction or diversity. And what he is this moment he ever has been and ever will be, without any new judgment, sentiment, or operation. He stands fixed in one simple, perfect state; nor can you ever say, with any propriety, that this act of his is different from that other, or that this judgment or idea has been lately formed and will give place, by succession, to any different judgment or idea.

I can readily allow, said Cleanthes, that those who maintain the perfect simplicity of the Supreme Being, to the extent in which you have explained it, are complete mystics, and chargeable with all the consequences which I have drawn from their opinion. They are, in a word, atheists, without knowing it. For though it be allowed that the Deity possesses attributes of which we have no comprehension, yet ought we never to ascribe to him any attributes which are absolutely incompatible with that intelligent nature essential to him. A mind whose acts and sentiments and ideas are not distinct and successive, one that is wholly simple and totally immutable, is a mind which has no thought, no reason, no will, no sentiment, no love, no hatred; or, in a word, is no mind at all. It is an abuse of terms to give it that appellation, and we may as well speak of limited extension without figure, or of number without composition.

Pray consider, said Philo, whom you are at present inveighing against. You are honouring with the appellation of *atheist* all the sound, orthodox divines, almost, who have treated of this subject; and you will at last be, yourself, found, according to your reckoning, the only sound theist in the world. But if idolaters be atheists, as, I think, may justly be asserted, and Christian theologians the same, what becomes of the argument, so much celebrated, derived from the universal consent of mankind?

But, because I know you are not much swayed by names and authorities, I shall endeavour to show you, a little more distinctly, the inconveniences of that anthropomorphism which you have embraced, and shall prove that there is no ground to suppose a plan of the world to be formed in the Divine mind, consisting of distinct ideas, differently arranged, in the same manner as an architect forms in his head the plan of a house which he intends to execute.

It is not easy, I own, to see what is gained by this supposition, whether we judge of the matter by *reason* or by *experience*. We are still obliged to mount higher in order to find the cause of this cause which you had assigned as satisfactory and conclusive.

If *reason* (I mean abstract reason derived from inquiries *a priori*) be not alike mute with regard to all questions concerning cause and effect, this sentence at least it will venture to pronounce: that a mental world or universe of ideas requires a cause as much as does a material world or universe of objects, and, if similar in its arrangement, must require a similar cause. For what is there in this subject which should occasion a different conclusion or inference? In an abstract view, they are entirely alike; and no difficulty attends the one supposition which is not common to both of them.

Again, when we will needs force *experience* to pronounce some sentence, even on these subjects which lie beyond her sphere, neither can she perceive any material difference in this particular between these two kinds of worlds, but finds them to be governed by similar principles, and to depend upon an equal variety of causes in their operations. We have specimens in miniature of both of them. Our own mind resembles the one; a vegetable or animal body the other. Let experience, therefore, judge from these samples. Nothing seems more delicate, with regard to its causes, than thought; and as these causes never operate in two persons after the same manner, so we never find two persons who think exactly alike. Nor indeed does the same person think exactly alike at any two different periods of time. A difference of age, of the disposition of his body, of weather, of food, of company, of books, of passions—any of these particulars, or others more minute, are sufficient to alter the curious machinery of thought and communicate to it very different movements and operations. As far as we can judge, vegetables and animal bodies are not more delicate in their motions, nor depend upon a greater variety or more curious adjustment of springs and principles.

How, therefore, shall we satisfy ourselves concerning the cause of that Being whom you suppose the Author of nature, or, according to your system of anthropomorphism, the ideal world into which you trace the material? Have we not the same reason to trace that ideal world into another ideal world or new intelligent principle? But if we stop and go no farther, why go so far? why not stop at the material world? How can we satisfy ourselves without going on *in infinitum*? And, after all, what satisfaction is there in that infinite progression? Let us remember the story of the Indian philosopher and his elephant. It was never more applicable than to the present subject. If the material world rests upon a similar ideal world, this ideal world must rest upon some other, and so on without end. It were better, therefore, never to look beyond the present material world. By supposing it to contain the principle of its order within itself, we really assert it to be God; and the sooner we arrive at that Divine Being, so much the better. When you go one step beyond the mundane system, you only excite an inquisitive humour which it is impossible ever to satisfy.

To say that the different ideas which compose the reason of the Supreme Being fall into order of themselves and by their own nature is really to talk without any precise meaning. If it has a meaning, I would fain know why it is not as good sense to say that the parts of the material world fall into order of themselves and by their own nature. Can the one opinion be intelligible, while the other is not so?

We have, indeed, experience of ideas which fall into order of themselves and without any *known* cause. But, I am sure, we have a much larger experience of matter which does the same, as in all instances of generation and vegetation where the accurate analysis of the cause exceeds all human comprehension. We have also experience of particular systems of thought and of matter which have no order; of the first in madness, of the second in corruption. Why, then, should we think that order is more essential to one than the other? And if it requires a cause in both, what do we gain by your system, in tracing the universe of objects into a similar universe of ideas? The first step which we make leads us on for ever. It were, therefore, wise in us to limit all our inquiries to the present world, without looking farther. No satisfaction can ever be attained by these speculations which so far exceed the narrow bounds of human understanding.

It was usual with the Peripatetics, you know, Cleanthes, when the cause of any phenomenon was demanded, to have recourse to their *faculties* or *occult qualities*, and to say, for instance, that bread nourished by its nutritive faculty, and senna purged by its purgative. But it has been discovered that this subterfuge was nothing but the disguise of ignorance, and that these philosophers, though less ingenuous, really said the same thing with the sceptics or the vulgar who fairly confessed that they knew not the cause of these phenomena. In like manner, when it is asked, what cause produces order in the ideas of the Supreme Being, can any other reason be assigned by you, anthropomorphites, than that it is a *rational* faculty, and that such is the nature of the Deity? But why a similar answer will not be equally satisfactory in accounting for the order of the world, without having recourse to any such intelligent creator as you insist on, may be difficult to determine. It is only to say that *such* is the nature of material objects, and that they are all originally possessed of a *faculty* of order and proportion. These are only more learned and elaborate ways of confessing our ignorance; nor has the one hypothesis any real advantage above the other, except in its greater conformity to vulgar prejudices.

You have displayed this argument with great emphasis, replied

Cleanthes: You seem not sensible how easy it is to answer it. Even in common life, if I assign a cause for any event, is it any objection, Philo, that I cannot assign the cause of that cause, and answer every new question which may incessantly be started? And what philosophers could possibly submit to so rigid a rule?—philosophers who confess ultimate causes to be totally unknown, and are sensible that the most refined principles into which they trace the phenomena are still to them as inexplicable as these phenomena themselves are to the vulgar. The order and arrangement of nature, the curious adjustment of final causes, the plain use and intention of every part and organ—all these bespeak in the clearest language an intelligent cause or author. The heavens and the earth join in the same testimony: The whole chorus of nature raises one hymn to the praises of its Creator. You alone, or almost alone, disturb this general harmony. You start abstruse doubts, cavils, and objections; you ask me what is the cause of this cause? I know not; I care not; that concerns not me. I have found a Deity; and here I stop my inquiry. Let those go farther who are wiser or more enterprising.

I pretend to be neither, replied Philo; and for that very reason I should never, perhaps, have attempted to go so far, especially when I am sensible that I must at last be contented to sit down with the same answer which, without further trouble, might have satisfied me from the beginning. If I am still to remain in utter ignorance of causes and can absolutely give an explication of nothing, I shall never esteem it any advantage to shove off for a moment a difficulty which you acknowledge must immediately, in its full force, recur upon me. Naturalists indeed very justly explain particular effects by more general causes, though these general causes themselves should remain in the end totally inexplicable, but they never surely thought it satisfactory to explain a particular effect by a particular cause which was no more to be accounted for than the effect itself. An ideal system, arranged of itself, without a precedent design, is not a whit more explicable than a material one which attains its order in a like manner; nor is there any more difficulty in the latter supposition than in the former.

Part · V

But to show you still more inconveniences, continued Philo, in your anthropomorphism, please to take a new survey of your principles. *Like effects prove like causes.* This is the experimental argument; and this, you say too, is the sole theological argument. Now it is certain that the liker the effects are which are seen and the liker the causes which are inferred, the stronger is the argument. Every departure on either side diminishes the probability and renders the experiment less conclusive. You cannot doubt of the principle; neither ought you to reject its consequences.

All the new discoveries in astronomy which prove the immense grandeur and magnificence of the works of nature are so many additional arguments for a Deity, according to the true system of theism; but, according to your hypothesis of experimental theism, they become so many objections, by removing the effect still farther from all resemblance to the effects of human art and contrivance. For if Lucretius, even following the old system of the world, could exclaim:

> Quis regere immensi summam, quis habere profundi
> Indu manu validas potis est moderanter habenas?
> Quis pariter cœlos omnes convertere? et omnes
> Ignibus ætheriis terras suffire feraces?
> Omnibus inque locis esse omni tempore præsto? [1]

If Tully [Cicero] esteemed this reasoning so natural as to put it into the mouth of his Epicurean:

> Quibus enim oculis animi intueri potuit vester Plato fabricam illam tanti operis, qua construi a Deo atque ædificari mundum facit? quæ molitio? quæ ferramenta? qui vectes? quæ machinæ? qui minstri tanti muneris fuerunt? quemadmodum autem obedire et parere voluntati architecti aer, ignis, aqua, terra potuerunt? [2]

If this argument, I say, had any force in former ages, how much greater must it have at present when the bounds of Nature are so infinitely enlarged and such a magnificent scene is opened to us? It is still more unreasonable to form our idea of so unlimited a cause from our experience of the narrow productions of human design and invention.

The discoveries by microscopes, as they open a new universe in miniature, are still objections, according to you, arguments, according to me. The further we push our researches of this kind, we are still led

---

[1] [De Rerum Natura], lib. XI [II], 1094. [Who can rule the sum, who hold in his hand with controlling force the strong reins, of the immeasurable deep? Who can at once make all the different heavens to roll and warm with ethereal fires all the fruitful earths, or be present in all places at all times? (Translation by H. A. J. Munro, G. Bell & Sons, 1920.)]

[2] De Natura Deorum, lib. I; [cap. VIII.] [For with what eyes could your Plato see the construction of so vast a work which, according to him, God was putting together and building? What materials, what tools, what bars, what machines, what servants were employed in such gigantic work? How could the air, fire, water, and earth pay obedience and submit to the will of the architect?]

to infer the universal cause of all to be vastly different from mankind, or from any object of human experience and observation.

And what say you to the discoveries in anatomy, chemistry, botany? . . . These surely are no objections, replied Cleanthes; they only discover new instances of art and contrivance. It is still the image of mind reflected on us from innumerable objects. Add a mind *like the human*, said Philo. I know of no other, replied Cleanthes. And the liker, the better, insisted Philo. To be sure, said Cleanthes.

Now, Cleanthes, said Philo, with an air of alacrity and triumph, mark the consequences. *First*, by this method of reasoning you renounce all claim to infinity in any of the attributes of the Deity. For, as the cause ought only to be proportioned to the effect, and the effect, so far as it falls under our cognizance, is not infinite, what pretensions have we, upon your suppositions, to ascribe that attribute to the Divine Being? You will still insist that, by removing him so much from all similarity to human creatures, we give in to the most arbitrary hypothesis, and at the same time weaken all proofs of his existence.

Secondly, you have no reason, on your theory, for ascribing perfection to the Deity, even in his finite capacity, or for supposing him free from every error, mistake, or incoherence, in his undertakings. There are many inexplicable difficulties in the works of nature which, if we allow a perfect author to be proved *a priori*, are easily solved, and become only seeming difficulties from the narrow capacity of man, who cannot trace infinite relations. But according to your method of reasoning, these difficulties become all real, and, perhaps, will be insisted on as new instances of likeness to human art and contrivance. At least, you must acknowledge that it is impossible for us to tell, from our limited views, whether this system contains any great faults or deserves any considerable praise if compared to other possible and even real systems. Could a peasant, if the *Æneid* were read to him, pronounce that poem to be absolutely faultless, or even assign to it its proper rank among the productions of human wit, he who had never seen any other production?

But were this world ever so perfect a production, it must still remain uncertain whether all the excellences of the work can justly be ascribed to the workman. If we survey a ship, what an exalted idea must we form of the ingenuity of the carpenter who framed so complicated, useful, and beautiful a machine? And what surprise must we feel when we find him a stupid mechanic who imitated others, and copied an art which, through a long succession of ages, after multiplied trials, mistakes, corrections, deliberations, and controversies, had been gradually improving? Many worlds might have been botched and bungled, throughout an eternity, ere this system was struck out; much labour lost, many fruitless trials made, and a slow but continued improvement carried on during infinite ages in the art of world-making. In such subjects, who can determine where the truth, nay, who can conjecture where the probability lies, amidst a great number of hypotheses which may be proposed, and a still greater which may be imagined?

And what shadow of an argument, continued Philo, can you produce from your hypothesis to prove the unity of the Deity? A great number of men join in building a house or ship, in rearing a city, in framing a commonwealth; why may not several deities combine in contriving and framing a world? This is only so much greater similarity to human affairs. By sharing the work among several, we may so much further limit the attributes of each, and get rid of that extensive power and knowledge which must be supposed in one diety, and which, according to you, can only serve to weaken the proof of his existence. And if such foolish, such vicious creatures as man can yet often unite in framing and executing one plan, how much more those deities or demons, whom we may suppose several degrees more perfect!

To multiply causes without necessity is indeed contrary to true philosophy, but this principle applies not to the present case. Were one deity antecedently proved by your theory who were possessed of every attribute requisite to the production of the universe, it would be needless, I own, (though not absurd) to suppose any other deity existent. But while it is still a question whether all these attributes are united in one subject or dispersed among several independent beings, by what phenomena in nature can we pretend to decide the controversy? Where we see a body raised in a scale, we are sure that there is in the opposite scale, however concealed from sight, some counterpoising weight equal to it; but it is still allowed to doubt whether that weight be an aggregate of several distinct bodies or one uniform united mass. And if the weight requisite very much exceeds anything which we have ever seen conjoined in any single body, the former supposition becomes still more probable and natural. An intelligent being of such vast power and capacity as is necessary to produce the universe, or, to speak in the language of ancient philosophy, so prodigious an animal exceeds all analogy and even comprehension.

But further, Cleanthes: Men are mortal, and renew their species by generation; and this is common to all living creatures. The two great sexes of male and female, says Milton, animate the world. Why must this circumstance, so universal, so essential, be excluded from those numerous and limited deities? Behold, then, the theogeny of ancient times brought back upon us.

And why not become a perfect anthropomorphite? Why not assert the deity or deities to be corporeal, and to have eyes, a nose, mouth, ears, etc.? Epicurus maintained that no man had ever seen reason but in a human figure; therefore, the gods must have a human figure. And this argument, which is deservedly so much ridiculed by Cicero, becomes, according to you, solid and philosophical.

In a word, Cleanthes, a man who follows your hypothesis is able, perhaps, to assert or conjecture that the universe sometime arose from something like design; but beyond that position he cannot ascertain one single circumstance, and is left afterwards to fix every point of his theology by the utmost license of fancy and hypothesis. This world, for aught he knows, is very faulty and imperfect, compared to a superior standard, and was only the first rude essay of some infant deity who afterwards abandoned it, ashamed of his lame performance; it is the work only of some dependent, inferior deity, and is the object of derision to his superiors; it is the production of old age and dotage in some superannuated deity, and ever since his death has run on at adventures, from the first impulse and active force which it received from him. You justly give signs of horror, Demea, at these strange suppositions; but these, and a thousand more of the same kind, are Cleanthes' suppositions, not mine. From the moment the attributes of the Deity are supposed finite, all these have place. And I cannot, for my part, think that so wild and unsettled a system of theology is, in any respect, preferable to none at all.

These suppositions I absolutely disown, cried Cleanthes: they strike me, however, with no horror, especially when proposed in that rambling way in which they drop from you. On the contrary, they give me pleasure when I see that, by the utmost indulgence of your imagination, you never get rid of the hypothesis of design in the universe, but are obliged at every turn to have recourse to it. To this concession I adhere steadily; and this I regard as a sufficient foundation for religion.

Part · V I

It must be a slight fabric, indeed, said Demea, which can be erected on so tottering a foundation. While we are uncertain whether there is one deity or many, whether the deity or deities, to whom we owe our existence, be perfect or imperfect, subordinate or supreme, dead or alive, what trust or confidence can we repose in them? What devotion or worship address to them? What veneration or obedience pay them? To all the purposes of life the theory of religion becomes altogether useless; and even with regard to speculative consequences its uncertainty, according to you, must render it totally precarious and unsatisfactory.

To render it still more unsatisfactory, said Philo, there occurs to me another hypothesis which must acquire an air of probability from the method of reasoning so much insisted on by Cleanthes. That like effects arise from like causes—this principle he supposes the foundation of all religion. But there is another principle of the same kind, no less certain and derived from the same source of experience, that, where several known circumstances are observed to be similar, the unknown will also be found similar. Thus, if we see the limbs of a human body, we conclude that it is also attended with a human head, though hid from us. Thus, if we see, through a chink in a wall, a small part of the sun, we conclude that were the wall removed we should see the whole body. In short, this method of reasoning is so obvious and familiar that no scruple can ever be made with regard to its solidity.

Now, if we survey the universe, so far as it falls under our knowledge, it bears a great resemblance to an animal or organized body, and seems actuated with a like principle of life and motion. A continual circulation of matter in it produces no disorder; a continual waste in every part is incessantly repaired; the closest sympathy is perceived throughout the entire system; and each part or member, in performing its proper offices, operates both to its own preservation and to that of the whole. The world, therefore, I infer, is an animal; and the Deity is the *soul* of the world, actuating it, and actuated by it.

You have too much learning, Cleanthes, to be at all surprised at this opinion which, you know, was maintained by almost all the theists of antiquity, and chiefly prevails in their discourses and reasonings. For though, sometimes, the ancient philosophers reason from final causes, as if they thought the world the workmanship of God, yet it appears rather their favourite notion to consider it as his body whose organization renders it subservient to him. And it must be confessed that, as the universe resembles more a human body than it does the works of human art and contrivance, if our limited analogy could ever, with any propriety, be extended to the whole of nature, the inference seems juster in favour of the ancient than the modern theory.

There are many other advantages, too, in the former theory which recommended it to the ancient theologians. Nothing more repugnant to all their notions because nothing more repugnant to common experience than mind without body, a mere spiritual substance which fell not under their senses nor comprehension, and of which they had not observed one single instance throughout all nature. Mind and body they knew because they felt both; an order, arrangement, organization, or internal machinery, in both they likewise knew, after the same manner; and it could not but seem reasonable to transfer this experience to the universe, and to suppose the divine mind and body to be also coeval and to have, both of them, order and arrangement naturally inherent in them and inseparable from them.

Here, therefore, is a new species of *anthropomorphism*, Cleanthes, on which you may deliberate, and a theory which seems not liable to any considerable difficulties. You are too much superior, surely, to *systematical prejudices* to find any more difficulty in supposing an animal body to be, originally, of itself or from unknown causes, possessed of order and organization, than in supposing a similar order to belong to mind. But the *vulgar prejudice* that body and mind ought always to accompany each other ought not, one should think, to be entirely neglected; since it is founded on *vulgar experience*, the only guide which you profess to follow in all these theological inquiries. And if you assert that our limited experience is an unequal standard by which to judge of the unlimited extent of nature, you entirely abandon your own hypothesis, and must thenceforward adopt our mysticism, as you call it, and admit of the absolute incomprehensibility of the Divine Nature.

This theory, I own, replied Cleanthes, has never before occurred to me, though a pretty natural one; and I cannot readily, upon so short an examination and reflection, deliver any opinion with regard to it. You are very scrupulous, indeed, said Philo, were I to examine any system of yours, I should not have acted with half that caution and reserve, in starting objections and difficulties to it. However, if anything occur to you, you will oblige us by proposing it.

Why then, replied Cleanthes, it seems to me that, though the world does, in many circumstances, resemble an animal body, yet is the analogy also defective in many circumstances the most material: no organs of sense; no seat of thought or reason; no one precise origin of motion and action. In short, it seems to bear a stronger resemblance to a vegetable than to an animal, and your inference would be so far inconclusive in favour of the soul of the world.

But, in the next place, your theory seems to imply the eternity of the world; and that is a principle which, I think, can be refuted by the strongest reasons and probabilities. I shall suggest an argument to this purpose which, I believe, has not been insisted on by any writer. Those who reason from the late origin of arts and sciences, though their inference wants not force, may perhaps be refuted by considerations derived from the nature of human society, which is in continual revolution between ignorance and knowledge, liberty and slavery, riches and poverty; so that it is impossible for us, from our limited experience, to foretell with assurance what events may or may not be expected. Ancient learning and history seem to have been in great danger of entirely perishing after the inundation of the barbarous nations; and had these convulsions continued a little longer or been a little more violent, we should not probably have now known what passed in the world a few centuries before us. Nay, were it not for the superstition of the popes, who preserved a little jargon of Latin in order to support the appearance of an ancient and universal church, that tongue must have been utterly lost; in which case the Western world, being totally barbarous, would not have been in a fit disposition for receiving the Greek language and learning, which was conveyed to them after the sacking of Constantinople. When learning and books had been extinguished, even the mechanical arts would have fallen considerably to decay; and it is easily imagined that fable or tradition might ascribe to them a much later origin than the true one. This vulgar argument, therefore, against the eternity of the world seems a little precarious.

But here appears to be the foundation of a better argument. Lucullus was the first that brought cherry-trees from Asia to Europe, though that tree thrives so well in many European climates that it grows in the woods without any culture. Is it possible that, throughout a whole eternity, no European had ever passed into Asia and thought of transplanting so delicious a fruit into his own country? Or if the tree was once transplanted and propagated, how could it ever afterwards perish? Empires may rise and fall, liberty and slavery succeed alternately, ignorance and knowledge give place to each other; but the cherry-tree will still remain in the woods of Greece, Spain, and Italy, and will never be affected by the revolutions of human society.

It is not two thousand years since vines were transplanted into France, though there is no climate in the world more favourable to them. It is not three centuries since horses, cows, sheep, swine, dogs, corn, were known in America. Is it possible that during the revolutions of a whole eternity there never arose a Columbus who might open the communication between Europe and that continent? We may as well imagine that all men would wear stockings for ten thousand years, and never have the sense to think of garters to tie them. All these seem convincing proofs of the youth or rather infancy of the world, as being founded on the operation of principles more constant and steady than those by which human society is governed and directed. Nothing less than a total convulsion of the elements will ever destroy all the European animals and vegetables which are now to be found in the Western world.

And what argument have you against such convulsions? replied Philo. Strong and almost incontestable proofs may be traced over the whole earth that every part of this globe has continued for many ages entirely covered with water. And though order were supposed inseparable from matter, and inherent in it, yet may matter be susceptible of

many and great revolutions, through the endless periods of eternal duration. The incessant changes to which every part of it is subject seem to
intimate some such general transformations; though, at the same time,
it is observable that all the changes and corruptions of which we have
ever had experience are but passages from one state of order to another;
nor can matter ever rest in total deformity and confusion. What we see
in the parts, we may infer in the whole; at least, that is the method of
reasoning on which you rest your whole theory. And were I obliged to
defend any particular system of this nature, which I never willingly
should do, I esteem none more plausible than that which ascribes an
eternal inherent principle of order to the world, though attended with
great and continual revolutions and alterations. This at once solves all
difficulties; and if the solution, by being so general, is not entirely complete and satisfactory, it is at least a theory that we must sooner or later
have recourse to, whatever system we embrace. How could things have
been as they are, were there not an original inherent principle of order
somewhere, in thought or in matter? And it is very indifferent to which
of these we give the preference. Chance has no place, on any hypothesis,
sceptical or religious. Everything is surely governed by steady, inviolable
laws. And were the inmost essence of things laid open to us, we should
then discover a scene of which, at present, we can have no idea. Instead
of admiring the order of natural beings, we should clearly see that it
was absolutely impossible for them, in the smallest article, ever to admit of any other disposition.

   Were anyone inclined to revive the ancient pagan theology which
maintained, as we learn from Hesiod, that this globe was governed by
30,000 deities, who arose from the unknown powers of nature, you
would naturally object, Cleanthes, that nothing is gained by this hypothesis; and that it is as easy to suppose all men animals, beings more
numerous but less perfect, to have sprung immediately from a like origin.
Push the same inference a step further, and you will find a numerous
society of deities as explicable as one universal deity who possesses
within himself the powers and perfections of the whole society. All these
systems, then, of Scepticism, Polytheism, and Theism, you must allow,
on your principles, to be on a like footing, and that no one of them has
any advantage over the others. You may thence learn the fallacy of
your principles.

Part · V I I

But here, continued Philo, in examining the ancient system of the soul
of the world there strikes me, all on a sudden, a new idea which, if just,

must go near to subvert all your reasoning, and destroy even your first inferences on which you repose such confidence. If the universe bears a greater likeness to animal bodies and to vegetables than to the works of human art, it is more probable that its cause resembles the cause of the former than that of the latter, and its origin ought rather to be ascribed to generation or vegetation than to reason or design. Your conclusion, even according to your own principles, is therefore lame and defective.

Pray open up this argument a little further, said Demea, for I do not rightly apprehend it in that concise manner in which you have expressed it.

Our friend Cleanthes, replied Philo, as you have heard, asserts that, since no question of fact can be proved otherwise than by experience, the existence of a Deity admits not of proof from any other medium. The world, says he, resembles the works of human contrivance; therefore its cause must also resemble that of the other. Here we may remark that the operation of one very small part of nature, to wit, man, upon another very small part, to wit, that inanimate matter lying within his reach, is the rule by which Cleanthes judges of the origin of the whole; and he measures objects, so widely disproportioned, by the same individual standard. But to waive all objections drawn from this topic, I affirm that there are other parts of the universe (besides the machines of human invention) which bear still a greater resemblance to the fabric of the world, and which, therefore, afford a better conjecture concerning the universal origin of this system. These parts are animals and vegetables. The world plainly resembles more an animal or a vegetable than it does a watch or a knitting-loom. Its cause, therefore, it is more probable, resembles the cause of the former. The cause of the former is generation or vegetation. The cause, therefore, of the world we may infer to be something similar or analogous to generation or vegetation.

But how is it conceivable, said Demea, that the world can arise from anything similar to vegetation or generation?

Very easily, replied Philo. In like manner as a tree sheds its seed into the neighbouring fields and produces other trees, so the great vegetable, the world, or this planetary system, produces within itself certain seeds which, being scattered into the surrounding chaos, vegetate into new worlds. A comet, for instance, is the seed of a world; and after it has been fully ripened, by passing from sun to sun, and star to star, it is, at last, tossed into the unformed elements which everywhere surround this universe, and immediately sprouts up into a new system.

Or if, for the sake of variety (for I see no other advantage), we should suppose this world to be an animal: a comet is the egg of this animal; and in like manner as an ostrich lays its egg in the sand, which, without any further care, hatches the egg and produces a new animal, so. . . . I understand you, says Demea. But what wild, arbitrary suppositions are these! What *data* have you for such extraordinary conclusions? And is the slight, imaginary resemblance of the world to a vegetable or an animal sufficient to establish the same inference with regard to both? Objects which are in general so widely different ought they to be a standard for each other?

Right, cries Philo: This is the topic on which I have all along insisted. I have still asserted that we have no *data* to establish any system of cosmogony. Our experience, so imperfect in itself and so limited both in extent and duration, can afford us no probable conjecture concerning the whole of things. But if we must needs fix on some hypothesis, by what rule, pray, ought we to determine our choice? Is there any other rule than the greater similarity of the objects compared? And does not a plant or an animal, which springs from vegetation or generation, bear a stronger resemblance to the world than does any artificial machine, which arises from reason and design?

But what is this vegetation and generation of which you talk? said Demea. Can you explain their operations, and anatomize that fine internal structure on which they depend?

As much, at least, replied Philo, as Cleanthes can explain the operations of reason, or anatomize that internal structure on which it depends. But without any such elaborate disquisitions, when I see an animal, I infer that it sprang from generation; and that with as great certainty as you conclude a house to have been reared by design. These words *generation, reason* mark only certain powers and energies in nature whose effects are known, but whose essence is incomprehensible; and one of these principles, more than the other, has no privilege for being made a standard to the whole of nature.

In reality, Demea, it may reasonably be expected that the larger the views are which we take of things, the better will they conduct us in our conclusions concerning such extraordinary and such magnificent subjects. In this little corner of the world alone, there are four principles, *reason, instinct, generation, vegetation*, which are similar to each other, and are the causes of similar effects. What a number of other principles may we naturally suppose in the immense extent and variety of the universe could we travel from planet to planet, and from system to system, in order to examine each part of this mighty fabric? Any one of these four principles above mentioned (and a hundred others which lie open to our conjecture) may afford us a theory by which to judge of the origin of the world; and it is a palpable and egregious partiality to confine our view entirely to that principle by which our own minds operate. Were this principle more intelligible on that account, such a partiality might be somewhat excusable; but reason, in its internal fabric and structure, is really as little known to us as instinct or vegetation; and, perhaps, even that vague, undeterminate word *nature* to which the vulgar refer everything is not at the bottom more inexplicable. The effects of these principles are all known to us from experience; but the principles themselves and their manner of operation are totally unknown; nor is it less intelligible or less conformable to experience to say that the world arose by vegetation, from a seed shed by another world, than to say that it arose from a divine reason or contrivance, according to the sense in which Cleanthes understands it.

But methinks, said Demea, if the world had a vegetative quality and could sow the seeds of new worlds into the infinite chaos, this power would be still an additional argument for design in its author. For whence could arise so wonderful a faculty but from design? Or how can order spring from anything which perceives not that order which it bestows?

You need only look around you, replied Philo, to satisfy yourself with regard to this question. A tree bestows order and organization on that tree which springs from it, without knowing the order; an animal in the same manner on its offspring; a bird on its nest; and instances of this kind are even more frequent in the world than those of order which arise from reason and contrivance. To say that all this order in animals and vegetables proceeds ultimately from design is begging the question; nor can that great point be ascertained otherwise than by proving, *a priori*, both that order is, from its nature, inseparably attached to thought and that it can never of itself or from original unknown principles belong to matter.

But further, Demea, this objection which you urge can never be made use of by Cleanthes, without renouncing a defence which he has already made against one of my objections. When I inquired concerning the cause of that supreme reason and intelligence into which he resolves everything, he told me that the impossibility of satisfying such inquiries could never be admitted as an objection in any species of philosophy. *We must stop somewhere*, says he; *nor is it ever within the reach of human capacity to explain ultimate causes or show the last connections of any objects. It is sufficient if any steps, so far as we go, are supported by experience and observation.* Now that vegetation and generation, as well as reason, are experienced to be principles of order in nature is undeniable. If I rest my system of cosmogony on the former, preferably to the latter, it is at my choice. The matter seems entirely arbitrary. And when Cleanthes asks me what is the cause of my great vegetative or generative faculty, I am equally entitled to ask him the cause of his great reasoning principle. These questions we have agreed to forbear on both sides; and it is chiefly his interest on the present occasion to stick to this agreement. Judging by our limited and imperfect experience, generation has some privileges above reason; for we see every day the latter arise from the former, never the former from the latter.

Compare, I beseech you, the consequences on both sides. The world, say I, resembles an animal; therefore it is an animal, therefore it arose from generation. The steps, I confess, are wide, yet there is some small appearance of analogy in each step. The world, says Cleanthes, resembles a machine; therefore it is a machine, therefore it arose from design. The steps are here equally wide, and the analogy less striking. And if he pretends to carry on *my* hypothesis a step further, and to infer design or reason from the great principle of generation on which I insist, I may, with better authority, use the same freedom to push further *his* hypothesis, and infer a divine generation or theogony from his principle of reason. I have at least some faint shadow of experience, which is the utmost that can ever be attained in the present subject. Reason, in innumerable instances, is observed to arise from the principle of generation, and never to arise from any other principle.

Hesiod and all the ancient mythologists were so struck with this analogy that they universally explained the origin of nature from an animal birth, and copulation. Plato, too, so far as he is intelligible, seems to have adopted some such notion in his *Timæus*.

The Brahmins assert that the world arose from an infinite spider, who spun this whole complicated mass from his bowels, and annihilates afterwards the whole or any part of it, by absorbing it again and resolving it into his own essence. Here is a species of cosmogony which appears to us ridiculous because a spider is a little contemptible animal whose operations we are never likely to take for a model of the whole universe. But still here is a new species of analogy, even in our globe. And were there a planet wholly inhabited by spiders (which is very possible), this inference would there appear as natural and irrefragable as that which in our planet ascribes the origin of all things to design and intelligence, as explained by Cleanthes. Why an orderly system may not be spun from the belly as well as from the brain, it will be difficult for him to give a satisfactory reason.

I must confess, Philo, replied Cleanthes, that, of all men living, the task which you have undertaken, of raising doubts and objections, suits you best and seems, in a manner, natural and unavoidable to you. So great is your fertility of invention that I am not ashamed to acknowledge myself unable, on a sudden, to solve regularly such out-of-the-way difficulties as you incessantly start upon me, though I clearly see, in general, their fallacy and error. And I question not, but you are yourself, at present, in the same case, and have not the solution so ready as the objection, while you must be sensible that common sense and reason are entirely against you, and that such whimsies as you have delivered may puzzle but never can convince us.

Part · V I I I

What you ascribe to the fertility of my invention, replied Philo, is entirely owing to the nature of the subject. In subjects adapted to the narrow compass of human reason there is commonly but one determination which carries probability or conviction with it; and to a man of sound judgment all other suppositions but that one appear entirely absurd and chimerical. But in such questions as the present, a hundred contradictory views may preserve a kind of imperfect analogy, and invention has here full scope to exert itself. Without any great effort of thought, I believe that I could, in an instant, propose other systems of cosmogony which would have some faint appearance of truth, though it is a thousand, a million to one if either yours or any one of mine be the true system.

For instance, what if I should revive the old Epicurean hypothesis? This is commonly, and I believe justly, esteemed the most absurd system that has yet been proposed; yet I know not whether, with a few alterations, it might not be brought to bear a faint appearance of probability. Instead of supposing matter infinite, as Epicurus did, let us suppose it finite. A finite number of particles is only susceptible of finite transpositions; and it must happen, in an eternal duration, that every possible order or position must be tried an infinite number of times. This world, therefore, with all its events, even the most minute, has before been produced and destroyed, and will again be produced and destroyed, without any bounds and limitations. No one who has a conception of the powers of infinite, in comparison of finite, will ever scruple this determination.

But this supposes, said Demea, that matter can acquire motion without any voluntary agent or first mover.

And where is the difficulty, replied Philo, of that supposition? Every event, before experience, is equally difficult and incomprehensible; and every event, after experience, is equally easy and intelligible. Motion, in many instances, from gravity, from elasticity, from electricity, begins in matter, without any known voluntary agent; and to suppose always, in these cases, an unknown voluntary agent is mere hypothesis and hypothesis attended with no advantages. The beginning of motion in matter itself is as conceivable *a priori* as its communication from mind and intelligence.

Besides, why may not motion have been propagated by impulse through all eternity, and the same stock of it, or nearly the same, be still upheld in the universe? As much is lost by the composition of motion, as much is gained by its resolution. And whatever the causes are, the fact is certain that matter is and always has been in continual agitation, as far as human experience or tradition reaches. There is not probably, at present, in the whole universe, one particle of matter at absolute rest.

And this very consideration, too, continued Philo, which we have stumbled on in the course of the argument suggests a new hypothesis of cosmogony that is not absolutely absurd and improbable. Is there a system, an order, an economy of things, by which matter can preserve that perpetual agitation which seems essential to it, and yet maintain a constancy in the forms which it produces? There certainly is such an economy, for this is actually the case with the present world. The continual motion of matter, therefore, in less than infinite transpositions, must produce this economy or order, and, by its very nature, that order, when once established, supports itself for many ages if not to eternity. But wherever matter is so poised, arranged, and adjusted, as to continue in perpetual motion, and yet preserve a constancy in the forms, its situation must, of necessity, have all the same appearance of art and contrivance which we observe at present. All the parts of each form must have a relation to each other and to the whole; and the whole itself must have a relation to the other parts of the universe, to the element in which the form subsists, to the materials with which it repairs its waste and decay, and to every other form which is hostile or friendly. A defect in any of these particulars destroys the form, and the matter of which it is composed is again set loose, and is thrown into irregular motions and fermentations till it unite itself to some other regular form. If no such form be prepared to receive it, and if there be a great quantity of this corrupted matter in the universe, the universe itself is entirely disordered, whether it be the feeble embryo of a world in its first beginnings that is thus destroyed or the rotten carcase of one languishing in old age and infirmity. In either case, a chaos ensues till finite though innumerable revolutions produce, at last, some forms whose parts and organs are so adjusted as to support the forms amidst a continued succession of matter.

Suppose (for we shall endeavour to vary the expression) that matter were thrown into any position by a blind, unguided force; it is evident that this first position must, in all probability, be the most confused and most disorderly imaginable, without any resemblance to those works of human contrivance which, along with a symmetry of parts, discover an adjustment of means to ends and a tendency to self-preservation. If the actuating force cease after this operation, matter must remain for ever in disorder and continue an immense chaos, without any proportion or activity. But suppose that the actuating force, whatever it be, still continues in matter, this first position will immediately give place to a second which will likewise, in all probability, be as disorderly as the first, and so on through many successions of changes and revolutions. No particular order or position ever continues a moment unaltered. The original force, still remaining in activity, gives a perpetual restlessness to matter. Every possible situation is produced, and instantly destroyed. If a glimpse or dawn of order appears for a moment, it is instantly hurried away and confounded by that never-ceasing force which actuates every part of matter.

Thus the universe goes on for many ages in a continued succession of chaos and disorder. But is it not possible that it may settle at last, so as not to lose its motion and active force (for that we have supposed inherent in it), yet so as to preserve an uniformity of appearance, amidst the continual motion and fluctuation of its parts? This we find to be the case with the universe at present. Every individual is perpetually changing, and every part of every individual; and yet the whole remains, in appearance, the same. May we not hope for such a position or rather be assured of it from the eternal revolutions of unguided matter; and may not this account for all the appearing wisdom and contrivance which is in the universe? Let us contemplate the subject a little, and we shall find that this adjustment if attained by matter of a seeming stability in the forms, with a real and perpetual revolution or motion of parts, affords a plausible, if not a true, solution of the difficulty.

It is in vain, therefore, to insist upon the uses of the parts in animals or vegetables, and their curious adjustment to each other. I would fain know how an animal could subsist unless its parts were so adjusted? Do we not find that it immediately perishes whenever this adjustment ceases, and that its matter, corrupting, tries some new form? It happens indeed that the parts of the world are so well adjusted that some regular form immediately lays claim to this corrupted matter; and if it were not so, could the world subsist? Must it not dissolve, as well as the animal, and pass through new positions and situations till in great but finite succession it fall, at last, into the present or some such order?

It is well, replied Cleanthes, you told us that this hypothesis was suggested on a sudden, in the course of the argument. Had you had leisure to examine it, you would soon have perceived the insuperable objections to which it is exposed. No form, you say, can subsist unless it possess those powers and organs requisite for its subsistence; some new order or economy must be tried, and so on, without intermission, till at last some order which can support and maintain itself is fallen upon. But according to this hypothesis, whence arise the many conveniences and advantages which men and all animals possess? Two eyes, two ears are not absolutely necessary for the subsistence of the species. Human race might have been propagated and preserved without horses, dogs, cows, sheep, and those innumerable fruits and products which serve to our satisfaction and enjoyment. If no camels had been created for the use of man in the sandy deserts of Africa and Arabia, would the world have been dissolved? If no loadstone had been framed to give that wonderful and useful direction to the needle, would human society and the human kind have been immediately extinguished? Though the maxims of nature be in general very frugal, yet instances of this kind are far from being rare; and any one of them is a sufficient proof of design—and of a benevolent design—which gave rise to the order and arrangement of the universe.

At least, you may safely infer, said Philo, that the foregoing hypothesis is so far incomplete and imperfect, which I shall not scruple to allow. But can we ever reasonably expect greater success in any attempts of this nature? Or can we ever hope to erect a system of cosmogony that will be liable to no exceptions, and will contain no circumstance repugnant to our limited and imperfect experience of the analogy of nature? Your theory itself cannot surely pretend to any such advantage, even though you have run into *anthropomorphism*, the better to preserve a conformity to common experience. Let us once more put it to trial. In all instances which we have ever seen, ideas are copied from real objects, and are ectypal, not archetypal, to express myself in learned terms. You reverse this order and give thought the precedence. In all instances which we have ever seen, thought has no influence upon matter except where that matter is so conjoined with it as to have an equal reciprocal influence upon it. No animal can move immediately anything but the members of its own body; and, indeed, the equality of action and reaction seems to be an universal law of nature; but your theory implies a contradiction to this experience. These instances, with many more which it were easy to collect (particularly the supposition of a mind or system of thought that is eternal or, in other words, an animal ingenerable and immortal)—these instances, I say, may teach all of us sobriety in condemning each other, and let us see that as no system of this kind ought ever to be received from a slight analogy, so neither ought any to be rejected on account of a small incongruity. For that is an inconvenience from which we can justly pronounce no one to be exempted.

All religious systems, it is confessed, are subject to great and insuperable difficulties. Each disputant triumphs in his turn, while he carries on an offensive war, and exposes the absurdities, barbarities, and pernicious tenets of his antagonist. But all of them, on the whole, prepare a complete triumph for the *sceptic*, who tells them that no system ought ever to be embraced with regard to such subjects: for this plain reason that no absurdity ought ever to be assented to with regard to any subject. A total suspense of judgment is here our only reasonable resource. And if every attack, as is commonly observed, and no defence among theologians is successful, how complete must be *his* victory who remains always, with all mankind, on the offensive, and has himself no fixed station or abiding city which he is ever, on any occasion, obliged to defend?

Part · I X

But if so many difficulties attend the argument *a posteriori*, said Demea, had we not better adhere to that simple and sublime argument *a priori* which, by offering to us infallible demonstration, cuts off at once all doubt and difficulty? By this argument, too, we may prove the *infinity* of the Divine attributes, which, I am afraid, can never be ascertained with certainty from any other topic. For how can an effect which either is finite or, for aught we know, may be so—how can such an effect, I say, prove an infinite cause? The unity, too, of the Divine Nature it is very difficult, if not absolutely impossible, to deduce merely from contemplating the works of nature; nor will the uniformity alone of the plan, even were it allowed, give us any assurance of that attribute. Whereas the argument *a priori* . . .

You seem to reason, Demea, interposed Cleanthes, as if those advantages and conveniences in the abstract argument were full proofs of its solidity. But it is first proper, in my opinion, to determine what argument of this nature you choose to insist on; and we shall afterwards, from itself, better than from its *useful* consequences, endeavour to determine what value we ought to put upon it.

The argument, replied Demea, which I would insist on is the common one. Whatever exists must have a cause or reason of its existence, it being absolutely impossible for anything to produce itself or be the cause of its own existence. In mounting up, therefore, from effects to causes, we must either go on in tracing an infinite succession, without any ultimate cause at all, or must at last have recourse to some ultimate cause that is *necessarily* existent. Now that the first supposition is absurd may be thus proved. In the infinite chain or succession of causes and effects, each single effect is determined to exist by the power and efficacy of that cause which immediately preceded; but the whole eternal chain or succession, taken together, is not determined or caused by anything, and yet it is evident that it requires a cause or reason, as much as any particular object which begins to exist in time. The question is still reasonable why this particular succession of causes existed from eternity, and not any other succession or no succession at all. If there be no necessarily existent being, any supposition which can be formed is equally possible; nor is there any more absurdity in *nothing's* having existed from eternity than there is in that succession of causes which constitutes the universe. What was it, then, which determined *something* to exist rather than *nothing*, and bestowed being on a particular possibility, exclusive of the rest? *External causes*, there are supposed to be none. *Chance* is a word without a meaning. Was it *nothing*? But that can never produce anything. We must, therefore, have recourse to a necessarily existent Being who carries the *reason* of his existence in himself, and who cannot be supposed not to exist, without an express contradiction. There is, consequently, such a Being—that is, there is a Deity.

I shall not leave it to Philo, said Cleanthes, though I know that the starting objections is his chief delight, to point out the weakness of this metaphysical reasoning. It seems to me so obviously ill-grounded, and at the same time of so little consequence to the cause of true piety and religion, that I shall myself venture to show the fallacy of it.

I shall begin with observing that there is an evident absurdity in pretending to demonstrate a matter of fact, or to prove it by any arguments *a priori*. Nothing is demonstrable unless the contrary implies a contradiction. Nothing that is distinctly conceivable implies a contradiction. Whatever we conceive as existent, we can also conceive as nonexistent. There is no being, therefore, whose non-existence implies a contradiction. Consequently there is no being whose existence is demonstrable. I propose this argument as entirely decisive, and am willing to rest the whole controversy upon it.

It is pretended that the Deity is a necessarily existent being; and this necessity of his existence is attempted to be explained by asserting that, if we knew his whole essence or nature, we should perceive it to be as impossible for him not to exist, as for twice two not to be four. But it is evident that this can never happen, while our faculties remain the same as at present. It will still be possible for us, at any time, to conceive the non-existence of what we formerly conceived to exist; nor can the mind ever lie under a necessity of supposing any object to remain always in being; in the same manner as we lie under a necessity of always conceiving twice two to be four. The words, therefore, *necessary existence* have no meaning or, which is the same thing, none that is consistent.

But further, why may not the material universe be the necessarily existent Being, according to this pretended explication of necessity? We dare not affirm that we know all the qualities of matter; and, for aught we can determine, it may contain some qualities which, were they known, would make its non-existence appear as great a contradiction as that twice two is five. I find only one argument employed to prove that the material world is not the necessarily existent Being; and this argument is derived from the contingency both of the matter and the form of the world. "Any particle of matter," it is said, "may be *conceived* to be annihilated, and any form may be *conceived* to be altered. Such an annihilation or alteration, therefore, is not impossible." [1] But it seems a great partiality not to perceive that the same argument extends equally to the Deity, so far as we have any conception of him, and that the mind can at least imagine him to be non-existent or his attributes to be altered. It must be some unknown, inconceivable qualities which can make his non-existence appear impossible or his attributes unalterable; and no reason can be assigned why these qualities may not belong to matter. As they are altogether unknown and inconceivable, they can never be proved incompatible with it.

Add to this that in tracing an eternal succession of objects it seems absurd to inquire for a general cause or first author. How can anything that exists from eternity have a cause, since that relation implies a priority in time and a beginning of existence?

In such a chain, too, or succession of objects, each part is caused by that which preceded it, and causes that which succeeds it. Where then is the difficulty? But the *whole*, you say, wants a cause. I answer that the uniting of these parts into a whole, like the uniting of several distinct countries into one kingdom, or several distinct members into one body, is performed merely by an arbitrary act of the mind, and has no influence on the nature of things. Did I show you the particular causes of each individual in a collection of twenty particles of matter, I should think it very unreasonable should you afterwards ask me what was the cause of the whole twenty. This is sufficiently explained in explaining the cause of the parts.

Though the reasonings which you have urged, Cleanthes, may well excuse me, said Philo, from starting any further difficulties, yet I cannot forbear insisting still upon another topic. It is observed by arithmeticians that the products of 9 compose always either 9 or some lesser product of 9 if you add together all the characters of which any of the former products is composed. Thus, of 18, 27, 36, which are products

---

[1] Dr. Clarke.

of 9, you make 9 by adding 1 to 8, 2 to 7, 3 to 6. Thus 369 is a product also of 9; and if you add 3, 6, and 9, you make 18, a lesser product of 9.[2] To a superficial observer so wonderful a regularity may be admired as the effect either of chance or design; but a skilful algebraist immediately concludes it to be the work of necessity, and demonstrates that it must for ever result from the nature of these numbers. Is it not probable, I ask, that the whole economy of the universe is conducted by a like necessity, though no human algebra can furnish a key which solves the difficulty? And instead of admiring the order of natural beings, may it not happen that, could we penetrate into the intimate nature of bodies, we should clearly see why it was absolutely impossible they could ever admit of any other disposition? So dangerous is it to introduce this idea of necessity into the present question! and so naturally does it afford an inference directly opposite to the religious hypothesis!

But dropping all these abstractions, continued Philo, and confining ourselves to more familiar topics, I shall venture to add an observation that the argument *a priori* has seldom been found very convincing, except to people of a metaphysical head who have accustomed themselves to abstract reasoning, and who, finding from mathematics that the understanding frequently leads to truth through obscurity, and contrary to first appearances, have transferred the same habit of thinking to subjects where it ought not to have place. Other people, even of good sense and the best inclined to religion, feel always some deficiency in such arguments, though they are not perhaps able to explain distinctly where it lies—a certain proof that men ever did and ever will derive their religion from other sources than from this species of reasoning.

Part · X

It is my opinion, I own, replied Demea, that each man feels, in a manner, the truth of religion within his own breast, and, from a consciousness of his imbecility and misery rather than from any reasoning, is led to seek protection from that Being on whom he and all nature is dependent. So anxious or so tedious are even the best scenes of life that futurity is still the object of all our hopes and fears. We incessantly look forward and endeavour, by prayers, adoration, and sacrifice, to appease those unknown powers whom we find, by experience, so able to afflict and oppress us. Wretched creatures that we are! What resource for us amidst the innumerable ills of life did not religion suggest some methods of atonement, and appease those terrors with which we are incessantly agitated and tormented?

---

[2] *Republique des Lettres*, Aut 1685.

I am indeed persuaded, said Philo, that the best and indeed the only method of bringing everyone to a due sense of religion is by just representations of the misery and wickedness of men. And for that purpose a talent of eloquence and strong imagery is more requisite than that of reasoning and argument. For is it necessary to prove what everyone feels within himself? It is only necessary to make us feel it, if possible, more intimately and sensibly.

The people, indeed, replied Demea, are sufficiently convinced of this great and melancholy truth. The miseries of life, the unhappiness of man, the general corruptions of our nature, the unsatisfactory enjoyment of pleasures, riches, honours—these phrases have become almost proverbial in all languages. And who can doubt of what all men declare from their own immediate feeling and experience?

In this point, said Philo, the learned are perfectly agreed with the vulgar; and in all letters, *sacred* and *profane*, the topic of human misery has been insisted on with the most pathetic eloquence that sorrow and melancholy could inspire. The poets, who speak from sentiment, without a system, and whose testimony has therefore the more authority, abound in images of this nature. From Homer down to Dr. Young, the whole inspired tribe have ever been sensible that no other representation of things would suit the feeling and observation of each individual.

As to authorities, replied Demea, you need not seek them. Look round this library of Cleanthes. I shall venture to affirm that, except authors of particular sciences, such as chemistry or botany, who have no occasion to treat of human life, there is scarce one of those innumerable writers from whom the sense of human misery has not, in some passage or other, extorted a complaint and confession of it. At least, the chance is entirely on that side; and no one author has ever, so far as I can recollect, been so extravagant as to deny it.

There you must excuse me, said Philo: Leibniz has denied it, and is perhaps the first [1] who ventured upon so bold and paradoxical an opinion; at least, the first who made it essential to his philosophical system.

And by being the first, replied Demea, might he not have been sensible of his error? For is this a subject in which philosophers can propose to make discoveries especially in so late an age? And can any man hope by a simple denial (for the subject scarcely admits of reasoning) to bear down the united testimony of mankind, founded on sense and consciousness?

And why should man, added he, pretend to an exemption from the lot of all other animals? The whole earth, believe me, Philo, is cursed

---

[1] That sentiment had been maintained by Dr. King and some few others before Leibniz, though by none of so great fame as that German philosopher.

and polluted. A perpetual war is kindled amongst all living creatures. Necessity, hunger, want stimulate the strong and courageous; fear, anxiety, terror agitate the weak and infirm. The first entrance into life gives anguish to the new-born infant and to its wretched parent; weakness, impotence, distress attend each stage of that life, and it is, at last, finished in agony and horror.

Observe, too, says Philo, the curious artifices of nature in order to embitter the life of every living being. The stronger prey upon the weaker and keep them in perpetual terror and anxiety. The weaker, too, in their turn, often prey upon the stronger, and vex and molest them without relaxation. Consider that innumerable race of insects, which either are bred on the body of each animal or, flying about, infix their stings in him. These insects have others still less than themselves which torment them. And thus on each hand, before and behind, above and below, every animal is surrounded with enemies which incessantly seek his misery and destruction.

Man alone, said Demea, seems to be, in part, an exception to this rule. For by combination in society he can easily master lions, tigers, and bears, whose greater strength and agility naturally enable them to prey upon him.

On the contrary, it is here chiefly, cried Philo, that the uniform and equal maxims of nature are most apparent. Man, it is true, can, by combination, surmount all his *real* enemies and become master of the whole animal creation; but does he not immediately raise up to himself *imaginary* enemies, the demons of his fancy, who haunt him with superstitious terrors and blast every enjoyment of life? His pleasure, as he imagines, becomes in their eyes a crime; his food and repose give them umbrage and offence; his very sleep and dreams furnish new materials to anxious fear; and even death, his refuge from every other ill, presents only the dread of endless and innumerable woes. Nor does the wolf molest more the timid flock than superstition does the anxious breast of wretched mortals.

Besides, consider, Demea: This very society by which we surmount those wild beasts, our natural enemies, what new enemies does it not raise to us? What woe and misery does it not occasion? Man is the greatest enemy of man. Oppression, injustice, contempt, contumely, violence, sedition, war, calumny, treachery, fraud—by these they mutually torment each other, and they would soon dissolve that society which they had formed were it not for the dread of still greater ills which must attend their separation.

But though these external insults, said Demea, from animals, from men, from all the elements, which assault us from a frightful catalogue of woes, they are nothing in comparison of those which arise within ourselves, from the distempered condition of our mind and body. How many lie under the lingering torment of diseases? Hear the pathetic enumeration of the great poet.

> Intestine stone and ulcer, colic-pangs,
> Demoniac frenzy, moping melancholy,
> And moon-struck madness, pining atrophy,
> Marasmus, and wide-wasting pestilence.
> Dire was the tossing, deep the groans: Despair
> Tended the sick, busiest from couch to couch.
> And over them triumphant Death his dart
> Shook: but delay'd to strike, though oft invok'd
> With vows, as their chief good and final hope.[2]

The disorders of the mind, continued Demea, though more secret, are not perhaps less dismal and vexatious. Remorse, shame, anguish, rage, disappointment, anxiety, fear, dejection, despair—who has ever passed through life without cruel inroads from these tormentors? How many have scarcely ever felt any better sensations? Labour and poverty, so abhorred by everyone, are the certain lot of the far greater number; and those few privileged persons who enjoy ease and opulence never reach contentment or true felicity. All the goods of life united would not make a very happy man, but all the ills united would make a wretch indeed; and any one of them almost (and who can be free from every one?), nay, often the absence of one good (and who can possess all?) is sufficient to render life ineligible.

Were a stranger to drop on a sudden into this world, I would show him, as a specimen of its ills, an hospital full of diseases, a prison crowded with malefactors and debtors, a field of battle strewed with carcases, a fleet foundering in the ocean, a nation languishing under tyranny, famine, or pestilence. To turn the gay side of life to him and give him a notion of its pleasures—whether should I conduct him? To a ball, to an opera, to court? He might justly think that I was only showing him a diversity of distress and sorrow.

There is no evading such striking instances, said Philo, but by apologies which still further aggravate the charge. Why have all men, I ask, in all ages, complained incessantly of the miseries of life? . . . They have no just reason, says one: these complaints proceed only from their discontented, repining, anxious disposition. . . . And can there possibly, I reply, be a more certain foundation of misery than such a wretched temper?

But if they were really as unhappy as they pretend, says my antagonist, why do they remain in life? . . .

---

[2] [Milton: Paradise Lost, Bk. XI.]

Not satisfied with life, afraid of death—

this is the secret chain, say I, that holds us. We are terrified, not bribed to the continuance of our existence.

It is only a false delicacy, he may insist, which a few refined spirits indulge, and which has spread these complaints among the whole race of mankind. . . . And what is this delicacy, I ask, which you blame? Is it anything but a greater sensibility to all the pleasures and pains of life? And if the man of a delicate, refined temper, by being so much more alive than the rest of the world, is only so much more unhappy, what judgment must we form in general of human life?

Let men remain at rest, says our adversary, and they will be easy. They are willing artificers of their own misery. . . . No! reply I: an anxious languor follows their repose; disappointment, vexation, trouble, their activity and ambition.

I can observe something like what you mention in some others, replied Cleanthes, but I confess I feel little or nothing of it in myself, and hope that it is not so common as you represent it.

If you feel not human misery yourself, cried Demea, I congratulate you on so happy a singularity. Others, seemingly the most propserous, have not been ashamed to vent their complaints in the most melancholy strains. Let us attend to the great, the fortunate emperor, Charles V, when, tired with human grandeur, he resigned all his extensive dominions into the hands of his son. In the last harangue which he made on that memorable occasion, he publicly avowed *that the greatest prosperities which he had ever enjoyed had been mixed with so many adversities that he might truly say he had never enjoyed any satisfaction or contentment.* But did the retired life in which he sought for shelter afford him any greater happiness? If we may credit his son's account, his repentance commenced the very day of his resignation.

Cicero's fortune, from small beginnings, rose to the greatest lustre and renown; yet what pathetic complaints of the ills of life do his familiar letters, as well as philosophical discourses, contain? And suitably to his own experience, he introduces Cato, the great, the fortunate Cato protesting in his old age that had he a new life in his offer he would reject the present.

Ask yourself, ask any of your acquaintance, whether they would live over again the last ten or twenty years of their life. No! but the next twenty, they say, will be better:

> *And from the dregs of life, hope to receive*
> *What the first sprightly running could not give.*[3]

---

[3] [John Dryden, *Aureng-Zebe*, Act IV, sc. 1.]

Thus, at last, they find (such is the greatness of human misery, it recon-
ciles even contradictions) that they complain at once of the shortness of
life and of its vanity and sorrow.

And is it possible, Cleanthes, said Philo, that after all these reflections, and infinitely more which might be suggested, you can still persevere in your anthropomorphism, and assert the moral attributes of the
Deity, his justice, benevolence, mercy, and rectitude, to be of the same
nature with these virtues in human creatures? His power, we allow, is
infinite; whatever he wills is executed; but neither man nor any other
animal is happy; therefore, he does not will their happiness. His wisdom
is infinite; he is never mistaken in choosing the means to any end; but
the course of nature tends not to human or animal felicity; therefore, it
is not established for that purpose. Through the whole compass of human knowledge there are no inferences more certain and infallible
than these. In what respect, then, do his benevolence and mercy resemble the benevolence and mercy of men?

Epicurus' old questions are yet unanswered.

Is he willing to prevent evil, but not able? then is he impotent. Is he
able, but not willing? then is he malevolent. Is he both able and willing?
whence then is evil?

You ascribe, Cleanthes, (and I believe justly) a purpose and intention to nature. But what, I beseech you, is the object of that curious artifice and machinery which she has displayed in all animals—the preservation alone of individuals, and propagation of the species? It seems
enough for her purpose, if such a rank be barely upheld in the universe,
without any care or concern for the happiness of the members that compose it. No resource for this purpose: no machinery in order merely to
give pleasure or ease; no fund of pure joy and contentment; no indulgence without some want or necessity accompanying it. At least, the few
phenomena of this nature are overbalanced by opposite phenomena of
still greater importance.

Our sense of music, harmony, and indeed beauty of all kinds, gives
satisfaction, without being absolutely necessary to the preservation and
propagation of the species. But what racking pains, on the other hand,
arise from gouts, gravels, megrims, toothaches, rheumatisms, where the
injury to the animal machinery is either small or incurable? Mirth,
laughter, play, frolic seem gratuitous satisfactions which have no further
tendency; spleen, melancholy, discontent, superstition are pains of the
same nature. How then does the Divine benevolence display itself, in
the sense of you anthropomorphites? None but we mystics, as you were
pleased to call us, can account for this strange mixture of phenomena, by
deriving it from attributes infinitely perfect but incomprehensible.

And have you, at last, said Cleanthes smiling, betrayed your intentions, Philo? Your long agreement with Demea did indeed a little surprise me, but I find you were all the while erecting a concealed battery against me. And I must confess that you have now fallen upon a subject worthy of your noble spirit of opposition and controversy. If you can make out the present point, and prove mankind to be unhappy or corrupted, there is an end at once of all religion. For to what purpose establish the natural attributes of the Deity, while the moral are still doubtful and uncertain?

You take umbrage very easily, replied Demea, at opinions the most innocent and the most generally received, even amongst the religious and devout themselves; and nothing can be more surprising than to find a topic like this—concerning the wickedness and misery of man— charged with no less than atheism and profaneness. Have not all pious divines and preachers who have indulged their rhetoric on so fertile a subject, have they not easily, I say, given a solution of any difficulties which may attend it? This world is but a point in comparison of the universe; this life but a moment in comparison of eternity. The present evil phenomena, therefore, are rectified in other regions, and in some future period of existence. And the eyes of men, being then opened to larger views of things, see the whole connection of general laws, and trace, with adoration, the benevolence and rectitude of the Deity through all the mazes and intricacies of his providence.

No! replied Cleanthes, no! These arbitrary suppositions can never be admitted, contrary to matter of fact, visible and uncontroverted. Whence can any cause be known but from its known effects? Whence can any hypothesis be proved but from the apparent phenomena? To establish one hypothesis upon another is building entirely in the air; and the utmost we ever attain by these conjectures and fictions is to ascertain the bare possibility of our opinion, but never can we, upon such term, establish its reality.

The only method of supporting Divine benevolence—and it is what I willingly embrace—is to deny absolutely the misery and wickedness of man. Your representations are exaggerated; your melancholy views mostly fictitious; your inferences contrary to fact and experience. Health is more common than sickness; pleasure than pain; happiness than misery. And for one vexation which we meet with, we attain, upon computation, a hundred enjoyments.

Admitting your position, replied Philo, which yet is extremely doubtful, you must at the same time allow that, if pain be less frequent than pleasure, it is infinitely more violent and durable. One hour of it is often able to outweigh a day, a week, a month of our common insipid enjoyments; and how many days, weeks, and months are passed by several in the most acute torments? Pleasure, scarcely in one instance, is ever able to reach ecstasy and rapture; and in no one instance can it continue for any time at its highest pitch and altitude. The spirits evaporate, the nerves relax, the fabric is disordered, and the enjoyment quickly degenerates into fatigue and uneasiness. But pain often, good God, how often! rises to torture and agony; and the longer it continues, it becomes still more genuine agony and torture. Patience is exhausted, courage languishes, melancholy seizes us, and nothing terminates our misery but the removal of its cause or another event which is the sole cure of all evil, but which, from our natural folly, we regard with still greater horror and consternation.

But not to insist upon these topics, continued Philo, though most obvious, certain, and important, I must use the freedom to admonish you, Cleanthes, that you have put the controversy upon a most dangerous issue, and are unawares introducing a total scepticism into the most essential articles of natural and revealed theology. What! no method of fixing a just foundation for religion unless we allow the happiness of human life, and maintain a continued existence even in this world, with all our present pains, infirmities, vexations, and follies, to be eligible and desirable! But this is contrary to everyone's feeling and experience; it is contrary to an authority so established as nothing can subvert. No decisive proofs can ever be produced against this authority; nor is it possible for you to compute, estimate, and compare all the pains and all the pleasures in the lives of all men and of all animals; and thus, by your resting the whole system of religion on a point which, from its very nature, must for ever be uncertain, you tacitly confess that that system is equally uncertain.

But allowing you what never will be believed, at least, what you never possibly can prove, that animal or, at least, human happiness in this life exceeds its misery, you have yet done nothing; for this is not, by any means, what we expect from infinite power, infinite wisdom, and infinite goodness. Why is there any misery at all in the world? Not by chance, surely. From some cause then. Is it from the intention of the Deity? But he is perfectly benevolent. Is it contrary to his intention? But he is almighty. Nothing can shake the solidity of this reasoning, so short, so clear, so decisive, except we assert that these subjects exceed all human capacity, and that our common measures of truth and falsehood are not applicable to them—a topic which I have all along insisted on, but which you have, from the beginning, rejected with scorn and indignation.

But I will be contented to retire still from this intrenchment, for I deny that you can ever force me in it. I will allow that pain or misery in man is *compatible* with infinite power and goodness in the Deity, even in your sense of these attributes: what are you advanced by all these concessions? A mere possible compatibility is not sufficient. You must *prove* these pure, unmixt, and uncontrollable attributes from the present mixed and confused phenomena, and from these alone. A hopeful undertaking! Were the phenomena ever so pure and unmixed, yet, being finite, they would be insufficient for that purpose. How much more, where they are also so jarring and discordant!

Here, Cleanthes, I find myself at ease in my argument. Here I triumph. Formerly, when we argued concerning the natural attributes of intelligence and design, I needed all my sceptical and metaphysical subtilty to elude your grasp. In many views of the universe and of its parts, particularly the latter, the beauty and fitness of final causes strike us with such irresistible force that all objections appear (what I believe they really are) mere cavils and sophisms; nor can we then imagine how it was ever possible for us to repose any weight on them. But there is no view of human life or of the condition of mankind from which, without the greatest violence, we can infer the moral attributes or learn that infinite benevolence, conjoined with infinite power and infinite wisdom, which we must discover by the eyes of faith alone. It is your turn now to tug the labouring oar, and to support your philosophical subtilties against the dictates of plain reason and experience.

Part · X I

I scruple not to allow, said Cleanthes, that I have been apt to suspect the frequent repetition of the word *infinite*, which we meet with in all theological writers, to savour more of panegyric than of philosophy, and that any purposes of reasoning, and even of religion, would be better served were we to rest contented with more accurate and more moderate expressions. The terms *admirable, excellent, superlatively great, wise,* and *holy*—these sufficiently fill the imaginations of men, and anything beyond, besides that it leads into absurdities, has no influence on the affections or sentiments. Thus, in the present subject, if we abandon all human analogy, as seems your intention, Demea, I am afraid we abandon all religion and retain no conception of the great object of our adoration. If we preserve human analogy, we must forever find it impossible to reconcile any mixture of evil in the universe with infinite attributes; much less can we ever prove the latter from the former. But supposing the Author of nature to be finitely perfect, though far exceeding mankind, a satisfactory account may then be given of natural and moral evil, and every untoward phenomenon be explained and adjusted. A less evil may then be chosen in order to avoid a greater; inconveniences be submitted to in order to reach a desirable end; and, in a word, benevolence, regulated by wisdom and limited by necessity, may produce just such a world as the present. You, Philo, who are so prompt at starting views and reflections and analogies, I would gladly hear, at length, without interruption, your opinion of this new theory; and if it deserve our attention, we may afterwards, at more leisure, reduce it into form.

My sentiments, replied Philo, are not worthy being made a mystery of; and, therefore, without any ceremony, I shall deliver what occurs to me with regard to the present subject. It must, I think, be allowed that, if a very limited intelligence whom we shall suppose utterly unacquainted with the universe were assured that it were the production of a very good, wise, and powerful Being, however finite, he would, from his conjectures, form *beforehand* a different notion of it from what we find it to be by experience; nor would he ever imagine, merely from these attributes of the cause of which he is informed, that the effect could be so full of vice and misery and disorder, as it appears in this life. Supposing now that this person were brought into the world, still assured that it was the workmanship of such a sublime and benevolent Being, he might, perhaps, be surprised at the disappointment, but would never retract his former belief if founded on any very solid argument, since such a limited intelligence must be sensible of his own blindness and ignorance, and must allow that there may be many solutions of those phenomena which will for ever escape his comprehension. But supposing, which is the real case with regard to man, that this creature is not antecedently convinced of a supreme intelligence, benevolent, and powerful, but is left to gather such a belief from the appearances of things—this entirely alters the case, nor will he ever find any reason for such a conclusion. He may be fully convinced of the narrow limits of his understanding, but this will not help him in forming an inference concerning the goodness of superior powers, since he must form that inference from what he knows, not from what he is ignorant of. The more you exaggerate his weakness and ignorance, the more diffident you render him, and give him the greater suspicion that such subjects are beyond the reach of his faculties. You are obliged, therefore, to reason with him merely from the known phenomena, and to drop every arbitrary supposition or conjecture.

Did I show you a house or palace where there was not one apartment convenient or agreeable, where the windows, doors, fires, passages, stairs, and the whole economy of the building were the source of noise, confusion, fatigue, darkness, and the extremes of heat and cold, you would certainly blame the contrivance, without any further examination. The architect would in vain display his subtilty, and prove to you that, if this door or that window were altered, greater ills would ensue.

What he says may be strictly true: the alteration of one particular, while the other parts of the building remain, may only augment the inconveniences. But still you would assert in general that, if the architect had had skill and good intentions, he might have formed such a plan of the whole, and might have adjusted the parts in such a manner as would have remedied all or most of these inconveniences. His ignorance, or even your own ignorance of such a plan, will never convince you of the impossibility of it. If you find any inconveniences and deformities in the building, you will always, without entering into any detail, condemn the architect.

In short, I repeat the question: Is the world considered in general and as it appears to us in this life, different from what a man or such a limited being would, *beforehand*, expect from a very powerful, wise, and benevolent Deity? It must be strange prejudice to assert the contrary. And from thence I conclude that, however consistent the world may be, allowing certain suppositions and conjectures with the idea of such a Deity, it can never afford us an inference concerning his existence. The consistency is not absolutely denied, only the inference. Conjectures, especially where infinity is excluded from the Divine attributes, may perhaps be sufficient to prove a consistency, but can never be foundations for any inference.

There seem to be *four* circumstances on which depend all or the greatest part of the ills that molest sensible creatures; and it is not impossible but all these circumstances may be necessary and unavoidable. We know so little beyond common life, or even of common life, that, with regard to the economy of a universe, there is no conjecture, however wild, which may not be just, nor any one, however plausible, which may not be erroneous. All that belongs to human understanding, in this deep ignorance and obscurity, is to be sceptical or at least cautious, and not to admit of any hypothesis whatever, much less of any which is supported by no appearance of probability. Now this I assert to be the case with regard to all the causes of evil and the circumstances on which it depends. None of them appear to human reason in the least degree necessary or unavoidable, nor can we suppose them such, without the utmost license of imagination.

The *first* circumstance which introduces evil is that contrivance or economy of the animal creation by which pains, as well as pleasures, are employed to excite all creatures to action, and make them vigilant in the great work of self-preservation. Now pleasure alone, in its various degrees, seems to human understanding sufficient for this purpose. All animals might be constantly in a state of enjoyment; but when urged by any of the necessities of nature, such as thirst, hunger, weariness, instead of pain, they might feel a diminution of pleasure by which they might be prompted to seek that object which is necessary to their subsistence. Men pursue pleasure as eagerly as they avoid pain; at least, they might have been so constituted. It seems, therefore, plainly possible to carry on the business of life without any pain. Why then is any animal ever rendered susceptible of such a sensation? If animals can be free from it an hour, they might enjoy a perpetual exemption from it, and it required as particular a contrivance of their organs to produce that feeling as to endow them with sight, hearing, or any of the senses. Shall we conjecture that such a contrivance was necessary, without any appearance of reason, and shall we build on that conjecture as on the most certain truth?

But a capacity of pain would not alone produce pain were it not for the *second* circumstance, viz., the conducting of the world by general laws; and this seems nowise necessary to a very perfect Being. It is true, if everything were conducted by particular volitions, the course of nature would be perpetually broken, and no man could employ his reason in the conduct of life. But might not other particular volitions remedy this inconvenience? In short, might not the Deity exterminate all ill, wherever it were to be found, and produce all good, without any preparation or long progress of causes and effects?

Besides, we must consider that, according to the present economy of the world, the course of nature, though supposed exactly regular, yet to us appears not so, and many events are uncertain, and many disappoint our expectations. Health and sickness, calm and tempest, with an infinite number of other accidents whose causes are unknown and variable, have a great influence both on the fortunes of particular persons and on the prosperity of public societies; and indeed all human life, in a manner, depends on such accidents. A being, therefore, who knows the secret springs of the universe might easily, by particular volitions, turn all these accidents to the good of mankind and render the whole world happy, without discovering himself in any operation. A fleet whose purposes were salutary to society might always meet with a fair wind. Good princes enjoy sound health and long life. Persons born to power and authority be framed with good tempers and virtuous dispositions. A few such events as these, regularly and wisely conducted, would change the face of the world, and yet would no more seem to disturb the course of nature or confound human conduct than the present economy of things where the causes are secret and variable and compounded. Some small touches given to Caligula's brain in his infancy might have converted him into a Trajan. One wave, a little higher than the rest, by burying Caesar and his fortune in the bottom of the ocean, might have restored liberty to a considerable part of mankind. There may, for aught we know, be good reasons why

Providence interposes not in this manner, but they are unknown to us; and, though the mere supposition that such reasons exist may be sufficient to *save* the conclusion concerning the Divine attributes, yet surely it can never be sufficient to *establish* that conclusion.

If everything in the universe be conducted by general laws, and if animals be rendered susceptible of pain, it scarcely seems possible but some ill must arise in the various shocks of matter and the various concurrence and opposition of general laws; but this ill would be very rare were it not for the *third* circumstance which I proposed to mention, viz., the great frugality with which all powers and faculties are distributed to every particular being. So well adjusted are the organs and capacities of all animals, and so well fitted to their preservation, that, as far as history or tradition reaches, there appears not to be any single species which has yet been extinguished in the universe. Every animal has the requisite endowments, but these endowments are bestowed with so scrupulous an economy that any considerable diminution must entirely destroy the creature. Wherever one power is increased, there is a proportional abatement in the others. Animals which excel in swiftness are commonly defective in force. Those which possess both are either imperfect in some of their senses or are oppressed with the most craving wants. The human species, whose chief excellence is reason and sagacity, is of all others the most necessitous, and the most deficient in bodily advantages, without clothes, without arms, without food, without lodging, without any convenience of life, except what they owe to their own skill and industry. In short, nature seems to have formed an exact calculation of the necessities of her creatures, and, like a *rigid master,* has afforded them little more powers or endowments than what are strictly sufficient to supply those necessities. An *indulgent parent* would have bestowed a large stock in order to guard against accidents, and secure the happiness and welfare of the creature in the most unfortunate concurrence of circumstances. Every course of life would not have been so surrounded with precipices that the least departure from the true path, by mistake or necessity, must involve us in misery and ruin. Some reserve, some fund, would have been provided to ensure happiness, nor would the powers and the necessities have been adjusted with so rigid an economy. The Author of nature is inconceivably powerful; his force is supposed great, if not altogether inexhaustible, nor is there any reason, as far as we can judge, to make him observe this strict frugality in his dealings with his creatures. It would have been better, were his power extremely limited, to have created fewer animals, and to have endowed these with more faculties for their happiness and preservation. A builder is never esteemed prudent who undertakes a plan beyond what his stock will enable him to finish.

In order to cure most of the ills of human life, I require not that man should have the wings of the eagle, the swiftness of the stag, the force of the ox, the arms of the lion, the scales of the crocodile or rhinoceros; much less do I demand the sagacity of an angel or cherubim. I am contented to take an increase in one single power or faculty of his soul. Let him be endowed with a greater propensity to industry and labour, a more vigorous spring and activity of mind, a more constant bent to business and application. Let the whole species possess naturally an equal diligence with that which many individuals are able to attain by habit and reflection, and the most beneficial consequences, without any allay of ill, is the immediate and necessary result of this endowment. Almost all the moral as well as natural evils of human life arise from idleness; and were our species, by the original constitution of their frame, exempt from this vice or infirmity, the perfect cultivation of land, the improvement of arts and manufactures, the exact execution of every office and duty, immediately follow; and men at once may fully reach that state of society which is so imperfectly attained by the best regulated government. But as industry is a power, and the most valuable of any, nature seems determined, suitably to her usual maxims, to bestow it on men with a very sparing hand, and rather to punish him severely for his deficiency in it than to reward him for his attainments. She has so contrived his frame that nothing but the most violent necessity can oblige him to labour; and she employs all his other wants to overcome, at least in part, the want of diligence, and to endow him with some share of a faculty of which she has thought fit naturally to bereave him. Here our demands may be allowed very humble, and therefore the more reasonable. If we required the endowments of superior penetration and judgment, of a more delicate taste of beauty, of a nicer sensibility to benevolence and friendship, we might be told that we impiously pretend to break the order of nature, that we want to exalt ourselves into a higher rank of being, that the presents which we require, not being suitable to our state and condition, would only be pernicious to us. But it is hard, I dare to repeat it, it is hard that, being placed in a world so full of wants and necessities, where almost every being and element is either our foe or refuses its assistance . . . we should also have our own temper to struggle with, and should be deprived of that faculty which can alone fence against these multiplied evils.

The *fourth* circumstance whence arises the misery and ill of the universe is the inaccurate workmanship of all the springs and principles of the great machine of nature. It must be acknowledged that there are few parts of the universe which seem not to serve some purpose, and whose removal would not produce a visible defect and disorder in the whole. The parts hang all together, nor can one be touched without affecting the rest, in a greater or less degree. But at the same time, it must be observed that none of these parts or principles, however useful, are so accurately adjusted as to keep precisely within those bounds in which their utility consists; but they are, all of them, apt, on every occasion, to run into the one extreme or the other. One would imagine that this grand production had not received the last hand of the maker—so little finished is every part, and so coarse are the strokes with which it is executed. Thus the winds are requisite to convey the vapours along the surface of the globe, and to assist men in navigation; but how often, rising up to tempests and hurricanes, do they become pernicious? Rains are necessary to nourish all the plants and animals of the earth; but how often are they defective? how often excessive? Heat is requisite to all life and vegetation, but is not always found in the due proportion. On the mixture and secretion of the humours and juices of the body depend the health and prosperity of the animal; but the parts perform not regularly their proper function. What more useful than all the passions of the mind, ambition, vanity, love, anger? But how often do they break their bounds and cause the greatest convulsions in society? There is nothing so advantageous in the universe but what frequently becomes pernicious, by its excess or defect; nor has nature guarded, with the requisite accuracy, against all disorder or confusion. The irregularity is never perhaps so great as to destroy any species, but is often sufficient to involve the individuals in ruin and misery.

On the concurrence, then, of these *four* circumstances does all or the greatest part of natural evil depend. Were all living creatures incapable of pain, or were the world administered by particular volitions, evil never could have found access into the universe; and were animals endowed with a large stock of powers and faculties, beyond what strict necessity requires, or were the several springs and principles of the universe so accurately framed as to preserve always the just temperament and medium, there must have been very little ill in comparison of what we feel at present. What then shall we pronounce on this occasion? Shall we say that these circumstances are not necessary, and that they might easily have been altered in the contrivance of the universe? This decision seems too presumptuous for creatures so blind and ignorant. Let us be more modest in our conclusions. Let us allow that, if the goodness of the Deity (I mean a goodness like the human) could be established on any tolerable reasons *a priori*, these phenomena, however untoward, would not be sufficient to subvert that principle, but might easily, in some unknown manner, be reconcilable to it. But let us still assert that, as this goodness is not antecedently established but must be inferred from the phenomena, there can be no grounds for such an inference while there are so many ills in the universe, and while these ills might so easily have been remedied, as far as human understanding can be allowed to judge on such a subject. I am sceptic enough to allow that the bad appearances, notwithstanding all my reasonings, may be compatible with such attributes as you suppose, but surely they can never prove these attributes. Such a conclusion cannot result from scepticism, but must arise from the phenomena, and from our confidence in the reasonings which we deduce from these phenomena.

Look round this universe. What an immense profusion of beings, animated and organized, sensible and active! You admire this prodigious variety and fecundity. But inspect a little more narrowly these living existences, the only beings worth regarding. How hostile and destructive to each other! How insufficient all of them for their own happiness! How contemptible or odious to the spectator! The whole presents nothing but the idea of a blind nature, impregnated by a great vivifying principle, and pouring forth from her lap, without discernment or parental care, her maimed and abortive children!

Here the Manichaean system occurs as a proper hypothesis to solve the difficulty; and, no doubt, in some respects it is very specious and has more probability than the common hypothesis, by giving a plausible account of the strange mixture of good and ill which appears in life. But if we consider, on the other hand, the perfect uniformity and agreement of the parts of the universe, we shall not discover in it any marks of the combat of a malevolent with a benevolent being. There is indeed an opposition of pains and pleasures in the feelings of sensible creatures; but are not all the operations of nature carried on by an opposition of principles, of hot and cold, moist and dry, light and heavy? The true conclusion is that the original Source of all things is entirely indifferent to all these principles, and has no more regard to good above ill than to heat above cold, or to drought above moisture, or to light above heavy.

There may *four* hypotheses be framed concerning the first causes of the universe: that they are endowed with perfect goodness; that they have perfect malice; that they are opposite and have both goodness and malice; that they have neither goodness nor malice. Mixed phenomena can never prove the two former unmixed principles; and the uniformity and steadiness of general laws seem to oppose the third. The fourth, therefore, seems by far the most probable.

What I have said concerning natural evil will apply to moral with little or no variation; and we have no more reason to infer that the rectitude of the Supreme Being resembles human rectitude than that his benevolence resembles the human. Nay, it will be thought that we have still greater cause to exclude from him moral sentiments, such as we feel them, since moral evil, in the opinion of many, is much more predominant above moral good than natural evil above natural good.

But even though this should not be allowed, and though the virtue which is in mankind should be acknowledged much superior to the vice, yet, so long as there is any vice at all in the universe, it will very much puzzle you anthropomorphites how to account for it. You must assign a cause for it, without having recourse to the first cause. But as every effect must have a cause, and that cause another, you must either carry on the progression *in infinitum* or rest on that original principle, who is the ultimate cause of all things. . . .

Hold! hold! cried Demea: Whither does your imagination hurry you? I joined in alliance with you in order to prove the incomprehensible nature of the Divine Being, and refute the principles of Cleanthes, who would measure everything by human rule and standard. But I now find you running into all the topics of the greatest libertines and infidels, and betraying that holy cause which you seemingly espoused. Are you secretly, then, a more dangerous enemy than Cleanthes himself?

And are you so late in perceiving it? replied Cleanthes. Believe me, Demea, your friend Philo, from the beginning, has been amusing himself at both our expense; and it must be confessed that the injudicious reasoning of our vulgar theology has given him but too just a handle of ridicule. The total infirmity of human reason, the absolute incomprehensibility of the Divine Nature, the great and universal misery, and still greater wickedness of men—these are strange topics, surely, to be so fondly cherished by orthodox divines and doctors. In ages of stupidity and ignorance, indeed, these principles may safely be espoused; and perhaps no views of things are more proper to promote superstition than such as encourage the blind amazement, the diffidence, and melancholy of mankind. But at present . . .

Blame not so much, interposed Philo, the ignorance of these reverend gentlemen. They know how to change their style with the times. Formerly, it was a most popular theological topic to maintain that human life was vanity and misery, and to exaggerate all the ills and pains which are incident to men. But of late years, divines, we find, begin to retract this position and maintain, though still with some hesitation, that there are more goods than evils, more pleasures than pains, even in this life. When religion stood entirely upon temper and education, it was thought proper to encourage melancholy, as, indeed, mankind never have recourse to superior powers so readily as in that disposition. But as men have now learned to form principles and to draw consequences, it is necessary to change the batteries, and to make use of such arguments as will endure at least some scrutiny and examination. This variation is the same (and from the same causes) with that which I formerly remarked with regard to scepticism.

Thus Philo continued to the last his spirit of opposition, and his censure of established opinions. But I could observe that Demea did not at all relish the latter part of the discourse; and he took occasion soon after, on some pretence or other, to leave the company.

Part · XII

After Demea's departure, Cleanthes and Philo continued the conversation in the following manner. Our friend, I am afraid, said Cleanthes, will have little inclination to revive this topic of discourse while you are in company; and to tell the truth, Philo, I should rather wish to reason with either of you apart on a subject so sublime and interesting. Your spirit of controversy, joined to your abhorence of vulgar superstition, carries you strange lengths when engaged in an argument; and there is nothing so sacred and venerable, even in your own eyes, which you spare on that occasion.

I must confess, replied Philo, that I am less cautious on the subject of Natural Religion than on any other; both because I know that I can never, on that head, corrupt the principles of any man of common sense and because no one, I am confident, in whose eyes I appear a man of common sense will ever mistake my intentions. You, in particular, Cleanthes, with whom I live in unreserved intimacy, you are sensible that, notwithstanding the freedom of my conversation and my love of singular arguments, no one has a deeper sense of religion impressed on his mind, or pays more profound adoration to the Divine Being, as he discovers himself to reason in the inexplicable contrivance and artifice of nature. A purpose, an intention, a design strikes everywhere the most careless, the most stupid thinker; and no man can be so hardened in absurd systems as at all times to reject it. *That nature does nothing in vain* is a maxim established in all the schools, merely from the contemplation of the works of nature, without any religious purpose; and, from a firm conviction of its truth, an anatomist who had observed a new organ or canal would never be satisfied till he had also discovered its use and intention. One great foundation of the Copernican system is the maxim *that nature acts by the simplest methods, and chooses the most proper means to any end;* and astronomers often, without thinking of it, lay this strong foundation of piety and religion. The same thing is observable in other parts of philosophy; and thus all the sciences almost lead us insensibly to acknowledge a first intelligent Author; and their authority is often so much the greater as they do not directly profess that intention.

It is with pleasure I hear Galen reason concerning the structure of the human body. The anatomy of a man, says he,[1] discovers above 600 different muscles; and whoever duly considers these will find that, in each of them, nature must have adjusted at least ten different circumstances in order to attain the end which she proposed: proper figure, just magnitude, right disposition of the several ends, upper and lower position of the whole, the due insertion of the several nerves, veins, and arteries, so that, in the muscles alone, above 6000 several views and intentions must have been formed and executed. The bones he calculates to be 284; the distinct purposes aimed at in the structure of each above forty. What a prodigious display of artifice, even in these simple and homogeneous parts! But if we consider the skin, ligaments, vessels, glandules, humours, the several limbs and members of the body, how must our astonishment rise upon us, in proportion to the number and intricacy of the parts so artificially adjusted! The further we advance in these researches, we discover new scenes of art and wisdom; but descry still, at a distance, further scenes beyond our reach: in the fine internal structure of the parts, in the economy of the brain, in the fabric of the seminal vessels. All these artifices are repeated in every different species of animal, with wonderful variety, and with exact propriety, suited to the different intentions of nature in framing each species. And if the infidelity of Galen, even when these natural sciences were still imperfect, could not withstand such striking appearances, to what pitch of pertinacious obstinacy must a philosopher in this age have attained who can now doubt of a Supreme Intelligence!

Could I meet with one of this species (who, I thank God, are very rare), I would ask him: Supposing there were a God who did not discover himself immediately to our senses, were it possible for him to give stronger proofs of his existence than what appear on the whole face of nature? What indeed could such a Divine Being do but copy the present economy of things, render many of his artifices so plain that no stupidity could mistake them, afford glimpses of still greater artifices which demonstrate his prodigious superiority above our narrow apprehensions, and conceal altogether a great many from such imperfect creatures? Now, according to all rules of just reasoning, every fact must pass for undisputed when it is supported by all the arguments which its nature admits of, even though these arguments be not, in themselves, very numerous or forcible—how much more in the present case where no human imagination can compute their number, and no understanding estimate their cogency!

I shall further add, said Cleanthes, to what you have so well urged, that one great advantage of the principle of theism is that it is the only

---

[1] *De Formatione Fœtus.*

system of cosmogony which can be rendered intelligible and complete, and yet can throughout preserve a strong analogy to what we every day see and experience in the world. The comparison of the universe to a machine of human contrivance is so obvious and natural, and is justified by so many instances of order and design in nature, that it must immediately strike all unprejudiced apprehensions and procure universal approbation. Whoever attempts to weaken this theory cannot pretend to succeed by establishing in its place any other that is precise and determinate; it is sufficient for him if he start doubts and difficulties, and, by remote and abstract views of things, reach that suspense of judgment which is here the utmost boundary of his wishes. But, besides that this state of mind is in itself unsatisfactory, it can never be steadily maintained against such striking appearances as continually engage us into the religious hypothesis. A false, absurd system, human nature, from the force of prejudice, is capable of adhering to with obstinacy and perseverance; but no system at all, in opposition to a theory supported by strong and obvious reason, by natural propensity, and by early education, I think it absolutely impossible to maintain or defend.

So little, replied Philo, do I esteem this suspense of judgment in the present case to be possible that I am apt to suspect there enters somewhat of a dispute of words into this controversy, more than is usually imagined. That the works of nature bear a great analogy to the productions of art is evident, and, according to all the rules of good reasoning, we ought to infer, if we argue at all concerning them, that their causes have a proportional analogy. But as there are also considerable differences, we have reason to suppose a proportional difference in the causes, and, in particular, ought to attribute a much higher degree of power and energy to the supreme cause than any we have ever observed in mankind. Here, then, the existence of a *Deity* is plainly ascertained by reason; and if we make it a question whether on account of these analogies, we can properly call him a *mind* or *intelligence*, notwithstanding the vast difference which may reasonably be supposed between him and human minds, what is this but a mere verbal controversy? No man can deny the analogies between the effects; to restrain ourselves from inquiring concerning the causes is scarcely possible. From this inquiry the legitimate conclusion is that the causes have also an analogy; and if we are not contented with calling the first and supreme cause a *God* or *Deity*, but desire to vary the expression, what can we call him but *Mind* or *Thought* to which he is justly supposed to bear a considerable resemblance?

All men of sound reason are disgusted with verbal disputes, which abound so much in philosophical and theological inquiries; and it is found that the only remedy for this abuse must arise from clear definitions, from the precision of those ideas which enter into any argument, and from the strict and uniform use of those terms which are employed. But there is a species of controversy which, from the very nature of language and of human ideas, is involved in perpetual ambiguity, and can never, by any precaution or any definitions, be able to reach a reasonable certainty or precision. These are the controversies concerning the degrees of any quality or circumstance. Men may argue to all eternity whether Hannibal be a great, or a very great, or a superlatively great man, what degree of beauty Cleopatra possessed, what epithet of praise Livy or Thucydides is entitled to, without bringing the controversy to any determination. The disputants may here agree in their sense and differ in the terms, or *vice versa*, yet never be able to define their terms so as to enter into each other's meaning; because the degrees of these qualities are not, like quantity or number, susceptible of any exact mensuration, which may be the standard in the controversy. That the dispute concerning theism is of this nature, and consequently is merely verbal, or, perhaps, if possible, still more incurably ambiguous, will appear upon the slightest inquiry. I ask the theist if he does not allow that there is a great and immeasurable, because incomprehensible, difference between the *human* and the *divine* mind; the more pious he is, the more readily will he assent to the affirmative, and the more will he be disposed to magnify the difference; he will even assert that the difference is of a nature which cannot be too much magnified. I next turn to the atheist, who, I assert, is only nominally so and can never possibly be in earnest, and I ask him whether, from the coherence and apparent sympathy in all the parts of this world, there be not a certain degree of analogy among all the operations of nature, in every situation and in every age; whether the rotting of a turnip, the generation of an animal, and the structure of human thought, be not energies that probably bear some remote analogy to each other. It is impossible he can deny it; he will readily acknowledge it. Having obtained this concession, I push him still further in his retreat, and I ask him if it be not probable that the principle which first arranged and still maintains order in this universe bears not also some remote inconceivable analogy to the other operations of nature and, among the rest, to the economy of human mind and thought. However reluctant, he must give his assent. Where then, cry I to both these antagonists, is the subject of your dispute? The theist allows that the original intelligence is very different from human reason; the atheist allows that the original principle of order bears some remote analogy to it. Will you quarrel, Gentlemen, about the degrees, and enter into a controversy which admits not of any precise meaning, nor consequently of any determination? If you should be so obstinate, I should not be surprised to find you insensibly change sides; while the theist, on the one hand, exaggerates the dissimilarity between the Supreme Being and frail, imperfect, variable, fleeting, and mortal creatures; and the atheist, on the other, magnifies the analogy among all the operations of nature, in every period, every situation, and every position. Consider then where the real point of controversy lies; and if you cannot lay aside your disputes, endeavour, at least, to cure yourselves of your animosity.

And here I must also acknowledge, Cleanthes, that, as the works of nature have a much greater analogy to the effects of *our* art and contrivance than to those of *our* benevolence and justice, we have reason to infer that the natural attributes of the Deity have a greater resemblance to those of men than his moral have to human virtues. But what is the consequence? Nothing but this, that the moral qualities of man are more defective in their kind than his natural abilities. For, as the Supreme Being is allowed to be absolutely and entirely perfect, whatever differs most from him departs the farthest from the supreme standard of rectitude and perfection.[2]

These, Cleanthes, are my unfeigned sentiments on this subject; and these sentiments, you know, I have ever cherished and maintained. But in proportion to my veneration for true religion is my abhorrence of vulgar superstitions; and I indulge a peculiar pleasure, I confess, in pushing such principles sometimes into absurdity, sometimes into impiety. And you are sensible that all bigots, notwithstanding their great aversion to the latter above the former, are commonly equally guilty of both.

My inclination, replied Cleanthes, lies, I own, a contrary way. Religion, however corrupted, is still better than no religion at all. The doctrine of a future state is so strong and necessary a security to morals that we never ought to abandon or neglect it. For if finite and temporary rewards and punishments have so great an effect, as we daily find, how much greater must be expected from such as are infinite and eternal?

How happens it then, said Philo, if vulgar superstition be so salutary to society, that all history abounds so much with accounts of its pernicious consequences on public affairs? Factions, civil wars, persecutions,

---

[2] It seems evident that the dispute between the sceptics and dogmatists is entirely verbal, or, at least, regards only the degrees of doubt and assurance which we ought to indulge with regard to all reasoning; and such disputes are commonly, at the bottom, verbal and admit not of any precise determination. No philosophical dogmatist denies that there are difficulties both with regard to the senses and to all science, and that these difficulties are, in a regular, logical method, absolutely insolvable. No sceptic denies that we lie under an absolute necessity, notwithstanding these difficulties, of thinking, and believing, and reasoning, with regard to all kinds of subjects, and even of frequently assenting with confidence and security. The only difference, then, between these sects, if they merit that name, is that the sceptic, from habit, caprice, or inclination, insists most on the difficulties, the dogmatist, for like reasons, on the necessity.

subversions of government, oppression, slavery—these are the dismal consequences which always attend its prevalence over the minds of men. If the religious spirit be ever mentioned in any historical narration, we are sure to meet afterwards with a detail of the miseries which attend it. And no period of time can be happier or more prosperous than those in which it is never regarded or heard of.

The reason of this observation, replied Cleanthes, is obvious. The proper office of religion is to regulate the heart of men, humanize their conduct, infuse the spirit of temperance, order, and obedience; and, as its operation is silent and only enforces the motives of morality and justice, it is in danger of being overlooked and confounded with these other motives. When it distinguishes itself, and acts as a separate principle over men, it has departed from its proper sphere and has become only a cover to faction and ambition.

And so will all religion, said Philo, except the philosophical and rational kind. Your reasonings are more easily eluded than my facts. The inference is not just—because finite and temporary rewards and punishments have so great influence that therefore such as are infinite and eternal must have so much greater. Consider, I beseech you, the attachment which we have to present things, and the little concern which we discover for obects so remote and uncertain. When divines are declaiming against the common behaviour and conduct of the world, they always represent this principle as the strongest imaginable (which indeed it is), and describe almost all human kind as lying under the influence of it, and sunk into the deepest lethargy and unconcern about their religious interests. Yet these same divines, when they refute their speculative antagonists, suppose the motives of religion to be so powerful that, without them, it were impossible for civil society to subsist, nor are they ashamed of so palpable a contradiction. It is certain, from experience, that the smallest grain of natural honesty and benevolence has more effect on men's conduct than the most pompous views suggested by theological theories and systems. A man's natural inclination works incessantly upon him; it is for ever present to the mind, and mingles itself with every view and consideration; whereas religious motives, where they act at all, operate only by starts and bounds, and it is scarcely possible for them to become altogether habitual to the mind. The force of the greatest gravity, say the philosophers, is infinitely small, in comparison of that of the least impulse, yet it is certain that the smallest gravity will, in the end, prevail above a great impulse because no strokes or blows can be repeated with such constancy as attraction and gravitation.

Another advantage of inclination: it engages on its side all the wit and ingenuity of the mind, and, when set in opposition to religious principles, seeks every method and art of eluding them; in which it is almost always successful. Who can explain the heart of man, or account for those strange salvos and excuses with which people satisfy themselves when they follow their inclinations in opposition to their religious duty? This is well understood in the world; and none but fools ever repose less trust in a man because they hear that, from study and philosophy, he has entertained some speculative doubts with regard to theological subjects. And when we have to do with a man who makes a great profession of religion and devotion, has this any other effect upon several who pass for prudent than to put them on their guard, lest they be cheated and deceived by him?

We must further consider that philosophers, who cultivate reason and reflection, stand less in need of such motives to keep them under the restraint of morals, and that the vulgar, who alone may need them, are utterly incapable of so pure a religion as represents the Deity to be pleased with nothing but virtue in human behaviour. The recommendations to the Divinity are generally supposed to be either frivolous observances or rapturous ecstasies or a bigoted credulity. We need not run back into antiquity or wander into remote regions to find instances of this degeneracy. Amongst ourselves, some have been guilty of that atrociousness, unknown to the Egyptian and Grecian superstitions, of declaiming, in express terms, against morality, and representing it as a sure forfeiture of the Divine favour if the least trust or reliance be laid upon it.

But even though superstition or enthusiasm should not put itself in direct opposition to morality, the very diverting of the attention, the raising up a new and frivolous species of merit, the preposterous distribution which it makes of praise and blame, must have the most pernicious consequences, and weaken extremely men's attachment to the natural motives of justice and humanity.

Such a principle of action likewise, not being any of the familiar motives of human conduct, acts only by intervals on the temper, and must be roused by continual efforts in order to render the pious zealot satisfied with his own conduct and make him fulfil his devotional task. Many religious exercises are entered into with seeming fervour where the heart, at the time, feels cold and languid. A habit of dissimulation is by degrees contracted, and fraud and falsehood become the predominant principle. Hence the reason of that vulgar observation that the highest zeal in religion and the deepest hypocrisy, so far from being inconsistent, are often or commonly united in the same individual character.

The bad effects of such habits, even in common life, are easily imagined, but, where the interests of religion are concerned, no morality can be forcible enough to bind the enthusiastic zealot. The sacredness of the cause sanctifies every measure which can be made use of to promote it.

The steady attention alone to so important an interest as that of eternal salvation is apt to extinguish the benevolent affections, and beget a narrow, contracted selfishness. And when such a temper is encouraged, it easily eludes all the general precepts of charity and benevolence.

Thus the motives of vulgar superstition have no great influence on general conduct, nor is their operation favourable to morality, in the instances where they predominate.

Is there any maxim in politics more certain and infallible than that both the number and authority of priests should be confined within very narrow limits, and that the civil magistrate ought, for ever, to keep his *fasces* and *axes* from such dangerous hands? But if the spirit of popular religion were so salutary to society, a contrary maxim ought to prevail. The greater number of priests and their greater authority and riches will always augment the religious spirit. And though the priests have the guidance of this spirit, why may we not expect a superior sanctity of life and greater benevolence and moderation from persons who are set apart for religion, who are continually inculcating it upon others, and who must themselves imbibe a greater share of it? Whence comes it then that, in fact, the utmost a wise magistrate can propose with regard to popular religions is, as far as possible, to make a saving game of it, and to prevent their pernicious consequences with regard to society? Every expedient which he tries for so humble a purpose is surrounded with inconveniences. If he admits only one religion among his subjects, he must sacrifice, to an uncertain prospect of tranquillity, every consideration of public liberty, science, reason, industry, and even his own independence. If he gives indulgence to several sects, which is the wiser maxim, he must preserve a very philosophical indifference to all of them and carefully restrain the pretensions of the prevailing sect, otherwise he can expect nothing but endless disputes, quarrels, factions, persecutions, and civil commotions.

True religion, I allow, has no such pernicious consequences; but we must treat of religion as it has commonly been found in the world, nor have I anything to do with that speculative tenet of theism which, as it is a species of philosophy, must partake of the beneficial influence of that principle, and, at the same time, must lie under a like inconvenience of being always confined to very few persons.

Oaths are requisite in all courts of judicature, but it is a question whether their authority arises from any popular religion. It is the solemnity and importance of the occasion, the regard to reputation, and the reflecting on the general interests of society, which are the chief restraints upon mankind. Customhouse oaths and political oaths are but little regarded even by some who pretend to principles of honesty and religion; and a Quaker's asseveration is with us justly put upon the same footing with the oath of any other person. I know that Polybius [3] ascribes the infamy of Greek faith to the prevalence of the Epicurean philosophy; but I know also that Punic faith had as bad a reputation in ancient times as Irish evidence has in modern, though we cannot account for these vulgar observations by the same reason. Not to mention that Greek faith was infamous before the rise of the Epicurean philosophy; and Euripides,[4] in a passage which I shall point out to you, has glanced a remarkable stroke of satire against his nation, with regard to this circumstance.

Take care, Philo, replied Cleanthes, take care: push not matters too far, allow not your zeal against false religion to undermine your veneration for the true. Forfeit not this principle—the chief, the only great comfort in life and our principal support amidst all the attacks of adverse fortune. The most agreeable reflection which it is possible for human imagination to suggest is that of genuine theism, which represents us as the workmanship of a Being perfectly good, wise, and powerful; who created us for happiness; and who, having implanted in us immeasurable desires of good, will prolong our existence to all eternity, and will transfer us into an infinite variety of scenes, in order to satisfy those desires and render our felicity complete and durable. Next to such a Being himself (if the comparison be allowed), the happiest lot which we can imagine is that of being under his guardianship and protection.

These appearances, said Philo, are most engaging and alluring, and, with regard to the true philosopher, they are more than appearances. But it happens here, as in the former case, that, with regard to the greater part of mankind, the appearances are deceitful, and that the terrors of religion commonly prevail above its comforts.

It is allowed that men never have recourse to devotion so readily as when dejected with grief or depressed with sickness. Is not this a proof that the religious spirit is not so nearly allied to joy as to sorrow?

But men, when afflicted, find consolation in religion, replied Cleanthes. Sometimes, said Philo; but it is natural to imagine that they will form a notion of those unknown beings, suitable to the present gloom and melancholy of their temper, when they betake themselves to the contemplation of them. Accordingly, we find the tremendous images to predominate in all religions; and we ourselves, after having employed the most exalted expression in our descriptions of the Deity,

---

[3] Lib. vi. cap. 54.
[4] *Iphigenia in Tauride.*

fall into the flattest contradiction in affirming that the damned are infinitely superior in number to the elect.

I shall venture to affirm that there never was a popular religion which represented the state of departed souls in such a light as would render it eligible for human kind that there should be such a state. These fine models of religion are the mere product of philosophy. For as death lies between the eye and the prospect of futurity, that event is so shocking to nature that it must throw a gloom on all the regions which lie beyond it, and suggest to the generality of mankind the idea of Cerberus and Furies, devils, and torrents of fire and brimstone.

It is true, both fear and hope enter into religion because both these passions, at different times, agitate the human mind and each of them forms a species of divinity suitable to itself. But when a man is in a cheerful disposition, he is fit for business, or company, or entertainment of any kind; and he naturally applies himself to these and thinks not of religion. When melancholy and dejected, he has nothing to do but brood upon the terrors of the invisible world, and to plunge himself still deeper in affliction. It may indeed happen that, after he has, in this manner, engraved the religious opinions deep into his thought and imagination, there may arrive a change of health or circumstances which may restore his good humour and, raising cheerful prospects of futurity, make him run into the other extreme of joy and triumph. But still it must be acknowledged that, as terror is the primary principle of religion, it is the passion which always predominates in it, and admits but of short intervals of pleasure.

Not to mention that these fits of excessive, enthusiastic joy, by exhausting the spirits, always prepare the way for equal fits of superstitious terror and dejection, nor is there any state of mind so happy as the calm and equable. But this state it is impossible to support where a man thinks that he lies in such profound darkness and uncertainty, between an eternity of happiness and an eternity of misery. No wonder that such an opinion disjoints the ordinary frame of the mind and throws it into the utmost confusion. And though that opinion is seldom so steady in its operation as to influence all the actions, yet it is apt to make a considerable breach in the temper, and to produce that gloom and melancholy so remarkable in all devout people.

It is contrary to common sense to entertain apprehensions or terrors upon account of any opinion whatsoever, or to imagine that we run any risk hereafter, by the freest use of our reason. Such a sentiment implies both an *absurdity* and an *inconsistency*. It is an absurdity to believe that the Deity has human passions, and one of the lowest of human passions, a restless appetite for applause. It is an inconsistency to believe that, since the Deity has this human passion, he has not others also, and, in particular, a disregard to the opinions of creatures so much inferior.

To know God, says Seneca, *is to worship him.* All other worship is indeed absurd, superstitious, and even impious. It degrades him to the low condition of mankind, who are delighted with entreaty, solicitation, presents, and flattery. Yet is this impiety the smallest of which superstition is guilty. Commonly, it depresses the Deity far below the condition of mankind, and represents him as a capricious demon who exercises his power without reason and without humanity! And were that Divine Being diposed to be offended at the vices and follies of silly mortals, who are his own workmanship, ill would it surely fare with the votaries of most popular superstitions. Nor would any of human race merit his *favour* but a very few, the philosophical theists, who entertain or rather indeed endeavour to entertain suitable notions of his Divine perfections. As the only persons entitled to his *compassion* and *indulgence* would be the philosophical sceptics, a sect almost equally rare, who, from a natural diffidence of their own capacity, suspend or endeavour to suspend all judgment with regard to such sublime and such extraordinary subjects.

If the whole of natural theology, as some people seem to maintain, resolves itself into one simple, though somewhat ambiguous, at least undefined, proposition, *That the cause or causes of order in the universe probably bear some remote analogy to human intelligence*—if this proposition be not capable of extension, variation, or more particular explication, if it affords no inference that affects human life, or can be the source of any action or forbearance, and if the analogy, imperfect as it is, can be carried no further than to the human intelligence, and cannot be transferred, with any appearance of probability, to the other qualities of the mind, if this really be the case, what can the most inquisitive, contemplative, and religious man do more than give a plain, philosophical assent to the proposition, as often as it occurs, and believe that the arguments on which it is established exceed the objections which lie against it? Some astonishment, indeed, will naturally arise from the greatness of the object, some melancholy from its obscurity, some contempt of human reason that it can give no solution more satisfactory with regard to so extraordinary and magnificent a question. But believe me, Cleanthes, the most natural sentiment which a well-disposed mind will feel on this occasion is a longing desire and expectation that Heaven would be pleased to dissipate, at least alleviate, this profound ignorance by affording some more particular revelation to mankind, and making discoveries of the nature, attributes, and operations of the Divine object of our faith. A person, seasoned with a just sense of the imperfections of natural reason, will fly to revealed truth with the greatest avidity, while the haughty dogmatist, persuaded that he can erect a complete system of theology by the mere help of philosophy, disdains any further aid and rejects this adventitious instructor. To be a philosophical sceptic is, in a man of letters, the first and most essential step towards being a sound, believing Christian—a proposition which I would willingly recommend to the attention of Pamphilus; and I hope Cleanthes will forgive me for interposing so far in the education and instruction of his pupil.

Cleanthes and Philo pursued not this conversation much further; and as nothing ever made greater impression on me than all the reasonings of that day, so I confess that, upon a serious review of the whole, I cannot but think that Philo's principles are more probable than Demea's, but that those of Cleanthes approach still nearer to the truth.

KANT

INTRODUCTION TO

Kant

LIFE

At the eastern end of Germany, in the Prussian port city of Königsberg (now called Kaliningrad), Immanuel Kant was born on April 22, 1724. Strangely enough, his father, who was a saddler by trade, was of Scotch origin. The original name was "Cant" but the son changed the spelling in order to avoid mispronunciation in German. Both of Kant's parents were devout pietistic Lutheran Protestants, described later in life by their son as gentle and humane and by no means without a love of the beauties of nature; but their primary attitudes toward life, and necessarily among their strongest influences on their son, were resignation, inwardness, acceptance, and reverence for the life of the spirit.

As a bright student in elementary school, Kant excelled at classical languages and quickly demonstrated a universal curiosity. He entered the University of Königsberg as a student in the Faculty of Theology, but, becoming especially attracted to study of the natural sciences, he did not pursue that direction. At an early age he had to begin to support himself, and he earned what money he could by private tutoring; this brought him into the homes of several noble families of East Prussia. He is remembered in the memoirs of some of the leaders in the movement against serfdom in the next generation, as having been a most impressive tutor to them in their early years. Kant began to write and to embark on the career of a university teacher at thirty-one, upon returning to Königsberg in the year 1755. He had previously published one short work on a problem of physics, and, it is interesting to note, he began by giving lectures on physical geography and empirical psychology. It may well be a classic example of the difference between the temperament of a man speaking and a man writing that Kant, who is often criticized as being one of the most difficult writers in philosophy, was one of the most popular of the University of Königsberg lecturers. Even in this first period of his public development he was no "dogmatist" but a teacher who argued that helping students to learn to philosophize for themselves is vastly more valuable than instructing them in a "ready-made" philosophy.

In a series of works written in 1762–3, he begins to show a loss of faith in the Continental rationalist techniques, and at this time, he records, he was considerably influenced by the works of both Jean-Jacques Rousseau and David Hume. Until the age of forty-six, he remained a *Privat-Dozent* and held only a poorly paid sublibrarianship, although a chair of poetry was offered to him at the University. It was not until 1770 that he was appointed Professor of Philosophy, and in that year he published one of the earliest works in which he formulates the basic conceptions of his philosophy, *On The Form And Principles Of The Sensible And Intelligible World.* The crucial idea making its initial appearance here is that the forms which the mind supplies as "the conditions for anything whatever becoming an object of our knowledge" must be valid for all experience. What this means is that Kant had arrived at the insight into a system of thought based on the proposition that human understanding, no less than sensory perception, has certain universal presuppositions, and that these cannot have their source in experience, since they make all mental experience possible.

The full-blown formulation of this position appears in A *Critique Of Pure Reason* (1781). The work is difficult to read, not only because the organization of the work reveals the combination of earlier versions with later versions, but also because Kant wrote in German instead of Latin and, in many cases, he originated German equivalents for certain Latin terms, and no "perfect" English equivalents for these exist. Two years after this great work appeared, Kant produced the *Prolegomena To Every Future Metaphysics,* a shorter, more compact, and more readable introduction to the argument in the *Critique.* It was Kant's purpose, after having constructed what he believed to be a solid basis for epistemology and methodology, to proceed with comparable critical works on ethical and aesthetic judgments as well. These analyses followed in 1785, 1788, and 1790.

While Kant spent the whole of his life in East Prussia, it would be extremely misleading to consider him a "provincial" in any sense except that he had not traveled in much of the geographical world. Socially, he was familiar with the manner of life of the aristocrats of his day; and politically, once his fame had been established, he was a public figure of concern—both of praise and of disapprobation—to the Prussian government. His fame was such that Mme de Staël made a trip to Königsberg to see him, and she included an interpretation of his philosophy in her early-nineteenth-century book about Germany. In his last years, Kant's mental powers wavered and failed him at times, but he maintained his good temper and dignity with his friends until the last. He died February 12, 1804.

The scope of Kant's interests and the originality of his thought are comparable only to Aristotle's. His contributions to the natural sciences [1], to theories of law, government, the concept of religion, academic freedom, and aesthetics, and his support of both the French and the American Revolutions, to which he was a contemporary, place him in a position along with perhaps only two or three other men of universal genius, the ramifications of whose thoughts have been gargantuan and continue with varying degrees of power through the present time.

METAPHYSICS AND THEORY OF KNOWLEDGE

Kant believed he had accomplished a revolution in philosophy comparable to the revolution that Nicolaus Copernicus had brought about in astronomy. Prior to Copernicus, astronomers assumed that the earth was the center of the universe and that it was stable, whereas other planets, the sun, and all the stars revolved around the earth. Copernicus offered the hypothesis that a great deal more of our information concerning celestial movement could be explained by assuming that the sun was the center of the universe, and that the earth and other planets moved around it. By comparison, Kant made use of this metaphor to imply that, prior to his analysis of knowledge, it was believed that the formulations of the human mind are true only insofar as they conform to the nature of the objects of our experience. It is Kant's revolution to reverse that order and urge upon us the hypothesis that a great deal more of our information of both nature and knowledge can be explained by assuming that the objects of our experience must conform to the nature of the human mind.

In the Preface to the Second Edition of his *Critique Of Pure Reason,* Kant wrote:

> Until now it was assumed that all our knowledge must conform
> or be adjusted to objects. But upon this assumption all attempts

---

[1] Kant's contribution to astronomy involved the first application of a "principle of evolution" to the origin of the solar system.

to figure out a priori by concepts anything regarding such objects, that is, anything which would enlarge our knowledge, were failures. Therefore let us try to see whether we can get ahead better with the tasks of metaphysics, if we assume that the objects should conform or be adjusted to our knowledge.

In essence, Kant urges upon us the idea that the mind can experience only what conforms with the conditions of mental activity and that science can comprehend only what it can examine and interpret according to its own plan. As he summarizes it in the *Prolegomena:* "The intellect does not derive its laws (a priori) from nature, but prescribes them to nature."

The stated intention of the *Prolegomena* is not to write metaphysics but to indicate the conditions under which metaphysics is possible at all. It is in this sense that Kant's proposal is a prolegomenon, a "foreword" or a preliminary, introductory study. It must be recognized that the essay itself is a critical examination of the epistemological, methodological problems that would have to be solved if there is to be *any* "scientific" metaphysics. Kant readily agreed with Hume that all previous metaphysical speculations were based on presuppositions that could not stand the test of Hume's searching analysis of causality and substance.

As many a philosopher before him, Kant begins by examining the nature of human thought. Mind must discover how it came into possession of its most basic conceptions, and what logical justification it has to employ them, before it may reasonably draw implications from them. Kant's approach to the questions of epistemology, then, amounts to subjecting the fundamental concepts or categories within which the mind operates to a strict examination, in order to establish them deductively and exhaustively.

Essential to this analysis is Kant's distinction between two classifications for all possible *judgments* that the human mind makes. The first is of judgments that are either *analytic* or *synthetic*. This is concerned with the *meaning* of a judgment. A judgment consists of a stated relationship between a subject and a predicate. In order to understand what a judgment *means* we must understand both the subject and the predicate. If we do, we can determine whether the judgment is analytic or synthetic. If, in understanding the predicate, we merely make more explicit an idea already contained in the subject, then the judgment is analytical—that is, its meaning is an analysis of a complex idea. The predicate adds no *new* information about the subject; it only makes knowledge of the subject better articulated. On the other hand, if in understanding the predicate, we *add* new information to our idea of the subject, then the judgment is synthetical—that is, its meaning is a synthesis, a putting together, of different ideas. Consider an example. The judgment "a bachelor is an unmarried adult male" does not add any new information to the meaning of the subject "bachelor." On the other hand, "Immanuel Kant was a bachelor" is a synthetical judgment, since we can know who Immanuel Kant was without knowing that he remained unmarried.

The second classification, concerned not with the meaning of judgments but with the grounds on which they can be justified, consists of a difference between what is a priori and a posteriori. A judgment is a priori when it is possible to determine whether it is true or false without relying upon the evidence of experience. We can know this by the operation of reason alone, and our knowledge of it is absolutely certain, or logically necessary. (In Kant's terminology, such a judgment is "apodictic.") On the other hand, a judgment is a posteriori when we can know whether it is true or false only upon the evidence of experience. We can, likewise, call an a posteriori judgment simply an empirical judgment. An example of the first would be the statement, "Two and two make four." An example of a true or false a posteriori judgment would be "Immanuel Kant had red hair."

It is obvious that there are four possible combinations of the different kinds of judgments, namely: (1) Analytic a priori, (2) Analytic a posteriori, (3) Synthetic a priori, (4) Synthetic a posteriori.

Kant's position is that all analytical judgments are a priori, and therefore there are no judgments of type 2. However, he believes that synthetical judgments may be either a posteriori or a priori. All synthetical a posteriori judgments are ordinary statements and the judgments of the empirical sciences. Synthetical a priori judgments belong to two branches of knowledge: metaphysics and mathematics (and, subsequent to Kant's own writings, the judgments arrived at through the critical method examining these two.) In effect, for Kant the primary methodological questions are concerned with the nature of synthetic a priori judgments.

If one makes the Copernican-like reversal of thought and asks how nature conforms with our knowledge, then the idea of nature will not be divided between "appearances" (changeable impressions) and "reality" (the unchanging something that endures independent of the impressions and is imagined to be the thing-in-itself). Kant takes the position that when the subject matter for examination is knowledge of nature, then all that we can know are the phenomena that we are able to experience. The "noumena" (or whatever the thing might be "in itself") can never be experienced. One way of putting it, using the terms that go back through the history of philosophy to Plato, would be to say that, for Kant, "appearances" are the only "reality" that we can know scientifically. It is a matter of considerable significance, now, to follow the outline of Kant's epistemology in order to locate the synthetic a priori judgments of metaphysics in his systematic thought.

Kant begins with the division between what nature offers for our knowledge and what the mind contributes to this. This is a distinction of matter and form. The phrase "what nature offers" is a metaphor for the inchoate sensory impressions that we experience. It is the mind that organizes such impressions, and the conditions for these organizations consist of the forms of our experience. The content of our impressions is given by nature; the forms are already in the mind; they are not derived from our impressions of nature. They are directly intuited; we never experience them independent of sensory data. Likewise, we never perceive sensory data without them. It is in this sense that Kant says, "Perceptions without conceptions are blind; conceptions without perceptions are empty."

What Kant calls a Transcendental Aesthetic explains how the mind organizes our perceptions of outer experiences through the form of space; and how it organizes our inner experiences through the form of time.

The term "transcendental" is, as Professor Friedrich points out, "most unfortunate . . . since it suggests an other-worldly emphasis," whereas "what Kant has in mind, primarily, is . . . expounding a *method* which transcends the customary dichotomies by stressing the *mode* of knowing rather than what is known." [2] "Transcendental" is in this instance being used to emphasize the independence of the mind from the passive condition that philosophers of empiricism believe it to have. This enables Kant to stress the independent, creative, formative powers of the mind in the process of knowing.

To proceed with the analysis of the modes by which the mind organizes its experience, Kant then goes on from the Transcendental Aesthetic, which is the mode of organizing perceptions, to the Transcendental Logic, the mode of organizing our concepts. These are the forms of abstract thought—such as substance and causality—again not derived from experience, and of which we do not become conscious unless we examine judgments. Imagination is the key to understanding how the concepts are related to the forms of intuition (in perception). While the concepts of the Transcendental Logic are not themselves judgments, they are the conditions for all transcendental judgments to be made. Just as space and time are the formal conditions (the modes

[2] Carl J. Friedrich, ed: *The Philosophy of Kant* (New York: The Modern Library; 1949), p. xxix–xxx.

or the ways) by which the mind organizes perceptions given in sensation, so the concepts of the Transcendental Logic are the forms for all subsequent judgments. The latter are analyzed in Kant's Transcendental Analytic and Transcendental Dialectic. It is through them that he arrives at the examination of synthetic a priori judgments. It should be obvious now that "Pure Reason" can achieve certainty of only the *forms* of thought—the modes by which the mind organizes its experience, concepts, and judgments. These are certainly not empirical but, in Kant's language, apodictic.

Given this analysis, the only possible metaphysics would be that of *phenomena*, never the possibility of a metaphysics of noumena (or things in themselves). Although the tone, the arguments, and the specific intention of the *Prolegomena* indicate that a future metaphysics is possible, the overwhelming effect of this critical interpretation is to see this analysis of the conditions of knowledge itself as the outer limit that the mind can legitimately arrive at in pursuit of a "scientific" metaphysics.

While a metaphysics of noumena, or that which cannot be experienced, is palpably impossible in Kant's view, the tendency of the mind to grasp "totalities of conditions" remains aesthetically powerful. Out of the contrast set up between the limits of our understanding and the longings for such "totalities," there result concepts by which the mind tends to synthesize the highest cognitions of which reason is capable. While Kant calls these "ideas," it might be more effective to think of them as ideals. Insofar as they relate to the possibility of grasping the totality of the conditions for all inner experience, there is the idea of Soul; insofar as they apply to the outer sense, there is the idea of World; and insofar as they refer to the conditions of all experience in general, the idea of God. Kant considers it a "transcendental illusion" to mistake these ideas as "given," whereas they are imposed upon or presented to the mind as *regulative principles*. These are not constitutive principles, through which objects of knowledge are produced, but "regulative" in the sense that they lead the mind to formulate such questions as might be answered within the limits of the sciences.

In pointing out the dangers involved in reifying the ideas, Kant notes that any supposed deduction drawn from these ideas themselves is as incapable of being proved as it is of being refuted. These are what Kant terms the "antinomies" of pure reason. By this he expresses the interpretation of the transcendental dialectic that, when the universe is treated as the object of knowledge, propositions that are mutually contradictory can be maintained with equal right. Whenever thinkers have attempted to formulate propositions concerning a subject matter not within the realm of experience, they have overstepped the boundary beyond which it is neither possible to prove their theses nor to disprove the antitheses.

In all that has preceded, it will be seen that there are similarities and differences in Kant's thinking in relation to both rationalism and empiricism. (1) Kant is a rationalist in the sense that he is concerned with establishing the universal, eternal, and necessary features in human knowledge. (2) He operates as an empiricist insofar as he concentrates on establishing the actual conditions for possible knowledge; but in contrast to the British empiricists—such as Hobbes, Locke, and Hume, who make it appear that the mind is essentially passive and receptive to change by impressions of nature independent of the mind—Kant makes the activity, the operation of the mind itself, an absolutely indispensable cooperating condition, not only for all sensory perception but for all forms of understanding as well. "Perception without conception is blind; conception without perception is empty."

Kant cannot thereby be said to have solved Hume's problem concerning the nature of causality, if the question of its "legitimacy" remains in Hume's terms. What Kant has done is to shift the focus of Hume's concern to the formal conditions through which the mind functions, regardless of particular subject matters. He thereby eliminated the problem in respect to objective nature, and found the concept of causality in the faculty of consciousness itself. The relation of cause and effect is not a fact in nature but a necessary form of thought. The mind is not passive to objects of nature; it is at least "half" of what constitutes the possibility of all experience. This Copernican-like revolution in epistemology, discovering a new way of seeing the activities of thought—and which assigns infinitely more power, dignity, freedom, and grandeur to the human mind—is likewise reflected in Kant's overwhelming respect for the freedom and independence of man's self-determination in action as well as in thought.

ETHICS

The metaphysics of nature is a critical examination of pure *speculative* reason. A metaphysics of morals, then, would be a critical examination of pure *practical* reason. What they share is the identity of the common principle, reason, whereas they are ultimately distinguished by their applications. While pure reason seeks to discover the laws according to which things *must* happen, practical reason seeks to discover the laws according to which things *ought to* happen. The first is the realm of science; the second is the realm of freedom.

For Plato, it appears that what is good in human behavior depends on what is true in reality; therefore, Plato's ethics is called dianoetic. For Aristotle, what is good in human behavior is what leads to human happiness; the name for this approach is eudemonian. In both cases, the *end* to be achieved is what determines the means employed. One leads to greater knowledge of one's "real" self; the other leads to greater happiness in practical life. For Kant, however, it is neither the end of knowledge nor of happiness that characterizes morality; it is an understanding of the *motive* and the *structure of action*.

Kant hopes thereby to make moral philosophy a purely rational science. Applying the distinction between form and matter, reason and experience, in the sphere of moral behavior, Kant concludes that the laws of ethics are purely formal laws. And the power of ethics lies in the opportunity for human beings to exercise their freedom and rationality.

The influence of Kant's metaphysics of nature shows itself in his theory of ethics, in which he conceives of the moral law as analogous with the natural laws. "The validity of the will as a general law for possible actions," he writes, "is analogous with the general interconnection of the existence of things according to general laws, which is the formula of nature."

The basis of all objectivity is law; but such law cannot be established a posteriori, on the basis of experience (as Hume had assumed). Rather, moral law springs from that element in man which has to do with freedom rather than from the results of psychological or social conditioning. Therefore the moral law, seen as purely formal, will not give instructions for specific action (in the sense that etiquette does) but only the form that the will must assume in order to be good in action. It must be valid for all rational beings. It will be seen that the logical essence of Kant's argument rests on the assumption that only when an action is based on a law that can be universalized without achieving self-contradiction can it be shown to be, properly speaking, moral. In this respect it aims at both logical universality and the ideal of the noblest aspects of human freedom. Herein the fundamental category is not that of objects of knowledge but the activities of human will.

For Kant it is clear that the activity of pure reason in proposing ends to itself must appear as a command—in the form of an imperative. When the will is concerned with particular objects or relations of experience, then it is determined by those and dependent upon them; whereas the *pure* rational will can be determined only through and by itself. Therefore, it is necessarily directed toward something other than the objects of natural impulses. It is the independence from such objects or purposes which characterises its "purity." The character of ethical judgment is concerned with disposition (attitude, motive) rather than with external consequences.

Kant says that nothing in the world can be called good without qualification, except a good will. In effect, anything else that might be called good (any power—for example, money or health) may be used for either moral or immoral purposes. They are not good *without* quali-fication, and the propositions of empirical morality (or ordinary pru-dence) which take as a rule "*If* you do so and so, *then* such and such will result" are only *hypothetical* imperatives. But the moral law cannot be dependent upon any object of will or any resulting experience. What constitutes the uniquely moral quality of ethical actions is that they are performed solely for the sake of the good motive. Moral law, therefore, is an absolute command, a *categorical* imperative, not a hypothetical one.

The principle of morality is the *good* will. It alone can be conceived as a source of what is good, not in terms of its results but in respect to its beginning (origin). Here again there may be seen a Copernican revo-lution in the theory of ethics. If the good will is *necessary* as the source for moral action, then it is also *sufficient*, since the question is not whether the acts that result are good in their effects—not relative to the ends attained by the action—but good for the volition itself.

To prove the goodness of the good will, Kant turns his attention to the workings of human nature, and asks why human beings should have been equipped with reason. If happiness were the end and the only good of human life, we would have been sufficiently equipped with in-stinct alone. Since we have been given reason by nature, and reason is a doubtful means toward happiness, reason must have been given for some other purpose. And this Kant relates to *respect for law*, which instincts cannot possibly supply. Good will, thereby, is practical reason as opposed to desire, with its appeal to the common experience of morality as means to fulfilling desires (within the forms of etiquette or within the restrictions of legality).

Whereas for Aristotle the central forces of morality are found in the desire to achieve happiness, for Kant the central forces of morality are found in respect for the law, in duty. Although the idea of duty im-plies a subjective restriction or hindrance, Kant uses it in order to point out the uniqueness of human freedom. This is seen constantly as a function of individuals who, it is never to be forgotten, are members of mankind. The dramatic tension in this view consists in the awareness that what makes any one man moral is necessarily the same as what makes mankind moral. Actions may therefore be divided or classified as inconsistent with duty or conforming to duty. If they conform to duty, they can then be subdivided as having been performed with an inclination to the action (Hume's moral sentiment) or without inclination to the action. If the latter, then either not from duty but rather from fear of punishment or from desire for reward; or from duty. In the latter case alone is found the moral situation per se, in which the good will acts in accordance with the law, action performed for the sake of the law and with full cognizance of the rationality that this implies.

To have moral worth, then, action must be performed from duty. For duty to have moral worth, it must be determined by a maxim, a subjective principle of volition—a formal, a priori principle of the will. Kant's point is that, if moral principles are to be necessary, they must have this abstract formal character. Duty, then, consists of the universal necessity of acting from respect for the moral law. Kant conceived that any alternative to this would be subjective, culturally relative, purely experiential, and therefore without logical necessity. Another way of putting it would be that pure reason offers us an insight into the intrinsic values of behavior, whereas an analysis based on experience offers us an understanding of only instrumental values.

If one asks: How is the basis of morality *rational*? Kant answers that it is its form. The idea of pure consistency or a lack of contradiction in itself is what constitutes the rationality of moral law. Each formulation that Kant offers of the categorical imperative is a statement of this form. For example, "Act as if the maxim from which you act were to become through your will a universal law of nature." Or again, "So act as to treat humanity, whether in thine own person or in that of any other, in every case as an end withal, never as a means only." If you ask how this categorical imperative is an example of self-consistency, the answer is that any action taken in violation of it would become self-destructive if it were universalized—that is, made the rule for mankind, rather than the explanation of the particular action for a particular person. For example, if one asks whether the act of murder can be condoned in particular instances, Kant would answer that it involves a lack of rationality if it were universalized; when the test for the ethical is seen as universalization, then condoning an act of murder would be equivalent to establishing the maxim that all men *should* kill. This is not an appeal to the way in which the desires of men may be thwarted but to logical coherence without which mankind would be self-destructive.

The first two pages of Kant's *Metaphysics Of Morals* offer the key to all that follows. Here he makes the fundamental distinction between viewing morals (a) in external action, from the point of view of legality or from respect for the consequences alone, and (b) in subjective experience through the maxims based on belief in duty. The latter follows from the idea of law itself universalized and stated in a universal, a priori form. It is therefore not "inclination" which is essential to morality. Inclination, rather, has to do with the matter of particular actions, known empirically (the subject matter of "popular morality"); it is reason—the logical form—that makes possible the understanding of ethics in the light of a metaphysics of morals. This does not mean that all men must become logicians. But it assumes that the philosopher must comprehend the abstract conditions which distinguish moral action from nonmoral action. For this, Kant finds that objective necessity is identified only with duty, which makes an action arise out of respect for the moral law. In this alone, morality is distinguished by a consideration of motivation rather than consideration of effects. The agreement of action with an empirical law, but without reference to the spring of action, would be legality, prudence, or propriety. Agreement of action with respect to the idea of duty, derived from the categorical imperative, would be morality. It is, in effect, the internalization of the conditions for morality, whereas legality is seen as purely external. Legislation is concerned with (civil) right action; ethics is concerned with moral virtue. There are, of course, certain duties in common between the duty of right and the duty of ethics, but what is not shared is the species of obligation and the motivation. The proper differentia of ethical legislation is to perform actions simply because they are duties, and to make the principle of duty itself a sufficient spring for the acts of the will.

The sense in which freedom is essential here has to do with Kant's conception of human rationality and spontaneity—the ability for human beings to work according to principles independent of the particular social or other external conditioning forces. If freedom is the power to originate actions, it is to be found uniquely in the intelligible world of human being; and Kant conceives this freedom identified with an idea of man's dignity as noble as he conceives the moral law itself to be.

MORRIS PHILIPSON

SELECTED BIBLIOGRAPHY

Kant's Works

The Philosophy of Kant: Immanuel Kant's Moral and Political Writings. Edited, with an Introduction, by Carl J. Friedrich. New York: The Modern Library; 1949. This volume contains: "The Sense of the Beautiful and of the Sublime," "Dreams of a Visionary Explained by Dreams of Metaphysics," "Critique of Pure Reason," "Prolegomena to Every Future Metaphysics That May Be Presented as a Science," "Idea for a Universal History with Cosmopolitan Intent," "What is Enlightenment?", "Metaphysical Foundations of Morals," "Critique of Pure Practical Reason," "Critique of Judgment," "Religion Within the Limits of Reason Alone," "Theory and Practice: Concerning the Common Saying: This May Be True in Theory But Does Not Apply to Practice," "Eternal Peace."

Critique of Pure Reason. Translated by Norman Kemp Smith. New York: St. Martin's Press; 1929. An abridged edition is available in The Modern Library.

Critique of Practical Reason and Other Writings in Moral Philosophy. Translated by Lewis W. Beck. Chicago: University of Chicago Press; 1949. This volume contains: "Foundations of the Metaphysics of Morals," "Critique of Practical Reason," "An Inquiry Into the Distinctness of the Principles of Natural Theology and Morals," "What is Enlightenment?", "What is Orientation in Thinking?", "Perpetual Peace: A Philosophical Sketch," "On a Supposed Right to Lie from Altruistic Motives," "Selections from The Metaphysics of Morals."

Critique of Aesthetic Judgment. Translated by James C. Meredith. Oxford: The Clarendon Press; 1911.

Works on Kant

Caird, E.: The Critical Philosophy of Immanuel Kant. 2 vols. Second edition. New York: Maclehose & Sons; 1889.

Ewing, A. C.: A Short Commentary on Kant's Critique of Pure Reason. Chicago: University of Chicago Press; 1938.

Jones, W. T.: Morality and Freedom in the Philosophy of Immanuel Kant. London: Oxford University Press; 1940.

Kroner, Richard: Kant's Weltanschauung. Translated by John F. Smith. Chicago: University of Chicago Press; 1956.

Lindsay, A. D.: Kant. London: Benn; 1934.

Paton, H. J.: The Categorical Imperative. Chicago: The University of Chicago Press; 1948.

Paulsen, Friedrich: Immanuel Kant, His Life and Doctrines. Translated from the revised German edition by J. E. Creighton and Albert Lefevre. New York: Scribner's; 1902.

Singer, Marcus George: Generalization in Ethics. New York: Alfred A. Knopf, Inc.; 1961.

PROLEGOMENA

TO EVERY FUTURE METAPHYSICS THAT MAY BE PRESENTED AS A SCIENCE

INTRODUCTION

These *Prolegomena* are not designed for the use of students, but for future teachers, and even for the latter they should serve not so much to provide the order of exposition of an already existing science as to create such a science.

There are scholars for whom the history of philosophy (ancient no less than modern) constitutes their own philosophy; for these the present *Prolegomena* are not written. These scholars must wait until the people who are endeavoring to tap the sources of reason have completed their work and then it will be the turn of the scholars to give an account to the world of what has been done by the others. Otherwise nothing can be said that, in their opinion, has not been said before. In fact, this may pass as an infallible prophecy for all future time. Since the human mind has speculated for so many centuries on countless subjects in so many ways, it is likely that for every new idea an old one can be found having some affinity with it.

My purpose is to convince all those caring to occupy themselves with metaphysics that for the present it is indispensably necessary that they suspend their work, look upon all that has gone before as non-existent and above all, first ask the question: "Whether such a thing as metaphysics is even possible at all?"

If metaphysics is a science, how does it happen that it cannot win for itself universal and lasting applause like other sciences? If it is not a science, how is it that under the semblance of a science it is ceaselessly boasting and holding out to the human mind hopes that are never extinguished and never fulfilled? Something definite must be worked out respecting the nature of this assumed science, whether it demonstrates our knowledge or our ignorance; for it is impossible that metaphysics should remain on the same footing any longer. It seems almost ridiculous that, while every other science moves forward ceaselessly, this one claiming to be wisdom itself, whose oracular pronouncements everyone consults, is continually revolving in one spot without advancing a step. Furthermore, its votaries have much decreased and we do not see that those who feel strong enough to shine in other sciences are willing to risk their fame in this one. On this science everyone, ignorant though he may be in all else, presumes to have a decided opinion just because in this sphere there is no certain weight and measure at hand by which to distinguish a thorough work from superficial chatter.

However, it is not an uncommon occurrence that, after long-continued work in a science in which wonders of progress are believed to have been made, the question occurs to someone: Whether and how such a science is possible at all? For human reason is so fond of building that many times it has reared up a lofty tower and then afterwards pulled it down to see how the foundation was laid. It is never too late to become reasonable and wise; but it is always more difficult when the insight for initiating it comes late.

To ask whether a science is possible presupposes a doubt as to its existence. But such a doubt would offend all those whose whole fortune may consist of this supposed treasure; anyone who raises such a doubt must anticipate resistance on all sides. Some people, in the proud consciousness of their ancient, and therefore what they consider legitimate, possession, will, with their metaphysical textbook in hand, look down with contempt upon him who raises such a doubt. Others, who never notice anything that does not coincide with what they have previously seen elsewhere, will not understand him, and so everything will remain for some time as though nothing at all had happened that could allow one to fear or to hope for an impending change.

At the same time I confidently dare to predict that the thoughtful reader of these *Prolegomena* will not only doubt his previous science, but will be quite convinced in the end that such a science cannot exist unless the demands made here have been satisfied; for upon them rests the possibility of metaphysics. Inasmuch as this has never happened, there is as yet no such thing as metaphysics. But, since the demand for metaphysics can never disappear because the interests of universal human reason are so intimately bound up with it, the thoughtful reader will confess that a complete reform, or rather a new birth, is inevitable according to a plan hitherto quite unknown, however much this may be resisted for a time.

Since the attempts of Locke and Leibnitz, or rather since the first rise of metaphysics, no event has occurred that could be more decisive for the fortunes of this science than the attack made upon it by David Hume. He contributed no new light to this kind of knowledge, but he struck a spark by which a light might have been kindled had it encountered receptive tinder whose glimmer could have been preserved and enlarged.

Hume took for his initial starting point a single but important conception of metaphysics, namely, that of the *connection of cause and effect* (together with the derivative conceptions of force and action, etc.). He demanded that reason, which pretends to have given metaphysics birth, give a reasoned answer to the question: By what right does reason think that something is of such a quality that on its being posited something else is thereby necessarily also posited? For that is the meaning of the concept of cause. Hume proved irrefutably that it is quite impossible for reason to imagine this connection *a priori* and based on a mere concept since this connection involves necessity. It is not at all apparent how, because something exists something else must necessarily exist, and thus how the concept of such a connection can be introduced *a priori*. Hence Hume concluded that reason completely deceived itself by this concept, that reason falsely claimed this concept as its own child, while it was nothing more than a bastard of the imagination which, conceived by experience, had brought certain representations under the law of association, and had substituted a resulting subjective necessity, i.e., habit, for an objective necessity based on insight. From this he concluded that reason possessed no faculty for thinking of such connections even in general terms, because [if it did] its concepts would then be mere constructs, and all its pretended *a priori* knowledge nothing but common experiences mislabeled; which is to say that no such thing as metaphysics exists at all and that there is no possibility of its ever existing.

However hasty and incorrect Hume's conclusion was, at least it was based on investigation and this investigation would have been worthwhile if the good brains of his time could have possibly united to solve, with happier results, the problem in the sense in which he had stated it. Then a speedy and complete reform of the science would have resulted.

But fate, always unfavorable to metaphysics, willed that Hume should be understood by no one. One cannot see, without feeling a certain regret, how completely his opponents: Reid, Oswald, Beattie, and lastly Priestley, missed the point of his task; for they took for granted precisely that which Hume doubted and then they proved heatedly and mostly quite immodestly what it had never entered his head to question. As a result, they so completely misunderstood his hint at improvement that everything remained in the same state as though nothing had happened. It was not a question whether the concept of cause was correct and useful, and indispensable in regard to the whole knowledge of nature, for Hume had never doubted this. It was a question whether this concept could be thought of *a priori* by reason, and in this way the concept would have inherent truth independent of all experience, and therefore also have a more extended usefulness which would not be limited to objects of experience; it was upon this problem that Hume desired clarification. The question was as to the origin of the concept, not as to its practical indispensability in use. As soon as the origin of the concept had been ascertained, the conditions of its use and the extent to which it is valid would have been settled of themselves.

To have done the problem full justice, the opponents of this celebrated man would have had to penetrate deeply into the nature of reason, in so far as it is occupied solely with pure thought, a course which was inconvenient for them. Therefore they invented a more convenient means by which they might defy him without any insight, namely, the appeal to the *common sense of mankind*. Common sense (or, as it has recently been called, plain sense) is indeed a great natural gift to possess. But it must be proved by acts, by the thoughtfulness and reasonableness of what one thinks and says, and not by appealing to it as to an oracle when one has nothing intelligent to adduce to justify oneself. When insight and knowledge are at a low ebb, then and not before, one of the subtle inventions of modern times is to appeal to common sense, by means of which the shallowest talker may calmly confront the profoundest thinker and hold out against him. But so long as there is a small remnant of insight left, one will be hesitant to use this crutch. Seen in its true light, that argument is nothing better than an appeal to the verdict of the multitude; an applause at which the philosopher blushes, but about which the popular smart-aleck boasts scornfully. But I should think that Hume can make as good a claim to the possession of common sense as Beattie, and furthermore, to something the latter certainly did not possess, namely, critical reason, which keeps common sense from overreaching itself in speculations. If we are merely concerned with speculations, a restrained common sense will then not seek to decide them, as common sense does not know how to justify its own principles; only in this way will common sense remain healthy. Chisel and hammer are quite sufficient for working on a piece of wood, but for copper-engraving an etching needle is necessary. In the same way, the common intellect, no less than the speculative philosophical intellect, is useful in itself; the former when we have to do with judgments having an immediate bearing on experience, but the latter when we have to judge universally on the basis of mere concepts, as for instance in metaphysics where the self-appointed, healthy common sense is capable of no judgment at all.

I readily confess that the reminder [challenge] of David Hume was what first interrupted my dogmatic slumber many years ago and gave my research in the field of speculative philosophy quite a different direction. I was quite far from accepting the consequences which resulted merely from his not having faced his problem squarely, but having only attacked a part of it which could not possibly afford a solution by itself. When one starts from a well-founded, though undeveloped, idea that a predecessor has left, one may well hope that by increased reflection one can bring it further than was possible for the acute man whom one has to thank for the original sparks of its light.

First of all, I tried to see whether Hume's observation could not be made general and soon found that the concept of the connection of cause and effect was not the only one, by a great deal, by which the intellect thinks *a priori* of the connections of things, but that metaphysics consists entirely of such concepts. I endeavored to ascertain their number, and as I succeeded in doing this to my satisfaction, namely, out of a single principle, I proceeded to the deduction of these concepts, which I was now assured could not be derived from experience as Hume had pretended, but must have originated in the pure intellect. This deduction that had seemed impossible to my acute predecessor and that had not even occurred to anyone except him, although everyone unconcernedly used these concepts (without asking on what their objective validity rested); this deduction, I say, was the most difficult problem that could ever be undertaken in the interests of metaphysics. The worst of it was that metaphysics, so far as it exists at all at present, could not afford me the least help because the above deduction was needed to make metaphysics possible in the first place. Having now succeeded in the solution of Hume's problem, not only in one particular case, but in respect to the entire capacity of pure reason, I could at least determine more surely, though still only by slow steps, the whole range of pure reason in its limits as well as in its content. I could determine it completely according to the universal principles which are required for metaphysics in order to construct its system on a secure plan.

However I am afraid that [my effort to resolve] the problem of

Hume to the greatest possible extent (namely, in the *Critique of Pure Reason*) will fare as the *problem* itself fared when it was first stated. My effort will be mistakenly judged because it is not understood; it will not be understood because people, though they may care to turn over the leaves of my book, will not care to think it through; and they will be unwilling to take this trouble with it because the work is dry, obscure, and, besides being diffuse, contrary to all accustomed conceptions. But I must confess that I was quite surprised to hear from a philosopher complaints as to the work not being popular, entertaining, and agreeably arranged. What is at stake is a branch of knowledge highly prized and indispensable to humanity which cannot be treated otherwise than according to the most strict rules of academic precision. Popularity may indeed follow in time but it can never be expected at the beginning. However, a grievance must be admitted as regards a certain obscurity which arises partly from the diffuseness of the plan, as a result of which the main points of the investigation are not so readily perceived. It is the task of the present *Prolegomena* to remove this difficulty.

The *Critique of Pure Reason*, which presents the capacity of pure reason in its whole range and limits, remains the foundation to which the *Prolegomena* are only preparatory. For the *Critique* must, as a science, be complete and systematic even down to the smallest detail before we can so much as think of presenting metaphysics, or of even allowing ourselves the most distant hope in this direction.

We have long been accustomed to seeing old and worn-out theories remodeled by being taken out of their former coverings and fitted to a systematic garment according to our own approved style but under new titles; the great majority of readers will expect nothing different from our *Critique*. But these *Prolegomena* will convince them that it is quite a new science of which no one had previously had the smallest conception, of which even the idea was unknown, and with reference to which all hitherto received knowledge was unavailable, with the exception of the hint afforded by Hume's doubt. But Hume never dreamt of a possible formal science of this nature, and in order to land his ship in safety, he ran it aground on the shore of scepticism where it might lie and rot. Instead of doing this, it is my purpose to furnish a pilot who, according to certain principles of seamanship derived from a knowledge of the globe, and supplied with a complete map and compass, may steer the ship with safety wherever it seems good to him. For were we not to do this we should only fancy, because the terms sound alike, that we saw everywhere what we had known already except that everything would appear misshapen, senseless and unintelligible because we would be basing our approach upon our own notions to which we have become habituated by long use, instead of basing our approach on the author's thought. But the diffuseness of the work and the ensuing unavoidable dryness and academic precision, however advantageous these may be objectively, are undoubtedly disadvantageous to the book in so far as this is a result of the nature of the science itself and not of its presentation.

Indeed, it is not given to everyone to write as subtly and at the same time as charmingly as David Hume, or as thoroughly and as elegantly as Moses Mendelssohn; but I flatter myself that I might have rendered my style popular had I only set out to sketch a plan and had left its completion to others, and if I had not had the interests of the science, with which I have been occupied so long, so much at heart. For it requires considerable persistence and not a little self-denial to choose a late but enduring fame in perference to the allure of an early and favorable reception.

Plan-making is often a luxurious and pretentious mental occupation, whereby one acquires the reputation of a creative genius by demanding what one cannot achieve oneself, by censuring what one cannot improve, and by proposing what one does not know how to find. But in a thorough plan of the general *Critique of Reason* something more is necessary that perhaps may be supposed, if the plan is not to be the usual mere declamation of pious wishes. For pure reason is so isolated, and is so closely-knit a sphere in itself, that no part of it can be touched upon without affecting the rest. Therefore, we can accomplish nothing without determining the position and influence of each part with regard to the others because there is nothing outside each part by which we can judge correctly as to anything inside. The validity and use of every part depends upon the relation in which the part stands in respect to this composition. The situation is *similar* to that of an organized body where the purpose of each member can only be deduced from a complete concept of the whole. Therefore it may be said that such a critique is never reliable unless it is quite complete down to the least of the elements of pure reason; and that in the sphere of this faculty one must determine and expound either *everything* or *nothing*.

A mere plan preceding the *Critique of Pure Reason* would be incomprehensible, unreliable and useless, but following the *Critique* it is much more useful. Then one is in a position to view the whole, to test one by one the main points upon which the science rests and to render the style better than was possible on the first execution of the work.

The following is such a plan which may be presented according to an analytical method, since the work is complete, whereas the work itself had to be constructed throughout according to synthetic method in order that the new science might exhibit all its articulations in their natural connection as the organization of a special faculty of knowledge. On the other hand, should anyone find that this plan which I am putting forward as a Prolegomena to any future system of metaphysics, is itself obscure, he must bear in mind that it is not necessary for *everyone* to study metaphysics. There is much talent which is perfectly adequate for investigating the thorough and even profound sciences which lie more in the field of observation, but this talent is apt to be unsuccessful in a species of research based solely on abstract conceptions. When this last happens, one's mental abilities should be turned in another direction. But he who undertakes to judge a system of metaphysics, or to construct one, must satisfy in every way the demands that will be made here. It may happen that he either accepts my solution or he utterly refutes it and offers another in its stead; but evade it, he cannot. Thus, the much-decried obscurity (though it is a frequent covering for indolence and stupidity) may have its uses in the end, since those who maintain a judicious silence in respect to other sciences speak masterfully and decide anew in questions of metaphysics because in this their ignorance does not contrast conspicuously with established scientific knowledge, although it certainly does with the principles of sound criticism. Of these one may claim, *Ignavum, fucos, pecus a praesepibus arcent.* (Virgil: They keep off from the hives the lazy swarm of drones.)

INTRODUCTORY REMARKS ON THE
SPECIFIC QUALITY OF ALL
METAPHYSICAL KNOWLEDGE

§ 1

Of the Sources of Metaphysics

In presenting a branch of knowledge as *science*, it is necessary to be able to define with precision its distinguishing characteristic, that which it possesses in common with no other branch and which is therefore specific to this science. Otherwise, the boundaries of all sciences run into one another and no one of them can be thoroughly treated according to its own nature.

Whether this specific quality consists in the distinction of its *object*, of its *sources of knowledge*, of its *kind of knowledge*, or lastly, of several if not all these points taken together, the idea of this possible science and of its sphere rests primarily upon this specific quality.

Firstly, as regards the *sources* of metaphysical knowledge, its very conception shows that these sources cannot be empirical. Its principles (which include not merely its axioms, but also its fundamental conceptions) consequently can never be taken from experience; since it is not *physical* but *metaphysical* knowledge, i.e., knowledge beyond experience, that is wanted. Thus neither external experience which is the source of physical science proper, nor internal experience which is the groundwork of empirical psychology, will constitute its foundation. Metaphysics consists, then, of *a priori* knowledge, that is, of knowledge derived from pure intellect and pure reason.

But there is nothing in this to distinguish it from pure mathematics; therefore metaphysics must be defined as *pure philosophical knowledge*. Regarding the meaning of this expression, I must refer the reader to the *Critique of Pure Reason* where the distinction between these two ways of using reason are clearly and adequately presented. So much for the sources of metaphysical knowledge.

§ 2

Of the only kind of Knowledge that can be termed Metaphysical

A. Of the difference between synthetic and analytic judgments in general

Metaphysical knowledge must only contain *a priori* judgments; that much is required by the specific quality of its sources. But all judgments, no matter what origin they may have, or how they are constructed in regard to logical form, differ according to their content, by virtue of which they are either simply *explanatory* and add nothing to the content of knowledge, or they are *extensive* and enlarge the given knowledge. The first may be termed *analytic* and the second *synthetic* judgments.

Analytic judgments say nothing in the predicate but what has already been thought of in the conception of the subject, although perhaps not so clearly, nor with the same degree of consciousness. When I say that all bodies are extended, I do not thereby in the least enlarge my concept of a body but have simply resolved it, inasmuch as extension, although not expressly stated, was already thought of in that conception; in other words the judgment is analytic. On the other hand, the proposition that some bodies are heavy contains something in the predicate which was not already thought of in the general conception of a body; that is to say, it enlarges my knowledge in so far as it adds something to my conception and therefore it must be termed a synthetic judgment.

B. The common principle of all analytic judgments is the principle of contradiction

All analytic judgments are based entirely on the principle of contradiction and are *a priori* cognitions by their nature, whether the concepts involved are empirical or not. Since the predicate of an affirmative analytic judgment is previously implied in the conception of the subject, such a predicate cannot be denied of the subject without contradiction. In the same way, and also in accordance with the principle of contradiction, the reverse of this subject must necessarily be denied in a negative analytic judgment. This is the situation with the propositions: every body is extended and no body is unextended (simple). For this reason all analytic propositions are *a priori* judgments, although their conceptions may be empirical. Let us take as an instance the proposition: gold is a yellow metal. Now in order to know this I require no further experience beyond my concept of gold which contains the propositions that this body is yellow and a metal. This precisely constitutes my concept and therefore I only have to analyze it without needing to look around for anything elsewhere.

C. Synthetic judgments demand a principle other than that of contradiction

There are synthetic *a posteriori* judgments whose origin is empirical, but there are also others which are certain and *a priori* and which spring from pure intellect and reason. Both kinds of judgments are alike in that they can never have their source solely in the principle of analysis, namely, the principle of contradiction. They require an altogether different principle in spite of the fact that no matter what principle they may be deduced from, they must always *conform to the principle of contradiction*, for nothing can be at variance with this principle, although not everything can be deduced from it. I shall now classify synthetic judgments.

(1) *Empirical judgments are always synthetic.* It would be absurd to found an analytic judgment on experience, as it is unnecessary to go beyond my own concept in order to construct the judgment, and therefore the confirmation of experience is unnecessary to it. That a body is extended is a proposition possessing *a priori* certainty; it is not an empirical judgment. For before I turn to experience I have all the conditions of my judgment already at hand in the conception from which I simply deduce the predicate in accordance with the principle of contradiction.

Thereby I may, at the same time, become conscious of the *necessity* of the judgment which experience could never teach me.

(2) *All mathematical judgments are synthetic.* Up till now this truth seems to have altogether escaped those who have analyzed human reason; indeed, it seems to be directly opposed to all their guesses, although it is indisputably certain and very important in its consequences. Because it was found that the conclusions of mathematicians all proceed according to the principle of contradiction, which the nature of every apodictic certainty demands, it was concluded that the axioms were also known through the principle of contradiction. This was a great error; for although a synthetic proposition can be viewed in the light of the principle of contradiction, this can only be done by presupposing another synthetic proposition from which the first proposition is derived, but such a proposition can never be derived from the principle of contradiction.

First of all it must be remarked that genuinely mathematical propositions are always judgments *a priori* and are never empirical because they involve necessity which cannot be derived from experience. Should anyone be unwilling to admit this, I will limit my proposition to *pure mathematics*, the very conception of which implies that it contains nothing empirical but simply pure, *a priori* knowledge.

At first sight, one might be disposed to think that the proposition $7 + 5 = 12$ is merely analytic resulting from the conception of a sum of seven and five according to the principle of contradiction. But if one considers it more closely one will find that the conception of the sum of 7 and 5 comprises nothing beyond the union of two numbers in a single one, and that there is nothing whatever implied in it as to what this single number is, which comprehends both the others. The concept of twelve is by no means already thought of when I think merely of the union of seven and five, and I may dissect my concept of such a possible sum as long as I please without discovering the number twelve in it. One must go beyond these concepts and seek the assistance from observing something which corresponds to one or the other of them, as for example, one's five fingers, and so gradually add the units of the five given in observation to the conception of the seven. One's conception is therefore really enlarged by the proposition $7 + 5 = 12$; to the first conception a new one is being added which was in no way implied in the former. In other words, arithmetical propositions are always synthetic. This is more clear when we take larger numbers, for then we will be clearly convinced that, turn and twist our concept as we may, we shall never find the sum required by the mere dissection of the original concept without calling observation to our aid.

A principle of pure geometry is not any more analytic than a principle of arithmetic. That a straight line is the shortest distance between two points is a synthetic proposition. For my concept of straight has no reference to size but only to quality. Therefore the concept of the "shortest" is quite additional and cannot be drawn from any analysis of the conception of a straight line. Therefore observation must again be brought to our aid; by means of it alone the synthesis is possible.

Indeed certain other principles which are postulated by geometricians are really analytic and rest on the principle of contradiction, but they only serve as links in the chain of method like identical propositions and are not true principles. For instance a = a, the whole is equal to itself, or (a + b) > a, i.e., the whole is greater than its part. But even these, although they are valid according to mere conceptions, are only admitted in mathematics because they can be presented in observation. What produces the common belief that the predicate of such apodictic judgments is already unified in our conception, and that therefore the judgment is analytic, is merely the ambiguity of expression. We ought to add in one thought a certain predicate to a given concept, for this necessity is implied in the concepts themselves. But the question is not what we *ought* to think, but what we actually, though obscurely, think in connection with them. This shows us that the predicate is implied in those conceptions necessarily though not immediately, and it must be added by means of an observation.

The essential feature distinguishing pure *mathematical* [1] knowledge from all other *a priori* knowledge is that it does not proceed from *concepts themselves* but always from the construction of concepts. (*Critique of Pure Reason*, p. 435) Therefore, since mathematics in its propositions must go beyond the concept to that which the corresponding observation contains, these propositions never can nor ought to arise from the analysis of the concepts, that is, arise analytically; in other words, these propositions are synthetic in their entirety.

I cannot refrain from remarking on the disadvantage which the neglect of this simple and apparently insignificant observation has brought on philosophy. Hume inadvertently severed from pure knowledge an entire and indeed more important province, namely that of pure mathematics, when he cast his eye over the whole field of pure, *a priori* knowledge in which the human intellect claims such extensive possessions. He was under the impression that the nature of pure mathematics rested on totally different principles; namely, that it rested solely on the

---

[1] Vaihinger has urged ("Eine Blattversetzung in Kant's Prolegomena" *Philosophische Monatshefte* XV, 1882) that the following six paragraphs belong in this section 2, rather than where they occur in section 4. The argument is convincing and they have therefore been shifted here.—Ed.

principle of contradiction. Although he did not undertake such a formal and general classification of propositions, nor in the same terms as I do here, yet what he did was like saying: pure mathematics contains merely analytic judgments, while metaphysics contains synthetic *a priori* judgments. Now he made a great mistake in this and this mistake had decidedly injurious consequences for his whole conception [of knowledge]. For if he had not made it, he would have broadened his question respecting the origin of our synthetic judgments far beyond his metaphysical concept of causality, and extended it [to include] the possibility of *a priori* mathematics; for he should have regarded this as synthetic also. But in the latter case, he could under no circumstances have based his metaphysical propositions on mere experience, as then he would have been obliged to subordinate the axioms of pure mathematics to experience, a proceeding for which he had too much insight.

The good company into which metaphysics would have thereby been brought would have ensured it against mean maltreatment; for the thrusts aimed at metaphysics would have also hit mathematics, and this neither was nor could have been Hume's opinion. Thus this keen man would have been led to reflections similar to those with which we are now occupied, but they would have gained infinitely by his inimitably beautiful style of presentation.

(3) *Metaphysical judgments proper are synthetic in their entirety.* We must distinguish between judgments belonging to *metaphysics* and metaphysical judgments. Among the former are included many that are analytic, but these only furnish the means for metaphysical judgments proper which form the entire purpose of the science and are all synthetic. For, when concepts belong to metaphysics, as does for instance that of substance, the judgments arising from the analysis of the concepts also belong to metaphysics. For example, [we say] substance is that which only exists as a subject, etc., and [by making] several analytic judgments of this kind we seek to approach the definition of the concept. However, since the analysis of a pure intellectual concept, such as those concepts continued in metaphysics, cannot proceed differently than the analysis of any other empirical concept which does not belong to metaphysics (e.g., air is an elastic fluid, the elasticity of which is not destroyed by any known degree of coldness), [it follows that] the concept but not the analytic judgment is peculiarly metaphysical. For this science exhibits something special and peculiar in the way it produces its intellectual knowledge *a priori*. This peculiar mode of production must be distinguished from what metaphysics has in common with all other intellectual knowledge. Thus, for example, the proposition that all that is substance in things persists is a synthetic and properly metaphysical proposition.

When the *a priori* concepts constituting the structural materials of metaphysics have been collected according to certain principles, the analysis of these concepts is of great value. They can then be presented as a special part (as it were, a *philosophia definitiva*), containing solely analytic propositions relating to metaphysics and this part would be separate from the synthetic propositions which constitute metaphysics itself. Actually, these analyses have nowhere any important use except in metaphysics, that is, no use in reference to the synthetic propositions which are constructed from these analyzed concepts.

Hence the conclusion to be drawn in this section is that metaphysics is properly concerned with *a priori* synthetic propositions, and that these alone constitute its task, but that metaphysics requires for this purpose some analyses of its concept or analytic judgments, the procedure in this respect being no different than in other kinds of knowledge in which concepts are sought to be made clear by analysis. But the *generation* of *a priori* knowledge which is derived as much from observation as from concepts, together with *a priori* synthetic propositions understood philosophically, finally constitute the essential content of metaphysics.

§ 3

A Footnote on the General Classification of Judgments into Analytic and Synthetic Judgments

This classification is indispensable in regard to the critique of the human mind and therefore deserves to be *classic* in this critique, but I do not know of any other considerable use for it. I also find here the reason why dogmatic philosophers, who, looking for the sources of metaphysical judgments in metaphysics itself (rather than outside it in the laws of pure reason in general), have neglected this classification which seems to offer itself so naturally. I see why men like the celebrated Wolff, or the acute Baumgarten who followed in his steps, have sought the proof of the principle of sufficient cause, which is obviously synthetic, in the principle of contradiction. I encountered a hint of this classification in Locke's "Essay on the Human Understanding." In the third chapter of the fourth book he discusses the association of different ideas (*Vorstellungen*) in judgments and their sources. He sees one of their sources in the principles of identity and contradiction while he sees the other source in the existence of such ideas in a subject (synthetic judgments). Locke then confesses that our *a priori* knowledge of the latter judgments is very limited, amounting to almost nothing. But there is so little that is definite and reduced to rules in what he says respecting this kind of knowledge that one cannot be surprised that no one, not even Hume, has undertaken to reflect upon this class of propositions. For such general yet definite principles as these are not easily learned from other men to whom they have only been dimly discernible. One must first discover them through one's own reflection and then one will find them elsewhere in places where otherwise one certainly would not have noticed them, since the authors themselves did not know that their own remarks were based upon such an idea. Once a point has been clarified, writers who do not think for themselves nevertheless possess the acumen to hunt it up in what has previously been said though no one could see it before.

THE GENERAL QUESTION OF THE
PROLEGOMENA

Is Metaphysics possible at all?

§ 4

Were metaphysics actually a viable science, one could say: here is metaphysics, you only have to learn it and it will convince you permanently and irresistibly of its truth. In that case the present question would be unnecessary and there would only remain the question: how is such metaphysics possible, and how is reason to set about attaining it? (This would be more a testing of our acuteness than a proof of the existence of metaphysics.) Unfortunately, in this case human reason is not in such a happy position. One cannot point to a single book like *Euclid* and say: this is metaphysics, in this is to be found the supreme purpose of this science, the knowledge of a supreme being and of a future world, demonstrated upon principles of pure reason. One can produce many propositions that are apodictically certain and that have never been contested. But these propositions are analytic in their entirety and concern more the materials and the elements of construction than the extension of knowledge which is our special object in the present case (§ 2, B, C above). Then there is the case of certain synthetic propositions, such as the principle of sufficient cause, which are readily conceded though they have never been proved by mere reason, that is, proved *a priori* as they ought to have been. In these cases, whenever someone attempted to make use of such propositions for the main purpose [of establishing a metaphysics], he ended up in such inadmissible and doubtful assertions that it has always happened that one system of metaphysics has contradicted another, either in respect to the assertions in it or their proofs, thus destroying all claim to a lasting recognition. Without doubt, the very attempts to establish such a science were the first cause of the scepticism that arose so soon. Scepticism is a mode of thought in which reason treats itself with such violence that this scepticism would never have arisen but for reason's utter despair of satisfying its [own] chief aspirations. For, long before man methodically began to question nature, he interrogated his own isolated reason, which had already become skilled to a certain extent by common experience, while the laws of nature must usually be laboriously discovered. So metaphysics floated to the surface like foam and also like foam no sooner was it gathered up than it dissolved, and more of it appeared on the surface which some people were always eager to gather, while others, instead of seeking to penetrate the cause of this phenomenon considered themselves wise in laughing at the futile endeavors of the former.

Wearied then of a dogmatism that teaches us nothing as well as of a scepticism that promises us nothing, not even the peace of a permissible ignorance, led on by the importance of the knowledge we need, yet rendered mistrustful by long experience regarding all knowledge that we believe ourselves to possess or that offers itself in the name of pure reason, we still face one critical question; *is metaphysics possible at all?* We shall adopt our future conduct in the light of the answer. But this question must be answered, not by sceptical objections to particular assertions of any actual system of metaphysics (for we do not admit of any at present), but from the as yet only problematical conception of such a science.

In the *Critique of Pure Reason* I went to work synthetically on this question by investigating pure reason itself and from this source I endeavored to determine according to principles the elements as well as the laws of the pure use of reason. This task is difficult and a resolute reader is needed to penetrate step by step into a system which presupposed nothing but itself and which consequently seeks to unfold knowledge from its original germs without depending upon any external fact. On the contrary the *Prolegomena* should be preparatory exercises designed to show what has to be done if possible to realize such a science, rather than to expound one. Therefore the *Prolegomena* must rely on something known as trustworthy from which we may proceed with confidence and ascend to the sources which are yet unknown to us and whose discovery will not only explain what we already know but will exhibit to us at the same time a range of many insights all arising from the same sources. Therefore the methodical procedure of the

Prolegomena will be analytic, especially those [parts of it] destined to prepare for a future system of metaphysics.

Now it fortunately happens that, although we cannot assume metaphysics to be an actual science, we may assert with confidence that certain pure synthetic insights are *a priori*, actual and given; namely, *pure mathematics* and *pure natural science*. Both contain propositions some of which are apodictically certain through mere reason and some of which are recognized as being in general accord with experience, though completely independent of such experience. At least we now have some *uncontested, a priori*, synthetic knowledge, and since such knowledge exists we should not ask whether it is possible, but only ask: *how is it possible?* [We should do this] in order to deduce from the principle of the possibility of such existing knowledge the possibility of all other such knowledge.

GENERAL QUESTION:

How is knowledge possible from pure reason?

§ 5

We have already seen the important distinction between analytic and synthetic judgments. The possibility of analytic propositions can be conceived very easily for they are simply based on the principle of contradiction. The possibility of synthetic *a posteriori* propositions, i.e. of such as are derived from experience, requires no particular explanation, for experience is nothing more than a continual fitting together (synthesis) of perceptions (*Wahrnehmungen*). There remain only synthetic *a priori* propositions, the possibility of which has yet to be discovered and examined because their possibility must rest on principles other than that of contradiction.

But we do not need to inquire into the possibility of such propositions, that is to ask whether they are possible, for there are enough of them actually given and given with unquestionable certainty. As the method we are following here is analytic, we shall assume at the outset that such synthetic but also pure knowledge exists based on reason. But we must investigate the grounds for this possibility and proceed to ask: how is this knowledge possible? We must do this so that we may be in a position to determine the conditions, scope and limits of the use of this knowledge from the principles of its possibility. Therefore the specific task on which everything turns will be the question, when expressed with academic precision: *How are synthetic, a* priori *propositions possible?*

A little earlier I expressed the problem somewhat differently for the sake of popularity; namely, as an inquiry into knowledge derived from pure reason. I could do this on that occasion without detriment to the desired insight. For, as we are simply concerned here with metaphysics and its sources, I hope that after the above remarks readers will constantly bear in mind that when we speak here of knowledge derived from pure reason, we invariably refer to synthetic and never to analytic knowledge.

The very existence of metaphysics depends upon the solution of this problem. It does not matter if anyone presents assertions however plausible with regard to this problem and piles conclusion upon conclusion. I have a right to say that, if he has not first been able to answer satisfactorily the above question, this is all vain, baseless philosophy and false wisdom. You speak through pure reason and claim to create *a priori* knowledge inasmuch as you not only dissect given conceptions but you pretend to establish new connections which do not rest on the principle of contradiction and which you still believe to understand quite independently of all experience. How do you arrive at the new connections and how will you justify such pretensions? You cannot be allowed to appeal to the concurrence of the general common sense of mankind for that is a witness whose reputation rests only on popular rumor. *Quodcumque ostendis mihi sic, incredulus odi.* (Horace: All that you thus show me, I unbelieving hate.)

While the answer to this question is indispensable, at the same time it is very difficult. The chief reason why men have not endeavored to answer it long before lies in the fact that it never occurred to them that anything of the kind could be asked. But a second cause is that the satisfactory answer to this one question demands a more persistent, deeper and more laborious reflection than did the most diffuse work on metaphysics that gave promise of immortal fame to its author on its first appearance. Every thoughtful reader, on attentively considering the requirements of this problem and frightened at the outset by its difficulty, would regard it as insoluble, and even as altogether impossible were it not for the actual existence of such pure, *a priori*, knowledge. This happened in the case of David Hume, although he did not place the problem before him in nearly as much generality as is done here, and as must be done if the answer is to be decisive for the whole of metaphysics. For how is it possible, said that acute man, that when I am given a concept, I can go beyond it and connect it with another which is not contained in it at all [but which is connected] in such a manner as if it necessarily belonged to it? He concluded from that difficulty which he mistook for an impossibility that only experience can present us with such associations and hence that all this presumed necessity (or what is the same thing, knowledge assumed to be *a priori*) is nothing but a long habit of believing something to be true, and therefore of believing the subjective necessity to be objective.

If the reader should complain of the difficulty and trouble I shall give him in solving this problem, then let him set about attempting to solve it in an easier way. Perhaps he will then feel obligated to one who has undertaken for him the labor of such searching inquiry. He may then show some surprise at the facility with which it has been possible to find the solution, considering the nature of the subject. It has cost years of trouble to solve this problem in a general way (taking the word "general" in the sense in which mathematicians use it, namely; sufficient for all cases), and finally to be able to present the solution in analytic form, such as the reader will find here.

Therefore all metaphysicians are solemnly and legally suspended from their business until they shall have answered adequately the question: *How is synthetic* a priori *knowledge possible?* For their answer alone can provide the credentials they must show if they have anything to present to us in the name of pure reason. In default of this, they can expect nothing else but to be rejected, without any further inquiry into their work, by sensible people who have been so often deceived.

On the other hand, should they want to carry on their business not as a *science*, but as an *art* of helpful persuasion that is suitable to the general common sense of mankind, this calling cannot in fairness be denied them. In that case they should use only the modest language of a reasonable belief, they should admit that it is not even allowed them to *conjecture*, much less to *know* anything respecting what lies beyond the boundaries of all possible experience, but merely to *assume* what is possible and even indispensable for directing the intellect and the will in life. Only in this way can they possibly acquire the reputation of wise and useful men and they will have it to a greater extent the more they renounce the title of metaphysicians. For metaphysicians want to be speculative philosophers, and, inasmuch as bare probabilities cannot be accepted, it cannot be allowed them to play with conjectures; their assertions must either be true knowledge, or they are nothing at all.

It may be said that the whole of transcendental philosophy, which necessarily precedes all metaphysics, is itself nothing more than the full solution, in systematic order and completeness, of the question propounded here. Therefore it may be said that we have no transcendental philosophy as yet. What bears its name is properly a part of metaphys-

ics, and since transcendental philosophy is to establish the possibility
of metaphysics, it must precede all metaphysics. Considering then that a
complete science, entirely new in itself and lacking assistance from
other sciences, is needed in order to answer a single question adequately, it is not surprising that the solving of this task is accompanied
by trouble and difficulty and even perhaps by some degree of obscurity.

As we now proceed to this solution according to the analytic
method, presupposing that such knowledge exists from pure reason, we
can only cite two *sciences* of theoretic knowledge, (with which we are
solely concerned here), namely; *pure mathematics* and *pure natural
science*. Only these can present to us objects in observation and therefore if *a priori* knowledge should occur in these sciences, they could
show the truth or agreement of such knowledge with the object *in
concreto*. In other words, these sciences can show the existence of such
objects. We can proceed analytically from this existence to the ground
of its possibility. This facilitates the matter very much as the general
considerations are not only applied to facts but even start from them
when otherwise they would have to be deduced by synthetic procedure
from concepts *in abstracto*.

But in order to ascend from these existing and well-grounded pure,
a priori insights to a possible knowledge such as we are seeking, namely,
to reach metaphysics as a science, we have to embrace that which
occasions it under our main question. For what occasions metaphysical
questions and forms the basis of metaphysics is given naturally, although as regards the truth in it, it is rather suspect *a priori* knowledge,
the treatment of which is usually called metaphysics without any
[prior] critical inquiry as to its possibility. In short we must comprise
within our main question the natural propensity of mankind toward
such a science [as metaphysics.] [If we do that then] the main transcendental question will be divided into four more questions which
will be answered step by step.

(1) How is pure mathematics possible?
(2) How is pure natural science possible?
(3) How is metaphysics in general possible?
(4) How is metaphysics as a science possible?

It will be seen that although the solution of these problems is
chiefly intended to present the essential contents of the *Critique of
Pure Reason*, the solution itself has something specific [to offer]. This
in itself is worthy of attention; for it is the task of discovering in reason
the sources of given sciences in order to explore and measure in the
process the faculty of reason for realizing something *a priori*. In this
way the sciences themselves should gain, if not in their content, at
least in regard to their proper use. These sciences should also gain from

greater clarification of their proper nature since the consideration of these problems [the four stated above] will provide a better insight into the common origin of these sciences.

FIRST PART OF THE MAIN
TRANSCENDENTAL QUESTION

How is pure Mathematics possible?

§ 6

Mathematics is a great and established branch of knowledge, already of remarkable compass and promising unlimited expansion in the future. Yet it carries with it a thoroughly apodictic certainty, i.e., an absolute necessity. Thus mathematics rests on no empirical grounds but is a pure product of reason, besides being thoroughly synthetic. "How is it possible for the human mind to create such knowledge entirely *a priori?*" Does not this capacity, since it does not and cannot rest on experience, presuppose some ground of *a priori* knowledge which lies deephidden, but which might manifest itself in these its effects, if only their first beginnings were diligently explored?

SECOND PART OF THE MAIN
TRANSCENDENTAL PROBLEM

How is Pure Natural Science Possible?

§ 14

Nature is the existence of things in so far as this existence is determined by universal laws. If Nature signified the existence of *things in themselves*, we could never know it either *a priori* or *a posteriori*. Not *a priori*, for how shall we know what applies to things in themselves since this can never be done by analyzing our concepts (analytic propositions)? For what I [would then] want to know is not what is contained in my concept of a thing (for that concerns its logical essence), but what, in the reality of the thing, is added to this concept, by which the thing itself is determined in its existence outside my concept. My intellect, which is subject to the conditions under which alone it can relate the qualities of things as they exist, prescribes no rules for the things in themselves; these things do not conform to my intellect, but my intellect must conform to them. These things would therefore have to be given me previously, in order for these qualities to be discovered in them; and in this case they would not be known *a priori*.

But such a knowledge of the nature of things in themselves would be equally impossible *a posteriori*. For if experience is to teach me laws to which the existence of things is subject, these laws would, in so far as they concerned things in themselves, necessarily also apply to them outside my experience. Now experience teaches me what exists and how it exists, but never that it exists necessarily in such a manner and no other. Therefore it can never teach the nature of things in themselves.

§ 15

Nevertheless, we are actually in possession of a pure natural science, which puts forward, *a priori* and with all the necessity requisite to apodictic propositions, laws to which nature is subordinated. I only need to call to witness here that introductory field which, under the title of general natural science, precedes all physics based on empirical principles. Therein we find mathematics applied to phenomena and also to those discursive principles derived from concepts which constitute the philosophical part of pure knowledge of nature. But this knowledge also contains some matters which are not pure and are not independent of experience, such as the concept of motion, impenetrability (on which the empirical concept of matter rests), inertia, and others. These matters prevent physics from being called a perfectly pure natural science. Besides, physics is only concerned with objects of the sense and thus furnishes no example of a pure natural science in the strict meaning. For, such a science must bring nature under general laws, irrespective of whether it concerns the object of the outer or of the inner sense; that of physics or that of psychology. But, among the principles of this universal physics are to be found some that really possess the universality we require, such as the proposition: *substance continues and is permanent*, and that, according to fixed laws: *all which happens is at all times previously determined by a cause*. These are really universal natural laws, existing completely *a priori*. Therefore a pure natural science actually exists, and now the question arises: *how is it possible?*

§ 16

However, the word *nature* can take on another meaning defining the *object*, whereas in the above meaning it suggested merely that *laws* determined the qualities of things as they exist. *Nature*, when considered *materialiter*, is the *sum-total of all the objects of experience.* We are only concerned with this nature here, since anyhow things which could never be objects of an experience, if they were known according to their nature, would force us to form concepts whose meaning could never be given *in concreto* (in an example of a possible experience). Therefore we would have to form concepts of which it could never be decided whether they really referred to objects or were mere figments of thought. The knowledge of that which cannot be an object of experience would be beyond the physical and we have nothing at all to do with such matters here. We are only concerned with that knowledge of nature whose reality can be confirmed by experience, even though it is possible *a priori*, and precedes all experience.

§ 17

In this narrower meaning the *formal* in nature are the laws of nature which regulate all the objects of experience, and, in so far as they are known *a priori*, these laws constitute the necessary regularity of nature. But it has just been demonstrated that the laws of nature can never be known *a priori* in objects when these objects are considered as things in themselves. . . . Hence we are not concerned here with things in themselves, but merely with things as the objects of a possible experience. The sum-total of these is what we properly call nature. Therefore, if the question concerns the possibility of *a priori* knowledge of nature, would it not be better to formulate the problem as follows? How is it possible to know *a priori* the necessary laws regulating things as objects of experience? Or, how can the necessary laws, which regulate experience itself in respect to all its objects, be known generally and *a priori?*

Seen in its true light, the solution of the problem of pure knowledge of nature (which constitutes the real point of the question) is all the same in the end, whether imagined in one form or another. For the subjective laws, under which alone a knowledge of things through experience is possible, are also valid for those things as objects of a possible experience. It does not matter then whether I say: No judgment based on observation can be considered experience without the law, that any event on being observed must invariably be referred to something preceding it upon which it follows according to a general rule; or whether I express myself thus: Everything that experience teaches as happening must have a cause.

However, it is advisable to choose the first statement. For we can have, *a priori* and before all given objects, a knowledge of those conditions under which alone an experience is possible. But we can never have knowledge of what laws those objects are subject to by themselves without reference to a possible experience. Therefore we shall not be able to study *a priori* the nature of things except by investigating the conditions and by investigating general, though subjective, laws, under which alone such a knowledge as experience is formally possible, and then by determining in accordance with this the possibility of things as objects of experience. Were I to choose the second mode of expression and were I to investigate the *a priori* conditions under which nature can possibly be an *object* of experience, I should easily be led into misunderstanding, and might then fancy I had to explain nature as a thing in itself, and I should then be fruitlessly involved in endless efforts to seek laws for things of which nothing is given me.

Therefore we shall simply be concerned here with experience and with the general and *a priori* given conditions of its possibility, and we shall thereby determine nature as the complete object of all possible experience. I think it will be understood that I am not referring to the rules for the *observation* of a nature already given, which [rules] presuppose experience, [nor am I referring to the procedure by which] we can arrive at the laws of nature through experience, for then these laws would not be laws *a priori* and they would give no pure science of nature. [What I do mean is to show] how the *a priori* conditions of the possibility of experience are at the same time the sources from which all the general laws of nature must be derived.

§ 18

First of all we must observe that while all judgments based on experience are empirical (i.e., have their foundation in immediate sense perception), on the other hand empirical judgments are not judgments based solely on experience, but that beyond the empirical, and beyond the perception given by the senses generally, special concepts must come into play. These concepts have their origin entirely *a priori* in the pure intellect; every perception is first of all subsumed under them and can then be transformed into experience by means of these concepts.

Empirical judgments, in so far as they have objective validity, are

JUDGMENTS BASED ON EXPERIENCE; but those which are merely *sub-jectively valid* I call judgments based on perception. . . .

All our judgments are at first mere judgments based on perception; they are valid simply for ourselves, as subject. Only subsequently do we give them a new reference, namely, to an object, and insist that they shall always be valid for ourselves as well as for everyone else. For, when a judgment agrees with an object, all judgments concerning the same object must agree with one another; hence the objective validity of a judgment based on experience means nothing more than its necessary general validity. Reversely, when we have to consider a judgment as necessarily and generally valid (a judgment which never rests on the perception but on the pure intellectual concept under which the perception is subsumed), we have to regard the judgment as objective, i.e., as expressing not merely the regulation of the perception to a subject but a quality of the object. For there would be no reason why the judgments of other persons must necessarily agree with mine, if it were not for the unity of the object to which they all refer, with which they agree; consequently, they must all agree with one another.

§ 19

Objective validity and necessary general validity are therefore inter-changeable notions. Although we do not know the object in itself, we regard a judgment as both general and necessary when objective validity is understood thereby. We know the object through this judgment by the general and necessary linking of given perceptions, though what it is in itself remains unknown. As this is the case with all objects of sense, judgments of experience owe their objective validity not to the direct knowledge of the object, but merely to the condition of the general validity of judgments. The object in itself always remains unknown; but when the linking of the images given to our imagination is by this intellectual concept determined as generally valid through the concept that the intellect provides, the object is determined by this relation and the judgment is objective.

We will illustrate this. That the room is warm,[2] the sugar sweet, the

---

[2] I readily admit that these instances do not present judgments of perception that could ever become judgments of experience, even if an intellectual concept came into play, because they refer to mere feeling, which everyone recognizes as merely subjective, and as such never predicable of the object, and thus never capable of becoming objective. At present I only wish to give an instance of a judgment that is subjectively valid, but that contains in itself no reason for necessary general validity and hence no reference to an object. An example of judgments of perception that become judgments of experience by the employment of an intellectual concept follows in the next footnote.

wormwood bitter, are merely subjectively valid judgments. I do not expect that I, or every other person, will always find them as I do now. They only express a relation of two sensations to the same subject, namely, myself, and they do so only in my present state of perception and are therefore not valid of an object. I call these judgments based on perception. With judgments based on experience the case is altogether different. What experience teaches me under certain circumstances, it must teach me, and every other person as well, at all times; its validity is not limited to the subject or to the state of such a subject at a particular time. All such judgments are stated as objectively valid. For instance, when I say that the air is elastic, this judgment is first of all a judgment of perception since I only link (associate) the two sensations with one another. If I wish it to be called a judgment of experience I must demand that this link (association) be so conditioned as to make it generally valid. I wish that I, and every other person shall at all times necessarily so associate the same perceptions under the same circumstances.

§ 20

Therefore, we must analyze experience, in order to see what is contained in this product of the senses and of the intellect, and how the judgment based on experience is itself possible. Such judgment is based on the thing-looked-at [*Anschauung*] of which I am conscious, the perception which merely belongs to the senses. But secondly, judging which is the sole province of the intellect is also a part of it. This [act of] judgment may be twofold; firstly, I may simply compare the perceptions in a particular state of my own consciousness; or secondly, I may link (associate) them in a general consciousness. The first judgment is a simple judgment based on perception and has [as we have seen] only subjective validity. . . . No general validity and necessity of the judgment can arise therefrom. . . .

Before a judgment of perception can become a judgment of experience, it is first of all necessary that the perception be subsumed under intellectual concepts [as stated above, § 18]. For instance, air may be subsumed under the concept of cause, which determines the judgment regarding its extension, as hypothetical.[3] In this way the extension

---

[3] The following may be taken as a more readily understandable example: When the sun shines on the stone it grows warm. This judgment [that the stone is warm] is a mere judgment of perception and contains no necessity no matter how often I or others have perceived it. These perceptions usually find themselves so linked (associated). If I say that the sun warms the stone, the intellectual concept, cause, comes into play in addition to the perception. The conception of sunshine

is represented not as merely belonging to my perception of air in my particular state, or in any of my states, or in a particular state of the perception of others, but as *necessarily* belonging thereto; and the judgment that the air is elastic becomes generally valid. It thereby becomes a judgment of experience, preceded by certain other judgments which subsume the thing-looked-at, air, under the concept of cause and effect. Thus these judgments determine the perceptions, not only with respect to one another in myself as subject, but with respect to the form of judgment generally (in this case an hypothetical judgment), and they thereby make the empirical judgment universally valid.

If we analyze all our synthetic judgments in so far as they are objectively valid, we shall find that they never consist of mere things-looked-at, which are linked, as is commonly believed, through comparison in a judgment, but that they would be impossible had there not been added, besides, to the concepts derived from looking at things, a pure intellectual concept under which the former concepts are subsumed and, only in this way, connected in an objectively valid judgment. Even the judgments of pure mathematics in its simplest axioms are not excepted from this condition. The axiom that the straight line is the shortest distance between two points presupposes that the line be subsumed under the concept of quantity, which is assuredly not a thing-looked-at, but which has its origin in the intellect. This concept serves to determine the thing-looked-at, the line, with respect to the judgments which may be made regarding it. Judgments about its quantity may be called *judicia plurativa* [4] inasmuch as it is understood through them that many similar things are comprehended under a given thing-looked-at (intuition) [*Anschauung*].

§ 21

In order to demonstrate the possibility of experience, in so far as it rests on pure, intellectual, *a priori* concepts, we must first present in a complete table what belongs to judgments generally and the various aspects of the intellect in these [judgments]. For the pure

---

necessarily becomes causally linked to that of warmth, and thereupon the synthetic judgment of necessity becomes generally valid, and consequently becomes objective: thus a perception is transformed into experience.

[4] I would prefer to call by this name those judgments which are known in logic as *particularia*, for this expression implies the notion that they are not general. When I start with unity in individual judgments and proceed to universality, I cannot include any reference to universality; I think merely of plurality without universality, not of an exception from universality. This is necessary if the logical aspects are to be the basis of the pure intellectual concept; in logical use the matter may be left as heretofore.

intellectual concepts will exactly parallel them, since they are nothing but concepts of things looked at in general, in so far as these [concepts] are determined in themselves by one or another of these aspects of judgment, that is, are necessarily and universally valid. In this way, the *a priori* principles of the possibility of all experience are precisely determined as an objectively valid empirical knowledge. For they are nothing but propositions which subsume all perception under the pure intellectual concepts in accordance with certain general conditions.

LOGICAL TABLE OF THE JUDGMENTS

1	2
According to Quantity	*According to Quality*
General	Affirmative
Particular	Negative
Single	Indefinite

3	4
According to Relation	*According to Modality*
Categorical	Problematical
Hypothetical	Assertive
Disjunctive	Apodictic

TRANSCENDENTAL TABLE OF THE INTELLECTUAL CONCEPTS

1	2
According to Quantity	*According to Quality*
Unity (the measure)	Reality
Plurality (the magnitude)	Negation
Universality (the whole)	Limitation

3	4
According to Relation	*According to Modality*
Substance	Possibility (potentiality)
Cause	Actuality (existence)
Togetherness (interaction)	Necessity

PURE PHYSIOLOGICAL TABLE OF THE UNIVERSAL PRINCIPLES OF NATURAL SCIENCE

1

Axioms of intuition [of looking at or envisaging things]

2	3
Anticipations of Perception	Analogies of Experience

4

Postulates of empirical thought in general

§ 22

The sum of all the above is this: the business of the senses is to look at (*anschauen*), that of the intellect to think. But to think is to bring together images in a consciousness. This bringing together is either merely related to the subject and is fortuitous and subjective, or it is necessary or objective. The bringing together of images in a consciousness is judgment. Thus thinking is the same as judging or referring images to judgments in general. Hence judgments are either merely subjective when images are referred to a single consciousness and brought together in it, or judgments are objective if they are brought together in the general consciousness. The logical aspects of all judgments are so many possible modes of bringing together images in a consciousness. But if they serve as concepts, they are concepts of the *necessary* togetherness of these images in a consciousness, and therefore are principles of objectively valid judgments. This togetherness in a consciousness is either analytic by identity, or synthetic by the combination and addition of different images to one another. Experience consists of the synthetic linking (associating) of phenomena (perceptions) in a consciousness, in so far as such association is necessary. Hence pure intellectual concepts are those under which all perceptions must be previously subsumed, before they can serve in judgments of experience.[5]

§ 23

Judgments, considered merely as the condition for bringing together given images in a consciousness, are rules. These rules, in so far as they present the togetherness as necessary, are *a priori*. In so far as there are none above these rules from which they can be derived, they are principles. Since there are no conditions of the judgments based on experience, in respect to the possibility of all experience when considered as a mere form of thought, beyond those conditions of the judgments which subsume the phenomena in their various forms under the pure intellectual concepts which make the empirical judgment objectively valid, these [principles] must be the *a priori* principles of all experience.

At the same time, the principles of possible experience are the

---

[5] As to how the perception came by this addition [of the concept], the *Critique of Pure Reason* may be consulted in the section dealing with the transcendental faculty of judgment, entitled, "Of the *Schematization* of Pure Intellectual Concepts," *Works*, vol. III, 137 ff. [All references to *Works* are made to the German original edited by Ernst Cassirer.]

universal laws of nature which may become known *a priori*. Thus the problem contained in our present second question (*How is pure natural science possible?*) is solved. For the systematic character required by the form of a science is completely met with here since beyond the above-named formal conditions of all judgments in general, that is, of all the general rules to be found in logic, there are none possible. These constitute a logical system; while the concepts founded upon them containing the *a priori* conditions of all synthetic and necessary judgments [constitute] a transcendental system, and the principles by means of which all phenomena are subsumed under the concepts, constitute a natural system preceding all empirical knowledge of nature and rendering this knowledge possible in the first place. Therefore such a system may properly be termed the general and pure science of nature.

§ 24

The first [6] of the above natural principles subsumes all phenomena, as things-looked-at in space and in time, under the conception of *quantity*, and to that extent it is a principle of the application of mathematics to experience. The second principle subsumes the sensation which is properly empirical and denotes the reality of things-looked-at, though not precisely, under the concept of *quantity* because sensation is not a looking-at-things which contains space and time although it places its corresponding object in both. But between the reality of a sensation and zero, i.e., the complete lack of anything felt, there is a quantitative difference. For between each given degree of light and darkness, between each degree of heat and complete coldness, each degree of weight and of absolute lightness, each degree of filling a space and the complete vacuum, progressively smaller degrees can be thought of, just as between consciousness and complete unconsciousness (psychological dark-ness) continually smaller [degrees] exist. Hence no perception is possible that would prove an absolute lack (of something); for instance, no psychological darkness which could not be viewed as a consciousness that is being surpassed by another stronger consciousness, and the same in all cases of sensation. In this way the intellect can even anticipate sensations which constitute the proper quality of empirical images (phenomena) by means of the principle that all these sensations (and

---

[6] The three following paragraphs will hardly be understood without referring to what the *Critique of Pure Reason* says on the principles, but it may be useful to have a general view of them, and to fix the attention on the main points. Cf. *Works*, vol. III, 137–224.

thus the reality of all phenomena) have degrees. This is the second application of mathematics (*mathesis intensorum*) to natural science.

§ 25

The determination of the relation of phenomena, if we consider merely their existence, is not mathematical but dynamic; it can never be objectively valid and therefore appropriate for an experience if it is not subordinated to *a priori* principles rendering their knowledge based on experience possible in the first place. Hence phenomena must be subsumed under [three concepts. Of these the first is] the concept of substance upon which is based all determination of existence as a concept of the thing itself. The second concept is that of cause and effect in so far as a succession of phenomena, that is, an event, is met with. The third concept is that of reciprocal action in so far as co-existence is to be known objectively. These *a priori* principles are those upon which objectively valid, though empirical, judgments are based. These principles are the proper laws of nature which may be termed dynamic.

Finally, there belong to judgments based on experience the knowledge and insight into the agreement and connection, not so much of phenomena in experience, as of the relation of phenomena to experience generally. This relation brings together in one concept either the agreement of phenomena with the formal conditions known by the intellect or their connection with the material of the senses and of perception, or both. Thus this relation comprises potentiality, actuality and necessity, according to the general laws of nature. [This knowledge then] constitutes the natural theory of method, the distinction between truth and hypotheses, and the limits of the reliability of the latter.

§ 26

The third table, that of the principles, is derived *from the nature of the intellect itself* according to the critical method; it shows a completeness that raises it far above every other table that has been deduced in a dogmatic way from things themselves, (although to no purpose) or that may be so attempted in the future. In this table, all synthetic *a priori* principles have been set forth completely and in accordance with a [higher] principle, the general capacity of judging, which constitutes the essence of experience as far as the intellect is concerned. Thus one can be certain that there are no additional principles—a satisfaction that cannot be obtained by the dogmatic method. Yet all this is by far not the greatest service of this table.

Attention must be paid to the grounds of proof that reveal the possibility of this *a priori* knowledge, and at the same time limit all such principles by a condition that must never be overlooked if this knowledge is not to be misunderstood and not to be extended further in use than the original meaning attached to the principles by the intellect will allow. These principles only contain the conditions of possible experience in general in so far as such experience is subordinated to *a priori* laws. Thus I do not say that *things in themselves* possess quantity, that their reality contains degrees, that their existence implies a connection of accidents in a substance, etc. For no one can prove these propositions since such a synthetic connection is simply impossible when based on mere concepts, where there is wanting on the one hand all reference to things felt by the senses, and on the other all linking of the same in a possible experience. Therefore the essential limitation of the concepts in these principles is that all things are only necessarily and *a priori* subject to the above-mentioned conditions when they are *objects of experience*.

In the second place there follows from this a specific and peculiar mode of proof of these principles. They do not refer directly to phenomena and their relation, but to the possibility of experience, of which phenomena constitute the matter but not the form. In other words, these principles refer to objective and universally valid synthetic propositions which is precisely the distinction between judgments based on experience and mere judgments based on perception. This results from the fact that the phenomena, as mere things-looked-at which occupy a part of space and time, are subsumed under the concept of quantity. This concept unites the manifold of these phenomena synthetically and *a priori* in accordance with rules. . . . [Here follows a restatement of § 24., Ed.] [7]

The reader must give the greatest attention to the mode of proof of the principles which go under the name of analogies of experience. For these principles do not concern the origin of impressions (*Anschauung*),

---

[7] The degree of heat, light, etc., is as great in a small space as in a large one. In the same way inward presentations (*Vorstellungen*), such as pain or consciousness in general, are not smaller in degree whether they last a long or a short time. Hence quantity is as great here at one point and at one moment as at any time or in any space however large. Therefore degrees are quantities, not in the looking at them, but only in the mere feeling of them. Degrees can only be estimated as quantity through the relation of 1 to 0, that is, by each one passing through infinitely small intermediate degrees to the point where it disappears, or by each one growing from zero through infinitely small momenta of increase to a definite feeling in a given time. *Quantitas qualitatis est gradus.* (The quantity of quality is a matter of degree.)

like the principles of the application of mathematics to natural science generally, but they do concern the connection of their existence in an experience. Since this experience can be nothing but the ascertaining of existence in time according to necessary laws, under which alone this experience is objectively valid and hence is [true] experience, it follows that the proof is not directed toward showing the synthetic unity of the connection of *things in themselves,* but [it is directed toward showing the synthetic unity of] *perceptions.* As far as these perceptions are concerned, the proof does not do this with respect to their content but with respect to their determination in time and to the relation of existence thereto according to universal laws. Therefore these general laws contain the necessary determination of existence in time and consequently according to an *a priori* rule of the intellect whenever the empirical determination in the relative time is to be objectively valid, that is, [whenever it is to be] experience. I cannot enter further into the matter here, in these *Prolegomena,* but I recommend that the reader, who has been long accustomed to regard experience as a mere empirical joining together of perceptions give close attention to this distinction between experience and a mere aggregate of perceptions.

§ 27

This is the place to remove Hume's doubt at its basic point. He maintained justly that we can in no way, through reason, understand the possibility of causation, that is to say, the reference of the existence of one thing to the existence of some other thing necessarily posited by the former. I may add to this that we can just as little understand the conception of subsistence [substance], i.e., the necessity for a subject lying at the basis of the existence of things which is itself no predicate of any other thing. [I would even say] that we can form no conception of the possibility of such a thing (though we can point out examples of its use in experience). In the same way, this incomprehensibility even attaches to the togetherness of things since it is not possible to see how, from the state of one thing, a consequence can be drawn as to the state of some totally different thing external to it, and vice versa; and how substances, of which each has its own separate existence, are necessarily dependent on one another. At the same time I am far from regarding these conceptions [of causation, substance and togetherness] as merely borrowed from experience, and [equally far] from regarding the necessity that is imagined through them as fictitious and mere illusion, by which we are deluded through long habit. Rather have I shown sufficiently that both they and the principles deduced from them are *a priori* certain before all experience, and that they possess indubitable objective validity, although unquestionably only in respect of experience.

§ 28

Although I do not have the slightest notion of the connection of things in themselves, or how they exist as substances, how they work as causes, or how they co-exist together as parts of a real whole, I can even less conceive of such properties in phenomena *as* phenomena because these concepts contain nothing that is inherent in the phenomena, but do contain something the intellect must conceive of by itself. But we do have a conception of how such a connection may exist between the images in our mind, in general judgments. [These general judgments may take the form of saying that] in one kind of judgment images appear as subjects in relation to predicates, in another kind as cause in relation to effect, and in a third as parts that together constitute a whole. Furthermore, we know *a priori* that without looking upon the image of an object as something definite with regard to one or another of these aspects, we could have no knowledge that could be valid of such an object. If we occupied ourselves with the object in itself there would be no single criterion by which I could know whether it was determined in respect of one or another of the above-mentioned aspects. . . . But then our question is not how things in themselves, but how knowledge based on experience of things in regard to the aforementioned judgments is arrived at, that is, how things as objects of experience can and should be subsumed under the above intellectual concepts. Hence it is clear that I fully understand not only the possibility but also the necessity of subsuming all phenomena under these concepts, that is, of using them as principles of the possibility of experience.

§ 29

In making an attempt to [analyze] Hume's problematical concept (his *crux metaphysicorum*), namely, the concept of Cause, I am first given generally, *a priori*, and by means of logic, the form of a conditional judgment [which consists in] using one thing known (*Erkenntnis*) as cause and another as effect. But it is possible to meet with a regularity of relation in perception which amounts to saying that one phenomenon always follows another (though the reverse does not happen). If so, it would be a case in which to make use of the hypothetical [form of] judgment and, for instance, to say that if the sun shines long enough upon a body, the body will become warm. Certainly there is no necessary connection here; in other words no concept of cause is involved. But I continue: If the above proposition, which is a mere subjective linking of perceptions, is to become a proposition based on experience, it must be regarded as necessary and generally valid. Such a proposition would run: Sun is the cause of heat through its light. The above empirical regularity is now looked upon as a law, and indeed, not only as valid for phenomena, but valid for them in relation to any possible experience which requires generally, and therefore necessarily, valid rules. Therefore I understand perfectly the concept of cause as a concept belonging necessarily to the mere form of experience, and I understand its possibility as a synthetic linking of perceptions in a consciousness in general. But I do not understand at all how a thing in itself is a possible cause, because the concept of cause does not at all mean a condition attached to things, but only attached to experience. Experience can only be an objectively valid knowledge of phenomena and of their sequence in time, in so far as the antecedent can be united to the consequent according to the rule of hypothetical judgments.

§ 30

Therefore pure intellectual concepts have no meaning whatever when they refer to things in themselves (*noumena*) instead of the objects of experience. They serve, as it were, to "spell out" phenomena so that these may be "read" as experience. The principles that originate from relating these concepts to the realm of the senses are useful to the intellect merely in [interpreting] experience. It can never be known *a priori* whether such combinations are possible nor whether their reference to objects can be verified by an example or even made intelligible, because all examples are borrowed from some possible experience. Consequently the objects of those concepts may not be met with anywhere except in a possible experience.

This complete solution of Hume's problem, although it turns out to be contrary to the presumption of its originator, preserves for the pure intellectual concepts their *a priori* origin, and preserves for the general laws of nature, their validity as intellectual laws. But it does so in such a manner that the use of these concepts is limited to experience because their possibility is grounded solely in the relation of the mind to experience. This is true not because they are derived from experience, but because experience is derived from them. This completely reversed mode of linking [mind and experience] never occurred to Hume.

From this conclusion flows the following result of all previous researches: "All synthetic *a priori* principles are nothing more than principles of possible experience." The synthetic *a priori* principles can never refer to anything more than mere phenomena and can only represent that which makes experience in general possible, or which, inasmuch as experience is derived from these principles, must always be capable of being represented in some possible experience.

§ 31

Thus we at last have something definite upon which to depend in all metaphysical undertakings, which have hitherto boldly enough, but always blindly, tackled everything without discrimination. Dogmatic thinkers have never allowed themselves to imagine that the goal of their efforts was so near by. Nor did those men who were conceited about their supposed common sense or their sane reason realize this. These latter started with concepts and principles of mere reason which, it is true, are legitimate and natural, but are intended merely for use in experience in order to secure insight, for which these men neither knew nor could know any definite boundaries because they had neither reflected nor could reflect on the nature or even the possibility of any such pure intellectual concepts.

Many a naturalist of pure reason (by which I mean the man who considers himself capable of deciding questions of metaphysics without any systematic knowledge) may pretend that long before from the prophetic spirit of his common sense, he not only suspected but knew and comprehended that which has been propounded here with so much preparation, or, if he will have it so, with so much prolix and pedantic pomp: "That with all our reason, we can never get beyond the field of experience." But when he is eventually questioned about his rational principles, he must confess that among them there are many principles that are not drawn from experience and that are therefore valid independently of experience and *a priori*. How then and on what grounds will he restrain himself and the dogmatist who use these concepts and principles outside all possible experience, simply because they are recognized as independent of it? And this adept of sane reason, in spite of all his pretended and cheaply acquired wisdom, is not even proof against wandering unobserved beyond the objects of experience into the field of chimeras. Indeed, in an ordinary way, he is deeply enough involved in such chimeras, although by using popular language, and by putting everything forward as probability, reasonable supposition or analogy, he gives some color to his groundless presumptions.

§ 32

From the earliest days of philosophy students of pure reason have postulated, in addition to the beings known to sense (phenomena) constituting the world of sense, special intellectual beings (noumena) which are supposed to constitute an intellectual world. Since previous students held appearance and illusion [*Erscheinung und Schein*] to be identical, [an error] which may be excused in an undeveloped epoch, they conceded true existence only to the intellectual beings.

Indeed when we rightly regard the objects of sense as mere phenomena we thereby admit that each such object is based upon a thing-in-itself of which we are not aware as it is constituted in itself, but only as known through its appearances, that is, by the manner in which our senses are affected by this unknown something. Therefore the intellect, by assuming phenomena, admits the existence of things-in-themselves. We may even say that the imagining of such beings underlying the phenomena, such mere intellectual beings, is not only permissible, but unavoidable.

Our critical deduction does not exclude by any means such things (noumena), it rather limits the principles of aesthetic so that these principles shall not be extended to everything [as that would mean that] everything would be transformed into mere phenomena. Instead, these principles should only hold with objects of possible experience. Intellectual beings are hereby admitted but only after emphasizing this rule which admits of no exception: that we know nothing definite whatever about these pure intellectual beings, nor can we know anything about them. Our pure intellectual concepts, no less than our pure images, refer to nothing but objects of a possible experience, to mere beings of sense. As soon as we leave these beings of sense, the intellectual concepts retain no meaning whatever.

§ 33

There is indeed something seductive about our pure intellectual concepts which tempt us to a transcendent use; for so I call the use that transcends all possible experience. Not only are our concepts of substance, force, action, reality, etc., entirely independent of experience, but these concepts do not contain any phenomena of sense. They really seem to refer to things-in-themselves (noumena). What confirms this supposition is that they possess a necessary certainty in themselves that experience can never approach. The concept of cause implies a rule according to which one state follows from another in a necessary manner. Experience only teaches us that often, or at most usually, one state of things follows upon another. Therefore experience can produce neither strict universality nor necessity. . . .

§ 34

[In the light of the foregoing], two important and even altogether indispensable, albeit exceedingly dry, investigations are necessary. They have been undertaken in the *Critique of Pure Reason* (*Works*, pp. 141 ff. and pp. 276 ff.). In the first of these investigations it was shown that the senses do not, *in concreto*, furnish pure intellectual concepts, but only the pattern for their use, and that the object that conforms to this pattern is only encountered in experience which [as we have seen] is the product that the intellect fashions from materials of sense. In the second investigation it was shown that [our pure intellectual concepts] cannot be used for thinking about anything outside the field of experience because these concepts merely prescribe the logical form of judgment in respect to images or things-looked-at. But, since no image is given beyond the field of the senses, these pure concepts are entirely void of meaning inasmuch as they cannot be presented *in concreto* in any way. Consequently all these *noumena* together with their sum-total, an intelligible world,[8] are nothing but notions of a task, whose object is conceivable in itself, but whose execution is utterly impossible because of the nature of our intellect. Our intellect is not a faculty for looking at things, but is merely a faculty for joining given images into experience. Therefore experience must comprise all objects for our concepts; while, outside experience, all concepts will be without meaning as then they cannot be related to any images.

§ 36

How is Nature itself Possible?

This question is the highest point that transcendental philosophy can ever reach and so it must proceed to this point which is its boundary and completion. It properly comprises two questions.

First: How is nature possible at all in its material sense in accord-

---

[8] [The footnote justifies the term "intelligible" as contrasted with "intellectual" world.—Ed.]

ance with what is seen and observed? How are space, time, and what fills them both, namely the object of sensation, possible at all? The answer is that they are possible by means of the quality of our senses; in keeping with this quality our senses are affected in a particular manner by objects that are unknown in themselves and are entirely distinct from these phenomena. This answer has been given in the *Prolegomena* in the solution of the first general question and in the *Critique of Pure Reason* in the section on transcendental aesthetics.

Second: How is nature possible at all in its *formal* sense, as the sum-total of the rules to which all phenomena must be subject if they are to be considered as connected in experience? The answer has to be that nature is only possible in this sense by means of the quality of our mind. In keeping with this quality, all images resulting from sense impressions are necessarily referred to a consciousness. By means of this referring of images to a consciousness, the peculiar method of our thinking according to rules becomes possible, and in turn through this method experience is possible. This answer has been given in the *Critique of Pure Reason* in the section on transcendental logic and in these Prolegomena in the course of the solution of the second general question.

But the question of how this peculiar quality of our senses is possible or how the quality of the intellect and the quality of the necessary perception, upon which intellect and all thinking is based, are possible cannot be analyzed or answered further because we always require these qualities for all our answers and our thinking about objects.

There are many basic laws of nature which we can only know by means of experience, but we can never come to know through experience the fact that phenomena are linked according to laws in general because [the concept of] experience itself presupposes such laws, upon which its possibility is based *a priori*.

Therefore, the possibility of any experience at all is at the same time the universal law of nature, and the principles of that experience are at the same time the laws of nature. For, we only know nature as the sum-total of phenomena, i.e., as the sum-total of images or representations in our mind. Therefore we can derive the law of their connection only from the principles of the connection of images in ourselves, i.e., from the conditions of a necessary association in a consciousness which provides the possibility of experience.

Even the main proposition that general laws of nature can be known *a priori*, which has been expounded throughout the whole of this section, leads of itself to the further proposition that the highest law-making of nature must apply to ourselves, namely, to our mind, and that we must not seek nature's general laws by means of experience; but that, conversely, we must seek nature's conformity to law only in the conditions of the possibility of experience given by our senses and our mind. For how otherwise could it be possible to know these laws *a priori* since they are not rules of analytic knowledge, but are true synthetic extensions of such knowledge? Such a necessary agreement of the principles of possible experience with the laws of the possibility of nature can only result from one of two causes: That either the laws are borrowed from nature by means of experience, or conversely that nature [as a conceptual manifold] is derived from the laws of the possibility of experience generally and is entirely identical with the mere general conformity to law of such experience. The first hypothesis contradicts itself, for the universal laws of nature can and must be known *a priori*, i.e., known independently of all experience, and be posited as the basis of the empirical use of the intellect; hence only the second [hypothesis] remains to us.

But we must distinguish the empirical laws of nature, which always presuppose particular perceptions, from the pure or universal laws of nature, which, without being based upon any particular perceptions, merely contain the conditions of the necessary association of such perceptions in experience; in respect of the last, nature and possible experience are the same thing. Since in this, nature's conformity to law rests on the necessary linking of phenomena in experience, without which we could not know any object of the world of the senses, in other words, such conformity rests on the original laws of the intellect, it sounds strange at first, but it is none the less true when I say in respect of these laws of the intellect: *The intellect does not derive its laws (a priori) from nature but prescribes them to nature.*

§ 38

If we consider the properties of the circle by which this figure combines in itself under a universal rule so many arbitrary determinations of space, one cannot help but attribute a specific character (*eine Natur*) to this geometrical thing. For instance, two lines that intersect one another and the circle, however they may be drawn, are yet always so regular that the rectangle constructed with the segments of one line is equal to that constructed with the segments of the other. Now I ask, "Does this law originate in the circle or in the intellect?" In other words, does this figure, independently of the intellect, contain the ground of the law itself, or does the intellect introduce this law, that chords cut one another in geometrical proportion, since the intellect itself has constructed the figure according to its own concepts, namely the equality of radii? When we follow the proofs of this law we soon perceive that it can only be derived from the condition upon which the intellect has based the construction of this figure, namely, the equality of radii. If, in order to pursue still further the unity of the manifold properties of geometrical figures under common laws, we extend the concept and consider the circle as a conic section subordinated to the same fundamental conditions of construction as other conic sections, we find that all chords that intersect within the ellipse (parabola and hyperbola) always intersect so that the rectangles under their segments, though indeed not equal, yet stand in the same ratio to one another. If we proceed still further to the fundamental laws or physical astronomy we find a physical law of reciprocal attraction at work over all material nature, whose rule it is that such attraction decreases inversely as the square of the distance from each attracting point, that is as the spherical surfaces increase over which this power radiates. This law seems to be necessarily inherent in the nature of things themselves and is therefore usually propounded as capable of being known *a priori*. Simple as the sources of this law may be, since they rest merely on the relations of spherical surfaces of different radii, its consequences are so valuable as regards the variety of their regularity and agreement that not only are all possible orbits of the celestial bodies [described] in conic sections, but such a relation of these orbits results, that no other law of attraction than that of the inverse square of the distance could be conceived as suitable for a cosmic system.

Therefore nature is resting here on laws that the intellect comes to know *a priori* and to know mainly from general principles for determining spatial relations. Now I ask: Are these natural laws inherent in space and does the intellect learn them by merely seeking to discover the full meaning contained therein, or are they inherent in the intellect and in the manner in which the intellect determines space according to the conditions of uniform synthesis toward which all the concepts of the intellect tend? Space is so uniform a thing and so indeterminate as regards all particular properties that certainly no one will seek any wealth of natural laws in it. But that which shapes space into circular form, the figure of the cone or of the sphere, is the intellect in so far as it contains the grounds of the unity of the construction of these figures. Therefore the mere general form of imagining called space is presumably the substratum of all particular objects of determinate images and this substratum certainly furnishes the condition of the possibility and variety of these images.

[Following this, Kant repeats what he said at the end of § 36. Then, in § 39 he briefly sketches his approach to "categories," rejecting the scheme of Aristotle.—Ed.]

THE THIRD PART OF THE MAIN
TRANSCENDENTAL PROBLEM

How is Metaphysics possible at all?

§ 40

For their own security and certainty pure mathematics and pure natural science do not require a deduction such as we have just concluded with respect to them both; for pure mathematics rests upon its own evidence while pure natural science, though arising from the pure sources of the intellect, is dependent upon complete verification by experience, a witness that pure natural science is unable to repudiate and to do altogether without, since, with all its certainty, it can never, when philosophically considered, rival mathematics. Both these sciences did not require the foregoing investigation for their own sake, but for the sake of another science: metaphysics.

Metaphysics has to do not only with concepts of nature which invariably have an application in experience, but also with pure rational concepts which can never be related to any possible experience. Therefore metaphysics has to do with concepts whose objective reality (that they are not mere chimeras) and with assertions whose truth or falsity cannot be confirmed or discovered by any experience. This part of metaphysics is precisely what constitutes its essential purpose, all else being merely a means thereto, and hence this science requires *for its own sake* such a deduction [as Kant has just given for mathematics and pure natural science]. The problem now before us concerns the core and specific nature of metaphysics: The occupation of reason with itself alone and the supposed acquaintance with objects arising from reason as it broods over its own concepts without having need of, nor indeed being able to achieve such knowledge through the meditation of experience.[9]

Reason can never fulfill its rôle without solving this problem. The empirical use to which reason limits pure intellect does not consummate reason's purpose to the utmost extent. Each single experience is

---

[9] If we may say that a science at least exists in all men's thought when it has been established that the problems leading to it are put to everybody by the nature of human reason and consequently that many, though faulty, attempts at solving these problems are constantly and inevitably being made, then we must say that metaphysics exists subjectively (and indeed necessarily). Hence we rightly ask: How is it (objectively) possible?

but a part of the whole sphere of the intellect's domain. But the *absolute totality of all possible experience is not itself* an experience but is a necessary problem for reason. In order to present this problem reason needs concepts quite different from the pure intellectual concepts [the categories]. The use of these intellectual concepts is only *immanent,* that is, related to experience in so far as it can be given. The rational [spiritual] concepts of reason aim toward complete knowledge, i.e., toward the collective unity of all possible experience and thereby transcending any given experience. Thus these concepts become transcendent.

As the intellect needs the categories for [the acquisition of] experience, so reason contains in itself the basis of ideas, by which I mean necessary concepts whose object *cannot* be given in any experience. These ideas are inherent in the nature of reason as much as the categories are inherent in the nature of the intellect. If these ideas involve an appearance that may mislead easily, this appearance is unavoidable, although we may very well guard ourselves against being misled by it.

Since all appearance consists in the subjective grounds of judgment being taken for objective, a self-knowledge of pure reason, in its transcendent use, will be the only protection against the aberrations into which reason falls when it misinterprets its function and relates to an *object,* or thing-in-itself that which only concerns its own *subject* and this subject's guidance in the immanent use of reason.

[In § 41 Kant states once again that the distinction between ideas as concepts of pure reason and categories as concepts of the pure intellect is extremely important and that this distinction itself renders the *Critique of Pure Reason* a major contribution to metaphysics. In § 42 Kant reasserts the important differences between ideas and categories as regards experience.—Ed.]

§ 43

It has always been my greatest aim in the *Critique of Pure Reason* not only to distinguish carefully between the ways of [acquiring] knowledge, but also to derive from their common source all the concepts pertaining to these several ways so that by being informed whence they are derived, I should not only be able to determine their [right] use with certainty, but that I should have the never-suspected and priceless advantage of knowing the number, classification and specification of these concepts *a priori,* that is, according to principle. Without this [survey] everything in metaphysics is mere rhetoric and one would never know if what one has is sufficient or if and where something may be wanting in it. We can certainly only have this advantage in pure philosophy, but it constitutes the essence of this philosophy.

Since I had found the origin of the categories in the four logical functions of all judgments of the intellect, it was only natural to seek the origin of the ideas in the three functions of the syllogisms of reason. For, when such concepts of pure reason (transcendental ideas) are once given, they cannot be found, unless they are supposed to be innate, elsewhere than in an act of reason. As far as mere form is concerned, such an act of reason constitutes the logical element of the syllogisms of reason, while it constitutes the transcendental concepts of pure reason, in so far as such an act presents the judgments of the intellect as determined *a priori* with respect to one or another form.

The formal differences in the syllogisms of reason render necessary their division into categorical, hypothetical and disjunctive syllogisms. The concepts of reason based on them contain: first, the idea of the complete subject (*Substantiale*), second, the idea of the complete series of conditions, and third, the determination of all concepts in [by?] the idea of a complete complex (*Inbegriff*) of the possible.[1] The first idea is psychological, the second cosmological, and the third theological. Since all three give rise to dialectics, although each does so in its own way, the classification of the entire Dialectics of pure reason is based upon these [three ideas]: it is divided into the paralogism, the antinomy, and finally the ideal of such a dialectics. By this division we are fully assured that all requirements of pure reason are completely presented here and that no further requirements can be missing because the capacity of reason is completely surveyed by these three syllogisms.

§ 44

In these general reflections it is noteworthy that rational ideas, unlike categories, are of no service to the intellect for interpreting experience,

---

[1] In disjunctive judgments we consider all possibility to be classified in relation to a particular concept. The ontological principle of the complete determination of a thing generally is that of all the possible contradictory predicates one must be attributed to this [given] thing. At the same time this is the principle of all disjunctive judgments and hence this ontological principle is based on the aggregate of all possibilities. This serves as a slight explanation of the above proposition: That the act of reason, in disjunctive syllogisms of reason, is the same, as far as form is concerned, as the act by which reason fashions the idea of an aggregate of all reality; for this idea contains in itself the positive [predicate] of all mutually contradictory predicates.

and can be wholly dispensed with in this connection. In fact, rational ideas are likely to be impediments to the maxims of a rational knowledge of nature, although they are needed for another purpose which has yet to be determined. The question of whether the soul is, or is not, a simple substance need not concern us in so far as the explanation of the soul's phenomena is concerned. We cannot make the concept of a simple being comprehensible by any possible experience related to the senses, i.e., *in concreto*. Hence this concept is quite empty as far as gaining any insight into the cause of phenomena is concerned. It cannot serve as a principle for explaining anything presented by either internal or external experience. The cosmological ideas of the beginning of the world or of the eternity of the world (*a parte ante*) can help us just as little to explain an occurrence in the world itself. Finally, in accordance with a just maxim of the philosophy of nature, we must refrain from all explanations of the order of nature that are derived from the will of a Supreme Being, because that would no longer be a philosophy of nature, but a confession that we are at the end of such a philosophy. Hence, these ideas are destined for quite a different use than the categories. By means of these ideas and the principles based upon them experience itself first becomes possible. But our laborious analysis of the intellect would be quite superfluous if our aim were nothing more than knowledge of nature such as can be provided through experience. Reason accomplishes its work certainly and well both in mathematics and natural science without any of this subtle deduction. Thus our critique of the pure intellect combines with the ideas of pure reason in a direction aiming beyond the empirical use of the intellect. Yet, as we have said above, such empirical use is quite impossible and without object or meaning. Nevertheless there must be an agreement between what belongs to the nature of reason and what belongs to the nature of the intellect and reason must contribute to the perfection of the intellect and cannot possibly confuse it.

The solution of the problem is as follows: Pure reason does not have particular objects in view which lie outside the field of experience, but has in view objects denoted by its ideas. Pure reason requires completeness in the use of the intellect in dealing with experience. This completeness can only be a completeness of principles, not one of images and objects. But in order to be able to present such principles as definite, reason conceives of them as the knowledge of an object. Such knowledge is completely determined in regard to these rules [principles]. But, this object is only an idea designed to bring the knowledge of the intellect as near as possible to the completeness indicated by that idea.

§ 57

The Determination of the Bounds of Pure Reason

After all the very clear proofs we have given above, it would be absurd for us to expect to know more of any object than what belongs to the possible experience of such an object. It would be equally absurd to lay claim to the least knowledge of any conceivable thing of which we can assume that it is not an object of possible experience; we cannot determine what its quality may be or what it is in itself. For how could we effect such a determination? Neither time, space, nor all the intellectual concepts [categories], and certainly not the concepts derived from empirical observation or *perception* in the world of sense have or could have any other use than merely to make experience possible. If we omit this condition from pure intellectual concepts, then these concepts determine no object whatever and have no meaning anywhere.

But it would be even more absurd not to admit [that there might be] things in themselves, or to suggest that our kind of experience is the only possible method of knowing objects, in other words, to pretend that our way of looking at things in space and time is the only possible way, and that our discursive intellect is the prototype of every possible intellect. [This would amount to] insisting that principles of the possibility of experience be considered general conditions of things-in-themselves.

Then our principles, which merely limit the use of reason to possible experience, might accordingly become *transcendent* themselves [which would mean that] the limits of reason would be held to be the limits of things themselves. The *Dialogues* of Hume may serve as an example of this error which results if no careful critique of the limits of our reason watches its empirical use and sets a limit to its pretensions. Scepticism originally arose from metaphysics and its uncontrolled dialectics. At first scepticism, in order to aid the empirical use of the mind, claimed that all that went beyond this empirical use was nugatory and deceptive. But as it gradually became evident that the very same principles that we use in experience were *a priori* and that these principles, imperceptibly and apparently with justification, carried the mind way beyond experience, a doubt began to be thrown on the principles of experience themselves. This doubt means no great danger, for common sense will always assert its rights. But then extraordinary confusion arose in all knowledge, for it could not be determined how far reason was to be trusted and why only so far and no farther. This confusion can only be remedied, and any future relapse prevented, by a formal determination of the limits derived from principles for using reason.

It is true that we cannot form any definite conception of things in themselves, yet we are not entirely free from avoiding an inquiry about them. Considering the nature of our soul, what man can stand attaining a clear consciousness of himself as a subject, and attaining the conviction that the soul's phenomena cannot be explained *materialistically*, without asking what the soul really is? If no concept based on experience suffices for [answering] this question, who can avoid at least assuming a rational concept, namely, that of a simple immaterial being, even though its objective reality cannot be demonstrated in any way? Who can be satisfied with mere knowledge [when it comes to] such cosmological questions as the size and duration of the world, of freedom, or of natural necessity? For, no matter how we start, every answer given according to the principles of experience will generate a new question requiring an answer just as urgently, thereby clearly demonstrating the inadequacy of all physical modes of explanation for satisfying reason. Finally, who does not see how impossible it is to stop with these empirical principles when confronted by the thoroughgoing contingency and dependence of all that he can assume and conceive according to principles based on experience? Who then does not feel himself, though prohibited from losing himself in transcendent ideas, constrained (*notgedrungen*) to go beyond all the concepts verifiable by experience to seek rest and contentment in the concept of a Being whose possibility cannot be perceived by itself but whose possibility cannot be refuted either? This idea is a mere rational being, but without its possibility reason would have to remain unsatisfied forever.

Boundaries, where extended beings are involved, always presuppose a space which is encountered outside a certain place and encloses it. Limits do not require this, since they are mere negations affecting a quantity so far as this quantity is not absolutely complete.[2] However, our reason sees, so to speak, around itself a space in which things-in-themselves might be known, but it can never have definite concepts of them, since it is limited to phenomena.

As long as knowledge corresponds to reason, no definite boundaries can be conceived for such knowledge. Human reason recognizes limits but no boundaries in mathematics and natural science. Reason recognizes that something exists outside itself to which it can never attain, but it does not recognize that it can ever be perfected itself in

---

[2] [The sharp dichotomy that Kant suggests here between *Grenzen* and *Schranken* does not exist in either German or English. The word *limit* denotes both, but so does *boundary*.—Ed.]

its inner progress. The extension of our insight into mathematics and the possibility of new discoveries reaches to infinity. The same can be said of the discovery of new qualities in nature, of new forces and laws through continued experience and the linking of such experience by reason. At the same time we cannot fail to acknowledge limits, for mathematics refers only to *phenomena* and that which cannot be an object of observation through the senses, such as the concepts of metaphysics and morals, lies wholly outside the sphere of mathematics. [It lies in a region] to which mathematics can never lead, but then mathematics does not require these concepts. Therefore there is no approach and no continuous progress toward this kind of knowledge. Natural science will never discover the inner [nature] of things; that which is not phenomenon but could serve as the final explanation of phenomena. But natural science does not require this [final solution] for its physical explanations; even if such solutions were offered from other sources, for example the influence of immaterial beings, natural science should reject such solutions and on no account bring them into its own analysis. Natural science should invariably base its analysis on that which is a part of experience, being an object of sense; [for such objects] can be related to our actual perceptions by laws based on experience.

But metaphysics carries us through the dialectical efforts of pure reason to limits [boundaries] which are not initiated arbitrarily or rashly, but which the nature of reason itself impels us [to discover]. Since we cannot deal with transcendental ideas and since transcendental ideas will never allow themselves to be realized, they serve to show us not only the actual boundaries of the use of pure reason, but also the way to determine the boundaries. Indeed, this is the end and use of the natural disposition of our reason, which has given birth to metaphysics as its pet child, whose begetting is not to be ascribed to chance like that of everything else in the world, but ascribed to an original germ, wisely organized for great ends. For, perhaps more than any other science, metaphysics, in its basic outline, is implanted in us by nature itself. Metaphysics can by no means be regarded as the product of an arbitrary choice or as an accidental extension [occurring] in the progress of experience.

Although all reason's concepts and laws of the intellect are adequate for empirical use, i.e., in the world of sense, reason does not find any satisfaction for itself in such, for it is deprived of all hope of completely solving some questions which recur *ad infinitum*. Such problems for reason are the transcendental ideas that aim at this completion [perfection—*Vollendung*]. Reason sees clearly that the world of sense cannot contain such perfection and so it can be contained just as little by those concepts which serve simply for understanding the world of sense, space and time, and by all the concepts we have mentioned under the heading of pure intellectual concepts. The world of sense is nothing but a chain of phenomena connected according to general laws and therefore, being not properly the thing in itself, has no existence by itself. Therefore this world necessarily refers to what provides the basis of this phenomenal world, to beings that cannot be known as things in themselves and cannot be known merely as phenomena. Only in the knowledge of these beings can reason hope to see some time its desire satisfied for completing the progress from the conditioned to its conditions.

We have indicated above (§§ 33, 34) the limits of reason in respect to all knowledge of mere thought beings [rational beings]. We can now determine the boundaries of pure reason, since transcendental ideas have necessitated the progress to these rational beings and they have thus led us, as it were, to the point where filled space is in contact with empty space of which (the *noumena*) we can know nothing. The limits described in the cited paragraphs are not yet sufficient, since we have found that something lies beyond them, even though we can never know what this may be in itself. For now the question is: How does our reason behave in this linking of what we know with what we do not know and never can know? Here is a real link of the known with a wholly unknown which will always remain unknown. Even if the unknown should not become better known in the least [degree]—which indeed is not to be expected—the concept of this link can be determined and made distinctive.

Therefore, it seems, we are to conceive of an immaterial being, of an intellectual world, and of a highest of all beings, all of them *noumena*, because only in these [concepts], as things in themselves, does reason meet with completeness [perfection] and satisfaction. This is because these concepts really refer to something distinct and therefore wholly different from themselves. . . .

Since we can never definitely come to know these intellectual beings [Ed. should read: rational beings] regarding what they may be in themselves and yet we must assume such beings in relation to the world of sense and since we must link these beings to the world of sense through reason, we should at least be able to conceive of this link by means of such concepts as express their relation to the world of sense. We will take an example from the concept of a Supreme Being.

The *deistic* concept [of God] is a very pure, rational concept, but it only represents a thing containing all reality without being able to determine a single [partial reality]. In order to do so, an illustration would have to be borrowed from the world of sense and in that case we would be dealing in every instance with an object of sense and not with something completely different, which cannot be an object of sense. For example, I might attribute intellect to the deistic concept [of God]; yet I have no concept whatever of any intellect other than one like my own, one to which images must be given through the senses, and one which occupies itself with subsuming these images under rules [springing from] the unity of the consciousness. But in that case the elements of my concept would necessarily be those inherent in a phenomenon. Yet it was the inadequacy of the phenomena which forced me [in the first place] to pass beyond the phenomena to the conception of a being in no way dependent on phenomena, or bound up with them as conditions of its definition. On the other hand, if I sever intellect from the senses in order to arrive at a pure intellect nothing remains but the mere form of thought without any images. By such mere form of thought I can know nothing determinate, hence no object. For this purpose I would have to conceive another mind that could look at such objects [things-in-themselves]. I have not the least notion of such a mind because the human mind is discursive and can only know through general concepts. The same happens if I attribute a will to the Supreme Being, for I have this concept only in so far as I derive it from my inner experience. This experience depends upon the satisfaction of [my desires and the] things which we need, and hence upon my senses. Such a dependence completely contradicts the pure concept of a Supreme Being.

The objections of Hume to Deism are weak, hitting upon no more than the proofs and never on the [central] proposition of the deistic assertion. But Hume's objections are very strong as regards Theism, [in which the conception of God] is supposed to be created by a more detailed determination of our concept of the Supreme Being [which] is merely transcendent. Depending on how the concept is constructed, Hume's objections are irrefutable. Hume always maintains that we are really thinking of nothing definite [when we employ] the mere concept of an original being to whom we can attribute none but the ontological predicates of eternity, omnipresence, and omnipotence, and that qualities constituting a concrete concept must be added. It is not enough, says Hume, to state that the original being is cause, but [we must also state] what its causality is like and whether [it operates] perhaps through intellect and will. At this point, Hume's attacks on Theism itself start in earnest, while before he had only assailed the grounds of proof for Deism, which does not constitute any special danger. His dangerous arguments refer entirely to the anthropomorphism which he holds to be inseparable from Theism and to make Theism self-contradictory. For, if this anthropomorphism is left out,

[Theism itself] would fall and nothing would remain but a Deism with which one could not accomplish anything that would be useful because it could not serve as a foundation for religion and morals. If it were certain that anthropomorphism were inescapable, the proofs of the existence of a Supreme Being might be what they will, and might all be conceded, the concept of this Being could never be determined by us without involving us in contradictions.

But suppose we combine the apparently contradictory command to proceed to concepts outside the field of the immanent (empirical) use [of the intellect] with the command to avoid all transcendent judgments of pure reason. We then become aware that both commands may prevail together, but just on the *boundary* of all admissible use of reason. This boundary belongs as much to the field of experience as to that of the beings [created by] thought. At the same time we are taught how those strange ideas merely serve to determine the boundaries of human reason. On the one hand, we must not seek to extend beyond all bounds knowledge based on experience, for then nothing but a mere [phenomenal] world remains for us to know. On the other hand, we must not seek to transcend the boundaries of experience and to judge things outside experience as things-in-themselves.

We are keeping to this boundary when we limit our judgment to the relation the world may have to a Being whose concept lies outside all that knowledge of which we are capable within this world. In this case we are not attributing to the Supreme Being itself any of the qualities by which we conceive the objects of experience and we are thus avoiding *dogmatic* anthropomorphism. But we do attribute these qualities to the relations of the Supreme Being to the world. We are thereby allowing ourselves a *symbolical* anthropomorphism which, as a matter of fact, only concerns the language and not the object.

When I say that we are impelled to regard the world *as if* it were the work of a supreme will and intellect, I am not really saying more than the following: As a watch, a ship, or a regiment is related to the craftsman, the shipbuilder or the general, so this world of sense, or all that constitutes the basis of this aggregate of phenomena, is related to the unknown, which I conceive, not according to what it is in itself, but according to what it is for me in regard to the world of which I am a part.

§ 58

An insight such as this is gained by *analogy*, not in the usual meaning of an imperfect resemblance of two things, but of a perfect resemblance of two relations between totally dissimilar things.[3] By means of this analogy there remains a conception of the Supreme Being which is adequately defined *for our purposes*, although we have left out everything that could determine this conception generally and *in itself*. For, we define this conception in respect of the world and therefore of ourselves and no more is necessary for us.

[Hereafter in this section Kant restates, with slightly different focus, the argument of the previous section.—Ed.]

§ 60

Thus we have fully set forth metaphysics as it is actually given in the natural propensity of human reason and in what constitutes the essential purpose of developing metaphysics. We have done this according to the subjective potentiality of man for metaphysics. We have found in the course of this inquiry that the *merely natural* use of such a propensity of our reason involves reason in extravagant dialectical syllogisms, some of which are illusion, some even [mutually] conflicting, unless discipline bridles our reason and keeps it within limits. This is only possible by means of scientific criticism. Furthermore, [we have found] this speculative metaphysics to be dispensable and even prejudicial to the promotion of the knowledge of nature. Nevertheless, it remains a task worthy of further inquiry to discover the *natural* ends aimed at by this propensity in our reason for [developing] transcendent concepts. For, everything in nature must have been originally designed for some useful purpose.

Such an inquiry is indeed difficult. Moreover I confess that all I say here respecting the primary ends of nature is only conjecture. But I may be permitted to do so in this case as the question does not con-

---

[3] Of this nature is an analogy between the legal relations of human actions and the mechanical relations of moving forces: I can do nothing to another without giving him the right, under the same conditions, to do the same to me; similarly, no body can act upon another body with its moving force without thereby causing that other body to react upon itself to the same extent. Here, right and moving force are quite dissimilar things, but there is complete resemblance in their relation. Hence, by means of an analogy such as this, I can give a relational concept of things absolutely unknown to me. For instance, as the promotion of the happiness of children is related to the love of parents, so the welfare of the human race is related to the unknown [quality] in God which we term love, not as though this unknown quality had the least resemblance to any human affection, but because we can conceive its relation to the world as similar to the relation that things of the world have to each other. But here the relational concept is a mere category; it is the concept of cause which has nothing to do with sense perception.

cern the objective validity of metaphysical judgments, but refers merely to the natural propensity to make such judgments. This inquiry is thus outside the system of metaphysics and belongs to anthropology.

Suppose one compares all transcendental ideas whose aggregate constitutes the peculiar task of natural, pure reason, compelling it to leave mere observation of nature and to pass beyond all possible experience, and in these efforts to produce the thing called metaphysics, whether it be knowledge or mere argumentation. I believe that I can discern that this natural propensity is meant to free our concepts from the restraints of experience and the limits of mere observation of nature enough so that it may at least see a field opened before it which merely contains objects for the pure intellect that cannot be arrived at by any of the senses. The purpose is not to occupy ourselves speculatively with these objects, because in this we can find no firm ground on which to stand. But we are to occupy ourselves with these objects because principles of action cannot claim general currency if they do not find scope for their necessary expectations and cannot spread and gain the general acceptance that reason requires as indispensable for moral purposes.

Thus the *psychological* idea may offer small insight into the pure nature of the human soul since this nature is beyond all concepts based on experience. But at least this idea reveals to me sufficiently the inadequacy of the concepts of experience and thereby preserves me from materialism. [This is important, because] materialism as a psychological concept is of no use in explaining nature, while it also narrowly restricts reason in its practical aspect [capacity for moral action]. In the same way *cosmological* ideas serve to keep us from a naturalism that proclaims nature to be self-sufficing by (showing) the obvious inadequacy of all possible knowledge of nature in satisfying reason in its justifiable inquiries. Finally, since all natural necessity in the world of sense is invariably conditioned [by antecedent causes] inasmuch as natural necessity always presupposes dependence of things on one another; unconditioned [absolute] necessity must be sought in the unity of a cause differentiated from the world of sense. Yet if the causality of this cause [of causes] were mere nature, it could never make the existence of the contingent comprehensible as its sequence. Therefore reason frees itself from fatalism by means of the *theological idea*, no matter whether such fatalism means a blind natural necessity devoid of a first principle in the context of nature, or whether it means the causality of this principle itself. Instead, reason leads to the conception of causation through freedom, in other words, to a supreme intelligence. Thus the transcendental ideas, if they do not instruct us positively, at least serve to repudiate the audacious assertions of *materialism, naturalism and fatalism* that narrowly restrict the field of reason. At the same time, these ideas procure a place for moral ideas outside the sphere of [mere] speculations. This achievement, it seems to me, will explain in some measure the natural propensity [of man to develop these ideas].

Whatever practical utility a merely speculative science may have lies outside the boundaries of this science and hence can be viewed merely as a scholium, and like all scholia, as not forming a part of the science itself. At the same time, the practical utility of a speculative science at least lies within the boundaries of [general] philosophy, especially in that [part] drawing from the sources of pure reason. Thus the speculative use of reason in metaphysics must necessarily be in concord with its practical use in morals. Hence, when the inescapable dialectics of pure reason in metaphysics are considered as a natural propensity, they deserve to be explained not merely as an illusion requiring to be resolved, but as a natural arrangement [designed] for a highly beneficial end [*überverdienstlich*]. However, as this task is more than meritorious, in justice it cannot be assigned to metaphysics proper.

The solution of these problems, which are discussed in the *Critique of Pure Reason*, might be regarded as a second scholium which is more closely related to the content of metaphysics. For certain principles of reason are expounded there that determine *a priori* the order of nature, or rather the intellect, which is discovering nature's laws through experience. These principles seem to be constitutive and legislative in respect to experience since they arise from mere reason which, like the intellect, cannot be regarded as a principle of possible experience. [It is a question] whether the agreement between intellect and reason rests upon the fact that the intellect can only achieve the thorough uniformity of its use in dealing with the entire possible experience (in a system) by referring to reason, and that therefore experience is directly subject to the laws of reason. . . . This question may be further considered by those who desire to explore the nature of reason apart from its use in metaphysics and how to systematize it in the general principles of a history of nature. This question I have indeed presented as important in the book [*Critique of Pure Reason*] itself, but I have not attempted to solve it.

Thus I conclude the analytical solution of the problem I had proposed myself—How is metaphysics possible at all? I have proceeded from where the use of metaphysics is at least really given in its consequences, to the reasons for the possibility of metaphysics.

SOLUTION OF THE GENERAL PROBLEM OF
THE PROLEGOMENA

How is Metaphysics Possible as a Science?

Metaphysics exists as a natural disposition of reason, but it is also dialectical and deceptive when taken by itself as proved in the analytical solution of the third main problem. Hence, attempting to take principles from it and using them to follow natural, but nevertheless misleading, illusions, can never produce science but only an empty dialectical art in which one school may indeed outdo another but none can ever attain a justifiable and lasting success.

In order that metaphysics, as a true knowledge or science, may claim not merely to persuade deceptively but to produce insight and conviction, a critique of reason must exhibit the whole stock of concepts *a priori*, in a complete system arranged according to their different sources: senses, intellect, and reason. Such a critique must also present a complete table of these concepts together with an analysis of them and all that can be deduced from it. But more especially it must present the possibility of synthetic knowledge *a priori* by means of the deduction of these concepts, the principles of their use, and finally the boundaries of such synthetic knowledge, and all of this in a complete system. Thus criticism contains, and it alone contains, the whole plan well tested and approved; indeed, it contains all the means whereby metaphysics may be perfected as a science; by other ways and means this is impossible. The question is now not how this business is possible but only how we are to go about it, how good heads are to be turned from their previous mistaken and fruitless path to a non-deceptive treatment and how such a group may be best directed toward the common end.

This much is certain; that he who has once tried criticism will be revolted forever by all the dogmatic glibness that he was compelled to put up with before because his reason needed something [in the way of general explanation] and could not find anything better with which to entertain itself. Criticism stands to ordinary, academic metaphysics in exactly the same relation as *chemistry* stands to *alchemy*, or as *astronomy* to fortune-telling *astrology*. I guarantee that no one who has comprehended and thought through the conclusions of criticism, even in these *Prolegomena* will ever return to the old sophistical pseudoscience. Instead, he will look forward with a kind of pleasure to a metaphysics which is now within his power and requires no more preparatory discoveries and which alone can procure permanent satisfaction for reason. For this is an advantage upon which metaphysics, alone among all possible sciences, can count with confidence; that metaphysics can be brought to completion and into a firm state where it cannot change any further and where it is not capable of any enlargement through new discoveries. Since the sources of the knowledge of reason are not in objects nor in the imagining of objects (by which it cannot be taught anything additional), these sources are in reason itself. Therefore when reason has presented the basic laws of its capacity completely and determinately (safe) from any interpretation, there remains no knowledge *a priori* for pure reason to seek or even reasonably to inquire after. The certain prospect of so definite and perfect a knowledge has a special attraction, even if all its advantage, of which I shall speak hereafter, be set aside.

All false art, all vain wisdom lasts its time, but it destroys itself in the end and its highest cultivation marks at the same time the period of its decline. That this time has now come for metaphysics is proved by the state to which metaphysics has declined among all cultivated nations, notwithstanding the zeal with which every other kind of science is being worked on. The old curriculum of university studies still preserves its shadow, a single academy of sciences bestirs itself now and then by offering prizes to induce another attempt to be made therein. But metaphysics is no longer counted among the fundamental sciences, and anyone may judge for himself how an intellectually gifted man, to whom the term great metaphysician was applied, would take this well-meant compliment.

Although the period of the decline of all dogmatic metaphysics has undoubtedly come, as yet we are far from being able to say that the time of its re-birth by means of a thorough and complete Critique of Reason has already appeared. All transitional phases from one tendency to its opposite pass through the state of indifference and this moment is the most dangerous for an author, but, it seems to me, the most favorable moment for the science. For, when party spirit is extinguished through the complete dissolution of former groups, men's minds are in the best mood for listening eventually to proposals for agreeing on another plan.

When I say that I hope that these *Prolegomena* will perhaps revive inquiry into the field of criticism, and that they will offer to the general spirit of philosophy, which seems to be wanting in nourishment on its speculative side, a new and very promising field for its entertainment, I can foresee already that everyone, who had trodden unwillingly and with vexation the thorny path I have led him in the

Critique, will ask me on what I base this hope. I answer: *on the ir-resistible law of necessity.*

It can be just as little expected that the spirit of man will ever wholly give up metaphysical investigations as that we should stop breathing in order not to be always breathing bad air. Metaphysics will always exist in the world, and what is more, will always [exist] for everyone, but more especially for thoughtful men, who, lacking a public standard, will each fashion it in his own way. What has been termed metaphysics up till now can satisfy no acute mind, but it is impossible to renounce it entirely. Hence, a critique of pure reason itself must be *attempted* at last, and if one exists it must be examined and subjected to general inquiry because there are no other means of relieving this pressing need which is something more than mere thirst for knowledge.

After finishing the perusal of a work on metaphysics, especially if it had entertained as well as instructed me by the definition of its conceptions, its variety and its orderly arrangement in conjunction with its easy style, I cannot, since I have known criticism, forbear asking: Has this author brought metaphysics one step farther? I beg forgive-ness of the learned men whose works have been useful to me in other respects and have contributed to the cultivation of my intellectual powers, if I confess that neither in their works, nor in my own lesser efforts in whose favor amour-propre inclines me, have I been able to find that the science has been advanced in the least, and this for the very natural reason that the science did not exist then, nor could it have been brought together piecemeal, for its core had first to be fully formed in the *Critique.* However, in order to avoid all misconception it must be remembered from what has gone before that while the intel-lect has benefited greatly by analytical treatment of our concepts, the science of metaphysics has not been advanced in the least because these analyses of concepts are only materials out of which the science has to be constructed. We may dissect and define the concept of sub-stance and accident or property as well as possible, for this is useful enough as preparation for its future use. But if I cannot know that in everything that exists substance continues and only the accidents change, science would not be furthered in the least by all this dissec-tion. Now metaphysics has not been able to prove either this proposi-tion *a priori* and validly nor that of sufficient cause, much less any more complex propositions such as those belonging to the doctrine of the soul or to cosmology, and certainly never any synthetic proposition *a priori.* Thus nothing has been accomplished by all this analysis, nothing has been created and nothing furthered and the science, after so much turmoil and noise, remains where it was in Aristotle's time. If only the clue to synthetic knowledge *a priori* had been found first, then [philosophical] efforts would indisputably have been much more effective than they have in fact been formerly.

Should anyone feel offended by what is said here then he can very easily nullify the accusation if he will only abduce a single synthetic proposition belonging to metaphysics which admits of being demonstrated dogmatically *a priori*. For only when he has achieved this shall I concede that he has really advanced the science [of metaphysics], even though the particular proposition may be sufficiently confirmed by common experience. No demand could be more fair and moderate nor, in the unquestionably certain event that the demand is not fulfilled, could any statement be juster than that metaphysics as a science has not hitherto existed at all.

In case the challenge should be accepted, I must forbid two things: First, any playing with *probability* and conjecture, which is as inappropriate to metaphysics as to geometry, and second, any solution by means of the magic rod of so-called *sound common sense* which does not work [alike] for everyone but shifts according to personal characteristics.

As *regards the first*, nothing could be more absurd in a system of metaphysics, a philosophy of pure reason, than wanting to base judgments on probability and conjecture. All that is to be known *a priori* is claimed as apodictically certain and must be proved as such. We might just as well undertake to found geometry or arithmetic on conjectures. As for calculating probability in the latter, such calculation contains not probable but perfectly certain propositions on the degree of probability in certain cases under given similar conditions which, in the sum of all possible cases, must infallibly occur in accordance with the rule, although the occurrence is not sufficiently determined in respect of any single event. Only in empirical natural science can conjectures be permitted by means of induction and analogy and only in such a manner that at least the possibility of what I assume must be quite certain.

With the *appeal to sound common sense* we are, if possible, still worse off when we are dealing with concepts and principles, not so far as they are allegedly valid for experience, but when these principles are supposedly valid outside the conditions of experience. For what is *sound sense?* It is *common sense* when it judges correctly. And what is common sense? It is the faculty for gathering knowledge and employing rules *in concrete situations* as distinguished from the *speculative sense* or *intellect* which is a faculty for gathering knowledge of rules *in abstract terms*. Thus, common sense will hardly comprehend or understand as a general proposition the rule: that all that happens is determined by means of its cause. Hence common sense demands an example from experience. But when common sense learns that the general [law of causation] means nothing more than what was always apparent when a window pane was broken or a household utensil lost, common sense understands the principle and admits it. Thus sense has no use beyond seeing its rules confirmed in experience, even though these rules are really inherent in it *a priori*. The comprehension of these rules, which is independent of experience, belongs to the speculative understanding and is wholly beyond the horizon of common understanding. Metaphysics is exclusively occupied with this latter kind of knowledge and it is certainly a poor sign of sound sense to appeal to a witness who has no right of judgment here.

METAPHYSICAL FOUNDATIONS OF
MORALS

FIRST SECTION

Transition from the Common Rational Knowledge of Morality to the Philosophical

Nothing can possibly be conceived in the world, or even out of it, which can be called good without qualification, except a GOOD WILL. Intelligence, wit, judgment, and the other *talents* of the mind, however they may be named, or courage, resolution, perseverance, as qualities of temperament, are undoubtedly good and desirable in many respects. But these gifts of nature may also become extremely bad and mischievous if the will which is to make use of these gifts, and which therefore constitutes what is called *character*, is not good. It is the same with the *gifts of fortune*. Power, riches, honor, even health, and the general well-being and contentment with one's condition which is called *happiness*, all inspire pride and often presumption if there is not a good will to correct the influence of these on the mind, and with this to rectify also the whole principle of acting and adapt it to its end. The sight of a being, not adorned with a single feature of a pure and good will, enjoying unbroken prosperity can never give pleasure to an impartial rational spectator. Thus a good will appears to constitute the indispensable condition for being even worthy of happiness.

Indeed, quite a few qualities are of service to this good will itself and may facilitate its action, yet have no intrinsic, unconditional value, but are always presupposing a good will; this qualifies the esteem that we justly have for these qualities and does not permit us to regard them as absolutely good. Moderation in the affections and passions, self-control and calm deliberation are not only good in many respects, but even seem to constitute part of the intrinsic worth of a person; but they are far from deserving to be called good without qualification, although they have been so unconditionally praised by the ancients. For without the principles of a good will, these qualities may become extremely bad. The coolness of a villain not only makes him far more dangerous, but also immediately makes him more abominable in our eyes than he would have been without it.

A good will is good not because of what it performs or effects, nor by its aptness for attaining some proposed end, but simply by virtue of the volition; that is, it is good in itself and when considered by itself is to be esteemed much higher than all that it can bring about in pursuing any inclination, nay even in pursuing the sum total of all inclinations. It might happen that, owing to special misfortune, or to the niggardly provision of a step-motherly nature, this will should wholly lack power to accomplish its purpose. If with its greatest efforts this will should yet achieve nothing and there should remain only good will (to be sure, not a mere wish but the summoning of all means in our power), then, like a jewel, good will would still shine by its own light as a thing having its whole value in itself. Its usefulness or fruitlessness can neither add to nor detract anything from this value. It would be, as it were, only the setting to enable us to handle it the more conveniently in common commerce and to attract to it the attention of those who are not yet experts, but not to recommend it to true experts or to determine its value.

However, there is something so strange in this idea of the absolute value of the mere will in which no account is taken of its utility, that notwithstanding the thorough assent of even common reason, a suspicion lingers that this idea may perhaps really be the product of mere high-flown fancy, and that we may have misunderstood the purpose of nature in assigning reason as the governor of the will. Therefore, we will examine this idea from this point of view:

We assume, as a fundamental principle, that no organ [designed] for any purpose will be found in the physical constitution of an organized being, except one which is also the fittest and best adapted for that purpose. Now if the proper object of nature for a being with reason and a will was its *preservation*, its *welfare*, in a word its happiness, then nature would have hit upon a very bad arrangement when it selected the reason of the creature to carry out this function. For all the actions which the creature has to perform with a view to this purpose, and the whole rule of its conduct would be far more surely prescribed by [its own] instinct, and that end [happiness] would have been attained by instinct far more certainly than it ever can be by reason. Should reason have been attributed to this favored creature over and above [such instinct], reason would only have served this creature for contemplating the happy constitution of its nature, for admiring it, and congratulating itself thereon, and for feeling thankful for it to the beneficent cause. But [certainly nature would not have arranged it so that] such a creature should subject its desires to that weak and deceptive guidance, and meddle with nature's intent. In a word, nature would have taken care that reason should not turn into *practical* exercise, nor have the presumption, with its feeble insight, to figure out for itself a plan of happiness and the means for attaining it. In fact, we find that the more a cultivated reason applies itself with deliberate purpose to enjoying life and happiness, so much more does the man lack true satisfaction. From this circumstance there arises in many men, if they are candid enough to confess it, a certain degree of *misology*; that is, hatred of reason, especially in the case of those who are most experienced in the use of reason. For, after calculating all the advantages they derive, not only from the invention of all the arts of common luxury, but even from the sciences (which then seem to them only a luxury of the intellect after all) they find that they have actually only brought more trouble upon themselves, rather than gained in happiness. They end by envying, rather than despising, the common run of men who keep closer to the guidance of mere instinct and who do not allow their reason to have much influence on their conduct. We must admit this much; that the judgment of those, who would diminish very much the lofty eulogies on the advantages which reason gives us in regard to the happiness and satisfaction of life, or would even deny these advantages altogether, is by no means morose or ungrateful for the goodness with which the world is governed. At the root of these judgments lies the idea that the existence of world order has a different and far nobler end for which, rather than for happiness, reason is properly intended. Therefore this end must be regarded as the supreme condition to which the private ends of man must yield for the most part.

Thus reason is not competent enough to guide the will with certainty in regard to its objects and the satisfaction of all our wants which it even multiplies to some extent; this purpose is one to which an implanted instinct would have led with much greater certainty. Nevertheless, reason is imparted to us as a practical faculty; that is, as one which is to have influence on the *will*. Therefore, if we admit that nature generally in the distribution of natural propensities has adapted the means to the end, nature's true intention must be to produce a *will*, which is not merely good as a *means* to something else but *good in itself*. Reason is absolutely necessary for this sort of will. Then this will, though indeed not the sole and complete good, must be the supreme good and the condition of every other good, even of the desire for happiness. Under these circumstances, there is nothing inconsistent with the wisdom of nature in the fact that the cultivation of the reason which is requisite for the first and unconditional purpose, does in many ways interfere, at least in this life, with the attainment of the second purpose: happiness, which is always relative. Nay, it may even reduce happiness to nothing without nature failing thereby in her purpose. For reason recognizes the establishment of a good will as its highest practical destintion, and is capable of only satisfying its own proper kind in attaining this purpose: the attainment of an end determined only by reason, even when such an attainment may involve many a disappointment over otherwise desirable purposes.

Therefore we must develop the notion of a will which deserves to be highly esteemed for itself and is good without a specific objective, a notion which is implied by sound natural common sense. This notion needs to be clarified rather than expounded. In evaluating our actions this notion always takes first place and constitutes the condition of all the rest. In order to do this we will take the notion of duty which includes that of a good will, although implying certain subjective restrictions and hindrances. However, these hindrances, far from concealing it or rendering it unrecognizable, rather emphasize a good will by contrast and make it shine forth so much the brighter.

I omit here all actions which are already recognized as inconsistent with duty, although they may be useful for this or that purpose. The question whether these actions are done *from duty* cannot arise at all since they conflict with it. I also leave aside those actions which really conform to duty but to which men have *no* direct *inclination*, performing them because they are impelled to do so by some other inclination. For in this case we can readily distinguish whether the action which agrees with duty is done *out of duty* or from a selfish point of view. It is much harder to make this distinction when the action accords with duty and when besides the subject has a *direct* inclination toward it. For example, it is indeed a matter of duty that a dealer should not overcharge an inexperienced purchaser, and wherever there is much commerce the prudent tradesman does not overcharge, but keeps a fixed price for everyone, so that a child buys of him as well as any other. Men are thus *honestly* served; but this is not enough to make us believe that the tradesman has acted from duty and from principles of honesty; his own advantage required it. It is out of the question in this case to suppose that he might have besides a direct inclination in favor of the buyers, so that out of love, as it were, he should give no advantage to one over another. Hence the action was done neither out of duty nor because of inclination but merely with a selfish view. On the other hand, it is a duty to maintain one's life; in addition everyone also has a direct inclination to do so. But on this account the often anxious care which most men take of their lives has no intrinsic worth and their maxim has no moral import. No doubt they preserve their life *as duty requires,* but not *because duty requires.* The case is different, when adversity and hopeless sorrow have completely taken away the relish for life; if the unfortunate one, strong in mind, indignant at his fate rather than despondent or dejected, longs for death and yet preserves his life without loving it. [If he does this] not from inclination or fear but from duty, then his maxim has a moral worth.

To be beneficent when we can is a duty; besides this, there are many minds so sympathetically constituted that without any other motive of vanity or self-interest, they find a pleasure in spreading joy [about them] and can take delight in the satisfaction of others so far as it is their own work. But I maintain that in such a case, however proper, however amiable an action of this kind may be, it nevertheless has no true moral worth, but is on a level with other inclinations; e.g. the inclination to honor which, if it is happily directed to that which is actually of public utility and accordant with duty and consequently honorable, deserves praise and encouragement but not respect. For the maxim lacks the moral ingredient that such actions be done *out of duty,* not from inclination. Put the case [another way and suppose] that the mind of that philanthropist were clouded by sorrow of his own, extinguishing all sympathy with the lot of others, and that while he still has the power to benefit others in distress he is not touched by their trouble because he is absorbed with his own; suppose that he now tears himself out of this deadening insensibility, and performs the action without any inclination for it, but simply from duty; only then has his action genuine moral worth. Furthermore, if nature has put little sympathy into the heart of this or that man, if a supposedly upright man is by temperament cold and indifferent to the sufferings of others, perhaps because in respect of his own sufferings he is provided with the special gift of patience and fortitude so that he supposes or even requires that others should have the same; such a man would certainly not be the meanest product of nature. But if nature had not specially shaped him to be a philanthropist, would he not find cause in himself for attributing to himself a value far higher than the value of a good-natured temperament could be? Unquestionably. It is just in this that there is brought out the moral worth of the character which is incomparably the highest of all; namely, that he is beneficent, not from inclination, but from duty.

To secure one's own happiness is a duty, at least indirectly; for discontent with one's condition under pressure of many anxieties and amidst unsatisfied wants might easily become a great *temptation to transgression from duty*. But here again, without reference to duty, all men already have the strongest and most intense inclination to happiness, because it is just in this idea that all inclinations are combined in one total. But the precept for happiness is often of such a sort that it greatly interferes with some inclinations. Yet a man cannot form any definite and certain conception of the sum of satisfying all of these inclinations, which is called happiness. It is not then to be wondered at that a single inclination, definite both as to what it promises and as to the time within which it can be gratified, is often able to overcome such a fluctuating idea [as the precept for happiness.] For instance, a gouty patient can choose to enjoy what he likes and to suffer what he may, since according to his calculation, at least on this occasion he has not sacrificed the enjoyment of the present moment for a possibly mistaken expectation of happiness supposedly found in health. But, if the general desire for happiness does not influence his will, and even supposing that in his particular case health was not a necessary element in his calculation, there yet remains a law even in this case, as in all other cases; that is, he should promote his happiness not from inclination but from duty. Only in following duty would his conduct acquire true moral worth.

Undoubtedly, it is in this manner that we are to understand those passages of the Scripture in which we are commanded to love our neighbor, even our enemy. For love, as an affection, cannot be commanded, but beneficence for duty's sake can be, even though we are not impelled to such kindness by any inclination, and may even be repelled by a natural and unconquerable aversion. This is *practical* love and not *psychological*. It is a love originating in the will and not in the inclination of sentiment, in principles of action, not of sentimental sympathy.

The second proposition is: That an action done from duty derives its moral worth, *not from the purpose* which is to be attained by it, but from the maxim by which it is determined. Therefore the action does not depend on the realization of its objective, but merely on the *principle* of volition by which the action has taken place, without regard to any object of desire. It is clear from what precedes that the purposes which we may have in view for our actions, or their effects as regarded as ends and impulsions of the will, cannot give to actions any unconditional or moral worth. Then in what can their worth consist if it does not consist in the will as it is related to its expected effect? It cannot consist in anything but the *principle of the will*, with no regard to the ends which can be attained by the action. For the will stands between its *a priori* principle which is formal, and its *a posteriori* impulse which is material, as between two roads. As it must be determined by something, it follows that the will must be determined by the formal principle of volition, as when an action is done from duty, in which case every material impulse has been withdrawn from it.

The third proposition, which is a consequence of the preceding two, I would express thus: *Duty is the necessity of an action, resulting from respect for the law.* I may have an *inclination* for an object as the effect of my proposed action, but I cannot have *respect* for an object just for this reason: that it is merely an effect and not an action of will. Similarly, I cannot have respect for an inclination, whether my own or another's; I can at most, if it is my own, approve it; if it is another's I can sometimes even cherish it; that is, look on it as favorable to my own interest. Only the law itself which is connected with my will by no means as an effect but as a principle which does not serve my inclination but outweighs it, or at least in case of choice excludes my inclination from its calculation; only such a law can be an object of respect and hence a command. Now an action done from duty must wholly exclude the influence of inclination, and with it every object of the will, so that nothing remains which can determine the will objectively except the *law*, and [determine the will] subjectively except *pure respect* for this practical law, and hence [pure respect] for the maxim[1] to follow this law even to the thwarting of all my inclinations.

Thus the moral worth of an action does not consist of the effect expected from it, nor from any principle of action which needs to borrow its motive from this expected effect. For, all these effects, agreeableness of one's condition and even the promotion of the happiness of others, all this could have also been brought about by other causes so that for this there would have been no need of the will of a rational being. However, in this will alone can the supreme and unconditional good be found. Therefore the pre-eminent good which we call moral can consist in nothing other than *the concept of law* in itself, *which is certainly only possible in a rational being*, in so far as this conception,

---

[1] A maxim is the subjective principle of volition. The objective principle, that is, what would also serve all rational beings subjectively as a practical principle if reason had full power over desire; this objective principle is the practical *law*.

and not the expected effect, determines the will. This is a good which is already present in the person acting according to it, and we do not have to wait for good to appear in the result.[2]

But what sort of law can it be the conception of which must determine the will, even without our paying any attention to the effect expected from it, in order that this will may be called good absolutely and without qualification? As I have stripped the will of every impulse which could arise for it from obedience to any law, there remains nothing but the general conformity of the will's actions to law in general. Only this conformity to law is to serve the will as a principle; that is, I am never to act in any way other than *so I could want my maxim also to become a general law*. It is the simple conformity to law in general, without assuming any particular law applicable to certain actions, that serves the will as its principle, and must so serve it, if duty is not to be a vain delusion and a chimerical notion. The common reason of men in their practical judgments agrees perfectly with this and always has in view the principle suggested here. For example, let the question be: When in distress may I make a promise with the intention of not keeping it? I readily distinguish here between the two meanings which the question may have: Whether it is prudent, or whether it is in accordance with duty, to make a false promise. The former undoubtedly may often be the case. I [may] see clearly that it is not enough to extricate myself from a present difficulty by means of this subterfuge, but that it must be carefully considered whether there may not result from such a lie a much greater inconvenience than that from which I am now freeing myself. But, since in

---

[2] Here it might be objected that I take refuge in an obscure feeling behind the word *respect* instead of giving a distinct solution of the question by a concept of reason. But, although respect is a feeling, it is not a feeling *received* through outside influence, but is self-generated by a rational concept, and therefore is specifically distinct from all feelings of the former kind, which may be related either to inclination or fear. What I recognize immediately as a law, I recognize with respect. This merely signifies the consciousness that my will is *subordinate* to a law, without the intervention of other influences on my sense. The immediate determination of the will by the law and the consciousness of this may be called *respect*, so that this may then be regarded as an effect of the law on the subject and not as the *cause* of it. In a word, respect is the conceiving of a value which reduces my self-love. Accordingly, respect is considered neither an object of inclination nor of fear, though it has something analogous to both. The *object* of respect is the *law*, only, a law that we impose on *ourselves* and yet recognize as necessary in itself. We are subjected to it as a law without consulting self-love; but as imposed by us on ourselves, it is a result of our will. In the former aspect it has analogy to fear, in the latter to inclination. Respect for a person is properly only respect for the law (of honesty, etc.) of which he gives us an example. Since we also look on the improvement of our talents as a duty we consider that we see in a person of talents the *example of a law*, as it were, to become like him in this by effort and this constitutes our respect. All so-called moral *interest* consists simply in *respect* for the law.

spite of all my supposed *cunning* the consequences cannot be foreseen easily; the loss of credit may be much more injurious to me than any mischief which I seek to avoid at present. That being the case, one might consider whether it would not be more *prudent* to act according to a general maxim, and make it a habit to give no promise except with the intention of keeping it. But, it is soon clear that such a maxim is still only based on the fear of consequences. It is a wholly different thing to be truthful from a sense of duty, than to be so from apprehension of injurious consequences. In the first case, the very conceiving of the action already implies a law for me; in the second case, I must first look about elsewhere to see what results may be associated with it which would affect me. For it is beyond all doubt wicked to deviate from the principle of duty; but to be unfaithful to my maxim of prudence may often be very advantageous to me, although it is certainly wiser to abide by it. However, the shortest way, and an unerring one, to discover the answer to this question of whether a lying promise is consistent with duty, is to ask myself, "Would I be content if this maxim of extricating myself from difficulty by a false promise held good as a general law for others as well as for myself?" Would I care to say to myself, "everyone may make a deceitful promise when he finds himself in a difficulty from which he cannot extricate himself otherwise"? Then I would presently become aware that while I can decide in favor of the lie, I can by no means decide that lying should be a general law. For under such a law there would be no promises at all, since I would state my intentions in vain in regard to my future actions to those who would not believe my allegation, or, if they did so too hastily, they would pay me back in my own coin. Hence, as soon as such a maxim was made a universal law, it would necessarily destroy itself.

Therefore I do not need any sharp acumen to discern what I have to do in order that my will may be morally good. [As I am] inexperienced in the course of the world and incapable of being prepared for all its contingencies, I can only ask myself: "Can you will that your maxim should also be a general law?" If not, then my maxim must be rejected, not because of any disadvantage in it for myself or even for others, but because my maxim cannot fit as a principle into a possible universal legislation, and reason demands immediate respect from me for such legislation. Indeed, I do not *discern* as yet on what this respect is based; into this question the philosopher may inquire. But at least I understand this much: that this respect is an evaluation of the worth that far outweighs all that is recommended by inclination. The necessity of acting from *pure* respect for the practical law [of right action;] is what constitutes duty, to which every other motive must yield, because it is the condition of a will being good *in itself*, and the value of such a will exceeds everything.

Thus we have arrived at the principle of moral knowledge of common human reason. Although common men no doubt do not conceive this principle in such an abstract and universal form, yet they really always have it before their eyes and use it as the standard for their decision. It would be easy to show here how, with this compass in hand, men are well able to distinguish, in every case that occurs, what is good, bad, conformable to duty or inconsistent with it. Without teaching them anything at all new, we are only, like Socrates, directing their attention to the principle they employ themselves and [showing] that we therefore do not need science and philosophy to know what we should do to be honest and good and even wise and virtuous. Indeed, we might well have understood before that the knowledge of what every man ought to do, and hence also [what he ought] to know is within the reach of every man, even the commonest. We cannot help admiring what a great advantage practical judgment has over theoretical judgment in men's common sense. If, in theoretical judgments, common reason ventures to depart from the laws of experience and from the perceptions of the senses, it plunges into many inconceivabilities and self-contradictions, [or] at any rate into a chaos of uncertainty, obscurity and instability. But in the practical sphere [of just action] it is right that, when one excludes all sense impulses from [determining] practical laws, the power of judgment of common sense begins to show itself to special advantage. It then even becomes a subtle matter as to whether common sense provides tricky excuses for conscience in relation to other claims regarding what is to be called right, or whether, for its own guidance, common sense seeks to determine honestly the value of [particular] actions. In the latter case, common sense has as good a hope of hitting the mark as any philosopher can promise himself. A common man is almost more sure of doing so, because the philosopher cannot have any other [better] principle and may easily perplex his judgment by a multitude of considerations foreign to the matter in hand, and so he may turn from the right way. Therefore would it not be wiser in moral matters to acquiesce in the judgment of common reason, or at most to call in philosophy only for rendering the system of morals more complete and intelligible and its rules more convenient for use, especially for disputation, but not to deflect common sense from its happy simplicity, or to lead it through philosophy into a new path of inquiry and instruction?

Innocence is indeed a glorious thing, only it is a pity that it cannot maintain itself well and is easily seduced. On this account even wisdom, which otherwise consists more in conduct than in knowledge, yet has need of science, not in order to learn from it, but to secure for its own precepts acceptance and permanence. In opposition to all the commands of duty that reason represents to man as so greatly deserving respect, man feels within himself a powerful counterpoise in his wants and inclinations, the entire satisfaction of which he sums up under the name of happiness. Reason issues its commands unyieldingly, without promising anything to the inclinations and with disregard and contempt, as it were, for these demands which are so impetuous and at the same time so plausible and which will not allow themselves to be suppressed by any command. Hence there arises a natural *dialectic*; that is, a disposition to argue against these strict laws of duty and to question their validity, or at least to question their purity and strictness. [There is also a disposition] to make them more accordant, if possible, with our wishes and inclinations; that is to say, to corrupt them at their very source and to destroy their value entirely, an act that even common practical reason cannot ultimately approve.

Thus the *common reason of man* is compelled to leave its proper sphere and to take a step into the field of a *practical philosophy*, but not for satisfying any desire to speculate, which never occurs to it as long as it is content to be mere sound reason. But the purpose is to secure on practical grounds information and clear instruction respecting the source of the principle [of common sense] and the correct definition of this principle as contrasted with the maxims which are based on wants and inclinations, so that common sense may escape from the perplexity of opposing claims, and not run the risk of losing all genuine moral principles through the equivocation into which it easily falls. Thus when practical, common reason cultivates itself, there arises insensibly in it a dialectic forcing it to seek aid in philosophy, just like what happens to practical reason in its theoretic use. Therefore in this case as well as in the other, [common sense] will find no rest but in a thorough critical examination of our reason.

SECOND SECTION

Transition from Popular Moral Philosophy to the Metaphysics of Morals

If hitherto we have drawn our concept of duty from the common use of our practical reason, it is by no means to be inferred that we have treated it as an empirical concept. On the contrary, if we attend to the experience of men's conduct, we meet frequent and, as we admit ourselves, just complaints that there is not to be found a single certain example of the disposition to act from pure duty. Although many things are done *in conformity* to what duty prescribes, it is nevertheless always doubtful whether they are done strictly *out of duty* [which would have to be the case if they are] to have a moral value. Hence, in all ages there have been philosophers who have denied altogether that this disposition actually exists in human actions at all, and who have ascribed everything to a more or less refined self-love. Not that they have on that account questioned the soundness of the conception of morality; on the contrary they have spoken with sincere regret of the frailty and corruption of human nature, which though noble enough to take as its law an idea so worthy of respect, is yet too weak to follow it, and employs reason, which ought to give it the law, only for the purpose of accommodating the inclinations, whether single or, at best, in the greatest possible harmony with one another. In fact it is absolutely impossible to ascertain by experience with complete certainty a single case in which the maxim of an action, however right in itself, rested simply on moral grounds and on the conception of duty. Sometimes it happens that with the sharpest self-examination we can find nothing, besides the moral principle of duty, powerful enough to move us to this or that action and to such a great sacrifice; yet we cannot infer from this with certainty that it was not some really secret impulse of self-love, under the false appearance of that idea [of the moral principle of duty] that was the actual determining cause of the will. We then like to flatter ourselves by falsely taking credit for a more noble motive. In fact we can never, even by the strictest self-examination, penetrate completely [to the causes] behind the secret springs of action, since when we ask about moral worth, we are not concerned with actions but with their inward principles which we do not see.

Moreover, we cannot better serve the wishes of those people, who ridicule all morality as a mere chimera of human imagination overstepping itself through vanity, than by conceding to them that concepts of duty must be drawn only from experience, just as people are ready to think out of indolence that this is also the case with all other notions; doing this would prepare a certain triumph for them. Out of love for humanity, I am willing to admit that most of our actions accord with duty, but on examining them more closely we encounter everywhere the cherished self which is always dominant. It is this self that men have considered for and not the strict command of duty which would often require self-denial. Without being an enemy to virtue, a cool observer who does not mistake an ardent wish for good for goodness itself, may sometimes doubt whether true virtue is actually found anywhere in the world, and do this especially as his years increase and his judgment is in part made wiser by experience and in part more acute by observation. This being so, nothing can save us from altogether abandoning our ideas of duty, nothing can maintain in our soul a well-grounded respect for the law; nothing but the clear conviction that, although there have never been actions really springing from such pure sources, yet . . . reason, by itself and independent of all experience, ordains what ought to be done. Accordingly actions, of which hitherto the world has perhaps never had an example and of which the feasibility might even be very much doubted by anyone basing everything on experience, are nevertheless inflexibly commanded by reason; e.g., even though a sincere friend might never have existed up till now, [just the same] pure sincerity in friendship is required of every man not a whit less, because above and beyond all experience this duty is obligatory in the idea of a reason that determines the will by *a priori* principles.

Unless we deny that the notion of morality has any truth or reference to any possible object, we must admit that its law must be valid not only for men, but for all *rational creatures generally*, not only under certain contingent conditions or with exceptions, but with *absolute necessity*. [When we admit this] then it is clear that no experience could enable us even to infer the possibility of such apodictic laws. What right have we to demand unbounded respect, as for a universal precept of every rational creature, for something that only holds true under the contingent conditions of humanity? Or, how could laws determining *our* will be regarded as laws determining the will of rational beings generally, if these laws were only empirical and did not originate wholly *a priori* from pure and practical reason?

Nor could anything be more ill-advised for morality than our wishing to derive it from examples. Every example set before me must first be tested by principles of morality [to determine] whether it is worthy of serving as an orignal example; that is, as a model or pattern. An example can by no means furnish authoritatively the concept of morality. Even the Holy One of the Gospels must first be compared with our ideal of moral perfection before we can recognize Him as such; and so He says of himself, "Why call ye Me (whom ye see) good? None is good (the model of good) but God only (whom ye do not see)!" But whence do we acquire the concept of God as the supreme good? Simply from the *idea* of moral perfection which reason sketches *a priori* and connects inseparably with the concept of a free will. Imitation has no place at all in morality, and examples serve only for encouragement; that is, they make feasible beyond any doubt what the law commands and they make visible what the practical rule expresses more generally, but they can never authorize us to set aside the true original existing in reason and to guide ourselves by examples. Therefore, if there is no genuine supreme principle of morality, but only that which rests on pure reason independent of all experience, I think it is unnecessary even to put the question as to whether it is good to exhibit these concepts in their generality (*in abstracto*) as they are established *a priori* along with the principles belonging to them, if our knowledge is to be distinguished from the *vulgar* and called philosophical. Indeed, in our times this question might perhaps be necessary; for if we collected votes on whether pure rational knowledge, apart from everything empirical, that is to say, a metaphysic of morals, is to be preferred to a popular practical philosophy; it is easy to guess which side would carry more weight.

This descent to popular notions is certainly very commendable if the ascent to the principles of pure reason has taken place first and has been accomplished satisfactorily. This implies that first we should establish ethics on metaphysics and, when it is firmly founded, procure a hearing for ethics by giving it a popular character. But it is quite absurd to try to be popular in the first inquiry on which the soundness of the principles depends. Not only can this procedure never lay claim to having the very rare merit of a true *philosophical popularity* for there is no sense in being intelligible if one renounces all thoroughness of insight, but this procedure also produces a disgusting medley of compiled observations and half-reasoned principles. Shallow pates enjoy this because it can be used for everyday chat, but those with deeper understanding find only confusion in this method and, being unsatisfied and unable to assist themselves, turn away their eyes, while philosophers, seeing quite clearly through this confusion, are little heeded when they call men away for a time from this pretended popularity, so they may be rightfully popular after attaining a definite insight.

We only need to look at the attempts of moralists in [using] that favorite fashion and we shall find [a variety of things:] at one point the special destination of human nature including the idea of a rational nature generally, at another point perfection, at another happiness, here moral sense, there fear of God, a little of this and a little of that, all in a marvelous mixture. It does not occur to them to ask whether the principles of morality are to be sought at all in the knowledge of human nature which we can have only from experience. If this is not so, if these principles are completely *a priori* and are to be encountered free from everything empirical only in pure rational concepts and nowhere else, not even in the smallest degree, shall we then adopt the method of making this a separate inquiry as a pure practical philosophy? Or [shall we construct], if one may use a name so decried, a metaphysic of morals [3] and complete it by itself and ask the public wishing for popular treatment to await the outcome of this undertaking?

Such a metaphysic of morals, completely isolated and unmixed with any anthropology, theology, physics, or hyperphysics, and still less with occult qualities which we might call superphysical, is not only an indispensable condition for all sound theoretical knowledge of duties, but at the same time it is a *desideratum* highly important to the actual fulfilment of the precepts of duties. For the pure concept of duty unmixed with any foreign element of experienced attractions, in a word, the pure concept of moral law in general, exercises an influence on the human heart through reason alone. . . . This influence is so much more powerful than all other impulses [4] which may be derived from the field of experience, that in the consciousness of its dignity it despises such impulses and by degrees can become their master. An eclectic ethics compounded partly of motives drawn from feelings and inclinations and partly from concepts of reason, will necessarily make the mind waver between motives which cannot be brought under any one principle, and will therefore lead to good only by mere accident, and may often lead to evil.

It is clear from what has been said that all moral concepts have their seat and origin completely *a priori* in the reason, and have it in the commonest reason just as truly as in what is speculative in the highest degree. Moral concepts cannot be obtained by abstraction from any empirical and hence merely contingent knowledge. It is exactly this purity in origin that makes them worthy of serving our supreme practical principle [for right action] and, as we add anything

---

[3] Just as pure mathematics is differentiated from applied and pure logic from applied, so, if we choose, we may also differentiate pure philosophy of morals (metaphysics) from applied (viz., applied to human nature). Also, by this designation we are at once reminded that moral principles are not based on properties of human nature, but must exist *a priori* of themselves; practical rules for every rational nature must be capable of being deduced from such principles and accordingly deduced for the rational nature of man.

[4] I have a letter from the late excellent Sulzer, in which he asks me what might be the reason for moral instruction accomplishing so little although it contains much that is convincing to reason. My answer was postponed in order that I might make it complete. But it is simply this: teachers themselves do not have their own notions clear, and when they endeavor to make up for this by suggesting all kinds of motives for moral goodness and in trying to make their medicine strong they spoil it. For, the most ordinary observations show that this is an act of honesty done with steadfast mind and without regard for any advantage in this world or another, and when [persisted in] even under the greatest temptations of need or allurement it will . . . elevate the soul and inspire one with the wish to be able to act in a like manner. Even fairly young children feel this impression and one should never represent duties to them in any other light.

empirical, we detract in proportion from their genuine influence and from the absolute value of actions. It is not only very necessary from a purely speculative point of view, but it is also of the greatest practical importance to derive these notions and laws from pure reason, to present them pure and unmixed, and even to determine the compass of this practical or pure rational knowledge; that is, to determine the entire faculty of pure practical reason. In doing so we must not make the principles of pure practical reason dependent on the particular nature of human reason, though in speculative philosophy this may be permitted and even necessary at times. Since moral laws ought to hold true for every rational creature we must derive them from the general concept of a rational being. Although morality has need of anthropology for its application to man, yet in this way, as in the first step, we must treat morality independently as pure philosophy; that is, as metaphysics, complete in itself. . . . We must fully realize that unless we are in possession of this pure philosophy not only would it be vain to determine the moral element of duty in right actions for purposes of speculative criticism, but it would be impossible to base morals on their genuine principles. This is true even for common practical purposes, but more especially for moral instruction which is to produce pure moral dispositions and to engraft them on men's minds for promoting the greatest possible good in the world.

Our purpose in this study must be not only to advance by natural steps from common moral judgment, which is very worthy of respect, to the philosophical, as has been done already, but also to progress from a popular philosophy which only gets as far as it can by groping with the help of examples, to metaphysics, which does not allow itself to be held back by anything empirical and which goes as far as ideal concepts in measuring the whole extent of this kind of rational knowledge wherever examples fail us. [In order to accomplish this purpose] we must clearly describe and trace the practical faculty of reason, advancing from general rules to the point where the notion of duty springs from it.

Everything in nature works according to laws. Rational beings alone have the faculty for acting according *to the concept* of laws; that is, according to principles. [In other words, rational beings alone] have a will. Since deriving actions from principles requires *reason*, the will is nothing more than practical reason. If reason infallibly determines the will, then the actions of such a being that are recognized as objectively necessary are also subjectively necessary. The will is a faculty for choosing *only that* which reason, independently of inclination, recognizes as practically necessary; that is, as good. But if reason does not sufficiently determine the will by itself, if the latter is also subject to the subjective conditioning of particular impulses which do not always coincide with the objective conditions; in a word, if the will *in itself* does not completely accord with reason, as is actually the case with men, then the actions which are objectively recognized as necessary are subjectively contingent. Determining such a will according to objective laws is compulsory (*Nötigung*). This means that the relation of objective laws to a will not thoroughly good is conceived as the determination of the will of a rational being by principles of reason which the will, because of its nature, does not necessarily follow.

The concept of an objective principle, in so far as it is compulsory for a will, is called a command of reason and the formulation of such a command is called an IMPERATIVE.

All imperatives are expressed by the word *ought* (or *shall*) and are indicating thereby the relation of an objective law of reason to a will, which, because of its subjective constitution, is not necessarily determined by this [compulsion]. Such imperatives may state that something would be good to do or to forbear from doing, but they are addressing themselves to a will which does not always do a thing merely because that thing is represented as good to do. The practically *good* determines the will by means of the concepts of reason, and consequently from objective, not subjective causes; that is, [it determines them] on principles which are valid for every rational being as such. The practically good is distinguishable from the *pleasant* which influences the will only by means of sensations from subjective causes and which is valid only for the particular sense of this or that man and is not a principle of reason holding true for everyone.[5]

Therefore a perfectly good will would be equally subject to objective laws of good [action], but could not be conceived thereby as *compelled* to act lawfully by itself. Because of its subjective constitution it can only

---

[5] The dependence of the desires on sensations is called inclination, and accordingly always indicates a *want*. The dependence of a contingently determinable will on principles of reason is called an *interest*. Therefore, this dependence is only found in the case of a dependent will, which of itself does not always conform to reason. We cannot conceive of the Divine will having any interest. But the human will can *take an interest* without necessarily acting *from interest*. The former signifies practical interest in the action, the latter *psychological* interest in the object of the action. The first merely indicates dependence of the will on principles of reason in themselves and the second merely indicates dependence on principles of reason for the sake of inclination, reason supplying only the practical rules of how the demands of inclination may be satisfied. In the first case the action interests me in the object of the action, inasmuch as it is pleasant for me. We have seen, in the first section, that in an action done from duty we must not look to the interest in the object but only to the interest in the action itself, and in its rational principle: the law.

be determined by the concept of the good. Consequently no imperatives hold true for the Divine will, or in general for a *holy* will. *Ought*
is out of place here because the act of willing is already necessarily in
unison with the law. Therefore imperatives are only formulations for expressing the relation of the objective laws of all volition to the subjective
imperfections of the will of this or that rational being; that is, the human
will.

All *imperatives* command either *hypothetically* or *categorically*.
. . . Since every practical law represents a possible action as good, and
on this account as necessary for a subject who can determine practically
by reason, all imperatives are formulations determining an action which
is necessary according to the principle of a will in some respects good. If
the action is good only as a means *to something else,* then the imperative is *hypothetical.* If the action is conceived as good *in itself* and consequently as necessarily being the principle of a will which of itself conforms to reason then it is *categorical.*

Thus the imperative declares what, of my possible actions, would be
good. It presents the practical rule in relation to a will which does not
perform an action forthwith simply because it is good. For, either the
subject does not always know that such action is good or, even should
the subject know this, its maxims might be opposed to the objective
principles of practical reason.

Consequently the hypothetical imperative only states that an action is good for some purpose, *potential* or *actual.* In the first case the
principle is *problematical,* in the second it is *assertorial* [positively asserting a claim and may be called a] practical principle. The categorical
imperative which declares an action to be objectively necessary in itself
without reference to any purpose, i.e., without any other end, is valid as
an *apodictic* (practical) principle.

Whatever is possible through the ability of some rational being
may also be considered as a possible purpose of some will. Therefore the
principles of action concerning the means needed to attain some possible purpose are really infinitely numerous. All sciences have a practical
aspect consisting of problems expressing that some end is possible for us,
and of imperatives directing how it may be attained. Therefore, these
may, in general, be called imperatives of *skill.* There is no question as to
whether the end is rational and good, but only as to what one must do
in order to attain it. The precepts for the physician to make his patient
thoroughly healthy, and for a poisoner to ensure certain death, are
equivalent in that each serves to effect its purpose perfectly. Since in
early youth it cannot be known what purposes are likely to occur to us
in the course of life, parents seek to have their children taught a *great*

many things and provide for their *skill* in using means for all sorts of purposes. They cannot be sure whether any particular purpose may perhaps hereafter be an objective for their pupil; it is possible that he might aim at any of them. This anxiety is so great that parents commonly neglect to form and correct their judgment on the value of the things which may be chosen as ends.

However there is *one* end which may actually be assumed to be an end for all rational beings, there is one purpose which they not only *may* have, but which we may assume with certainty that they all actually *do have* by natural necessity; that is *happiness*. The hypothetical imperative expressing the practical necessity of an action as a means for the advancement of happiness is assertorial. We are not presenting it as necessary for an uncertain and merely possible purpose, but for a purpose which we may presuppose with certainty and *a priori* for every man, because it belongs to his being. Now a man's skill in choosing the means to his own greatest well-being may be called *prudence* in the most specific sense.[6] Thus the imperative which refers to the choice of means to one's own happiness, that is, the precept of prudence, is still hypothetical. The action is not commanded absolutely but only as a means to another purpose. Whereas, the categorical imperative directly commands a certain conduct without being conditioned by any other attainable purpose. . . . This imperative may be called the imperative of morality (*Sittlichkeit*).

There is also a marked distinction among the acts of willing according to these three kinds of principles resulting from the *dissimilarity* in the obligation of the will. In order to differentiate them more clearly, I think they would be most suitably classified as either *rules* of skill, *counsels* of prudence, or *commands* or laws of morality. For it is only *law* that involves the concept of an *unconditional necessity* which is objective and hence universally valid. Commands are laws that must be obeyed; that is, must be adhered to even when inclination is opposed. Indeed, counsels involve [a certain kind of] necessity, but only one which can hold true under a contingent subjective condition. They depend on whether this or that man counts this or that [object] as essential to his happiness. By contrast, the categorical imperative is not limited by any condition. . . . We might also call the first kind of imperatives

---

[6] The word prudence is taken in two senses: In one it may mean knowledge of the world, in the other, private prudence. The first is a man's ability to influence others so as to use them for his own purposes. The second is the insight to combine all these purposes for his own lasting benefit. This latter is properly that to which the value of even the former is reduced, and when a man is prudent in the former sense, but not in the latter, we might better say of him that he is clever and cunning, but on the whole, imprudent.

technical as belonging to art, the second *pragmatic* [7] as belonging to welfare, and the third *moral* as belonging to free conduct generally, that is, to morals.

The question now arises: How are all these imperatives possible? This question is to ascertain, not how the action commanded by the imperative can be carried out, but merely how the compulsion of will expressed by the imperative can be conceived. I should think that no special explanation is needed to show how an imperative related to skill is possible. Whoever wills the end, also wills, so far as reason decisively influences his conduct, the means in his power which are indispensable for achieving this end. This proposition is analytical in regard to the volition. For, in willing an object as an effect, there is already implied therein that I myself am acting as a cause, that is, I make use of the means. From the concept of the willed end, the imperative derives the concept of the actions necessary for achieving this end. No doubt synthetic propositions will have to be employed in defining the means to a proposed end, but they do not concern the principle, the act of the will but only the object and its realization. To give an example: in order to bisect a line I must draw two intersecting arcs from its end points. Admittedly, this is taught by mathematics in synthetic propositions. But if I know that the intended operation can only be performed by this process, then it is an analytical proposition to say that in fully willing the operation, I also will the action required for it. For [assuming that I want a certain thing] it is just the same to conceive that thing as an effect which I can only produce in a certain way as to conceive of myself as acting in this way.

If it were equally easy to give a definite concept of happiness [as of simpler ends], the imperatives of prudence would correspond exactly with those of skill, and would likewise be analytical. It could then be said that whoever wills the end also wills the indispensable means thereto which are in his power. But unfortunately the notion of happiness is so indefinite that although every man wishes to attain it, he never can say definitely and consistently what it is that he really wishes and wills. The reason is that the elements belonging to the notion of happiness are altogether empirical; that is, they must be borrowed from experience. Nevertheless, the idea of happiness implies something absolute and whole; a maximum of well-being in my present and all future circum-

---

[7] It seems to me that the proper meaning of the word *pragmatic* may be most accurately defined in this way: *Sanctions* are called pragmatic when they flow properly not from the law of the states as necessary enactments, but from *precaution* for the general welfare. A history is composed pragmatically when it teaches *prudence*; i.e., instructs the world how it can better provide for its interests, or at least as well as did the men of former times.

stances. Now, it is impossible for even the most clear-sighted and most powerful being, as long as it is supposedly finite, to frame for itself a definite concept of what it really wills [when it wants to be happy]. If he wills riches, how much anxiety, envy, and snares might not be drawn upon his shoulders thereby? If he wills knowledge and discernment, perhaps such knowledge might only prove to be so much sharper sight showing him much more fearfully the unavoidable evils now concealed from him, or suggesting more wants for his desires which already give him concern enough. If he should will a long life, who can guarantee him that it will not be a long misery? If he should at least have health, how often has infirmity of the body restrained a man from excesses into which perfect health would have allowed him to fall? And so on. In short, a human being is unable with certainty to determine by any principle what would make him truly happy, because to do so he would have to be omniscient. Therefore, we cannot act on any definite principles to secure happiness, but only on counsels derived from experience; e.g., the frugality, courtesy, reserve, etc., which experience teaches us will promote well-being, for the most part. Hence it follows that the imperatives of prudence do not command at all, strictly speaking; that is, they cannot present actions objectively as practically *necessary* so that they are to be regarded as *counsels* (*consilia*) of reason rather than precepts (*praecepta*). The problem of determining certainly and generally which action would most promote the happiness of a rational being is completely insoluble. Consequently, no imperative respecting happiness is possible, for such a command should, in a strict sense, command men to do what makes them happy. Happiness is an ideal, not of reason, but of imagination resting solely on empirical grounds. It is vain to expect that these grounds should define an action for attaining the totality of a series of consequences that are really endless. However, this imperative of prudence could be an analytical proposition if we assume that the means to happiness could, with certainty, be assigned. For, this imperative is distinguished from the imperative of skill only by this; in the latter the end is merely possible [and available to be chosen]; in the former the end is given. However, both only prescribe the means to an end which we assume to have been willed. It follows that the imperative which calls for the willing of the means by him who wills the end is analytical in both cases. Thus there is no difficulty in regard to the possibility of this kind of imperative either.

On the other hand, the question of how the imperative of *morality* is possible is undoubtedly the only question demanding a solution as this imperative is not at all hypothetical, and the objective necessity it presents cannot rest on any hypothesis, as is the case with hypothetical imperatives. Only we must never leave out of consideration the fact that we *cannot* determine *by any example*, i.e., empirically, whether there is any such imperative at all. Rather is it to be feared that all those apparently categorical imperatives may actually be hypothetical. For instance, when you have a precept such as: thou shalt not promise deceitfully, and it is assumed that the [normative] necessity of this is not a mere counsel to avoid some other evil, [in which case] it might mean: you shall not make a lying promise lest it become known and your credit would be destroyed. On the contrary, an action of this kind should be regarded as evil in itself so that the imperative of the prohibition is categorical. Yet we cannot show with certainty in any instance that the will is determined merely by the law without any other source of action, although this may appear to be so. It is always possible that fear of disgrace, also perhaps obscure dread of other dangers, may have a secret influence on the will. Who can prove by experience the non-existence of a cause when all that experience tells us is that we do not perceive it? In such a case the so-called moral imperative, which appears to be categorical and unconditional, would really only be a pragmatic precept, drawing our attention to our own interests, and merely teaching us to take these interests into consideration.

Therefore we shall have to investigate *a priori* the possibility of a *categorical* imperative, since, in this case, we do not have the advantage that the imperative's reality is given in experience, so that the elucidation of its possibility would be needed only for explaining it, not for establishing it. It can be discerned that the categorical imperative has the purport of a practical law. All the rest may certainly be called *principles* of the will but not laws, since whatever is merely necessary for attaining some casual purpose may be considered contingent in itself, and at any time we can be free from the precept if we give up the purpose. However, the unconditional commmand leaves the will no liberty to choose the opposite, and consequently only the will carries with it that necessity we require in a law.

Secondly, in the case of this categorical imperative or law of morality the difficulty [of discerning its possibility] is very profound. It is *a priori*, a synthetic, practical proposition [8] and as there is so much difficulty in discerning the possibility of speculative propositions of this kind, it may readily be supposed that the difficulty will be no less with the practical. In [approaching] this problem we will first inquire whether the

---

[8] I connect the act with the will without presupposing a condition resulting from any inclination but *a priori*, and therefore necessarily (though only objectively; that is, assuming the idea of a reason possessing full power over all subjective motives). Therefore this is a practical proposition which does not analytically deduce the willing for an action from another already presupposed proposition (for we have not such a perfect will), but connects it immediately with the concept of the will of a rational being, as something not contained in it.

mere concept of a categorical imperative may not perhaps supply us with its formula also, which contains the proposition that alone can be a categorical imperative. Even if we know the tenor of such an absolute command, yet how it is possible will require further special and laborious study which we will postpone to the last section.

When I conceive of a hypothetical imperative at all, I do not know previously what it will contain until I am given the condition. But when I conceive of a categorical imperative I know at once what it contains. In addition to the law, the imperative contains only the necessity that the maxim [9] conform to this law. As the maxim contains no condition restricting the maxim, nothing remains but the general statement of the law to which the maxim of the action should conform, and it is only this conformity that the imperative properly represents as necessary.

Therefore there is only one categorical imperative, namely this: *Act only on a maxim by which you can will that it, at the same time, should become a general law.*

Now, if all imperatives of duty can be deduced from this one imperative as easily as from their principle, then we shall be able at least to show what we understand by it and what this concept means, although it would remain undecided whether what is called duty is not just a vain notion.

Since the universality of the law constitutes what is properly called *nature* in the most general sense [as to form]; that is, the existence of things as far as determined by general laws, the general imperative duty may be expressed thus: *Act as if the maxim of your action were to become by your will a general law of nature.*

We will now enumerate a few duties, adopting the usual division of duties to ourselves and to others, and of perfect and imperfect duties.[1]

1. A man, while reduced to despair by a series of misfortunes and feeling wearied of life, is still so far in possession of his reason that he can ask himself whether it would not be contrary to his duty to himself to take his own life. Now he inquires whether the maxim of his action could become a general law of nature. His maxim is: Out of self-love I consider it a principle to shorten my life when continuing it is likely to bring more misfortune than satisfaction. The question then simply is whether this principle of self-love could become a general law of nature.

---

[9] A maxim is a subjective principle of action and must be distinguished from an *objective principle;* namely, practical law. The former contains the practical rule set by reason according to the conditions of the subject (often its ignorance or its inclinations); hence it is the principle on which the subject *acts;* but the law is the objective principle valid for every rational being and is the principle on which the being *ought to act;* that is, an imperative.

[1] It must be noted here that I reserve the classification of duties for a future metaphysic of morals; so here I only give a few arbitrary duties as examples.

Now we see at once that a system of nature, whose law would be to destroy life by the very feeling designed to compel the maintenance of life, would contradict itself, and therefore could not exist as a system of nature; hence that maxim cannot possibly be a general law of nature and consequently it would be wholly inconsistent with the supreme principle of all duty.

2. Another man finds himself forced by dire need to borrow money. He knows that he will not be able to repay it, but he also sees that nothing will be lent him unless he promises firmly to repay it within a definite time. He would like to make this promise but he still has enough conscience to ask himself: Is it not unlawful and contrary to my duty to get out of a difficulty in this way? However, suppose that he does decide to do so, the maxim of his action would then be expressed thus: When I consider myself in want of money, I shall borrow money and promise to repay it although I know that I never can. Now this principle of self-love or of one's own advantage may perhaps be agreeable to my whole future well-being; but the question is now: Is it right? Here I change the suggestion of self-love into a general law and state the question thus: How would it be if my maxim were a general law? I then realize at once that it could never hold as a general law of nature but would necessarily contradict itself. For if it were a general law that anyone considering himself to be in difficulties would be able to promise whatever he pleases intending not to keep his promise, the promise itself and its object would become impossible since no one would believe that anything was promised him, but would ridicule all such statements as vain pretenses.

3. A third man finds himself a talent which with the help of some education might make him a useful man in many respects. But he finds himself in comfortable circumstances, and prefers to indulge in pleasure rather than to take pains in developing and improving his fortunate natural capacities. He asks, however, whether his maxim of neglecting his natural gifts, besides agreeing with his inclination toward indulgence, agrees also with what is called duty. He sees then that nature could indeed subsist according to such a general law, though men (like the South Sea Islanders) let their talents rust and devote their lives merely to idleness, amusement, and the propagation of their species, in a word, to enjoyment. But he cannot possibly *will* that this should be a general law of nature or be implanted in us as such by an instinct of nature. For, as a rational being, he necessarily wills that his faculties be developed, since they have been given to serve him for all sorts of possible purposes.

4. A fourth, prosperous man, while seeing others whom he could help having to struggle with great hardship thinks: What concern is it

of mine? Let everyone be as happy as heaven pleases or as he can make himself. I will take nothing from him nor even envy him, but I do not wish either to contribute anything to his welfare or assist him in his distress. There is no doubt that if such a way of thinking were a general law, society might get along very well and doubtless even better than if everyone were to talk of sympathy and good will or even endeavor occasionally to put it into practice, but then [were to] cheat when one could and so betray the rights of man or otherwise violate them. But although it is possible that a general law of nature might exist in terms of that maxim, it is impossible to *will* that such a principle should have the general validity of a law of nature. For a will which resolved this would contradict itself, inasmuch as many a time one would need the love and sympathy of others and by such a law of nature, sprung from one's own will, one would deprive himself of all hope of the aid he desires.

These are a few of the many actual duties, or at least what we regard as such, which derive clearly from the one principle that we have established. We must be *able to will* that a maxim of our action should be a general law. This is the canon of any moral assessment at all of such action. Some actions are such that their maxims cannot even be *conceived* as a general law of nature without contradiction, let alone that one could *will* that these maxims *should* become such laws. Other actions reveal no such intrinsic impossibility, but still it is impossible to *will* that their maxim should be elevated to the universality of a law of nature, since such a will would contradict itself. It can be easily seen that the former would conflict with strict or more specific, inexorable duty, the latter merely with a broader (meritorious) duty. Therefore, all duties, in regard to their compulsory nature (not the object of their action), depend on the same principle as the above illustrations conclusively show.

If we now watch ourselves for any transgression of duty, we shall find that we actually do not will that our maxim should be a general law in such cases. On the contrary, we will that the opposite should remain a general law. We merely take the liberty of making an *exception* in our own favor or (just for this time) in favor of our inclination. Consequently, if we considered all cases from the point of view of reason, we should find a contradiction in our own will; namely, that a certain principle is objectively necessary as a general law and yet is subjectively not general but has exceptions. In regarding our action on the one hand from the point of view of a will wholly conformed to reason, and on the other hand looking at the same action from the point of view of a will affected by inclination, there is really no contradiction but an antagonism on the part of inclination to the precept of reason which turns the universality of the principle into a mere generality, so that the principle of practical reason can meet the maxim half way.

Now although our own impartial judgment cannot justify this, it can prove that we do really acknowledge the validity of the categorical imperative and (with due respect) take just a few liberties with it, which we consider unimportant and at the same time forced upon us.

Thus we have at least established this much; that if duty is a concept which is to have any import and real controlling authority over our actions, it can only be expressed in a categorical and never in hypothetical imperatives. It is also of great importance that the content of the categorical imperative be presented clearly and definitely for every purpose; the categorical imperative must contain the principle of all duty if there is such a thing at all. However, we cannot yet prove *a priori* that such an imperative actually exists; that there is a practical law which commands absolutely by itself and without any other impulse and that compliance with this law is duty.

To be able to do that, it is extremely important to heed the warning that we cannot possibly think of deducing the reality of this principle from *particular attributes of human nature*. Duty is to be the practical, unconditional necessity for action; it must hold therefore for all rational beings (to whom an imperative can refer at all), and *for this reason only* it must also be a law for all human wills. On the other hand, whatever is deduced from the particular natural make-up of human beings, from certain feelings and propensities [2] and, if possible, even from any particular tendency of human reason proper which does not need to show in the will of every rational being. [Whatever is so deduced] may indeed furnish a maxim, but not a law. It may offer us a subjective principle on which we may act and may have propensities and inclinations, but [it does not give us] an objective principle by which we should be *constrained* to act, even though all our propensities, inclinations, and natural dispositions were opposed to it. In fact, the maxim evinces the sublime quality and intrinsic dignity of the command that the more clearly duty holds true, the less its subjective impulses favor it and the more they oppose such duty without being able in the slightest to weaken the binding character of the law, or to diminish its validity. . . .

Therefore, every empirical element is not only quite incapable of aiding the principle of morality, but is even highly prejudicial to the

---

[2] [Kant distinguishes *Hang* (propensity) from *Neigung* (inclination) as follows: *Hang* is a predisposition to the desire of some enjoyment; in other words, it is the subjective possibility of excitement of a certain desire preceding the concept of its object. When the enjoyment has been experienced it produces a *Neigung* (inclination) for it, which accordingly is defined "habitual, sensible desire."—Ed.]

purity of morals. For the proper and inestimable value of a genuine good will consists just in the principle of action being free from all contingent causes which experience alone can furnish. We cannot repeat our warning too often against this lax and even low habit of thought which searches empirical motives and laws for principles. Human reason when weary likes to rest on this cushion and in a dream of sweet illusions it substitutes for morality a bastard made up of limbs of quite different origin which appears as anything one chooses to see in it, save as virtue to one who has once beheld her in her true form.[3]

The question then is this: Is it a necessary law *for all rational beings* that they should always judge their actions by maxims which they can will themselves to serve as general laws? If this is so, then this must be related (altogether *a priori*) to the very concept of the will of a rational being. But in order to discover this relationship we must, however reluctantly, take a step into metaphysics, although into a domain of it distinct from speculative philosophy; namely, into the metaphysic of morals. In practical philosophy, where one is not concerned with the reasons of what *happens* but with the laws of what *ought to happen* though it never may, that is, with objective practical laws, we need not inquire into the reasons why anything pleases or displeases, how the pleasure of mere sensation differs from taste, and whether the latter differs from a general rational enjoyment. [There we need not ask] for the grounds of pleasure or pain, how desires and inclinations arise from it, and how through the influence of reason from these in turn arise maxims. All this belongs to an empirical psychology which would constitute the second part of the natural sciences viewed as the *philosophy of nature* so far as it is based on *empirical laws.*

However, here we are concerned with objective practical laws and consequently with the relation of the will to itself so far as it is determined by reason alone, in which case whatever refers to the empirical is necessarily excluded. For, if *reason of itself* determines conduct (which possibility we are about to investigate), it must necessarily do so *a priori.*

The will is conceived as a faculty impelling a man to action *in accordance with the concept of certain laws.* Such a faculty can be found only in rational beings. Now, that which serves the will as the objective ground for its self-determination is the *end,* and if the end is given by reason alone, it must be so given for all rational beings. On the other

---

[3] To behold virtue in her proper form is but to contemplate morality divested of all admixture of sensible things and of every spurious ornament of reward or self-love. To what extent she then eclipses everything else that charms the inclinations one may readily perceive with the least exertion of his reason, if it be not wholly spoiled for abstraction.

hand, that which merely contains the ground of a possibility of action is called the *means*. The subjective ground of desire is the *main-spring*, the objective ground of volition is the *motive*; hence the distinction [arises] between subjective ends resting on main-springs, and objective ends depending on motives that hold for every rational being. Practical principles are *formal* when they abstract from all subjective ends, they are *material* when they assume these and, therefore, particular main-springs of action. The ends which a rational being chooses to set himself as *effects* of his action (material ends) are altogether merely relative as only their relation to the specific capacity for desire of the subject gives them their value. Such value therefore cannot furnish general principles, i.e., practical laws valid and necessary for all rational beings and for every volition. Hence all these relative ends can only give rise to hypothetical imperatives. However, supposing that there were something *whose existence* was *in itself* of absolute value, something which, as an *end in itself*, could be a ground for definite laws, then this end and it alone, would be the ground for a possible categorical imperative, i.e., a practical law. Now I say that man, and generally every rational being, *exists* as an end in himself, *not merely as a means* for the arbitrary use of this or that will; he must always be regarded as an end in all his actions whether aimed at himself or at other rational beings. All objects of the inclinations have only a conditional value since, but for the inclinations and their respective wants, their object would be without value. But the inclinations themselves, being sources of want, are so far from having an absolute value that instead of relishing them it must rather be the general wish of every rational being to be wholly free from them. Hence the value of any object which *can be acquired* by our action is always conditional. Beings whose existence depends not on our will but on nature have, nevertheless, if they are irrational beings, only a relative value as means and are therefore called *things*; rational beings, on the other hand, are called *persons*. Their very nature constitutes them as ends in themselves; that is, as something which must not be used merely as means. To that extent, a person is limiting freedom of action and is an object of respect. Therefore persons are not merely subjective ends whose existence is an end for us as the result of our action, but they are objective ends; that is, things whose existence in itself is an end. No other end can be substituted (as a justification) for such an end, making it *merely* serve as a means, because otherwise nothing whatever could be found that would possess *absolute value*. If all value were conditional and therefore contingent, reason would have no supreme practical principle whatever.

Now, if a supreme practical principle ought to exist, or a categorical imperative with respect to the human will, it must be one which turns the concept of what is necessarily an end for everybody because it is *an end in itself* into an *objective* principle of the will which can serve as a general practical law. The basis of this principle is that *rational nature exists as an end in itself*. Man necessarily conceives his own existence as being this rational nature, to the extent that it is a *subjective* principle of human actions. But every other rational being regards its existence similarly for the same rational reason that holds true for me,[4] so at the same time it is an objective principle from which, as a supreme practical ground, all laws of the will must needs be deductible. Accordingly, the practical imperative will be as follows: *Act so as to treat man, in your own person as well as in that of anyone else, always as an end, never merely as a means.* We shall now inquire whether this principle can be realized.

To use the previous examples:

First: In regard to the concept of necessary duty to oneself, whoever contemplates suicide will ask himself whether his action is consistent with the idea of man as *an end in itself*. If he destroys himself to escape onerous conditions, he uses a person merely as a *means* to maintain a tolerable condition until life ends. But man is not a thing, that is to say, something which can be used *merely* as means, but in all his actions must always be considered as an end in itself. Therefore I cannot dispose in any way of man in my own person so as to mutilate, damage or kill him. (It is a matter of morals proper to define this principle more precisely to avoid all misunderstanding. Therefore I bypass such questions as that of the amputation of the limbs in order to preserve one's life, and of exposing one's life to danger with a view to preserving it, etc.)

Second: As regards necessary or obligatory duties toward others, whoever is thinking of making a lying promise to others will see at once that he would be using another man *merely as a means*, without the latter being the end in itself at the same time. The person whom I propose to use by such a promise for my own purposes cannot possibly assent to my way of acting toward him. . . . This conflict with the principle of duty toward others becomes more obvious if we consider examples of attacks on the liberty and property of others. Here it is clear that whoever transgresses the rights of men intends to use the person of others merely as means without considering that as rational beings they shall always be regarded as ends also; that is, as beings who could possibly be the end of the very same action.[5]

---

[4] This proposition is stated here as a postulate. Its grounds are to be found in the concluding section.

[5] This does not mean that the trite saying, *Quod tibi non vis fieri* etc., could serve here as the rule or principle. This saying is only a deduction from the above

Third: As regards contingent (meritorious) duties to oneself, it is not enough that the action does not violate humanity in our own person as an end in itself; [such action] must also *be congruous to it.* Now, there are in mankind capacities for greater perfection which belong to the end of nature regarding humanity. . . . To neglect these capacities might at best be consistent with the *survival* of humanity as an end in itself, but [it is not consistent] with the *promotion* of nature's end regarding humanity.

Fourth: As regards meritorious duties toward others, the natural end which all men have is their own happiness. Now, humanity might indeed subsist if no one contributed anything to the happiness of others as long as he did not deliberately diminish it; but this would be only negatively congruous to *humanity as an end in itself* if everyone does not also endeavor to promote the ends of others as far as he is able. For the ends of any subject which is an end in himself must be my ends too as far as possible, if that idea is to be *fully* effective in me.

This principle of man, and any rational creature, being *an end in itself*, which is the main limiting condition of every man's freedom of action, is not taken from experience for two reasons. First, its universal character, applying as it does to all rational beings whatever, is a fact which no experience can determine; second, because this principle does not present humanity as a subjective end of men; that is, as an object which actually we set ourselves as an end, but it [presents humanity as] an objective end which, whatever [subjective] ends we may have, is to constitute as a law the supreme limiting condition of all subjective ends. It must, therefore, derive from pure reason. In fact, according to the first principle, *the rule* and its universal character which enables [such legislation] to be some kind of law, for example, a law of nature, the *subjective* ground is the *end.* Since, according to the second principle the subject of all ends is some rational being, each being an end in itself, the third practical principle of the will follows as the ultimate prerequisite for the congruity [of will] with general practical reason; vix, the idea that *the will of every rational being is a will giving general laws.*

By virtue of this principle all maxims are rejected which cannot co-exist with the will as the general legislator. Thus the will is not being subjected simply to law, but is so subjected that it must be regarded *as giving itself the law*, and for this very reason is subject to the law of

---

rule, though with several limitations: It cannot be a general law, for it does not contain the principle of duties to oneself, nor the duties of charity to others (for many a person would gladly consent that others need do no good deeds for him, provided only that he might be excused from doing good deeds for them), nor finally, that of obligatory duties to one another; by this reasoning the criminal might argue against judges, and so on.

which it may consider itself the author. . . . Although a will *which is subject to laws* may be attached to such a law through interest, yet a will which is itself a supreme law-giver cannot possibly depend on any interest, since such a dependent will would still need another law which would restrict the interest of its self-love by the condition that it should be valid as general law.

Thus the principle that every human will *gives general laws through all its maxims* [6] if otherwise correct, could very well be *suited as* the categorical imperative because it is *not grounded in any interest* but rather in the idea of universal law-giving. Therefore, it alone among all possible imperatives can be *unconditional.* Or better still, to reverse the proposition: If there is a categorical imperative, i.e., a law for every [act of] willing by a rational being, it can only command that everything be done on account of maxims of a will which could at the same time consider itself the object of its general laws, because only then both the practical principle and the imperative which it obeys are unconditional, the latter not being based on any interest.

Looking back now on all previous efforts to discover the principle of morality, we need not wonder why they all failed. Man was seen to be bound to laws by duty, but no one realized that he is subject *only to his own general laws* and that he is only bound to act in conformity with his own will, a will designed by nature to make general laws. For, when man was conceived as being only subject to some kind of law, such a law had to be supplemented by some interest, by way either of attraction or of constraint, since it did not originate as a law from *his own* will. [In the absence of such autonomy of the will] the will was obliged by *something else* to act in some manner or other. Through this reasoning, as such entirely necessary, all labor spent in finding a supreme principle of *duty* was irrevocably lost. Its final conclusion was never that of duty, but only that of a necessity of acting from a certain interest, be it a personal or impersonal interest. The imperative had to turn out to be a conditional one and could not by any means serve as a moral command. I will therefore call this principle [of will based on no interest] the principle of *autonomy* of the will as contrasted with every other which I regard as *heteronomy.*

The idea of a rational being which must consider itself as giving general laws through all the maxims of its will in order to evaluate itself and its actions under it, this idea leads to another related and very fruitful idea, namely, that of a *realm of ends.*

---

[6] I may be excused from offering examples to elucidate this principle, as those which have explained the categorical imperative and its formula would all serve the same purpose here.

By a realm I understand the linking of different rational beings by a system of common laws. Since laws determine the ends and their general validity, we are able to conceive all ends as constituting a systematic whole of both rational beings as ends in themselves, and of the special ends of each being, if we disregard the personal differentiation of rational beings as well as the content of their private ends. In other words, we can conceive a realm of ends which is possible in accordance with principles stated previously. The reason is that all rational beings are governed by the *law* that each must treat itself and all other such beings, *never merely as means*, but also always *as ends in themselves*. This results in a systematic linking of rational beings through common objective laws, i.e., a realm which may be called a realm of ends. In such a realm (admittedly only an ideal) these laws are directed toward the relations of these beings to one another as ends and means.

A rational being belongs as a *member* to the realm of ends to the extent to which he is himself subject to these general laws, although giving them himself. He belongs to it *as ruler* (*Oberhaupt*) when, while giving laws, he is not subject to the will of any other.

A rational being must always regard himself as law-making in a realm of ends made possible by freedom of the will, be it as member or as ruler. He cannot, however, hold the latter position merely by the maxims of his will but only if he is completely independent, has no wants and possesses unrestricted power adequate for his will. . . . Reason then relates every maxim of the will, as general law-giving to every other will and also to every action toward oneself, not on account of any other practical motive or any future advantage, but because of the idea of the *dignity* of a rational being which obeys no law but that which he himself gives.

In the realm of ends everything has either a price or *dignity*. Whatever has a price can be replaced by something else which is *equivalent*; whatever is above all price, and therefore has no equivalent, has dignity.

Whatever is related to the general inclinations and needs of mankind has a *market price*; whatever answers, without presupposing a need, to a certain taste, that is, to pleasure in the mere purposeless play of our emotions (*Gemütskräfte*) has a *fancy price*. But that which constitutes the condition under which alone anything can be an end in itself has not merely a relative value or price, but has an intrinsic value; it has *dignity*.

Morality is the sole condition under which a rational being can be an end in himself, since only then can he possibly be a law-making member of the realm of ends. Thus, only good morals (*Sittlichkeit*) and mankind, so far as it is capable of it, have dignity. Skill and diligence in work have a market price; with, lively imagination and whims have a fancy price; but faithfulness to promise, good will as a matter of principle, not as a matter of instinct, have an intrinsic value. Neither nature nor art has anything which, if dignity were lacking, they could put in its place. For, such intrinsic value consists neither in its effects, nor in the utility and advantage which it makes possible, but in convictions; that is, in the maxims of will which are ready to manifest themselves in actions, even when such action does not have the desired effect. These actions need no urging by any subjective taste or sentiment to be regarded with immediate favor and pleasure. They need no immediate propensity or feeling; they represent the will that performs them as an object of an immediate respect. Nothing but reason is required to oblige them. Reason need not *flatter* the will into doing them, which in the case of duties would be a contradiction anyhow. This respect therefore shows that the value of such an outlook is dignity and places it infinitely above all price. Such dignity cannot for a moment be evaluated in terms of price or compared with it without, as it were, violating its sanctity.

What entitles virtue or moral disposition to make such high claims? It is nothing less than the share in the making of general laws which affords the rational being, qualifying him thereby to be a member of a possible realm of ends, for which he was already destined by his own nature. . . . The laws setting all value must for that very reason possess dignity; that is, an unconditional incomparable value. The word *respect* alone offers a fitting expression of the esteem in which a rational being must hold it. *Autonomy* lies at the root of the dignity of human and of every other rational nature.

The aforementioned three modes of presenting the principle of morality are at bottom only so many formulae of the very same law, of which one comprises the other two. There is, however, a difference between them, but it is rather subjective than objective and practical. What is involved is bringing an idea of reason closer to what can be looked at and visualized (*Anschauung*) and thereby closer to feeling. All maxims, in fact, have three aspects.

First, there is *form*, consisting in being generalizations (*Allgemeinheit*). The formula of the moral imperative is stated thus: the maxims must be chosen as if they were as valid as general laws of nature.

Second, there is content or substance (*Materie*), in other words, an end. The formula states that the rational being, as an end by its own nature and therefore as an end in itself, must be for every maxim the condition limiting all merely relative and arbitrary ends.

Third, there is a *complete definition* of all maxims by this formula [of the categorical imperative], to wit: All maxims by virtue of their own lawmaking ought to harmonize so as to constitute together a possible realm of ends as a realm of nature.[7] This progression takes place through the categories of *unity* in the form of will (its generality), of *plurality* of the content or substance (the objects or ends), and of *totality* of their system. In forming a moral *judgment* about actions it is always better to proceed on the strict method and to start with the general formula of the categorical imperative: *Act according to a maxim which can become a general law.* If, however, we wish to introduce the moral law, it is very useful to evaluate the same action by the three specified concepts and thereby let it approach, as far as possible, something that is clearly envisaged (*Anschauung*).

We can conclude with what we started from, namely, with the concept of an absolutely good will. *That will is thoroughly good* which cannot be evil, or, whose maxim, if made a general law, could never contradict itself. This principle is also its supreme law: Act always on such a maxim as you can will to be a general law. This is the only condition under which a will can never contradict itself; and such an imperative is categorical. Since the validity of the will as a general law for possible actions is analogous to the general linking of the existence of things by general laws which is the formal aspect of nature in general, the categorical imperative can also be expressed as follows: *Act on maxims which can have themselves for their own object as general laws of nature.* Such then is the formula of a thoroughly good will.

Rational nature is distinguished from the rest of nature by setting itself an end. This end would be the content of every good will. But since the idea of an absolutely good will is not limited by any condition of attaining this or that end we must completely disregard every end *to be effected* which would make every will only relatively good. The end here must be understood to be not an end to be effected but an *independently existing* end, consequently only a negative one, i.e., one against which we must never act and therefore every act of willing must never be regarded merely as means, but as an end as well. This end can be nothing but the subject of all possible ends, since it is also the subject of a possible absolutely good will; because such a will cannot be related to any other object without contradiction. The principle: So act toward every rational being (yourself and others), that he may for you always be an end in himself, is therefore essentially identical with this other: Act upon a maxim which is generally valid for every rational being. . . .

In this way an intelligible world (*mundus intelligibilis*) is possible as a realm of ends, by virtue of the lawmaking of all persons as members.

---

[7] Teleology considers nature as a realm of ends; morals regards a possible realm of ends as a realm of nature. In the first case, the realm of ends is a theoretical idea explaining what actually is. In the latter it is a practical idea bringing about that which is not yet, but which can be realized in conforming to this idea in our conduct.

. . . Such a realm of ends would be actually realized if maxims conforming to the canon of the categorical imperative for all rational beings *were universally followed*. But a rational being, though punctiliously following this maxim himself, cannot count upon all others being equally faithful to it, nor [can he be certain] that the realm of nature and its purposive design so accord with him as a proper member as to form a realm made possible by himself; that is, favoring his expectation of happiness. Still the law remains in full force: Act according to the maxims of a member of a merely possible realm of ends in making general law since this law commands categorically. Therein lies the paradox; that merely the dignity of man as a rational creature, in other words, respect for a mere idea, should serve as an inflexible precept without any other end or advantage. The sublime character [of this dignity] consists precisely in this independence of maxims from all such springs of action. This makes every rational subject worthy to be a law-making member of the realm of ends. Otherwise he would have to be imagined as subject only to the natural law of his wants. Although we would suppose the realm of nature and the realm of ends to be united under one ruler, so that the realm of ends thereby would no longer be a mere idea but acquire true reality, [such reality] would no doubt gain an additional strong incentive, but never any increase of its intrinsic value. For, this sole unlimited law-giver must nonetheless always be conceived as evaluating the value of rational beings only by their disinterested behavior, as prescribed by the idea of the dignity of man alone. The essence of things is not altered by their external conditions and man must be judged by whatever constitutes his absolute value, irrespective of these [conditions], whoever be the judge, even it be the Supreme Being. Morality then is the relation of actions to the autonomy of the will, that is, to the possible general laws made by its maxims. An action that is consistent with the autonomy of the will is *permissible*, one that is not congruous with it is *forbidden*. A will whose maxims necessarily are congruous with the laws of autonomy is a *sacred*, wholly good will. The dependence of a not absolutely good will on the principle of autonomy (moral compulsion) is [called] obligation. It cannot be applied to a holy being. The objective necessity of an action resulting from obligation is called *duty*.

It is easy to see, from what has been just said, why we ascribe a certain quality and sublime dignity to the person who fulfils all his duties, although we think of the concept of duty as implying subjection to the law. There is no sublime quality in him as far as he is *subject* to the moral law, but there is as far as he is at the same time a maker of that very law and on that account subject to it. Furthermore, we have shown above that neither fear nor inclination but simply respect for the law is the incentive which can give actions a moral value. Our own will, as far as it acts under the condition that its maxims may constitute possible general laws—and such a will is possible as an idea—is the real object of respect. The dignity of mankind consists just in this capacity of making general laws, always provided that it is itself subject to these laws.

The Autonomy of the Will as the Supreme Principle of Morality

Autonomy of the will is that property by which will is a law unto itself, independent of any property of the objects of volition. The principle of autonomy therefore is: always so to choose that in the same act of willing the maxims of this choice are formulated as a general law. We cannot prove by a mere analysis of its concepts that this practical rule is an imperative, i.e., that the will of every rational being is necessarily bound by it as a condition, since [such rule] is a synthetical proposition. We would have to go beyond the knowledge of objects to a critique of the subject; that is to pure practical reason. For this synthetic proposition which commands apodictically must be understood and known wholly *a priori*. This matter, however, does not belong to the present section. But it can readily be shown by mere analysis of the concepts of morality that the principle of autonomy is the sole principle of morals. We shall then find that its principle must be a categorical imperative and the latter commands neither more nor less than this very autonomy.

Heteronomy of the Will as the Source of all False Principles of Morality

If the will is concerned with *anything else* but the suitability of its maxims as general laws of its own making, that is, if it goes beyond itself and seeks a law by which it is to be determined in the qualities of any of its objects, *heteronomy* always is the result. The will in that case does not give itself the law, but the object is given it through its relation to the will. This relation only admits of hypothetical imperatives, whether the imperative rests on inclination or on concepts of reason: *I must do something because I want something else.* On the other hand, the moral and therefore categorical imperative says: I ought to do thus and so although I want nothing more. For instance, the hypothetical imperative says: I must lie if I want to retain my reputation; the latter says: I ought not to lie whether it brings me the least discredit or not. The latter therefore must disregard the objects to the extent that it has no *influence* on the will, so that practical reason (the will) may not merely administer an alien interest, but simply prove its own commanding authority as the supreme law-giver. Thus, e.g., I ought to endeavor to promote the happiness of others, not as if I had an interest in it by immediate inclination or by any pleasure indirectly gained through reason, but simply because a maxim which excludes [the happiness of others] cannot be comprised in one and the same volition as a general law.

Classification of all Possible Principles of Morality which can be Founded on the Basic Concept of Heteronomy

Human reason has here, as elsewhere in its pure pre-critical use, first tried all kinds of wrong ways before it succeeded in finding the one true way [through criticism]. As we have seen, all principles to be considered from this point of view are either *empirical* or *rational*. As the determining cause of our will, the empirical principles derived from the principle of *happiness* are based on physical or moral sentiments, rational principles derived from the principle of perfection are based as a possible effect either on the rational concept of perfection or on the concept of an autonomous perfection; that is, the will of God.

[Ed: After repeating what he has said concerning the unsuitability of happiness as a foundation for morals, Kant continues:]

Among the *rational* principles of morality, the ontological concept of *perfection*, in spite of its defects, is better than the theological concept which deduces morality from a Divine, absolutely perfect, will. The ontological concept is no doubt empty and indefinite and consequently useless for finding the highest degree [of perfection] in the boundless field of possible reality. Moreover, in attempting to distinguish specifically the reality of which we are now speaking from every other reality, it inevitably tends to go around in circles and cannot avoid presupposing tacitly the morality which this reality is to explain. Nevertheless it is better than the theological concept, not only because we cannot visualize (*anschauen*) the divine perfection and can only deduce it from our own concepts of which the most important is morality itself (and even then our explanation would involve a gross, roundabout, reasoning), but also because the remaining concept of a [divine] will, derived from the attributes of desire for glory and domination and combined with the terrible ideas of power and vengeance, would constitute the basis of a system of morals diametrically opposed to morality.

However, if I had to choose between the concept of moral sense and that of perfection in general (both of which at least do not weaken

morality though they are not at all qualified to serve as its foundation)
I would decide for the concept of perfection because it, at least, removes
the question from the senses and brings it before the court of pure reason. Although even here the concept of perfection decides nothing, at
all events it preserves, unadulterated, the indefinite idea of a will good
in itself for more precise definition. . . .

Wherever an [external] object of the will has to be supposed and
the rule is prescribed for determining it, that rule is simple heteronomy.
The imperative is conditional; namely, if, or *because*, one desires this
object, one should act in this or that way; hence it can never command
morally, that is, categorically. Whether the object determines the will
through inclination, as in the principle of private happiness, or through
reason directed at objects of our possible volition, as in the principle of
perfection, in either case the will never determines itself *immediately*
through the conceived action, but only through the influence which the
foreseen effect of the action has on the will: *I ought to do something
because* I am willing something else. Here yet another law must be assumed in me as its subject by means of which I necessarily will this other
thing, which law in turn requires an imperative restricting this maxim.
The impulse which the concept of an object within the reach of our
faculties can give the will of the subject depends on its natural properties, no matter whether the senses (inclination and taste), or intellect
and reason are satisfied through use. . . . Consequently, nature would,
properly speaking, give the law, and, as such, not only must the law be
known and proved by experience and therefore would be contingent and
useless as an apodictic practical rule as the moral rule must be, but the
law always implies a heteronomy of the will. The will does not give itself the law, the law is given by an extraneous impulse to which the
natural constitution of the subject is receptive.

[Ed: After once again stating his views on the autonomy of the
good will, Kant continues:]

The problem of how such a synthetic, practical, a priori *proposition
is possible and necessary* cannot be solved within the limits of the metaphysics of morals. We have not asserted its truth here, much less professed to have a proof of it. We have simply shown, by the development of the universally accepted concept of morality that autonomy of
the will is inevitably connected with this concept or, rather, is its basis.
Whoever considers morality real, and not a chimerical idea without
truth, must likewise admit its principle as discussed here. This section
then, like the first, was merely analytic. To prove that morality is no
mere creation of the brain, which it cannot be if the categorical imperative and with it the autonomy of the will are a true idea and are
absolutely necessary as an *a priori* principle, requires a synthetic use of

pure practical reason. However, we cannot venture into this without first undertaking a critique of this faculty of reason. In the concluding section we shall give the principal features of this critique as far as is necessary for our purpose.

THIRD SECTION

TRANSITION FROM THE METAPHYSICS OF MORALS TO THE CRITIQUE OF PURE PRACTICAL REASON

The Concept of Freedom Is the Key Explanation of the Autonomy of the Will

The *will* is a kind of causality of living beings in so far as they are rational, and *freedom* should be that quality of this causality through which it can be an efficient cause independent of extraneous *determining* causes; just as *physical necessity* is the peculiar quality of the causality of all non-rational beings as impelled into activity by extraneous causes.

The above definition of freedom is *negative* and therefore unsuitable for understanding its essence; but it leads to a *positive* concept which is all the more ample and fruitful. Since the concept of causality implies that of law, according to which something called a cause produces something else called an effect, freedom, though not a quality of the will in so far as it depends on natural laws, is not for that reason without law, but must rather be a causality acting in accordance with immutable laws of a peculiar kind; otherwise free will would be an absurdity. Natural necessity is a heteronomy of efficient causes because every effect if possible only according to the law [of natural causality:] some [antecedent cause] determines the efficient cause to act causally. What else can freedom of the will be but autonomy; that is, the property of the will to be a law unto itself? But the proposition: the will is a law unto itself in every action, only expresses the principle of acting on no other maxim than that which can also aim to be a general law. This is precisely the formula of the categorical imperative and of the principle of ethics, so that a free will and a will subject to moral laws are one and the same.

If freedom of the will is assumed, morality and its principle can be deduced from it by mere analysis of the concept. However, the latter is still a synthetic proposition: that an absolutely good will is one whose maxim can always be stated in terms of a general law, still is a synthetic proposition. This quality of the maxims can never be discovered by analyzing the concept of an absolutely good will. Such synthetic propositions are only possible by uniting both insights (*Erkenntnisse*) with a third in which they both can be found. The *positive* concept of freedom leads to this third [element] which cannot be the nature of the sensible world with its physical causes. This third [element], to which freedom leads us and of which we have an idea *a priori*, cannot be shown here as yet. Nor can we yet explain the deduction of the concept of freedom from pure practical reason, nor the possibility of a categorical imperative. Some further preparation is required.

Freedom Must Be Assumed to Be a Quality of the Will of All Rational Beings

It is not enough to attribute freedom, for whatever reason, to our own will if we have not sufficient grounds for attributing the same to all rational beings. For, as morality serves us as a law only because we are *rational beings*, it must also hold true for all rational beings. As morality must be deduced simply from the quality of freedom, it must be shown that freedom is also a quality of all rational beings. It is not enough then to expound it as derived from certain supposed experiences of human nature (which indeed is quite impossible and can only be shown *a priori*), but we must prove that morality is part of the activity of any and all rational beings endowed with a will. Now I say that every being who cannot act except *under the idea of freedom* is, in practical respects, really free for just that reason. That is to say; all laws inseparably connected with freedom are as valid for this being as though his will had been shown to be free in itself and accepted by theoretical philosophy.[8] I assert that we must necessarily attribute to every rational being having a will the idea of freedom under which alone it acts. In such a being we conceive reason which is practical; that is, which acts causally in reference to its objects. We cannot possibly conceive reason consciously permitting any other quarter to direct its judgments, since then the subject would attribute the control of its judgment not to reason, but to an impulse. Reason must regard itself as the author of its principles independent of extraneous influences; consequently, it, as practical reason or

---

[8] I adopt this method of assuming that freedom, merely *as an idea* upon which alone rational beings base their actions, is sufficient for our purpose, in order to avoid the necessity of proving freedom in its theoretical aspect also. Even though the latter is not ascertained, a being that cannot act except under the idea of freedom is bound by the same laws as a being who is actually free. Thus we can escape here from the burden which weighs upon the theory.

as the will of a rational being, must regard itself as free. That is to say; the will [of such a being] cannot be a will of its own except under the idea of freedom. Therefore this idea must, practically speaking, be attributed to all rational beings.

Of the Interest Attaching to the Ideas of Morality

At last we have reduced the definite concept of morality to the idea of freedom. However, we could not prove this idea to be actually a quality of ourselves and of human nature; we saw merely that we must presuppose it if we want to think of a being as rational and conscious of its causality in its actions, i.e., as endowed with a will. So we find that on the very same grounds we must attribute to every being endowed with reason and will this quality of obliging itself to act under the idea of its freedom.

Presupposing these ideas means becoming aware of a law that the subjective principles of action, i.e., maxims, must always be taken as being objective, i.e., universal principles, and so serve as universal laws of our own making. But why should I, simply as a rational being, subject myself to this principle and thus also [subject to this principle] all other beings endowed with reason? I will allow that no interest *urges* me to do this, for interest would not yield a categorical imperative. But I must *take* an interest in it and discern how this comes to pass, as this "I ought" is properly an "I will" which holds for every rational being, provided only that reason determine his actions without hindrance. But for beings that are affected also, as we are, by impulses of a different kind, i.e., our senses, and do not always act according to reason alike, necessity is only an "ought" and the subjective necessity differs from the objective one.

Therefore it seems as if moral law, that is, the principle of the autonomy of the will, were actually only presupposed in the idea of freedom and as if its reality and objective necessity could not be proved independently. Even then we would have gained considerably in at least determining the true principle more exactly than had previously been done. But in regard to the validity of the principle and the practical necessity of subjecting oneself to it, we would not have advanced a step. If we were asked why the universal validity of our maxim as a law must be the condition restricting our actions and on what we base the value which we assign to this way of acting, a value so great that there can be no higher interest, [and if we were asked further] why by this alone a man believes to feel his own value compared with which a pleasant or unpleasant condition must be regarded as nothing, to these questions we could give no satisfactory answer.

Sometimes, indeed, we find that we can take an interest in a personal quality not involving any interest or external condition, provided this quality enables us to participate in the condition, in case reason were to bring it about. It can interest us merely in deserving happiness even without sharing the motive [for this happiness]. However this judgment is actually only the effect of the moral law whose importance we have already assumed if we detach ourselves from every empirical interest through the idea of freedom. But we do not realize in this way that we ought to detach ourselves from these interests; that is, consider ourselves as free in action and yet as subject to certain laws, so as to find a value simply in our own person which can compensate us for the loss of everything that gives our condition a value. Nor do we see how all this is possible; in other words, *why moral law is obligatory.*

It must be freely admitted that there appears a sort of circular reasoning here that seems impossible to escape. We assume ourselves to be free in the order of efficient causes so that we may conceive ourselves to be subject to moral laws in the order of ends. Then we consider ourselves as subject to these laws because we have conferred upon ourselves freedom of will. Freedom and law-making of will are both autonomous and are therefore correlative concepts. For this very reason one concept cannot be used to explain the other or set forth its basis, [but can be used] at best to reduce, for the sake of logic, apparently different notions of the same object to one single concept (as we reduce different fractions of equal content to their lowest denominator).

One resource remains: to inquire whether we do not occupy different positions when we think of ourselves as causes efficient *a priori* through freedom and when we consider ourselves as effects of our actions which we see before our eyes.

The remark, which needs no subtle reflection and which can presumably be made by the most average mind (though after his fashion by an obscure discernment of judgment which he calls sentiment) is that all images (*Vorstellungen*) which we get without willing them, such as those of the senses, do not enable us to know objects except as they affect us. Whatever they are in themselves remains unknown. Consequently, regardless of the closest attention and clarity of which the mind is capable, "images" of this kind allow us only to acquire knowledge of *phenomena*, never of *things in themselves.* Once this distinction has been made, (even in just observing a difference between the images or ideas we receive passively from without, and those which we actively produce ourselves), it follows that we must admit and assume behind the phenomena something else that are not phenomena; namely, the things-in-themselves, although we must resign ourselves never to being able to approach them and never to knowing what they are in themselves, but only as they affect us. This must furnish a distinction, no matter how crude, between the world of sense and the world of reason. The former can be distinguished according to the difference of sense impressions in various observers, while the second always remains the same as the basis of the distinction. Man cannot even pretend to know what he is himself from the self-knowledge he has through internal sensation. Since he does not create himself, as it were, and comes by the concept [of man] not *a priori* but empirically, it is natural that he can obtain knowledge of himself only by his inner sense, and consequently only through the phenomena of his nature and the way in which his consciousness is affected. Nevertheless, beyond the structure of his own subject, as made up of mere phenomena, he must suppose something else as the basis of these phenomena; namely, his ego, whatever its nature may be. In regard to mere perception and receptivity of the senses, man must reckon himself as belonging to the *world of sense,* but in regard to what may be pure action in him (reaching consciousness directly and not by affecting the senses), he must reckon himself as belonging to the *world of the mind,* of which, however, he has no further knowledge. . . .

Man actually finds in himself a faculty which distinguishes him from all other things, even from himself as affected by objects, and that is *reason.* Reason, being pure and spontaneous, is superior even to the mind. Though the latter is spontaneous too and does not, like the sense, merely contain images that arise when we are affected by things (and are therefore passive), reason's activity cannot produce any other concepts than those designed *to bring the impressions or images based on sense rules,* to unite them in one consciousness. Without this activity of the senses, the [mind] could not think at all, whereas reason in the form of ideas displays such pure spontaneity that it far transcends anything that the senses can offer it and so proves its most important function in distinguishing the world of sense from that of the intellect, thereby setting the limits of the intellect itself.

A rational being must regard himself *as an intelligence* (not from the viewpoint of his lower faculties) belonging, not to the world of sense, but to that of the intellect. Hence man can regard himself from two points of view and similarly can come to know laws for the exercise of his faculties and consequently laws for all his actions. *First,* so far as he belongs to the world of sense, man is himself subject to laws of nature (heteronomy); *second,* so far as he belongs to the intelligible

world, [man is] under laws independent of nature which are founded
not on experience but on reason alone. . . .

The suspicion which we considered above is now removed. This
was the suspicion that our reasoning, from freedom to autonomy and
from this to moral law, was mysteriously circular and that we thought
the idea of freedom was basic only because of the moral law so that we
might then infer the latter from freedom and that then we could offer
no explanation at all for this law, but could only [present] it by *begging
a principle* which well-disposed minds would gladly concede to us, but
which we could never put forward as a provable proposition. Now we
see that when we conceive ourselves as free we transfer ourselves into the
world of the intellect and recognize the autonomy of the will with its
consequence, morality; whereas if we conceive ourselves as obliged we
are considering ourselves as belonging at the same time to the world of
sense and to the intellectual world (*Verstandeswelt*).

How Is a Categorical Imperative Possible?

Every rational being considers himself as belonging, as an intelligence, to
the world of intellect and he calls his causality a will simply as an efficient cause belonging to that world. On the other hand, he is also conscious of being a part of the world of sense in which his actions are displayed as mere phenomena of that causality. However, we cannot
discern how they are possible from this causality which we do not know.
Instead, these actions must be viewed as determined by other phenomena; namely, desires and inclinations belonging to the sensible world.
If I were only a member of the world of the intellect, all my actions
would conform perfectly to the principle of the autonomy of pure will;
if I were only a part of the world of sense they would be assumed to
conform wholly to the natural law of desires and inclinations, i.e., to
the heteronomy of nature. (The former would rest on the supreme principle of morality, the latter on that of happiness.) Since *the world of the
intellect contains the basis of the world of sense, and consequently of its
laws*, and so gives law directly to my will (as belonging entirely to the
world of the intellect), I, as an intelligence, must recognize myself as
subject to the law of the world of the intellect. [What this means is that
I am subject] to reason which contains this law in the idea of freedom,
and therefore as subject to the autonomy of the will, though otherwise
[I am] a being belonging to the world of sense. Consequently, I must
regard the laws of the world of the intellect as imperatives and the corresponding actions as duties.

Therefore categorical imperatives are possible because the idea of freedom makes me a member of an intelligible world whereby, were I nothing else, all my actions *would* always conform to the autonomy of the will. But, since I also see myself as a member of the world of sense, they *ought* so to conform, which *categorical* "ought" is a synthetic *a priori* proposition in so far as there is added to my will, as affected by sensible desires, the idea of the same will belonging to the world of the intellect, pure and practical in itself. . . .

The practical use of common human reason confirms this reflection. There is no one, not even the most consummate villain only provided that he is accustomed to the use of reason, who, when shown examples of honesty of purpose, of steadfastness in obeying good maxims, of sympathy and charity in the face of great sacrifices of advantages and comfort, would not wish that he might also possess these qualities. Only his inclinations and impulses prevent it and he wishes to be free from such troublesome inclinations. Therefore he proves that, with a will free from the impulses of the sense, he can imagine an order of things wholly different from that of his sensible desires. He believes himself to be this better person when he shifts to the viewpoint of a member of the world of the intellect into which he is prompted by the idea of freedom. . . . The moral "ought" is then the necessary "will" of a member of an intelligible world and he conceives it as an "ought" only to the same extent that he considers himself a member of the world of sense.

Of the Extreme Limit of all Practical Philosophy

All men attribute freedom of will to themselves. This explains all judgments of actions that *ought to have been done* but *were not*. Nevertheless this freedom is not a concept based on experience, nor can it be such since it persists even when experience shows the contrary of what are conceived to be its necessary consequences once freedom is presupposed. On the other hand, it is equally necessary that every event should be firmly determined according to laws of nature. This necessity of nature is likewise not an empirical concept in that it involves the notion of necessity; that is, of *a priori* knowledge. But this concept of nature is confirmed by experience and must be presupposed if experience itself is to be possible; that is, if it is to be a coherent knowledge in terms of general laws of sensory objects. Therefore freedom is only an *idea* of reason and its objective reality as such is doubtful, while nature is a *concept* of the *intellect* which proves, and must necessarily prove, its reality in examples of experience.

Although this results in a dialectic of reason since the freedom attributed to the will appears to contradict the necessity of nature, and reason at this parting of the ways for *speculative purposes* finds the road of physical necessity much better trodden and more appropriate than that of freedom, yet for *practical purposes* the narrow path of freedom is the only one by which it is possible to make use of reason in our conduct. Hence it is impossible for the subtlest philosophy as well as for the commonest human reason to argue away freedom. Philosophy must assume that no real contradiction will be found between the freedom and physical necessity of the same human actions, for it cannot give up the concept of nature any more than that of freedom.

It is impossible to escape this contradiction if the subject, thinking itself free, thought of itself *in the same sense* or *in the very same relation* when it calls itself free as when it assumes itself subject to the law of nature with respect to the same action. It is an inescapable problem of speculative philosophy to show at least that this seeming contradiction rests on our thinking of man in a different sense and relation when we call him free, from that when we regard him as part and parcel of nature, and as subject to its laws. It must therefore show not only that both *can* co-exist very well, but that both must be thought of *as necessarily united* in the same subject, since otherwise no explanation could be given for burdening reason with an idea which entangles us in a perplexity sorely embarrassing reason in its theoretic use, though it may be reconciled *without contradiction* with another idea that is sufficiently established. However, this task belongs to speculative philosophy by which it may clear the way for practical philosophy. The philosopher has no option; he must remove the apparent contradiction since if he left it untouched the theory about it would be *bonum vacans* and the fatalist would have a right to acquire it and expel all morality from its supposed domain as occupying it without title.

The title to freedom of will, even that of common reason, is founded on the consciousness and the admitted assumption that reason is independent of mere subjectively determined causes which, as a whole, belong only to sensation, and which consequently come under the general designation of the senses. . . . Man soon realizes that both can hold true, nay even must hold true at the same time. There is not the least contradiction in saying that a *thing-in-appearance* or phenomenon (belonging to the world of sense) is subject to certain laws, of which the very same thing *as a thing* or being *in itself* is independent. [The fact] that he must conceive and think of himself in this two-fold way rests, in regard to the first [way], on his consciousness of being an object affected through the senses, and in regard to the second [way], on his consciousness of being an intelligence; that is, [of being] independent from sense impressions in using his reason and so belonging to the world of the intellect. This explains man claiming the possession of a will which allows nothing to be charged against it merely belonging to his desires and inclinations and, on the other hand, a will which conceives actions as being possible and even necessary that can happen only through disregard of all desires and sensible inclinations. The causality of such actions lies in man as an intelligence, and in the laws of effects and actions according to the principles of an intelligible world, of which he may know nothing other than that there pure reason alone makes the law, independent of the senses. Moreover, since he is his proper self as an intelligence only in that world (as man is only the phenomenon of himself), those laws concern him directly and categorically, so that the incitements of inclinations and appetites (the whole nature of the world of sense) cannot impair the laws of his volition as an intelligence. Furthermore, he does not even hold himself responsible for the former or ascribe them to his proper self, i.e., his will; he only ascribes to his will any indulgence toward them if he allowed them to influence his maxims to the prejudice of the rational laws of the will.

When practical reason *thinks* itself into a world of the intellect it does not thereby transgress its own limits, as it would if it tried to enter it by *looking* at or *sensing* it. This is only a negative thought in respect to the world of sense, which does not give reason any laws to determine the will, and is positive only in the single respect that this freedom as a negative condition is combined with a (positive) faculty and even with a causality of reason, which we call a will, a will of acting so that the principle of the actions conforms to the essential character of a rational motive; i.e., to the condition that the maxim have universal validity as a law. But if practical reason were to borrow an *object* of *will*, that is, a motive from the world of the intellect, it would overstep its bounds and would venture to be acquainted with something of which it knows nothing. The concept of a world of the intellect is only a *position* outside the phenomena which reason finds itself compelled to take in order to *conceive itself as practical*, which would not be possible if the influences of the senses had a determining power over man, but which is necessary unless he is denied the consciousness of himself as an intelligence; that is, as a rational cause acting freely and through reason. This thought certainly involves the idea of an order and a system of laws different from that of the mechanism of nature which governs the sensible world, and it requires the concept of an intelligible world; that is to say, of a whole system of rational beings as things in themselves. But this thought does not in the least entitle us to consider it in terms other than those of its *formal* condition; that is, the autonomy of this intelligible world which alone can co-exist with its freedom. On the other hand, all laws that refer to an object give heteronomy, which is only found in laws of nature and can only apply to the sensible world.

But reason would be overstepping all its bounds if it undertook to *explain how* pure reason could be practical; this would be exactly the same task as explaining *how freedom is possible*.

We can explain nothing but that which we can reduce to laws, whose object can be given in some possible experience. But freedom is a mere idea, whose objective reality can never be shown through laws of nature nor, consequently, through possible experience; therefore it can never be comprehended or even visualized, because we cannot support it by any sort of example or analogy. It is valid only as a necessary hypothesis of reason in a being that believes itself conscious of a will. Where impulse ceases according to laws of nature, there ceases all *explanation* also, leaving nothing but defense, i.e., the removal of the objections of those who pretend to have seen deeper into the nature of things, and who thereupon boldly declare freedom impossible. We can only show them that the contradiction that they believe to have discovered arises only from man having to be considered as a phenomenon in order to apply the law of nature to human actions. When we demand of them that they should also think of him as an intelligence, as a thing-in-itself, they still persist in considering him as [only] phenomenon. [If that were so], to cut off the causality of the same subject, that is, his will, from all the natural laws of the sensible world would unquestionably be a contradiction. But this contradiction disappears if one bethinks oneself and admits as reasonable that beneath the phenomenon must lie at their root [so to speak] the hidden things-in-themselves, and that we cannot expect the laws of these to be identical to those that govern their appearances.

The subjective impossibility of explaining the freedom of the will as identical with the impossibility of discovering and explaining an interest[9] which man could take in the moral law. Nevertheless he does actually take an interest in it, the basis of which in ourselves we call the moral sentiment, which some have falsely pronounced the standard of our moral judgment, whereas it must rather be viewed as the *subjective*

---

[9] Interest is that which makes reason practical; that is, a cause determining the will. Hence we say of rational beings only that they take an interest in something; irrational beings only feel sensual appetites. Reason takes a direct interest in action only if the universal validity of its maxims is sufficient to determine the will. Such an interest alone is pure. But if it can determine the will only by means of another object of desire or on the assumption of a particular sentiment in the subject, reason takes only an indirect interest in the action. As reason without experience cannot discover either objects of the will or a special sentiment actuating it, this latter interest would only be empirical, and not a pure rational interest. The scholarly interest of reason, for extending its insight, is never direct, but it presupposes purposes for which reason is employed.

effect that the law exercises on the will, for which reason alone furnishes the objective principle.

In order that a rational being, also affected through the senses, should will what reason alone directs such beings to will, reason must have a power *to infuse a sensation of pleasure* or satisfaction in the fulfilment of duty; that is, it should have a causality by which it determines the sensibility according to its own principles. But it is quite impossible to realize, i.e., to make it intelligible *a priori*, how a mere thought, itself containing nothing sensible, can produce a sensation of pleasure or pain; for this is a particular kind of causality of which, as of any causality, we can determine *a priori* nothing whatever; we can consult only experience about it. But as experience cannot supply us with any relation of cause and effect as between two objects of experience, whereas in this case the cause is supposed to be pure reason acting through mere ideas which offer no object to experience, although the effect produced lies within experience, it is quite impossible that we human beings explain how and why the *universality of the maxim as a law*, that is, morality, can interest [man]. This much is certain, that it has validity for us not just *because it interests* us, for that would be heteronomy and dependence of practical reason on the senses or a sentiment as its principle, in which case it could never give moral laws. The universal maxim interests us because it is valid for us as human beings as it has its source in our will as intelligences; in other words, in our proper self. *Whereas whatever belongs to mere appearance, reason necessarily subordinates to the nature of the thing in itself.*

The question of how a categorical imperative is possible can be answered to the extent that we can state the only hypothesis on which it is possible, namely, the idea of freedom, and we can also perceive the necessity of this hypothesis which is sufficient for the practical exercise of reason; that is, for convincing us of the *validity of this imperative* and hence of the moral law, but how this hypothesis itself is possible can never be discerned by any human reason. However, on the hypothesis that the will of an intelligence is free, its autonomy is a necessary consequence as the essential formal condition of its determination. Moreover, this freedom of will is not only quite possible as a hypothesis without involving any contradiction to the principle of physical necessity in the nexus of phenomena of the sensible world, as speculative philosophy can show, but a rational being who is conscious of causality through reason, that is to say, of a will distinct from desires, must of *necessity* make it, as an idea, the condition of practically all his voluntary actions. But how pure reason can be practical of itself without the aid of any impulse to action, no matter where such impulse is derived, i.e., how the mere principle of the *universal validity of its maxims as laws* (which would certainly be the form of a pure practical reason) can supply an impulse of itself without any object of the will in which one could antecedently take any original interest; and how it can produce an interest which would be called purely moral; or, in other words, *how pure reason can be practical*, [all this] is beyond the power of human reason to explain and all the labor and pains of seeking an explanation for this are in vain.

The same applies to the attempt to find out how freedom itself is possible as the causality of a will. Here I quit the ground of philosophical explanation and I have no other to go upon. I might revel in the world of intelligences which still remains [open] to me, but though I have an *idea* of it which is well founded, yet I have not the least *knowledge* of it, nor can I ever attain it with all the efforts of my natural faculty of reason. Freedom signifies only a something that remains when I have eliminated everything belonging to the world of sense from the actuating principles of my will, serving merely to restrict the principle of such motives as are taken from the field of sensibility by fixing its limits and showing that it does not contain everything, but that there is more beyond it; but of this "more" I know nothing. After the abstraction of all matter, i.e., knowledge of objects, there remains of pure reason which conceives this ideal nothing but the form, namely, the practical law of the universality of the maxims, and congruous with it the concept of reason in reference to a pure world of the intellect as a possible efficient cause, i.e., a cause determining the will. There must be here a total absence of impulses, unless this idea of an intelligible world is itself the impulse, or the primary interest of reason; but to make this intelligible is precisely the problem that we cannot solve.

This is the extreme limit of all moral inquiry. Yet it is of great importance to determine this limit on this account: that reason may not on the one hand search about in the world of sense to the prejudice of morals for the supreme motive and an interest comprehensible but empirical; and on the other hand so that reason may not impotently raise its wings in the empty space of transcendent concepts which we call the intelligible world without being able to move and so lose itself amidst chimeras. For the rest, the idea remains of a pure world of the intellect as a whole [comprising] all intelligences, to which we ourselves belong [insofar as we are] rational beings, although otherwise we are members of the sensible world. It is a useful and legitimate idea for the purposes of rational belief, even though all knowledge stops at its threshold. It produces in us a lively interest in the moral law by means of the magnificent ideal of a universal realm of *ends in themselves* (of rational beings) to which we can belong as members only when we carefully conduct ourselves according to the maxims of freedom as if they were laws of nature.

Conclusion

The speculative use of reason *with respect to nature* leads to the absolute necessity of some supreme cause for *the world*. The practical use of reason *with a view to freedom* also leads to absolute necessity, but only *for the laws of the actions* of a rational being as such. It is an essential *principle* of reason, however used, to push its knowledge to a consciousness of its *necessity* (without which it would not be rational knowledge). It is, however, an equally essential *restriction* of the same reason that it can neither discern the *necessity* of what is, or of what happens, or of what ought to happen, unless a condition is supposed on which it is, or happens, or ought to happen. By constant inquiry into this condition, the satisfaction of reason is only further and further postponed. Hence reason searches unceasingly for the unconditionally necessary and finds itself forced to assume it without any means of making it comprehensible to itself; reason is fortunate if it can discover a concept which suits this assumption. Therefore our deduction of the supreme principle of morality cannot be blamed but human reason in general should be reproached for not enabling us to conceive the absolute necessity of an unconditional practical law, such as the categorical imperative must be. Reason cannot be blamed for refusing to explain this necessity by a condition; that is to say, by means of some interest assumed as a basis, since the law would then cease to be a supreme law of reason. Thus we do not comprehend the practical, unconditional necessity of the moral imperative, but we comprehend its *incomprehensibility* which is all that, in fairness, can be demanded of a philosophy which aims to carry its principles to the very limit of human reason.

A NOTE ON THE TYPE

THIS BOOK is set in *Electra*, a Linotype face designed by W. A. Dwiggins (1880–1956). This face
cannot be classified as either modern or old-style. It
is not based on any historical model, nor does it
echo any particular period or style. It avoids the
extreme contrasts between thick and thin elements
that mark most modern faces, and attempts to give
a feeling of fluidity, power, and speed.

Composed, printed, and bound by
Kingsport Press, Inc., Kingsport, Tennessee.
Typography and binding design by
VINCENT TORRE

➤➤❯❮❮❮